1996

SPECULATIONS

SPECULATIONS

Readings in Culture, Identity, and Values

Second Edition

Edited by

Charles I. Schuster
University of Wisconsin—Milwaukee

William V. Van Pelt
University of Wisconsin—Milwaukee

A Blair Press Book

Prentice Hall, Upper Saddle River, NJ 07458

Library of Congress Cataloging-in-Publication Data

Speculations : readings in culture, identity, and values / edited by
  Charles I. Schuster, William V. Van Pelt.—2nd ed.
    p. cm.
  "A Blair Press book."
  Includes index.
  1. Readers—United States.   2. United States—Civilization—
  Problems, exercises, etc.   3. English language—Rhetoric.
  4. College readers.   I. Schuster, Charles I.   II. Van Pelt, William
V.
PE1127.HS77   1996   95–32126
808'.0427—dc20   CIP

Editorial Production Service: Electronic Publishing Services Inc.
Cover Designer: Wendy Alling Judy
Cover Art: Diane Ong "Crowd," b. 1940. Chinese/USA.
Buyer: Robert Anderson
Photo Credits: p. 5—Jose Luis Banus/FPG International; p. 123—AP/Wide
World Photos; P. 207—Paul Conklin/Monkmeyer Press Photos; p. 331—Joel
Gordon; p. 469—Stock Boston.
Acknowledgments appear on pages 629–632, which constitute a continuation
of the copyright page.

A Blair Press Book

© 1996, 1993 by Prentice-Hall, Inc.
Simon & Schuster/A Viacom Company
Upper Saddle River, New Jersey 07458

Printed in the United States of America
10 9 8 7 6 5 4 3 2 1

ISBN 0-13-442294-5

Prentice-Hall International (UK) Limited, *London*
Prentice-Hall of Australia Pty. Limited, *Sydney*
Prentice-Hall Canada Inc., *Toronto*
Prentice-Hall Hispanoamericana, S.A., *Mexico*
Prentice-Hall of India Private Limited, *New Delhi*
Prentice-Hall of Japan, Inc., *Tokyo*
Simon & Schuster Asia Pte. Ltd., *Singapore*
Editora Prentice-Hall do Brasil, Ltda., *Rio de Janeiro*

PREFACE

We hold as an article of faith that college courses should invite students to engage in productive intellectual work—rigorous, challenging, surprising, unsettling, thoughtful, and richly satisfying to the mind. It is around this principle that we designed this second edition of *Speculations: Readings in Culture, Identity, and Values.* Although we are pleased with the results, you and your students will provide the real test of our success, for no matter how much we approve of the changes we made in this second edition, what finally matters is the kind of teaching and learning that *Speculations* makes possible for you and your students.

Speculations began life as a homegrown reader for the first-year composition program at the University of Wisconsin—Milwaukee. Small as it was—the original anthology contained only fifteen or so selections—the book rested on the assumption that students would be best served if invited to examine their beliefs and values in the context of the culture around them, an approach that has become known as "cultural studies" or "cultural literacy." With this second edition, we reaffirm our original assumption: one of the most effective ways to transform the writing classroom into an intellectually exciting space is to engage students in reading and writing about issues that are centered in their lives, issues that affect their choices, perspectives, and possibilities. In this second edition, those issues have been collected under five major themes: Growing Up, Music and Morality, Crime and Punishment, Gender Matters, and Struggling toward Success. We believe students will be engaged by these subjects and that they will write about them with energy and vigor.

Within each of the five thematic chapters we have created "focus sections" which examine a specific cultural issue in greater depth: Videos and Violence, Rap Music, Date Rape, Gay/Lesbian Identities, and Opportunity and Otherness. Having taught these focus sections while working on the second edition, we can say that they allow students both to elaborate and to clarify their spoken and written arguments. They produce debate. They stimulate discussion. They provide the means by which students will produce richer, more textured, and more complex essays—the ultimate goal of first-year composition courses.

In putting together the second edition of *Speculations* we again looked for selections—essays primarily, but also a few stories—that engage readers with the issues, that cry out to be read and reread. We tried hard to select works that have broad appeal, that capture the interests of undergraduates and faculty, majority and minority students, men and women, theorists and practitioners. We hope that the choices in *Speculations* reward your first reading, but even more importantly we hope that they reward subsequent readings. There isn't a selection included that we haven't read at least four or five times, discussed, debated, argued through. That, in fact, was our main test for including a work; if it sustained itself over multiple readings, arguments, and conversations—then it was something we wanted to share with students.

We wanted to create a book that was eminently teachable. In order to allow for more flexibility in the second edition, we included the focus sections—which can be taught entirely on their own—and thereby greatly expanded the range of topics for discussion and consideration. In effect, *Speculations* now features ten thematic units, with essays that amplify and augment each other's analyses and arguments, sometimes quite explicitly. Thus we see Ellis Cose referring directly to Stephen Carter, Katharine Greider responding to Katie Roiphe.

We feel positive as well about the apparatus. The headnotes that introduce selections are as full and informative as we could make them. Because a number of the authors included in *Speculations* are likely to be unfamiliar to instructors as well as to students, we worked doubly hard to provide biographical, historical, and bibliographic information. We also wanted the headnotes to function as windows that open onto the selections that follow. In describing the openings of his own literary journalistic essays, John McPhee has said that a lead should shine a light into the piece. We have similarly tried to shine such a light with our headnotes.

The questions and assignment sequences offer a substantial departure from those in more typical composition anthologies. The questions that accompany selections focus primarily on structure, argument, style, and content. We struggled to articulate fundamental issues by asking questions that do not have simple or correct answers, so as to invite discussion and debate. The end-of-section assignment sequences represent the kind of pedagogy that we have used for years. "Situational sequencing," as we refer to it, asks students to situate themselves within a specific rhetorical context, to engage with the text through role playing and imaginative speculation. For virtually all students, such serious but playful writing is powerful and productive. It forces them to experiment with styles and voices, to write from someone else's point of view, to explore alternative perspectives. As they work their way through a sequence, students engage in what might best be described as conceptual revision; that is, they write an essay and then write on the same subject but from a different perspective or for a different audience, or they work their way through one argument and then apply that same argument to a different text. Given the richness of the selections in this book, we felt that assignment sequences offered the greatest potential for students and instructors to mine the depths.

Most textbook revisions do not change more than a small percentage of the original book. Our revision of *Speculations* breaks that tradition: more than 50 percent of the selections are new. Frankly, making such a sweeping revision in a successful anthology is risky business, but we remain convinced that the changes strengthen the book and create richer opportunities for reading, writing, and discussion. Susan Douglas and Elayne Rapping, for example, offer complementary feminist takes on music and television that are both trenchant and humorous, while Cannon, Krasny, Males, and Leonard offer evidence and argument concerning the moral value of film and television. Venise Berry offers a rare and insightful scholarly analysis of the socio-political and aesthetic dimensions of rap music, one that is complemented by bell hooks but strongly opposed by Arthur Cribb and Jerry Adler. Camille Paglia, Katie Roiphe, Mary Gaitskill, and Katharine Greider provide highly articulate and widely differing approaches to date rape—and they do so using significantly different rhetorical strategies. The same is true in section after section: we have tried to include compelling authors writing about compelling issues in compellingly different and successful ways. Moreover, all the essays and writing sequences included here are timely: we were still inserting selections and assignments even as the book was going into production.

No project of this enormity can be completed without a great deal of help. We have many to whom we owe a debt, but to no one more than Nancy Perry, publisher of Blair Press, who, as always, helped us stay true to course. We greatly appreciate her work and wisdom. As well, we wish to express our thanks to Nancy's assistant, Rosanna Rodriguez, for her indefatigable grace under pressure. René Steinke deserves special mention for her helpful readings of our work and for her research that contributed so much to the author headnotes. We want to thank the dedicated graduate students and staff in the English and Comparative Literature Department at the University of Wisconsin—Milwaukee who provided much needed feedback and support, especially Alice Gillam and Mary Cyrulik. We also want to thank the reviewers and questionnaire respondents, who helped give the book shape and definition: Margo Axsom, Indiana University, South Bend; Richard Batteiger, Oklahoma State University; Jon Beasley-Murray, University of Wisconsin—Milwaukee; Dianne Blaesing, Shasta College; Belinda Bruner, Oklahoma State University; Sandy Camilly, Finger Lakes Community College; Jo Chern, University of Wisconsin—Green Bay; Arlene Clarke, American River

College; Tami L. Conner, Oklahoma State University; James Cooper, Oklahoma State University; Patricia Couillard, University of Wisconsin—Milwaukee; Anna Creadick, Boston College; Steve DeCaroli, University of Wisconsin—Milwaukee; Jana French, University of Wisconsin—Madison; Gwenette Gaddis, Tennessee Technological University; Mike Geurin, University of Oklahoma; Judith I. Hall, Monroe Community College; Mark M. Hammer, Oklahoma State University; Lee Hartman, Howard Community College; Ruth J. Heflin, Oklahoma State University; Janet Henderson, Bergen Community College; Douglas Hesse, Illinois State University; Dorothy Howell, University of North Carolina—Charlotte; Suzanne Kaibnick, State University of New York at Stony Brook; Scott Kelley, University of Oklahoma; Jeff Kersh, Oklahoma State University; Paul Kosidowski, University of Wisconsin—Milwaukee; Patricia W. LaCoste, University of Wisconsin—Milwaukee; Eric Leuschner, Oklahoma State University; Valery E. Neiswonger, Clarion University of Pennsylvania; Stacy Papakonstantino, City College of San Francisco; Christopher J. Parker, Finger Lakes Community College; Brooke Patrick, Oklahoma State University; Lisa Rohrbach, Oklahoma State University; Robert Rosen, William Paterson College; Hephzibah Roskelly, University of North Carolina—Greensboro; Karen Smith, Clarion University of Pennsylvania; Lily Iona Soucie, University of San Francisco; Joan Spangler, California State University—Fullerton; Donna Strickland, University of Wisconsin—Milwaukee; Heidemarie Z. Weidner, Tennessee Technological University; Paul Williams, University of Wisconsin— Milwaukee; and Kristi Yager, University of Wisconsin—Milwaukee.

We owe a great debt as well to the freshmen and sophomores at UWM who inspired us always to rethink our assignments and return one more time to the library to find that elusive essay we needed. In particular, we want to thank the students of English 101, Section 101 (Fall 1994) who tested many of these essays, and assignments in class; in alphabetical order, they are: Ryan Anderson, Shirin Botros, Kevin Budsberg, Tina Carlson, Barrett Dowell, Anna Ferriter, Ahmad Harris, Chris Jordan, Cari Kauth, Brenda Kertscher, Zoran Krecak, Jay Kuntsman, Steve Lindner, Ben Meyer, Mark Nielsen, Elizabeth Polansky, and Jaime Young. They proved to be a smart and demanding pedagogical review board.

Finally we want to thank our families: Patricia Ellis and Jacob Schuster, Mary Mullins and Elizabeth Van Pelt. Anyone who has completed a book knows how all-enveloping the work can be. Our wives and children had to suffer weeks and months of long absences and vacant stares on the part of their husbands and fathers. Perhaps more significantly, they were our first audience, our primary support staff. And they were our inspiration. Without them, *Speculations* would have remained a bunch of scattered pages sitting on a back table.

Charles I. Schuster
William V. Van Pelt

CONTENTS

CHAPTER 4

Gender Matters   335

INTRODUCTION

Speculations provides a diverse collection of readings for students who want to learn more about themselves, their culture, and the changing values of the 1990s. In creating this anthology, our first goal was to find selections that you would enjoy reading and that you would want to read more than once. We tried to create a book that you would keep on your bookshelf long after completing the course for which it was required. Our second goal was to include readings that would challenge you intellectually and stimulate you to think critically about your own cultural history, social background, and personal identity. Many of the ideas presented in this book are controversial and intended to provoke argument and debate. The selections, then, should give you not only pleasure in reading but also pleasure in debating and writing about ideas and issues that are fundamental to the future of our country and our culture. We believe that you and your classmates will have a lot to say about the five areas of modern life that the readings address: Growing Up, Music and Morality, Crime and Punishment, Gender Matters, and Struggling toward Success.

One of the innovative features of this text is that it offers five or six readings on a general theme and then zeroes in on a specific issue related to that theme. Our intention was to offer you and your instructor a wide array of options for reading. You can read generally about the problems of growing up, for example, and then focus on the critics' argument over whether the violent images in our media are contributing to the increasing trend of violence among children and young adults. Or you can read about the struggles of working people to obtain material success, and then focus on a specific debate about affirmative action, race, and prejudice. We think the specificity and the variety of themes will make for exciting discussions and excellent essays based on close reading and analysis.

As you read and write, it is important for you to keep an open mind and study the various essays closely, both for what they say and for how they say it. We encourage you not to form an opinion or argument too quickly; one of the complexities offered by a text like this is that writers with strongly varying views present reasonable and persuasive analyses. It is important for you to read the essays carefully, sorting out fact from opinion, logical argument from emotional appeal and to realize as well that any idea worth arguing over is one that will generate a wide spectrum of responses. Thus, there is no easy answer to whether we should censor television and rap lyrics or what it means to be a criminal or whether certain classes of people should be given job preferences in response to a history of prejudicial treatment. These are subjects that we have debated for years—and which have once again risen to the forefront of our national conversation.

The opening section, Growing Up, presents teenage as well as adult perspectives on how and why parents and children have trouble getting along. Many of you will identify with the stories of resistance to parental and social domination told by writers like Jamaica Kincaid and Amy Tan, both of whom display strong egos and powerful wills to succeed on their own. Other selections may reflect experiences different from yours, but they deal with subjects that you have heard a good deal about, such as Léon Bing's "When You're a Crip (or a Blood)," which vividly describes, in their own words, the lives of gang members in Los Angeles. The focus section that follows Growing Up considers media violence and encourages you to enter into a complex debate that involves issues of morality, censorship, and cause/effect relationships. You will enter into an argument concerning whether a causal relationship exists between TV and movie violence and the violence on our streets and in our neighborhoods, an argument which does not have a simple "yes" or "no" answer.

Music and Morality invites you to consider a range of issues including the argument that rock music ruins the moral education of modern youth, the attitude of rock music toward women, and the suicide of Kurt Cobain. The focus section treats the most controversial of musical forms—rap—with a wide range of critics offering attacks and defenses of this urban, black musical form. Because popular music has become central to American culture, we have devoted Music and Morality entirely to rock and rap—music that most students in first-year composition know a good bit about. We think this knowledge will help you to write with more understanding and authority about a subject that we hope you find compelling.

Crime and Punishment looks at our national obsession with crime and its consequences. What is the nature of crime and criminals? Are these categories of law, or does our definition of the word "criminal" derive from prejudice and socio-economic factors? Jessica Mitford's "The Criminal Type," for example, examines our perceptions of who criminals are and how they are created within our society. Are the causes of criminal behavior biological, behavioral, economic, or social? In "Senseless Crimes," Rick Telander looks at teenage murderers and asks us to ponder difficult questions. Why do kids kill for sports clothes? Should professional athletes promote such products? What is the role of advertising in a society where kids kill for clothes? The focus section considers a topic that has disturbing implications for all college students: date rape. The essayists included here—Ellen Sweet, Camille Paglia, Kate Roiphe, Mary Gaitskill, and Katharine Greider—offer a surprising array of perspectives about this controversial subject. We think you'll want to enter this debate with some writing of your own.

Gender Matters is new to this edition, and it is included in response to many requests from teachers and students who wanted to consider the issue of gender, particularly the subject of gay/lesbian identity. The pun in the title is intentional. Gender matters a great deal, as the essays in this opening section illustrate. From Maxine Hong Kingston's richly imagined account of her aunt's ostracism and suicide in "No Name Woman" to Naomi Wolf's description of the horrifying effects of anorexia and bulimia, the essays examine what it means to be gendered "male" or "female" within contemporary American culture. The focus on Gay/Lesbian Identities invites you to enter into one of the most divisive debates in contemporary society—the debate on homosexuality. Our intention here, quite frankly, is not to question whether gays and lesbians pervert moral and spiritual values; such a question is foolish and it dehumanizes gay and lesbians: our sons and daughters, brothers and sisters. Rather, we have let a variety of voices speak to the essential human bond that exists among all of us regardless of our sexual orientation and to the limits, if any, that should be applied to gays and lesbians in the matters of raising children, serving in the military, and job protection. Given these subjects, we know that you will find a great deal to debate as you read about the consequences of homophobia and heterosexism, the shifting definitions of male and female sexuality, and the treatment of a gay man in the Navy.

Struggling Toward Success examines the world of work with readings that ask you to think about what it means not just to work but to succeed in terms that mean something to you. What are the pleasures as well as the material gains to be derived from work? What is the future work for young people in the United States? Is there an invisible cultural barrier that holds back women, blacks, and other minorities? You'll find many opportunities for discussing these and other questions as you read selections such as Barbara Garson's "McDonald's—We Do It All for You," Studs Terkel's "Mike LeFevre, Steelworker," and Susan Fraker's "Why Women Aren't Getting to the Top." Many of these essays ask you to consider issues of equity and equality, of fairness and value that the focus on Opportunity and Otherness examines in greater detail. The debate here—where the issues revolve around race, affirmative action, and preferential treatment for certain classes of individuals—closely mirrors similar debates that are occurring in state legislatures and in our federal government as the American public considers the benefits, drawbacks, and future of affirmative action legislation.

In addition to the rich diversity of perspectives on American culture in *Speculations*, you will find essays that reflect a variety of genres and styles: personal essays, scholarly essays, newspaper articles, interviews, speeches, short stories, and song lyrics. We chose these diverse forms of writing not just to enhance your pleasure in reading, important as that is, but also because each form has its own way of communicating and making its point. The writing sequences at the end of each section invite you to compose your thoughts and responses in different forms and styles in order to allow you to expand your rhetorical repertoire as a writer and thinker. Some invite you to adopt a particular persona; others ask you to consider a topic from one perspective and then another; still others invite you to do additional research so that you can enter into a particular debate with more authority. Most of the writing suggestions in the sequences build on issues, ideas, or points of view first articulated in the "Speculations" questions that follow each reading selection. Therefore, you should find it useful to return to the "Speculations" questions when considering specific readings that you decide to use in your essays.

As with the reading selections, the writing sequences in this book are designed to encourage you to respond critically to issues and ideas about which you already have some knowledge and understanding. *Speculations* seeks to connect your knowledge and voice to a new experience of academic writing and a new understanding of your identity within the changing values of our society. We encourage you to draw on your personal experience as you voice your own opinion, enter the debate, and learn more about what others have to say. Most importantly, we hope you enjoy reading and speculating about the ideas and perspectives you encounter in this book.

1

GROWING

UP

Most of us experience a paradox about growing up—we can't wait to be finished with it, yet once we've become adults we tend to look back on our childhood as the happiest times of our lives. Unfortunately, this nostalgic image of childhood, this memory of growing up within a loving family with caring parents and affectionate if occasionally pesky siblings, may be more myth than reality. Increasingly we are living with the perception that the difficulties of growing up—poverty, drugs, AIDS, teenage pregnancy, gangs, anger, alienation—reach into every community, regardless of race, color, geography, or income. Even a casual reading of the daily newspaper reminds us of the perils of growing up; of babies abandoned, children abused, parents who seem never to have learned certain fundamental principles of mothering and fathering.

For many critics, the problem is a shift in values that occurred during the past 25 years. Divorce became acceptable. Fathers and mothers abandoned their children, psychologically and sometimes physically. Young adults focused on their own needs, neglecting parental obligations. Extended families were torn apart. Economic strains forced both fathers and mothers to work, creating generations of latch-key, daycare, and home-alone children. Television and Hollywood rotted the minds of young children who stared into TV and movie screens, awash in images of violence, sexuality, and blatant commercialism. Cities were abandoned by the middle class, thus dissolving into economically blighted ghettoes where large numbers of children and their parents found little comfort, no safety, and increasing amounts of despair. The emotional bonds of love among family members became transformed into dubious legal relationships: children and parents wound up in court, accusing each other of emotional abuse, acts of violence, and financial irresponsibility. Or worse yet, antagonisms flared into physical violence and a blunting of emotional sensibilities.

To offer such a stark picture is not to engage in hopelessness. The problems of growing up are real, but so are the solutions. And there is still much to celebrate: America possesses great resources and an almost unlimited reservoir of optimism and resiliency. The selections in this section address both the challenges we face and the means by which we can improve the quality of life for America's greatest resources: its families and its children.

With a range of topics from growing up as an African-American woman, confronting the horror of homelessness, struggling to achieve independence, and articulating the brutality and horrors of gang-life, the writers included here powerfully and eloquently inspire readers to react, respond, and reconsider values and assumptions. We invite you to be part of that discussion.

GIRL

Jamaica Kincaid

Antigua, a small Caribbean island that remained a British colony until 1967, is a sun-drenched exotic locale visited by rich tourists but inhabited by impoverished black families. Jamaica Kincaid described it as "a small place" in her defiant book by that title (1988), one of four that she has published since 1983. Her books offer a collection of brilliantly evoked impressions—of an angry childhood in Antigua, a young girl's sense of betrayal, the relationship between mother and daughter, the experiences of a young black woman hired into a wealthy family in New York City as a live-in housekeeper and childsitter.

Although Kincaid publishes her work as fiction, much of it closely follows the outlines of her own life. As described in a 1990 article in *The New York Times Sunday Magazine,* Kincaid "was born into tropical poverty. Her father was a carpenter and her mother kept house. They had no electricity, no bathroom, no running water. Every Wednesday he registered their outhouse at the Public Works Department so that the 'night soil men,' as they were called, would take away their full tub and replace it with a clean one. And every morning she went to a public pipe and drew four pails of water for her mother—more if it was a washday." These and other duties occupied much of Kincaid's life, even during her school years when she learned to love to read, pursuing her desire to own books past the point of recklessness. "Books," she said, "brought me the greatest satisfaction . . . I stole books, and I stole money to buy them."

In her writing, Kincaid manages to be defiant and outraged about life's injustices and yet celebratory and lyrical. A meticulous stylist who may spend hours choosing the right word, Kincaid has crafted some of the most beautiful sentences in the English language. "Girl," set in Antigua, is the first piece Jamaica Kincaid ever published; it appeared in *The New Yorker,* which has published her work ever since.

Wash the white clothes on Monday and put them on the stone heap; wash the color clothes on Tuesday and put them on the clothesline to dry; don't walk barehead in the hot sun; cook pumpkin fritters in very hot sweet oil; soak your little cloths right after you take them off; when buying cotton to make yourself a nice blouse, be sure that it doesn't have gum on it, because that way it won't hold up well after a wash; soak salt fish overnight before you cook it; is it true that you sing benna in Sunday school?; always eat your food in such a way that it won't turn someone else's stomach; on Sundays try to walk like a lady and not like the slut you are so bent on becoming; don't sing benna in

Sunday school; you mustn't speak to wharf-rat boys, not even to give directions; don't eat fruits on the street—flies will follow you; *but I don't sing benna on Sundays at all and never in Sunday school;* this is how to sew on a button; this is how to make a button-hole for the button you have just sewed on; this is how to hem a dress when you see the hem coming down and so to prevent yourself from looking like the slut I know you are so bent on becoming; this is how you iron your father's khaki shirt so that it doesn't have a crease; this is how you iron your father's khaki pants so that they don't have a crease; this is how you grow okra—far from the house, because okra tree harbors red ants; when you are growing dasheen, make sure it gets plenty of water or else it makes your throat itch when you are eating it; this is how you sweep a corner; this is how you sweep a whole house; this is how you sweep a yard; this is how you smile to someone you don't like too much; this is how you smile to someone you don't like at all; this is how you smile to someone you like completely; this is how you set a table for tea; this is how you set a table for dinner; this is how you set a table for dinner with an important guest; this is how you set a table for lunch; this is how you set a table for breakfast; this is how to behave in the presence of men who don't know you very well, and this way they won't recognize immediately the slut I have warned you against becoming; be sure to wash every day, even if it is with your own spit; don't squat down to play marbles—you are not a boy, you know; don't pick people's flowers—you might catch something; don't throw stones at blackbirds, because it might not be a blackbird at all; this is how to make a bread pudding; this is how to make doukona; this is how to make pepper pot; this is how to make a good medicine for a cold; this is how to make a good medicine to throw away a child before it even becomes a child; this is how to catch a fish; this is how to throw back a fish you don't like, and that way something bad won't fall on you; this is how to bully a man; this is how a man bullies you; this is how to love a man, and if this doesn't work there are other ways, and if they don't work don't feel too bad about giving up; this is how to spit up in the air if you feel like it, and this is how to move quick so that it doesn't fall on you; this is how to make ends meet; always squeeze bread to make sure it's fresh; *but what if the baker won't let me feel the bread?;* you mean to say that after all you are really going to be the kind of woman who the baker won't let near the bread?

Speculations

1. In "Girl," Jamaica Kincaid presents a relationship between a mother and daughter. How does she accomplish this portrayal? Why do you think Kincaid chooses this particular form to ex-

press this relationship? Who do you think is speaking? Who is the listener?

2. What kind of a life is being described here? What is the scene that is described? How important is the locale to "Girl"?

3. How does "advice" function in "Girl"? What does it suggest about the relationship?

4. What do you think is intended by the words in italics? Why do you think Kincaid wrote "Girl" all as one sentence, using italics, not using any paragraphs? What is the effect of this form on you as a reader?

5. How does repetition function in the piece to establish both rhythm and meaning?

6. What genre do you think best describes "Girl"? That is, is "Girl" an essay, a story, a prose poem? Is it fiction or nonfiction? Does its form influence the way you read and understand it?

TWO KINDS

Amy Tan

Amy Tan was born in 1952 in Oakland, California, shortly after her parents arrived in the United States from China. Like the children of most immigrants to America, Tan had to come to terms with living on the outside of two cultures—that is, being neither Chinese nor American—and yet identifying strongly with both. Typically, Tan's mother held high aspirations for her daughter: she wanted her to become a neurosurgeon. Instead, Tan, who resides in San Francisco, has become one of the brightest stars on the literary horizon. Her books include *The Joy Luck Club* (1989), which was made into a highly acclaimed motion picture in 1993; *The Moon Lady* (1992); *The Kitchen God's Wife* (1992); and *The Chinese Siamese Cat* (1994).

During her adolescence, Tan discovered that she had two half-sisters, left behind, by her mother, in China, after the Red Army invaded Beijing. Twenty-two years later, Amy Tan wrote about her family in *The Joy Luck Club*. Through sixteen interconnected stories told by four Chinese-born mothers and their four American-born daughters, Tan presents two generations of tough, intelligent, resourceful women trying to come to terms with their identities, aspirations, losses, and successes.

The central character of *The Joy Luck Club* is Jing-mei (June) Woo, who closely resembles Amy Tan. Ultimately June must travel to Shanghai to meet with her half-sisters and answer their inevitable questions about their mother—about June's mother. In the following selection from the book, Jing-mei Woo and her mother struggle over their conflicting notions of identity, ambition, success, and selfhood.

My mother believed you could be anything you wanted to be in America. You could open a restaurant. You could work for the government and get good retirement. You could buy a house with almost no money down. You could become rich. You could become instantly famous.

"Of course you can be prodigy, too," my mother told me when I was nine. "You can be best anything. What does Auntie Lindo know? Her daughter, she is only best tricky."

America was where all my mother's hopes lay. She had come here in 1949 after losing everything in China: her mother and father, her family home, her first husband, and two daughters, twin baby girls. But she never looked back with regret. There were so many ways for things to get better.

We didn't immediately pick the right kind of prodigy. At first my mother thought I could be a Chinese Shirley Temple. We'd watch Shirley's old movies on TV as though they were training films. My mother would poke my arm and say, *"Ni Kan"*—You watch. And I would see Shirley tapping her feet, or singing a sailor song, or pursing her lips into a very round O while saying, "Oh my goodness."

"Ni kan," said my mother as Shirley's eyes flooded with tears. "You already know how. Don't need talent for crying!"

Soon after my mother got this idea about Shirley Temple, she took me to a beauty training school in the Mission district and put me in the hands of a student who could barely hold the scissors without shaking. Instead of getting big fat curls, I emerged with an uneven mass of crinkly black fuzz. My mother dragged me off to the bathroom and tried to wet down my hair.

"You look like Negro Chinese," she lamented, as if I had done this on purpose.

The instructor of the beauty training school had to lop off these soggy clumps to make my hair even again. "Peter Pan is very popular these days," the instructor assured my mother. I now had hair the length of a boy's, with straight-across bangs that hung at a slant two inches above my eyebrows. I liked the haircut and it made me actually look forward to my future fame.

In fact, in the beginning, I was just as excited as my mother, maybe even more so. I pictured this prodigy part of me as many different images, trying each one on for size. I was a dainty ballerina girl standing by the curtains, waiting to hear the right music that would send me floating on my tiptoes. I was like the Christ child lifted out of the straw manger, crying with holy indignity. I was Cinderella stepping from her pumpkin carriage with sparkly cartoon music filling the air.

In all of my imagingings, I was filled with a sense that I would soon become *perfect*. My mother and father would adore me. I would be beyond reproach. I would never feel the need to sulk for anything.

But sometimes the prodigy in me became impatient. "If you don't hurry up and get me out of here, I'm disappearing for good," it warned. "And then you'll always be nothing."

Every night after dinner, my mother and I would sit at the Formica kitchen table. She would present new tests, taking her examples from stories of amazing children she had read in *Ripley's Believe It or Not*, or *Good Housekeeping, Reader's Digest*, and a dozen other magazines she kept in a pile in our bathroom. My mother got these magazines from people whose houses she cleaned. And since she cleaned many houses each week, we had a great assortment. She would look through them all, searching for stories about remarkable children.

The first night she brought out a story about a three-year-old boy who knew the capitals of all the states and even most of the European countries. A teacher was quoted as saying the little boy could also pronounce the names of the foreign cities correctly.

"What's the capital of Finland?" my mother asked me, looking at the magazine story.

All I knew was the capital of California, because Sacramento was the name of the street we lived on in Chinatown. "Nairobi!" I guessed, saying the most foreign word I could think of. She checked to see if that was possibly one way to pronounce "Helsinki" before showing me the answer.

The tests got harder—multiplying numbers in my head, finding the queen of hearts in a deck of cards, trying to stand on my head without using my hands, predicting the daily temperatures in Los Angeles, New York, and London.

One night I had to look at a page from the Bible for three minutes and then report everything I could remember. "Now Jehosphaphat had riches and honor in abundance and . . . that's all I remember, Ma," I said.

And after seeing my mother's disappointed face once again, something inside of me began to die. I hated the tests, the raised hopes and failed expectations. Before going to bed that night, I looked in the mirror above the bathroom sink and when I saw only my face staring back—and that it would always be this ordinary face—I began to cry. Such a sad, ugly girl! I made high-pitched noises like a crazed animal, trying to scratch out the face in the mirror.

And then I saw what seemed to be the prodigy side of me—because I had never seen that face before. I looked at my reflection, blinking so I could see more clearly. The girl staring back at me was angry, powerful. This girl and I were the same. I had new thoughts, willful thoughts, or rather thoughts filled with lots of won'ts. I won't let her change me, I promised myself. I won't be what I'm not.

So now on nights when my mother presented her tests, I performed listlessly, my head propped on one arm. I pretended to be bored. And I was. I got so bored I started counting the bellows of the foghorns out on the bay while my mother drilled me in other areas. The sound was comforting and reminded me of the cow jumping over the moon. And the next day, I played a game with myself, seeing if my mother would give up on be before eight bellows. After a while I usually counted only one, maybe two bellows at most. At last she was beginning to give up hope.

Two or three months had gone by without any mention of my being a prodigy again. And then one day my mother was watching "The Ed Sullivan Show" on TV. The TV was old and the sound kept shorting out. Every time my mother got halfway up from the sofa to adjust the set, the sound would go back on and Ed would be talking. As soon as she sat down, Ed would go silent again. She got up, the TV broke into loud piano music. She sat down. Silence. Up and down, back and forth, quiet and loud. It was like a stiff embraceless dance between her and the TV set. Finally she stood by the set with her hand on the sound dial.

She seemed entranced by the music, a little frenzied piano piece with this mesmerizing quality, sort of quick passages and then teasing lilting ones before it returned to the quick playful parts.

"*Ni kan*," my mother said, calling me over with hurried hand gestures. "Look here."

I could see why my mother was fascinated by the music. It was being pounded out by a little Chinese girl, about nine years old, with a Peter Pan haircut. The girl had the sauciness of a Shirley Temple. She was proudly modest like a proper Chinese child. And she also did this fancy sweep of a curtsy, so that the fluffy skirt of her white dress cascaded slowly to the floor like the petals of a large carnation.

In spite of these warnings signs, I wasn't worried. Our family had no piano and we couldn't afford to buy one, let alone reams of sheet music and piano lessons. So I could be generous in my comments when my mother bad-mouthed the little girl on TV.

"Play note right, but doesn't sound good! No singing sound," complained my mother.

"What are you picking on her for?" I said carelessly. "She's pretty good. Maybe she's not the best, but she's trying hard." I knew almost immediately I would be sorry I said that.

"Just like you," she said. "Not the best. Because you not trying."
She gave a little huff as she let go of the sound dial and sat down on
the sofa.

The little Chinese girl sat down also to play an encore of "Anitra's
Dance" by Grieg. I remember the song, because later on I had to learn
how to play it.

Three days after watching "The Ed Sullivan Show," my mother told
me what my schedule would be for piano lessons and piano practice.
She had talked to Mr. Chong, who lived on the first floor of our apartment building. Mr. Chong was a retired piano teacher and my mother
had traded housecleaning services for weekly lessons and a piano for
me to practice on every day, two hours a day, from four until six.

When my mother told me this, I felt as though I had been sent to
hell. I whined and then kicked my foot a little when I couldn't stand it
anymore.

"Why don't you like me the way I am? I'm *not* a genius! I can't play
the piano. And even if I could, I wouldn't go on TV if you paid me a
million dollars!" I cried.

My mother slapped me. "Who ask you be genius?" she shouted.
"Only ask you be your best. For you sake. You think I want you be genius? Hnnh! What for! Who ask you!"

"So ungrateful," I heard her mutter in Chinese. "If she had as much
talent as she has temper, she would be famous now."

Mr. Chong, whom I secretly nicknamed Old Chong, was very
strange, always tapping his fingers to the silent music of an invisible
orchestra. He looked ancient in my eyes. He had lost most of the hair
on top of his head and he wore thick glasses and had eyes that always
looked tired and sleepy. But he must have been younger than I
thought, since he lived with his mother and was not yet married.

I met Old Lady Chong once and that was enough. She had this peculiar smell like a baby that had done something in its pants. And her
fingers felt like a dead person's, like an old peach I once found in the
back of the refrigerator; the skin just slid off the meat when I picked it
up.

I soon found out why Old Chong had retired from teaching piano.
He was deaf. "Like Beethoven!" he shouted to me. "We're both listening only in our head!" And he would start to conduct his frantic silent
sonatas.

Our lessons went like this. He would open the book and point to
different things, explaining their purpose: "Key! Treble! Bass! No
sharps or flats! So this is C major! Listen now and play after me!"

And then he would play the C scale a few times, a simple chord,
and then, as if inspired by an old, unreachable itch, he gradually added

more notes and running trills and a pounding bass until the music was really something quite grand.

I would play after him, the simple scale, the simple chord and then I just played some nonsense that sounded like a cat running up and down on top of garbage cans. Old Chong smiled and applauded and then said, "Very good! But now you must learn to keep time!"

So that's how I discovered that Old Chong's eyes were too slow to keep up with the wrong notes I was playing. He went through the motions in half-time. To help me keep rhythm, he stood behind me, pushing down on my right shoulder for every beat. He balanced pennies on top of my wrists so I would keep them still as I slowly played scales and arpeggios. He had me curve my hand around an apple and keep that shape when playing chords. He marched stiffly to show me how to make each finger dance up and down, staccato like an obedient little solider.

He taught me all these things, and that was how I also learned I could be lazy and get away with mistakes, lots of mistakes. If I hit the wrong notes because I hadn't practiced enough, I never corrected myself. I just kept playing in rhythm. And Old Chong kept conducting his own private reverie.

So maybe I never really gave myself a fair chance. I did pick up the basics pretty quickly, and I might have become a good pianist at that young age. But I was so determined not to try, not to be anybody different that I learned to play only the most ear-splitting preludes, the most discordant hymns.

Over the next year, I practiced like this, dutifully in my own way. And then one day I heard my mother and her friend Lindo Jong both talking in a loud bragging tone of voice so others could hear. It was after church, and I was leaning against the brick wall wearing a dress with stiff white petticoats. Auntie Lindo's daughter, Waverly, who was about my age, was standing farther down the wall about five feet away. We had grown up together and shared all the closeness of two sisters squabbling over crayons and dolls. In other words, for the most part, we hated each other. I thought she was snotty. Waverly Jong had gained a certain amount of fame as "Chinatown's Littlest Chinese Chess Champion."

"She bring home too many trophy," lamented Auntie Lindo that Sunday. "All day she play chess. All day I have no time do nothing but dust off her winnings." She threw a scolding look at Waverly, who pretended not to see her.

"You lucky you don't have this problem," said Auntie Lindo with a sigh to my mother.

And my mother squared her shoulders and bragged: "Our problem worser than yours. If we ask Jing-mei wash dish, she hear nothing but music. It's like you can't stop this natural talent."

And right then, I was determined to put a stop to her foolish pride.

A few weeks later, Old Chong and my mother conspired to have me play in a talent show which would be held in the church hall. By then, my parents had saved up enough to buy me a secondhand piano, a black Wurlitzer spinet with a scarred bench. It was the showpiece of our living room.

For the talent show, I was to play a piece called "Pleading Child" from Schumann's *Scenes from Childhood.* It was a simple, moody piece that sounded more difficult than it was. I was supposed to memorize the whole thing, playing the repeat parts twice to make the piece sound longer. But I dawdled over it, playing a few bars and then cheating, looking up to see what notes followed, I never really listened to what I was playing. I daydreamed about being somewhere else, about being someone else.

The part I liked to practice best was the fancy curtsy: right foot out, touch the rose on the carpet with a pointed foot, sweep to the side, left leg bends, look up and smile.

My parents invited all the couples from the Joy Luck Club to witness my debut. Auntie Lindo and Uncle Tin were there. Waverly and her two older brothers had also come. The first two rows were filled with children both younger and older than I was. The littlest ones got to go first. They recited simple nursery rhythms, squawked out tunes on miniature violins, twirled Hula Hoops, pranced in pink ballet tutus, and when they bowed or curtsied, the audience would sigh in unison, "Awww," and then clap enthusiastically.

When my turn came, I was very confident. I remember my childish excitement. It was as if I knew, without a doubt, that the prodigy side of me really did exist. I had no fear whatsoever, no nervousness. I remember thinking to myself, This is it! This is it! I looked out over the audience, at my mother's blank face, my father's yawn, Auntie Lindo's stiff-lipped smile, Waverly's sulky expression. I had on a white dress layered with sheets of lace, and a pink bow in my Peter Pan haircut. As I sat down I envisioned people jumping to their feet and Ed Sullivan rushing up to introduce me to everyone on TV.

And I started to play. It was so beautiful. I was so caught up in how lovely I looked that at first I didn't worry how I would sound: So it was a surprise to me when I hit the first wrong note and I realized something didn't sound quite right. And then I hit another and another followed that. A chill started at the top of my head and began to trickle down. Yet I couldn't stop playing, as though my hands were bewitched. I kept thinking my fingers would adjust themselves back, like a train switching to the right track. I played this strange jumble through two repeats, the sour notes staying with me all the way to the end.

When I stood up, I discovered my legs were shaking. Maybe I had just been nervous and the audience, like Old Chong, had seen me go through the right motions and had not heard anything wrong at all. I swept my right foot out, went down on my knee, looked up and smiled. The room was quiet, except for Old Chong, who was beaming and shouting, "Bravo! Bravo! Well done!" But then I saw my mother's face, her stricken face. The audience clapped weakly, and as I walked back to my chair, with my whole face quivering as I tried not to cry, I heard a little boy whisper loudly to his mother, "That was awful," and the mother whispered back, "Well, she certainly tried."

And now I realized how many people were in the audience, the whole world it seemed. I was aware of eyes burning into my back. I felt the shame of my mother and father as they sat stiffly throughout the rest of the show.

We could have escaped during intermission. Pride and some strange sense of honor must have anchored my parents to their chairs. And so we watched it all: the eighteen-year-old boy with a fake mustache who did a magic show and juggled flaming hoops while riding a unicycle. The breasted girl with white makeup who sang from *Madama Butterfly* and got honorable mention. And the eleven-year-old boy who won first prize playing a tricky violin song that sounded like a busy bee.

After the show, the Hsus, the Jongs, and the St. Clairs from the Joy Luck Club came up to my mother and father.

"Lots of talented kids," Auntie Lindo said vaguely, smiling broadly.

"That was somethin' else," said my father, and I wondered if he was referring to me in a humorous way, or whether he even remembered what I had done.

Waverly looked at me and shrugged her shoulders. "You aren't a genius like me," she said matter-of-factly. And if I hadn't felt so bad, I would have pulled her braids and punched her stomach.

But my mother's expression was what devastated me: a quiet, blank look that said she had lost everything. I felt the same way, and it seemed as if everybody were now coming up, like gawkers at the scene of an accident, to see what parts were actually missing. When we got on the bus to go home, my father was humming the busy-bee tune and my mother was silent. I kept thinking she wanted to wait until we got home before shouting at me. But when my father unlocked the door to our apartment, my mother walked in and then went to the back, into the bedroom. No accusations. No blame. And in a way, I felt disappointed. I had been waiting for her to start shouting, so I could shout back and cry and blame her for all my misery.

I assumed by talent-show fiasco meant I never had to play the piano again. But two days later, after school, my mother came out of the kitchen and saw me watching TV.

"Four clock," she reminded me as if it were any other day. I was stunned, as though she were asking me to go through the talent-show torture again. I wedged myself more tightly in front of the TV.

"Turn off TV," she called from the kitchen five minutes later.

I didn't budge. And then I decided. I didn't have to do what my mother said anymore. I wasn't her slave. This wasn't China. I had listened to her before and look what happened. She was the stupid one.

She came out from the kitchen and stood in the arched entryway of the living room. "Four clock," she said once again, louder.

"I'm not going to play anymore," I said nonchalantly. "Why should I? I'm not a genius."

She walked over and stood in front of the TV. I saw her chest was heaving up and down in an angry way.

"No!" I said, and I now felt stronger, as if my true self had finally emerged. So this was what had been inside me all along.

"No! I won't!" I screamed.

She yanked me by the arm, pulled me off the floor, snapped off the TV. She was frighteningly strong, half pulling, half carrying me toward the piano as I kicked the throw rugs under my feet. She lifted me up and onto the hard bench. I was sobbing by now, looking at her bitterly. Her chest was heaving even more and her mouth was open, smiling crazily as if she were pleased I was crying.

"You want me to be someone that I'm not!" I sobbed. "I'll never be the kind of daughter you want me to be!"

"Only two kinds of daughters," she shouted in Chinese. "Those who are obedient and those who follow their own mind! Only one kind of daughter can live in this house. Obedient daughter!"

"Then I wish I wasn't your daughter. I wish you weren't my mother," I shouted. As I said these things I got scared. I felt like worms and toads and slimy things were crawling out of my chest, but it also felt good, as if this awful side of me had surfaced, at last.

"Too late change this," said my mother shrilly.

And I could sense her anger rising to its breaking point. I wanted to see it spill over. And that's when I remembered the babies she had lost in China, the ones we never talked about. "Then I wish I'd never been born!" I shouted. "I wish I were dead! Like them."

It was as if I had said the magic words. Alakazam!—and her face went blank, her mouth closed, her arms went slack, and she backed out of the room, stunned, as if she were blowing away like a small brown leaf, thin, brittle, lifeless.

It was not the only disappointment my mother felt in me. In the years that followed, I failed her so many times, each time asserting my own will, my right to fall short of expectations. I didn't get straight A's. I didn't become class president. I didn't get into Stanford. I dropped out of college.

For unlike my mother, I did not believe I could be anything I wanted to be. I could only be me.

And for all those years, we never talked about the disaster at the recital or my terrible accusations afterward at the piano bench. All that remained unchecked, like a betrayal that was now unspeakable. So I never found a way to ask her why she had hoped for something so large that failure was inevitable.

And even worse, I never asked her what frightened me the most: Why had she given up hope?

For after our struggle at the piano, she never mentioned my playing again. The lessons stopped. The lid to the piano was closed, shutting out the dust, my misery, and her dreams.

So she surprised me. A few years ago, she offered to give me the piano, for my thirtieth birthday. I had not played in all those years. I saw the offer as a sign of forgiveness, a tremendous burden removed.

"Are you sure?" I asked shyly. "I mean, won't you and Dad miss it?"

"No, this your piano," she said firmly. "Always your piano. You only one can play."

"Well, I probably can't play anymore," I said. "It's been years."

"You pick up fast," said my mother, as if she knew this was certain. "You have natural talent. You could been genius if you want to."

"No I couldn't."

"You just not trying," said my mother. And she was neither angry nor sad. She said it as if to announce a fact that could never be disproved. "Take it," she said.

But I didn't at first. It was enough that she had offered it to me. And after that, every time I saw it in my parents' living room, standing in front of the bay windows, it made me feel proud, as if it were a shiny trophy I had won back.

Last week I sent a tuner over to my parents' apartment and had the piano reconditioned, for purely sentimental reasons. My mother had died a few months before and I had been getting things in order for my father, a little bit at a time. I put the jewelry in special silk pouches. The sweaters she had knitted in yellow, pink, bright orange—all the colors I hated—I put those in moth-proof boxes. I found some old Chinese silk dresses, the kind with little slits up the sides. I rubbed the old silk against my skin, then wrapped them in tissue and decided to take them home with me.

After I had the piano tuned, I opened the lid and touched the keys. It sounded even richer than I remembered. Really, it was a very good piano. Inside the bench were the same exercise notes with handwritten scales, the same secondhand music books with their covers held together with yellow tape.

I opened up the Schumann book to the dark little piece I had played at the recital. It was on the left-hand side of the page. "Pleading Child." It looked more difficult than I remembered. I played a few bars, surprised at how easily the notes came back to me.

And for the first time, or so it seemed, I noticed the piece on the right-hand side. It was called "Perfectly Contented." I tried to play this one as well. It had a lighter melody but the same flowing rhythm and turned out to be quite easy. "Pleading Child" was shorter but slower; "Perfectly Contented" was longer but faster. And after I played them both a few times, I realized they were two halves of the same song.

Speculations

1. Why is the mother in this story so determined to make her daughter into a prodigy? What attitudes are typical of immigrants? of Chinese parents? of most or all parents?
2. Tan uses a lot of detail in this story: Shirley Temple, the Formica kitchen table, "The Ed Sullivan Show," magazine titles, descriptions of various characters, titles of musical compositions. Why do you think she does this? What effects do these kinds of details have on you as you read?
3. Throughout "Two Kinds," there is a debate between mother and daughter as to whether the daughter is trying hard enough. How would you analyze her motivations, seriousness, willingness to please her mother? What are her qualifications to be a genius as the mother tells her long after she has grown up? Do you believe that the narrator at the end of the story was actually able to play "Pleading Child" and "Perfectly Contended"—and what does she mean by saying that "they were two halves of the same song?"
4. The narrator's mother states that there are two kinds of daughters: "Those who are obedient and those who follow their own mind!" How does the narrator react? How would you react? When the daughter retorts, "I wish I were dead! Like them," why is the mother stunned, silenced, defeated?
5. Can you describe your own relation to what your parent(s) want(s) for you? How do you sort out what you want for yourself from what your mother or father wants for you?

CHILDHOOD'S END

David Elkind

A specialist in child development, David Elkind is a professor of psychology and chair of the Department of Child Study at Tufts University. Educated at UCLA, Elkind is a member of the American Psychological Association and other professional organizations, including the Society for the Scientific Study of Religion.

Born in Michigan in 1931, David Elkind has devoted his professional life to the study of children. His list of publications includes translating and editing the work of famed child researcher Jean Piaget and authoring books of his own such as *Exploitation in Middle Class Delinquency: Issues in Human Development* (1971), *Child Development and Education* (1976), *The Child and Society* (1979), *Mis-Education: Preschoolers at Risk* (1987), *Images of the Young Child: Collected Essays* (1993), *Parenting Your Teenager in the Nineties* (1994), and *The Ties that Stress: The New Family Imbalance* (1994).

The selection reprinted here is an excerpt from *The Hurried Child*, a book published in 1989 that analyzes the American family's obsession with pushing children headlong into adulthood without taking the necessary time to allow children to enjoy childhood for its own sake.

The concept of childhood, so vital to the traditional American way of life, is threatened with extinction in the society we have created. Today's child has become the unwilling, unintended victim of overwhelming stress—the stress borne of rapid, bewildering social change and constantly rising expectations. The contemporary parent dwells in a pressure-cooker of competing demands, transitions, role changes, personal and professional uncertainties, over which he or she exerts slight direction. We seek release from stress whenever we can, and usually the one sure ambit of our control is the home. Here, if nowhere else, we enjoy the fact (or illusion) of playing a determining role. If child-rearing necessarily entails stress, then by hurrying children to grow up, or by treating them as adults, we hope to remove a portion of our burden of worry and anxiety and to enlist our children's aid in carrying life's load. We do not mean our children harm in acting thus—on the contrary, as a society we have come to imagine that it is good for young people to mature rapidly. Yet we do our children harm when we hurry them through childhood.

The principal architect of our modern notion of childhood was the French philosopher Jean-Jacques Rousseau. It was he who first criticized the educational methods for presenting materials from a uniquely adult perspective, reflecting adult values and interests. Classical *paideia*—that is, the value of transmitting a cultural-social heritage—was a good thing, said Rousseau, but the learning process must take the child's perceptions and stage of development into account. In his classic work *Emile*, Rousseau wrote, "Childhood has its own way of seeing, thinking, and feeling, and nothing is more foolish than to try to substitute ours for theirs." More specifically, he observed that children matured in four stages, and just as each stage had its own characteristics, it should also have a corresponding set of appropriate educational objectives.[1]

---

[1] J.-J. Rousseau, *Emile*. New York: Dutton, 1957.

This idea of childhood as a distinct phase preceding adult life became inextricably interwoven with the modern concepts of universal education and the small, nuclear family (mother, father, children—not the extended family of earlier eras) in the late eighteenth and early nineteenth centuries, the heyday of the original Industrial Revolution. The transition is well explained by futurologist Alvin Toffler: "As work shifted out of the fields and the home, children had to be prepared for factory life. . . . If young people could be prefitted in the industrial system, it would vastly ease the problems of industrial discipline later on. The result was another central structure of all [modern] societies: mass education."[2]

In addition to free, universal, public education, the emergent society tended to create smaller family units. Toffler writes, "To free workers for factory labor, key functions of the family were parcelled out to new specialized institutions. Education of the child was turned over to schools. Care of the aged was turned over to the poor houses or old-age homes or nursing homes. Above all, the new society required mobility. It needed workers who would follow jobs from place to place. . . . Torn apart by migration to the cities, battered by economic storms, families stripped themselves of unwanted relatives, grew smaller, more mobile, more suited to the needs of the [work place].[3]

Miniature Adults

Today's pressures on middle-class children to grow up fast begin in early childhood. Chief among them is the pressure for early intellectual attainment, deriving from a changed perception of precocity. Several decades ago precocity was looked upon with great suspicion. The child prodigy, it was thought, turned out to be a neurotic adult; thus the phrase "early ripe, early rot!" Trying to accelerate children's acquisition of academic skills was seen as evidence of bad parenting.

A good example of this type of attitude is provided by the case of William James Sidis, the son of a psychiatrist. Sidis was born at the turn of the century and became a celebrated child prodigy who entered Harvard College at the age of eleven. His papers on higher mathematics gave the impression that he would make major contributions in this area. Sidis soon attracted the attention of the media, who celebrated his feats as a child. But Sidis never went further and seemed to move aimlessly from one job to another. In 1930 James Thurber wrote a profile of Sidis in the *New Yorker* magazine entitled "Where Are They Now?"; he described Sidis's lonely and pitiful existence in which his major preoccupation was collecting streetcar transfers from all over the world.

---

[2] A. Toffler, *The Third Wave.* New York: Bantam, 1980.
[3] *Ibid.*

Such attitudes, however, changed markedly during the 1960s when parents were bombarded with professional and semiprofessional dicta on the importance of learning in the early years. If you did not start teaching children when they were young, parents were told, a golden opportunity for learning would be lost. Today, tax-supported kindergartens are operating in almost every state, and children are admitted at increasingly earlier ages. (In many cities a child born before January 1 can enter kindergarten the preceding September, making his or her effective entrance age four.) Once enrolled in kindergarten, children are now often presented with formal instruction in reading and math once reserved for the later grades.

How did this radical turnabout in attitudes happen? There are probably many reasons, but a major one was the attack on "progressive" education that occurred in the fifties and that found much educational material dated. The Russian launching of the Sputnik in 1957 drove Americans into a frenzy of self-criticism about education and promoted the massive curriculum movement of the 1960s that brought academics from major universities into curriculum writing. Unfortunately, many academics knew their discipline but didn't know children and were unduly optimistic about how fast and how much children could learn. This optimism was epitomized in Jerome Bruner's famous phrase. "That any subject can be taught effectively in some intellectually honest form to any child at any stage of development."[4] What a shift from "early ripe, early rot"!

One consequence of all this concern for the early years was the demise of the "readiness" concept. The concept of readiness had been extolled by developmental psychologists such as Arnold Gesell who argued for the biological limitations on learning.[8] Gesell believed that children were not biologically ready for learning to read until they had attained a Mental Age (a test score in which children are credited with a certain number of months for each correct answer) of six and one-half years. But the emphasis on early intervention and early intellectual stimulation (even of infants) made the concept of readiness appear

---

[4] J. Bruner, *The Process of Education*. Cambridge, Massachusetts: Harvard University Press, 1960.

The trend toward early academic pressure was further supported by the civil rights movement, which highlighted the poor performance of disadvantaged children in our schools. Teachers were under attack by avant-garde educators such as John Holt,[5] Jonathan Kozol,[6] and Herbert Kohl,[7] and they were forced to defend their lack of success by shifting the blame. Their children did not do well because they came inadequately prepared. It was not what was going on in the classroom but what had not gone on at home that was the root of academic failure among the disadvantaged; hence Headstart, hence busing, which by integrating students would equalize background differences.

[5] J. C. Holt, *How Children Fail*. New York: Pitman, 1964.

[6] J. Kozol, *Death at an Early Age*. Boston: Houghton Mifflin, 1967.

[7] H. R. Kohl, *36 Children*. New York: New American Library, 1967.

[8] Arnold L. Gesell, Louise B. Ames, and Frances L. Ilg, *Infant and Child in the Culture of Today*. New York: Harper & Row, 1943.

dated and old-fashioned. In professional educational circles readiness, once an honored educational concept, is now in disrepute.

The pressure for early academic achievement is but one of many contemporary pressures on children to grow up fast. Children's dress is another. Three or four decades ago, prepubescent boys wore short pants and knickers until they began to shave; getting a pair of long pants was true rite of passage. Girls were not permitted to wear make-up or sheer stockings until they were in their teens. For both sexes, clothing set children apart. It signaled adults that these people were to be treated differently, perhaps indulgently; it made it easier for children to act as children. Today even preschool children wear miniature versions of adult clothing. From overalls to LaCoste shirts to scaled-down designer fashions, a whole range of adult costumes is available to children. (Along with them is a wide choice of corresponding postures such as those of young teenagers modeling designer jeans.) Below is an illustration from a recent article by Susan Ferraro entitled "Hotsy Totsy."

> It was a party like any other; ice cream and cake, a donkey poster and twelve haphazard tails, and a door prize for everyone including Toby, the birthday girl's little brother who couldn't do anything but smear icing.
>
> "Ooh," sighed seven-year-old Melissa as she opened her first present. It was Calvin Klein jeans. "Aah," she gasped as the second box revealed a bright new top from Gloria Vanderbilt. There were Christian Dior undies from grandma—a satiny little chemise and matching bloomer bottoms—and mother herself had fallen for a marvelous party outfit from Yves St. Laurent. Melissa's best friend gave her an Izod sports shirt, complete with alligator emblem. Added to that a couple of books were, indeed, very nice and predictable—except for the fancy doll one guest's eccentric mother insisted on bringing.[9]

When children dress like adults they are more likely to behave as adults do, to imitate adult actions. It is hard to walk like an adult male wearing corduroy knickers that make an awful noise. But boys in long pants can walk like men, and little girls in tight jeans can walk like women. It is more difficult today to recognize that children are children and not miniature adults, because children dress and move like adults.

Another evidence of the pressure to grow up fast is the change in the programs of summer camps for children. Although there are still many summer camps that offer swimming, sailing, horseback riding, archery, and camp fires—activities we remember from our own childhood—an increasing number of summer camps offer specialized training in many different areas, including foreign languages, tennis, baseball, dance, music, and even computers.

---

[9] S. Ferraro, "Hotsy Totsy," *American Way Magazine*, April, 1981, p. 61.

Among such camps the most popular seem to be those that specialize in competitive sports: softball, weight training, tennis, golf, football, basketball, hockey, soccer, lacrosse, gymnastics, wrestling, judo, figure skating, surfing. "Whatever the sport there's a camp (or ten or a hundred of them) dedicated to teaching the finer points. Often these camps are under the direction, actual or nominal, of a big name in a particular sport, and many have professional athletes on their staffs. The daily routine is rigorous, with individual and/or group lessons, practice sessions and tournaments, complete with trophies. And, to cheer the athletes on with more pep and polish, cheerleaders and song girls can also attend."[10]

The change in the programs of summer camps reflects the new attitude that the years of childhood are not to be frittered away by engaging in activities merely for fun. Rather, the years are to be used to perfect skills and abilities that are the same as those of adults. Children are early initiated into the rigors of adult competition. Competitive sports for children are becoming ever more widespread and include everything from Little League to Pee Wee hockey. The pressure to engage in organized, competitive sports at camp and at home is one of the most obvious pressures on contemporary children to grow up fast.

There are many other pressures as well. Many children today travel across the country, and indeed across the world, alone. The so-called unaccompanied minor has become so commonplace that airlines have instituted special rules and regulations for them. The phenomenon is a direct result of the increase in middle-class divorces and the fact that one or the other parent moves to another part of the country or world. Consequently, the child travels to visit one parent or the other. Children also fly alone to see grandparents or to go to special camps or training facilities.

Other facets of society also press children to grow up fast. Lawyers, for example, are encouraging children to sue their parents for a variety of grievances. In California, four-and-one-half-year-old Kimberely Ann Alpin, who was born out of wedlock, is suing her father for the right to visit with him. The father, who provides support payments, does not want to see Kimberely. Whatever the decision, or the merits of the case, it illustrates the tendency of child-advocates to accord adult legal rights to children. In West Hartford, Connecticut, David Burn, age 16, legally "divorced" his parents under a new state law in 1980. While such rights may have some benefits, they also put children in a difficult and often stressful position vis-à-vis their parents.

---

[10] C. Emerson, "Summer Camp, It's Not the Same Anymore," *Sky,* March 1981, 29–34.

The media too, including music, books, films, and television, increasingly portray young people as precocious and present them in more or less explicit sexual or manipulative situations. Such portrayals force children to think they should act grown up before they are ready. In the movie *Little Darlings* the two principals—teenage girls—are in competition as to who will lose her virginity first. Similarly, teen music extols songs such as "Take Your Time (Do It Right)" and "Do That to Me One More Time," which are high on the charts of teen favorites. Television also promotes teenage erotica with features detailing such themes as teenage prostitution. According to some teenagers, the only show on television where playing hard to get is not regarded as stupid is "Laverne and Shirley."

The media promote not only teenage sexuality but also the wearing of adult clothes and the use of adult behaviors, language, and interpersonal strategies. Sexual promotion occurs in the context of other suggestions and models for growing up fast. A Jordache jean commercial, which depicts a young girl piggyback on a young boy, highlights clothing and implicit sexuality as well as adult expressions, hairstyles, and so on. Likewise, in the film *Foxes*, four teenage girls not only blunder into sexual entanglements but also model provocative adult clothing, make-up, language, and postures. Thus the media reinforce the pressure on children to grow up fast in their language, thinking, and behavior.

But can young people be hurried into growing up fast emotionally as well? Psychologists and psychiatrists recognize that emotions and feelings are the most complex and intricate part of development. Feelings and emotions have their own timing and rhythm and cannot be hurried. Young teenagers may look and behave like adults but they usually don't feel like adults. (Watch a group of teenagers in a children's playground as they swing on the swings and teeter on the teeter-totters.) Children can grow up fast in some ways but not in others. Growing up emotionally is complicated and difficult under any circumstances but may be especially so when the children's behavior and appearance speak "adult" while their feelings cry "child."

The Child Inside

Some of the more negative consequences of hurrying usually become evident in adolescence, when the pressures to grow up fast collide with institutional prohibitions. Children pushed to grow up fast suddenly find that many adult prerogatives—which they assumed would be their prerogative—such as smoking, drinking, driving, and so on, are denied them until they reach a certain age. Many adolescents feel betrayed by a society that tells them to grow up fast but also to remain a child. Not surprisingly, the stresses of growing up fast often result in troubled and troublesome behavior during adolescence.

In a recent article, Patricia O'Brien gave some examples of what she called "the shrinking of childhood." Her examples reflect a rush to experiment that is certainly one consequence of growing up fast:

> Martin L (not his real name) confronted his teenager who had stayed out very late the night before. The son replied, "Look, Dad, I've done it all—drugs, sex, and booze, there is nothing left I don't know about." This young man is twelve years old!
>
> In Washington, D.C. area schools administrators estimate that many thousands of teenagers are alcoholics, with an estimated 30,000 such young people in Northern Virginia alone.[11]

The rush to experiment is perhaps most noticeable in teenage sexual behavior. Although survey data are not always as reliable as one might wish, the available information suggests that there has been a dramatic increase in the number of sexually active teenage girls in the last decade. Melvin Zelnick and John F. Kanther, professors of public health at Johns Hopkins University in Baltimore, conclude that nearly 50 percent of the total population of teenage girls between the ages of fifteen and nineteen (about 10.3 million females) have had premarital sex. The percentage has nearly doubled since the investigators first undertook their study in 1971. "Things that supported remaining a virgin in the past—the fear of getting pregnant, being labelled the 'town pump,' or whatever have disappeared," observes Zelnick.[12]

Young people themselves are very much aware of this trend. "I'd say half the girls in my graduating class are virgins," says an eighteen-year-old high school senior from New Iberia, Louisiana. "But you wouldn't believe those freshmen and sophomores. By the time they graduate there aren't going to be any virgins left."[13]

There are a number of disturbing consequences of this sexual liberation. The number of teenage pregnancies is growing at a startling rate. About 10 percent of all teenage girls, one million in all, get pregnant each year and the number keeps increasing. About 600,000 teenagers give birth each year, and the sharpest increase in such births is for girls under fourteen! In addition, venereal disease is a growing problem among teenagers, who account for 25 percent of the one million or so cases of gonorrhea each year.

The causes of this enhanced sexual activity among young people today are many and varied. The age of first menstruation, for example, has dropped from age seventeen about a century ago to age twelve and a half today. Fortunately this seems to be the lower limit made possible by good health care and nutrition. However, this age of first men-

---

11 Patricia O'Brien, "Dope, Sex, Crime, What Happened to Childhood," *Chicago Tribune,* March 8, 1981.
12 "The Games Teen Agers Play," *Newsweek,* September 1, 1980.
13 *Ibid.*

struation has remained stable over the past decade, so it cannot account for the increased sexual activity of young women during this period. Other contributing factors include rapid changes in social values, women's liberation, the exploding divorce rate, the decline of parental and institutional authority, and the fatalistic sense, not often verbalized, that we are all going to die in a nuclear holocaust anyway, so "what the hell, have a good time."

Although the media are quick to pick up these sexual trends and exploit them for commercial purposes (for example, the cosmetics for girls four to nine years old currently being marketed by toy manufacturers), the immediate adult model is perhaps the most powerful and the most pervasive. Married couples are generally discreet about their sexuality in front of their offspring—in part because of a natural tendency to avoid exposing children to what they might not understand, but also because by the time the children are born, much of the romantic phase of the relationship for many couples is in the past.

But single parents who are dating provide a very different model for children. Quite aside from confrontations such as that in *Kramer vs. Kramer* wherein the son encounters the father's naked girlfriend, single parents are likely to be much more overtly sexual than married couples. With single parents, children may witness the romantic phase of courtship—the hand-holding, the eye-gazing, the constant touching and fondling. This overt sexuality, with all the positive affection it demonstrates, may encourage young people to look for something similar.

It is also true, as Professor Mavis Hetherington of the University of Virginia has found in her research, that daughters of divorced women tend to be more sexually oriented, more flirtatious with men than daughters of widowed mothers or daughters from two-parent homes.[14] Because there are more teenage daughters from single-parent homes today than ever before, this too could contribute to enhanced sexual activity of contemporary teenage girls.

While it is true that some young people in every past generation have engaged in sex at an early age, have become pregnant, contracted venereal disease, and so on, they were always a small proportion of the population. What is new today are the numbers, which indicate that pressures to grow up fast are social and general rather than familial and specific (reflecting parental biases and needs). The proportion of young people who are abusing drugs, are sexually active, and are becoming pregnant is so great that we must look to the society as a whole for a full explanation, not to just the parents who mirror it.

---

[14] E. M. Hetherington, M. Cos, and R. Cox, "The Aftermath of Divorce." In J. H. Stevens, Jr. & M. Mathews (Eds.) *Mother-child, father-child relations.* Washington, D.C.: NAEYC, 1978.

Paralleling the increased sexuality of young people is an increase in children of what in adults are known as stress diseases. Pediatricians report a greater incidence of such ailments as headaches, stomachaches, allergic reactions, and so on in today's youngsters than in previous generations. Type A behavior (high-strung, competitive, demanding) has been identified in children and associated with heightened cholesterol levels. It has also been associated with parental pressure for achievement.

Another negative reflection of the pressure to grow up fast is teenage (and younger) crime. During 1980, for example, New York police arrested 12,762 children aged sixteen and under on felony charges. In Chicago the figure for the same period was 18,754 charges. Having worked for juvenile courts, I am sure that these figures are underestimated. Many children who have committed felonies are released without a formal complaint so that they will not have a police record. The children who are "booked" have usually had several previous encounters with the law.

The following examples, recent cases from the New York Police Department, illustrate the sort of activities for which children get arrested:

- On 27 February 1981, a boy who had to stand on tiptoes to speak to the bank teller made off with $118 that he had secured at gunpoint. He was nine years old, the youngest felon ever sought by the F.B.I.
- A ten-year-old Brooklyn girl was apprehended in December after she snatched a wallet from a woman's purse. Police said it was the girl's nineteenth arrest.
- One of four suspects captured in the murder of a policeman in Queens on 12 January 1981 was a fifteen-year-old youth.
- A thirteen-year-old Bronx boy was arrested in March 1981 on charges that he killed two elderly women during attempted purse snatchings.
- Another thirteen-year-old boy had a record of thirty-two arrests when seized last year on a charge of attempted murder. He later confessed to an incredible 200 plus felonies.[15]

Such crimes are not being committed just by poor disadvantaged youth who are acting out against a society prejudiced against them. Much teenage crime is committed by middle-class youngsters. However, it tends to be concealed because police and parents try to protect

---

[15] Michael Coakley, "Robert, a Robber at Age 9, and Just One of Thousands," *Chicago Tribune*, March 8, 1981.

the children; but sometimes this is not possible. One case involved a thirteen-year-old Long Island boy who was killed by three teenagers who stomped on him and strangled him by stuffing stones down his throat. He was attacked because he accidentally discovered that the other boys had stolen an old dirt bike worth only a couple of dollars. It was one of the most brutal and gruesome murders to be committed on Long Island.

There are many . . . solutions to [the] pressure to achieve early. One such solution is to join a cult, such as the "Moonies." What characterizes such cults is that they accept young people unconditionally, regardless of academic success or failure. The cults, in effect, provide an accepting family that does not demand achievement in return for love, although cults do demand obedience and adherence to a certain moral ethic. Even rebellious young people find it easy to adhere to these rules in the atmosphere of acceptance and lack of pressure and competition offered by the cult group. Cult membership is [a] form of negative identity in which young people adopt a group identity rather than an individual one.

A case in point is the Christ Commune (a pseudonym), a branch of the best-organized and most rapidly growing sect of what has been called the Jesus movement. The Commune is a summer camp where members come from their homes for a few months each year. The population (about one hundred) consists of young adults between the ages of fifteen and thirty (average age twenty-one) who are white and come from large (four to eight children), middle-class families. Most have completed high school and some have done college work. One gets the impression they are young people who have not distinguished themselves socially, academically, or athletically and who have held boring, low-paying jobs.

The group offers a strict moral code, a rigid behavioral program, and a sense of mission, of being chosen by and working for God through the mediation of Christ. The members work hard—they get up at 4:30 A.M. and go to sleep at 11:00 P.M. They seem happy with simple food (little meat, water to drink, peanut butter sandwiches for lunch) and strenuous work six days a week. Entertainment and recreation are limited to sitting in a common room, talking, singing spirituals, and engaging in spontaneous prayer.

Such communes, the Jesus movement, and other religious groups are attractive to young people whose personal styles are at variance with those of the larger society. Such groups offer recognition and status to young people who tend to be noncompetitive, anti-intellectual, and spiritual in orientation. Thus the groups provide a needed haven from the pressure to grow up fast, to achieve early, and to make a distinctive mark in life.

The last phenomenon in relation to hurrying to be discussed here is teenage suicide. Currently, suicide is the third leading cause of death during the teen years—preceded only by death via accidents and homicide. An American Academy of Pediatrics report on teenage suicide indicates a large increase in the number of suicides by adolescents in the last decade—the number is now about 5000 per year. For young people between the ages of fifteen to nineteen, the number of suicides per year doubled during the period from 1968 to 1976. The data for young adolescents of ages ten to fourteen are even more distressing: The number of suicides was 116 in 1968 and rose to 158 by 1976.

For every suicide completed, some 50 to 200 are attempted but not successful. Adolescents from all walks of life, all races, religions, and ethnic groups commit or attempt to commit suicide. Boys are generally more successful than girls because they use more lethal methods—boys tend to shoot or hang themselves whereas girls are more likely to overdose on pills or to cut their wrists. "For most adolescents," the pediatric report concludes, "suicide represents an attempt to resolve a difficult conflict, escape an intolerable living arrangement, or punish important individuals in their lives."

To illustrate how hurrying can contribute to teenage suicide, consider the data from the most affluent suburbs of Chicago, a ten-mile stretch of communities along Chicago's northside lakefront that is one of the richest areas in the country. It is the locale chosen by director Robert Redford for the movie *Ordinary People*. The median income per family is about $60,000. Children in these areas attend excellent schools, travel about the world on vacations, are admitted to the best and most prestigious private colleges, and often drive their own cars (which can sometimes be a Mercedes). These are children of affluence who would seem to have it made.

And yet, this cluster of suburbs has the highest number of teenage suicides per year in the state, and almost in the nation. There has been a 250 percent increase in suicides per year over the past decade. These figures are dismaying not only in and of themselves but because the community has made serious efforts at suicide prevention, including the training of teachers in suicide detection and the provision of a twenty-four-hour hot line. One hot line, provided by Chicago psychoanalyst Joseph Pribyl, receives some 150 calls per month. But the suicides continue.

A nineteen-year-old from Glencoe, Illinois, says, "We have an outrageous number of suicides for a community our size." One of this teenager's friends cut her wrist and two others drove their cars into trees. "Growing up here you are handed everything on a platter, but something else is missing. The one thing parents don't give is love, understanding, and acceptance of you as a person." And Isadora Sherman, of Highland Park's Jewish Family and Community Service says, "People give their kids a lot materially, but expect a lot in return. No one sees his kids as average, and those who don't perform are made to feel like failures."[16]

Chicago psychiatrist Harole Visotsky succinctly states how pressure to achieve at an early age, to grow up and be successful fast can contribute to teenage suicide: "People on the lower end of the social scale expect less than these people. Whatever anger the poor experience is acted out in antisocial ways—vandalism, homicide, riots—and the sense of shared misery in the lower income groups prevents people from feeling so isolated. With well-to-do kids, *the rattle goes in the mouth and the foot goes on the social ladder.* The competition ethic takes over, making a child feel even more alone. He's more likely to take it out on himself than society.[17]

Adolescents are very audience conscious. Failure is a public event, and the adolescent senses the audience's disapproval. It is the sense that "everyone knows" that is so painful and that can lead to attempted and successful suicides in adolescents who are otherwise so disposed. Hurrying our children has, I believe, contributed to the extraordinary rise in suicide rates among young people over the past decade.

All Grown Up and No Place to Go

Sigmund Freud was once asked to describe the characteristics of maturity, and he replied: *lieben und arbeiten* ("loving and working"). The mature adult is one who can love and allow himself or herself to be loved and who can work productively, meaningfully, and with satisfaction. Yet most adolescents, and certainly all children, are really not able to work or to love in the mature way that Freud had in mind. Children love their parents in a far different way from how they will love a real or potential mate. And many, probably most, young people will not find their life work until they are well into young adulthood.

When children are expected to dress, act, and think as adults, they are really being asked to playact, because of the trappings of adulthood do not in any way make them adults in the true sense of *lieben und arbeiten*. It is ironic that the very parents who won't allow their children to believe in Santa Claus or the Easter Bunny (because they are fantasy and therefore dishonest) allow their children to dress and behave as

---

[16] "Suicide Belt," *Time* Magazine, September 1, 1980.
[17] *Ibid.*

adults without any sense of the tremendous dishonesty involved in allowing children to present themselves in this grown-up way.

It is even more ironic that practices once considered the province of lower-class citizens now have the allure of middle-class chic. Divorce, single parenting, dual-career couples, and unmarried couples living together were common among the lower class decades ago. Such arrangements were prompted more often than not by economic need, and the children of low-income families were thus pressured to grow up fast out of necessity. They were pitied and looked down upon by upper- and middle-class parents, who helped provide shelters like the Home for Little Wanderers in Boston.

Today the middle class has made divorce its status symbol. And single parenting and living together without being married are increasingly commonplace. Yet middle-class children have not kept pace with the adjustments these adult changes require. In years past a child in a low-income family could appreciate the need to take on adult responsibilities early; families needed the income a child's farm or factory labor would bring, and chores and child-rearing tasks had to be allocated to even younger members of the family. But for the middle-income child today, it is hard to see the necessity of being relegated to a baby sitter or sent to a nursery school or a day care center when he or she has a perfectly nice playroom and yard at home. It isn't the fact of parents being divorced that is so distressing to middle-class children, but rather that often it seems so unnecessary, so clearly a reflection of parent and not child need. . . . It is the feeling of being used, of being exploited by parents, of losing the identity and uniqueness of childhood without just cause that constitutes the major stress of hurrying and accounts for so much unhappiness among affluent young people today.

It is certainly true that the trend toward obscuring the divisions between children and adults is part of a broad egalitarian movement in this country that seeks to overcome the barriers separating the sexes, ethnic and racial groups, and the handicapped. We see these trends in unisex clothing and hairstyles, in the call for equal pay for equal work, in the demands for affirmative action and in the appeals and legislation that provide the handicapped with equal opportunities for education and meaningful jobs.

From this perspective, the contemporary pressure for children to grow up fast is only one symptom of a much larger social phenomenon in this country—a movement toward true equality, toward the ideal expressed in our Declaration of Independence. While one can only applaud this movement with respect to the sexes, ethnic and racial groups, and the handicapped, its unthinking extension to children is unfortunate.

Children need time to grow, to learn, and to develop. To treat them differently from adults is not to discriminate against them but rather to recognize their special estate. Similarly, when we provide bilingual programs for Hispanic children, we are not discriminating against them but are responding to the special needs they have, which, if not attended to, would prevent them from attaining a successful education and true equality. In the same way, building ramps for handicapped students is a means to their attaining equal opportunity. Recognizing special needs is not discriminatory; on the contrary, it is the only way that true equality can be attained.

All children have, vis-à-vis adults, special needs—intellectual, social, and emotional. Children do not learn, think, or feel in the same way as adults. To ignore these differences, to treat children as adults, is really not democratic or egalitarian. If we ignore the special needs of children, we are behaving just as if we denied Hispanic or Indian children bilingual programs, or denied the handicapped their ramps and guideposts. In truth, the recognition of a group's special needs and accommodation to those needs are the only true ways to ensure equality and true equal opportunity.

Speculations

1. Elkind argues that children are different from adults. In what ways do you think he means this? What should children be doing—and not doing—that is different from adults?
2. What does Elkind mean by "the child inside"? What does he think happens to that child as young people grow up? In what ways do you support his argument? Express your point of view in terms of the "child" inside you.
3. Elkind's first sentence argues that "the concept of childhood, so vital to the traditional American way of life, is threatened with extinction in the society we have created." What parts of this statement do you agree with? In what ways do you think childhood has changed?
4. Elkind illustrates his argument with numerous examples drawn from cases of teenage suicide, violent crime, litigation, films, television, music, etc. Which examples are persuasive? Since most of them are over ten years old, are they too out-of-date to provide useful support for his argument? Can you think of more recent examples? Explain.
5. Based on Elkind's assumptions, how would you characterize the difference between a "child" and an "adult"?
6. How do Elkind's criticisms of fashion and dress work in this essay? Do you think his criticisms are valid and up-to-date? Explain your response.

RACHEL AND HER CHILDREN

Jonathan Kozol

"I'm not a violent person," Jonathan Kozol remarked during an interview in 1985 with the *Chicago Tribune* about the growing problems of illiteracy and poverty in America, "but I do think we will be faced with some form of extraordinary upheaval in our society, possibly extremely violent, if we let this go another fifteen years. If we allow this to smolder, there will simply not be enough people earning money to support those who can't."

Born into an affluent family in Boston in 1936, Kozol grew up as the son of a physician in a neighborhood devoid of crime, drugs, and poverty. His only contact with poor and black America was in the car with his father when driving their live-in maid back to Roxbury, Boston's black ghetto. Only much later did he realize, as he writes in his introduction to *Illiterate America* (1985), "with a wave of shame and fear," that the maid's children "had been denied the childhood and happiness and care that had been given to me by their mother."

The main theme to Kozol's writing is his outrage at the injustices that exist within our society. In 1964–65, his social conscience awakened while he worked as a permanent substitute fourth-grade teacher in an elementary school in Roxbury. There, he heard white teachers describe their black pupils as "animals" and then saw black children whipped for failing to show those same teachers proper "respect." In defiance of the Boston School Committee, Kozol introduced his students to the black poet Langston Hughes. Fired for "curriculum deviation," he was told that he would never again work in the Boston public school system.

Kozol described this experience in *Death at an Early Age: The Destruction of the Hearts and Minds of Negro Children in the Boston Public Schools* (1967), which won the 1968 National Book Award. He donated the $1,000 prize to Roxbury's community leaders. Kozol went on to write *The Night Is Dark and I Am Far from Home* (1975), an indictment of middle-class American values; *Illiterate America* (1985), an account of the plight of millions of Americans who cannot read; and *Savage Inequalities* (1991), in which he argues that America denies education to the poor. In 1992, Kozol appeared on the PBS television series, "Listening to America with Bill Moyers," in a segment called "Failing Our Children"; his most recent books include *Blueprint for a Democratic Education* (1992) and *On Being a Teacher* (1993).

Rachel and her Children (1988) is a study of the homeless in America. Like Kozol's other work, the theme of injustice is eloquently invoked.

Houses can be built without a number of ingredients that other ages viewed as indispensable. Acrylics, plastics, and aluminum may substitute for every substance known to nature. Parental love cannot be synthesized. Even the most earnest and methodical foster care demonstrates the limits of synthetic tenderness and surrogate emotion. So it seems of keen importance to consider any ways, and *every* way, by which a family, splintered, jolted and imperiled though it be by loss of home and subsequent detention in a building like the Martinique, may nonetheless be given every possible incentive to remain together.

The inclination to judge harshly the behavior of a parent under formidable stress seems to be much stronger than the willingness to castigate the policies that undermine the competence and ingenuity of many of these people in the first place.

"Men can be unequal in their needs, in their honor, in their possessions," writes historian Michael Ignatieff, "but also in their rights to judge others." The king's ultimate inequality, he says, "is that he is never judged." An entire industry of scholarship and public policy exists to judge the failing or defective parent; if we listen to some of these parents carefully we may be no less concerned by their impaired abilities, but we may be less judgmental or, if we remain compelled to judge, we may redirect our energies in more appropriate directions.

New Year's Eve.

She stalks into the room. Her eyes are reddened and her clothes in disarray. She wears a wrinkled and translucent nightgown. On her feet: red woolen stockings. At her throat: a crucifix. Over her shoulders is a dark and heavy robe. Nothing I have learned in the past week prepares me for this apparition.

She cries. She weeps. She paces left and right and back and forth. Pivoting and turning suddenly to face me. Glaring straight into my eyes. A sudden halt. She looks up toward the cracked and yellowish ceiling of the room. Her children stand around her in a circle. Two little girls. A frightened boy. They stare at her, as I do, as her arms reach out—for what? They snap like snakes and coil back. Her hair is gray—a stiff and brushlike Afro.

Angelina is twelve years old, Stephen is eleven, Erica is nine. The youngest child, eleven months, is sitting on the floor. A neighbor's child, six years old, sits in my lap and leans her head against my chest; she holds her arms around my neck. Her name or nickname (I do not know which) is Raisin. When she likes she puts her fingers on my mouth and interrupts the conversation with a tremolo of rapid words. There are two rooms. Rachel disappears into the second room, then returns and stands, uneasy, by the door.

Angie: "Ever since August we been livin' here. The room is either very hot or freezin' cold. When it be hot outside it's hot in here. When it be cold outside we have no heat. We used to live with my aunt but then it got too crowded there so we moved out. We went to welfare and they sent us to the shelter. Then they shipped us to Manhattan. I'm scared of the elevators. 'Fraid they be stuck. I take the stairs."

RAISIN: "Elevator might fall down and you would die."

RACHEL: "It's unfair for them to be here in this room. They be yellin'. Lots of times I'm goin' to walk out. Walk out on the street and give it up. No, I don't do it. BCW [Bureau of Child Welfare] come to take the children. So I make them stay inside. Once they walk outside that door they are in danger."

ANGIE: "I had a friend Yoki. They was tryin' to beat her. I said: 'Leave her.' They began to chase me. We was runnin' to the door. So we was runnin'. I get to the door. The door was stuck. I hit my eye and it began to bleed. So I came home and washed the blood. Me and my friends sat up all night and prayed. Prayin' for me. 'Dear Lord, can you please help me with my eye? If you do I promise to behave.' I was askin' God why did this happen. I wish someone in New York could help us. Put all of the money that we have together and we buy a building. Two or three rooms for every family. Everybody have a kitchen. Way it is, you frightened all the time. I think this world is coming to the end."

STEPHEN: "This city is rich."

ANGIE: "Surely is!"

ERICA: "City and welfare, they got something goin'. Pay $3,000 every month to stay in these here rooms . . ."

RACHEL: "I believe the City Hall got something goin' here. Gettin' a cut. They got to be. My children, they be treated like chess pieces. Send all of that money off to Africa? You hear that song? They're not thinking about people starvin' here in the United States. I was thinkin': Get my kids and all the other children here to sing, 'We are the world. We live here too.' How come do you care so much for people you can't see? Ain't we the world? Ain't we a piece of it? We are so close they be afraid to see. Give us a shot at something. We are something! Ain't we *something*? I'm depressed. But we are *something*! People in America don't want to see."

ANGIE: "Christmas is sad for everyone. We have our toys. That's not the reason why. They givin' you toys and that do help. I would rather that we have a place to be."

ERICA: "I wrote a letter to Santa Claus. Santa say that he don't have the change."

RAISIN: "I saw Santa on the street. Then I saw Santa on another street. I pulled his beard and he said something nasty."

ANGIE: "There's one thing I ask: a home to be in with my mother. That was my only wish for Christmas. But it could not be."

RAISIN: "I saw Mr. Water Bug under my mother's bed. Mr. Rat be livin' with us too."

ANGIE: "It's so cold right now you got to use the hot plate. Plug it in so you be warm. You need to have a hot plate. Are you goin' to live on cold bologna all your life?"

RAISIN: "Mr. Rat came in my baby sister's crib and bit her. Nobody felt sorry for my sister. Then I couldn't go to sleep. I started crying. All of a sudden I pray and went to sleep and then I woke up in the mornin', make my bed, and took a bath, and ate, and went to school. So I came back and did my homework. And all of a sudden there was something *irritatin'* at my hand. I looked out the window and the moon was goin' up. And then—I had a dream. I went to sleep and I was dreamin' and I dreamed about a witch that bit me. I felt *dead*. When I woke back up I had a headache."

ANGIE: "School is bad for me. I feel ashamed. They know we're not the same. My teacher do not treat us all the same. They know which children live in the hotel."

ERICA: "My teacher isn't like that. She treats all of us the same. We all get smacked. We all get punished the same way."

STEPHEN: "I'm in sixth grade. When I am a grown-up I be a computer."

ERICA: "You're in the fifth. You lie."

RAISIN: "When I grow up I want to be multiplication and subtraction and division."

ANGIE: "Last week a drug addict tried to stab me. With an ice pick. Tried to stab my mother too. Older girls was botherin' us. They try to make us fight. We don't fight. We don't start fires. They just pickin' on us. We ran home and got our mother. They ran home and got their mother."

RAISIN: "Those girls upstairs on the ninth floor, they be bad. They sellin' crack."

ERICA: "Upstairs, ninth floor, nine-o-five, they sellin' crack."

RAISIN: "A man was selling something on the street. He had some reefers on him and the po-lice caught him and they took him to the jail. You know where the junkies put the crack? Put the crack inside the pipe. Smoke it like that. They take a torch and burn the pipe and put it in their mouth. They go like this." [Puffs.]

I ask: "Why do they do it?"

ERICA: "Feel good! Hey! Make you feel fine!"

ANGIE: "This girl I know lives in a room where they sell drugs. One day she asks us do we want a puff. So we said: 'No. My mother doesn't let us do it.' One day I was walkin' in the hall. This man asked me do I want some stuff. He said: 'Do you want some?' I said no and I ran home."

RAISIN: "One day my brother found these two big plastic bags inside his teddy bear. Po-lice came up to my room and took that teddy bear." She's interrupted. "I ain't finished! And they took it. One day we was by my uncle's car and this man came and he said: 'Do you want some?' We said no. We told my uncle and he went and found the man and he ran to the bar and went into the women's bathroom in the bar. And so we left."

ANGIE: "I think this world is ending. Yes. Ending. Everybody in this city killin' on each other. Countries killin' on each other. Why can't people learn to stick together? It's no use to fightin'. Fightin' over nothin'. What they fightin' for? A flag! I don't know what we are fightin' for. President Reagan wants to put the rockets on the moon. What's he doin' messin' with the moon? If God wanted man and woman on the moon He would of put us there. They should send a camera to the moon and feed the people here on earth. Don't go messin' there with human beings. Use that money to build houses. Grow food! Buy seeds! Weave cloth! Give it to the people in America!"

ERICA: "When we hungry and don't have no food we borrow from each other. Her mother [Raisin's] give us food. Or else we go to Crisis. In the mornin' when we wake up we have a banana or a cookie. If the bus ain't late we have our breakfast in the school. What I say to President Reagan: Give someone a chance! I believe he be a selfish man. Can't imagine how long he been president."

RAISIN: "Be too long."

ANGIE: "Teacher tell us this be a democracy. I don't know. I doubt it. Rich people, couldn't they at least give us a refund?"

RAISIN: "This man say his son be gettin' on his nerves. He beat his little son 'bout two years old. A wooden bat. He beat him half to death. They took him to the hospital and at five-thirty he was dead. A little boy." [Interrupted.] "Let me talk!"

ERICA: "The little boy. He locked himself into the bathroom. He was scared. After he died police came and his father went to jail. His mother, she went to the store."

RAISIN, in a tiny voice: "People fight in here and I don't like it. Why do they do it? 'Cause they're sad. They fight over the world. I ain't finished!"

ERICA: "One time they was two cops in the hall. One cop pulled his gun and he was goin' shoot me. He said did I live there? I said no. So I came home."

RAISIN: "I was in this lady room. She be cryin' because her baby died. He had [mispronounced] pneumonia. He was unconscious and he died." Soft voice: "Tomorrow is my birthday."

The children are tended by a friend. In the other bedroom, Rachel, who is quieter now, paces about and finally sits down.

"Do you know why there's no carpet in the hall? If there was a carpet it would be on fire. Desperate people don't have no control. You have to sleep with one eye open. Tell the truth, I do not sleep at night.

"Before we lived here we were at the Forbell shelter [barracks shelter on Forbell Street in Brooklyn]. People sleep together in one room. You sleep across. You have to dress in front of everybody. Men and women. When you wake, some man lookin' at you puttin' on your clothes. Lookin' at your children too. Angelina, she be only twelve years old. . . .

"There's one thing. My children still are pure. They have a concept of life. Respect for life. But if you don't get 'em out of here they won't have anything for long. If you get 'em out right now. But if you don't . . . My girls are innocent still. They are unspoiled. Will they be that way for long? Try to keep 'em in the room. But you can't lock 'em up for long.

"When we moved here I was forced to sign a paper. Everybody has to do it. It's a promise that you will not cook inside your room. So we lived on cold bologna. Can you feed a child on that? God forgive me but nobody shouldn't have to live like this. I can't even go downstairs and get back on the elevator. Half the time it doesn't work. Since I came into this place my kids begun to get away from me."

There's a crucifix on the wall. I ask her: "Do you pray?"

"I don't pray! Pray for what? I been prayin' all my life and I'm still here. When I came to this hotel I still believed in God. I said: 'Maybe God can help us to survive.' I lost my faith. My hopes. And everything. Ain't nobody—no God, no Jesus—gonna help us in no way.

"God forgive me. I'm emotional. I'm black. I'm in a blackness. Blackness is around me. In the night I'm scared to sleep. In the mornin' I'm worn out. I don't eat no breakfast. I don't drink no coffee. If I eat, I eat one meal a day. My stomach won't allow me. I have ulcers. I stay in this room. I hide. This room is safe to me. I am afraid to go outside.

"If I go out, what do I do? People drink. Why do they drink? A person gets worn out. They usin' drugs. Why they use drugs? They say: 'Well, I won't think about it now.' Why not? You ain't got nothin' else to do, no place to go. 'Where I'm gonna be tomorrow or the next day?'

They don't know. All they know is that they don't have nothin'. So they drink. And some of them would rather not wake up. Rather be dead. That's right.

"Most of us are black. Some Puerto Rican. Some be white. They suffer too. Can you get the government to know that we exist? I know that my children have potential. They're intelligent. They're smart. They need a chance. There's nothin' wrong with them for now. But not for long. My daughter watches junkies usin' needles. People smokin' crack in front a them. Screwin' in front a them. They see it all. They see it everywhere. What is a man and woman gonna do when they are all in the same room?

"I met a girl the other day. She's twelve years old. Lives on the fourteenth floor. She got a baby the same age as mine. Her mother got five children of her own. I don't want my daughter havin' any baby. She's a child. Innocent. Innocent. No violence. She isn't bitter. But she's scared. You understand? This is America. These children growin' up too fast. We have no hope. And you know why? Because we all feel just the same way deep down in our hearts. Nowhere to go . . . I'm not a killer. My kids ain't no killers. But if they don't learn to kill they know they're goin' to die.

"They didn't go to school last week. They didn't have clean clothes. Why? Because the welfare messed my check. It's supposed to come a week ago. It didn't come. I get my check today. I want my kids to go to school. They shouldn't miss a day. How they gonna go to school if they don't got some clothes? I couldn't wash. I didn't have the money to buy food.

"Twice the welfare closed my case. When they do it you are s'posed to go for a fair hearing. Take some papers, birth certificates. So I went out there in the snow. Welfare worker wasn't there. They told me to come back. Mister, it ain't easy to be beggin'. I went to the Crisis. And I asked her, I said, 'Give me somethin' for the kids to eat. Give me *somethin'!* Don't turn me away when I am sittin' here in front of you and askin' for your help!' She said she had nothin'. So my kids went out into the street. That's right! Whole night long they was in Herald Square panhandlin'. Made five dollars. So we bought bologna. My kids is good to me. We had bread and bologna.

"Welfare, they are not polite. They're personal. 'Did you do this? Did you do that? Where your husband at?' Understand me? 'Cause they sittin' on the other side of this here desk, they think we're stupid and we do not understand when we're insulted. 'Oh, you had another baby?' Yeah! I had another baby! What about it? Are you goin' to kill that baby? I don't say it, but that's what I feel like sayin'. You learn to be humble.

"I'm here five miserable months. So I wonder: Where I'm goin'? Can't the mayor give us a house? A part-time job? I am capable of doin' *somethin'*.

"You go in the store with food stamps. You need Pampers. You're not s'posed to use the stamps for Pampers. Stores will accept them. They don't care about the law. What they do is make you pay a little extra. They know you don't have no choice. So they let you buy the Pampers for two dollars extra.

"Plenty of children livin' here on nothin' but bread and bologna. Peanut butter. Jelly. Drinkin' water. You buy milk. I bought one gallon yesterday. Got *this* much left. They drink it fast. Orange juice, they drink it fast. End up drinkin' Kool Aid.

"Children that are poor are used like cattle. Cattle or horses. They are owned by welfare. They know they are bein' used—for what? Don't *use* them! Give 'em somethin'!

"In this bedroom I'm not sleepin' on a bed. They won't give me one. You can see I'm sleepin' on a box spring. I said to the manager: 'I need a bed instead of sleepin' on a spring.' Maid give me some blankets. Try to make it softer."

The Bible by her bed is opened to the Twenty-third Psalm.

"I do believe. God forgive me. I believe He's there. But when He sees us like this, I am wonderin' where is He? I am askin': Where the hell He gone?

"Before they shipped us here we lived for five years in a basement. Five years in a basement with no bathroom. One small room. You had to go upstairs two floors to use the toilet. No kitchen. It was fifteen people in five rooms. Sewer kept backing up into the place we slept. Every time it flooded I would have to pay one hundred dollars just to get the thing unstuck. There were all my children sleepin' in the sewage. So you try to get them out and try to get them somethin' better. But it didn't get no better. I came from one bad place into another. But the difference is this is a place where I cannot get out.

"If I can't get out of here I'll give them up. I have asked them: 'Do you want to go away?' I love my kids and, if I did that, they would feel betrayed. They love me. They don't want to go. If I did it, I would only do it to protect them. They'll live anywhere with me. They're innocent. Their minds are clean. They ain't corrupt. They have a heart. All my kids love people. They love life. If they got a dime, a piece of bread, they'll share it. Letting them panhandle made me cry. I had been to welfare, told the lady that my baby ain't got Pampers, ain't got nothin' left to eat. I got rude and noisy and it's not my style to do that but you learn that patience and politeness get you nowhere.

"When they went out on the street I cried. I said: 'I'm scared. What's gonna happen to them?' But if they're hungry they are goin' to do *something*. They are gonna find their food from somewhere. Where I came from I was fightin' for my children. In this place here I am fightin' for my children. I am tired of fightin'. I don't want to fight. I want my kids to live in peace.

"I was thinkin' about this. If there was a place where you could sell part of your body, where they buy an arm or somethin' for a thousand dollars, I would do it. I would do it for my children. I would give my life if I could get a thousand dollars. What would I lose? I lived my life. I want to see my children grow up to live theirs.

"A lot of women do not want to sell their bodies. This is something that good women do not want to do. I will sell mine. I *will*. I will solicit. I will prostitute if it will feed them."

I ask: "Would you do it?"

"Ain't no 'would I?' I would do it." Long pause . . . "Yes. I *did*.

"I had to do it when the check ain't come. Wasn't no one gonna buy my arm for any thousand dollars. But they's plenty gonna pay me twenty dollars for my body. What was my choice? Leave them out there on the street, a child like Angelina, to panhandle? I would take my life if someone found her dead somewhere. I would go crazy. After she did it that one time I was ashamed. I cried that night. All night I cried and cried. So I decided I had one thing left. In the mornin' I got up out of this bed. I told them I was goin' out. Out in the street. Stand by the curb. It was a cold day. Freezin'! And my chest is bad. I'm thirty-eight years old. Cop come by. He see me there. I'm standin' out there cryin'. Tells me I should go inside. Gives me three dollars. 'It's too cold to be outside.' Ain't many cops like that. Not many people either . . .

"After he's gone a man come by. Get in his car. Go with him where he want. Takin' a chance he crazy and kill me. Wishin' somehow that he would.

"So he stop his car. And I get in. I say a price. That's it. Go to a room. It's some hotel. He had a lot of money so he rented a deluxe. Asked me would I stay with him all night. I tell him no I can't 'cause I have kids. So, after he done . . . whatever he did . . . I told him that I had to leave. Took out a knife at me and held it at my face. He made me stay. When I woke up next day I was depressed. Feel so guilty what I did. I feel real scared. I can understand why prostitutes shoot drugs. They take the drugs so they don't be afraid.

"When he put that knife up to my throat, I'm thinkin' this: What is there left to lose? I'm not goin' to do any better in this life. If I be dead at least my kids won't ever have to say that I betrayed them. I don't like to think like that. But when things pile up on you, you do. 'I'm better if I'm dead.'

"So I got me twenty dollars and I go and buy the Pampers for the baby and three dollars of bologna and a loaf of bread and everyone is fed.

"That cross of Jesus on the wall I had for seven years. I don't know if I believe or not. Bible say Jesus was God's son. He died for us to live here on this earth. See, I believe—Jesus was innocent. But, when He died, what was it for? He died for nothin'. Died in vain. He should a let us die like we be doin'—we be dyin' all the time. We dyin' every day.

"God forgive me. I don't mean the things I say. God had one son and He gave His son. He gave him up. I couldn't do it. I got four. I could not give any one of them. I couldn't do it. God could do it. Is it wrong to say it? I don't know if Jesus died in vain."

She holds the Bible in her hands. Crying softly. Sitting on the box spring in her tangled robe.

"They laid him in a manger. Right? Listen to me. I didn't say that God forsaken us. I am confused about religion. I'm just sayin' evil over-rules the good. So many bad things goin' on. Lot of bad things right here in this buildin'. It's not easy to believe. I don't read the Bible no more 'cause I don't find no more hope in it. I don't believe. But yet and still . . . I know these words." She reads aloud: "'Lie down in green pastures . . . leadeth me beside still waters . . . restores my soul . . . I shall not want.'

"All that I want is somethin' that's my own. I got four kids. I need four plates, four glasses, and four spoons. Is that a lot? I know I'm poor. Don't have no bank account, no money, or no job. Don't have no noth-in'. No foundation. Then and yet my children have a shot in life. They're innocent. They're pure. They have a chance." She reads: "'I shall not fear . . .' I fear! A long, long time ago I didn't fear. Didn't fear for nothin'. I said God's protectin' me and would protect my children. Did He do it?

"Yeah. I'm walkin'. I am walkin' in the wilderness. That's what it is. I'm walkin'. Did I tell you that I am an ex-drug addict? Yeah. My children know it. They know and they understand. I'm walkin'. Yeah!"

The room is like a chilled cathedral in which people who do not be-lieve in God ask God's forgiveness. "How I picture God is like an old man who speaks different languages. His beard is white and He has angels and the instruments they play are white and everything around is white and there is no more sickness, no more hunger for nobody. No panhandlin'. No prostitutes. No drugs. I had a dream like that.

"There's no beauty in my life except two things. My children and"—she hesitates—"I write these poems. How come, when I write it down, it don't come out my pencil like I feel? I don't know. I got no dic-tionary. Every time I read it over I am finding these mistakes.

> Deep down in my heart
> I do not mean these things I said.
> Forgive me. Try to understand me.
> I love all of you the same.
> Help me to be a better mother.

"When I cry I let 'em know. I tell 'em I was a drug addict. They know and they try to help me to hold on. They helpin' me. My children is what's holdin' me together. I'm not makin' it. I'm reachin'. And they see me reachin' out. Angelina take my hand. They come around. They ask me what is wrong. I do let them know when I am scared. But certain things I keep inside. I try to solve it. If it's my department, I don't want them to be sad. If it be too bad, if I be scared of gettin' back on drugs, I'll go to the clinic. They have sessions every other night.

"Hardest time for me is night. Nightmares. Somethin's grabbin' at me. Like a hand. Some spirit's after me. It's somethin' that I don't forget. I wake up in a sweat. I'm wonderin' why I dream these dreams. So I get up, turn on the light. I don't go back to sleep until the day is breakin'. I look up an' I be sayin': 'Sun is up. Now I can go to sleep.'

"After the kids are up and they are dressed and go to school, then I lay down. I go to sleep. But I can't sleep at night. After the sun go down makes me depressed. I want to turn the light on, move around.

"Know that song—'Those Monday Blues'? I had that album once."

I say the title: "'Monday Blues'?"

"I got 'em every day. Lots of times, when I'm in pain, I think I'm goin' to die. That's why I take a drink sometimes. I'm 'fraid to die. I'm wonderin': Am I dying?"

Speculations

1. "Rachel and Her Children" is the title both of one chapter and of the entire book. Obviously, the title carries great significance for Jonathan Kozol. What is the significance of the title, and how does it relate to the subject of children, families, and homelessness in America?
2. Kozol says that "the inclination to judge harshly the behavior of a parent under formidable stress seems to be much stronger than the willingness to castigate the policies that undermine the competence and ingenuity of many of these people in the first place." What does he mean by this analysis? What is your opinion? What policies is he referring to?
3. Kozol presents Rachel and her children through the use of dialogue and monologue, as if they were characters in a play. Why do you think Kozol chooses this way of presenting them? What other ways could he have told their story?
4. Explain which expressions or ideas from Rachel or her children are especially powerful and eloquent and why you think so.
5. Homeless people are part of many cities and towns. What is your reaction to them? How do you identify with them? Would you react differently if you knew that it was children who were homeless rather than adults?
6. Rachel confesses that she engages in prostitution in order to support her children. She also states that she has a problem with alcohol and that she is an ex-drug addict. Why do you think Kozol

includes those statements in this section when he could have ended it a few paragraphs earlier? Who are the victims in this story?

THE LESSON

Toni Cade Bambara

A distinguished writer, lecturer, and civil rights activist, Toni Cade Bambara is perhaps best known for her collections of short stories, *Gorilla, My Love* (1972) and *The Sea Birds Are Still Alive* (1977), vignettes of African-American life in the North and the South. *The Salt Eaters* (1980), a dream-like novel, explores a developing relationship between two women who suffer intense emotional turmoil. The critic John Leonard described it as "an incantation, poem-drunk, myth-happy, mud-caked, jazz-ridden, prodigal in meanings, a kite and a mask. . . . It is as if she jived the very stones to groan." This comment captures the rich blend of inspirational, political, and street-smart colloquial talk that characterizes Bambara's prose.

Unlike many writers, Bambara has not been content to lead the quiet life of the writer in her study. Since the urban turmoil and civil rights struggles of the 1960s, Bambara has worked to promote equal rights for blacks. Born in New York City in 1939, she began her professional life as a social investigator for the New York State Department of Welfare where she gained many insights concerning poverty and possibility. It is clear that her experiences in that job influenced "The Lesson."

Bambara has worked tirelessly with community centers, local writers in cities across the country, and public service organizations. She has lectured and read her work in museums, prisons, libraries, and universities. Winner of numerous awards including the Black Rose Award from *Encore* and *Ebony*'s Achievement in the Arts Award, Bambara has been described in *The New York Times Book Review* as able to tell "more about being black through her quiet, proud, silly, tender, hip, acute, loving stores than any amount of literary polemicizing could hope to do. She writes about love: a love for one's family, one's friends, one's race, one's neighborhood and it is the sort of love that comes with maturity and inner peace." Much of that love is in evidence in "The Lesson," a story of discovery by a young, poor, black girl in New York City who takes a trip to the most famous toy store in the world.

Back in the days when everyone was old and stupid or young and
foolish and me and Sugar were the only ones just right, this lady
moved on our block with nappy hair and proper speech and no make-
up. And quite naturally we laughed at her, laughed the way we did at
the junk man who went about his business like he was some big-time
president and his sorry-ass horse his secretary. And we kinda hated
her too, hated the way we did the winos who cluttered up our parks
and pissed on our handball walls and stank up our hallways and stairs
so you couldn't halfway play hide-and-seek without a goddamn gas
mask. Miss Moore was her name. The only woman on the block with
no first name. And she was black as hell, cept for her feet, which were
fish-white and spooky. And she was always planning these boring-ass
things for us to do, us being my cousin, mostly, who lived on the block
cause we all moved North the same time and to the same apartment
then spread out gradual to breathe. And our parents would yank our
heads into some kinda shape and crisp up our clothes so we'd be pre-
sentable for travel with Miss Moore, who always looked like she was
going to church, though she never did. Which is just one of things the
grown-ups talked about when they talked behind her back like a dog.
But when she came calling with some sachet she'd sewed up or some
gingerbread she'd made or some book, why then they'd all be too embarrassed to turn her down and we'd get handed over all spruced up.
She'd been to college and said it was only right that she should take responsibility for the young ones' education, and she not even related by
marriage or blood. So they'd go for it. Specially Aunt Gretchen. She
was the main gofer in the family. You got some ole dumb shit foolish-
ness you want somebody to go for, you send for Aunt Gretchen. She
been screwed into the goalong for so long, it's a blood-deep natural
thing with her. Which is how she got saddled with me and Sugar and
Junior in the first place while our mothers were in a la-de-da apartment
up the block having a good ole time.

So this one day Miss Moore rounds us all up at the mailbox and it's
puredee hot and she's knocking herself out about arithmetic. And
school suppose to let up in summer I heard, but she don't never let up.
And the starch in my pinafore scratching the shit outta me and I'm really hating this nappy-head bitch and her goddamn college degree. I'd
much rather go to the pool or to the show where it's cool. So me and
Sugar leaning on the mailbox being surly, which is a Miss Moore word.
And Flyboy checking out what everybody brought for lunch. And Fat
Butt already wasting his peanut-butter-and-jelly sandwich like the pig
he is. And Junebug punchin on Q.T.'s arm for potato chips. And Rosie
Giraffe shifting from one hip to the other waiting for somebody to step
on her foot or ask her if she from Georgia so she can kick ass, prefer-
ably Mercedes's. And Miss Moore asking us do we know what money
is, like we a bunch of retards. I mean real money, she say, like it's only

poker chips or monopoly papers we lay on the grocer. So right away I'm tired of this and say so. And would much rather snatch Sugar and go to the Sunset and terrorize the West Indian kids and take their hair ribbons and their money too. And Miss Moore files that remark away for next week's lesson on brotherhood, I can tell. And finally I say we oughta get to the subway cause it's cooler and besides we might meet some cute boys. Sugar done swiped her mama's lipstick, so we ready.

So we heading down the street and she's boring us silly about what things cost and what our parents make and how much goes for rent and how money ain't divided up right in this country. And then she gets to the part about we all poor and live in the slums, which I don't feature. And I'm ready to speak on that, but she steps out in the street and hails two cabs just like that. Then she hustles half the crew in with her and hands me a five-dollar bill and tells me to calculate 10 percent tip for the driver. And we're off. Me and Sugar and Junebug and Fly-boy hangin out the window and hollering to everybody, putting lipstick on each other cause Flyboy a faggot anyway, and making farts with our sweaty armpits. But I'm mostly trying to figure how to spend this money. But they all fascinated with the meter ticking and Junebug starts laying bets as to how much it'll read when Flyboy can't hold his breath no more. Then Sugar lay bets as to how much it'll be when we get there. So I'm stuck. Don't nobody want to go for my plan, which is to jump out at the next light and run off to the first bar-b-que we can find. Then the driver tells us to get the hell out cause we there already. And the meter reads eight-five cents. And I'm stalling to figure out the tip and Sugar say give him a dime. And I decide he don't need it bad as I do, so later for him. But then he tries to take off with Junebug's foot still in the door so we talk about his mama something ferocious. Then we check out that we on Fifth Avenue and everybody dressed up in stockings. One lady in a fur coat, hot as it is. White folks crazy.

"This is the place," Miss Moore say, presenting it to us in the voice she uses at the museum. "Let's look in the windows before we go in."

"Can we steal?" Sugar asks very serious like she's getting the ground rules squared away before she plays. "I beg your pardon," say Miss Moore, and we fall out. So she leads us around the windows of the toy store and me and Sugar screamin, "This is mine, that's mine, I gotta have that, that was made for me, I was born for that," till Big Butt drowns us out.

"Hey, I'm going to buy that there."

"That there? You don't even known what it is, stupid."

"I do so," he say punchin on Rosie Giraffe. "It's a microscope."

"Whatcha gonna do with a microscope, fool?"

"Look at things."

"Like what, Ronald?" ask Miss Moore. And Big Butt ain't got the first notion. So here go Miss Moore gabbing about the thousands of bacteria in a drop of water and the somethinorother in a speck of blood and the million and one living things in the air around us is invisible to the naked eye. And what she say that for? Junebug go to town on that "naked" and we rolling. Then Miss Moore ask what it cost. So we all jam into the window smudgin it up and the price tag say three hundred dollars. So then she ask how long'd take for Big Butt and Junebug to save up their allowances. "Too long," I say. "Yeh," adds Sugar, "outgrown it by that time." And Miss Moore say no, you never outgrow learning instruments. "Why, even medical students and interns and," blah, blah, blah. And we ready to choke Big Butt for bringing it up in the first damn place.

"This here costs four hundred eighty dollars," say Rosie Giraffe. So we pile up all over her to see what she pointin out. My eyes tell me it's a chunk of glass cracked with something heavy, and different-color inks dripped into the splits, then the whole thing put into a oven or something. But for $480 it don't make sense.

"That's a paperweight made of semi-precious stones fused together under tremendous pressure," she explains slowly, with her hands doing the mining and all the factory work.

"So what's a paperweight?" asks Rosie Giraffe.

"To weigh paper with, dumbbell," say Flyboy, the wise man from the East.

"Not exactly," say Miss Moore, which is what she say when you warm or way off too. "It's to weigh paper down so it won't scatter and make your desk untidy." So right away me and Sugar curtsy to each other and then to Mercedes who is more the tidy type.

"We don't keep paper on top of the desk in my class," say Junebug, figuring Miss Moore crazy or lyin one.

"At home, then," she say. "Don't you have a calendar and a pencil case and a blotter and a letter-opener on your desk at home where you do your homework?" And she know damn well what our homes look like cause she nosys around in them every chance she gets.

"I don't even have a desk," say Junebug, "Do we?"

"No. And I don't get no homework neither," says Big Butt.

"And I don't even have a home," say Flyboy like he do at school to keep the white folks off his back and sorry for him. Send this poor kid to camp posters, is his specialty.

"I do," says Mercedes. "I have a box of stationery on my desk and a picture of my cat. My godmother bought the stationery and the desk. There's a big rose on each sheet and the envelopes smell like roses."

"Who wants to know about your smelly-ass stationery," say Rosie Giraffe fore I can get my two cents in.

"It's important to have a work area all your own so that . . ."

"Will you look at this sailboat, please," say Flyboy, cuttin her off and pointin to the thing like it was his. So once again we tumble all over each other to gaze at this magnificent thing in the toy store which is just big enough to maybe sail two kittens across the pond if you strap them to the posts tight. We all start reciting the price tag like we in assembly. "Handcrafted sailboat of fiberglass at one thousand one hundred ninety-five dollars."

"Unbelievable," I hear myself say and am really stunned. I read it again for myself just in case the group recitation put me in a trance. Same thing. For some reason this pisses me off. We look at Miss Moore and she lookin at us, waiting for I dunno what.

"Who'd pay all that when you can buy a sailboat set for a quarter at Pop's, a tube of glue for a dime, and a ball of string for eight cents? It must have a motor and a whole lot else besides," I say. "My sailboat cost me about fifty cents."

"But will it take water?" say Mercedes with her smart ass.

"Took mine to Alley Pond Park once," say Flyboy. "String broke. Lost it. Pity."

"Sailed mine in Central Park and it keeled over and sank. Had to ask my father for another dollar."

"And you got the strap," laugh Big Butt. "The jerk didn't even have a string on it. My old man whaled on his behind."

Little Q.T. was staring hard at the sailboat and you could see he wanted it bad. But he too little and somebody'd just take it from him. So what the hell. "This boat for kids, Miss Moore?"

"Parents silly to buy something like that just to get all broke up," say Rosie Giraffe.

"That much money it should last forever," I figure.

"My father'd buy it for me if I wanted it."

"Your father, my ass," say Rosie Giraffe getting a chance to finally push Mercedes.

"Must be rich people shop here," say Q.T.

"You are a very bright boy," say Flyboy. "What was your first clue?" And he rap him on the head with the back of his knuckles, since Q.T. the only one he could get away with. Though Q.T. liable to come up behind you years later and get his licks in when you half expect it.

"What I want to know is," I says to Miss Moore though I never talk to her, I wouldn't give the bitch that satisfaction, "is how much a real boat costs? I figure a thousand'd get you a yacht any day."

"Why don't you check that out," she says, "and report back to the group?" Which really pains my ass. If you gonna mess up a perfectly good swim day least you could do is have some answers. "Let's go in," she say like she got something up her sleeve. Only she don't lead the way. So me and Sugar turn the corner to where the entrance is, but when we get there I kinda hang back. Not that I'm scared, what's there to be afraid of, just a toy store. But I feel funny, shame. But what I got to be shamed about? Got as much right to go in as anybody. But somehow I can't seem to get hold of the door, so I step away for Sugar to lead. But she hangs back too. And I look at her and she looks at me and this is ridiculous. I mean, damn, I have never ever been shy about doing nothing or going nowhere. But then Mercedes steps up and then Rosie Giraffe and Big Butt crowd in behind and shove, and next thing we all stuffed into the doorway with only Mercedes squeezing past us, smoothing out her jumper and walking right down the aisle. Then the rest of us tumble in like a glued-together jigsaw done all wrong. And people lookin at us. And it's like the time me and Sugar crashed into the Catholic church on a dare. But once we got in there and everything so hushed and holy and the candles and the bowin and the handker-chiefs on all the drooping heads, I just couldn't go through with the plan. Which was for me to run up to the altar and do a tap dance while Sugar played the nose flute and messed around in the holy water. And Sugar kept givin me the elbow. Then later teased me so bad I tied her up in the shower and turned it on and locked her in. And she'd be there till this day if Aunt Gretchen hadn't finally figured I was lying about the boarder takin a shower.

Same thing in the store. We all walkin on tiptoe and hardly touch-in the games and puzzles and things. And I watched Miss Moore who is steady watchin us like she waiting for a sign. Like Mama Drewery watches the sky and sniffs the air and takes note of just how much slant is in the bird formation. Then me and Sugar bump smack into each other, so busy gazing at the toys, 'specially the sailboat. But we don't laugh and go into our fat-lady bump-stomach routine. We just stare at that price tag. Then Sugar ran a finger over the whole boat. And I'm jealous and want to hit her. Maybe not her, but I sure want to punch somebody in the mouth.

"Whatcha bring us here for, Miss Moore?"

"You sound angry, Sylvia. Are you mad about something?" Givin me one of them grins like she tellin a grown-up joke that never turns out to be funny. And she's lookin very closely at me like maybe she plannin to do my portrait from memory. I'm mad, but I won't give her that satisfaction. So I slouch around the store bein very bored and say, "Let's go."

Me an Sugar at the back of the train watchin the tracks whizzin by large then small then gettin gobbled up in the dark. I'm thinkin about this tricky toy I saw in the store. A clown that somersaults on a bar then does chin-ups just cause you yank lightly at his leg. Cost $35. I could see me askin my mother for a $35 birthday clown. "You wanna who that costs what?" she'd say, cocking her head to the side to get a better view of the hole in my head. Thirty-five dollars could buy new bunk beds for Junior and Gretchen's boy. Thirty-five dollars and the whole household could go visit Granddaddy Nelson in the country. Thirty-five dollars would pay for the rent and the piano bill too. Who are these people that spend that much for performing clowns and $1,000 for toy sailboats? What kinda work they do and how they live and how come we ain't in on it? Where we are is who we are, Miss Moore always pointin out. But it don't necessarily have to be that way, she always adds then waits for somebody to say that poor people have to wake up and demand their share of the pie and don't none of us know what kind of pie she talkin about in the first damn place. But she ain't so smart cause I still got her four dollars from the taxi and she sure ain't getting it. Messin up my day with this shit. Sugar nudges me in my pocket and winks.

Miss Moore lines us up in front of the mailbox where we started from, seem like years ago, and I got a headache for thinkin so hard. And we lean all over each other so we can hold up under the draggy-ass lecture she always finishes us off with at the end before we thank her for borin us to tears. But she just looks at us like she readin tea leaves. Finally she say, "Well, what do you think of F.A.O. Schwarz?"

Rosie Giraffe mumbles, "White folks crazy."

"I'd like to go there again when I get my birthday money," says Mercedes, and we shove her out the pack so she has to lean on the mailbox by herself.

"I'd like a shower. Tiring day," says Flyboy.

Then Sugar surprises me by sayin, "You know, Miss Moore, I don't think all of us here put together eat in a year what that sailboat costs." And Miss Moore lights up like somebody goosed her. "And?" she say, urging Sugar on. Only I'm standin on her foot so she don't continue.

"Imagine for a minute what kind of society it is in which some people can spend on a toy what it would cost to feed a family of six or seven. What do you think?"

"I think," say Sugar pushing me off her feet like she never done before, cause I whip her ass in a minute, "that this is not much of a democracy if you ask me. Equal chance to pursue happiness means an equal crack at the dough, don't it?" Miss Moore is besides herself and I am disgusted with Sugar's treachery. So I stand on her foot one more time to see if she'll shove me. She shuts up, and Miss Moore looks at me, sorrowfully I'm thinkin. And somethin weird is goin on. I can feel it in my chest.

"Anybody else learn anything today?" lookin dead at me. I walk away and Sugar has to run to catch up and don't even seem to notice when I shrug her arm off my shoulder.

"Well, we got four dollars anyway," she says.

"Uh-hunh."

"We could go to Hascombs and get half a chocolate layer and then go to the Sunset and still have plenty money for potato chips and ice cream sodas."

"Uh-hunh."

"Race you to Hascombs," she say.

We start down the block and she gets ahead which is OK by me cause I'm going to the West End and then over to the Drive to think this day through. She can run if she want to and even run faster. But ain't nobody gonna beat me at nuthin.

Speculations

1. This story appears as if it is spoken by one person in a literary form known as a dramatic monologue. How would you characterize the speaker? How would you describe her value system, her neighborhood, her attitudes toward herself and her culture?
2. Why does Miss Moore take the kids to F.A.O. Schwarz on Fifth Avenue in New York City, the most expensive toy store in America if not the world? What is "the lesson?"
3. When you see "things" that you want in stores, magazines, or on television that you cannot afford, what is your response? How do you work through your frustration at not being able to attain something you want very much?
4. This is a first person narrative written in black dialect or black English vernacular. What grammatical and stylistic differences do you see between the dialect in which this story is written and edited American English, the standard dialect of writing and publishing? Why do you think Bambara chose to tell this story using black dialect? What kind of effect does it create?
5. Once in F.A.O. Schwarz, the narrator and Sugar bump into each other while staring at the sailboat. The narrator says:

   > We just stare at that price tag. Then Sugar ran a finger over the whole boat. And I'm jealous and want to hit her. Maybe not her, but I sure want to punch somebody in the mouth.

   Why is the narrator angry? Whom does she want to punch?

WHEN YOU'RE A CRIP
(OR A BLOOD)

Léon Bing

The author of *Do or Die*, a gripping study of the teenage culture of gangs and violence in America, Léon Bing is a writer compelled by the teenage subculture, the "disenfranchised kids of America."

A Californian by birth, Bing's interest in American youth originates from her view that "the way we treat our kids in this country is clearly the way we treat our future, and that treatment seems to me to be the trashing of the American dream. I wrote *Do or Die* to focus attention on the African-American gangs because it doesn't get much more disenfranchised than to grow up black in America."

Bing's writing drew notice in 1985 with an article entitled "Slow Death in Venice" in the *L.A. Weekly.* Her career launched, Bing continued to research and write essays about teenage gangs. Her next essay, entitled "Caged Kids," (*L.A. Weekly,* 1985) was nominated for the H.L. Mencken award; it offered a warning to teenagers that "you better behave or Mom and Dad will put you in the nuthouse." She followed up with pieces on the Crips and the Bloods, street gangs in Los Angeles. *Harper's* asked to reprint her work and requested the Forum piece, "When You're a Crip (or a Blood)," which appeared in 1989. This in turn led to a book contract for *Do or Die,* which won the American Library Award in 1992. One year later, she published *Smoked: A True, Shocking Story of Murder and the American Dream* (1993).

Bing loves to work with children and teenagers because "Kids tell you the truth. What they say is not filtered through the layers of calluses that build up with adults; kids are much less self-serving—and even when they are, you are going to get an extraordinary answer." A good bit of that unfiltered honesty is present in "When You're a Crip (or a Blood)."

The drive-by killing is the sometime sport and occasional initiation rite of city gangs. From the comfort of a passing car, the itinerant killer simply shoots down a member of a rival gang or an innocent bystander. Especially common among L.A.'s Bloods and Crips, the drive-by killing is the parable around which every telling of the gang story revolves. Beyond that lies a haze of images: million-dollar drug deals, ominous graffiti, and colorfully dressed marauders armed with Uzis. The sociologists tell us that gang culture is the flower on the vine of single-parent life in the ghetto, the logical result of society's indifference. It would be hard to write a morality play more likely to strike terror into the hearts of the middle class.

Many questions, though, go unasked. Who, really, are these people? What urges them to join gangs? What are their days like? To answer these questions, Harper's Magazine recently asked Léon Bing, a journalist who has established relations with the gangs, to convene a meeting between two Bloods and two Crips and to talk with them about the world in which the drive-by killing is an admirable act.

The following forum is based on a discussion held at the Kenyon Juvenile Justice Center in south central Los Angeles. Parole Officer Velma V. Stevens assisted in the arrangements. Léon Bing served as moderator.

LÉON BING is a Los Angeles-based journalist. She is currently writing a book about teenage life in Los Angeles.

LI'L MONSTER was a member of the Eight-Trey Gangsters
set of the Crips. He is twenty-three years old and currently on
probation; he has served time for first-degree murder, four
counts of attempted murder, and two counts of armed
robbery.

RAT-NECK was a member of the 107-Hoover Crips. He is
twenty-eight years old and currently on probation after serving time for attempted murder, robbery with intent to commit
grave bodily harm, assault and battery, burglary, and carrying
concealed weapons.

TEE RODGERS founded the first Los Angeles chapter of the
Chicago-based Blackstone Rangers, affiliated with the Bloods.
He is currently the resident "gangologist" and conflict specialist at Survival Education for Life and Family, Inc., and an actor
and lecturer.

B-DOG is a pseudonym for a twenty-three-year-old member of
the Van Ness Gangsters set of the Bloods. After this forum was
held, his telephone was disconnected, and he could not be located to supply biographical information.

Getting Jumped In

Léon Bing: Imagine that I'm a thirteen-year-old guy, and I want
to get into a gang. How do I go about it? Am I the right age?

Li'l Monster: There's no age limit. It depends on your status
coming into it. It's like, some people get jumped in, some people
don't.

Bing: Jumped in?

Li'l Monster: Beat up.

B-Dog: Either beat up or put some work in.

Rat-Neck: Put some work in, that's mandatory, you know, a little mis [misdemeanor]—small type of thing, you know.

It's like this: say I get this guy comin' up and he says, "Hey, Cuz, I
wanna be from the set." Then I'm like, "Well, what you *about*, man? I
don't know you—you might be a punk." So I might send him somewhere, let him go and manipulate, send him out on a burg' or—

Bing: is that a burglary?

LI'L MONSTER: Yeah. But then, you might know some person who's got a little juice, and, like, I might say, "You don't got to go through that, come on with me. You *from* the set."

TEE RODGERS: If you click with somebody that's already from a set, then you clicked up, or under his wing, you his protégé, and you get a ride in. Now, even though you get a ride in, there's gonna come a time when you got to stand alone and hold your own.

BING: Stand alone and hold your own? Does that mean I might have to steal a car or beat up somebody or commit a burglary?

RAT-NECK: Right.

BING: Is there another way?

RAT-NECK: You can be good from the shoulders.

LI'L MONSTER: Yeah. Fighting.

TEE: That's one of *the* best ways. A homeboy says:

I'm young and mean and my mind's more keen
And I've earned a rep with my hands
And I'm eager to compete with the bangers on the street
'Cause I've got ambitious plans.

LI'L MONSTER: See, when Tee was comin' up—he's *first* generation and we *second* generation. Now, if he saw me, he wouldn't be comin' from the pants pocket with a gat or a knife, he'd be comin' from his shoulders like a fighter. That's what it was established on. Then, later on, come a whole bunch of cowards that *can't* come from the shoulders, so they come from the pocket—

RAT-NECK: —he unloads!

BING: What's the most popular weaponry?

B-DOG: Whatever you get your hands on.

TEE: Keep in mind we don't have no target ranges and shit where we get prolific with these guns.

B-DOG: Shoot 'til you out of bullets, then back up.

RAT-NECK: Bullet ain't got no name, hit whatever it hit.

TEE: Wait a minute! That was a hell of a question, 'cause the mentality of the people that gonna read this be thinkin'—

LI'L MONSTER: every gang member walks around with that type of gun—

TEE: and I can hear the police chief saying, "That's why we need bazookas!" Look, put it on the record that everybody ain't got a mother-fuckin' bazooka—or an Uzi. Okay?

BING: It's all on the record.

B-DOG: There *are* some people still believe in .22s.

TEE: Or ice picks. And don't forget the bat.

RAT-NECK: And the lock in the sock!

BING: Are there little peewees, say, nine- to ten-year-olds, in the sets?

RAT-NECK: Yeah, but we say "Li'l Loc" or "Li'l Homie" or "Baby Homie." We never use "peewee" because then people think you're a Mexican. Mexicans say "peewee."

TEE: If it's a Blood set, they use a *k* instead of a *c*. Li'l lok with a *k*. See, Bloods don't say *c*'s and Crips don't say *b*'s. To a Blood, a cigarette is a "bigarette." And Crips don't say "because," they say "cecause."

BING: What prompted you to join, Li'l Monster?

LI'L MONSTER: Say we're white and we're rich. We're in high school and we been buddies since grammar school. And we all decide to go to the same *college*. Well, *we* all on the same street, all those years, and we all just decide to—

RAT-NECK: —join the gang.

TEE: What I think is formulating here is that human nature wants to be accepted. A human being gives less of a damn what he is accepted into. At that age—eleven to seventeen—all kids want to belong. They are un-people.

BING: If you move—can you join another set?

LI'L MONSTER: A couple weeks ago I was talking to a friend 'bout this guy—I'll call him "Iceman." He used to be from Eight-Trey, but he moved to Watts. Now he's a Bounty Hunter.

B-DOG: Boy, that stinks, you know?

BING: He went from the Crips to the Bloods!

LI'L MONSTER: Yeah. And he almost lost his life.

TEE: When you switch sets, when you go from Cuz to Blood, or Blood to Cuz, there's a jacket on you, and you are really pushed to prove yourself for that set. Sometimes the set approves it, and other times they cast you out. If you don't have loyalty to the first set you belong to, what the fuck makes us think that you gonna be loyal to us? That's just too much information. Shit, we kickin' it, we hangin', bangin', and slangin'. But who the fuck are you, and where are you really at? Where your heart at?

B-DOG: Perpetrated is what he is!

BING: What does that mean?

TEE: A perpetrator is a fraud, a bullshitter.

BING: How can someone prove himself?

LI'L MONSTER: All right, like the cat Iceman. They might say, "To prove yourself as a Bounty Hunter you go hit somebody from Eight-Trey."

B-DOG: If you got that much love.

BING: Hit somebody from the very set he was in?

RAT-NECK: Yeah. Then his loyalty is there.

BING: But is it really? Wouldn't someone say, "Hey, he hit his homeboy, what's to say he won't hit us if he changes his mind again?"

TEE: Look, when he changes sets, he's already got a jacket on his ass. And when he goes back and takes somebody else out, that cuts all ties, all love.

B-DOG: Can't go to no 'hood. Can't go nowhere.

RAT-NECK: There it is.

TEE: The highest honor you can give for your set is death. When you die, when you go out in a blaze of glory, you are respected. When you kill for your set, you earn your stripes—you put work in.

RAT-NECK: But once you a Crip—no matter what—you can't get out. No matter what, woo-wah-wham, you still there. I can leave here for five years. Then I get out of jail, I gets a new haircut, new everything. Then, "Hey, there goes Rat-Neck!" You can't hide your face. You can't hide nothin'! All that immunity stuff—that's trash. Nobody forgets you.

TEE: That's how it goes. Just like L.A.P.D.—once he retire and shit, that fool still the police! He's still strapped, carrying a gun. He's *always* a cop. Same with us. If you know the words, sing along: "When you're a Jet, you're a Jet all the way, from your first cigarette to your last dying day."

LI'L MONSTER: There you go.

Hangin', Bangin', Slangin'

BING: Once you're a Blood or a Crip, do you dress differently? We hear about guys with their jeans riding low, their underwear showing up top, wearing colors, and having a certain attitude.

TEE: See, a lot of that is media shit. A brother will get up, take his time, spray his hair, put his French braids in, fold his rag, press his Pendleton or his khaki top, put creases in his pants, lace his shoes, and hit the streets.

LI'L MONSTER: He's dressed to go get busy!

TEE: He's dressed, pressed, he's down!

BING: Is that the way you dress after you're in?

TEE: The reason a lot of brothers wear khaki and house slippers and shit like that is because it's cheap and comfortable.

B-DOG: Ain't no dress code nowadays.

LI'L MONSTER: Look, Rat-Neck got on a blue hat, I got on this hat, we Crips. B-Dog's a Blood: he got red stripes on his shoes, and *that* is that. Now I can be in the mall, look at his shoes, and know he's a Blood. He can look at *my* shoes—these B-K's I got on—and say, "He's a Crip."

RAT-NECK: But then again, might be none of that. Might just be ordinary guys.

BING: I've always thought that B-K stands for "Blood Killers" and that's why Crips wear them.

LI'L MONSTER: It stands for British Knights. I don't buy my clothes because they blue. My jacket and my car is red and white. I wear the colors I want to wear. I don't have no blue rag in my pocket. I don't have no blue rubber bands in my hair. But I can be walking down the street and, nine times out of ten, the police gonna hem me up, label me a gangbanger—

RAT-NECK: —or a dope dealer.

LI'L MONSTER: There's only one look at that you got to have. Especially to the police. You got to look black. *That's* the look. Now B-Dog here's a Blood, and he doesn't even have to be gangbanging because if I'm in a mall with some of my homeboys, nine times out of ten we gonna look at him *crazy*. That's how you know. He don't have to have no red on, we gonna look at him crazy. *That's* the mentality.

TEE: Let me give up this, and you correct me if I'm wrong: police officers can recognize police officers, athletes can recognize athletes, gay people can recognize gay people. Well, we can recognize each other. It's simple.

BING: When someone insults you, what happens?

LI'L MONSTER: Depends on what he saying.

BING: Say he calls you "crab" or "E-ricket." Or, if you're a Blood, he calls you a "slob." These are fighting words, aren't they?

RAT-NECK: It's really just words. Words anybody use. But really, a lot of that word stuff don't get people going nowadays.

LI'L MONSTER: That's right.

TEE: There was a time when you could say something about somebody's mama, and you got to fight. Not so anymore.

LI'L MONSTER: Now just ignore the fool.

TEE: But if somebody say, "Fuck your dead homeboys," oh, *now* we got a problem.

LI'L MONSTER: Yeah, that's right.

TEE: Somebody call me "oo-lah" or "slob," fuck 'em. My rebuttal to that is "I'm a super lok-ed out Blood." There's always a cap back, see what I'm saying? But when you get down to the basics, like, "Fuck your dead homeboy," and you *name* the homeboy, that is death. Oh man, we got to take *this* to the grave.

BING: Well, let's say you're with your homeboys and someone does say, "Fuck your dead homeboys." What happens then?

B-DOG: That's it. The question of the matter is on, right there, *wherever* you at.

LI'L MONSTER: He's dead. And if he's not, he's gonna—

B-DOG: —wish he was.

BING: What does that mean?

TEE: I cannot believe the readers of this magazine are that naive. The point of the matter is, if he disrespects the dead homeboys, his ass is gonna get got. Period. Now let your imagination run free; Steven Spielberg does it.

BING: Why this intensity?

TEE: Because there's something called dedication that we got to get into—dedication to the gang mentality—and understanding where it's coming from. It's like this: there's this barrel, okay? All of us are in it together, and we all want the same thing. But some of us are not so highly motivated to be educated. So we have to get ours from the blood, the sweat, and the tears of the street. And if a homeboy rises up—and it is not so much jealousy as it is the fear of him *leaving* me— I want to come up *with* him, but when he reaches the top of the barrel, I grab him by the pants leg and I—

TEE and LI'L MONSTER:—pull him back down.

TEE: It's not that I don't want to see you go home, but *take me with you!* As a man, I'm standing alone as an individual. But I can't say that to him! I got that manly pride that won't let me break down and say, "Man, I'm scared! Take me with you—I want to go with you!" Now, in-side this barrel, we are in there so tight that every time we turn around we are smelling somebody's ass or somebody else's stinky breath. There's so many people, I got to leave my community to change my fuckin' mind!

RAT-NECK: Yeah!

TEE: That's how strong peer pressure is! It's that crab-in-the-bar-rel syndrome. We are just packed in this motherfucker, but I want to feel good. So how? By bustin' a nut. So I fuck my broad, she get pregnant, and now I got *another* baby. So we in there even tighter. In here, in this room, we can relax, we can kick it, we can laugh, we can say, "Well, shit—homeboy from Hoover's all right." Because we in a setting now, and nobody's saying, "FUCK HIM UP, BLOOD! FUCK HIS ASS! I DON'T LIKE HIM—*KICK* HIS ASS!" You know what I'm saying? That's *bullshit!* We can't just sit down and enjoy each other and say, "Are you a man? Do you wipe your ass like I wipe my ass? Do you cut? Do you bleed? Do you cry? Do you die?" There's nowhere where we can go and just experience each other as *people*. And then, when we *do* do that, everybody's strapped.

RAT-NECK: Seems like nothin' else . . .

BING: You make it sound inescapable. What would you tell someone coming along? What would you tell a younger brother?

RAT-NECK: I had a younger brother, fourteen years old. He's dead now, but we never did talk about it. He was a Blood and I am a Crip, and I *know* what time it is. I couldn't socialize with him on what he do. All he could do is ask me certain things, like, "Hey, bro, do you think I'm doing the right thing?" And, well, all I could say is, "Hey, man, choose what you wanna be. What can I do? I love you, but what do I look like, goin' to my mama, tellin' her I *smoked* you, *smoked* my brother? What I look like? But why should I neglect you because you from there? Can't do that. You my love." And if I don't give a fuck about my love, and I don't give a fuck about my brother, then I don't give a fuck about my mama. And then your ass out, when you don't give a fuck about your mama.

Like some people say, "I don't give a fuck, I'll *smoke* my mama!" Well, you know, that's stupidity shit.

BING: I realize that loyalty is paramount. But what I want to know is, if a rival set has it out for someone, does it always mean death?

LI'L MONSTER: Before anybody go shooting, it's going to be, "What is the problem?" Then we are going to find the root of the problem. "Do you personally have something against Eight-Trey?" You say, "No, I just don't like what one of your homeboys did." Then you all beat him up.

B-DOG: Beat him up, yeah.

LI'L MONSTER: Just head it up. Ain't nobody else going to get in this.

BING: Head it up?

LI'L MONSTER: Fight. One on one. You know, head up. And then it's over.

BING: Are you friends after that?

LI'L MONSTER: Well, you not sending each other Christmas cards.

BING: What if you just drive through another gang's turf? Are you in danger?

LI'L MONSTER: Yeah. I mean, I could be sitting at a light, and somebody say, "That's that fool, Li'l Monster," and they start shooting. That could be anywhere. Bam! Bam! Bam!

BING: Are you targeted by reputation?

LI'L MONSTER: Yeah. That's my worst fear, to be sitting at a light.

B-DOG: That's one of mine, too.

LI'L MONSTER: So I don't stop. I don't pull up right behind a car. And I am always looking around.

B-DOG: Always looking.

LI'L MONSTER: That's my worst fear because *we* did so much of it. You know, you pull up, man, block him in, and—

B-DOG: —that was it.

LI'L MONSTER: They put in work. That is my worst fear. And if you ever ride with me, you notice I always position myself where there is a curb. That middle lane is no-man's land.

B-DOG: That's dangerous.

LI'L MONSTER: You know how they say, "Look out for the other guy?" Well, I *am* the other guy. Get out of my way. Give me the starting position. You know, because I can—phew! Claustrophobia. I see that shit happenin', man. I *be* that shit happenin', man, and I don't *never* want that to happen to me, just to be sitting at the light and they take your whole head off.

BING: Say everybody's fired up to get somebody from an enemy set, but there's this young kid who says, "I can't do that. I don't feel right about it—this is a friend of mine." What's going to happen?

LI'L MONSTER: There's many ways that it can be dealt with. Everybody can disown him, or everybody can just say, "Okay, *fine,* but you gotta do something else." See what I'm saying?

B-DOG: But he's gonna be disciplined one way or the other.

RAT-NECK: 'Cause he know everything, man, and he think he gonna ride on up outta here?

LI'L MONSTER: So you go home and say, "Yeah, mama. I got out, mama. Everything's cool." And mama looking at *you* like—"Son, are you sure?" 'Cause she knows damn well those motherfuckers ain't gonna let you go that easy.

TEE: Now that's the flip side to those motherfuckers who say, "I smoke *anybody*—I'll smoke my mama!" We, as homeboys, look at him and say, "Your mama carried you nine months and shitted you out, and if you'll kill your mama, I know you don't give two shakes of a rat's rectum about me!"

RAT-NECK: He'll kill me. He'll smoke me.

BING: What's going to happen in 1989? Los Angeles has the highest body count ever. More deaths than in Ireland.

RAT-NECK: Not more than New York. In New York they kill you for just a penny. I took a trip to New York one time. This guy wanted me to see what it was like.

BING: You mean gang life in New York City?

RAT-NECK: No, to see how people live—gang life, the whole environment, the whole everything. I was there for two days, right? He took us to Queens, Harlem, the Bronx—everywhere. We talked about going out strapped. He said, "What the fuck, you can't go out there strapped! What's wrong with you?" But I say I gotta let 'em know what time it is and carry *something,* you know, 'cause we don't really know what's going on in New York. But we hear so *much* about New York, how they operate, how rough it's supposed to be. So, okay, we decide we gonna carry a buck knife—something. So we kickin', walkin', cruisin' the street, everything. And then I see a homeboy standin' right here next to me.

And he come up to us and do some shit like this: he take three pennies, shake 'em, and throw 'em down in front of his shoe. We, like, what the fuck is this? Is it, you got a beef? Like, he knew we weren't from there. So we not lookin' at him, but, like, why the fuck he throw three pennies down there? Like, was it, "Get off our turf"? But we didn't understand his language. Out here, it's like, "What's happenin'? What's up, Cuz? What's up, Blood?" But in New York, you lookin' at the damn pennies, and maybe he come back and hit you. Maybe if you pick up the pennies, then you got a beef with him. Maybe if you don't pick 'em up, then you supposed to walk off. But shit, we lookin' at the pennies, and lookin' at him, and it's like god*damn!* So we walks off and leaves the Bronx and goes to Harlem.

Oh, man—*that's* what you call a gutter. You get to lookin' around there and thinking, "God*damn,* these my people? Livin' like *this?* Livin' in a cardboard box?" I mean, skid row got it goin' *on* next to Harlem. Skid row look like *Hollywood* to them.

Kickin' It

BING: Did you vote in the last election?

TEE: Yeah, I voted. But look at the choice I had: Bush bastard and Dumb-kakis.

RAT-NECK: A bush and a cock.

BING: Why didn't you vote for Jesse in the primary?

TEE: I truly believe that shit rigged. Everybody I know voted for Jesse, but—

B-DOG: Jesse was out.

RAT-NECK: It's different for us. Like, what's that guy's name shot President Reagan? What happened to that guy? *Nothin'!*

BING: He's in prison.

LI'L MONSTER: Oh no he's not. He's in a *hospital.*

TEE: They're *studyin'* him.

RAT-NECK: See, they did that to cover his ass. They say he retarded or something.

B-DOG: See, if I had shot Reagan, would they have put *me* in a mental facility?

RAT-NECK: They would have put you away right there where you shot him. Bam—judge, jury, executioner.

TEE: Why is it they always study white folks when they do heinous crimes, but they never study us? *We* got black psychiatrists.

BING: What about all this killing, then?

TEE: I'm gonna shut up now, because the way the questions are coming, you portray us as animals. Gangbanging is a way of life. You got to touch it, smell it, feel it. Hearing the anger, the frustration, and the desperation of all of us only adds to what the media's been saying—and it's worse, coming out of *our* mouths. There has to be questions directed with an understanding of our point of view. Sorry.

BING: All right. Ask one.

TEE: It's not my interview.

BING: I'm trying to understand your motives. Let me ask a different question: If a homeboy is killed, how is the funeral conducted?

TEE: You got four different sets here in this room, and each set has its own rules and regulations.

RAT-NECK: Okay, like, my little brother just got killed. You talkin' funeralwise, right? At this funeral, Bloods *and* Crips was there. But didn't nobody wear nothin', just suits. *Every* funeral you go to is not really colors.

TEE: Thank you! Yeah!

RAT-NECK: You just going to give your last respect. Like my little brother, it really tripped me out, the way I seen a big "B" of flowers with red roses in it, and one tiny *blue* thing they brought. And these were *Bloods!*—goddamn! Like one of my homeboys asked me, "What's happenin', Rat?" and I said, "Hey, man—you tell *me*." And I looked around, saw some other guys there, you know? They ain't *us*, but they came and showed respect, so—move back. Couple of them walked by us, looked at us, and said, "That's our homeboy, that's Rat-Neck's brother."

When he got killed, you know, I had a whole lot of animosity. I'd smoke any damn one of 'em, but one thing—one thing about it—*it wasn't black people who did it.* That's the one thing that didn't make me click too much. Now, if a black person woulda did it, ain't no tellin' where I'd be right now, or what I'd do, or how I'd feel. I'd be so confused I might just straight out fuck my job, my wife, my kid, whatever, and say, "I don't give a fuck about you—bro got killed!"

BING: How did he get killed?

RAT-NECK: I don't really know the whole rundown.

TEE: What Rat-Neck's saying is the respect. We buried three of our own yesterday, and for each one we went to the mother to see how *she* wanted it—

LI'L MONSTER: —how she wanted it! That's it!

TEE: 'Cause the mother carried that baby for nine months—that's her *child*. It's *her* family, and we're the extended family. She got the first rights on what goes on there. It's the respect factor that lies there, and if the mother says there's no colors, you better believe ain't no colors!

RAT-NECK: And no cartridges in the coffin.

TEE: If he went out in a blaze of glory, and his mama say, "You all bury him like you want to bury him"—oh, then we *do* it."

BING: How would that be?

TEE: If he was a baller—you know what I'm saying—then everybody get suited and booted.

BING: Do you mean a sea of colors?

EVERYONE: *NO!* Suits and ties! Shined shoes!

LI'L MONSTER: Jump in the silk!

TEE: We own suits, you know. Brooks Brothers, C and R Clothiers! And some of the shit is tailored!

BING: You mention your mothers a lot, and I sense a love that's very real. If you do love your moms so much and you kill each other, then it has to be the mothers who ultimately suffer the worst pain. How do you justify that?

B-DOG: Your mother gonna suffer while you living, anyway. While you out there gangbanging, she's suffering. My mother's suffering right now. All my brothers in jail.

RAT-NECK: My mother's sufferin', sittin' in her living room, and maybe there's a bullet comin' in the window.

BING: What do you say to your mother when she says, "All your brothers are in jail, and you're out there in danger"?

B-DOG: We don't even get *into* that no more.

RAT-NECK: She probably don't think about that at all—just so she can cope with it.

B-DOG: Me and my mother don't discuss that no more, because I been into this for so long, you know. When me and my mother be together, we try to be happy. We don't talk about the gang situation.

LI'L MONSTER: Me and my mother are real tight, you know? We talk like sister and brother. I don't try to justify myself to her—any more than she tries to justify *her* work or how she makes her money to me. What I do *may* come back to hurt her, but what *she* does may also come back to hurt me. Say I'm thirteen and I'm staying with my mother, and she goes off on her boss and loses her job—how does she justify that to *me?*

BING: Well, the loss of a job is not quite the same as an actively dangerous life-style in the streets, wouldn't you agree?

TEE: "An actively dangerous life-style"—that really fucks me up. Okay, here we go. "Woman" is a term that means "of man." Wo*man*. My mother raised me, true enough. Okay? And she was married. There was a male figure in the house. But I never accepted him as my father. My mother can only teach me so much 'bout being a man-child in the Promised Land. If, after that, there is nothing for me to take pride in, then I enter into manhood asshole backwards, and I stand there, a warrior strong and proud. But there is no outlet for that energy, for me or my brothers, so we *turn on each other*.

So, Mom sends us to the show, and all we get is Clint Eastwood, *Superfly*, and *Sweet Sweet Bad Ass*. Now what goes up on the silver screen comes down into the streets, and now you got a homeboy. And mama says, "I don't want you to go to your grave as a slave for the minimum wage." So you say, "I am going to go get us something, make this better, pay the rent."

The first thing a successful athlete does—and you can check me out—is buy his mama a big-ass house. That's what we want. And if we have to get it from the streets, that's where we go.

BING: Why?

TEE: It's the same *everywhere*. A sorority, a fraternity, the Girl Scouts, camping club, hiking club, L.A.P.D., the Los Angeles Raiders, are all the same. Everything that you find in those groups and institutions you find in a gang.

BING: So are you saying there's no difference between the motives of you guys joining a gang and, say, a young WASP joining a fraternity?

RAT-NECK: You got a lot of gangbangers out there who are smart. They want it. They *got* what it takes. But the difference is they got no money.

TEE: I know a homie who had a scholarship to USC. But he left school because he found prejudice *alive* in America, and it cut him out. He said, "I don't have to stand here and take this. As a matter of fact, you owe my great-grandfather forty acres and a mule."

LI'L MONSTER: Forget the mule, just give me the forty acres.

TEE: So he took to the streets. He got a Ph.D. from SWU. That's a Pimp and Hustler Degree from Sidewalk University.

BING: If it went the other way, what would your life be like?

RAT-NECK: I'm really a hardworking man. I make bed mattresses now, but I would like to straight out be an engineer, or give me a daycare center with little kids coming through, and get me the hell away as far as I can. All I want to do is be myself and not perpetrate myself, try not to perpetrate my black people. Just give me a job, give me a nice house—everybody dream of a nice home—and just let me deal with it.

BING: And how do drugs figure into this?

LI'L MONSTER: Wait a minute. I just want to slide in for a minute. I want to set the record straight. People think gangs and drugs go hand in hand, but they don't. If I sell drugs, does that make me a gangbanger? No. If I gangbang, does that make me sell drugs? No. See, for white people—and I am not saying for all white people, just like what I say about black people is not for all black people—they go for college, the stepping-stone to what they want to get. And some black people look to drugs as a stepping-stone to get the same thing.

B-DOG: They want to live better. To buy what they want. To get a house.

RAT-NECK: Not worry about where the next meal come from.

TEE: To live comfortable and get a slice of American Pie, the American Dream.

B-DOG: There it is.

TEE: The Army came out with a hell of a slogan: "Be all you can be." And that's it. We all want the same thing. We've been taught by television, the silver screen, to grow up and have a chicken in every pot, two Chevys, 2.3 kids in the family. So we have been taught the same thing that you have been taught, but there is certain things that we can hold on to and other things that—we see them, but we just cannot reach them. Most of us are dealing with the reality of surviving as opposed to, "Well, my dad will take care of it."

BING: Are you saying that gangbanging is just another version of the American Dream?

LI'L MONSTER: It's like this. You got the American Dream over there, and you reaching for it. But you can't get it. And you got dope right here, real close. You can grab it easy. Dealing with the closer one, you might possibly make enough money to grab the other one. Then you throw away the dope. That's a big *if* now.

BING: Seriously, does anybody ever stop dealing?

B-DOG: If you was making a million dollars off of drugs, you know what I'm saying, are you gonna give that up for a legitimate business?

TEE: This goes back to it. You started out for need, and now you stuck in it because of greed. That's when you play your life away. There comes a time when you have to stop playing, but as far as the streets go, you are a *street player*. Now there may come a time when you say, all right, I've played. I've had time in the gang, now I got to raise up. But if you is so greedy that you cannot smell the coffee, then you're cooked.

BING: But if you do get out, do you always have to come back when your homeboys call?

LI'L MONSTER: It ain't like you gonna be called upon every month.

B-DOG: But if you gets called, then you must be needed, and you must come.

LI'L MONSTER: It's like this—and I don't care who you are, where you started, or how far you got—you *never* forget where you come from.

TEE: That's it.

B-DOG: You *never* forget where you come from.

A Gangbanger's Glossary

Baller: a gangbanger who is making money; also *high roller*

Cap: a retort

Click up: to get along well with a homeboy

Crab: insulting term for a Crip; also *E-ricket*

Cuz: alternative name for a Crip; often used in a greeting, e.g., "What's up, Cuz?"

Down: to do right by your homeboys; to live up to expectations; to protect your turf, e.g., "It's the job of the homeboys to be down for the 'hood"

Gangbanging: the activities of a gang

Gat: gun

Give it up: to admit to something

Hangin', bangin', and slangin': to be out with the homeboys, talking the talk, walking the walk; slangin' comes from "slinging" or selling dope

Head up: to fight someone one-on-one

Hemmed up: to be hassled or arrested by the police

'Hood: neighborhood; turf

Homeboy: anyone from the same neighborhood or gang; a friend or an accepted person; in a larger sense, a person from the inner city; also *homie*

Jacket: a record or a reputation, both within the gang and at the police station

Jumped in: initiated into a gang; getting jumped in typically entails being beaten up by the set members

Kickin' it: kicking back, relaxing with your homeboys

Loc-ed out: also *lok-ed out;* from "loco," meaning ready and willing to do anything

Make a move: commit a crime; also *manipulate*

Mark: someone afraid to commit a crime; also *punk*

O.G.: an abbreviation for Original Gangster; i.e., a gang member who has been in the set for a long time and has made his name

Oo-lah: insulting term for a Blood; also *slob*

Perpetrate: betray your homeboys; bring shame on yourself and your set

Put in work: any perilous activity from fighting to murder that benefits the set or the gang

Set: any of the various neighborhood gangs that fit within the larger framework of Bloods and Crips

Smoke: to kill someone

Top it off: to get along well with someone; reach an understanding

Speculations

1. According to this article, why do kids join gangs? What do they receive from gangs that they need—and otherwise would be lacking?
2. The language in this selection can be described as offensive. What would have been lost if the swearing and expletives had been deleted? What would have been gained in terms of the reader's response? Aside from the coarseness of the language, evaluate what is said and the ability of the gang members to communicate.
3. The gang members are well aware that their conversation is being recorded by *Harper's Magazine* and that it will be published. Where do you detect evidence of this awareness? How do you think it influences what they say and how they say it? How do you think the gang members are responding to Bing? What is her interest in what they have to say?
4. What parallels, if any, would you draw between your own experiences growing up and those of gang members as repre-

sented in this essay? What kind of rapport would you have with the Crips and Bloods? What are your "gang" or group experiences as far as loyalty to the group and respect for your family?

5. Li'l Monster, B-Dog, Rat-Neck, and Tee all talk about the relationship between gangs, drugs, television, and images of success. How have these elements influenced your goals and future plans? Why do you think these elements were particularly influential on the Crips and Bloods?

ASSIGNMENT SEQUENCES

Sequence One: Family Life

1. You are a researcher, interested in discovering and collecting data about college students and their family experiences. Your job is to develop a questionnaire that you can give to 15 to 20 college students, from which you will draw some conclusions about the family experiences of those particular students.

   Creating a questionnaire is not easy; you will need to develop a clear sense of purpose, focus on just one or two specific areas of interest, and write questions that are clear and unambiguous. Such work might best be done in teams, with lots of in-class workshopping, sharing, and revising. You will want to make sure that your questionnaire is complete enough to provide you the information you want, yet short enough that students not known to you will be willing to fill it out easily and completely.

   Once you have developed this questionnaire, give it to at least 15 to 20 college students whom you do not know. You might simply find students in another class, in the student union, in the cafeteria, and the like. Make sure that you get full responses.

2. Now that you have responses to your questionnaire, the next step is to compile the data and draw some conclusions in a thoughtful, well-reasoned report. Your assignment, either individually or in groups (as designated by your instructor), is to draft a report on "the family experience of college students" based on the data from your questionnaire.

3. In *Rachel and Her Children,* Jonathan Kozol writes:

   It is a commonplace that a society reveals its reverence or contempt for history by the respect or disregard that it displays for older people. The way we treat our children tells us something of our moral disposition too. Kozol implies in this quote that young people may not be adequately valued in our society. Consider what this implies about the roles children are given in family life. Using the insights from the selections by Kozol and Léon Bing, write an essay that analyzes societal values among families and young people.

In your essay, you might want to focus on the particular problems of teenagers, single-parent families, gangs, or the homeless, drawing upon the works that you have read in *Speculations* as well as additional research that you do outside of class. Once you have analyzed your subject closely, draw some conclusions about the general "moral disposition" of society, based on what you discover.

4. What is it that enables successful families to thrive? What is a successful family? Based on selections by Jamaica Kincaid, Amy Tan, David Elkind, and others, offer your view of what it takes to create successful family life. You may use information gathered in Assignments 1–3 above or read ahead to other selections in *Specualtions* to form your ideas. Consider what principles you think families should adhere to and how conflicts should be resolved. You might also consider nontraditional family situations, single-parent families, families that have only one child, gay and lesbian parenting, adoption, and mixed-race famlies. As you develop your idea of what makes a successful family, remember that other readers may hold views very strongly opposed to your own.

5. You are now an expert on the particular subject you have just written about in Assignment 4. Write an editorial comment for your local newspaper on the Op-Ed page.

Before you write your editorial comment, make sure that you have a strong commitment toward a specific position. You will also need to make sure that you have enough facts, data, and information to be persuasive. You will also need to consider factors such as potential audience, appropriate tone, desirable length, etc. You might share drafts of this comment in class before handing in the final copy—which should go not only to your instructor but in the mail to your local newspaper as well.

Sequence Two: Using Language

1. In "Girl," Jamaica Kincaid explores what it means to be a particular girl in a particular family and culture. Taking this selection as your inspiration and model, write your own account of what it means to be a child in a specific family or culture. Entitle your essay "Girl" or "Boy" as appropriate. Although you do not have to imitate Kincaid's "Girl," do your best to emulate its sense of style, coherence, voice, and drama.

2. The experience of language that one has in families, neighborhoods, and among friends can make a major difference in the ways one perceives and uses words. We see such language use in selections by Kincaid, Bing, Bambara, and others. After brainstorming about the different contexts and uses of language in your own life, write an essay which describes some specific words, phrases, or usages that you remember with great pleasure and affection. They might have been words expressed by grandparents, parents, siblings, friends, neighbors. In your essay, consider as well why words/phrases/language usage are so important to you. What kinds of values do they represent? How do they see things differently than you?

3. "When You're a Crip (or a Blood)" presents an entirely different kind of language use. How do you explain the idiomatic and frequently profane use of language by Li'l Monster, Rat-Neck, Tee Rodgers, and B-Dog? Why do you think they speak the way they do? In a short essay, present your analysis; be prepared to share your essay with the rest of the class.

4. Toni Cade Bambara's story "The Lesson" is notable for its use of black dialect or black English vernacular. As a research project, investigate dialect in American society. What effect does dialect, black dialect in particular, have upon its audience? How did such a dialect develop in America? In what ways does it differ from the dialect known as edited American English? Is one dialect "superior" or "inferior" to another? What is the relation between dialect and class? Dialect and influence? Dialect and the speaker's place in society? Any one of these topics—when researched—can provide material for a thoughtful and substantial essay.

5. The previous questions focus on the relationship between language and reality. They suggest that language does not simply describe reality but actually gives shape to it. Thus the words people use influence what they see—and what they don't see. Drawing upon at least three of the selections in "Growing Up," explore the relationship between words and perception. Include your own personal insights and experiences as well.

Sequence Three: Parent and Child

1. In "Girl," Jamaica Kincaid portrays events from her childhood to draw out certain truths and feelings about her family experience. In an exploratory essay, use that same technique to write about a feeling, an experience, an event, a truth that has meaning for you. Remember that the past event or experience that you revisit does

not have to be anything momentous, although it can be. It can, however, also be an event that seemed insignificant at the time, but that you know now was important. Remember that you will want to write about that "you" of the past as if she/he were someone else, yet you will also want to establish for the reader a deep psychic connection between that "you" of the past and yourself as the author of this essay.

2. Many of the essays in this section focus on the relation between parents and children. What responsibilities do parents have for their children? What should parents do to help their children? What must they do? Look particularly at the selections by Jamaica Kincaid, Amy Tan, David Elkind, or Jonathan Kozol. What kinds of issues are raised by the way the parents in these selections relate to their children? What insights or comments would you want to offer them?

3. Now consider the same question from the other vantage point—namely, what responsibilities do children have to their parents? In this case, look at other selections from "Growing Up" as well as those mentioned in question 2. Do children owe their parents anything? If so, in what ways are they obligated to their parents? How would you describe a healthy child–parent relationship?

4. Compare Jamaica Kincaid's sense of *identity* and family life to Amy Tan's view of herself and her family. How are the family situations of these two women alike or different, especially in relation to their mothers? How do you think their experiences while growing up contribute to their sense of themselves as artists? Based on your reading of these two selections, write an essay that describes what these two writers hold in common.

Sequence Four: Family Values

1. Amy Tan and Jamaica Kincaid write about parent–child relationships from the child's point of view. Write an essay about family values and parent–child relationships from the parents' point of view. Base your essay on your reading of Amy Tan, Jamaica Kincaid, or a similar selection from this book, focusing on the same themes as the author you select.

2. "The Lesson" focuses on that "quintessential" American experience—looking at and buying things in stores. Based on your reading of this story, what is the political and cultural significance of going to stores, whether they are toy stores or shopping malls? What do stores offer us? What kinds of values are embodied in

them? What do they tell us about American society—both good and bad? What do they tell us about families?

3. David Elkind argues that:

> ... the trend toward obscuring the divisions between children and adults is part of a broad egalitarian movement in this country that seeks to overcome the barriers separating the sexes, ethnic and racial groups, and the handicapped.... From this perspective, the contemporary pressure for children to grow up fast is only one symptom of a much larger social phenomenon in this country—a movement toward true equality, toward the ideal expressed in our Declaration of Independence. While one can only applaud this movement with respect to the sexes, ethnic and racial groups, and the handicapped, its unthinking extension to children is unfortunate.

In a carefully reasoned essay, analyze this statement and the various assumptions that Elkind makes. Is there a movement toward equality? How so? Does such a movement include the collapse of difference between child and adult? How do children's rights compare to those of an adult? In your essay, attempt to formulate a set of family values that preserve the rights of children without forcing them, in Elkind's terms, to forsake their childhoods.

4. National leaders often call for Americans to return to traditional family values, especially during election years. Basing your views on the selections in "Growing Up," write an essay that explores contemporary family values. What do the families of 1990s America believe in? What's right—and what's wrong—with family life?

FOCUS ON

Video and Violence

As the diverse perspectives in this section demonstrate, many people are appalled at the overwhelming number of video images that regularly portray violence on television and in film while others suggest that to condemn these representations is to miss the point: Real violence has always been part of our culture, and its causes run deeper than images on a screen. Some of these critics argue that violent behavior goes hand-in-hand with childhood abuse, economic despair, emotional deprivation, racial divisions, and gender prejudices and that attacking media images rather than the real causes of violence wastes valuable time and resources. What is undeniable is that the mass media has insinuated itself into the fabric of our everyday lives with a profusion of provocative, alluring, aggressive, and disturbing images that seem unprecedented and unmanageable. Furthermore, we know that television shows and films are deliberately designed for our consumption and carry specific messages about how we can or should participate in our culture.

Do violent images display what we have become? To what degree do they shape our thinking and self-images? Does repeatedly viewing representations of mayhem, rape, and murder in the entertainment media desensitize us and perhaps even encourage us to enjoy such violence? Or does seeing such acts as high drama trigger a cathartic reaction that releases repressed desires and keeps people from acting out violent fantasies? Is it possible that dramatic violence can even engender critical awareness and compassion? And what about children? What effect does violence in film and television have on them, and how do we measure it?

These are the kinds of questions that the authors in this section consider as they sort through the complex issues surrounding film and television content, and its relationship to the emotional and psychological well-being of American children. We note as well that the authors here raise at least indirectly some disturbing questions about many of us as consumers and our seemingly insatiable craving for sex and violence within the entertainment industry. We think you will find these selections of significant interest and expect that you will have a great deal to reflect on in your own discussions and in your writing.

WHERE THE GIRLS ARE

Susan Douglas

Susan Douglas, a professor of media and American studies at Hampshire College, lives in Amherst, Massachusetts, with her husband and daughter. She writes a regular column as a media critic for *The Progressive* magazine and has authored two books: *Where the Girls Are: Growing Up Female with the Mass Media* (1994) and *Inventing American Broadcasting: 1899–1922* (1987). A graduate of Elmira College (B.A.) and Brown University (M.A. and Ph.D.) Douglas has lectured at colleges and universities throughout the United States and has written for *The Nation, The Village Voice, In These Times, The Washington Post,* and *TV Guide.* She has appeared on "The Today Show," "Working Woman," NPR's "Fresh Air," "Weekend Edition," and "Talk of the Nation," and various radio talk shows around the country. Widely praised, *Where the Girls Are* was chosen as one of the top ten books of 1994 by National Public Radio, *Entertainment Weekly,* and *The McLaughlin Group.* Currently cowriting a book on motherhood and the media, Douglas's next projects include a book about the history of radio listening in America, commissioned by the Alfred P. Sloan Foundation, and an examination of how motherhood has been portrayed in the mass media from the late 1960s to the present.

In her "Preface" to *Inventing American Broadcasting,* Douglas explains that she wrote about the history of media broadcasting so as "to understand better the rise of and impact of the communications systems that have so insinuated themselves into American thought and life . . . [and] to analyze intellectually as adults what has gripped us emotionally since childhood." In the following selection, taken from *Where the Girls Are,* she describes the influence of television on young girls, including her four-year-old daughter. Expressing her concern for how young women's identities are being shaped, Douglas suggests strategies for addressing the negative effects of mass media on children.

"Mommy, Mommy, hurry, come quickly, now!" implores my daughter at 8:16 a.m. on Saturday. This is the one time of the week she's allowed to watch commercial television, and the price is heavy. I drag my hungover and inadequately caffeinated butt over to the TV set. Her eyes shine like moonstones as I see what's on the screen. "Can I get that, Mommy, can I, puleeze? Please, Mommy." I see before me some hideous plastic doll, or pony, or troll, being pitched by a combination of elated little girls, flashing lights, and rap music. Everything seems to be colored hot pink or lilac. Sometimes it's one of these dolls you can put fake jewels all over, other times it's a troll doll in a wedding dress, or it's something really bad, like Kitty Surprise or Cheerleader Skipper. It is always something specifically targeted to little girls. She is four years old, and she understands, completely, the semiotics of gender differentiation. She never calls me when they're selling Killer Commando Unit, G.I. Joe, and all the other Pentagon-inspired stuff obviously for boys. She knows better. She knows she's a girl, and she knows what's for her. Twenty years of feminist politics and here I am, with a daughter who wants nothing more in the whole wide world than to buy Rollerblade Barbie.

Having grown up with the mass media myself, and considering what that has done for me and to me, I bring all that to bear as I raise my own little girl, who will, in her own way, and with her own generation, have her hopes and fears shaped by the mass media too. Ever since she was old enough to understand books, kids' movies, and *Sesame Street,* I have looked, in vain, for strong and appealing female characters for her to identify with. With a few exceptions, like *The Paperbag Princess,* shrewd, daring girls who outsmart monsters and value their freedom and self-esteem more than marrying some prince are hard to find. There's Maria, who knows how to fix toasters and stereos, on *Sesame Street.* But little kids are, at first, most drawn to the Muppets, and until recently, not one of the main stars—Big Bird, Kermit, the Count, Elmo, Snuffy, or Oscar—was female. Children's books are not much better. Even if they feature animals as the main protagonists, stories for kids too readily assume, automatically, that the main actor is male. Television cartoons, from Winnie the Pooh (no females except Kanga, and she's always doing laundry or cooking), to Garfield to Doug, not to mention the more obnoxious superhero action ones, still treat females either as nonexistent or as ancillary afterthoughts. We have the cartoon *James Bond, Jr.,* but no *Emma Peel, Jr.* And it goes without saying that nearly all the little girls she sees on TV and elsewhere are white.

And then there are the movies. When mothers cling to *The Little Mermaid* as one of the few positive representations of girls, we see how far we have not come. Ariel, the little mermaid in question, is indeed brave, curious, feisty, and defiant. She stands up to her father, saves Prince Eric from drowning, and stares down great white sharks as she hunts for sunken treasure. But her waist is the diameter of a chive, and her salvation comes through her marriage—at the age of sixteen, no less—to Eric. And the sadistic, consummately evil demon in the movie is, you guessed it, an older, overweight woman with too much purple eyeshadow and eyeliner, a female octopus who craves too much power and whose nether regions evoke the dreaded vagina dentate.

Belle, in *Beauty and the Beast,* dreams of escaping from the narrow confines of her small town, of having great adventures, and has nothing but contempt for the local cleft-chinned lout and macho beefcake Gaston. Her dreams of a more interesting, exciting life, however, are also fulfilled through marriage alone. The most important quality of these characters remains their beauty, followed closely by their self-lessness and the ability to sing. There are gestures to feminism—Ariel's physical courage, Belle's love of books, and, in *Aladdin,* Jasmine's defiance of an arbitrary law that dictates when and whom she must marry. These are welcome flourishes, and many of us milk them for all they're worth—"See how *strong* she is, honey?"—but they are still only flourishes, overwhelmed by the age-old narrative that selfless, beautiful girls are rewarded by the love of a prince they barely know. Nonanimated movies for kids are no better. Hollywood simply takes it for granted that little heroes, like big ones, are always boys. So little girls get *Home Alone* and who knows how many sequels, *Cop and a Half, The Karate Kid, Rookie of the Year, Free Willy,* and *Dennis the Menace,* all with little boy leads, little boy adventures, and little boy heroism, while gutsy, smart, enterprising, and sassy little girls remain, after all this time, absent, invisible, denied. Even my daughter, at the age of four, volunteered one day, "Mommy, there should be more movies with girls."

The one movie that I was happy to have my daughter embrace was made over fifty years ago, and judging from anecdotal evidence, it's been enjoying an enormous resurgence among the preschool set. No narrative has gripped my daughter's imagination more than *The Wizard of Oz.* And why not? Finally, here's a *girl* who has an adventure and doesn't get married at the end. She runs away from home, flies to Oz in a cyclone, kills one wicked witch and then another—although never on purpose—and helps Scarecrow get a brain, Tin Man get a heart, and Lion get some courage, all of which Dorothy already has in spades. Throughout the movie, Dorothy is caring, thoughtful, nurturing, and empathetic, but she's also adventuresome, determined, and courageous. She tells off Miss Gulch, slaps the lion while her male friends cower in the bushes, refuses to give the witch her slippers, and chastises the Wizard himself when she feels he is bullying her friends. Of course, when she's older, my daughter will learn the truth about Dorothy: that Judy Garland had to have her breasts strapped down for the part and was fed bucketfuls of amphetamines so she'd remain as slim as the studio wanted. This, too, I think, will speak to my daughter.

Shortly after seeing a few of the Disney fairy tales, both old and new, my daughter announced, at age three and a half, that she would no longer wear the unisex sweat suits and overalls I'd been dressing her in. It was dresses or nothing. Her favorite pretend games became "wedding" and "family," with her as either the bride or the mom. She loved playing Wizard of Oz—she was always Dorothy, of course—but she also loved playing Snow White, dropping like a sack of onions to the kitchen floor after she'd bitten into the pretend apple. The blocks, the Tinkertoys, and the trucks I had gotten her lay neglected, while the Barbie population began to multiply like fruit flies.

One of the things that feminist moms, and dads, for that matter, confront is the force of genetics. In the 1970s, I was convinced that most of the differences between men and women were the results of social-ization. In the nature-nurture debate, I gave nature very little due. But now, as a parent, I have seen my daughter, long before she ever watched television, prefer dolls to trucks, use blocks to build enclo-sures instead of towers, and focus on interpersonal relationships in her play rather than on hurling projectiles into things. But at the same time, I have seen children's television (which, if anything, is even more ret-rograde than it was in the 1970s) reinforce and exaggerate these gender differences with a vengeance as if there were no overlap of traits at all between boys and girls.

Back in the 1970s, when Action for Children's Television, under the leadership of Peggy Charren, and feminist activists were pressuring advertisers, the FCC, and the networks to reduce TV violence, elimi-nate sexism, and stop pushing pink and purple sugar balls as a nutri-tious breakfast, there seemed to be a few moments when it actually looked like children's television might improve. After all, "Free to Be You and Me" was one of the biggest hit records for kids, and *Sesame Street* was drawing viewers away from commercial television.

But if you turn on Saturday morning TV now, it's as if none of that ever happened. In fact, kids' TV is worse than ever, and certainly more crass, more sexist, and more nutritionally criminal than much of the programming pitched to adults. In addition to all the war toys that train little boys to be cannon fodder and/or gun collectors, and the makeup kits and dolls that train little girls to be sex objects and/or moms, the overall message is about regarding yourself and everyone else you know as a commodity to be bought and sold. Ads geared to each gender encourage kids to dehumanize themselves and one anoth-er, to regard people as objects to be acquired or discarded. "Get the right boyfriend! Get the right friends!" commands an ad for a game for girls, Spring Valley High School (or maybe it was called Shop 'Til You Drop). To be a desirable commodity, a little girl must herself consume the right goods so she can make herself pretty and ornament herself properly. Being able to sing and smile admiringly at boys is highly de-sirable. Being smart, brave, or assertive isn't. On Saturday morning, boys are "cool"; girls are their mirrors, flat, shiny surfaces whose func-tion is to reflect all this coolness back to them and on them. Girls watch boys be "awesome" and do "awesome" things. Girls aren't awesome; they're only spectators.

Already I see my little girl, at the age of four, managing the mixed messages around her. I see her process them, try to control them, and allow them into her sense of her place in the world. She wants to be at the center of the action, and she dictates the precise direction of her pretend games with the authority of a field marshal. In the books she has about rabbits, cats, alligators, and the like, she insists that I change all the pronouns from he to she so the story will be about a girl, not a boy. Already, she is resisting, without yet knowing it, certain sexist presumptions of the media. But she succumbs to them too. For it is also important to her that she be pretty, desired, and the one who beats out the ugly stepsisters for the prince's attention. She wants control and she wants love, and she is growing up in a culture as confused about how much of each a woman can have as it was in the 1950s and '60s. So she will be surrounded by media imagery that holds out promises of female achievement with one hand and slaps her down with the other. Already she knows we have a smart, accomplished first lady, because that's what her mother tells her. What she doesn't know yet, but will soon learn, is the price that first lady has had to pay simply for refusing to sit by the sidelines, cheerlead once in a while, and serve refreshments to the boys. My little girl will have to learn that if she wants nothing more than the same opportunities, access to power, freedom, and autonomy as any little boy in her preschool, sooner or later, she will pay a price never expected of them.

Because of the women's movement, and the ongoing vitality of feminism in the United States, my daughter will also grow up seeing women reporting the nightly news, women on the Supreme Court, women in the House and the Senate. She already has a female doctor, and when we go into town she sees female police officers, shop owners, and mail carriers. She knows women who are lawyers, reproductive rights activists, writers, college professors, corporate vice presidents, filmmakers, and video artists. Some of them are married, and some of them are not, some of them are straight, and some of them are lesbian or bisexual. She has seen women change a flat tire, assemble bookshelves, and operate a power saw. I never knew women like this as a child. When I was her age, all of this was nonexistent, completely unimaginable. As she grows up, she'll get to know these women, my friends whom I regard with awe and pride, and she will learn about the routes they have taken, the many accomplishments they have achieved, and she will learn that it wasn't all easy, but that it was worth the fight. This was something most of our mothers were unable to give us, and it is a precious legacy we can bequeath to their granddaughters.

It is especially important that we protect this legacy because the other lesson our daughters will learn from the mass media is that if they aren't pretty and aren't thin, no matter what their other gifts, they will be thought of as less than they are. If my daughter wants to be a journalist, an actress, a politician, or a tennis champion, looks will matter much more for her than they will for any boy aspiring to the same occupations. It will still make a big difference if she's pretty. It will also make a difference, as it won't for the little boys she plays with now, if she is outspoken, honest about her needs, expectations and desires, and willing to fight for principles she values. For most of the media images that will surround her as she grows up will equate not just thinness and beauty but also a soft-spoken, deferential voice with her right to be loved, admired, respected. She will learn that to be listened to, she will be expected to speak politely and in a noninflammatory manner, but she will also learn that whether she shouts or whispers (and how many ad campaigns have urged women to whisper?), she'll barely be listened to at all, because she's just a girl.

I see her now, so unself-conscious about her body, so completely happy and comfortable in it, and already I grieve for the time which will come all too soon when she regards that body with self-hate, no matter how fit and healthy it is, and will not get rid of that self-hate for the rest of her life. She and her little girlfriends cavort about nakedly with glee, so beautiful, so free, so unaware of what is to come, of the alienation they will learn to feel against the bodies that now give them so much pleasure and joy. But when they watch *Fern Gully* together, and see the fairy Crysta's waist, even narrower than Ariel's, or play with their Barbies, the campaign on them has begun. Mothers who intervene—"Isn't her waist really silly and *way* too small? No real person has a waist like that and always walks on her toes"—do so fearing that this is an ideological battle they can't win. We read (with knowing resignation) of the major drop in self-esteem among girls once they reach adolescence, and we know all too well where much of this comes from. And instead of giving our daughters less emaciated heroines, the media moguls just tell us smugly to shut off the TV and don't buy what you don't like, as if it's so easy to insulate your child from the semiotic sea in which she and all her friends swim. Nor do we have the money, technology, or access to fill in the representational blanks in their lives, to give them the heroines they deserve.

One recourse we do have is to teach our daughters how to talk back to and make fun of the mass media. This is especially satisfying since, thanks to Nickelodeon, we sometimes see them watching the same stuff we grew up with. In an episode of *Lassie* my daughter and I watched one morning, a ranger comes to the house to warn the mom that there are some mountain lions in the area. As he tries to show her, on a map, where they'd been spotted, she demurs, confessing that she can't read maps and they just confuse her. Then, on her way to meet Dad and Timmy at a Grange dinner, she gets a flat—which, of course, she hasn't a clue how to change—and then gets caught in one of the traps set for the mountain lions. Lassie—a dog—has more brains than she does and has to save her. Such scenes provide the feminist mom with an opportunity to impart a few words of wisdom about how silly and unrealistic TV can be when it comes to women.

But this was an exception. I don't want to monitor my daughter's TV viewing on Saturday morning, I want to go back to bed. How many mothers have the time or the energy for such interventions? Why should such interventions be so constantly necessary? And even the most conscientious and unharried mom can't compensate for the absences, the erasures, of what their daughters don't see, may never see, about women and bravery, intelligence, and courage. And this is just what little white girls don't see. What of my little girl's best friend, who is Asian? She will confront even more erasures, and more glib stereotypes. Of one thing I am certain. Like us, our daughters will make their own meanings out of much that they see, reading between the lines, absorbing exhortations to be feisty side by side with exhortations to be passive. Like us, they will have to work hard to fend off what cripples them and amplify what empowers them. But why, after all these years, should they still have to work so hard and to resist so much?

What will be dramatically different for my little girl is that she will be less sheltered from images of violence against women than I was. Rape was virtually unheard of in the mainstream media in the 1950s and '60s. Now the actual or threatened violation of women permeates the airwaves and is especially rampant on a channel like MTV, which caters, primarily, to adolescents. The MTV that initially brought us Culture Club, "Beat It," and Cyndi Lauper switched, under the influence of market research, to one of the most relentless showcases of misogyny in America. If MTV is still around in ten years, and if its images don't change much, my daughter will see woman after woman tied up, strapped down, or on her knees in front of some strutting male hominid, begging to service him forever. These women are either garter-belt-clad nymphomaniacs or whip-wielding, castrating bitches: they all have long, red fingernails, huge breasts, buns of steel, and no brains; they adore sunken-chested, sickly looking boys with very big guitars. Worse, they either want to be or deserve to be violated. Anyone who doesn't think such representations matter hasn't read any headlines recently recounting the hostility with which all too many adolescent boys treat girls, or their eagerness to act on such hostilities, especially when they're in groups with names like Spur Posse.

To be fair, in between these little pieces of corporate sewage on MTV, my daughter may also see female performers with guts and talent who defy such imagery. If she is lucky, she'll have her own generation's version of Annie Lennox, En Vogue, Tina Turner, Cyndi Lauper, Salt 'n' Pepa, and Mary-Chapin Carpenter. Her generation may even have girl groups like we did, young women singing together about the ongoing importance of girls sticking together and giving a name to what hurts women.

The other drama my little girl has already witnessed, and has enacted in her own pretend play, is the silencing of the female voice, the amputation of voice from desire. In *The Little Mermaid*, the central story involves Ariel's bargain with the sea witch Ursula: Ariel gets to be a human to meet the prince Eric, but, in exchange, Ursula takes away her voice. Feeling voiceless, and experiencing a severing between their true feelings and their own voices, is also, it turns out, a central psychological drama for adolescent girls in America. But the culprits are hardly individual women. Rather, they are an entire system, buttressed by media imagery, that urges young girls to learn how to mute themselves. It is therefore especially incumbent on my generation to help our daughters claim their voices. This is why music for women continues to be so important. Thirty years after "Will You Love Me Tomorrow," I remain convinced that singing certain songs with a group of friends at the top of your lungs sometimes helps you say things, later, at the top of your heart. I want to introduce my daughter to the music that got me through, because it is through this music that female resilience, camaraderie, and wisdom are often most powerfully and genuinely expressed. For every time she hears "Someday My Prince Will Come" I want her to hear "Sisters Are Doing It for Themselves."

I want my daughter to listen to Martha and the Vandellas, the Chiffons, and the Marvelettes, and I want her to know that girl talk didn't die out when the Shirelles stopped making hits. The early and mid-1970s (and beyond) would have been a lot bleaker and lonelier for me if it hadn't been for Laura Nyro, Joni Mitchell, Aretha Franklin, Bonnie Raitt, Bette Midler, the Pointer Sisters, LaBelle, Melissa Manchester, and Carole King. When I got totally fed up with news stories documenting women's "fear of success," or the endless rapes on prime time, or the ads that used the words *freedom* and *liberation* to sell douches, I could listen to women sing about the sexual passions, political outrage, strength, and defiance we shared like a secret pledge. All these singers were acknowledging that with the women's movement, girl talk mattered more than ever. Some of these women wrote their own music and played their own instruments; their music was more knowing, more sexually frank, and more politically inflected than girl group music had been. But it shared that same sense of irrepressible optimism that, no matter what, women would endure and prevail, and this is a powerful tradition to pass on to little girls who all too soon will be awash in the misogyny of heavy metal and rap.

This music will do nothing less than help my daughter survive. Women's music has acknowledged that we would indeed bob below the surface from time to time, sometimes feeling as if we wouldn't rise again, but then up we'd come, resurfaced, renewed. Melissa Manchester insisted, in songs like "This Lady's Not Home," "Home to Myself," and "Talkin' to Myself (And Feelin' Fine)," that certain women (and a lot more women than men thought) craved solitude and that they needed to be alone as much as, and sometimes more than, they needed or wanted to be with any man. The Divine Miss M exuded a totally confident, authoritative sexuality, not just in her music but also in her costumes, stage talk, and infamous retelling of those bawdy Sophie Tucker jokes. Long before Madonna, Bette Midler trashed the notion that women had to be or should be sexually innocent and demure. Bonnie Raitt, by covering the Sippie Wallace songs "Women Be Wise (Don't Advertise Your Man)," "Mighty Tight Woman," and "You Got to Know How," reintroduced us to a female blues tradition that demanded recognition and preservation because of its exuberant assertion of female sexual desire. In songs like "Give It Up or Let Me Go" and "Ain't Nobody Home," she made it clear that women like her expected men to cut the bullshit or take a hike. In "I'm a Radio," Joni Mitchell indicated that women like her were just as comfortable with casual, nonbinding relationships as men were. These were take-control women, at least in their music, reinforcing in positive terms what the rest of the mass media were castigating as negative.

The most poetic of these women was Laura Nyro, and already one of my daughter's favorite songs is what she calls "Wash You Up and Down," her title for Nyro's feminist call to arms, "Save the Country." Nyro's songs affirmed that women usually found themselves in the grip of forces beyond their control but that women also shared a form of knowledge, a wisdom combined of fatalism and feistiness, that helped them assume an ironic stance toward fate and helped them triumph over its cruelties. The exuberance of her piano playing and the unyielding survivalism of her lyrics insisted that women, despite the odds, were simply too resilient, too dogged, too optimistic, to be kept down. Twenty years later, Mary-Chapin Carpenter makes the same claims for women in "I Feel Lucky," "I Take My Chances," and "The Hard Way." Women do have to struggle and put up with suffocating stereotypes, but we often get lucky as well, usually because of our spirit, our willingness to try again, and our capacity for love.

These are the voices I want my daughter to sing along with. This is what I want her to know about the women who came before her. These are women who claimed their voices, and sang about what too many of us have felt we couldn't say in regular speech: our pride in ourselves, our anger, our sexual desires, our weariness of always having to compromise. I hope that she will relate this music to real women she knows, to her grandmothers who never quit, to her mother's friends who gamely dance around the living room with her to this music, and to her mother, who periodically turns this music up to house-shaking levels to blow out the self-doubt, the guilt, and the fear.

I don't believe I can insulate my daughter from the mass media, nor do I want to. There are pleasures there for her, ones she already knows and ones she will learn. The sitcoms, records, magazines, and movies she grows up with will form, for better and for worse, the culture she will share with other people she barely knows. Yet there is much in this culture I find pernicious, revolting, and, increasingly, dangerous, especially since she is a girl. She will be treated a certain way precisely because of how boys—and even other girls—apply their media lessons to everyday life. I will try to teach her to be a resistant, back-talking, bullshit-detecting media consumer, and to treasure the strong, funny, subversive women she does get to see. I will also remind her that any time a performer or a cultural form especially loved by young girls is ridiculed and dismissed, she and her friends should not be embarrassed. Instead, they should be suspicious about just who is feeling threatened, or superior, and why.

Yet despite my interventions—and, given how kids are, probably because of them—I fear that she will experience the same amputations I have experienced, between my mind and my body, my desires and my voice, my past and my present, my old self and my current self. And I know that what she sees and hears on television, on the radio, in magazines, newspapers, and movies, will reinforce and justify the political, economic, and social realities she will live with when she becomes a woman. But I also suspect that she and her generation may get wiser to all this sooner than we did—look at what she knows already, and she's only four—and that they will be less patient and less willing to compromise. This, at least, is my hope. For she will see with her eyes and feel in her spirit that despite all this, women are not helpless victims, they are fighters. And she will want to be a fighter too.

Speculations

1. What specific kinds of negative influences does Douglas object to in contemporary television and film? How does she see these influences shaping her own daughter's desires and self-image?
2. How does Douglas use the "nature-nurture" debate to develop her argument about women's role models, how they are received by young girls, and the effectiveness of parents' attempts to insulate children from mass media?
3. What do you think of the strategy of teaching "our daughters how to talk back to and make fun of the mass media?" Do you think this strategy of "parental intervention" will work to

strengthen young women's self-identities and their resistance to negative media images? Explain your answers.

4. Douglas mentions Barbie dolls, Belle in *Beauty and the Beast,* and Ariel in *The Little Mermaid:* How does she describe these female characters and what is the message they send to young women? Explain why you agree or disagree with Douglas's assessment of these characters and how they affect young women.

5. At the end of the article, what kind of woman does Douglas see her daughter becoming and in what ways does this vision fulfill Douglas's own image of the kind of woman she has struggled to become?

6. How does Douglas use humor and a wry tone to gain a different perspective on the issues that concern her? How does her tone and sense of humor affect you as a reader?

IN PRAISE OF ROSEANNE

Elayne Rapping

A professor of communications at Adelphi University, Long Island, New York, Elayne Rapping has had a distinguished career as a scholarly and popular writer on issues of gender politics and the media. Having published in *The Nation, The Village Voice,* and *The Women's Review of Books,* she is also a regular columnist for *The Progressive* magazine and *On the Issues: The Progressive Women's Journal.* Her books include *The Looking Glass World of Nonfiction Television* (1987), *The Movie of the Week* (1992), and *Media-tions: Forays into the Culture and Gender Wars* (1994).

Rapping writes to the general television audience, and in her preface to *Movie of the Week,* she describes her stance as that of "a public intellectual, a writer who wishes to engage a large public with a common stake in public life and in public media." Rejecting what she calls the "doom-and-gloom mongers" who portray individuals as helpless consumers entirely shaped by the designs of powerful media interests, Rapping argues that the public—all of us—must become more "media literate" by educating ourselves and learning to read critically what we see and hear. She believes that television viewers are individuals with a great variety of interests, ideas, and personal conflicts of their own making, and that they can respond intelligently and effectively to what they see on television. In a September, 1994, column entitled "Culture: Cable's Silver Lining," written for *The Progressive,* Rapping states:

> We need to stop accepting the media's own hype about how
> "powerless" we are over TV's impact, and start teaching
> viewers to understand how its images and messages func-
> tion—socially, economically, politically, culturally—so they
> won't be powerless but empowered, as viewers and citizens.

The following selection, also taken from Rapping's column on "Culture" in *The Progressive*, develops her argument further by examining
the ways in which the television character "Roseanne" has become a
complex, imperfect, yet affirmative image of the modern, working
class woman.

The other night, while flipping among the three nightly network
news broadcasts, I stopped—as I often do—to check out the *Roseanne*
rerun Fox cleverly schedules during that time slot in New York. And,
as often happens, I found myself sticking around longer than I intended, watching the Conners wiggle their way through whatever crisis
had hit their Kmart window fan that day.

On the three more respectable networks, the Dow Jones averages
rise and fall; Congress and the courts hand down weighty decisions in
lofty prose; the official weapons of state are deployed, around the
globe and in the inner cities, to preserve democracy and the American
way. But in the Conner residence, where most things are either in dis-
repair or not yet paid for, it is possible to glimpse—as it rarely is on the
newscasts themselves—how the fallout from such headlines might actually affect those who are relatively low in the pecking order.

On CBS, NBC, ABC, and CNN, the problems of the women who
make headlines are not likely to sound familiar to most of us. Zoë Baird
may be struggling with the servant issue. Hillary may have misplaced
her capital-gains records. The Queen of England may be embroiled in
royal-family dysfunction. But Roseanne, matriarch of the shabby Conner household, will be coping with less glamorous trauma—unemployment, foreclosure, job stress, marital power struggles, unruly and
unmotivated kids—in a less dignified but more realistic style.

I am a big fan of Roseanne—Barr, Arnold, Conner, whatever. So
are my female and working-class students, who invariably claim her as
their own and hang on to her for dear life as they climb the ladder of
class and professional achievement—an effort in which their parents
have so hopefully invested everything they own. But it recently occurred to me that I have never—in the many years I've regularly analyzed and commented on American popular culture—written a single
word about her. Nor have I read many, outside the trashy tabloids,
where her personal life and public persona are regularly recorded and
described.

In the last year, I've read dozens of academic and popular articles,
and two whole books, about *The Cosby Show*. Archie Bunker and *All in*

the Family have been praised and analyzed endlessly. Even *Murphy Brown* and *The Mary Tyler Moore Show* are taken seriously in ever-broadening academic and journalistic circles. Not to mention the well-structured, post-structural Madonna, long the darling of feminist critics and academics.

What is it about these other media icons that makes them somehow more "respectable" subjects of intellectual analysis, more suitable to "serious" discourse? What is it about Roseanne that makes her so easy to ignore or write off, despite her (to me) obvious talent, originality, political *chutzpah*, and power? Gender and appearance are surely part of it; but I suspect that class—position as well as attitude—is the major factor. Bill Cosby's Cliff Huxtable, Mary Tyler Moore's Mary Richards, Candice Bergen's Murphy Brown are all well-turned out, well-educated liberal professionals. And the grungy, working-class Archie Bunker, far from scoring points for his class, is always beaten down by the liberal, professional mentality of everyone else on the show. As for Madonna, while she is certainly not respectable, she makes up for it by being blond, chic, and gorgeous, which, in our culture, covers a multitude of social sins.

But Roseanne is a different story, far more unassimilable into mainstream-media iconography than any of these others. Fat, sloppy, foul-mouthed, and bossy, she is just a bit too unrepentantly, combatively proud of her gender and class position and style to be easily molded into the "movin' on up" mode of American mass media. She isn't "movin' up" to anywhere. She is standing pat, week after week on her show—and a lot of the rest of the time in a lot of other places—speaking out for the dignity and the rights of those the media have set out to shame into invisibility or seduce into endless, self-hating efforts at personal transformation. With her bad hair and baggy pants and oversized shirts from the lower level of the mall, with her burned meat loaf and tuna casseroles and Malomars, with her rough language and politically incorrect child-rearing methods, with her dead-end minimum-wage jobs, Roseanne has gone further than Madonna or almost anyone else I can think of at turning the hegemonic norms of the corporate media on their heads. But few of the intellectual writing classes have seen fit to credit, much less celebrate, her for it. So I will.

To appreciate Roseanne's unlikely ascent into prime-time stardom, it's useful to place her within the generic traditions of the family sitcom. Roseanne is not a descendant of the pristine line of virginal wife/mothers who have set the norms for such characters from the days of June Cleaver to the present. No sweetly submissive smiles or politely helpful suggestions to hubby and kids for her. She is one of a rarer breed, the one invented and defined by Lucille Ball in *I Love Lucy*, in which the female protagonist is more Helpmeet from Hell than from Heaven.

The parallels between these two women are interesting, and reveal a lot about what has and hasn't changed for the women—white, working-class, and poor—who make up the female majority in this country (although you'd never know it from watching TV). Both were, and are, popular and powerful beyond the dreams of almost any woman performer of their times. And yet both eschewed the traditional feminine, white, middle-class persona dictated by the norms of their days, preferring to present themselves as wild women, out of bounds, loud, funny, and noisy—all attributes which sexist culture beats out of most of us very early on. In a world in which females are enjoined not to take up too much space, not to make "spectacles" of ourselves, not to "disturb" but to contain "the peace," women like Roseanne and Lucy have always been frightening, repulsive, even indecent. That's why they so appall us even as, consciously or subconsciously, we are drawn to them.

I used to cringe when I watched *I Love Lucy* as a child. She filled me with embarrassment because she was so stereotypically "hysterical," so much a failure in her endless efforts to move out of the confines of traditional femininity and its many indignities (indignities otherwise kept hidden by the Stepford-like types of Donna Reed and June Cleaver).

I was far more comfortable, as a middle-class girl, with the persona created by Mary Tyler Moore—first as the frustrated dancer/wife in *The Dick Van Dyke Show* and later as the first real career woman in her own show. Unlike Lucy, Mary Richards was perfectly groomed and mannered. She was sweetly deferential in her apologetic efforts at assertiveness; embarrassingly grateful for every nod of respect or responsibility from her boss, "Mr. Grant." Ambitious, yes, but never forgetful of the "ladylike" way of moving up the corporate ladder, one dainty, unthreatening step at a time. Where Lucy embarrassed, Mary was soothing. No pratfalls of dumb disguises for her.

But through Roseanne, I've come to see the very improper Lucy differently. For her time, after all, she was a real fighter against those feminine constraints. She tried to *do* things and she tried to do them with other women, against the resistance of every man on the show. She was not well groomed, did not live in tasteful elegance, did not support and help her husband at business and social affairs—far from it. She was full of energy and rebelliousness and, yes, independence— to a point.

But of course she always failed, and lost, and made a fool of herself. Her show was pure slapstick fantasy, because, back then, the things she was trying to achieve were so far from imaginable that someone like her could only exist in a farcical mode. But, as Roseanne's very different way of playing this kind of woman shows, that is no longer true.

Like Lucy, Roseanne is loud, aggressive, messy, and ambitiously bossy. Roseanne, too, has close relationships with other women. And Roseanne, too, is larger than life, excessive, to many frightening and repulsive. But her show is no fantasy. It is the most realistic picture of gender, class, and family relations on television today. And that's because Roseanne herself is so consciously political, so gender- and class-conscious, in every detail of her show.

No more the harried husband rolling his eyes at his wife's antics. Where other sitcoms either ignore feminism and reproduce traditional relations or, perhaps worse, present perfectly harmonious couples—like the Huxtables—for whom gender equity comes as naturally as their good looks, Roseanne and Dan duke it out over gender and power issues as equals who seem really to love, respect, and—not least—get angry at each other.

Nor does Roseanne need to think up crazy schemes for achieving the impossible—a project outside the home. Roseanne, like most of us, needs to work. The jobs she is forced to take—sweeping in a hair salon, waiting tables in malls and diners, working on an assembly line—are very like the ones Lucy nabbed and then messed up, to the wild laughter of the audience. But for Roseanne the humor is different. Roseanne fights with sexist, overbearing bosses, lashes out at her kids because she's stressed out at work, moonlights to get them through the rough days when Dan is out of work. And if these things are funny to watch, they are also deeply revealing of social and emotional truths in the lives of women and working-class families today.

The most touching and impressive thing about this series—and the main reason for its popularity—is its subtle presentation of progressive "messages" in a way that is neither preachy nor condescending to audiences. Much was made of the famous episode in which Roseanne was kissed by a lesbian character. (And it is surely a tribute to Roseanne's integrity and clout that this first lesbian kiss got past Standards and Practices because of her.) But the kiss itself was really no big deal. Lots of shows will be doing this kind of one minute/one scene "Wow, did you see that?" thing soon enough.

Sitcoms are, indeed, informed by liberal values, and they do, indeed, tend to preach to us about tolerance and personal freedom. Lesbianism, as an idea, an abstraction, a new entry on the now very long list of liberal tolerances to which the professional middle classes must pay lip service, was bound to hit prime time soon anyway. What made the Roseanne "lesbian episode" remarkable and radically different from the usual liberal sitcom style of tackling such issues was not the kiss itself but the startlingly honest discussions about homosexuality that followed the kiss, between Dan and his young son D.J.; and then between Dan and Roseanne, in bed.

This segment was politically audacious because it *did not* lecture the vast majority of Americans who are, yes, queasy about homosexuality. It presented them with a mirror image of their own confusion and anxiety, and led them to a position of relative comfort about it all, by sympathizing with their very real concern about radical social and sexual change.

This is how the show attacks all its difficult issues, sensational and mundane. Much has been made of Roseanne's way of yelling at her kids, even hitting them on at least one occasion. Clearly, this is not how parents, since Dr. Spock, have been told to behave, and for obvious and good reason. Nonetheless, we all do these things on occasion. (And those who don't, ever, probably have other serious parenting problems.) To pretend that parents don't do that—as most sitcoms do—is to condescend to viewers who know that this goes on everywhere, and who have, themselves, done it or at least fought the urge.

On *Roseanne*, such behavior is neither denied nor condemned; it is talked about and analyzed. After hitting her son, for example, Roseanne apologizes and confesses, heartbreakingly, that she was herself beaten as a child and that it was wrong then and wrong now. It is this kind of honesty about negative feelings—especially when they are placed in the kind of social and economic context this show never slights—that makes the positive feelings of love and mutual respect within this battered, battling family so very believable.

Which brings me, unavoidably, to the issue of Roseanne Arnold herself, as a public persona—surely the major factor in the public unease about her. There are two "Roseannes"—both media images constructed cleverly and carefully by Arnold herself. "Roseanne Conner" is, as Arnold herself says, "much nicer." She is the sitcom version of how someone overcomes personal and economic difficulty and not only survives but thrives. She comes from a long line of show-business satirists whose humor was based on social and political truth. Like the Marx Brothers and Charlie Chaplin, she is the lovable outsider sneaking into the polite world to expose its hypocrisy and phoniness.

That is the fictional "Roseanne" of sitcom fame. The other persona, "Roseanne Barr Arnold"—the woman who appears in tabloids, talk shows, news shows, and comedy clubs—is far more outrageous, more dangerous. She is the ultimate bad girl, the woman who shouts out to the entire world every angry, nasty, shameful truth and emotion she feels about the lives of women, especially poor women, in America today.

Much of what Roseanne confesses to—about incest, wife abuse, mental illness, obesity, prostitution, lesbianism—makes people uncomfortable. It's tacky, embarrassing, improper, déclassé to discuss these issues in public. But so was much of what we Second Wave feminists and student activists and antiwar protesters and others insisted upon talking about and confessing to and doing in the 1960s. So is what Anita Hill insisted—in much classier style but to no less shock and outrage—on throwing at us from the Senate hearing rooms. So is almost every political statement and action that rocks the reactionary boats of institutionalized power and authority.

And like those other actions and statements, Roseanne's antics are inherently political, radical, salutary. For in speaking out about her hidden demons and ghosts and scars—as a woman, a working-class person, a victim of family and institutional abuse—she speaks *for* the myriad damaged and disempowered souls, mostly still silent and invisible, who also bear the scars of such class, gender, and age abuse.

My timing, as I write this, couldn't be worse, of course. The tabloids are currently ablaze with the latest, and most unfortunate, of Arnold brouhahas. Roseanne, having loudly accused her husband of infidelity and spousal abuse, filed for divorce, then almost immediately rescinded the statements and reconciled with her husband, only to file for divorce again a few weeks later.

I am neither shocked nor disillusioned by this. Every abused woman I have ever known has attempted, unsuccessfully, to leave her destructive relationship many times, before finally finding the strength and support to make the break. This, after all, is the very essence of the abuse syndrome. Only Roseanne, as usual, has chosen to play it out, in all its gory details, in the spotlight.

I'm a Roseanne fan. I like her show and marvel at her compassion and intelligence, at what she manages to get away with. I like her style—even when she offends me and makes me nervous (which she often does)—because the world needs loud-mouthed unattractive women with brains, guts, a social conscience, and a sense of humor. There are few enough of them who make it through puberty with their spirits and energies intact.

Speculations

1. In the first three paragraphs of her article, Rapping compares the Conners' household and its concerns to world events displayed on other television channels and the concerns of Roseanne to those of famous women in the news. Why? What point is Rapping driving home here?
2. Rapping mentions many of Roseanne's negative qualities ("Fat, sloppy, foul-mouthed, and bossy . . ."), but what qualities re-

deem this image of Roseanne and why does Rapping value these qualities?

3. How does the comparison between "Roseanne" and "I Love Lucy" form a pivotal turn in this essay? What is Rapping arguing by making this comparison?

4. What message was being sent to viewers in the "lesbian episode" of "Roseanne"? Explain why you disagree or agree with Rapping's argument about the political and cultural effectiveness of this message.

5. What distinctions does Rapping make between the fictional character of Roseanne on the television show and the real Roseanne? Why does she make these distinctions?

HONEY I WARPED THE KIDS

Carl M. Cannon

Carl M. Cannon has covered the White House for the *Baltimore Sun* since Bill Clinton took office in 1992. Before that, he worked in the Washington bureau of Knight-Ridder Newspapers for eleven years, first as a California regional correspondent for the *San Jose Mercury News* and later as a chief political reporter on Knight-Ridder's national staff. Cannon has written many news stories covering the last three presidential elections for Knight-Ridder, and he was one of the reporters on the news team that won the Pulitzer Prize for the *San Jose Mercury News* coverage of the Lomas Prieta earthquake.

A native of San Francisco, Cannon received his bachelor's degree in journalism from the University of Colorado. Before going to work in San Jose in 1981, he worked for three years at the *San Diego Union,* covering stories on the courts and police. He has also worked as a reporter at various newspapers in the eastern part of the United States, including Georgia, Virginia, Maryland, and Washington D.C., and he has written articles for more than a dozen magazines including *Mother Jones,* the *Washington Journalism Review,* and *Forbes Media Critic.*

While working at eight different newspapers throughout the country, Cannon served on several task forces, committees, and "groups of reporters and editors," all of whom have become increasingly concerned about the declining readership of daily newspapers. In a letter to the editors of *Speculations,* he explains that newspapers have not come to grips with their failure to maintain a loyal and appreciative reading audience:

By and large, the solutions that newspapers typically embrace (shorter and shorter stories about fluffier subjects with more and more graphics) are beside the point and are even counterproductive. Better story-telling, more compelling writing, breaking stories about life-and-death subjects is what news reporting needs to offer the public.

Cannon's hard-hitting, direct style of writing in the following selection constructs a compelling indictment of television networks and Hollywood producers, who, in his view, exploit violent images in order to expand their marketing power and viewing audiences.

Tim Robbins and Susan Sarandon implore the nation to treat Haitians with AIDS more humanely. Robert Redford works for the environment. Harry Belafonte marches against the death penalty.

Actors and producers seem to be constantly speaking out for noble causes far removed from their lives. They seem even more vocal and visible now that there is a Democrat in the White House. But in the one area over which they have control—the excessive violence in the entertainment industry—Hollywood activists remain silent.

This summer, Washington was abuzz with talk about the movie *Dave,* in which Kevin Kline stars as the acting president. But every time I saw an ad featuring Kline, the movie I couldn't get out of my head was *Grand Canyon.* There are two scenes in it that explain much of what has gone wrong in America.

Kline's character has a friend, played by Steve Martin, who is a producer of the B-grade, violent movies that Hollywood euphemistically calls "action" films. But after an armed robber shoots Martin's character in the leg, he has an epiphany.

"I can't make those movies any more," he decides. "I can't make another piece of art that glorifies violence and bloodshed and brutality. . . . No more exploding bodies, exploding buildings, exploding anything. I'm going to make the world a better place."

A month or two later, Kline calls on Martin at his Hollywood studio to congratulate him on the "new direction" his career has taken.

"What? Oh that," Martin says dismissively. "Fuck that. That's over. I must have been delirious for a few weeks there."

He then gins up every hoary excuse for Hollywood-generated violence you've ever heard, ending with: "My movies reflect what's going on; they don't make what's going on."

This is Hollywood's last line of defense for why it shows murder and mayhem on the big screen and the little one, in prime time and early in the morning, to children, adolescents, and adults:

We don't cause violence, we just report it.

Four years ago, I joined the legion of writers, researchers, and parents who have tried to force Hollywood to confront the more disturbing truth. I wrote a series of newspaper articles on the massive body of evidence that establishes a direct cause-and-effect relationship between violence on television and violence in society.

The orchestrated response from the industry—a series of letters seeking to discredit me—was something to behold.

Because the fact is, on the one issue over which they have power, the liberals in Hollywood don't act like progressive thinkers; they act like, say, the National Rifle Association:

Guns don't kill people, people kill people.

We don't cause violence in the world, we just reflect it.

The first congressional hearings into the effects of television violence took place in 1954. Although television was still relatively new, its extraordinary marketing power was already evident. The tube was teaching Americans what to buy and how to act, not only in advertisements, but in dramatic shows, too.

Everybody from Hollywood producers to Madison Avenue ad men would boast about this power—and seek to utilize it on dual tracks: to make money and to remake society along better lines.

Because it seemed ludicrous to assert that there was only one area—the depiction of violence—where television did not influence behavior, the television industry came up with this theory: Watching violence is cathartic. A violent person might be sated by watching a murder.

The notion intrigued social scientists, and by 1956 they were studying it in earnest. Unfortunately, watching violence turned out to be anything but cathartic.

In the 1956 study, one dozen four-year-olds watched a "Woody Woodpecker" cartoon that was full of violent images. Twelve other preschoolers watched "Little Red Hen," a peaceful cartoon. Then the children were observed. The children who watched "Woody Woodpecker" were more likely to hit other children, verbally accost their classmates, break toys, be disruptive, and engage in destructive behavior during free play.

For the next thirty years, researchers in all walks of the social sciences studied the question of whether television causes violence. The results have been stunningly conclusive.

"There is more published research on this topic than on almost any other social issue of our time," University of Kansas Professor Aletha C. Huston, chairwoman of the American Psychological Association's Task Force on Television and Society, told Congress in 1988. "Virtually all independent scholars agree that there is evidence that television can cause aggressive behavior."

There have been some three thousand studies of this issue— eighty-five of them major research efforts—and they all say the same thing. Of the eighty-five major studies, the only one that failed to find a causal relationship between television violence and actual violence was paid for by NBC. When the study was subsequently reviewed by three independent social scientists, all three concluded that it actually did demonstrate a causal relationship.

Some highlights from the history of TV violence research:

- In 1973, when a town in mountainous western Canada was wired for television signals, University of British Columbia researchers observed first- and second-graders. Within two years, the incidence of hitting, biting, and shoving increased 160 percent in those classes.

- Two Chicago doctors, Leonard Eron and Rowell Huesmann, followed the viewing habits of a group of children for twenty-two years. They found that watching violence on television is the single best predictor of violent or aggressive behavior later in life, ahead of such commonly accepted factors as parents' behavior, poverty, and race.

  "Television violence effects youngsters of all ages, of both genders, at all socioeconomic levels and all levels of intelligence," they told Congress in 1992. "The effect is not limited to children who are already disposed to being aggressive and is not restricted to this country."

- Fascinated by an explosion of murder rates in the United States and Canada that began in 1955, after a generation of North Americans had come of age on television violence, University of Washington Professor Brandon Centerwall decided to see if the same phenomenon could be observed in South Africa, where the Afrikaner-dominated regime had banned television until 1975.

  He found that eight years after TV was introduced—showing mostly Hollywood-produced fare—South Africa's murder rate skyrocketed. His most telling finding was that the crime rate increased first in the white communities. This mirrors U.S. crime statistics in the 1950s and especially points the finger at television, because whites were the first to get it in both countries.

  Bolder than most researchers, Centerwall argues flatly that without violent television programming, there might be as many as ten thousand fewer murders in the United States each year.

- In 1983, University of California, San Diego, researcher David P. Phillips wanted to see if there was a correlation between televised boxing matches and violence in the streets of America.

Looking at crime rates after every televised heavyweight championship fight from 1973 to 1978, Phillips found that the homicide rate in the United States rose by an average of 11 percent for approximately one week. Phillips also found that the killers were likely to focus their aggression on victims similar to the losing fighter: if he was white, the increased number of victims were mostly white. The converse was true if the losing fighter was black.

- In 1988, researchers Daniel G. Linz and Edward Donnerstein of the University of California, Santa Barbara, and Steven Penrod of the University of Wisconsin studied the effects on young men of horror movies and "slasher" films.

   They found that depictions of violence, not sex, are what desensitizes people.

   They divided male students into four groups. One group watched no movies, a second watched nonviolent, X-rated movies, a third watched teenage sexual-innuendo movies, and a fourth watched the slasher films *Texas Chainsaw Massacre, Friday the 13th Part 2, Maniac,* and *Toolbox Murders.*

   All the young men were placed on a mock jury panel and asked a series of questions designed to measure their empathy for an alleged female rape victim. Those in the fourth group measured lowest in empathy for the specific victim in the experiment—and for rape victims in general.

The anecdotal evidence is often more compelling than the scientific studies. Ask any homicide cop from London to Los Angeles to Bangkok if television violence induces real-life violence and listen carefully to the cynical, knowing laugh.

Ask David McCarthy, police chief in Greenfield, Massachusetts, why nineteen-year-old Mark Branch killed himself after stabbing an eighteen-year-old female college student to death. When cops searched his room they found ninety horror movies, as well as a machete and a goalie mask like those used by Jason, the grisly star of *Friday the 13th.*

Ask the families of thirty-five young men who committed suicide by playing Russian roulette after seeing the movie *The Deer Hunter.*

Ask George Gavito, a lieutenant in the Cameron County, Texas, sheriff's department, about a cult that sacrificed at least thirteen people on a ranch west of Matamoros, Mexico. The suspects kept mentioning a 1986 movie, *The Believers,* about rich families who engage in ritual sacrifice. "They talk about it like that had something to do with changing them," Gavito recalled later.

Ask LAPD lieutenant Mike Melton about Angel Regino of Los Angeles, who was picked up after a series of robberies and a murder in which he wore a blue bandanna and fedora identical to those worn by Freddy, the sadistic anti-hero of *Nightmare on Elm Street*. In case anybody missed the significance of his disguise, Regino told his victims that they would never forget him, because he was another Freddy Krueger.

Ask Britain Home Secretary Douglas Hurd, who called for further restrictions on U.S.-produced films after Michael Ryan of Hungerford committed Britain's worst mass murder in imitation of *Rambo*, massacring sixteen people while wearing a U.S. combat jacket and a bandoleer of ammunition.

Ask Sergeant John O'Malley of the New York Police Department about a nine-year-old boy who sprayed a Bronx office building with gunfire. The boy explained to the astonished sergeant how he learned to load his Uzi-like firearm: "I watch a lot of TV."

Or ask Manteca, California, police detective Jeff Boyd about thirteen-year-old Juan Valdez, who, with another teenager, went to a man's home, kicked him, stabbed him, beat him with a fireplace poker, and then choked him to death with a dog chain.

Why, Boyd wanted to know, had the boys poured salt in the victim's wounds?

"Oh, I don't know," the youth replied with a shrug. "I just seen it on TV."

Numerous groups have called, over the years, for curbing television violence: the National Commission on the Causes and Prevention of Violence (1969), the U.S. Surgeon General (1972), the Canadian Royal Commission (1976), the National Institute of Mental Health (1982), the U.S. Attorney General's Task Force on Family Violence (1984), the National Parents Teachers Association (1987), and the American Psychological Association (1992).

During that time, cable television and movie rentals have made violence more readily available while at the same time pushing the envelope for network TV. But even leaving aside cable and movie rentals, a study of television programming from 1967 to 1989 showed only small ups and downs in violence, with the violent acts moving from one time slot to another but the overall violence rate remaining pretty steady—and pretty similar from network to network.

"The percent of prime-time programs using violence remains more than seven out of ten, as it has been for the entire twenty-two-year period," researchers George Gerbner of the University of Pennsylvania Annenberg School for Communication and Nancy Signorielli of the University of Delaware wrote in 1990. For the past twenty-two years, they found, adults and children have been entertained by about sixteen violent acts, including two murders, in each evening's prime-time programming.

They also discovered that the rate of violence in children's programs is three times the rate in prime-time shows. By the age of eighteen, the average American child has witnessed at least eighteen thousand simulated murders on television.

By 1989, network executives were arguing that their violence was part of a larger context in which bad guys get their just desserts.

"We have never put any faith in mechanical measurements, such as counting punches or gunshots," said NBC's Alan Gerson. "Action and conflict must be evaluated within each specific dramatic context."

"Our policy," added Alfred R. Schneider of ABC, ". . . makes clear that when violence is portrayed [on TV], it must be reasonably related to plot development and character delineation."

Of course, what early-childhood experts could tell these executives is that children between the ages of four and seven simply make no connection between the murder at the beginning of a half-hour show and the man led away in handcuffs at the end. In fact, psychologists know that very young children do not even understand death to be a permanent condition.

But all of the scientific studies and reports, all of the wisdom of cops and grief of parents have run up against Congress's quite proper fear of censorship. For years, Democratic Congressman Peter Rodino of New Jersey chaired the House Judiciary Committee and looked at calls for some form of censorship with a jaundiced eye. At a hearing five years ago, Rodino told witnesses that Congress must be a "protector of commerce."

"Well, we have children that we need to protect," replied Frank M. Palumbo, a pediatrician at Georgetown University Hospital and a consultant to the American Academy of Pediatrics. "What we have here is a toxic substance in the environment that is harmful to children."

Arnold Fege of the national PTA added, "Clearly, this committee would not protect teachers who taught violence to children. Yet why would we condone children being exposed to a steady diet of TV violence year after year?"

Finally there is a reason to hope for progress.

Early this summer, Massachusetts Democrat Edward Markey, chair of the House Energy and Commerce subcommittee on telecommunications, said that Congress may require manufacturers to build TV sets with a computer chip so that parents could block violent programs from those their children could select.

He joins the fight waged by Senator Paul Simon, a liberal Democrat from Illinois. Nine years ago, Simon flipped on a hotel television set hoping to catch the late news. "Instead," he has recalled many times, "I saw a man being sawed in half with a chainsaw in living color."

Simon was unsettled by the image and even more unsettled when he wondered what repeatedly looking at such images would do to the mind of a fourteen-year-old.

When he found out, he called television executives, who told him that violence sells and that they would be at a competitive disadvantage if they acted responsibly.

Why not get together and adopt voluntary guidelines? Simon asked.

Oh, that would be a violation of antitrust law, they assured him.

Simon called their bluff in 1990 by pushing through Congress a law that allowed a three-year moratorium on antitrust considerations so that the industry could discuss ways to jointly reduce violence.

Halfway through that time, however, they had done nothing, and an angry Simon denounced the industry on the Senate floor. With a push from some prominent industry figures, a conference was set for this August 2 in Los Angeles.

This spring, CBS broadcast group president Howard Stringer said his network was looking for ways to cut back on violence in its entertainment, because he was troubled by the cost to society of continuing business-as-usual.

"We must admit we have a responsibility," he said.

Jack Valenti, the powerful head of the Motion Picture Association of America, wrote to producers urging them to participate in the August 2 conference. "I think it's more than a bunch of talk," Simon said. "I think this conference will produce some results. I think the industry will adopt some standards."

The federal government, of course, possesses the power to regulate the airwaves through the FCC, and Simon and others believe that this latent power to control violence—never used—has put the fear of God in the producers. He also thinks some of them are starting to feel guilty.

"We now have more people in jail and prison per capita than any country that keeps records, including South Africa," Simon says. "We've spent billions putting people behind bars, and it's had no effect on the crime rate. None. People realize there have to be other answers, and as they've looked around, they have settled on television as one of them."

Maybe Simon is right. Maybe Hollywood executives will get together and make a difference.

Or maybe, like Steve Martin's character in *Grand Canyon*, producers and directors from New York to Beverly Hills will wake up after Simon's antitrust exemption expires December 1, shake off the effects of their holiday hangovers, and when asked about their new commitment to responsible filmmaking, answer:

"What? Oh that. Fuck that. That's over. We must have been delirious for a few weeks there."

Speculations

1. What analogy does Cannon use to compare the Hollywood producer's explanation of violence in the media to that of the National Rifle Association? What is the rhetorical effect of this analogy for his argument as a whole and how well do you think it works?
2. Cannon cites several research reports on violence in the media. Name the three specific research results that you find the most compelling and explain why you chose these three.
3. What does Cannon mean when he says "anecdotal evidence is often more compelling than scientific evidence?" How does he present these anecdotes for maximum effect on the reader? Explain why you agree or disagree with his assertion that this evidence is more compelling than scientific studies.
4. What strategies does Cannon offer for curbing television violence and what are the strengths and weaknesses of each of these strategies?
5. Which outcome do you think will prevail over future media violence: the positive responsiveness proposed by Senator Paul Simon or the cynical pessimism articulated by Steve Martin's character in *Grand Canyon?* Describe a third, alternative kind of outcome of your own liking. Speaking from your own experience of violence in the media, explain why you would argue that one outcome is more likely than another.

PASSING THE BUCK
IN TINSEL TOWN

Michael Krasny

Born in 1944 and raised in Cleveland, Ohio, Michael Krasny is now happily settled in the San Francisco Bay Area. He has published essays and fiction widely in a number of publications, including *The New Republic, Mother Jones,* and *American Fiction Quarterly.* An English professor at San Francisco State University since 1970, Krasny teaches twentieth-century literature and literary theory. For many years, he has simultaneously worked in broadcasting and at the University, and this combination has influenced his teaching, writing, and research.

Krasny worked in commercial broadcasting and for several years was the co-host of "Night Focus," a highly celebrated television talk show that focused on culturally significant topics and attracted an educated audience. He currently hosts "Forum," on San Francisco's public radio station KQED, a weekday talk show covering current events, politics, the arts, and culture. As the following selection demonstrates, Krasny's writing style imitates that of his talk show success: He seeks out the opinions of the professionals who actually produce the movies and television shows containing violent images and he succinctly relates their ideas without editorializing or reacting to their responses. As a result, the sense of moral responsibility held by each of these producers, executives, and directors comes through loud and clear in their own voices.

Editors' Note: Michael Krasny was commissioned by *Mother Jones* magazine to explore the trend toward excess, particularly excess violence, in the entertainment industry. Krasny spoke to film and TV producers, directors, and writers, asking them how First Amendment rights can be reconciled with the cost to society of viewing media violence—and whether they feel personally responsible for the societal effects—if any—of their violent movies and television shows. Here are the responses Krasny received.

BRIAN GRAZER, Ron Howard's partner, has produced more than twenty movies. "Most of my films have been sweet-spirited: *Parenthood. Splash. My Girl.* I'm proud of them. Others I'm not so proud of. I learned a big lesson with *Kindergarten Cop.* No one objected to the violent confrontation scene, and there was no problem with it in our focus groups. Then I showed it to my five-year-old, and all of a sudden, reflexively, I put my hand over his eyes. I knew at that point that we'd made a mistake. It was too late to cut the scene, but I would cut it now.

"Usually bad movies aren't hits. I don't see Freddy Krueger [*Nightmare on Elm Street*] movies, and I wouldn't want my kids to see them. I don't know why people make such movies. They're sick."

BOB SHAYE, chief executive officer of New Line Cinema, is responsible for the *Nightmare on Elm Street* horror films. "There's an almost sardonic or dour humor to Freddy Krueger [the *Elm Street* killer], especially to fantasy horror buffs. The tales are useful and cautionary. They suggest that evil and harm are everywhere and that we need to be prepared. They're not intended for kids.

"We create a product. People buy it or they don't. It pains my aesthetic judgment, but I often feel a good movie is one that makes money.

My interest is in entertaining people. *The Killers* and *Batman?* Too much for kids. I can draw my lines. Not everyone can."

SAM HAMM shares screenwriting credit for *Batman* and *Batman Returns.* "It was probably a bad idea to excite small children to see *Batman Returns.* The tie-in to McDonald's was the idea of marketing people.

"But I'm ambivalent about all of this. I can remember being scared as a kid at horror films and developing a craving for that sort of thing, but that's what may form imagination in a strong way and that's what creates narrative and inner life. It teaches you to look for stuff that's not safe in the art you enjoy later on.

"I'm not arguing to expose kids to *Friday the 13th* movies or porno, but I feel there's too much caution about what kids see. Gravitating toward the forbidden is a natural part of growing up.

"I'm dubious of stimulation and effect, wary of speaking of anyone's experience but my own. I knew as a kid very clearly the distinction between real violence and cartoon or film violence. I'm waiting for the legions of those affected by what they see to give testimony."

VIVIENNE VERDON-ROE directed the documentary film *Women For America, For The World.* "I can't go to most popular movies without checking them out with friends first, because I can't physically sit through [violent ones]. My body will not allow it. People really ought to think about the effects. They may not faint like I do, but they're getting desensitized to violence, and it contributes to the social violence of gangs and the like.

"It's incredibly difficult when there are so few alternatives. Teens go to movies because there's often nothing else for them to do, and if they are gruesome or bad movies, no one in society seems to be saying so.

"I'm not an insider. I'm not living down there. But I know enough. It's all money. Everything's money. It's horrible."

RICHARD DONNER directed the *Lethal Weapon* movies, *Superman, The Omen,* and *The Goonies,* among others. "If people see gratuitous violence in any of the *Lethal Weapon* movies, I wonder if they've seen the same movie. It's entertainment. That's my obligation. I brought social issues into the *Lethal Weapon* movies, like when Danny Glover's family comes down on him for eating tuna, or the 'Stamp out the NRA' sign up in the LA police station. In the last one the daughter wears a pro-choice T-shirt.

"You've got to prove [a connection between film violence and real violence] to me. Movies do provoke. I won't do gratuitous or animal violence. We went a little too far in the first *Lethal Weapon,* but I wanted to move more after that toward a less real and more comic-book effect, despite the great reaction we had.

"Public trust comes into filmmaking. The filmmaker is ultimately accountable. I can defend my own work only on personal grounds. If I'm a provocateur of anything, I hope it's good emotion and humor. Censorship is in the ratings system. It works."

CALLIE KHOURI won an Academy Award for her screenplay of *Thelma and Louise*. "I have a hard time with violence just to entertain, but I believe it can be very effective in getting a point across. I resorted to it in my film, but there was a conscience to it. Thelma and Louise felt they had done something wrong, and there were big consequences— including psychic consequences.

"Outlaw movies have always been a catharsis for men, but denied to women. I was extremely frustrated with the literal interpretation of *Thelma and Louise*. Doesn't anyone read anymore or understand metaphor? The film was supposed to be complex, without easy answers, and with flawed characters. I thought when Louise shot that guy that there'd be dead silence in the theater. That scene was written carefully: it was an attempted rape, and I wanted to make what she did wrong. And yet people cheered. I was stunned."

LESLIE MOONVES is head of Lorimar Studios, often called the fifth network, which produced the TV movies "Jack the Ripper" and "Deliberate Strangers" (about serial killer Ted Bundy), as well as shows that Moonves has considerably more pride in, such as "I'll Fly Away" and "Home Front." "I'd love to do another 'I'll Fly Away,' but the corporate bosses won't let me. When you get burned with quality programming you get gun-shy—you feel you need to stick to the shows that make money. You know what the problem is? Network change. Somebody like Bill Paley [former chairman of CBS] used to say that he didn't care if he got a twelve share, because there was a public trust and social responsibility to put on an 'I'll Fly Away.' GE buys a network, and you've got a different agenda.

"Network presidents don't keep their jobs based on the number of Emmy awards. Let's face it: there is more sensation and violence because it works. The movie of the week has become the killer of the week story.

"Do we have a responsibility to our public? Of course. I honestly don't know what to do about it. How's that for an answer?"

JOE ESZTERHAS has written the scripts for such major Hollywood films as *Betrayal, Jagged Edge, Basic Instinct,* and *Sliver*. His work has been criticized as sexist and homophobic. "I don't like to be a Monday morning quarterback on my own work."

DAWN STEEL became the first woman to head a major studio when she was made president of Columbia Pictures in 1987. During her career, she has worked on such films as *Top Gun, Beverly Hills Cop II, Casualties of War, When Harry Met Sally,* and *Look Who's Talking*. She now runs her own production company. "I believe I've never made a movie in bad taste or with excessive violence. But for profit, I've had to make movies not from my soul. If I want to make a film for passion, I have to make it for less money.

"I'm more cynical about the violence in LA than about violence in our business. It's unanswerable whether movies reflect the culture or vice versa. I monitor my kid's movies and won't let her see what's not appropriate for her. There's no way you can censor any movie in this country that's being made. That's our First Amendment."

MATT GROENING is creator and executive producer of the TV hit "The Simpsons." "Anytime you visualize something, it's difficult not to glorify it. Every antiwar film is pro-war, because its violence is stylized and an audience can be removed from it and enjoy it. Stylistically, violence is almost invariably glorified, even when you have an anti-violent point of view. Look at *Platoon*. Violence is invariably used in movies and TV as punctuation, and it does have a numbing effect on people after a time.

"Most TV, most movies, really, are less pernicious than tedious and boring. What's bad for kids is bad storytelling. Tell better stories."

BARRY DILLER, ex-chief executive officer and chairman of Fox and Matt Groening's former boss, now heads QVC Network. He couldn't disagree more with Groening about television's being mostly bad. "I can't imagine why he would say that. Pound for pound, the hour and half-hour television series are very good. There's a lot of junk, but much more in the movie business, the record business, even legitimate theater. It's snobbery to call a show like 'Roseanne' lowbrow or vulgar. It's funny and interesting and has a good moral value and tone.

"TV movies are crummy. 'Hard Copy' is a lying, thieving, lowlife program of hideous, cynical purpose. It's not serious television. There are only a few tabloid shows, but they speak loudly.

"I think you look at society, and you see what is reflected on television in terms of violent action. Absolutely, [there is too much violence]. But we can be thoughtful and reasonable and change that, reduce it. I think plans over the last few years will help. Senator Simon's work with the networks will help."

PHILIP KAUFMAN co-wrote and directed *The Wanderers*, *The Unbearable Lightness of Being*, and *Henry and June*, and wrote and directed *The Right Stuff*. "There is a fascist edge to a lot of the violence we see. I'm in favor of pushing the envelope, but when you push it in romance or eroticism you get an NC-17 rating. It's easier to get an R rating if you use senseless violence, because the ratings board is largely conservative and embraces violence before sex."

JOSH BRAND, along with his partner, has produced the TV hits "St. Elsewhere" and "Northern Exposure." "If something gets a high rating, say, 'The Amy Fisher Story,' then advertisers pay more money. Now, did the networks create the audience for it, or do they pander to what the audience wanted? Is it okay to pollute the emotional and spiritual environment?

"Now there are studies [that show] that violent images don't affect people, just as the tobacco industry has studies showing that cigarette smoking doesn't cause cancer. And they use the First Amendment to evoke their rights and get into this study versus that study, and the whole thing becomes a wash, a miasma of moral mud. But I think that there is absolutely no question that the profusion of these kinds of images has a negative effect, not only on children but on human beings in general.

"But regulations are dangerous, particularly when dealing with the free expression of ideas. I do believe that some of those ideas are like pollutants, but there isn't one thing you can do. A panacea doesn't exist."

Speculations

1. Why did Krasny choose the title "Passing the Buck in Tinseltown," and what does it tell you about the opinions expressed by the individuals he interviewed?
2. Compare Brian Gazer's response to that of Bob Shaye and explain the difference. Why did Krasny place these two next to each other? What is your opinion of their responses?
3. Why does Sam Hamm say that it was "probably a bad idea to excite small children to see *Batman Returns*"? In what ways do you think that "gravitating to the forbidden" is natural (or unnatural) in children, and what does Hamm mean when he says "waiting for the legions of those affected" to bear witness will answer these questions? Explain why you agree or disagree with his thinking.
4. Compare Verdon Roe's response to those of Callie Khouri and Dawn Steel and explain which responses you find most convincing, which least convincing, and why.
5. After reading each response in this section, what overall grade would you give these people for their explanations concerning their work and their efforts at producing good programming? Justify the grade you give with your own opinion of their responses.
6. Pick one respondent in this section and explain how and why you would defend that individual's response as more honest and illuminating than the responses of the others.

PUBLIC ENEMY NUMBER ONE

Mike Males

Mike Males was born in 1950, in Oklahoma City, where he grew up. He received his B.A. in political science from Occidental College in Los Angeles in 1972, and is currently a doctoral student in social ecology at the University of California–Irvine. For eight years, he was a reporter at the *Bozeman Chronicle*, a newspaper in Bozeman, Montana, where he also served as an environmental lobbyist.

Males's background suggests a strong sense of social conscience and fair play: he has worked as a crew leader in the Youth Conservation corps in the National Parks, has worked with troubled adolescents, and in his writing he consistently defends those most misunderstood or abused by popular mythologies—especially adolescents who rarely have the opportunity to speak for themselves. In articles written for *The New York Times,* he has sympathetically explored the problems of youthful suicide and life-threatening behavior and has exposed the reality behind the myth of teenage pregnancy, that is, that most of these pregnancies are caused by adult men who fail to step forward and take responsibility for their action. Males has also published articles in *The Progressive* and in professional journals like *Adolescence* and *The Journal of School Health*. The media watchdog group, Project Censored, named his May 20, 1992, article from *In These Times,* a report on the myths of the war on drugs, as one of the year's top ten under-reported stories. As Males explained in an interview:

> I spend a lot of time disputing negative myths about adolescents . . . and my advice for aspiring writers is: Don't believe anything official. Most of my writing disputes official statements or commonly held beliefs about adolescents and shows how easily these beliefs can be exposed as groundless.

In the following article from *In These Times* (September 20, 1993), we see Males's methodology working relentlessly to correct what he considers to be faulty research and misdirected moral judgements. His goal is to expose the negative myths about public media that confuse offensive representations of violence with the far more devastating realities of violence itself.

Forget about poverty, racism, child abuse, domestic violence, rape. America, from Michael Medved to *Mother Jones,* has discovered the real cause of our country's rising violence: television mayhem, Guns N' Roses, Ice-T and Freddy Krueger.

No need for family support policies, justice system reforms or grappling with such distressing issues as poverty and sexual violence against the young. Today's top social policy priorities, it seems, are TV lockout gizmos, voluntary restraint, program labeling and (since everyone agrees these strategies won't work) congressionally supervised censorship. Just when earnest national soul-searching over the epidemic violence of contemporary America seemed unavoidable, that traditional scapegoat—media depravity—is topping the ratings again.

What caused four youths to go on a "reign of terror" of beating, burning and killing in a New York City park in August 1954? Why, declared U.S. Sen. Robert Hendrickson, chair of the Juvenile Delinquency Subcommittee, the ringleader was found to have a "horror comic" on his person—proof of the "dangers inherent in the multimillion copy spate of lurid comic books that are placed upon the newsstands each month."

And what caused four youths to go on a brutal "wilding" spree, nearly killing a jogger in a New York City park in May 1989? Why, Tipper Gore wrote in *Newsweek*, the leader was humming the rap ditty "Wild Thing" after his arrest. Enough said.

Today, media violence scapegoating is not just the crusade of censorious conservatives and priggish preachers, but also of those of progressive stripe—from Sen. Paul Simon (D-IL) and Rep. Edward Markey (D-MA) to *Mother Jones* and columnist Ellen Goodman. "The average American child," Goodman writes, "sees 8,000 murders and 10,000 acts of violence on television before he or she is out of grammar school." Goodman, like most pundits, expends far more outrage on the sins of TV and rock 'n' roll than on the rapes and violent abuses millions of American children experience before they are out of grammar school.

The campaign is particularly craven in its efforts to confine the debate to TV's effects on children and adolescents even though the research claims that adults are similarly affected. But no politician wants to tell voters they can't see *Terminator II* because it might incite grownups to mayhem.

Popular perceptions aside, the most convincing research, found in massive, multi-national correlational studies of thousands of people, suggests that, at most, media violence accounts for 1 to 5 percent of all violence in society. For example, a 1984 study led by media-violence expert Rowell Huesmann of 1,500 youth in the U.S., Finland, Poland and Australia, found that the amount of media violence watched is associated with about 5 percent of the the violence in children, as rated by peers. Other correlational studies have found similarly small effects.

But the biggest question media-violence critics can't answer is the most fundamental one: is it the *cause,* or simply one of the many *symp-*

toms, of this unquestionably brutal age? The best evidence does not exonerate celluloid savagery (who could?) but shows that it is a small, derivative influence compared to the real-life violence, both domestic and official, that our children face growing up in '80s and '90s America.

When it comes to the genuine causes of youth violence, it's hard to dismiss the 51 percent increase in youth poverty since 1973, 1 million rapes and a like number of violently injurious offenses inflicted upon the young every year, a juvenile justice system bent on retribution against poor and minority youth, and the abysmal neglect of the needs of young families. The Carter-Reagan-Bush eras added 4 million youths to the poverty rolls. The last 20 years have brought a record decline in youth well-being.

Despite claims that media violence is the best-researched social phenomenon in history, social science indexes show many times more studies of the effects of rape, violence and poverty on the young. Unlike the indirect methods of most media studies (questionnaires, interviews, peer ratings and laboratory vignettes), child abuse research includes the records of real-life criminals and their backgrounds. Unlike the media studies, the findings of this avalanche of research are consistent: child poverty, abuse and neglect underlie every major social problem the nation faces.

And, unlike the small correlations or temporary laboratory effects found in media research, abuse-violence studies produce powerful results: "Eighty-four percent of prison inmates were abused as children," the research agency Childhelp USA reports in a 1993 summary of major findings. Separate studies by the Minnesota State Prison, the Massachusetts Correctional Institute and the Massachusetts Treatment Center for Sexually Dangerous Persons (to cite a few) find histories of childhood abuse and neglect in 60 to 90 percent of the violent inmates studied—including virtually all death row prisoners. The most conservative study, that by the National Institute of Justice, indicates that some half-million criminally violent offenses each year are the result of offenders being abused as children.

Two million American children are violently injured, sexually abused or neglected every year by adults whose age averages 32 years, according to the Denver-based American Humane Association. One million children and teenagers are raped every year, according to the 1992 federally funded *Rape in America* study of 4,000 women, which has been roundly ignored by the same media outlets that never seem short of space to berate violent rap lyrics.

Sensational articles in *Mother Jones* ("Proof That TV Makes Kids Violent"), *Newsweek* ("The Importance of Being Nasty") and *U.S. News and World Report* ("Fighting TV Violence") devoted pages to blaming music and media for violence—yet all three ignored this study of the rape of millions of America's children. CNN devoted less than a minute to the study; *Time* magazine gave it only three paragraphs.

In yet another relevant report, the California Department of Justice tabulated 1,600 murders in 1992 for which offenders' and victims' ages are known. It showed that half of all teenage murder victims, six out of seven children killed, and 80 percent of all adult murder victims were slain by adults over age 20, not by "kids." But don't expect any cover stories on "Poverty and Adult Violence: The Real Causes of Violent Youth," or "Grownups: Wild in the Homes." Politicians and pundits know who not to pick on.

Ron Harris' powerful August 1993 series in the *Los Angeles Times*— one of the few exceptions to the media myopia on youth violence—details the history of a decade of legal barbarism against youth in the Reagan and Bush years—which juvenile justice experts now link to the late '80s juvenile crime explosion. The inflammatory, punishment-oriented attitudes of these years led to a 50 percent increase in the number of youths behind bars. Youth typically serve sentences 60 percent longer than adults convicted for the same crimes. Today, two-thirds of all incarcerated youth are black, Latino, or Native American, up from less than half before 1985.

Ten years of a costly "get tough" approach to deter youth violence concluded with the highest rate of crime in the nation's history. Teenage violence, which had been declining from 1970 through 1983, doubled from 1983 through 1991. It is not surprising that the defenders of these policies should be casting around for a handy excuse for this policy disaster. TV violence is perfect for their purposes.

This is the sort of escapism liberals should be exposing. But too many shrink from frankly declaring that today's mushrooming violence is the predictable consequence of two decades of assault, economic and judicial, against the young. Now, increasingly, they point at Jason, 2 Live Crew, and *Henry: Portrait of a Serial Killer.*

The insistence by such liberal columnists as Goodman and Coleman McCarthy that the evidence linking media violence to youth violence is on par with that linking smoking to lung cancer represents a fundamental misunderstanding of the difference between biological and psychological research. Psychology is not, despite its pretensions, a science. Research designs using human subjects are vulnerable to a bewildering array of confusing factors, many not even clear to researchers. The most serious (but by no means only) weakness is the tendency by even the most conscientious researchers to influence subjects to produce the desired results. Thus the findings of psychological studies must be swallowed with large grains of salt.

Consider a few embarrassing problems with media violence research. First, many studies (particularly those done under more realistic "field conditions") show no increase in violence following exposure to violent media. In fact, a significant number of studies show no effect, or even decreased aggression. Even media-violence critic Huesmann has written that depriving children of violent shows may actually increase their violence.

Second, the definitions of just what constitutes media "violence," let alone what kind produces aggression in viewers, are frustratingly vague. Respected researchers J. Singer and D. Singer found in a comprehensive 1986 study that "later aggressive behavior was predicted by earlier heavy viewing of public television's fast-paced *Sesame Street.*" The Parent's Music Resource Center heartily endorsed the band U2 as "healthy and inspiring" for youth to listen to—yet U2's song "Pistol Weighing Heavy" was cited in psychiatric testimony as a key inspiration for the 1989 killing of actress Rebecca Schaeffer.

Third, if, as media critics claim, media violence is the, or even just a, prime cause of youth violence, we might expect to see similar rates of violence among all those exposed to similar amounts of violence in the media, regardless of race, gender, region, economic status, or other demographic differences. Yet this is far from the case.

Consider the issue of race. Surveys show that while black and white families have access to similar commercial television coverage, white families are much more likely to subscribe to violent cable channels. Yet murder arrests among black youth are are now 12 times higher than among white, non-Hispanic youth, and increasing rapidly. Are blacks genetically more susceptible to television violence than whites? Or could there be other reasons for this pattern—perhaps the 45 percent poverty rates and 60 percent unemployment rates among black teenagers?

And consider also the issue of gender. Girls watch as much violent TV as boys. Yet female adolescents show remarkably low and stable rates of violence. Over the last decade or so, murders by female teens (180 in 1983, 171 in 1991) stayed roughly the same, while murders by boys skyrocketed (1,476 in 1983, 3,435 in 1991). How do the media-blamers explain that?

Finally, consider the issue of locale. Kids see the same amount of violent TV all over, but many rural states show no increases in violence, while in Los Angeles, to take one example, homicide rates have skyrocketed.

The more media research claims are subjected to close scrutiny, the more their contradictions emerge. It can be shown that violent people do indeed patronize more violent media, just as it can be shown that urban gang members wear baggy clothes. But no one argues that baggy clothes cause violence. The coexistence of media and real-life violence suffers from a confusion of cause and effect: is an affinity for violent media the result of abuse, poverty and anger, or is it a prime cause of the more violent behaviors that just happen to accompany those social conditions? In a 1991 study of teenage boys who listen to violent music, the University of Chicago's Jeffrey Arnett argues that "[r]ather than being the cause of recklessness and despair among adolescents, heavy metal music is a reflection of these [behaviors]."

The clamor over TV violence might be harmless were it not for the fact that media and legislative attention are rare, irreplaceable resources. Every minute devoted to thrashing over issues like violence in the media is one lost to addressing the accumulating, critical social problems that are much more crucial contributors to violence in the real world. In this regard, the media-violence crusade offers distressing evidence of the profound decline of liberalism as America's social conscience, and the rising appeal (even among progressives) of simplistic Reaganesque answers to problems that Reaganism multiplied many times over.

Virtually alone among progressives, columnist Carl T. Rowan has expressed outrage over the misplaced energies of those who have embraced the media crusade and its "escapism from the truth about what makes children (and their parents and grandparents) so violent." Writes Rowan: "I'm appalled that liberal Democrats . . . are spreading the nonsensical notion that Americans will, to some meaningful degree, stop beating, raping and murdering each other if we just censor what is on the tube or big screen. . . . The politicians won't, or can't, deal with the real-life social problems that promote violence in America . . . so they try to make TV programs and movies the scapegoats! How pathetic!"

Without question, media-violence critics are genuinely concerned about today's pandemic violence. As such, it should alarm them greatly to see policy-makers and the public so preoccupied with an easy-to-castigate media culprit linked by their research to, at most, a small part of the nation's violence—while the urgent social problems devastating a generation continue to lack even a semblance of redress.

Speculations

1. What specific distinctions does Males make between commentators' outrage over the violence portrayed in media and the actual violence itself? How do these distinctions form the crux of his argument?
2. What causes of actual crime and violence does Males suggest we should examine? How are these causes related or unrelated to the portrayal of violence in the media?

3. What distinction does Males make between biological and psychological research and how does this distinction support his argument? If you are not persuaded by this distinction, explain why.

4. How do issues of race, gender, and regional differences affect the results of national research studies on representations of violence in the media?

5. After reading Males along with several of the other selections in this section (especially those by Cannon, Krasny, and Leonard), do you agree or disagree with the view that research studies reveal conflicting results on this issue? Explain your position by using examples from the text.

6. Explain Males's argument about wasting valuable legislative resources. Based on your own sense of the effectiveness of passing laws to regulate media expression, state why this argument seems valid or mistaken to you.

7. What distinctions does Males make between the effects of violent images on adults and the effects of violent images on children? What differences do you think are important? Explain your responses.

TV AND THE DECLINE OF CIVILIZATION

John Leonard

Critic, reviewer, public intellectual, John Leonard was born in Washington, D.C. in 1939, and earned his B.A. from the University of California at Berkeley in 1962. His long and successful career as a writer began in 1959 with an editorial apprenticeship for the *National Review* in Boston. His next job was book reviewer and drama and literature producer for KPFA-Radio in Berkeley. He began writing for *The New York Times* in 1967, working his way up the ladder from staff member to book review editor and finally, in 1977, to chief cultural critic, where he stayed until leaving to become an editor at *Variety* in 1983.

Leonard is a prolific writer. In addition to publishing a multitude of articles for literary magazines, he has written six books, including: *The Naked Martini* (1964), *Crybaby of the Western World* (1969), *Black Conceit* (1973) which was nominated for the *National Book Award*, *This Pen for Hire* (1973), and *Private Lives in the Imperial City* (1979), a collection of sixty-nine columns written for the *Times*. Anstiss Drake, in his review of *Private Lives,* declared that Leonard "can write like a wizard; he wraps his self-analysis in witty wisdom so that the excellent pieces in this collection become delectable and memorable morsels." Another critic described him as "singing the praises of honor and parenthood, the courage of domesticity, and the glory of ordinariness." Leonard himself says more simply:

> I hope to ask moral questions: How do you want your children to grow up? What do you think is decent and fair? Who are your friends, and why? How do you behave when nobody's looking?

In the following essay from *The Nation,* Leonard displays a remarkable range of insight into the relations among modern and ancient cultures, classical literature and popular culture, and established critics versus ordinary viewers of television and film.

Like a warrior-king of Sumer, daubed with sesame oil, gorged on goat, hefting up his sword and drum, Senator Ernest Hollings looked down November 23 from a ziggurat to lament, all over the Op-Ed page of the *New York Times,* the destruction of a fabled Ur: "If the TV and cable industries have no sense of shame, we must take it upon ourselves to stop licensing their violence-saturated programming."

Hollings, of course, is co-sponsor in the Senate, with Daniel Inouye, of a ban on any of act of violence on television before, say, midnight. Never mind whether this is constitutional, or what it would do to the local news. Never mind, either, that in Los Angeles this past August, in the International Ballroom of the Beverly Hilton, in front of 600 industry executives, the talking heads—a professor here, a producer there, a child psychologist and a network veep for program standards—couldn't even agree on a definition of violence. (Is it only bad if it hurts or kills?) And they disagreed on which was worse, a "happy" violence that sugarcoats aggressive behavior or a "graphic" violence that at least suggests consequences. (How, anyway, does TV manage somehow simultaneously to *desensitize* and to *incite?*) Nor were they really sure what goes on in the dreamy heads of our children as they crouch in the dark to commune with the tube while their parents aren't around, if they have any. (*Roadrunner?* Beep-beep.) Nor does the infamous scarlet *V* "parent advisory" warning even apply to cartoons, afternoon soaps or Somalias.

Never mind, because everybody agrees—even Robert Scheer in *The Nation* ("Violence Is Us," November 15)—that watching television causes antisocial behavior, especially among the children of the poor; that there seems to be more violent programming on the air now than there ever was before; that *Beavis and Butt-head* inspired an Ohio 5-year-old to burn down the family trailer; that in this blue druidic light we will have spawned generations of toadstools and triffids; and that fluoridated water causes brown teeth and Alaskan concentration camps.

In fact, there is less violence on network TV than there used to be; because of ratings, it's mostly sitcoms. The worst stuff is the Hollywood splatterflicks found on premium cable, which means the poor are less likely to be watching. Everywhere else on cable, not counting the Court channel or home shopping and not even to think about blood sports and Pat Buchanan, the fare is innocent to the point of stupefaction (Disney, Discovery, Family, Nickelodeon). That Ohio trailer wasn't even wired for cable, so the littlest firebird must have got his MTV elsewhere in the dangerous neighborhood. (And kids have been playing with matches since, at least, Prometheus. I recall burning down my very own bedroom when I was 5 years old. The fire department had to tell my mother.) Since the sixties, according to statistics cited by Douglas Davis in *The Five Myths of Television Power,* more Americans than ever before are going out to eat in restaurants, see films, plays and baseball games, visit museums, travel abroad, jog, even *read.* (A *Consumer Research Study on Book Purchasing* tells us that Americans in 1992 purchased 822 million adult books, an increase of 7 percent over 1991.) Watching TV, everybody does *something else* at the same time. While our children are playing with their Adobe Illustrators and Domark Virtual Reality Toolkits, the rest of us eat, knit, smoke, dream, read magazines, sign checks, feel sorry for ourselves, think about Hillary and plot shrewd career moves or revenge.

Actually watching TV, unless it's C-SPAN, is usually more interesting than the proceedings of Congress. Or what we read in hysterical books like Jerry Mander's *Four Arguments for the Elimination of Television,* or George Gilder's *Life After Television,* or Marie Winn's *The Plug-In Drug,* or Neal Postman's *Amusing Ourselves to Death,* or Bill McKibben's *The Age of Missing Information.* Or what we'll hear at panels discussions on censorship, where right-wingers worry about sex and left-wingers worry about violence. Or at symposiums on "The Apocalypse Trope in Television News" and seminars on "Postmodern Styles of Sadomasochism and Unkindness to Small Animals in Heavy Metal Music Videos." Or just lolling around an academic deepthink-tank, trading mantras like "frame analysis" (Erving Goffman), "waning of affect" (Fredric Jameson), "social facsimiles" (Kenneth Gergen), "pseudo realism" (T.W. Adorno), "violence profiles" (George Gerbner), "processed culture" (Richard Hoggart), "iconography of rooms" (Horace Newcomb), "narcoleptic joys" (Michael Sorkin) or "glass teat" (Harlan Ellison), not to mention "masturbation" (Michael Arlen, Allan Bloom, David Mamet). You'd think the talking furniture was somehow entropic, a heat-death of the culture.

Of *course* something happens to us when we watch TV; networks couldn't sell their millions of pairs of eyes to advertising agencies, nor would ad agencies buy more than $21 billion worth of commercial time each year, if speech (and sound, and motion) didn't somehow modify action. But what happens is far from clear and won't be much clarified by lab studies, however longitudinal, of habits and behaviors isolated from the larger feedback loop of a culture full of gaudy contradictions. The only country in the world that watches more television than we do is Japan, and you should see its snuff movies and pornographic comic books; but the Japanese are pikers compared with us when we compute per capita rates of rape and murder. Some critics in India tried to blame the recent rise in communal violence there on a state-run television series dramatizing the *Mahabharata,* but not long ago they were blaming Salman Rushdie, as in Bangladesh they have decided to blame the writer Taslima Nasrin. No Turk I know of attributes skinhead violence to German TV. It's foolish to pretend that all behavior is mimetic, and that our only model is Spock or Brokaw. Or Mork and Mindy. Why, after so many years of *M*A*S*H,* weekly in prime time and nightly in reruns, aren't all of us out there hugging trees and morphing dolphins? Why, with so many sitcoms, aren't all of us comedians?

But nobody normal watches TV the way Congressmen, academics, symposiasts and Bill McKibbens do. We are less thrilling. For instance:

Last March 3, a Wednesday, midway through the nine-week run of *Homicide* on NBC, in an episode written by Tom Fontana and directed by Martin Campbell, Baltimore detectives Bayliss (Kyle Secor) and Pembleton (Andre Braugher) had twelve hours to wring a confession out of "Arab" Tucker (Moses Gunn) for the strangulation and disemboweling of an 11-year-old girl. In the dirty light and appalling intimacy of a single claustrophobic room, with a whoosh of wind-sound like some dread blowing in from empty Gobi spaces, among maps, library books, diaries, junk food, pornographic crime-scene photographs and a single black overflowing ashtray, these three men seemed as nervous as the hand-held cameras—as if their black coffee were full of jumping beans, amphetamines and spiders; as if God Himself were jerking them around.

Pembleton, the black guy, played Good Cop. Bayliss, the white guy, played Bad Cop. Then, according to cop torque, they reversed themselves. This bearded "Arab," a peddler of fruits and vegetables, whose fiancée dumped him, whose horse died, whose barn burned down, was attacked in his Mad Dog alcoholism, his polygraph readings, his lapsed Baptist churchgoing and his sexuality. About to crack, he struck back. To Pembleton: "You hate niggers like me cuz you hate the inner nigger, you hate being who you really are." And to Bayliss: "You got your dark side and it terrifies you. . . . You look into the mirror and all you see is an *amateur.*" Finally the detectives got a confession, but not to the murder of the girl to whom "Arab," as if from the prodigal riches of Africa, gave peaches, pomegranates and an avocado:

"I never touched her, not once." But 11-year-old Adena was neverthe-less "the one great love" of this old man's wasted life.

Well, you may think the culture doesn't really need another cop show. And, personally, I'd prefer a weekly series in which social prob-lems are solved through creative nonviolence, after a Quaker meeting, by a collective of vegetarian carpenters. But in a single hour last March, for which Tom Fontana eventually won an Emmy, I learned more about the behavior of fearful men in small rooms than from any num-ber of better-known movies, plays and novels on the topic by the likes of Don DeLillo, Mary McCarthy, Alberto Moravia, Heinrich Böll and Doris Lessing.

This, of course, was an accident, as it usually is when those of us who watch television like normal people are startled in our expecta-tions. We leave home expecting, for a lot of money, to be exalted, and almost never are. But staying put, slumped in an agnosticism about sentience itself, suspecting that our cable box is just another bad-faith credit card enabling us to multiply our opportunities for disappoint-ment, we are ambushed in our hebetude. And not so much by "event" television, like Ingmar Bergman's *Scenes From a Marriage,* originally a six-hour miniseries for Swedish television; or Marcel Ophüls's *The Sor-row and the Pity,* originally conceived for French television; or Rainer Werner Fassbinder's *Berlin Alexanderplatz,* commissioned by German television; or *The Singing Detective;* or *The Jewel in the Crown.* On the contrary, we've stayed home on certain nights to watch TV, the way on other nights we'll go out to a neighborhood restaurant, as if on Mon-days we ordered in for laughs, as on Fridays we'd rather eat Italian. We go to television—message center, mission control, Big Neighbor, elec-tronic Elmer's Glue-All—to look at Oscars, Super Bowls, moon shots, Watergates, Pearlygates, ayatollahs, dead Kings, dead Kennedys; and also, perhaps, to experience some "virtual" community as a nation. But we also go because we are hungry, angry, lonely or tired, and TV is al-ways there for us, a twenty-four-hour user-friendly magic box grind-ing out narrative, novelty and distraction, news and laughs, snippets of high culture, remedial seriousness and vulgar celebrity, an incitement and a sedative, a place to celebrate and a place to mourn, a circus and a wishing well.

And suddenly Napoleon shows up, like a popsicle, on *Northern Ex-posure,* while Chris on the radio is reading Proust. Or it turns out *Law & Order* isn't laughing at the Mayflower Madam, not when her sorori-ty sisters, who'd really rather eat buttered popcorn than go out and get paid for doing something *icky,* are also retail merchants of HIV. Or *Roseanne* is about lesbianism instead of bowling. Or *Picket Fences* has moved on, from serial bathers and elephant abuse to euthanasia and gay-bashing. Or between Inspector Morse and Zoe Wanamaker on *Mystery!* there is enough static cling to hydroelectrify the Yangtze. Or, on *The Young Indiana Jones Chronicles*, no sooner has young Indy finished consorting with Hemingways and Bolsheviks than he is being advised on his sexual confusions, in Vienna, by Dr. Freud and Dr. Jung.

Kurt Vonnegut on Showtime! David ("Masturbation") Mamet on TNT! Mailer wrote the TV screenplay for *The Executioner's Song*, and Gore Vidal gave us *Lincoln* with Mary Tyler Moore as Mary Todd. In just the past five years, if I hadn't been watching television, I'd have missed *Tanner '88*, when Robert Altman and Garry Trudeau ran Michael Murphy for President of the United States; *A Very British Coup*, in which socialists and Mozart took over England; *My Name Is Bill W.*, with James Woods as the founding father of Alcoholics Anonymous; *Roe vs. Wade*, with Holly Hunter as a Supreme Court case; *The Final Days*, with Theodore Bikel as Henry Kissinger; *No Place Like Home*, where there wasn't one for Christine Lahti and Jeff Daniels, as there hadn't been for Jane Fonda in *The Dollmaker* and Mare Winningham in *God Bless the Child*; *Eyes on the Prize*, a home movie in two parts about America's second Civil War; *The Last Best Year*, with Mary Tyler Moore and Bernadette Peters learning to live with their gay sons and HIV; *Separate But Equal*, with Sidney Poitier as Thurgood Marshall; *Seize the Day*, with Robin Williams as a fictionalized Saul Bellow; *High Crimes and Misdemeanors*, the Bill Moyers special on Irangate and the scandal of our intelligence agencies; *Sessions*, where Billy Crystal used Elliott Gould to take on psychoanalysis; not only Larry Gelbart's *Mastergate*, a deconstruction of the Reagan/Babar text, but also *Barbarians at the Gate*, his take on venture capitalism; Julie Dash's painterly meditation on Gullah culture off the Carolina coast, *Daughters of the Dust*; *The Caine Mutiny Court Martial*, set by Robert Altman on a basketball court; Evelyn Waugh's *Scoop*; Bette Midler's *Gypsy*; Graham Greene, John Updike, Philip Roth, Gloria Naylor, Arthur Miller and George Eliot, plus Paul Simon and Stephen Sondheim. Not to mention—guiltiest of all our secrets—those hoots without which any popular culture would be as tedious as a John Cage or an Anaïs Nin, like Elizabeth Taylor in *Sweet Bird of Youth* and the Redgrave sisters in a remake of *Whatever Happened to Baby Jane?*

What all this television has in common is narrative. Even network news—which used to be better than most newspapers before the bean counters started closing down overseas bureaus and the red camera lights went out all over Europe and Asia and Africa—is in the storytelling business. And what do we know about narrative? Well, we know what Christa Wolf told us, in *Cassandra*: "Only the advent of property, hierarchy, and patriarchy extracts a blood-red thread from the fabric of human life . . . and this thread is amplified at the expense of the web as a whole, at the expense of its uniformity. The blood-red thread is the narrative and struggle and victory of the heroes, or their doom. The plot is born." And what Don DeLillo told us in *Libra*: "There is a tendency of plots to move toward death. . . . the idea of death is woven into the nature of every plot. A narrative plot no less than a conspiracy of armed men. The tighter the plot of a story, the more likely it will come to death."

In other words, either the Old Testament or the *Iliad* was the first Western, and the *Mahabharata* wasn't such a big improvement. Think of Troy and Masada as warm-ups for the Alamo. This frontier sex-and-violence stuff runs deep, from Hannibal to Attila to El Cid to Sergio Leone. What all Westerns have always been about is clout and turf and sexual property rights and how to look good dying. But so far no one in Congress has suggested banning narrative.

Because I watch all those despised network TV movies, I know more about racism, ecology, homelessness, gun control, child abuse, gender confusion, date rape and AIDS than is dreamt of by, say, Katie Roiphe, the Joyce Maynard of Generation X, or than Hollywood has ever bothered to tell me, especially about AIDS. Imagine, Jonathan Demme's *Philadelphia* is just opening in theaters around the country, after at least a dozen TV movies on the subject that I can remember without troubling my hard disk. And I've learned something else, too:

We were a violent culture before TV, from Wounded Knee to the lynching bee, and we'll be one after all our children have disappeared by video game into the pixels of cyberspace. Before TV, we blamed public schools for what went wrong with the Little People back when classrooms weren't overcrowded in buildings that weren't falling down in neighborhoods that didn't resemble Beirut, and whose fault is that? *The A-Team?* We can't control guns, or drugs, and each year 2 million American women are assaulted by their male partners, who are usually in an alcoholic rage, and whose fault is that? *Miami Vice?* The gangs that menace our streets aren't home watching Cinemax, and neither are the sociopaths who make bonfires, in our parks, from our homeless, of whom there are at least a million, a supply-side migratory tide of the deindustrialized and dispossessed, of angry beggars, refugee children and catatonic nomads, none of them traumatized by *Twin Peaks.* So cut Medicare, kick around the Brady bill and animadvert Amy Fisher movies. But children who are loved and protected long enough to grow up to have homes and respect and lucky enough to have jobs don't riot in the streets. Ours is a tantrum culture that measures everyone by his or her ability to produce wealth, and morally condemns anybody who fails to prosper, and now blames Burbank for its angry incoherence. Why not recessive genes, angry gods, lousy weather? The mafia, the zodiac, the *Protocols of the Elders of Zion?* Probability theory, demonic possession, Original Sin? George Steinbrenner? Sunspots?

Speculations

1. In what ways is the title of Leonard's article ironic? Identify specific passages that play off this irony by drawing connections between modern and ancient cultures.
2. Describe what Leonard thinks "happens to us when we watch TV." How does his description develop from a simple recognition of obvious attempts at manipulation on the part of advertisers to more complex social insights about ourselves. Provide specific examples of the latter.
3. What does Leonard mean by "narrative" and how does his definition connect television to cultures of the past? How does he use specific examples to relate coherence of plot to violence and human compassion?
4. Based on your experience of watching TV, describe an instance in which you learned something significant about "racism, ecology, hopelessness, gun control, child abuse, gender confusion, date rape, [or] AIDS. . . ." Does your experience support Leonard's argument? Explain.
5. Do you agree with Leonard's assertion that "Ours is a tantrum culture that measures everyone by his or her ability to produce wealth, and morally condemns anybody who fails to prosper, and now blames Burbank for its angry incoherence." Why or why not? Support your response with specifics.
6. Do you agree with Leonard that "We were a violent culture before TV, from Wounded Knee to the lynching bee, and we'll be one after all our children have disappeared by video game into the pixels of cyberspace"? Has Leonard sufficiently justified his position? Does his diction and tone support or undercut his celebration of the media's place in our society? Explain your responses.

ASSIGNMENT SEQUENCES

Sequence One: Identities, Values, and Influences

1. Identify three important role models, characters, heroes, or heroines that you encountered in television, film, or mass media during your early years or adolescence. Write an essay that describes what you admired or found memorable in these figures and how you think they have influenced you for better or worse.

2. Write an essay that identifies, compares, and contrasts the kind of television role models that Susan Douglas and Elayne Rapping use in each of their essays. Explain how you agree or disagree with

both the negative and positive influences of these television role models.

3. Select a popular television show—a situation comedy or drama—that you, your friends, or classmates have often watched. Interview three people you know who watch this show by asking what characters they like and dislike, what values they think are operating, and how they think the show influences the opinions and ideas of viewers. Write an analysis of your findings and respond to what others have said with your own opinions and conclusions.

4. Identify a children's television show or film and write an essay describing and analyzing the content of the show, the assumptions it makes about its viewers, and how you think it will influence children for better or worse.

5. Each selection in this section presents arguments and evidence suggesting one of the following: 1) that media images have an overall negative effect on the viewers' development of values and their relationship to society, or 2) that this relationship is highly complex, not always negative, and that individuals can respond critically to what they see and hear in order to shape their own identities and values. Identify arguments for both these positions by selecting quotations, points of view, and specific examples from several selections in this section. Write an essay that organizes what you discover, analyzes each argument, and identifies positions you think are most effective. Conclude by presenting your own evaluation the evidence and your own examples from mass media to support your views on the subject.

6. Based on what you have learned from writing one or more of the above assignments, write an editorial for your local newspaper that expresses your opinion of current values in the media and what people should or should not be doing about it.

Sequence Two: Anecdotes, Research Sources, and Arguments

1. Notice that Susan Douglas and Elayne Rapping base their views primarily on personal experience—their own observations concerning what they feel is most important about television and film. Using the same approach, select a television show or a film that has had a personal impact on you, and write an essay about its representation of cultural values and social problems (gender differences, criminal justice, family loyalties, abusive relationships, etc.). What are the positive and negative values of the characters in the film or show, and how do their actions support or deny those val-

ues? Use personal observations and anecdotes from your own experience to explain how you see those values working or not working around you. How do you see your family and friends accepting or rejecting the societal values you have identified in this film or television show?

2. Susan Douglas, Carl Cannon, and Michael Krasny come down on one side of the argument about video and violence while Elayne Rapping, Mike Males, and John Leonard come down on the other. Decide where you stand in this debate and formulate an argument for that stance by selecting examples, evidence, and quotations from the authors in this section.

3. As a follow up to writing assignment 2, pick two authors from this section and write an analysis of their research methods: Where do they get their facts and observations? What makes their sources seem persuasive, authentic, or compelling? How do their presentations of research work rhetorically to build an argument based on their sources? What makes their research findings and their presentation of those materials more persuasive than other authors in this section?

4. Take Carl Cannon's and Mike Males's selections to the library and find one of the research sources mentioned by each of them. Read the original source and write an evaluation of how each adapted the original to his argument. If you have difficulty finding their sources, consult a reference librarian on how to find the sources cited by these authors. You may include an account of the difficulties you have locating the sources in your evaluation of how the authors use their sources.

5. As a follow up to assignment 4, do some of your own research on violence in television, film, and mass media. Look for sources that relate to those you found in assignment 4 and collect three that you think effectively support, contradict, or somehow alter your sense of the original sources you have already seen. Use these new sources to construct your own argument about the conflicting views of the effect of images of violence in television and film on the viewing audience.

6. In the spirit of Michael Krasny's methodology, interview two or three media, film, mass communications, or even English professors on your campus. You might find teaching assistants or graduate students working in these areas more accessible than professors. Ask them to respond to the same questions that Krasny asks at the beginning of his article (that is: the issue of freedom of expression and the issue of who is responsible for violent

movies and television shows). Write up their responses. Based on what you learn, formulate your own opinion about how to resolve the conflict between free expression and excessive violence in entertainment.

7. Notice that Elayne Rapping and John Leonard rely on their own feelings and thoughts about the structures of television shows they admire. In a way, they treat these shows as if they were literary texts worthy of close examinations. They even find redeeming social lessons in the shows. Following their leads, write an essay about a television show that you think teaches us something valuable about ourselves and society.

2

MUSIC
— AND —
MORALITY

Music is as old as history. Human beings sang, danced, and played instruments long before they wrote books or watched NFL football on Super Sunday. The ancient Greeks understood that music embodies *ethos*, the fundamental character and values of a people, and that music possesses the power to influence the listener's emotions, behavior, and morals. At the same time, music is perhaps the most pervasive of the arts, permeating all levels of culture. It plays an essential role in celebrations, dance, and worship; it can be heard in virtually every aural medium—radio, television, film, or theater. Clearly, the human psyche has some need to move to instrumentation, rhythm, and beat, and to marry words to musical notes. The explosion of musical genres in the twentieth century alone testifies to music's universal appeal: ballads, folk music, blues, jazz, big band, rock 'n' roll, pop, punk, heavy metal, and rap, to mention only a few.

Music is an idiom that speaks to virtually everyone who hears it. Rock 'n' roll, for example, appeals strongly to rebellious teenagers. Jazz is an expression for playful sophisticates. Rap music tests the boundaries of middle-class conventions. Folk music fuels the muscle underlying political struggle. Country music tells life stories and appeals to the audience's emotions. Although such statements are broad generalizations, they reflect perceptions shared by many within our culture.

Because music is such a broad subject, this section of *Speculations* focuses on only a few key themes and individuals that intersect music, culture, and the politics of expression. In particular, the real and presumed dangers of music and their significance as cultural and political markers are examined. For many critics, music is a clear and present danger to society, something that needs to be regulated, supervised, and occasionally banned. Such responses are nothing new; over 2,000 years ago in Book III of the *Republic*, Plato warned that "innovations in music" could corrupt "the fundamental political and social conventions" of his idealized Republic. Philosophers, politicians, educators, parents—they all have expressed strong concerns about the nature and role of music within society.

The selections that follow illustrate the complexity of our view of music. Is its current formulation within culture destructive? Does it isolate individuals and make its listeners into cultural zombies or defiant outlaws? How can the genius of certain forms of music be explained? Is music sexist, racist, ageist? What roles, positive or negative, do musical icons play within youth culture? What does it mean to be a fan or a groupie, transfixed within a mindless gaze toward an adored object? The writers included here raise these kinds of questions as they speculate on the relations between music and morality.

MUSIC

Allan Bloom

Allan Bloom described his childhood the following way in an interview with *Contemporary Authors:* "I was a kind of intellectual kid. . . . Self-understanding was always my goal, a scholarly goal, even when I was little." Born in 1930 in Indiana, Bloom entered college after his second year of high school and went on to earn B.A., M.A., and Ph.D. degrees at the University of Chicago. He taught at Yale, Cornell, Toronto, Tel Aviv and Chicago universities, and published several books, including translations of Plato's *Republic* and two books by Rousseau, a co-authored book on *Shakespeare's Politics* (1964), *The Closing of the American Mind: How Higher Education Has Failed Democracy and Impoverished the Souls of Today's Students* (1987), which contains the chapter "Music," reprinted here, and *Love and Friendship* (1993). Bloom died in 1992.

Throughout his career, Bloom expressed strong concern about what he considered irresponsible politics and policies in education. In 1969, two years after winning the Clark Distinguished Teaching Award at Cornell University, he resigned his position in protest of Cornell's failure to protect teachers' academic freedoms and their right to teach unpopular views. His resignation came in the wake of a campus uprising in which a group of rifle-wielding students took over the administration building. Bloom felt strongly that administrators had acted cowardly by giving in to the students' radical demands and by failing to protect professors who had received death threats for opposing them.

In 1987, Bloom provoked an intense debate with the publication of *The Closing of the American Mind,* a critique of the way American universities are educating students. According to Bloom, tolerance has become an end in itself, which means accepting everything and denying reason's power to make distinctions between important and superficial ideas. Bloom believed that a philosophy of complete equality and openness may limit learning by undermining traditional educational values. He favored a "Great Books" approach to education, which focuses on authors such as as Plato, Shakespeare, Rousseau, Hegel, and others in the Western tradition.

Many critics of *The Closing of the American Mind* charged Bloom with elitism and antiquarianism, while others celebrated its message as a return to fundamental American values. As one critic said, this book "will provoke nearly everyone." "Music" examines rock music as an example of how modern culture undermines our intellectual foundations, and may prevent young people from developing insights into a fuller life.

Though students do not have books, they most emphatically do have music. Nothing is more singular about this generation than its addiction to music. This is the age of music and the states of soul that accompany it. To find a rival to this enthusiasm, one would have to go back at least a century to Germany and the passion for Wagner's operas. They had the religious sense that Wagner was creating the meaning of life and that they were not merely listening to his works but experiencing that meaning. Today, a very large proportion of young people between the ages of ten and twenty live for music. It is their passion; nothing else excites them as it does; they cannot take seriously anything alien to music. When they are in school and with their families, they are longing to plug themselves back into their music. Nothing surrounding them—school, family, church—has anything to do with their musical world. At best that ordinary life is neutral, but mostly it is an impediment, drained of vital content, even a thing to be rebelled against. Of course, the enthusiasm for Wagner was limited to a small class, could be indulged only rarely and only in a few places, and had to wait on the composer's slow output. The music of the new votaries, on the other hand, knows neither class nor nation. It is available twenty-four hours a day, everywhere. There is the stereo in the home, in the car; there are concerts; there are music videos, with special channels exclusively devoted to them, on the air nonstop; there are the Walkmans so that no place—not public transportation, not the library—prevents students from communing with the Muse, even while studying. And, above all, the musical soil has become tropically rich. No need to wait for one unpredictable genius. Now there are many geniuses, producing all the time, two new ones rising to take the place of every fallen hero. There is no dearth of the new and the startling.

The power of music in the soul—described to Jessica marvelously by Lorenzo in the *Merchant of Venice*—has been recovered after a long period of desuetude. And it is rock music alone that has effected this restoration. Classical music is dead among the young. This assertion will, I know, be hotly disputed by many who, unwilling to admit tidal changes, can point to the proliferation on campuses of classes in classical music appreciation and practice, as well as performance groups of all kinds. Their presence is undeniable, but they involve not more than 5 to 10 percent of the students. Classical music is now a special taste, like Greek language or pre-Columbian archeology, not a common culture of reciprocal communication and psychological shorthand. Thirty years ago, most middle-class families made some of the old European music a part of the home, partly because they liked it, partly because they thought it was good for the kids. University students usually had some early emotive association with Beethoven, Chopin and Brahms, which was a permanent part of their makeup and to which they were likely to respond throughout their lives. This was probably the only regularly recognizable class distinction between educated and uneducated in America. Many, or even most, of the young people of that generation also swung with Benny Goodman, but with an element of self-consciousness—to be hip, to prove they weren't snobs, to show solidarity with the democratic ideal of a pop culture out of which would grow a new high culture. So there remained a class distinction between high and low, although private taste was beginning to create doubts about whether one really liked the high very much. But all that has changed. Rock music is as unquestioned and unproblematic as the air the students breathe, and very few have any acquaintance at all with classical music. This is a constant surprise to me. And one of the strange aspects of my relations with good students I come to know well is that I frequently introduce them to Mozart. This is a pleasure for me, inasmuch as it is always pleasant to give people gifts that please them. It is interesting to see whether and in what ways their studies are complemented by such music. But this is something utterly new to me as a teacher; formerly my students usually knew much more classical music than I did.

Music was not all that important for the generation of students preceding the current one. The romanticism that had dominated serious music since Beethoven appealed to refinements—perhaps overrefinements—of sentiments that are hardly to be found in the contemporary world. The lives people lead or wish to lead and their prevailing passions are of a different sort than those of the highly educated German and French bourgeoisie, who were avidly reading Rousseau and Baudelaire, Goethe and Heine, for their spiritual satisfaction. The music that had been designed to produce, as well as to please, such exquisite sensibilities had a very tenuous relation to American lives of any kind. So romantic musical culture in America had had for a long time the character of a veneer, as easily susceptible to ridicule as were Margaret Dumont's displays of coquettish chasteness, so aptly exploited by Groucho Marx in *A Night At The Opera*. I noticed this when I first started teaching and lived in a house for gifted students. The "good" ones studied their physics and then listened to classical music. The students who did not fit so easily into the groove, some of them also serious, were looking for things that really responded to their needs. Almost always they responded to the beat of the newly emerging rock music. They were a bit ashamed of their taste, for it was not respectable. But I instinctively sided with this second group, with real, if coarse, feelings as opposed to artificial and dead ones. Then their musical sans-culotteism won the revolution and reigns unabashed today. No classical music has been produced that can speak to this generation.

Symptomatic of this change is how seriously students now take the famous passages on musical education in Plato's *Republic*.[1] In the

---

[1] See Book III of Plato's *Republic,* paragraphs 397 through 404. [Eds.]

past, students, good liberals that they always are, were indignant at the censorship of poetry, as a threat to free inquiry. But they were really thinking of science and politics. They hardly paid attention to the discussion of music itself and, to the extent that they even thought about it, were really puzzled by Plato's devoting time to rhythm and melody in a serious treatise on political philosophy. Their experience of music was as an entertainment, a matter of indifference to political and moral life. Students today, on the contrary, know exactly why Plato takes music so seriously. They know it affects life very profoundly and are indignant because Plato seems to want to rob them of their most intimate pleasure. They are drawn into argument with Plato about the experience of music, and the dispute centers on how to evaluate it and deal with it. This encounter not only helps to illuminate the phenomenon of contemporary music, but also provides a model of how contemporary students can profitably engage with a classic text. The very fact of their fury shows how much Plato threatens what is dear and intimate to them. They are little able to defend their experience, which had seemed unquestionable until questioned, and it is most resistant to cool analysis. Yet if a student can—and this is most difficult and unusual—draw back, get a critical distance on what he clings to, come to doubt the ultimate value of what he loves, he has taken the first and most difficult step toward the philosophic conversion. Indignation is the soul's defense against the wound of doubt about its own; it reorders the cosmos to support the justice of its cause. It justifies putting Socrates to death. Recognizing indignation for what it is constitutes knowledge of the soul, and is thus an experience more philosophic than the study of mathematics. It is Plato's teaching that music, by its nature, encompasses all that is today most resistant to philosophy. So it may well be that through the thicket of our greatest corruption runs the path to awareness of the oldest truths.

Plato's teaching about music is, put simply, that rhythm and melody, accompanied by dance, are the barbarous expression of the soul. Barbarous, not animal. Music is the medium of the *human* soul in its most ecstatic condition of wonder and terror. Nietzsche, who in large measure agrees with Plato's analysis, says in *The Birth of Tragedy* (not to be forgotten is the rest of the title, *Out of the Spirit of Music*) that a mixture of cruelty and coarse sensuality characterized this state, which of course was religious, in the service of gods. Music is the soul's primitive and primary speech and it is *alogon*,[2] without articulate speech or reason. It is not only not reasonable, it is hostile to reason. Even when articulate speech is added, it is utterly subordinate to and determined by the music and the passions it expresses.

---

[2] *Alogon* is the Greek word for that which is beyond or without words or rational thought. [Eds.]

Civilization or, to say the same thing, education is the taming or domestication of the soul's raw passions—not suppressing or excising them, which would deprive the soul of its energy—but forming and informing them as art. The goal of harmonizing the enthusiastic part of the soul with what develops later, the rational part, is perhaps impossible to attain. But without it, man can never be whole. Music, or poetry, which is what music becomes as reason emerges, always involves a delicate balance between passion and reason, and, even in its highest and most developed forms—religious, warlike and erotic—that balance is always tipped, if ever so slightly, toward the passionate. Music, as everyone experiences, provides an unquestionable justification and a fulfilling pleasure for the activities it accompanies: the solider who hears the marching band is enthralled and reassured; the religious man is exalted in his prayer by the sound of the organ in the church; and the lover is carried away and his conscience stilled by the romantic guitar. Armed with music, man can damn rational doubt. Out of the music emerge the gods that suit it, and they educate men by their example and their commandments.

Plato's Socrates disciplines the ecstasies and thereby provides little consolation or hope to men. According to the Socratic formula, the lyrics—speech and, hence, reason—must determine the music—harmony and rhythm. Pure music can never endure this constraint. Students are not in a position to know the pleasures of reason; they can only see it as a disciplinary and repressive parent. But they do see, in the case of Plato, that that parent has figured out what they are up to. Plato teaches that, in order to take the spiritual temperature of an individual or a society, one must "mark the music." To Plato and Nietzsche, the history of music is a series of attempts to give form and beauty to the dark, chaotic, premonitory forces in the soul—to make them serve a higher purpose, an ideal, to give man's duties a fullness. Bach's religious intentions and Beethoven's revolutionary and humane ones are clear enough examples. Such cultivation of the soul uses the passions and satisfies them while sublimating them and giving them an artistic unity. A man whose noblest activities are accompanied by a music that expresses them while providing a pleasure extending from the lowest bodily to the highest spiritual, is whole, and there is no tension in him between the pleasant and the good. By contrast a man whose business life is prosaic and unmusical and whose leisure is made up of coarse, intense entertainments, is divided, and each side of his existence is undermined by the other.

Hence, for those who are interested in psychological health, music is at the center of education, both for giving the passions their due and for preparing the soul for the unhampered use of reason. The centrality of such education was recognized by all the ancient educators. It is hardly noticed today that in Aristotle's *Politics* the most important passages about the best regime concern musical education, or that the *Poetics* is an appendix to the *Politics*. Classical philosophy did not censor the singers. It persuaded them. And it gave them a goal, one that was understood by them, until only yesterday. But those who do not notice the role of music in Aristotle and despise it in Plato went to school with Hobbes, Locke and Smith, where such considerations have become unnecessary. The triumphant Enlightenment rationalism thought that it had discovered other ways to deal with the irrational part of the soul, and that reason needed less support from it. Only in those great critics of Enlightenment and rationalism, Rousseau and Nietzsche, does music return, and they were the most musical of philosophers. Both thought that the passions—and along with them their ministerial arts—had become thin under the rule of reason and that, therefore, man himself and what he sees in the world have become correspondingly thin. They wanted to cultivate the enthusiastic states of the soul and to re-experience the Corybantic possession deemed a pathology by Plato. Nietzsche, particularly, sought to tap again the irrational sources of vitality, to replenish our dried-up stream from barbaric sources, and thus encouraged the Dionysian and the music derivative from it.

This is the significance of rock music. I do not suggest that it has any high intellectual sources. But it has risen to its current heights in the education of the young on the ashes of classical music, and in an atmosphere in which there is no intellectual resistance to attempts to tap the rawest passions. Modern-day rationalists, such as economists, are indifferent to it and what it represents. The irrationalists are all for it. There is no need to fear that "the blond beasts" are going to come forth from the bland souls of our adolescents. But rock music has one appeal only, a barbaric appeal, to sexual desire—not love, not *eros*, but sexual desire undeveloped and untutored. It acknowledges the first emanations of children's emerging sensuality and addresses them seriously, eliciting them and legitimating them, not as little sprouts that must be carefully tended in order to grow into gorgeous flowers, but as the real thing. Rock gives children, on a silver platter, with all the public authority of the entertainment industry, everything their parents always used to tell them they had to wait for until they grew up and would understand later.

Young people know that rock has the beat of sexual intercourse. That is why Ravel's *Bolero* is the one piece of classical music that is commonly known and liked by them. In alliance with some real art and a lot of pseudo-art, an enormous industry cultivates the taste for the orgiastic state of feeling connected with sex, providing a constant flood of fresh material for voracious appetites. Never was there an art form directed so exclusively to children.

Ministering to and according with the arousing and cathartic music, the lyrics celebrate puppy love as well as polymorphous attractions, and fortify them against traditional ridicule and shame. The words implicitly and explicitly describe bodily acts that satisfy sexual desire and treat them as its only natural and routine culmination for children who do not yet have the slightest imagination of love, marriage or family. This has a much more powerful effect than does pornography on youngsters, who have no need to watch others do grossly what they can so easily do themselves. Voyeurism is for old perverts; active sexual relations are for the young. All they need is encouragement.

The inevitable corollary of such sexual interest is rebellion against the parental authority that represses it. Selfishness thus becomes indignation and then transforms itself into morality. The sexual revolution must overthrow all the forces of domination, the enemies of nature and happiness. From love comes hate, masquerading as social reform. A worldview is balanced on the sexual fulcrum. What were once unconscious or half-conscious childish resentments become the new Scripture. And then comes the longing for the classless, prejudice-free, conflictless, universal society that necessarily results from liberated consciousness—"We Are the World," a pubescent version of *Alle Menschen werden Brüder*,[3] the fulfillment of which has been inhibited by the political equivalents of Mom and Dad. These are the three great lyrical themes: sex, hate and a smarmy, hypocritical version of brotherly love. Such polluted sources issue in a muddy stream where only monsters can swim. A glance at the videos that project images on the wall of Plato's cave since MTV took it over suffices to prove this. Hitler's image recurs frequently enough in exciting contexts to give one pause. Nothing noble, sublime, profound, delicate, tasteful or even decent can find a place in such tableaux. There is room only for the intense, changing, crude and immediate, which Tocqueville warned us would be the character of democratic art, combined with a pervasiveness, importance and content beyond Tocqueville's wildest imagination.

Picture a thirteen-year-old boy sitting in the living room of his family home doing his math assignment while wearing his Walkman headphones or watching MTV. He enjoys the liberties hard won over centuries by the alliance of philosophic genius and political heroism, consecrated by the blood of martyrs; he is provided with comfort and leisure by the most productive economy ever known to mankind; science has penetrated the secrets of nature in order to provide him with the marvelous, lifelike electronic sound and image reproduction he is enjoying. And in what does progress culminate? A pubescent child whose body throbs with orgasmic rhythms; whose feelings are made articulate in hymns to the joys of onanism or the killing of parents; whose ambition is to win fame and wealth in imitating the drag-queen

---

[3] All Men Are Brothers. [Eds.]

who makes the music. In short, life is made into a non-stop, commercially prepackaged masturbational fantasy.

This description may seem exaggerated, but only because some would prefer to regard it as such. The continuing exposure to rock music is a reality, not one confined to a particular class or type of child. One need only ask first-year university students what music they listen to, how much of it and what it means to them, in order to discover that the phenomenon is universal in America, that it begins in adolescence or a bit before and continues through the college years. It is *the* youth culture and, as I have so often insisted, there is now no other countervailing nourishment for the spirit. Some of this culture's power comes from the fact that it is so loud. It makes conversation impossible, so that much of friendship must be without the shared speech that Aristotle asserts is the essence of friendship and the only true common ground. With rock, illusions of shared feelings, bodily contact and grunted formulas, which are supposed to contain so much meaning beyond speech, are the basis of association. None of this contradicts going about the business of life, attending classes and doing the assignments for them. But the meaningful inner life is with the music.

This phenomenon is both astounding and indigestible, and is hardly noticed, routine and habitual. But it is of historic proportions that a society's best young and their best energies should be so occupied. People of future civilizations will wonder at this and find it as incomprehensible as we do the caste system, witch-burning, harems, cannibalism and gladiatorial combats. It may well be that a society's greatest madness seems normal to itself. The child I described has parents who have sacrificed to provide him with a good life and who have a great stake in his future happiness. They cannot believe that the musical vocation will contribute very much to that happiness. But there is nothing they can do about it. The family spiritual void has left the field open to rock music, and they cannot possibly forbid their children to listen to it. It is everywhere; all children listen to it; forbidding it would simply cause them to lose their children's affection and obedience. When they turn on the television, they will see President Reagan warmly grasping the daintily proffered gloved hand of Michael Jackson and praising him enthusiastically. Better to set the faculty of denial in motion—avoid noticing what the words say, assume the kid will get over it. If he has early sex, that won't get in the way of his having stable relationships later. His drug use will certainly stop at pot. School is providing real values. And popular historicism provides the final salvation: there are new life-styles for new situations, and the older generation is there not to impose its values but to help the younger one to find its own. TV, which compared to music plays a comparatively small role in the formation of young people's character and taste, is a consensus monster—the Right monitors its content for sex, the Left for violence, and many other interested sects for many other things. But the music has hardly been touched, and what efforts have been made are both ineffectual and misguided about the nature and extent of the problem.

The result is nothing less than parents' loss of control over their children's moral education at a time when no one else is seriously concerned with it. This has been achieved by an alliance between the strange young males who have the gift of divining the mob's emergent wishes—our versions of Thrasymachus, Socrates' rhetorical adversary—and the record-company executives, the new robber barons, who mine gold out of rock. They discovered a few years back that children are one of the few groups in the country with considerable disposable income, in the form of allowances. Their parents spend all they have providing for the kids. Appealing to them over their parents' heads, creating a world of delight for them, constitutes one of the richest markets in the postwar world. The rock business is perfect capitalism, supplying to demand and helping to create it. It has all the moral dignity of drug trafficking, but it was so totally new and unexpected that nobody thought to control it, and now it is too late. Progress may be made against cigarette smoking because our absence of standards or our relativism does not extend to matters of bodily health. In all other things the market determines the value. (Yoko Ono is among America's small group of billionaires, along with oil and computer magnates, her late husband having produced and sold a commodity of worth comparable to theirs.) Rock is very big business, bigger than the movies, bigger than professional sports, bigger than television, and this accounts for much of the respectability of the music business. It is difficult to adjust our vision to the changes in the economy and to see what is really important. McDonald's now has more employees than U.S. Steel, and likewise the purveyors of junk food for the soul have supplanted what still seem to be more basic callings.

This change has been happening for some time. In the late fifties, De Gaulle gave Brigitte Bardot one of France's highest honors. I could not understand this, but it turned out that she, along with Peugeot, was France's biggest export item. As Western nations became more prosperous, leisure, which had been put off for several centuries in favor of the pursuit of property, the means to leisure, finally began to be of primary concern. But, in the meantime, any notion of the serious life of leisure, as well as men's taste and capacity to live it, had disappeared. Leisure became entertainment. The end for which they had labored for so long has turned out to be amusement, a justified conclusion if the means justify the ends. The music business is peculiar only in that it caters almost exclusively to children, treating legally and naturally imperfect human beings as though they were ready to enjoy the final or complete satisfaction. It perhaps thus reveals the nature of all our entertainment and our loss of a clear view of what adulthood or maturity is, and our incapacity to conceive ends. The emptiness of *values* results in the acceptance of the natural *facts* as the ends. In this case infantile sexuality is the end, and I suspect that, in the absence of other ends, many adults have come to agree that it is.

It is interesting to note that the Left, which prides itself on its critical approach to "late capitalism" and is unrelenting and unsparing in its analysis of our other cultural phenomena, has in general given rock music a free ride. Abstracting from the capitalist element in which it flourishes, they regard it as a people's art, coming from beneath the bourgeoisie's layers of cultural repression. Its antinomianism and its longing for a world without constraint might seem to be the clarion of the proletarian revolution, and Marxists certainly do see that rock music dissolves the beliefs and morals necessary for liberal society and would approve of it for that alone. But the harmony between the young intellectual Left and rock is probably profounder than that. Herbert Marcuse appealed to university students in the sixties with a combination of Marx and Freud. In *Eros and Civilization* and *One Dimensional Man* he promised that the overcoming of capitalism and its false consciousness will result in a society where the greatest satisfactions are sexual, of a sort that the bourgeois moralist Freud called polymorphous and infantile. Rock music touches the same chord in the young. Free sexual expression, anarchism, mining of the irrational unconscious and giving it free rein are what they have in common. The high intellectual life . . . and the low rock world are partners in the same entertainment enterprise. They must both be interpreted as parts of the cultural fabric of late capitalism. Their success comes from the bourgeois' need to feel that he is not bourgeois, to have undangerous experiments with the unlimited. He is willing to pay dearly for them. The Left is better interpreted by Nietzsche than by Marx. The critical theory of late capitalism is at once late capitalism's subtlest and crudest expression. Anti-bourgeois ire is the opiate of the Last Man.

This strong stimulant, which Nietzsche called Nihiline, was for a very long time, almost fifteen years, epitomized in a single figure, Mick Jagger. A shrewd, middle-class boy, he played the possessed lower-class demon and teen-aged satyr up until he was forty, with one eye on the mobs of children of both sexes whom he stimulated to a sensual frenzy and the other eye winking at the unerotic, commercially motivated adults who handled the money. In his act he was male and female, heterosexual and homosexual; unencumbered by modesty, he could enter everyone's dreams, promising to do everything with everyone; and, above all, he legitimated drugs, which were the real thrill that parents and policemen conspired to deny his youthful audience. He was beyond the law, moral and political, and thumbed his nose at it. Along with all this, there were nasty little appeals to the suppressed inclinations toward sexism, racism and violence, indulgence in which is not now publicly respectable. Nevertheless, he managed not to appear to contradict the rock ideal of a universal classless society founded on love, with the distinction between brotherly and bodily blurred. He was the hero and the model for countless young persons in universities, as well as elsewhere. I discovered that students who boasted of having no heroes secretly had a passion to be like Mick Jagger, to live his life, have his fame. They were ashamed to admit this in a university, although I am not certain that the reason has anything to do with a higher standard of taste. It is probably that they are not supposed to have heroes. Rock music itself and talking about it with infinite seriousness are perfectly respectable. It has proved to be the ultimate leveler of intellectual snobbism. But it is not respectable to think of it as providing weak and ordinary persons with a fashionable behavior, the imitation of which will make others esteem them and boost their own self-esteem. Unaware and unwillingly, however, Mick Jagger played the role in their lives that Napoleon played in the lives of ordinary young Frenchmen throughout the nineteenth century. Everyone else was so boring and unable to charm youthful passions. Jagger caught on.

In the last couple of years, Jagger has begun to fade. Whether Michael Jackson, Prince or Boy George can take his place is uncertain. They are even weirder than he is, and one wonders what new strata of taste they have discovered. Although each differs from the others, the essential character of musical entertainment is not changing. There is only a constant search for variations on the theme. And this gutter phenomenon is apparently the fulfillment of the promise made by so much psychology and literature that our weak and exhausted Western civilization would find refreshment in the true source, the unconscious, which appeared to the late romantic imagination to be identical to Africa, the dark and unexplored continent. Now all has been explored; light has been cast everywhere; the unconscious has been made conscious, the repressed expressed. And what have we found? Not creative devils, but show business glitz. Mick Jagger tarting it up on the stage is all that we brought back from the voyage to the underworld.

My concern here is not with the moral effects of this music—whether it leads to sex, violence or drugs. The issue here is its effect on education, and I believe it ruins the imagination of young people and makes it very difficult for them to have a passionate relationship to the art and thought that are the substance of liberal education. The first sensuous experiences are decisive in determining the taste for the whole of life, and they are the link between the animal and spiritual in us. The period of nascent sensuality has always been used for sublimation, in the sense of making sublime, for attaching youthful inclinations and longings to music, pictures and stories that provide the transition to the fulfillment of the human duties and the enjoyment of the human pleasures. Lessing, speaking of Greek sculpture, said "beautiful men made beautiful statues, and the city had beautiful statues in part to thank for beautiful citizens." This formula encapsulates the fundamental principle of the esthetic education of man. Young men and women were attracted by the beauty of heroes whose very bodies expressed their nobility. The deeper understanding of the meaning of nobility comes later, but is prepared for by the sensuous experience and is actually contained in it. What the senses long for as well as what reason later sees as good are thereby not at tension with one another. Education is not sermonizing to children against their instincts and pleasures, but providing a natural continuity between what they feel and what they can and should be. But this is a lost art. Now we have come to exactly the opposite point. Rock music encourages passions and provides models that have no relation to any life the young people who go to universities can possibly lead, or to the kinds of admiration encouraged by liberal studies. Without the cooperation of the sentiments, anything other than technical education is a dead letter.

Rock music provides premature ecstasy and, in this respect, is like the drugs with which it is allied. It artificially induces the exaltation naturally attached to the completion of the greatest endeavors—victory in a just war, consummated love, artistic creation, religious devotion and discovery of the truth. Without effort, without talent, without virtue, without exercise of the faculties, anyone and everyone is accorded the equal right to the enjoyment of their fruits. In my experience, students who have had a serious fling with drugs—and gotten over it—find it difficult to have enthusiasms or great expectations. It is as though the color has been drained out of their lives and they see everything in black and white. The pleasure they experienced in the beginning was so intense that they no longer look for it at the end, or as the end. They may function perfectly well, but dryly, routinely. Their energy has been sapped, and they do not expect their life's activity to produce anything but a living, whereas liberal education is supposed to encourage the belief that the good life is the pleasant life and that the best life is the most pleasant life. I suspect that the rock addiction, particularly in the absence of strong counterattractions, has an effect similar to that of drugs. The students will get over this music, or at least the exclusive passion for it. But they will do so in the same way Freud says that men accept the reality principle—as something harsh, grim and essentially unattractive, a mere necessity. These students will assiduously study economics or the professions and the Michael Jackson costume will slip off to reveal a Brooks Brothers suit beneath. They will want to get ahead and live comfortably. But this life is as empty and false as the one they left behind. The choice is not between quick fixes and dull calculation. This is what liberal education is meant to show them. But as long as they have the Walkman on, they cannot hear what the great tradition has to say. And, after its prolonged use, when they take it off, they find they are deaf.

Speculations

1. Allan Bloom writes: "Today, a very large portion of young people between the ages of ten and twenty live for music. It is their passion; nothing else excites them as it does; they cannot take seriously anything alien to music." Discuss this opinion. What do you think he means by "music" as young people's "passion"?

2. What is extraordinary about music for you? How do you compare the importance and value of music to other daily activities such as school, work, watching television, dating?

3. Consider the kinds of music you like and listen to the most. How would you describe the benefits, educational qualities, and entertainment value of your music? Or put another way, how does music affect you and your peers?

4. Notice that Bloom refers to Richard Wagner's operas, the classical music of Beethoven, Chopin, and Brahms, the philosophy of Plato and Nietzsche, and many other literary figures in our culture. Why does he do this? How do these figures help us to better understand present-day culture?

5. What is Bloom's attitude toward students in this essay? How does he talk about them? What tone does he use? How do you feel about his attitude toward "today's students"? Would you take a class from this teacher? Why or why not?

6. Bloom states that "Young people know that rock has the beat of sexual intercourse" and that the lyrics from rock songs "implicitly and explicitly describe bodily acts that satisfy sexual desire." He goes on to connect rock music with "pornography," "voyeurism," and "life . . . made into a nonstop commercially prepackaged masturbational fantasy." Do you agree? Explain your response.

7. Assume you are a parent of a teenage daughter and a teenage son: How would you respond to the effects of rock music on teenagers described by Bloom? Are these effects that you would want your own teenage son and daughter to experience? Why or why not?

THE WAR ON ROCK
AND RAP MUSIC

Barbara Dority

Barbara Dority is a committed activist in politics and social reform. President of the Humanists of Washington, Executive Director
of the Washington Coalition Against Censorship, and a member of
the Washington Board of the American Civil Liberties Union, she is
familiar with the legal ramifications of censorship and its history in
the popular music world. Writing for *The Humanist* magazine, Dority
upholds an unequivocal stand in defense of "intellectual freedom and
free speech." Her activism also extends to the feminist movement and
the terminally ill as co-chair of the Northwest Feminists Anti-Censorship Taskforce and board member of the Hemlock Society—a non-
profit organization which seeks "to promote a climate of public opinion which is tolerant of the right of people who are terminally ill to
end their own lives in a planned manner."

Dority's article pinpoints specific legal actions and political figures responsible for the war against rock and rap. Like Jerry Adler in
"The Rap Attitude," she identifies the FBI's criticism of the rap group
NWA's album *Straight Outta Compton* as a response to specific musical lyrics—something worthy of our analysis and attention. But unlike Adler, Dority sees the powerful force of rap music among young
people as "a new form of communication and protest" by the disenfranchised. She and Adler offer a kind of point and counterpoint debate about the complex issue surrounding free speech as guaranteed
by the First Amendment of the Bill of Rights.

All music lovers, including those who prefer classical music and
opera to more modern sounds, should be vitally concerned about the
censorship of rock and rap music. As a long-time anti-censorship activist, I am alarmed by recent events which make a mockery of our Bill
of Rights. I am convinced that we must take a stand against this strong-
arm suppression of intellectual freedom and free speech.

A nationwide movement to restrict access to music began in
1985 with the founding of the Parents' Music Resource Center by
Susan Baker, wife of Secretary of State James Baker, and Tipper
Gore, wife of Senator Albert Gore. After a series of sensational congressional hearings failed to convince Congress to pass legislation
mandating government labeling of "objectionable" music, the
PMRC shifted its pressure tactics to the record companies. Insisting
that rock and rap lyrics cause violence and sexual irresponsibility,
the PMRC demanded that record producers institute a system of
"voluntary" labeling.

Persistence pays off. On May 9, 1990, the Recording Industry Association of America announced the coming of a uniform warning label system on "all possibly objectionable materials" beginning in July.

This alarming concession, however, still falls woefully short of what pro-censorship activists really want. Many states are considering repressive legislation that would ban the sale of recordings containing lyrics about adultery, incest, illicit drug or alcohol use, murder, or suicide. Opera lovers will note that such works as *Madame Butterfly, Tosca, Carmen, La Traviata,* and many others would fall victim to these standards.

In Missouri, Representative Jean Dixon, with help from Phyllis Schlafly's Eagle Forum, has fashioned a model anti-rock-and-rap bill that would make labeling mandatory for music containing "unsuitable" lyrics. Proposed measures in 20 other states would prohibit the sale of stickered recordings to those under 18. Some would prohibit minors from attending live concerts by the targeted groups. Many would provide for awarding damages to persons injured by someone "motivated" by a recording.

Such proposals have frightened retailers into requiring proof of age for purchases, pulling labeled recordings altogether, or applying their own stickers. (Meyer Music Markets have gone so far as to apply a warning label to Frank Zappa's *Jazz from Hell,* an all-instrumental album.)

This year we witnessed the first two music obscenity trials ever held in the United States. In February, an Alabama retailer was arrested and charged for selling a purportedly obscene rap album by the group 2 Live Crew to a police officer. An Alabama jury acquitted him after a four-day trial in which experts traced the musical and cultural developments of rap music. The high cost of defending against such prosecutions has, of course, created a chilling effect on the content of creative works.

After a grand jury in Volusia County, Florida, declared 2 Live Crew's best-selling *As Nasty As They Wanna Be* obscene, another record store clerk in Sarasota was arrested for selling the album to a minor. He faces up to five years in prison and a $5,000 fine. At least six other Florida counties have banned 2 Live Crew's recordings.

In June, a U.S. district court judge in Fort Lauderdale ruled that a second 2 Live Crew album was obscene. The ruling was followed within days by the arrest of a record shop owner and the Gestapo-style arrest of two members of the band. That picture is engraved forever behind my eyes: two young black musicians being led away in handcuffs in the middle of the night. As Frank Zappa says, "Is this really the Land of the Free and the Home of the Brave? Then where the hell are we, Wanda?"

Meanwhile, the Federal Communications Commission is cracking down on what it calls "indecency" in broadcast music. Last October, KLUC in Las Vegas was fined $2,000 for playing Prince's "Erotic City"; WTZA in Miami was fined $2,000 for playing "Penis Envy" by the folk group Uncle Bonsai; and WIOD in Miami was fined $10,000 for various broadcast music infractions.

Late last year, the FBI became a formidable rock critic when its chief spokesperson, Milt Ahlerich, sent a letter on Department of Justice stationery to the president of Priority Records, which had just released the million-selling album *Straight Outta Compton* by the rap group NWA. The letter, referring to a song from the album called "----tha police" (dashes in the official title), states that the song "encourages violence against and disrespect for law enforcement officers. I wanted you to be aware of the FBI's position. . . . I believe my views reflect the opinion of the entire law enforcement community."

The FBI's letter is historic; the bureau has never before taken an official position on a work of art. Although direct FBI action wasn't specifically threatened, it was hardly necessary. Local police departments faxed a version of the song from city to city. When NWA attempted to perform the song at a concert in Detroit, police moved toward the stage and ended the set.

Rap music is a powerful force for young people. This new form of communication and protest is the voice of the disenfranchised. NWA and other rap groups—almost exclusively young black musicians—are deliberately provocative. These people are expressing the reality of their lives and their culture, which includes drug use, sexual activity, and violence. In today's climate of hostility and violence between police and the black community, these songs illuminate a harsh reality—a reality we must confront. This cannot be accomplished by silencing bands. In fact, this draconian suppression will only further enflame the situation.

"----tha police" is part of a long tradition of literature and art that question authority. So far, the FBI seems concerned only when those expressing anti-authority sentiments are young, black, and amplified. Certainly this music from the streets and ghettos of America makes many people uncomfortable. That's what it's supposed to do. The First Amendment itself makes many people uncomfortable. But it doesn't exist to promote comfort. It exists to promote freedom.

Rockers, rappers, and free speech advocates are organizing to fight back. Music in Action, a coalition of artists, retailers, fans, and concerned citizens, is forming local affiliates and has held several rallies in Washington, D.C. At one rally, rock critic and journalist Dave Marsh told the crowd, "It's shameful that on this day we live in a climate of fear. We are here to serve notice that free speech is for everyone, not just the elite." You can contact MA at 705 President Street, Brooklyn, NY 11215. Rock & Roll Confidential, another group keeping members informed and fighting music censorship, can be contacted at Box 15052, Long Beach, CA 90815.

If the state is given license to require producers and retailers to label and restrict access to commercial recordings, it's a small step to requiring publishers and booksellers to label and restrict access to books. New forms of music have always served as the cutting-edge voice of youth and have long been attacked due to sex, drugs, and obscenity. But the current campaign goes beyond past efforts and involves many powerful people. Why? I believe, along with Dave Marsh, that suppression tactics have increased because of the explosion of social and political comment in pop music and the growing social and political involvement of musicians and their audiences.

These heavy-handed attacks on the freedom of expression of young musicians are direct assaults on everyone's First Amendment rights of free speech and political dissent. We *must not tolerate* government censorship. We must stand together against this tyranny!

Speculations

1. What parts of Dority's argument that we should be concerned about the censorship of rock and rap music appeal to you? Describe her assertion that we must take a stand against this strong-arm suppression of intellectual freedom and censorship.
2. Compare rap music with other art forms. How do the lyrics represent artistic self-expression and social commentary? Cite examples that support your answers.
3. What political, cultural, or social assumptions support Dority's assertion that the FBI's letter condemning *Straight Outta Compton* by the rap group NWA is "historic" because "the bureau has never before taken an official position on a work of art"? Why do you think the FBI took action now?
4. Why is it important to Dority's argument for us to understand rap music as a form of "protest" and "political comment" voiced by "the disenfranchised"? Who are these disenfranchised? In what ways does rap music communicate a statement? Based on this article, who listens to rap? Explain why rap does or does not cause you discomfort.

THE DEGRADATION OF WOMEN

Marion Meade

Marion Meade in an interview with *Contemporary Authors* confessed: "I am a feminist and my writings reflect a feminist point of view." As a novelist and biographer, her published works reflect that ideological commitment; they focus on famous women and their places in history: *Bitching* (1973), *Free Woman: The Life and Times of Victoria Woodhull* (1976), *Eleanor of Aquitaine* (1977), *Stealing Heaven: The Love Story of Héloïse and Abélard* (1979), and *Madame Blavatsky: The Woman Behind the Myth* (1980).

Born in Pittsburgh in 1934, Meade earned a bachelor's degree at Northwestern University and a master's at Columbia University. She currently resides and works in New York City.

The following selection, taken from an article entitled "Does Rock Degrade Women?", was written for the *New York Times* in 1971. Her indictment of rock music's misogynist lyrics, attitudes, and politics echoes many similar remarks from other writers in this section. Meade's position sees through the allure of rebellion and social protest that is sometimes attributed to rock music, and she condemns male rock musicians for their unrelenting reinforcement of "old-fashioned sex-role stereotypes." At the same time, she refuses to indulge in endless diatribe and pessimism. The women's movement represents to her signs of hope.

Last spring I sat through three hours of the film *Woodstock* alternating between feelings of enchantment and repulsion. Sure, there was all that magnificent music, along with the generous helpings of peace and love and grass. And yet I found something persistently disturbing about the idyllic spectacle on the screen. For one thing, with the exception of a pregnant Joan Baez who couldn't seem to stop talking about her husband, all the musicians were men. Sweaty, bearded men were busy building the stage, directing traffic, shooting the film, and running the festival. *Brother*hood was repeatedly proclaimed, both on stage and off. Woodstock Nation was beginning to look ominously like a fantasyland which only welcomed men. How about the women? Barefooted and sometimes barebreasted, they sprawled erotically in the grass, looked after their babies, or dished up hot meals. If this was supposed to be the Aquarian Utopia,[1] it reminded me more of a Shriners' picnic at which the wife and kiddies are invited to participate once a year.

Looking back, I think the movie confirmed an uneasiness I'd felt for some time but had refused to admit: Rock music, in fact the entire rock "culture," is tremendously degrading to women. I reached this conclusion reluctantly and with a good deal of sadness because rock has been important to me. And while I still dig the vitality of the sound, I find myself increasingly turned off in nearly every other respect.

---

[1] *Aquarian Utopia* refers to the notion that the earth is passing under the influence of Aquarius, the eleventh sign of the zodiac, which will bring about a new age of love, peace, harmony, and understanding as proclaimed in the song "Aquarius" from the popular 1968 rock musical "Hair" [Eds.]

Stokely Carmichael[2] recalls that as a child he loved Westerns and always cheered wildly for the cowboys to triumph over the Indians until one day he realized *he* was an Indian. All along he'd been rooting for the wrong side. More and more, women rock fans are discovering themselves in the same curiously surprised position. For those who have taken the trouble to listen carefully, rock's message couldn't be clearer. It's a man's world, baby, and women have only one place in it. Between the sheets or, if they're talented like Arlo Guthrie's Alice, in the kitchen.

The paradox is that rock would appear to be an unlikely supporter of such old-fashioned sex-role stereotypes. In fact, its rebellion against middle-class values, its championing of the unisex fashions and long hair styles for men seem to suggest a blurring of the distinctions between male and female. But for all the hip camouflage sexism flourishes.

The clearest indication of how rock music views womankind is in its lyrics. Women certainly can't complain that the image presented there is one-dimensional. On the contrary, the put-downs are remarkably multifaceted, ranging from open contempt to sugar-coated condescension. Above all, however, women are always-available sexual objects whose chief function is to happily accommodate any man who comes along. This wasn't always the case. Elvis's pelvis notwithstanding, the popular songs of the fifties and early sixties explored such innocuous adolescent pastimes as dancing around the clock, the beach, going steady, and blue suede shoes. In those days before the so-called sexual revolution, the typical woman portrayed in rock was the nice girl next door with whom the Beatles only wanted to hold hands. Then suddenly came the nice girl's metamorphosis into "groovy chick," the difference being that a groovy chick is expected to perform sexually. In rock songs, she never fails.

The worst picture of women appears in the music of the Rolling Stones, where sexual exploitation reaches unique heights. A woman is a "Stupid Girl" who should be kept "Under My Thumb," a "Honky Tonk Woman" who gives a man "Satisfaction." In "Yesterday's Papers," where women are equated with newspapers, the dehumanization is carried to an extreme. Who wants yesterday's papers, the song arrogantly demands, who wants yesterday's girl? The answer: Nobody. Once used, a woman is as valuable as an old newspaper, presumably good only for wrapping garbage.

But the Stone's album *Let It Bleed* is surely unrivaled when it comes to contempt for women, as well as lewdness in general. One cut in particular, "Live With Me," is explicit about woman's proper place:

> Doncha' think there's a place for you in-between the sheets?

---

[2] Stokely Carmichael (b. 1942) is a black political activist. [Eds.]

And only an extraordinarily masochistic woman could listen to the album's title song with any sense of pleasure whatsoever. There a woman is represented as a drive-in bordello, a one-stop sexual shopping center offering all the standard services plus a few extras casually thrown in as a kind of shopper's Special of the Day.

The Stone's next album has been tentatively titled "Bitch." It figures.

Misogyny is only slightly more disguised in the music of Bob Dylan who, in his early work at least, tended to regard nearly every female as a bitch. For example, in "Like a Rolling Stone," Dylan apparently feels so threatened by Miss Lonely (whose only sin as far as I can tell is that she has a rather shallow life style) that he feels compelled to destroy her. First he takes away her identity, then he puts her out on the street without shelter or food, and in the end—obliteration, as he makes her invisible. "How does it feel?" he asks.

There's no more complete catalogue of sexist slurs than Dylan's "Just Like a Woman," in which he defines woman's natural traits as greed, hypocrisy, whining, and hysteria. But isn't that cute, he concludes, because it's "just like a woman." For a finale, he throws in the patronizing observation that adult women have a way of breaking "just like a little girl."

These days a seemingly mellowed Dylan has been writing about women with less hatred, but the results still aren't especially flattering. Now he calls his females ladies and invites them to lay across his big brass bed. In short, he has more or less caught up with Jim Morrison's request to "Light my fire" and with John Lennon's suggestion, "Why don't we do it in the road?"

Again and again throughout rock lyrics women emerge either as insatiable, sex-crazed animals or all-American emasculators. Although one might think these images indicate a certain degree of aggressiveness in women, oddly enough they still wind up in a servile position where they exist only to enhance the lives of men.

As for romance, rock hasn't rejected it entirely. Rock love songs exhibit a regular gallery of passive, spiritless women, sad-eyed ladies propped on velvet thrones as the private property of a Sunshine Superman. From the Beatles we get motherly madonnas whispering words of wisdom ("Let it be, let it be") or pathetic spinsters like Eleanor Rigby who hang around churches after weddings to collect the rice. Leonard Cohen's romantic ideal is the mystical Suzanne who wears rags from the Salvation Army and acts, the composer asserts, "half crazy." Seldom does one run across a mature, intelligent woman or, for that matter, a woman who is capable enough to hold a job (one exception is the Beatles' meter maid, Rita). Only the Stones' Ruby Tuesday insists on an independent life of her own.

Since rock is written almost entirely by men, it's hardly surprising to find this frenzied celebration of masculine supremacy. But it's also understandable in terms of the roots from which rock evolved. In both blues and country music, attitudes toward women reflected a rabid machismo: men always dominated and women were fickle bitches who ran off with other men. Often they were seen in relationship to the wandering superstud who recounts his conquests in every town along the road, a fantasy which remains fashionable in rock today.

Apart from the myths of female inferiority proclaimed by rock lyricists, the exploitation and dehumanization of women also extends into the off-stage rock scene. How else can one account for a phenomenon like the groupies? That these aggressive teenage camp followers could possibly be regarded as healthy examples of sexual liberation is certainly a cruel joke. In fact, groupies service the needs of the male musicians and further symbolize rock's impersonal view of women as cheap commodities which can be conveniently disposed of after use. The Stones said it: nobody in the world wants yesterday's papers.

Finally, rock is a field from which women have been virtually excluded as musicians. Not only is it rare to find an integrated band, but the few all-female groups have been notably unsuccessful. The very idea of a women's rock band is looked upon as weird, in the same category as Phil Spitalny's all-girl orchestra, a freak show good for a few giggles.

The problem is that women have been intimidated from even attempting a career in rock. Women, the myth says, aren't smart enough to understand the complexities of electronics or tough enough to compose music of sufficient intensity or physically strong enough to play drums. The guitar is acceptable but the electric guitar is unfeminine.

As for female rock singers, you can count them on a few fingers. We did have Janis Joplin, a blueswoman in the finest tradition of Bessie Smith and Billie Holiday. When Janis wailed about love as a ball and chain and women being losers, now there were ideas with which women could identify. At least we knew what she meant. The soul sounds of Tina Turner and Laura Nyro also radiate the feeling that they know what it's like to be a woman. Otherwise, just about the only rock queen left is Grace Slick. Although some may regard her private life as liberated in that she decided to have an illegitimate child and generally appears to care little for society's conventions, even her work with the Jefferson Airplane is hardly oriented toward women.

Which leaves us with Joan Baez, Judy Collins and Joni Mitchell, who specialize in the bland folk-rock deemed appropriate for a delicate sex.

At this point, what does rock offer women? Mighty little.

Recently, however, rock bands have reported strange happenings at concerts. Instead of the usual adoring screams from the women, every so often they've been hearing boos and unladylike shouts of "male chauvinist pigs." Because the bands tend to regard these disturbances as a puzzling but passing phenomenon, they've made little effort so far to understand the changes taking place in their audience. What they fail to recognize is that the condescending swaggering which worked for Elvis in the fifties and the sadistic, anti-woman sneers of Mick Jagger in the sixties are no longer going to make it in the seventies.

There's no question that rock is already in trouble. The current spiritual and economic malaise has been variously attributed to the Hendrix-Joplin deaths, the general tightness of money, as well as lackluster albums and tired performances from the popular stars. Whatever the reasons, rock listeners today are plainly bored. Does anyone really care if John, Paul, Ringo, and George ever get together again? Not me.

On the other hand, isn't it about time for women to band together and invade the chauvinistic rock scene? Only then will the vicious stereotypes be eliminated and, one hopes, some fresh energy generated as well. For too long we've sat wistfully on the sidelines, acting out our expected roles as worshipful groupies.

Women have always constituted an important segment of the rock audience. Unless the industry is willing to alienate us completely, they'd better remember what Bob Dylan said about not needing a weatherman to know which way the wind blows. For the times they are a-changin', eh, fellas?

Speculations

1. In what ways do you agree or disagree with Marion Meade's basic thesis that "rock music, in fact the entire rock 'culture,' is tremendously degrading to women"? What specific examples support your view?
2. How does the emergence of MTV and images of women in rock videos affect Meade's thesis about the degradation of women?
3. Meade's essay first appeared in the *New York Times,* one of America's greatest newspapers. What parts of her essay are characteristic of a newspaper column? Describe the aspects of her style, tone, form, and argument that suggest she wrote it for a newspaper audience.
4. How does Meade's use of specific words and detailed examples support her argument? What effect do these examples have on you? In what ways are you surprised by them? What additional examples would you add to the argument?
5. What is Meade's point when she recalls Stokely Carmichael's account of how he had always rooted for the cowboys as a child

until one day he realized he was an Indian himself and had been rooting for the wrong side all along? Have you ever cheered the wrong side? When it comes to rock music, are you rooting for the "wrong" side or the "right" side now? Explain your side of the female rock musician issue and how you got there.

6. Writing in 1971, Meade states that "rock is a field from which women have been virtually excluded as musicians." Have women become more included in the field of rock music today? Support your response with specific examples of how things have changed or remained the same.

TORI AMOS KEEPS HER HEAD

Elysa Gardner

Born in 1967 in the Bronx, Elysa Gardner grew up in New York state. A prolific writer on the contemporary music scene, she now lives in New York City and regularly contributes to *The New Yorker, Rolling Stone, Spin, Musician,* and other magazines. She wrote the forward to *U2: the Rolling Stone Files* and has worked extensively on the forthcoming *Rolling Stone Encyclopedia.* Displaying remarkable modesty about her writing, Gardner told *Speculations* that she always makes a point of saying, "The only difference between the journalist and the fan is that the journalist gets paid to express his or her views in print." In the same vein, she emphasized that writing about pop music is not primarily an intellectual endeavor: "It should be a visceral thing. You can't get too intellectual or too arrogant. You have to be careful about being a political pundit."

Gardner's ability to look inside the character and social purpose of musicians and their work comes through clearly in the following interview with Tori Amos, which was published in 1993 in *Musician* magazine. One gets the feeling from this piece that you are indeed sitting across from Tori Amos herself while she expostulates prophetically on the contemporary music scene and suggests that female musicians have changed the relationship between women and rock'n'roll. With regard to the interview, Gardner said, "Tori Amos was fun to interview. At a time when a lot of women in rock strive to be wacky and iconoclastic, she really is wacky and iconoclastic. She's very genuine."

Tori Amos looks you straight in the eye when she speaks to you. "We're living on a very sick planet," she announces. "And it's getting more sick, in a sense, because we're not pressing our freedoms home.

Especially in the art community—painters, writers, dancers, musicians. There is a numbness that is happening. It's as if a sleeping drug has been given." Amos is wide awake at the moment, and digging into a bowl of pasta in a dimly lit Italian restaurant on New York's Lower West Side. The topic of discussion is what the singer describes as the "intimidation" of today's pop music community. "We musicians have turned our self-worth over to those who listen to our music. The troubadour thing was that if they didn't like you, you'd hope you didn't lose your head and then move on to the next castle. But these days we turn over our music like puppies: 'Please love us, please tell us it's okay.' I mean, not all of us do that, but I know I've had that tendency in me."

Amos' *Little Earthquakes,* a collection of dramatic, starkly introspective ballads, has made her a favorite on college radio and MTV and led critics to herald her as one of the most promising new singer/songwriters of our young decade. "The exposure on alternative radio has been really good fun," Amos says, "because, as a piano player, you wouldn't think I'd be up their street." Conversely, you wouldn't think Nirvana's "Smells Like Teen Spirit" would be up Amos' street, but on an EP released this year, she gave that song the acoustic piano treatment. Far from an irreverent spoof, Amos' version is as earnestly tender as the original is wickedly catchy.

Amos points to Nirvana, Pearl Jam, and Ice-T's Body Count as examples of "outbreaks"—indignant and necessary reactions to the malaise she believes is afflicting our pop climate. "These artists are saying, like it or not, this is the truth from my point of view; this is what I have to say, with no fear of repercussions. It provides the thread between chaos and vision; it centers us, it brings us back *into* our bodies. Because about 90 percent of the time, most of us are *just not present.* We're just floating around, trying to avoid confrontation—trying to avoid the fact that we don't have the guts to say what we really feel. So, yes, artists have a responsibility to come from the heart—to come from the tummy."

Many of Amos' songs address concerns and experiences common to women. "Me and a Gun," a graphic first-person account of rape, delivered a cappella, deals unsparingly with dangerous assumptions about female sexuality. The daughter of a second-generation Methodist preacher, Amos is neither as calculated in using sexual imagery as Madonna nor as rash in her comments about abuses of power as Sinéad O'Connor—whose actions on "Saturday Night Live," tearing a photo of the Pope to shreds, Amos chooses not to condemn: "She wanted to express that, and felt she had to. I respect that."

For all her colorful outspokenness, in fact, Amos is a study in postfeminist—and, given her upbringing and her preoccupation with all things spiritual, post-Christian—ambivalence. Her assertions, whether in lyrics or over linguine, reveal complex, often conflicting feelings about sex, God and other matters prevalent in pop music and dinner conversation.

"I've been reading the account of a woman from the Middle East who became a free spirit and as a result was put in solitary confinement for the rest of her life. This is an example of a person's spirit not being honored, and it makes me sad. And I'll tell you another thing that saddens me, that makes me lose my temper. I have such respect for a lot of today's rap poets; I think that theirs is the music most committed to telling the truth. But if they were more comfortable with women, these poets wouldn't always need to be *demeaning* them. No matter who you are—man or woman, whatever your race—you *honor* another spirit. That's where the Native Americans were coming from."

Amos should know: Her great-grandmother was a full-blooded Cherokee, and passed many of her beliefs concerning nature and spirituality on to her son, Amos' grandfather, who the singer says "trained me every day, teaching me about life."

"My dad can tell you all about how, after giving birth to Jesus, the Virgin Mary did it and had, like, three or four kids. Nobody wants to talk about that fact, but my parents didn't hide it from me. And I'm totally proud of Mary! If you look back at mythology, you'll find that the goddesses represented in most cultures were not cut off from their sexuality. Now, Mary is the Christian version of a goddess. And Mary— the Virgin Mary—has been the role model of Christian women for almost two thousand years. Well, we can't be the Virgin Mary—we've messed *that* up—so now what? Hmmm . . .

"I wonder what would happen if certain people allowed themselves to admit what they were really feeling—what's really going on in their minds when they think about sex. Do they think any woman who would throw a man against a wall and lick every inch of his body couldn't prove as capable a mother as a woman who believes that such action goes against God? Now, there's the far left as well as the far right; they're not that much apart."

Amos' flirtatious smile and penchant for caressing the piano bench with her hips and thighs are trademarks of her performance style. It's easy to detect a wry, self-knowing humor in that swivel and grin. "Really good tragedy has to have a giggle in it," she insists. "It's like, with loud music, you have to have a moment—just a moment—of silence. You have to alter the dynamics so you can appreciate the loudness again. So that it *means* something."

Which brings Amos back—again—to the need for honest, purposeful statements in art and in life. "We have all these communications systems all over the world, and we can fill that space with thoughts; we can fill it with possibilities. We need truth now, we really need truth. It doesn't have to come with a sword. Why can't it simply come as truth?"

Speculations

1. Gardner begins this piece with a direct quote from Tori Amos: "'We're living on a very sick planet,' she announces." Gardner also briefly describes the scene of the interview in a New York restaurant. What sense do you get of Tori Amos, her manner, and her way of speaking? How does this character portrayal permeate the entire interview and what does it make you think of Tori Amos as a person?
2. Gardner describes the opening topic as "'intimidation' of today's pop music community." What does she mean by intimidation here and who is being intimidated by whom? Based on your own experience with and attitudes toward popular singers, explain why you agree or disagree with the idea that intimidation is a problem for the community of singers and listeners.
3. What point does this article try to make about "outbreaks" in popular music, especially with regard to the music of Nirvana, Pearl Jam, and Ice-T? Explain why you think such "outbreaks" are either worthwhile or unimportant. Or explain why you disagree. Provide specific examples from popular music to support your views.
4. What specific concerns does Tori Amos have about women's issues and feminism? What does Gardner mean by referring to Amos as "a study in post-feminism?"
5. Describe how Tori Amos's relationship to and understanding of Christianity is different from what you might expect from most traditional Christians. How do you feel about her description of the Virgin Mary? How does this alter or confirm your perception of Amos as an iconoclastic critic of popular culture?

"CRUCIFY" AND "ME AND A GUN"

Tori Amos

Born in North Carolina in 1964 and raised in Maryland by her Methodist minister father, Edison, and her homemaker mother, Mary Ellen, Tori Amos was the youngest of three children. As a two-year-old, she is reputed to have climbed up to the family piano and started playing, and by the age of four she rebuked a six-year-old girl's teasing by boasting "I can play Mozart." Her parents supported her precocious talent by sending her to the Peabody Institute of Music at Johns Hopkins University in Maryland, where she studied a strict course in classical music. By the tender age of eleven, however, she rebelled against the classical tradition by composing her own pop-based music, prompting her father to escort her to piano bars and clubs that would hire her to play. By thirteen, she had a steady job playing in a Georgetown lounge.

Asserting that she is more comfortable playing the piano than doing anything else, Amos explained to *Rolling Stone* that the piano "... is where I was able to express some kind of freedom without guilt. Guilt for passion. . . . I suppressed many things because I wanted respect and put all my passion into music." In her early twenties, Amos was raped by an acquaintance, an incident she wrote about in her song "Me and a Gun," reprinted in the following selections. As part of the album, *Little Earthquakes,* which sold over a million copies in 1992, "Me and a Gun" became Amos's opening signature at concerts and won a 1994 "Visionary Award" from the Washington, D.C., Rape Crisis Center. The song has been called "an anthem for thousands of female Amos fans," and Tori Amos refers to it as her "flashlight, the thing that has taken me by the hand down a very, very, very long recovery path." Like the lyrics to "Crucify" and like Amos herself, the lyrics to "Me and a Gun" are powerfully ambiguous, complex, passionate, and rich with the possibility of many meanings.

CRUCIFY every finger in the room is pointing at me I wanna spit in their faces then I get afraid of what that could bring I got a bowling ball in my stomach I got a desert in my mouth figures that my COURAGE would choose to sell out now I've been looking for a savior in these dirty streets looking for a savior beneath these dirty sheets I've been raising up my hands drive another nail in just what GOD needs one more victim *why do we crucify ourselves every day I crucify myself nothing I do is good enough for you crucify myself every day and my HEART is sick of being in chains* got a kick for a dog beggin' for LOVE I gotta have my suffering so that I can have my cross I know a cat named Easter he says will you ever learn you're just an empty cage girl if you kill the bird I've been looking for a savior in these dirty streets looking for a savior beneath these dirty sheets I've been raising up my hands drive another nail in got enough GUILT to start my own religion please be save me I CRY . . .

ME AND A GUN 5am friday morning thursday night far from sleep I'm still up and driving can't go home obviously so I'll just change direction cause they'll soon know where I live and I wanna live got a full tank and some chips it was me and a gun and a man on my back and I sang "holy holy" as he buttoned down his pants *me and a gun and a man on my back but I haven't seen BARBADOS so I must get out of this* yes I wore a slinky red thing does that mean I should spread for you, your friends your father, Mr Ed and I know what this means me and Jesus a few years back used to hang and he said "it's your choice babe just re-

member I don't think you'll be back in 3 days time so you choose well"
tell me what's right is it my right to be on my stomach of Fred's Seville
and do you know CAROLINA where the biscuits are soft and sweet
these things go through your head when there's a man on your back
and you're pushed flat on your stomach it's not a classic cadillac . . .

Speculations

1. How would you describe the situation of the speaker in these
   lines from "Crucify"? What anxiety is expressed in the phrase
   "every finger in the room is pointing at me"? In what ways can
   you relate to the feelings she expresses and her longing to be
   saved from those feelings?
2. Explain how "Crucify" can be interpreted as a failure of love. In
   what ways is that failure spiritual, physical, or social? Support
   your response.
3. What specific Christian imagery and terminology does Amos use
   in "Crucify" to tell a story of anxiety, fear, and the need for self-
   fulfillment? Why has she chosen to express a personal narrative
   through religious terms and what impact does it have on you as
   a listener?
4. "Me and a Gun" tells us a story in the form of a traditional, lyric
   ballad, which almost always ends tragically. In your own words,
   summarize the story told and describe the plight of the storyteller.
5. What choices does the speaker of "Me and a Gun" have when her
   attacker confronts her? What choices does she have after the
   rape? What do these choices tell us about how female sexuality is
   perceived by society?
6. Tori Amos concluded her interview with Elysa Gardner by saying, "We need truth now, we really need truth. It doesn't have to
   come with a sword. Why can't it simply come as truth?" Explain
   how "Crucify" and "Me and A Gun" attempt to give us truth.
   What kind of truths do these songs offer? How well do you think
   the songs succeed or fail in delivering Amos's message?

SUICIDAL TENDENCIES: KURT DID NOT DIE FOR YOU

Donna Gaines

Born in 1951 in Brooklyn, New York, Donna Gaines received her
B.A. from Binghamton State University (1974), her M.S.W. from Adelphi University (1977), and her Ph.D. (1990) from State University of

New York at Stony Brook. In addition to maintaining a private practice as a social worker since 1976, Gaines has been a research associate at SUNY Institute for Social Research, a workshop presenter, a
guest on several television shows such as "USA Today," and a contributing writer to *Village Voice, Long Island Monthly, Newsday, Spin,*
and *Rolling Stone.* Her books include *Teenage Wasteland: Suburbia's
Dead End Kids* (1991) and her forthcoming *Suburbia, 1992–93,* which
examines problems of youth and violence, advocacy, criminal justice,
music in the youth culture, and women, pornography, and war. In an
interview with *Contemporary Authors,* Gaines remarked that, "It never
occurred to me to become a writer. I am a sociologist and an advocate.
My desire to write is motivated by having something to say that
might uplift the human race."

In *Teenage Wasteland,* Gaines articulates the exploitation of the
oppressed, acknowledges the alienation that Americans feel toward
their culture, and attempts to break down the walls separating
teenagers from one another and from their parents:

> History is always written by those who survive, rarely by
> those silenced by it. The radical pedagogue Paulo Freire has
> said about the United States, "This is one of the most alien-
> ated of all countries and people know they are exploited and
> dominated, but they feel incapable of breaking down the de-
> humanized wall." . . . The radical educator begins by vali-
> dating the dominated person's local, intuitive knowledge of
> the world. Likewise, therapeutic intervention must reinforce
> this knowledge, acknowledge it, constitute it as truth. That
> means—to borrow my neighbor Scott's words—"calling out
> the bullshit" when and how you see it coming down.
>
> I wanted to do that for every kid who survived "the
> decade of greed," and for all the ones who didn't.

In the selection reprinted here from *Rolling Stone,* Gaines acknowledges the oppression of Kurt Cobain's generation with terrifying clarity, and she begins the therapeutic work of calling out the
truth that others like him need to know in order to survive.

LIFE IN AMERICA can kill young people. Kurt Cobain was the
Great White Hope for many kids trapped in bad lives. Growing up as
an average teen in 1980s America, he shared a sad social history too
common among members of his generation. A *lumpen*-prole hero, he
not only made it out of teen-age wasteland alive, he soared to the highest ground. Cobain's triumph gave kids hope, faith that you could be
yourself, be human and not get totally destroyed for it. He was the outcast kid's proof that in the end, truth would be revealed, and justice
would prevail. In Nirvana, Cobain moved a kid's private hell to a generation's collective howl. He was not supposed to commit suicide.

In 1987, I investigated a teen-age suicide pact among four close
friends who lived in a small, predominantly white, nonaffluent, suburban turnpike town. Like many places across America, Bergenfield, N.J.,

was economically depressed, offering limited opportunity to kids who didn't play the game. Like Cobain, the two boys and two girls were labeled as outcasts. Three out of the four came from families fractured by divorce; they all had lost loved ones suddenly and tragically. When things got too rough at home, the kids stayed with friends. The guys failed at several attempts at detox, rehab and recovery. Three of the four kids dropped out of high school and worked at dead-end jobs. They cherished their friends, and they lived for rock & roll. In their collective suicide note, the four kids said they felt unloved. Like Cobain, they offered their love to anyone who would accept it. If they had lived, the two boys would now have been about Cobain's age.

Although girls attempt suicide with greater frequency, it is mainly a disease of white, nonurban males. Teenage suicide was a virtually nonexistent category before 1960, but between 1950 and 1980 it nearly tripled. While America as a whole became less suicidal during the 1980s, people under 30 became dramatically more suicidal. While adolescents remain the most frequent attempters of suicide—an estimated 400,000 a year—the actual rates of suicide are higher once people enter their 20s. At the time of the Bergenfield suicide pact, suicide was the second leading killer of young people, after accidents, accounting for around 12 percent of youth mortalities. By the 1990s, suicide had been displaced by homicide. Today, suicide is the third leading method of destruction for young people. Firearms and alcohol are crucial elements in suicides, especially for boys.

The 1980s offered young people an experience of unsurpassed social violence and humiliation. Traumatized by absent or abusive parents, educators, police and shrinks, stuck in meaningless jobs without a livable wage, disoriented by disintegrating institutions, many kids felt trapped in a cycle of futility and despair. Adults fucked up across the board, abandoning an entire generation by failing to provide for or protect them or prepare them for independent living. Yet when young people began to exhibit symptoms of neglect, reflected in their rates of suicide, homicide, substance abuse, school failure, recklessness and general misery, adults condemned them as apathetic, illiterate, amoral losers.

Even the media couldn't resist capitalizing on "youth atrocities"—but we rarely bothered to ask the kids what was going on. When kids did seize the opportunity to speak, an existential terror too horrific to put into words was reduced to sound bites. Add to this the creepy litany of AIDS, global warming, unemployment and homelessness, and a gruesome landscape emerges. For more than a decade, taking on the brutality agenda—exposing the lies, fighting the bullshit—has been the central project of the Fucked Generation.

Throughout the worst years of our lives, the kids' music—hardcore, thrash metal and hip-hop—expressed the brutal truth of coming of age in Reagan's America. Since adults didn't get it, it was through the youth underground that kids created opportunities to explore the grim social realities they struggled against. Across music paradigms, artists as diverse as Slayer, N.W.A, Henry Rollins, Axl Rose, Suzanne Vega, Courtney Love and Morrissey have tried to work out this experience of humiliation and *objec*tification. By now, young people acknowledge alienation, deep loss and rage as normative conditions of living. To his credit, Kurt Cobain pushed the brutality agenda from the margins to the mainstream, disseminating it through mass culture like rapid fire. For a while, it seemed like history was on the side of the righteous.

Some kids don't make it out of high school alive. They give up before they even try. Others stick around, wounded, just to see what happens. Introverted and depressed, Cobain maybe was born with a morbid disposition. Maybe he had a chemical imbalance that made him too sensitive to live in the world, so that even true love, a beautiful daughter, a brilliant band, detox, family life and his wholesome Northwestern community rootedness couldn't fill the hole in his soul. At 27, Cobain was tired of being alive.

Maybe Cobain's anger and moral outrage kept him alive through his early, wasted years. Like most kids growing up in dying towns in dysfunctional-family situations, his expectations were pretty low. But the suicidal imagination has a dramatic flair. Like everyone with a rock & roll heart, he probably figured he would die young, go down in flames. He lived hard and fast, blew off school, relished his music, his friends, his recreational chemicals. If he didn't kill himself back then, it was probably because he had plans. He was busy painting, cutting demos, writing—certain that something good would kick in sooner or later.

Many of the guys who live in white, nonaffluent dead-end towns from coast to coast grow up feeling they're gonna die young. When some guys I know heard about Cobain, they made note of his age— the dreaded age of rocker mortality, when Jimi, Janis and Jim crash-burned from too much too soon. For the average 27-year-old, though, life today isn't so glamorous. They're struggling with rent, college tuition, health insurance and car payments. But their dreams haven't died. They're still playing music, making plans and working hard. Bands rehearse, lovers fantasize about weddings, kids, a nice place to live. They strive for serenity and sobriety. To keep life simple and honest, to live decently. Friends huddle together, helping each other, and little by little, they keep moving forward.

Kurt Cobain and Courtney Love knew they had problems. They understood themselves as unloved children, as codependents. They took turns rescuing and protecting each other from exploitation, illness, bad publicity. They said they wanted a better emotional life for their daughter, Frances Bean; they wanted her to feel loved. They saw where their parents' generation had failed.

I remember reading how Love held Cobain's hand, soothing him through his heroin withdrawal in the delivery room while she was giving birth to their child. She once said all she wanted was to make Cobain happy. The same week all her rocker dreams came true, Mrs. Kurt Cobain was again preoccupied with her husband's needs. After he died, she said she didn't know what more she could have done to help him. Nothing worked: not true love, not tough love, not Frances Bean, detox, rehab, therapy or prayer. Nothing Love could have done would have prevented Cobain's suicide. No one person can be an ongoing life-support system for another. Anyone on either side of the suicide game knows this.

Yet some people blame Love for destroying Cobain. Others blame the media for crucifying the couple or the state (child welfare authorities, for example) for labeling them unfit parents and unnecessarily worrying them again about losing their daughter. Was it pressure from the band, the biz, the jolting anomie of massive fame? The drugs, the chronic stomach pain? Was Cobain a gifted, troubled soul whose misery was so deep that nothing would ever make him happy? No matter how far we travel in life, are we always at risk of feeling worthless, hopeless and helpless? Does anybody ever really get out of teen-age wasteland?

We've heard endless public discussion about the low self-esteem suffered by young Americans, the supposed root of all the self-destructive "acting out" behaviors. An entire generation of de facto abused and neglected children have been remanded to psychotherapy to cure the results of a collapsed social order. Young people resisted this panacea with a keen political instinct, viewing shrink-o-rama as just one more fixture on the brutality landscape. The anarchist's soul will resist normative proscriptives for daily living as social control. Despite the genuine intentions of an army of helping professionals, many young people would just rather have a beer and talk things over with a friend.

"I still can't get out the frustration, the guilt and the empathy I have for everyone. There's good in all of us, and I simply love people too much, so much that it makes me feel too fucking sad. . . . I love and feel for people too much." In her widow's wail, as Love read portions of Cobain's suicide note at the Seattle Center, she challenged him: If he loved everyone so much, why the *hell* didn't he just stick around? Sarcastically, she referred to him as "the sad little sensitive Pisces Jesus man," as if he was some self-absorbed martyr so tormented by his love of the world that he chose to blow it off rather than deal with it.

Kurt Cobain was a Pisces, the sign known as the dustbin of the zodiac. That made him a psychic sponge for collective feelings, able to intuit and absorb everything around him. With the archetype of Jesus

Christ, we ushered in the Piscean Age, whose attributes are self-sacrifice, surrender and martyrdom. According to lore, the Pisces would rather self-destruct than cause harm to others, in effect, is willing to die for the sins of others. There is a dark side to Pisces that can motivate self-pity, defeatism, alcoholism and suicide. The Pisces soul is tender and has difficulty filtering out the negative. Most Pisceans waver between extremes. Apparently, Cobain had an affinity for Jesus. Maybe he had a martyr complex and saw himself as a humble servant who absorbed our human pain, even against his own will. Cobain's "burning, nauseous stomach" was his bleeding heart.

In his way, Kurt Cobain tried to show us how to live—he prayed for the racist, the homophobe, the misogynist. But he wasn't Jesus, and he couldn't save us. Despite his compassion, he wasn't an altruist who died for anybody's sins. His suicide was a betrayal; it negated an unspoken contract among members of a generation who depended on one another to reverse the parental generation's legacy of neglect, confusion and frustration. Cobain broke that promise. He just walked.

From Jesus to Cobain in 2,000 years. There's no Mommy or Daddy, no great savior coming down to walk us through the millenium. As the Aquarian Age seeps into our collective consciousness, we'll need to be a nation of messiahs, individuals working together, looking out for one another. The Fucked Generation has already figured that out. It's been doing it for years.

Speculations

1. At the end of the first paragraph of this selection, Gaines asserts that Kurt Cobain "was not supposed to commit suicide." Why does she say this and what does she mean?
2. Gaines draws a portrait of what it was like to grow up in the 1980s for kids who "felt trapped in a cycle of futility and despair." What facts, statistics, social conditions, and other details does she use to support this picture? Draw up a short list of the facts you think are most important and explain your choices.
3. Gaines mentions several bands and musicians whom she describes as part of a "youth underground" that enables kids to struggle against the "grim social realities" of our time. Using examples from Gaines's list, Kurt Cobain's music, or a musician or band that you are familiar with, describe how you think the music challenges our culture's values.
4. How did Cobain try to overcome his despair? What role did Courtney Love play in trying to help him? What does Gaines suggest about why nothing seemed to work?
5. Gaines ends this selection with Cobain's own statements about how much he loved people and Courtney Love's reference to

Cobain as "the sad little sensitive Pisces Jesus Man." How does this comparison work and what does it have to do with loving others? Explain why you find this comparison either convincing or unpersuasive.

6. In her conclusion, Gaines asserts that Cobain's generation made a promise among themselves and that "Cobain broke that promise. He just walked." Do you agree or disagree with her final assessment of Cobain's suicide? Explain your response.

—————— ASSIGNMENT SEQUENCES ——————

Sequence One: Music and Value

1. Write an essay in which you agree or disagree with the position put forth by Allan Bloom's "Music." Consider your own experience of music and how it corresponds to or contradicts Bloom's main points about the effects of rock music. Consider, for example, his statements that "When [young people] are in school and with their families, they are longing to plug themselves back into their music. Nothing surrounding them—school, family, church—has anything to do with their musical world. At best that ordinary life is neutral, but mostly it is an impediment, drained of vital content, even a thing to be rebelled against." What do you think? As you consider this quotation, analyze what you think Bloom considers to be the effects of rock music, how these effects differ from the effects of other forms of music, and why Bloom associates rock music with escape, rebellion against parental authority, and premature sexuality. Use specific examples of music that illustrate your views and build your own idea of music's place among young people today.

2. Assume you are a parent of a teenage daughter and a teenage son. How would you respond to Bloom's arguments? Would you find yourself in agreement with the negative effects rock music has on teenagers as described by Bloom? What effects do you believe your own teenage son and daughter would experience? Write an essay from the point of view of a parent concerned about music and your own children. Try not to create a stereotype of a parent; to prevent this, you might want to speak to some parents or read some "letters to the editor" or other statements written by parents about music and music lyrics.

3. Select a piece of music that illustrates, responds to, contradicts, or adds something new to one or more of the positions articulated in the essays in this section. Write your own essay in which you iden-

tify the message, values, and effects of the piece of music you have selected on young people today. You may consider the examples of rap music in relation to issues of freedom of expression, or the way the blues represents a specific attitude or view of life, or a song that expresses a specific political message as suggested in Barbara Dority's or Donna Gaines's essays, or you may explore a song that speaks to differences between men and women as in Marion Meade's, Elysa Gardener's, or Tori Amos's work. Or you may choose a piece of music that represents a worthwhile perspective you think has been neglected in these essays altogether. Your job is to write an essay that presents your chosen piece of music to your classmates as representative of some meaningful idea, value, or experience in our culture. After completing the essay, you should be prepared to play a taped selection of the music for class and to summarize orally the arguments in your paper.

4. You are Tori Amos. You have recently been compared to a combination of Tracy Chapman and Madonna. The *Los Angeles Times* Sunday music section is doing a retrospective on recent rock music and has asked you to write about what you were driving at in the lyrics for "Crucify," "Me and a Gun," or another lyric of your own choosing. Write a short piece that explains or comments on your intentions—what you were striving to say and how well you said it.

5. Imagine that you have been selected as a student representative on the Chancellor's Committee for Improving Undergraduate Curriculum at your university. Allan Bloom has been advising the committee and has strongly recommended a course in the great musical culture of the West that would include many of the philosophers, operas, and musicians mentioned in his article and would, in his view, remedy the negative influence of rock music. He concludes his argument with the statement that "My concern here is not with the moral effects of rock music—whether it leads to sex, violence or drugs. The issue here is its effect on education, and I believe it ruins the imagination of young people and makes it very difficult for them to have a passionate relationship to the art and thought that are the substance of liberal education. . . . [A]s long as they have the Walkman on, they cannot hear what the great tradition has to say. And, after its prolonged use, when they take it off, they find they are deaf." Donna Gaines, who wrote the essay "Suicidal Tendencies: Kurt Did Not Die for You," is also on the committee. She argues that such a course should include a final unit on popular culture which critically examines rock music as a real and vital part of the Western cultural tradition. Since you are the student member of the committee, the chancellor asks you to

write a statement of several paragraphs that would examine this issue from the students' perspective and argue for specific recommendations on what should or should not be included in the new course. Your paper will be distributed to the other members of the committee, and you will be asked to speak in support of your ideas at the committee's next meeting.

Sequence Two: Music and Culture

1. Consider Barbara Dority's essay on the "The War on Rock and Rap." Dority suggests that rock music and rap often contain political messages from the disenfranchised and that we should be vitally concerned about the censorship of rock and rap music. Where do you stand on these issues? What rights do artists have to protest and free expression, even when those expressions may be hurtful or damaging to others? Write a paper that argues your position on the freedom of musical expression versus censorship using examples from your own experience and your reading.

2. Imagine that you have been asked to write a music review for the student newspaper about some form of popular music or a musical event. You may choose a specific kind of music, an individual performer, a local band, or a nationally known group that may be playing in town. The paper's editor wants you to write about both the performance and the music itself, but she also wants you to provide some commentary on the kind of music you are reviewing, its history, and its reception by differing audiences. If you can, provide information about the musicians involved. Ideally, you should go hear a concert in person and interview the musician(s). You might also do library research. Write that review.

3. Dority compares rap music to opera and argues that banning song lyrics that talk about adultery, incest, illicit drug or alcohol use, murder, or suicide, would also require banning operas such as *Madame Butterfly, Tosca, Carmen, La Traviata,* all of which contain descriptions or depictions of many of the same kinds of "offensive behavior." How is this comparison valid or invalid for you? How would you justify or deny different standards for music which comes out of and speaks to a different cultural background? How can rap music be censored, if opera is not? Write a paper supporting your position with specific examples.

4. Create an anthology of ten to fifteen of your favorite song lyrics. You can include any lyrics at all—from opera to rock opera, from blues to easy listening. Then write an introduction to your anthol-

ogy in which you explain your rationale for what you included. What makes these lyrics worth reading as forms of poetry or expressions of political and cultural sentiments? Do not include any of the lyrics in this section.

5. According to Allan Bloom and Marion Meade, popular music, especially rock music, is destructive to basic cultural values, including education, the individual, and respect for women. Bloom compares rock music to drug addiction and states that it "ruins the imagination of young people and makes it difficult for them to have a passionate relationship to the art and thought that are the substance of liberal education." Marion Meade argues that rock music has traditionally been written by men, that it is riddled with misogyny, sexism, a "frenzied celebration of masculine supremacy," and that this "exploitation and dehumanization of women also extends into the off-stage rock scene." Barbara Dority, Donna Gaines, and Elysa Gardener take a different view in which they see rock music as upholding certain values of freedom of expression and the right to protest social injustice. Drawing on these essays, offer your own argument as to the effects of popular music. Is popular music a positive or negative influence on young people? What does it tell us about our cultural values? Be sure to include appropriate quotations by authors you read in *Speculations*.

Sequence Three: Heroes, Heroines, and Values in the Youth Culture

1. At the end of her interview with Elysa Gardner, Tori Amos says "We need truth now, we really need truth. It doesn't have to come with a sword. Why can't it simply come as truth?" Similarly, at the end of her essay, Donna Gaines suggests that Kurt Cobain's suicide was the wrong way to announce the truth about his generation and that we must find another way to acknowledge the truths he confronted and to deal with the cultural alienation he suffered. Write an essay that answers Tori Amos's question and responds to Kurt Cobain's suicide.

2. What contemporary musicians would you describe as having musical, cultural, or political influence similar to that of Kurt Cobain? Describe some ideals, beliefs, or controversies that surround today's popular singers. How do these singers generate a "culture hero" or even "anti-hero" status that may have influence in our society? What specific political, social, or moral influence do these figures have and how have you been influenced in particular?

3. Marion Meade's "The Degradation of Women" is a powerful indictment of rock music's treatment of women. Since the writing of

this essay in 1971, how have things changed for the better or gotten worse? Consider Elysa Gardner's account of Tori Amos or Gaines's description of Courtney Love's substantial influence on the rock music scene. Write your own essay that picks up where Meade left off, providing an account of how you think women rock musicians have influenced the rock music scene in recent years. Use specific examples to support your arguments.

4. Use your personal experience with music to write an essay that accounts for the complexities with which the youth culture responds to rock stars. Consider issues of gender, including how men and women respond differently to male versus female rock stars. How does your evaluation of gender roles, sexuality, and gender stereotypes compare with what authors have said in this section? Select specific pieces of music to make your point. How has this music had a positive influence in your life or helped you appreciate certain emotions, values, or a new awareness of musical style? Be prepared to bring a recording of the music or the lyrics to class and to talk about your essay.

5. You are the poetry editor for a book entitled *The American Book of Modern Poetry*. The assistant editor has submitted the two song lyrics by Tori Amos reprinted in this section for publication. You must decide if they are poetry and worthy of inclusion in *The American Book of Modern Poetry*. Write an analysis that includes your final judgment. You can take into account any criteria that you think are relevant such as cultural significance, poetic structure, metaphor, style, form, rhyme. In what ways are these song lyrics expressions of poetry? Show whether they retain their power and significance once they are divorced from the music.

FOCUS ON

Rap Music and Social Responsibility

Ice-T is regarded as one of the most talented rap singers because of his clever rhymes and powerful voice, but he is controversial because of his association with "gangsta rap"—a strain of rap music despised by many who see it as glamorizing gangs, drugs, guns, and fast sex. His 1992 song "Cop Killer" created furor about the influence of gangsta rap in our culture and was pulled off the market by Time-Warner Records. In his book *Ice-Opinion* (1994), he argues that rap music isn't responsible for violence because violence is caused by repressive social conditions, not music; if you take violence out of music and videos, you won't take violence out of the ghetto:

> The fact that I don't have money in my pockets and you do creates a situation in which I want what you've got in your pocket. That's what's going on in the ghetto: everybody's crab's trying to crawl out of a barrel. But out in the suburbs, there's no great increase in drive-by shootings. Instead, a lot of parents are yelling "My kid's talking like you!" All right, that's cool. People in the world want power, so these parents scream "Oh! Oh! I don't like it because my kids won't listen to me. They listen to y'all instead, so I'm mad!". . . . But in the ghetto, you've got real problems because people become accustomed to the prospect of a bleak future. If you try to talk to them about a positive future they don't really see it. It's too dim, too untouchable.

This argument helps frame the issues and counter arguments in the following section: rap music has been associated with violence, sexism, racism, and nihilism, but it also expresses the frustrations, hopes, and political voice of an oppressed segment of our urban black population. At the same time, elements of rap music culture have been rapidly assimilated into mainstream styles of dress, speech, and advertising, while rap groups have multiplied and diversified their messages, gender appeals, and political outlooks. Will rap music continue to grow as a music subculture? Has its influence been mostly negative or positive? Will rap music's outspoken and often offensive lyrics create a backlash among parents, radio stations, and record producers? Who benefits from the growing profits amassed in this market? Are rap musicians really creative artists who have become agents of social change or are they mostly angry young men whose machismo impulses are exploited for profit by clever and unscrupulous capitalists willing to reinforce negative stereotypes of black men? Or does the truth reside somewhere in between this flurry of cultural opposition and emotional contraries? Will rap be completely assimilated into mainstream culture? And if it is, how will this alter our dominant culture and what will rap have achieved for a subculture of oppressed urban blacks? These are just a few of the questions raised by authors in the following section, and we hope that your reading will help you formulate a more knowledgeable response to questions about the values and controversies that surround rap music.

THE RAP ATTITUDE

Jerry Adler

Jerry Adler's stance in "The Rap Attitude" might best be described as hard-hitting, a kind of "frontal assault—take no prisoners" approach to argument. This strategy can be effective, but Adler does more than just slash and burn. His considerable understanding of the arts can be seen from his informed allusions to opera, jazz artist Jelly Roll Morton, and folk singer Woody Guthrie. This depth of knowledge establishes Adler as someone who knows his subject, an authority worth listening to. What characterizes his point of view is his abiding concern for the moral impact of music on youth, similar in some ways to the concerns expressed by Allan Bloom.

Well known in the New York theater community, Jerry Adler is a graduate of Syracuse University and has spent most of his career as a director, stage manager, and producer of Broadway musical theater and television, including *My Fair Lady, Camelot, California Suite,* and *Little Murders.* In 1992, Adler moved to California where he began a new career as an actor in Hollywood and wrote his first book, *High Rise: How 10,000 Men and Women Worked Around the Clock for Five Years and Lost 200 Million Building a Skyscraper* (1993).

To his credit, Adler's commentary on rap and heavy metal music, originally published in *Newsweek* magazine, takes into account both sides of the story behind the recent evolution of negative attitudes in our society. He presents the conservative reactions of organizations such as the Parents' Music Resource Center and the FBI as well as the liberal sentiments of the American Civil Liberties Union and the rap groups' own attempts to defend themselves against criticism. Perhaps the most telling and disturbing aspect of his indictment, however, is his analysis of the band members' public statements and his close readings of the song lyrics themselves.

Let's talk about "attitude." And I don't mean a good attitude, either. I mean "attitude" by itself, which is always bad, as in, you'd better not be bringing any attitude around here, boy, and, when that bitch
gave me some attitude, I cut her good. I mean attitude as a cultural
style, marrying the arrogance of Donald Trump to the vulgarity of
Roseanne Barr. Comedians have attitude, rock bands have attitude, in
America today even *birthday cards* have attitude. In the rap-music
group NWA, which stands for Niggas With Attitude, you don't have
to guess what kind of attitude they mean: jaunty and sullen by turns;
showy but somehow furtive, in glasses as opaque as a limousine window and sneakers as white as a banker's shirt. Their music is a rhythmic chant, a rhyme set to a drum solo, a rant from the streets about
gunning down cops. Now *that's* attitude.

OK, here it is: the first important cultural development in America
in 25 years that the baby-boom generation didn't pioneer: The Culture
of Attitude. It is heard in the thundering cacophony of heavy metal and
the thumping, clattering, scratching assault of rap—music so postin-
dustrial it's mostly not even *played,* but pieced together out of prere-
corded sound bites. It is the culture of American males frozen in various stages of adolescence: their streetwise music, their ugly macho
boasting and joking about anyone who hangs out on a different
block—cops, other races, women and homosexuals. Its most visible
contribution has been the disinterment of the word nigger, a generation after a national effort to banish it and its ugly connotations from
the American language. Now it is back, employed with savage irony
by black rappers and dumb literal hostility by their white heavy-metal
counterparts. *Nigger! Faggot!* What ever happened to the idea that rock
and roll would make us free?

Although most Americans may never have heard of them, these are
not obscure bands playing in garages and afterhours clubs. In the '70s,
urban rappers performed in parks, plugging loudspeakers into lamp-
posts. Now they fill major arenas—although more and more arenas
won't have rap concerts any longer, because of fear that the violence can
spill over from the stage to the crowd. Public Enemy, a rap group
caught up in a protracted anti-Semitic controversy, and NWA, have had
platinum albums, with more than a million in sales. The heavy-metal
group Guns N' Roses sold more than 4 million copies worldwide of the
"G N' R Lies" record, whose lyrics insult blacks, homosexuals and "immigrants" inside 10 lines. Major companies are behind them: Public
Enemy's releases for the Def Jam label are distributed by CBS/Colum-
bia Records; Guns N' Roses parades its prejudices on Geffen Records,
headed by the noted AIDS philanthropist David Geffen.

Attitude! Civilized society abhors attitude, and perpetuates itself
by keeping it under control. There are entire organizations devoted to
this job, most notably the Parents' Music Resource Center in Arlington,

Va. The center has an extensive file of lyrics in rap and heavy-metal music, describing every imaginable perversity from unsafe sex to Devil worship. (The Satanist influence on heavy metal called down a condemnation last week from New York's Cardinal John O'Connor as well.) But executive director Jennifer Norwood is careful to point out that the center takes "no position on any specific type of music." There are rap ballads whose sentiments would not have brought a blush to the cheek of Bing Crosby, and rap acts that promote an anti-drug message. The center does support printing song lyrics on album jackets for the information of parents—although such a step might also make it easier for kids to learn them—and a warning label, which some record companies already apply voluntarily, about "explicit lyrics."

Others who stand against attitude include Florida Gov. Bob Martinez, who asked the statewide prosecutor to investigate the Miami rap group The 2 Live Crew for alleged violations of obscenity laws in the album "As Nasty as They Want to Be." "If you answer the phone one night and the voice on the other end begins to read the lyrics of one of those songs, you'd say you received an obscene phone call," reasoned Martinez. This proved to be outside the governor's jurisdiction. But a Broward County judge last week cleared the way for prosecutors to charge record-shop owners who *sell* the album; courts would then rule on whether the material was obscene. And the Kentucky-based chain that operates 121 Disc Jockey record stores announced that it would no longer carry records with warning stickers. In part, says company executive Harold Guilfoil, this is a move to preempt mandatory-labeling and sales-restriction laws under consideration in at least 10 states. A Pennsylvania bill that has already passed in one House would require labels for lyrics describing or advocating suicide, incest, sodomy, morbid violence or several other things. "That about takes care of every opera in the world," observes Guilfoil.

Particularly concerned is the Anti-Defamation league, whose civil-rights director, Jeffrey Sinensky, sees evidence in popular music that "hatred is becoming hip." The rap group Public Enemy was the most notorious offender, not even for anything in their music, but for remarks by a nonsinging member of the group, Professor Griff, a hanger-on and backup dancer with the grandiloquent but meaningless title of Minister of Information. Griff, a follower of Louis Farrakhan's Nation of Islam, gave an interview last spring in which he parroted some Farrakhanesque nonsense about Jews being behind "the majority of wickedness that goes on across the globe." After the predictable outcry Griff was fired and the group disbanded; but soon it re-formed, and Griff came back as "Supreme Allied Chief of Community Relations," a position in which he is not allowed to talk to the press. And Public Enemy proceeded to discuss the episode in ominous, if somewhat obscure, terms in "Welcome to the Terrordome," a single prereleased from its forthcoming album, "Fear of a Black Planet". . . .

"I mean, I made the apology, but people are still trying to give me hell," elaborates Public Enemy's lead rapper, Chuck D. "The media crucified me, comparable to another brother who caught hell." If you add up all the Jewish blood that has been spilled over the slander of deicide, it makes Chuck D's sufferings at the hands of his critics seem mild by comparison. The ADL reacted swiftly to what appeared to be a gratuitous incitement to anti-Semitism, and took its protest to where it would do the most good, CBS Records. CBS Records Inc. president Walter Yetnikoff responded with a commitment to police future releases for "bigotry and intolerance." While "it goes without saying that artists have the right of freedom of expression," Yetnikoff wrote in a memo to the rest of the company, "when the issue is bigotry, there is a fine line of acceptable standards which no piece of music should cross." And once again, Chuck D is saying that Professor Griff will leave the group . . . maybe later this year.

NWA's attitude even got it into trouble with the FBI. In a letter last summer to NWA's distributor, FBI Assistant Director Milt Ahlerich observed that the groups' album "Straight Outta Compton" "encourages violence against and disrespect for the law-enforcement officer." But Ahlerich couldn't do much more than make the company "aware of the FBI's position" on lyrics in a song ("F--- Tha Police") he couldn't bring himself to name:

> Pullin' out a silly club so you stand
> With a fake-ass badge and a gun in your hand
> Take off the gun so you can see what's up
> And we'll go at it, punk, and I'm 'af--- you up . . .
> I'm a sniper with a hell of a 'scope . . .
> Takin' out a cop or two . . .

Are even such appalling expressions of attitude protected by the First Amendment? Yes, according to an American Civil Liberties Union official, who told The Village Voice that "the song does not constitute advocacy of violence as that has been interpreted by the courts." (Although in plain English, it's hard to imagine what else it might be advocating.) Asked whether his music doesn't give the impression that the gang culture in the sorry Los Angeles slum of Compton is fun, Eazy-E, the group's coleader, replied, "It is fun," "'F--- tha police' was something people be wanting to say for years but they were too scared to say it," he says. "The next album might be 'F--- tha FBI'".

Yes, having an attitude means it's always someone else's fault: cops who disrespect (or "dis") you when you walk through a housing project with a gold chain that could lock up a motorcycle, immigrants so dumb they can't speak the language, women who are just asking for it anyway.

The outrageous implication is that to *not* sing about this stuff would be to do violence to an artistic vision as pure and compelling as Bach's. The viler the message, the more fervent the assertion of honesty that underlies it. Eazy sometimes calls himself a "street historian" to deflect the charge that he is a rabble-rouser. "We're like underground reporters," he says; "We just telling it like it is, we don't hold back." The fact is, rap grows out of a violent culture in which getting shot by a cop is a real fear. But music isn't reportage, and the way to deal with police brutality is not to glorify "taking out a cop or two." By way of self-exculpation, Eazy denies any aspirations toward being a role model. As he puts it, "I don't like anybody want to look at me and stop being theyself."

Even so, Eazy sounds like Edmund Wilson, compared with Axl Rose of Guns N' Roses trying to explain the lyrics to "One in a Million." He says he's mad at immigrants because he had a run-in with a Middle Eastern clerk at a 7-Eleven. He hates homosexuals because one once made advances to him while he was sleeping. This is a textbook definition of bigotry. "I used words like . . . niggers because you're not allowed to use the word nigger," he told his "authorized biographer," Del James, in an interview printed in *Rolling Stone.* "I don't like being told what I can and what I can't say. I used the word *nigger* because it's a word to describe somebody that is basically a pain in your life, a problem. The word nigger doesn't necessarily mean black."

Oh, no? This is an example of what Todd Gitlin, director of the mass-communications program at the University of California, Berkeley, calls the "free-floating rancor" of the youth culture, the "tribal acrimony" that leads to fights over turf, real and psychic. Attitude primarily is a working-class and underclass phenomenon, a response to the diminishing expectations of the millions of American youths who forgot to go to business school in the 1980s. *If* they had ever listened to anything except the homeboys talking trash, *if* they had ever studied anything but the strings of a guitar, they might have some more interesting justifications to offer. They could quote the sainted Woody Guthrie about "Pretty Boy Floyd," who "laid [a] deputy down" (for disrespecting his wife, as it happened in the song). Apropos of their penchant for exaggerated sexual braggadocio, they could point out that the great jazz pianist Jelly Roll Morton didn't get his nickname because he liked pastry. They could point out that as recently as a generation ago, racial epithets that today would make Morton Downey, Jr., swoon with embarrassment came tripping innocently off the tongues of educated, decent people. *Then* we might have a sensible discussion with them; but they haven't, so we can't.

But of course attitude resists any such attempt at intellectualizing. To call it visceral is to give it the benefit of the doubt. It has its origins in parts of the body even less mentionable, as the pioneering California rapper Ice-T puts it: "Women have some eerie connection with gangsters. They always want the rebel more than the brain. Girls want somebody who can beat everybody up." . . .

This is the height of gallantry for Ice-T: no one gets killed. More often, when attitude meets woman, woman is by far the worse for it. If she's lucky, she gets made love to with a flashlight ("Shut Up, Be Happy" by Ice-T). Otherwise, she finds herself in the even less healthy company of Eazy-E:

> Now back on the street and
> my records are clean
> I creeped on my bitch with my
> Uzi machine
> Went to the house and kicked
> down the door
> Unloaded like hell, cold
> smoked the ho'.

It is not just that romance has gone out of music—attitude has done the seemingly impossible and taken sex out of teenage culture, substituting brutal fantasies of penetration and destruction. Girls who want to have fun this way need to have their heads examined.

But that's the point. The end of attitude is nihilism, which by definition leads nowhere. The culture of attitude is repulsive, but it's mostly empty of political content. As Gitlin puts it, "There's always a population of kids looking to be bad. As soon as the establishment tells them what's bad this season, some of them are going to go off and do it." And that's not good, but it's probably not a case for the FBI, either. If we learned one thing from the '60s, it's how *little* power rock and roll has to change the world.

Speculations

1. In "The Rap Attitude," Adler makes the argument that in much of today's music, particularly rap music, it is acceptable and even desirable to be offensive and insulting. Can you provide examples beyond the article? Is this a new phenomenon or do we find similar instances in the history of popular music, such as Elvis, the Beatles, and the Rolling Stones?

2. Why does Adler assert that "civilized society abhors attitude, and perpetuates itself by keeping it under control. There are entire organizations devoted to this job, most notably the Parents' Music Resource Center. . . ."? Why should attitude be kept under control? What do you think "civilized society" is afraid of here? Discuss Adler's "attitude" in this essay.

3. What does Adler's analysis of Ice-T's music say about this kind of rap music and sexuality? What attitude toward women and

sex does this music express and what lies behind that attitude?
Discuss whether this attitude is appropriate and realistic or dangerous.

4. How have you been frightened or threatened by other people's
strongly expressed feelings or "attitudes"? Draw on your own
personal experiences to explain what you think people should be
free to say and what you think the limits of free expression are.
Who gets hurt when such limits are either imposed or violated?

5. Adler finally argues that rock and roll has "little power" to change
the world. Why does he make this final argument? Do you agree
or disagree? What specific examples from your own experience or
observations about rock and roll support your view?

GANGSTA RAPPERS SING WHITE RACISTS' TUNE

Arthur Lawrence Cribbs, Jr.

Born and raised in what he calls a "bilingual barrio-ghetto" of
Los Angeles, the Reverend Arthur Lawrence Cribbs, Jr. became associate pastor at his father's Golden Rule Missionary Baptist Church
when he was just thirteen. Receiving his B.A. in political science from
the University of California-Berkeley in 1986, he became a lay minister at Morningside United Church of Christ in Inglewood, California,
and in 1971, he combined his career as a minister with a broadcasting
career. As a news writer, producer, and researcher at KHJ-TV in Los
Angeles and other stations, he traveled widely to report stories on the
debt crisis in Mexico, the rise of Corazon Aquino in the Philippines,
the independence of Belize, Indian affairs and politics in Reno, and a
prison riot in Canada. Having worked for more than a dozen radio
and television stations and as an officer in the United Church of
Christ, Cribbs currently is a reporter for KPIX-TV in San Francisco,
California.

In 1993, the United Church of Christ sent Reverend Cribbs to Los
Angeles to help overcome the tensions, bigotry, and economic breakdown that plague the city. Convinced that Los Angeles's racial problems affect people of many races, he now works with Asian and Latino communities as well as with African-Americans and whites. In the
following editorial, Cribbs decries the vulgarity and misogyny of
gangsta rap as a violation of the dignity of African-American culture
and as exploitation by large record companies making a profit from
racial stereotyping.

It is one of the most ironic and pathetic trends to hit the black community: Gyrating "gangsta" rappers who demean African daughters by promoting vulgarity and violence against them without restraint.

Too often, their depiction of life in the so-called ghetto is more fantasy and regurgitation of racial stereotyping than expressions of personal experience.

The ill-fitting clothing that hangs off their bodies, displaying underwear not designed for external use, is just another step backward and away from opportunities for employment and service to humanity.

Half-cocked caps and oversized, pricey sneakers do nothing to improve the image of the person donning such attire.

Gangsta rap is often performed by criminals.

A Top Ten hit on the charts today is by rapper Snoop Doggy Dogg, a man charged with first-degree murder after his bodyguard shot a man in September.

Rapper Flavor Flav, of the group Public Enemy, has been charged with firing a gun at a neighbor.

Abuse against women is more than mere musical lyrics and artistic expression, as some gangsta rappers and their supporters try to argue. Their advocacy in music has been carried out in real life. Rapper Tupac Shakur faces charges of shooting two off-duty police officers and sexually assaulting a female fan.

This genre of popular culture is nothing more than the latest assault on African and African-American heritage. The fact that the principal participants are the lost children of the mother continent is insufficient evidence to justify its practice.

In the twin traditions of African and African-American societies, women are honored and vulgarity is uttered in a whisper, if at all, and definitely away from polite company. Under no circumstances is it recorded, produced, promoted and peddled as a commercial product.

This would not be widespread if white, megarecord companies did not put filth on sale for big dollars.

But it is both worthy of note and applause that radio stations across the nation recently decided to limit, edit or ban violent and vulgar lyrics on the air.

WBLS-FM in New York and KACE-FM in Los Angeles will ban rap songs that encourage violence. KPWR-FM in Los Angeles will mask or delete words like "nigga" or "bitch" that are used negatively in a song. WCKZ-FM in Charlotte, N.C., decided to limit gangsta rap to late-night hours.

A new message must go across the nation that challenges any promotion of assault, abuse and exploitation of women and youth.

As a junior high school student in Compton, Calif., I remember trying out new "bad words" with my friends. Despite this adventure into the lingual jungle, we knew enough about our cultural ties not to scream those words out loud. We knew that while we were experimenting, it was too great a risk to speak those words loud enough for any adult along the route home to hear us. So, we cursed quietly among ourselves.

That is in complete contrast to the blaring streams of obscenities coming from mouths, tape decks and radios on public streets.

If this were simply restricted to music and media hype, that would be bad enough. But we also hear the repetition of those words spoken in front of and directed at toddlers. Worse, young children have learned them and fire them at adults and elders.

Gangsta rappers have slipped to a level of base behavior that is not recognized within African and African-American cultures.

Even the new action movies that are presented as virtual reality in the black community are nothing more than horror stories based on sensational episodes that come from racially biased news reports. Even if they are true according to the life of a gang-banger, is it the kind of story black people want or need to tell about themselves?

As a high school journalism student, I was both shocked and angered by the depiction of my community during the 1965 Watts riots. For the most part, we were an ignored people until the fires began to burn.

We watched as all the vile fears of white America roared across our television screens with reports and commentary that included terms like "savage," "jungle," "beasts" and "massacre" to describe the people, places and activities in our neighborhood.

Then, we labeled the reporting racist without qualification because the reporters were insensitive whites who came into our community from suburbs and the far West Side.

Today, the commentary is still racist, only now it's in black-face. Like their white counterparts, gangsta rappers come into our communities with a narrow life-view.

If these "artists" want to redeem themselves and reclaim their true African and African-American legacies, let me suggest they read a few books as primers: *They Came Before Columbus, Before the Mayflower, When and Where I Enter* and *Black Skins/White Masks.*

As a second suggestion, they need to spend some time *listening* to elders in the 'hood who know their own history. Then, maybe they can return to rapping and making money off Africans and African-Americans but with new messages of hope and truth.

Speculations

1. Cribbs makes a strong argument about the appearance and dress of the gangsta rappers. Do you agree with his argument? Based on your own experience, how do you think the fashions adopted by rap musicians or other popular singers influence young people and their stylistic choices? Support your responses with specific examples and details.

2. How does Cribbs portray "the twin traditions of African and African-American societies"? What values does he find worthwhile in these societies? How are these values similar to or dissimilar to your own? Explain why you would agree or disagree with endorsing the specific values he describes.

3. Based on his experience as "a junior high school student in Compton, California," what argument does Cribbs make about language use? Based on your own junior high school experience, respond to Cribbs's argument about why and how we use "bad words."

4. What comparisons does Cribbs make between news reports of the Watts riots and the music of the rap "artists"? What does this comparison say about the relationship of rap to the African-American community?

5. What two recommendations to gangsta rappers does Cribbs make at the end of his argument? Imagining yourself to be a rap musician or an ardent fan of rap music, how would you respond to Cribbs's recommendations? Why would you respond that way?

VOX POPULI

Francis Davis

Primarily a jazz journalist, Francis Davis lives in Philadelphia, where he was born and raised and where he now teaches a course on jazz and blues at the University of Pennsylvania. Awarded a Guggenheim Fellowship in 1993 and a Pew Fellowship in the Arts for literary nonfiction last year, Davis has written prolifically about music for *The Village Voice, The Philadelphia Enquirer, The Atlantic, Rolling Stone,* and many other newspapers and magazines; his books include *In The Moment: Jazz in the 1980s* (1986), *Outcats: Jazz Composers, Instrumentalists, and Singers* (1990), *The History of Blues* (1995), and the forthcoming *Bebop and Nothingness* (1996). His current project is a biography of John

Coltrane. Book reviewer Ronald M. Radano has aptly described Davis's writing:

> Jazz journalists, like the improvisers they so often admire, exemplify the art of creative, quick thinking. As deadline writers, they often rely on instinct rather than reflection, making rapid musical choices that test their critical skills and literary imagination. Both the writer and the musician are actors of immediacy, creators who work in the moment. . . . Davis's strength is as an essayist, a storyteller who uses his narrative gifts to explain a musical subculture that stands outside the realm of general understanding and appreciation.

Davis himself describes his work as "a brand of advocacy journalism," and as indicated by the title of this selection, *"Vox Populi"* (a Latin phrase meaning "voice of the people"), he advocates a complex understanding and recognition of rap music as an expression of the fears, anger, alienation, and desires of a diverse people.

Rock-and-roll has outlived its usefulness to most of us who grew up with it. The current hits aren't about us anymore, but that's all right—we're no longer crowding the clubs and record stores. Pop has always existed primarily for the young, the only ones who have time for it. The source of disenchantment is in realizing that the favorite songs of our high school and college years are no longer about us either—they reflect where we were in our lives then, not where we are now.

This may be why so many of my friends have developed a sudden interest in country, a style of pop whose subject matter is less often adolescent sensuality than adult wreckage. It may also explain why so many aging rock singers, on finding themselves in a reflective mood, have turned to songs given their definitive interpretations by Frank Sinatra in the 1950s, when our parents were our current age. With notable exceptions, including Neil Young, Richard Thompson, and Loudon Wainwright III, the pop singers of our own generation have given us no clue as to how grownups of our day are supposed to feel and behave as they enter middle age. This is because these pop singers know no better than we do.

I sense, too, that the first full generation after ours might be more disenchanted with rock than we are: between their favorites and ours exists no clear line of demarcation like the one that existed between the big-band crooners our parents had enjoyed and our yowling idols. Pop today, in other words, has something to alienate everyone. People in their late thirties and older are put off because it's not just theirs anymore, younger people because it never was just theirs.

No other subgenre of pop alienates as many people as deeply as rap does, despite what I sense to be a suspicion—even on the part of those who profess to find rap indistinguishable from random gunfire—that it is the only thing happening right now, the only kind of pop with the sort of larger cultural significance taken for granted in pop since Woodstock.

By the time a rap song first made the national charts—"Rapper's Delight," by the Sugar Hill Gang, in 1979—rap was already something of an old story, having started about five years earlier as an underground offshoot of disco. Its origins as a kind of dance music are hinted at in its other name, "hip-hop," which is preferred by those for whom it is not just music but a look, an attitude, and a lifestyle, although even they frequently use the terms interchangeably. The "rap" is the lead vocal or vocals; "hip-hop" is the vocal plus everything else on the record—the background chants and disjunct instrumental sounds that initiates call the "beats," which are sometimes supplied by live singers and musicians but are more frequently the result of a disc jockey's sampling bits and pieces of other records.

In the beginning the rap was optional. Hip-hop's first heroes were its DJs, who provided a nonstop groove for dancers by isolating, electronically boosting, and repeating ad infinitum bass lines and drum breaks from 1970s funk and glam-rock hits. Although vilified by some as plagiarists and scavengers, these hip-hop DJs (Grandmaster Flash and Afrika Bambaataa became the most famous of them) were essentially grass-roots successors to Phil Spector, Brian Wilson, and George Martin, the 1960s rock producers who pioneered the use of the recording studio as an instrument in its own right. A sociological study that attempted to link the rise of hip-hop to the decreased availability of musical instruments in public schools in the 1970s would be right on target. In the meantime, what needs to be acknowledged about hip-hop, apart from its paradoxical origins as a roots music dependent on electronic technology, is its remarkable staying power. It has outlasted graffiti, break dancing, and every other manifestation of the black-teen Zeitgeist of which it was initially seen as only one component.

Rap remains dance music, and on the most basic level a catchy rap song wins you over in much the same manner any good pop song does: by virtue of its hooks—those vocal refrains and stupid instrumental riffs you can't get out of your head. The DJs have been relegated to the background, but the most imaginative of the record producers who have succeeded them—Teddy Riley (Wreckx-N-Effect, Kool Moe Dee, and Heavy D. and the Boyz), Prince Paul (Queen Latifah, Big Daddy Kane, 3rd Bass, and De La Soul), and Hank Shocklee (Ice Cube and Public Enemy)—are responsible for the only formal innovation in pop since the punk minimalism of Talking Heads and the Ramones in the late 1970s.

The controversy surrounding rap, however, usually concerns its lyrics, not its hooks or its merits as a music for dancing. In Michael Small's informative 1992 rap scrapbook, *Break It Down* (Citadel Press), Afrika Bambaataa includes on his list of rap's possible antecedents African call and response, the insult game called the dozens, Cab Calloway, chitlin-circuit comedians, be-bop scat singing, black nationalist oratory, Jamaican dance-hall "toasts," and the "political awareness rap" of the Last Poets, a spoken-word group popular in the 1970s. Others have mentioned the influence of jive-talking radio disc jockeys, the singing poet Gil Scott-Heron, and the jump-rope game double dutch.

Rap can also be compared to 1950s a cappella or doo-wop, with which it shares a street-corner male ethic, a delight in onomatopoeia, and an ingenuity in making do with very little. The difference is that doo-wop's young singers were forever trying on courtly feelings much too large for them, on already popular songs such as "Red Sails in the Sunset" and "A Sunday Kind of Love." Rap has no dreamy side—unless you accept, as an indication of how times have changed, a song like Ice Cube's "It Was a Good Day," from his recent CD *The Predator*, in which Ice Cube enjoys marathon sex, gets drunk without throwing up, doesn't get stopped and searched by the police, doesn't have to attend the funerals of any buddies, and goes the entire day without having to fire his AK-47. As if to show us what a fantasy all this is, the video for the song ends with Ice Cube in a Los Angeles SWAT team's crosshairs.

Ice Cube, a founding member of a group called NWA ("Niggas With Attitude"), epitomizes "gangsta," probably the most popular style of rap right now, and certainly the most truculent and ghettocentric—the style people have in mind when they condemn rap for its comic-book Afrocentrism, its monotonous profanity, its Uzi-brandishing, its anti-Semitism and intolerance of Asians, its homophobia and crotch-grabbing misogyny, and the seeming determination of many of its performers to conform to every negative black stereotype.

According to gangsta's apologists in the music press, these objectionable characteristics are symptoms of black disempowerment. It's difficult to argue with this at face value—difficult not to feel, on being subjected to a drive-by musical attack from a Jeep whose back seat has been torn out and replaced with speakers, that what one is hearing is the death rattle of Martin Luther King Jr.'s dream.

Just as there is something called alternative rock, which nobody in the music business seems quite able to define except by example, there is something called alternative rap—perhaps best exemplified by the group Arrested Development. Musically, the difference between gangsta and alternative is that alternative tends to be more playful, both in its rhymes and in its sampling. But the *perceived* difference between the two styles has almost nothing to do with music. One gains a sense of what both gangsta and alternative have come to stand for by listening to "People Everyday," a song from Arrested Development's debut album, *3 Years, 5 Months & 2 Days in the Life of. . . .* Speech, Arrested Development's leader, is spending the afternoon in the park with his girlfriend when along come "a group of brothers" swigging forty-ounce bottles of malt liquor, "goin' the nigga route," and "disrespecting my black queen." Speech at first ignores them, but after they make fun of his colorful garb (an Afrocentric variation on thrift-shop chic, to judge from the album cover) and start "squeezing parts of my date's anatomy," he springs into action. "I ain't Ice Cube," he tells us, "but I had to take the brother out for bein' rude."

It takes "three or four" cops to pull Speech off the gangsta (who evidently survives the encounter), and the story becomes one of "a black man, acting like a nigga and get stomped by an African." Speech, who tells us on another of the album's songs that he's "a bit shorter than the average man" and on yet another that "brothers" in possession of automatic weapons "need to learn how to correctly shoot them, [to] save those rounds for a revolution," has more in common with Ice Cube than he may care to admit. A machismo fantasy is still a machismo fantasy, even if it takes the form of an appeal to black pride rather than a call for retribution against the police. And shouldn't a songwriter who has been praised for leading one of the few sexually integrated rap groups know better than to put a woman on a pedestal as his "black queen"? At least she's not his "bitch" or his "ho," as she might be on a gangsta record. And at least Speech's politics are slightly more sophisticated than those of the gangstas, many of whom claim Malcolm X as their role model, although what they seem to find most admirable about him is that he was once a street hustler with the gift of gab, just like them.

Beyond complaining that rap isn't really music because so few of its performers play instruments or "sing" in the conventional sense of the word, middle-class whites who grew up dancing to Motown's three-minute assimilationist fantasies seem to be alienated by what they take to be rap's black-separatist agenda. A still deeper source of frustration might be a sense on the part of middle-aged whites that rap's tacit off-limits sign is generational, not racial.

But at whose young is rap aimed? In a nasty little cover piece on rap in a 1991 issue of *The New Republic*, David Samuels argued that the audience for rap now consists in large measure of white middle-class teenagers turned on by rap's "evocation of an age-old image of blackness: a foreign, sexually charged, and criminal underworld against which the norms of white society are defined and, by extension, through which they may be defiled." The cover of Ice-T's recent *Home Invasion*, which depicts a white tousle-top surrounded by the books of Malcolm X, Donald Goines, and Iceberg Slim, listening to music on headphones as he fantasizes that his mother is being ravished and his father is being beaten to death by muscular black intruders, suggests that there's some merit to Samuels's argument.

So what? Rap's young white fans are hardly the first of their race to get off on black music. The problem with focusing on what percentage of rap's listenership is white and whether its performers pander to white sexual fantasies is that such questions leave black adults out altogether. Reading any of the recent trendy books and magazine pieces contrasting the tastes and values of Boomers with those of their offspring, one might think that generation gaps were an exclusively white phenomenon. Yet a visit to a record store with one section for rap and another for soul makes clear that black America has its own generation gap, of which differing tastes in music are only the visible tip.

As the essayist Gerald Early has pointed out, each new generation [of African-Americans] views its elders with suspicion, thinking them failures who compromised and accommodated themselves in order to survive among the whites. And each generation, in some way, wishes to free itself from the generation that produced it.

African-Americans now in their late thirties or early forties, already resentful of their marginalization by mass media that tend to present black culture only in terms of new directions in jive, must sometimes feel as though everything they grew up believing is under attack in some of the music their children are listening to. "When we first started, everything was black-this and black-that—the whole positive black thing," Easy E, the former drug dealer who was a founder of NWA, once explained to an interviewer. "We said f . . . that—we wanted to come out in everybody's face. Something that would shock people."

This particular generational clash is exacerbated by class friction of a sort seldom experienced by whites. In *Juice*, an otherwise forgettable 1992 action movie directed by Ernest Dickerson (Spike Lee's cinematographer), a man named Quincy who is an aspiring hip-hop DJ from the projects introduces himself as "Q" (his street name) to the estranged husband of the older woman he's been sleeping with. "What, did names like Mustafah and Akbar become too hard to spell?" the husband sneers. His equal disdain for the African or Islamic names given to children by roots-conscious black parents in the 1970s and for the breezy street names many of those kids have since adopted is supposed to tip us off that this man is a member of the black bourgeoisie, or at least aspires to it. Both kinds of names reek of the ghetto to him, and this makes him an unsympathetic character in the movie's scheme of things. What gives the scene its power and surprising complexity is the glimpse it provides of the alienation felt by many middle-class African-Americans at a time when the ghetto street culture celebrated in rap is increasingly viewed as the only authentic black experience.

My own feelings about rap are so conflicted that I hardly know how to answer when somebody asks if I'm a fan. As a middle-aged white man, I'm in no position to think of rap as mine. As a music critic, I listen to a good deal of it out of professional obligation, and I enjoy much of what I hear—although even much of the rap I enjoy troubles or saddens me. The rapper most admired by my colleagues is Chuck D, of the group Public Enemy, who has, in effect, put a beat to the bluster of the Black Panthers and the Nation of Islam. Marshall Berman, a professor at the City University of New York and the author of *All That Is Solid Melts Into Air*, an influential text on modernism, has likened Public Enemy's "breakthroughs" in rap to "Picasso's in painting, Eliot's and Pound's in poetry, Faulkner's and Joyce's in the novel, Parker's in jazz." All I hear in Chuck D is a rapper whose delivery is too sententious to be convincing and whose worship by the pop intelligentsia is evidence of the extent to which black racism is now accepted as a legitimate response to white oppression.

The rap performers I enjoy are those who emphasize production values, songcraft, and that quality of playfulness endemic to all good pop. These include P. M. Dawn, Neneh Cherry, De La Soul, and a new group from Los Angeles called The Pharcyde. Another new group, the Digable Planets, are nothing if not playful in attempting to fuse rap with elements of bebop, but what finally turns me off about them is their reduction of jazz to walking bass lines, finger-snaps, and bohemian posturing.

These performers (I'll add Arrested Development, if only for their "Tennessee," an evocation of the agrarian South as a place filled with both harrowing and idyllic memories for black Americans) suggest the wide range of approaches possible in a genre as seemingly inflexible as rap. My favorite among all recent pop albums is one generally spoken of as an example of alternative rap, though it might not be if the young performer responsible for it weren't black and didn't employ sampling and other hip-hop studio conventions.

Michael Ivey is the leader of a group called Basehead, which—at least on its debut album, *Play With Toys*—turns out to be not a group at all but just Ivey on guitar and vocals, a drummer named Brian Hendrix, and a handful of other musicians drifting in and out of the studio. Ivey sings in a small voice as uvular as any we've heard since Donovan. When he isn't singing, he's speeding up and slowing down the tape to alter his speaking voice: what are presented as arguments between him and his friends are actually Ivey's stoned interior monologues. Although "basehead" is street slang for someone who freebases cocaine, the illegal substance of choice in Ivey's songs is marijuana, and even it takes second place to beer—Ivey or one of his imaginary friends is always popping the top off a cold one.

Ivey is a musical as well as a verbal ironist who delights in subverting both rock and gangsta-rap conventions. His guitar riffs demonstrate pop's boomerang effect: played a little faster and with more thunder, they could be the riffs that Led Zeppelin and other British proto-metal bands appropriated from the Delta bluesmen. The bass-heavy sound mix on *Play With Toys* is similar to those favored by the gangstas, but Ivey turns the tables on them by sampling NWA's "8 Ball" on a song called (what else?) "Ode to My Favorite Beer."

Ivey's melodies are slightly woozy and doggedly minimalistic; a key change is a big event. Not much happens in his lyrics either. Ivey, who recently graduated from Howard University with a degree in film, drinks beer, writes songs, broods over breaking up with his girlfriend, and frets over his own future and the fate of other young black men as he watches the evening news. Although compared by critics to the aimless post-adolescents in Richard Linklater's movie *Slacker,* Ivey can no more be said to represent a type than his music can be reduced to sociology.

Basehead's new *Not in Kansas Anymore* is a disappointing follow-up on which Ivey—whose cult listenership is mostly white, to judge from the audience that turned out for a show he gave in Philadelphia last winter—makes what sounds like a deliberate attempt to blacken up, at least in terms of his lyrics. Leaving his apartment for a change, he's treated as a potential shoplifter in a clothing store and stopped and frisked by the police for no apparent reason other than that he's young and black, and therefore assumed to be armed and dangerous. Though I don't doubt for a minute that Ivey is writing from experience, his touch is almost too light to convey his indignation.

This turf belongs to the gangstas, whose ghetto narratives forcefully express the rage a middle-class monologuist such as Ivey can't bring himself to feel. What gives a song like Ice-T's "Cop Killer" or Paris's "Coffee, Doughnuts & Death" its troubling power is the performer's sense and ours that he isn't speaking just for himself. These songs are the only ones on the radio now in which more seems at stake than a spot on next week's charts. But the fact of their social significance does not allow us to overlook all that is reprehensible about them; issues are rarely that simple, and neither is pop.

I am someone whose tolerance for such violent films as Quentin Tarantino's *Reservoir Dogs* and Abel Ferrara's *Bad Lieutenant* renders him vulnerable to charges of practicing a racial double standard in feeling such dismay over rap's bloodlust. And I do admit that rap troubles me in a way that movies rarely do. But there are differences between movies and pop music, perhaps the most obvious of which is that movies, by their very nature, are capable of presenting multiple points of view. In *Reservoir Dogs*, for example, Tarantino stops just short of showing us a cop having his ear sliced off by a sadistic, razor-wielding hood played by Michael Madsen. This is a scene that sickens some moviegoers and sends others stumbling for the exits, either in fear of what they're about to see or in fear of their response to it. The camera follows Madsen throughout the scene, and it's difficult not to become caught up in his delirium as he turns up the volume on the radio, does a series of graceful little dance steps to Stealers Wheel's "Stuck in the Middle With You," and closes in on his defenseless, screaming captive. "Was that as good for you as it was for me?" Madsen asks the cop afterward. Then he douses him with gasoline and pulls out his lighter. Madsen might also be asking those of us who sat through the scene without averting our eyes. But along with Madsen's dance steps, what stays in the mind are the cop's screams and his dazed reaction to his mutilation and imminent death.

Pop songs are theoretically as capable as film of providing this kind of emotional and moral complexity. Randy Newman and Lou Reed are among the pop songwriters who have provided it, or at least have come close. Rap is strictly first-person-singular at this point. Its young performers have yet to develop the artistic, and moral, gift of empathy. Maybe when they grow up. This, though, may be asking too much of pop.

Speculations

1. Throughout his essay, Davis evaluates what is good and bad about rap. Make two lists, one positive and one negative, and explain which points you find most persuasive.
2. Davis has been praised for his ability to "tell a story." If you think of this essay as a story about rap music, where does the story begin? What are the origins of rap and what are the most important moments in its development? How does this story help you to better understand rap music?
3. Explain why Davis says "A machismo fantasy is still a machismo fantasy, even if it takes the form of an appeal to black pride rather than a call for retribution against the police"? What point is he making? How does his retelling of specific rap lyrics support this idea? Do you agree? Explain your response.
4. Davis initiates his essay by comparing music that appeals to "adolescent sensuality" versus that which speaks to "adult wreckage." Later he discusses the inevitability of the generation gap among whites as well as blacks. How is his notion of the generation gap crucial to his argument about rap music and its critics? Describe how rap is viewed by young people as opposed to older people.

5. Explain why Davis says, "My own feelings about rap are so conflicted that I hardly know how to answer when somebody asks if
I am a fan." What draws him to rap and what repels him?

6. Davis likes Michael Ivey's rap music the best, yet why does he insist that the ghetto gangsta rappers are better at expressing rage?
Why does this trouble him? What moral conflict does he sense
between rap's social significance and its reprehensibility? Compare your own moral sense of rap music to Davis's.

GANGSTA CULTURE—SEXISM, MISOGYNY: WHO WILL TAKE THE RAP?

bell hooks

bell hooks is the pen name of Gloria Watkins, who was born in
1955, attended Stanford University, and became a professor of
African-American studies at Yale University. Besides having been
published in dozens of magazines and scholarly journals, hooks has
also written many books, including: *Ain't I A Woman: Black Women and
Feminism, Feminist Theory: From Margin to Center, Talking Back: Thinking Feminist, Thinking Black, Yearning: Race, Gender, and Cultural Politics, Black Looks: Race and Representation,* and *Sisters of the Yam: Black
Women and Self-Recovery.* In these works, hooks reinterprets the feminist movement from the perspective of black women. Using the
metaphor of marginality, which she describes as being "part of the
whole but outside the main body," hooks questions whether traditional feminism, which "emerges from privileged women who live at
the center," addresses the needs of working-class, poor, and minority
women.

hooks grew up in the 1950s in a small Kentucky town whose railroad tracks symbolized the marginality of the black townspeople's
lives. In the preface to *Feminist Theory: From Margin to Center* (1984),
she describes how blacks could cross the tracks to work, but only in
service jobs. They could not live there.

Living as we did—on the edge—we developed a particular
way of seeing reality. We looked both from the outside in
and from the inside out. We focused our attention on the
center as well as on the margin. We understood both. This
mode of seeing reminded us of the existence of a whole uni-

verse, a main body made up of both margin and center. Our survival depended on an ongoing public awareness of the separation between margin and center and an ongoing private acknowledgment that we were a necessary, vital part of that whole.

This dual perspective gives hooks a "willingness to explore all possibilities." She remains convinced that feminism "must become a mass based political movement if it is to have a revolutionary, transformative impact on society. . . . As we educate one another to acquire critical consciousness, we have the chance to see how important airing diverse perspectives can be for any progressive political struggle that is serious about transformation." Precisely that kind of critical exploration and awareness characterizes her stance in this selection from her most recent book, *Outlaw Culture: Resisting Representations* (1994). In this essay she argues that problems of gender and race are not isolated from one another and that gender issues in rap music are further complicated by the crossing and mixing of values, attitudes, and concerns between the black youth culture and the larger white majority.

For the past several months, the white mainstream media has been contacting me to hear my views on gangsta rap. Whether major television networks, or small independent radio shows, they seek me out for the black and feminist take on the issue. After I have my say, I am never called back, never invited to do the television shows, the radio spots. I suspect they call me, confident that when we talk they will hear the hardcore "feminist" trash of gangsta rap. When they encounter instead the hardcore feminist critique of white supremacist capitalist patriarchy, they lose interest.

To the white-dominated mass media, the controversy over gangsta rap makes great spectacle. Besides the exploitation of these issues to attract audiences, a central motivation for highlighting gangsta rap continues to be the sensationalist drama of demonizing black youth culture in general and the contributions of young black men in particular. It's a contemporary remake of *Birth of a Nation*—only this time we are encouraged to believe it is not just vulnerable white womanhood that risks destruction by black hands, but everyone. When I counter this demonization of black males by insisting that gangsta rap does not appear in a cultural vacuum, that it is not a product created in isolation within a segregated black world but is rather expressive of the cultural crossing, mixings, and engagement of black youth culture with the values, attitudes, and concerns of the white majority, some folks stop listening.

The sexist, misogynist, patriarchal ways of thinking and behaving that are glorified in gangsta rap are a reflection of the prevailing values in our society, values created and sustained by white supremacist capitalist patriarchy. As the crudest and most brutal expression of sexism, misogynistic attitudes tend to be portrayed by the dominant culture as always an expression of male deviance. In reality, they are part of a sexist continuum, necessary for the maintenance of patriarchal social order. While patriarchy and sexism continue to be the political and cultural norm in our society, feminist movement has created a climate where crude expressions of male domination are likely to be called into question, especially if they are made by men in power. It is useful to think of misogyny as a field that must be labored in and maintained both to sustain patriarchy but also to nourish an antifeminist backlash. And what better group to labor on this "plantation" than young black men?

To see gangsta rap as a reflection of dominant values in our culture rather than as an aberrant pathological standpoint does not mean that a rigorous feminist critique and interrogation of the sexist and misogyny expressed in this music is not needed. Without a doubt black males, young and old, must be held politically accountable for their sexism. Yet this critique must always be contextualized or we risk making it appear that the problems of misogyny, sexism, and all the behaviors this thinking supports and condones, including rape, male violence against women, is a black male thing. And this is what is happening. Young black males are forced to take the heat for encouraging via their music the hatred of and violence against women that is a central core of patriarchy.

Witness the recent piece by Brent Staples in the *New York Times*, entitled "The Politics of Gangster Rap: A Music Celebrating Murder and Misogyny." Defining the turf, Staples writes, "For those who haven't caught up, gangster rap is that wildly successful music in which all women are 'bitches' and 'whores' and young men kill each other for sport." No mention of white supremacist capitalist patriarchy in this piece. Not a word about the cultural context that would need to exist for young males to be socialized to think differently about gender. No word about feminism. Staples unwittingly assumes that black males are writing their lyrics off in the "jungle," faraway from the impact of mainstream socialization and desire. At no point does he interrogate why it is huge audiences, especially young white male consumers, are so turned on by this music, by the misogyny and sexism, by the brutality. Where is the anger and rage at females expressed in this music coming from, the glorification of all acts of violence? These are the difficult questions that Staples feels no need to answer.

One cannot answer them honestly without placing accountability on larger structures of domination (sexism, racism, class elitism) and the individuals—often white, usually male, but not always—who are hierarchally placed to maintain and perpetuate the values that uphold these exploitative and oppressive systems. That means taking a critical look at the politics of hedonistic consumerism, the values of the men and women who produce gangsta rap. It would mean considering the seduction of young black males who find that they can make more money producing lyrics that promote violence, sexism, misogyny than with any other content. How many disenfranchised black males would not surrender to expressing virulent forms of sexism if they knew the rewards would be unprecedented material power and fame?

More than anything, gangsta rap celebrates the world of the material, the dog-eat-dog world where you do what you gotta do to make it even if it means fucking over folks and taking them out. In this world view killing is necessary for survival. Significantly, the logic here is a crude expression of the logic of white supremacist capitalist patriarchy. In his new book *Sexy Dressing Etc.*, privileged white male law professor Duncan Kennedy gives what he calls "a set of general characterizations of U.S. culture," explaining that "it is individual (cowboys), material (gangsters), and philistine." This general description of mainstream culture would not lead us to place gangsta rap on the margins of what this nation is about but at the center. Rather than seeing it as a subversion or disruption of the norm, we would need to see it as an *embodiment* of the norm.

That viewpoint was graphically highlighted in the film *Menace II Society*, a drama not only of young black males killing for sport, but which included scenes where mass audiences voyeuristically watched and in many cases enjoyed the kill. Significantly, at one point in the film we see that the young black males have learned their gangsta values from watching movies and television and shows where white male gangsters are center stage. The importance of this scene is how it undermines any notion of "essentialist" blackness that would have viewers believe that the gangsterism these young black males embraced emerged from some unique black cultural experience.

When I interviewed rap artist Ice Cube for *Spin* magazine recently, he talked about the importance of respecting black women, of communication across gender. In our conversation, he spoke against male violence against women, even as he lapsed into a justification for antiwoman lyrics in rap by insisting on the madonna/whore split where some females "carry" themselves in a manner that determines how they will be treated. But when this interview came to press it was sliced to ribbons. Once again it was a mass media set-up. Folks (mostly white and male) had thought that if the hardcore feminist talked with the hardened mack, sparks would fly; there would be a knock-down, drag-out spectacle. When Brother Cube and myself talked to each other with respect about the political, spiritual and emotional self-determination of black people, it did not make good copy. I do not know if his public relations people saw the piece in its entirety and were worried that it would be too soft an image, but clearly folks at the magazine did not get the darky spectacle they were looking for.

After this conversation, and after talking with other rappers and folks who listen to rap, it became clear that while black male sexism is real and a serious problem in our communities, some of the more misogynist stuff in black music was there to stir up controversy, to appeal to audiences. Nowhere is this more evident than in the image used with Snoop Doggy Dogg's record *Doggystyle*. A black male music and cultural critic called me from across the ocean to ask if I had checked this image out, sharing that for one of the first times in his music-buying life he felt he was seeing an image so offensive in its sexism and misogyny he did not want to take it home. That image—complete with doghouse, "Beware the Dog" sign, a naked black female head in the doghouse, her naked butt sticking out—was reproduced "uncritically" in the November 29, 1993, issue of *Time* magazine. The positive music review of this album written by Christopher John Farley titled "Gangsta Rap, Doggystyle" makes no mention of sexism and misogyny, or any reference to the cover. If a naked white female body had been inside the doghouse, presumably waiting to be fucked from behind, I wonder if *Time* would have reproduced an image of the cover along with their review. When I see the pornographic cartoon that graces the cover of *Doggystyle* I do not think simply about the sexism and misogyny of young black men, I think about the sexist and misogynist politics of the powerful white adult men and women (and folks of color) who helped produce and market this album.

In her book *Misogynies*, Joan Smith shares her sense that while most folks are willing to acknowledge unfair treatment of women, discrimination on the basis of gender, they are usually reluctant to admit that hatred of women is encouraged because it helps maintain the structure of male dominance. Smith suggests, "Misogyny wears many guises, reveals itself in different forms—which are dictated by class, wealth, education, race, religion, and other factors, but its chief characteristic is its pervasiveness." This point reverberated in my mind when I saw Jane Campion's widely acclaimed film *The Piano*, which I saw in the midst of the mass media's focus on sexism and misogyny in gangsta rap. I had been told by many friends in the art world that this was "an incredible film, a truly compelling love story." Their responses were echoed by numerous positive reviews. No one speaking about this film mentions misogyny and sexism or white supremacist capitalist patriarchy, which blithely ignores how the nineteenth-century world of the white invasion of New Zealand and the conquest of femininity are utterly romanticized in this film.

A racist white imagination assumes that most young black males, especially those who are poor, live in a self-created cultural vacuum, uninfluenced by mainstream cultural values. Yet it is the application of those values, largely learned through passive, uncritical consumption of the mass media, that is most revealed in gangsta rap. Brent Staples is willing to challenge the notion that "urban primitivism is romantic" when it suggests that black males become "real men" by displaying the will to do violence, yet he remains resolutely silent about that world of privileged white culture that has historically romanticized primitivism and erotized male violence. Contemporary films like *Reservoir Dogs* and *The Bad Lieutenant* celebrate urban primitivism. Many of the artistically less successful films create or exploit the cultural demand for graphic depictions of hardcore macks who are willing to kill for sport.

To take gangsta rap to task for its sexism and misogyny while accepting and perpetuating expressions of that ideology which reflect bourgeois standards (no rawness, no vulgarity) is not to call for a transformation of the culture of patriarchy. Ironically, many black male ministers who are themselves sexist and misogynist are leading the attacks against gangsta rap. Like the mainstream world that supports white supremacist capitalist patriarchy, they are most concerned with advancing the cause of censorship by calling attention to the obscene portrayals of women. For them, rethinking and challenging sexism both in the dominant culture and in black life is not the issue.

Mainstream white culture is not at all concerned about black male sexism and misogyny, particularly when it is mainly unleashed against black women and children. It *is* concerned when young white consumers utilize black vernacular popular culture to disrupt bourgeois values. A young white boy expresses his rage at his mother by aping black male vernacular speech (a true story); young white males (and middle-class men of color) reject the constraints of bourgeois bondage and the call to be "civilized" by acts of aggression in their domestic households. These are the audiences who feel such a desperate need for gangsta rap. It is much easier to attack gangsta rap than to confront the culture that produces that need.

Gangsta rap is part of the antifeminist backlash that is the rage right now. When young black males labor in the plantations of misogyny and sexism to produce gangsta rap, white supremacist capitalist patriarchy approves the violence and materially rewards them. Far from being an expression of their "manhood," it is an expression of their own subjugation and humiliation by more powerful, less visible forces of patriarchal gangsterism. They give voice to the brutal, raw anger and rage against women that it is taboo for "civilized" adult men to speak. No wonder, then, that they have the task of tutoring the young, teaching them to eroticize and enjoy the brutal expressions of that rage (both language and acts) before they learn to cloak it in middle-class decorum or Robert Bly-style reclaimings of lost manhood. The tragedy for young black males is that they are so easily duped by a vision of manhood that can only lead to their destruction.

Feminist critiques of the sexism and misogyny in gangsta rap, and in all aspects of popular culture, must continue to be bold and fierce. Black females must not allow ourselves to be duped into supporting shit that hurts us under the guise of standing beside our men. If black men are betraying us through acts of male violence, we save ourselves and the race by resisting. Yet our feminist critiques of black male sexism fail as meaningful political interventions if they seek to demonize black males, and do not recognize that our revolutionary work is to transform white supremacist capitalist patriarchy in the multiple areas of our lives where it is made manifest, whether in gangsta rap, the black church, or in the Clinton administration.

Speculations

1. What does bell hooks mean by "the demonizing of black youth culture"? How does this demonizing maintain a negative cultural view of black men, forcing them to participate in their oppression?
2. What is hooks's criticism of Brent Staples's position on gangsta rap? Do you find her criticism persuasive? Explain your response.
3. hooks states that "A racist white imagination assumes that most young black males . . . live in a self-created cultural vacuum, uninfluenced by mainstream cultural values." How does her essay work to disprove this assumption? What specific examples does she use to reveal how this assumption perpetuates racial prejudice against black men? From your own observation of the media (advertising, TV, film, etc.), describe some images that fit this pattern.
4. How does hooks regard black ministers who condemn gangsta rap? Do you agree? Taking the opinion of Reverend Arthur Cribbs in the selection "Gangsta Rappers Sing White" as an example, explain your response to hooks's argument.

5. Given the system of domination described by hooks, who are the real gangsters? Who rewards young black men for their sexist violence against women? How are young black men "duped" by these gangsters? Who benefits and who suffers from this arrangement? Explain your responses in terms of what you have learned about rap music in this section.

REDEEMING THE RAP MUSIC EXPERIENCE

Venise Berry

Born in Kansas City in 1955, Venise Berry grew up in Des Moines, Iowa, where she attended public school. Receiving her B.A. and M.A. degrees from the University of Iowa and a Ph.D. from the University of Texas in Austin, she is currently an assistant professor at the University of Iowa School of Journalism and Mass Communication. In an interview with *Speculations*, Berry explained that "Growing up as an African-American in an environment like Iowa where only about two percent of the population is African-American gave me a different perspective on culture—a perspective not only different from the larger population of Iowans but also different from that of African-Americans in larger urban areas of the United States." Having published several scholarly articles on African-American images in the media, particularly music, television, and film, she is co-editing a forthcoming book called *Mediated Messages and African-American Culture: Contemporary Issues* (1996), has written a novel entitled *So Good* (1996), and is currently working on an historical account of actor and civil rights activist, Joel Fluellen, called *Cultural Politics in the Early Film Industry: The Life of Joel Fluellen 1909–1990.*

Berry explains how working for eight years as a professional news broadcaster at three different radio stations (KTSU and KCOH in Houston and KAZI in Austin) helped shape her identity as a writer: "Everything that you do becomes a part of your writing style. My scholarly writing benefits from my creative writing and oral broadcasting style, and developing research skills enhances all of my writing. All of your experiences work together to make you the kind of writer you eventually become." As the following selection demonstrates, Berry has achieved a clarity, balance, and readability in her prose style which is unusual for most academic researchers. She strives for a balance of fluency and factual presentation that will enable her to reach a wide audience, so that her academic research will be accessible to the public and participate in a larger conversation about learning, culture, and society. Berry gained first-hand knowledge of how black youths received rap music in the mid-1980s when she worked with junior high and high school-age black students who participated in the Upward Bound program at Huston-Tillotson College in Austin. Recognizing how profoundly the emerging rap scene influenced young black lives and the music industry, Berry integrates both her research and personal knowledge into the following account of rap's history and impact on our culture.

You know—parents are the same no matter time nor place.
They don't understand that us kids are gonna make some mistakes.
So to you other kids all across the land, there's no need to argue—
PARENTS JUST DON'T UNDERSTAND!
(DJ Jazzy Jeff and The Fresh Prince 1988)

When rap music first appeared on the scene, music critics said it wouldn't last, record companies felt it was too harsh and black-oriented to cross over, and parents dismissed it as the latest fad. Ten years later, rap has become a powerful and controversial force in American popular culture. Rap music has grown significantly from its humble street beginnings in Harlem and the South Bronx. It now encompasses a dominant media paradigm through traditional music vehicles like cassettes and CDs, as well as television coverage in videos and talk shows, rappers as actors, film themes, concerts, advertising, and other promotional components.

On *Billboard*'s top 200 album list on January 18, 1992, rappers were found as high as #3 and as low as #184. Despite, or maybe because of, the controversies, groups such as Hammer, Public Enemy, Ice Cube, Ghetto Boyz, Salt 'N Pepa, 2 Live Crew, NWA, Tone Loc, and Queen Latifah have reached mainstream popularity, and each success pushes the rap genre into new directions. Rap music is constantly testing the boundaries of commercialism, sexism, radicalism, feminism, and realism, and a growing concern over the music's disrespect for traditional boundaries keeps it on the cutting edge.

Current literature on rap music has taken varied approaches, from content analyses which analyze and critique images and messages, to trade articles which offer promotional information on the artists and their music. One of the most important, yet least explored, areas in this discourse is the relationship between the music and its fans; particularly those whom it represents: black urban youths.

Rap Music, Urban Reality, and Popular Culture

Popular culture is made by subordinated peoples in their own interests out of resources that also, contradictorily, serve the economic interests of the dominant. Popular culture is made from within and below, not imposed from without and above as mass cultural theorists would have it. There is always an element of popular culture that lies outside of social control, that escapes or opposes hegemonic forces. (Fiske, 1989)

The power and promise of rap music rests in the bosom of urban America; an environment where one out of twenty-two black males will be killed by violent crimes, where the black high-school dropout rate is as high as 72 percent and where 86 percent of black children grow up in poverty. Years of degradation, welfare handouts, institutional racism, and discrimination have created a community where little hope, low self-esteem and frequent failure translate into drugs, teen pregnancy, and gang violence. These are the social, cultural, and economic conditions which have spurred rap's paradoxical position within American popular culture.

The relationship between low socioeconomic status and the negative self-evaluation of black urban youth results in problems of low self-esteem. These feelings are prominent because of limited opportunities, unsatisfied needs, instability, estrangement, racial prejudice, and discrimination (Hulbary, 1975). As these youth struggle with questions of independence and control in their environment, they embrace a sense of powerlessness. Mainstream society tends to view the lifestyles of low-income communities as deviant. The poor are believed to be perpetuating their own poverty because of their nonconforming attitudes and unconventional behavior (Gladwin, 1967). Poussaint and Atkinson (1972) suggest that the stereotypes of deviance, a lack of motivation, and limited educational achievements ultimately become a part of their identity.

The youth movement which is evident in popular culture has, therefore, brought about only illusions for many urban American youth. The term "youth," which came to mean a specific attitude including pleasure, excitement, hope, power, and invincibility, was not experienced by these kids. Their future was mangled by racism, prejudice, discrimination, and economic and educational stagnation. As Bernard (1991) suggests, they found themselves in a gloomy darkness without friendship, trust, or hope; backed into a corner where life is all about self.

As a product of the black urban community, rap music is indisputably entangled with the struggle for black identity and legitimacy within mainstream society. Although rap music is undergoing significant changes, much of it remains true to its aesthetic purpose of bringing to the forefront the problematic nature of urban American experience.

Cultural rap music is, therefore, often seen in a negative light. The "culture of rap music" has been characterized as a "culture of attitude" by Adler (1990), who suggests that attitude is something civilized society abhors and likes to keep under control. He concludes that the end of attitude is nihilism, which by definition leads nowhere, and that the culture of attitude is repulsive, mostly empty of political content.

Costello and Wallace (1990), in *Signifying Rappers,* say that vitalists have argued for forty years that postwar art's ultimate expression will be a kind of enormous psychosocial excrement and the real aesthetic (conscious or otherwise) of today's best serious rap may be nothing but the first wave of this great peristalsis.

Negative images of rap are dominant in the news. The 2 Live Crew controversy in Florida concerning sexually explicit lyrics made big headlines, along with the charity basketball game by rap artists in New York which resulted in nine kids being trampled to death. Violence has also been reported at movies where rap themes are prominent. And, the music of defiant rap groups like NWA (Niggas With Attitude) have been considered radical and extremist. They made history as the first musical group to receive a warning from the FBI about the negative content of their song, "Fuck the Police," which encourages a lack of respect for the system.

Urban black American culture exists within a large infrastructure, segmented by various negative individual and situational environments. The relationship between the rap fan and his or her music, therefore, involves the larger contextual environment of the urban street. At the same time, it is important to recognize how the mainstream success of the rap genre has made urban language, style, dance, and attitude viable components of popular cultural form.

The Issue of Sex

The 2 Live Crew appeared in the public eye in 1986 with their first album, *The 2 Live Crew Is What We Are.* Their most successful hit, which is now considered tame, was entitled, "Hey, We Want Some Pussy." It sold a half-million copies without the backing of a major record company. The Crew's next album took sexual rap to a new level. *Move Something* sold more than a million copies and included songs like, "Head," "Booty and Cock," and "Me So Horny."

It was their third album, *As Nasty as We Wanna Be,* which made the group a household name. On June 6, 1990, U.S. District Judge Jose Gonzales, Jr., said the album was "utterly without any redeeming social value." The obscenity issue created a media bonanza for 2 Live Crew and boosted the sale of their album to more than two million copies.

Luther Campbell, leader of the group, has been on a number of talk shows and in many articles defending his right to produce sexually explicit rap music. In an interview in *Black Beat* magazine, he called the lyrics funny. "The stuff on our X-rated albums is meant to be funny.

We sit down and laugh about our lyrics. We don't talk about raping women or committing violence against them or anything like that" (Henderson, February 1990).

An analysis by Peterson-Lewis (1991) presents a different perspective: ". . . their lyrics lack the wit and strategic use of subtle social commentary necessary for effective satire; thus they do not so much debunk myths as create new ones, the major one being that in interacting with black women 'anything goes.' Their lyrics not only fail to satirize the myth of the hypersexual black, they also commit the moral blunder of sexualizing the victimization of women, black women in particular."

Campbell adds that the group's lyrics are a reflection of life in America's black neighborhoods. Yet he admits he won't let his seven-year-old daughter listen to such music. While 2 Live Crew served as the thrust of the controversy, the negative images of women in this society have been a concern of feminists for many years, through various media forms.

Peterson-Lewis goes on to question the extent of the ethical and moral responsibilities of artists to their audiences and the larger public. She focuses her argument on the constitutionality and racially motivated persecution and prosecution of 2 Live Crew, which she feels overshadowed the real criticism—the sexually explicit nature of their lyrics and their portrayal of women as objects for sexual assault.

Frankel (1990) agrees that the 2 Live Crew situation took away the real focus. She says the attack on the 2 Live Crew group made it an issue of censorship, racism, and free speech, rather than an issue of disgust at how women are portrayed, especially since an act like Andrew Dice Clay, who also promotes women and sex from a negative perspective, has not been sanctioned by the law.

Even though the controversy about sexually explicit lyrics in rap music has become a heated issue, out of a list of the top fifty rap groups, only about 10 percent can actually be identified as using truly obscene and violent lyrics in relation to women. An analysis of the number of more generally negative images of females as loose and whorish would probably double that percentage.

In a discussion on the subject of sex in rap with a group of Upward Bound high school juniors and seniors, there was a split on the 2 Live Crew issue. Bené said their records contain too much profanity and are obscene, so maybe they should be sold in X-rated stores. Steve felt that fifteen- and sixteen-year-olds are able to drive, and if they can be trusted with their lives in a car, why not be trusted to select their own music? Tamara compared the group's lyrics to the Playboy channel or magazine, and wondered why access to 2 Live Crew's music is not limited as well. Marty said that teenagers are still going to get the album if they want it, despite warning labels. Finally, Dewan explained that the warning labels can't stop the sexual things teens think in their minds.

When asked about record censorship, most of them felt that some kind of censorship was acceptable for kids ages twelve and under. But they also cited television, movies, and magazines as the places where they usually receive new sexual information, rather than music.

Female rappers like Salt 'N Pepa, Queen Latifah, Yo Yo, and MC Lyte have stepped forward to dispel many of the negative images of women with their own lyrical rhetoric and aggressive performance style. Yo Yo, a popular nineteen-year-old female rapper, says that she got into rap to help improve women's self-esteem because a lot of black women don't believe in themselves. She has created an organization for teenage women called the Intelligent Black Women's Coalition (IBWC), which speaks on issues of social concern.

In direct opposition to positive female rappers are the controversial groups, Bytches wit' Problems and Hoes wit' Attitude. According to Lyndah and Michelle of Bytches wit' Problems, "There's a little bitch in all women, and even some men . . . and we're just the bitches to say it" (October 1991). Lyndah and Michelle's new album, *B.Y.T.C.H.E.S.*, reflects another side of black urban reality. They feel they can say what they want just like men do, which is evident from their songs "Two Minute Brother," "Fuck a Man," and "Is the Pussy Still Good." Their definition of a bitch is "a powerful woman in control of her life, going after what she wants and saying what's on her mind" (October 1991).

The female trio, Hoes wit' Attitude, has been called the raunchiest all-girl rap group. With hit songs like "Eat This," "Little Dick," and "Livin' in a Hoe House," they constantly test their motto, "If men can do it we can too." The girls, 2 Jazzy, Baby Girl, and D. Diva, argue that "hoein' is the oldest profession, whether you're sellin' your body or something else. A hoe is a business woman. We're in business, the business of selling records."

When asked about their perceptions of such aggressive female images, the discussion group of Upward Bound students again split. Lanietra said, "All women are not like that and the words they use to describe themselves are not necessary." Louis felt rappers don't actually use the lyrics they sing about as a personal thing with another person, they are using the lyrics to warn people about the females and males of today. Tonje added concern that such rap music makes females seem like sex objects that can only be used to satisfy a man's needs.

These youth easily identified specific popular songs which had messages that were positive and negative in relation to sex. The top three songs named as "good for moral thinking" were "Let's Wait Awhile" by Janet Jackson; "Growing Up" by Whodini; and "I Need

Love" by L L Cool J. The top three songs listed as "bad for moral thinking about sex" were "Hey, We Want Some Pussy" by the 2 Live Crew; "I Want Your Sex" by George Michael; and "Kanday" by L L Cool J.

The Issue of Violence

Another prominent issue which seems to follow the rap music phenomenon is violence. On December 28, 1991, nine youths were trampled to death at a charity basketball game with rap artists at City College in New York. On July 12, 1991, Alejandra Phillips, a supermarket clerk, was shot outside a theater showing of *Boyz N' the Hood.* Cultural rap is often connected with such negative images of the black underclass. Pictures of pimps, drug dealers, and gang members riding around with rap music blasting loudly are prevalent in the media. Scholars like Jon Spencer have questioned the link between rap and rape made by Tipper Gore's editorial in *The Washington Post,* "Hate, Rape, and Rap" and the juxtapositioning of the 2 Live Crew's lyrics with the rape of a New York jogger in Central Park. Spencer suggests that when people see the word "rap" they read the word "rape," and they often view "rappists" as rapists.

One of the groups most publicized when exploring violence are NWA. NWA consists of five L.A. rappers whose controversial lyrics include topics like gang banging, drive-by shootings, and police confrontations. MTV refused to air their video, "Straight Outta Compton," because they said it "glorified violence." The ex-leader of the group, Ice Cube, says the group's lyrics deal with reality and violence is their reality. "Our goals are to show the audience the raw reality of life. When they come out the other end they gonna say, 'damn, it's like that for real?' And, we're gonna make money" (Hochman, 1989).

Williams (1990) disagrees that rap images and music are representative of the beliefs and ethics of black communities. He says when women are treated like sex slaves and ideas like "materialism is God" are put forth, they are not true visions of black America or black culture, but a slice of the worst of a small element of black culture that is not emblematic of the black community at large.

The positive efforts of black rappers to eliminate violence in their music and neighborhoods have not received as much publicity as the negative. For example, various popular rap stars from the West Coast such as NWA, Hammer, Young MC, and Digital Underground came together to record a single entitled "We're All in the Same Gang." It was a rap song that spoke out against the senseless violence of gangs.

The East Coast's "Stop the Violence" campaign raised more than $300,000 for youth-oriented community programs in New York. More than a dozen rappers, like Ice T, Tone Loc, and King Tee participated in the "Self Destruction" record and video which addressed the need to end black-on-black crime. The powerful lyrics and images of the song brought a new positive black urban consciousness into focus. As the song points out:

> Back in the sixties our brothers and sisters
> were hanged, how could you gangbang?
> I never ran from the Ku Klux Klan, and I shouldn't have to
> run from a black man.
> 'Cause that's self-destruction, self-destruction, you're
> headed for self-destruction.

Kids are forced to learn from the rhythm of life around them. Rap songs often include graphic images of drug dealers. The drug dealer is a very real personality in low-income neighborhoods. When asked to write down three questions they would include on a drug survey, Tamara asked, "Why do they (adults, authorities) allow the pushers to sell drugs on the corner by my school?" She later told me that it was very obvious what happens on that corner, but nobody bothers to do anything about it, so kids come to accept it too.

There is an obvious struggle going on in these kids' lives that links them to the conflict-oriented nature of cultural rap. The violent urban environment which is a prominent theme in rap music is also a prominent reality. One example of that reality came from a worksheet concerning a rap tune called "Wild Wild West" by Kool Moe Dee. In the song, Kool Moe Dee raps about how he and his buddies stop others (including gangs) from coming into their neighborhoods and terrorizing people. He talks about taking control of his environment in a fashion appropriate to the Old West. In response to the song, Mary said she could relate to it because in her neighborhood, people are always getting into other people's personal business. Tim also knew what Kool Moe Dee was talking about because he and his homeboys (friends) were always scuffling (fighting) with somebody for respect. Michael said the song means that kids are growing up too hard in the streets. He added, "My school and neighborhood are a lot like that." Finally, James said he had a friend who got shot at a party "because of the way he looked at a guy and that's just how it is."

On a more positive side, several of the kids have come to understand and change these negatives through their own raps. The Get It Girl Crew, four young ladies who love to rap, wrote the rap below as a testimony of their spirit and hope for the future.

> Tricky B, Lady J, Lady Love and Kiddy B from up above,
> we're the Get it Girl Crew and we're doing the do.
> And, yes when we're on the mic we're talking to you,
> homeboys and homegirls, with your jheri curls,
> we'll blow you away, knock out those curls.

This is a rap for World Wide peace,
listen to my rhyme while my beat's released.
White and black, we're not the same color,
but in this world we're sisters and brothers.
I'll say this rhyme till my dying day,
I'd rather be dead, dead in my grave.
You talk about me and put my name down,
but when I take revenge I put your face in the ground.
This is Baby Rock in the place to be,
throwing a def rap on the M.I.C.
The Get it Girl Crew, there is none finer,
'cause we're the freshest and we're on fire.
We're the Get it Girl Crew with strength from above
We need peace, unity and love!

The Issue of Racism

The issue of race in America is not a silent one today. Separate ideologies of black power and white supremacy are prominent and dividing the nation even further as indicated by an ex-KKK leader, David Duke, running for public office, the travesty of Rodney King's beating and trial in Los Angeles that ignited riots, and the powerful slogan of Malcolm X, "By any means necessary," as reemerging popular black ideology.

According to Pareles (1992), rap often sounds like a young black man shouting about how angry he is and how he's going to hurt people. Pareles says, "Rap's internal troubles reflect the poverty, violence, lack of education, frustration and rage of the ghetto. . . . Hating rap can be a synonym for hating and fearing young black men who are also the stars of rap."

Samuels (1991) voices concern about the acceptance of racism in this country through rap. He writes, "Gangster and racist raps foster a voyeurism and tolerance of racism in which black and white are both complicit, particularly when whites treat gangster raps as a window into ghetto life."

Until recently, Public Enemy was the rap group who seemed to be in the middle of the racist controversy. In response to the negative environment in the United States concerning race relations, rapper Chuck D (1990) of Public Enemy makes statements such as "a black person is better off dealing with a Klansman than a liberal." He goes on to quote Neely Fuller, Jr.'s, definition of a white liberal: "a white person who speaks and/or acts to maintain, expand and/or refine the practice of white supremacy (racism) by very skillfully pretending not to do so." Public Enemy has also called for the reorganization of the Black Panther party, a group considered radical in the 1960s that advocated violence and racism.

Public Enemy emerged into the headlines as racist when an ex-member, Professor Griff, made several statements that were considered anti-Semitic in a speech. Griff's comment involved his belief that Jews financed the slave trade and are responsible for apartheid in South Africa. He went on to ask, "Is it a coincidence that Jews run the jewelry business and it's named jew-elry?" (Dougherty, 1990.)

After firing Professor Griff, Chuck D responded to his comments in *Billboard* magazine. "We aren't anti-Jewish. We're pro-black," he said. "We're pro-culture, we're pro-human race. You can't talk about attacking racism and be racist" (Newman, 1989). According to Chuck D, the group is not here to offend anyone, but to fight the system which works against blacks twenty-four hours a day, 365 days a year. He adds, "We're not racists, we're nationalists, people who have pride and want to build a sense of unity amongst our own" (Newman, 1989).

Ice Cube is the second most prominent rapper to be labeled racist because of several controversial songs on his hit album, *Death Certificate*. He calls Koreans "Oriental one-penny motherfuckers" and lambasts members of his old group, NWA, about their Jewish manager. He raps, "Get rid of that Devil, real simple, put a bullet in his temple, 'cause you can't be the nigger for life crew, with a white Jew telling you what to do." In response to the criticism, Ice Cube says people need to pay heed to the frustration as they [black men] demand respect.

Ideology from the Nation of Islam, which is often called racist, is a major part of the controversy. Many rappers are reviving the words of black leaders like Elijah Muhammad and Louis Farrakhan, calling the white society devils and snakes, and advocating a new black solidarity. Several popular rappers are actually emerging from the Nation of Islam calling themselves "The 5 Percenters." These artists base their raps on the Islamic belief that only about 5 percent of the black nation knows that the black man *is* God and it's their duty to teach others.

Finally, racism is sometimes attributed to the Afrocentric voice; the pro-black attitude. The controversial KRS-One (Knowledge Reigns Supreme over Nearly Everyone) condemns gang violence, poor educational systems, and drug use, but his attack on the "white system" has been called racially motivated. At fourteen, KRS One was a homeless runaway sleeping on steaming New York City sidewalk grates. At twenty-four, he has become a popular, positive rap star and educator. Queen Latifah is one of the most positive and powerful black female rappers. Her albums are rich in African cultural ideology and images as she dresses in African garb and tells kids that all black men and women are kings and queens. Queen Latifah believes that the only way to fight bigotry is to teach black children their history.

Cultural rap is so direct and angry that it can be frightening to those who don't understand the frustration of these storytellers. For example, the decision not to honor the birthday of Martin Luther King, Jr., as a holiday in Arizona brought forth a rap from NWA with the theme "Gonna find a way to make the state pay" and the video portrayed the violent murders of several Arizona officials. Militant rapper Paris, on his album debut, *The Devil Made Me Do It*, presents a powerful, hard-edged commentary on the murder of Yousuf Hawkins in Bensonhurst called "The Hate that Hate Made." And the logo of Public Enemy shows the black male youth as a hunted animal with the motto "Kill or Be Killed." The image of a black silhouette is chilling within the crosshairs of a gun.

When Upward Bound students were asked to respond to the worksheet question, "How has growing up black, in your opinion, made a difference in your life?" a theme ran through the responses: the need to struggle or fight. Carlos, for instance, said being black causes him to struggle more for what he wants. He said, "At school, on TV, everywhere, other people get the things they want, but not me." Titus and Karon felt they had to fight a lot because of the color of their skin. "Fighting," according to Titus, "not only with people of other races." Damon explained, "Color really doesn't matter, but just because I'm black people expect me to be able to play sports and fight." When Damon went on to list the things which he felt might hinder him in his future success, his list included skin color, money, and friends.

As a whole, the group split on the issue of whether or not they felt their skin color would affect their future. About half agreed with the statement "In the past, my skin color would have hindered my success, but that is not true today," and the other half disagreed.

When asked if they see Public Enemy, NWA, and other black-conscious rappers as role models and heroes, the group said yes unanimously. As William explained, "They say what's going on in their hearts and that's what needs to be said." John added, "When brothers keep the pain inside they explode and that happens a lot around here." Nichole says she owns all of Public Enemy's tapes and she feels their music is important to help white people understand how black people feel about what's happening in black communities.

Conclusion

The history of black music is a history of adaptation, rebellion, acculturation, and assimilation. An essential part of black music rests inherently in black experience. As we look closely, we realize that black music has always been a communicative response to the pressures and challenges within black American society.

The cultural rap music experience exists within the realm of specific environmental contexts. For the black urban adolescent, the environment manifests itself through their most popular music choice: rap. As they listen, they construct both shared and personal realities. Rappers rising from this context are empowering storytellers. Their oral wit and unique street style create a purposeful presence for inner-city ideology. Rap music has become the champion of an otherwise ignored and forgotten reality. Through critical spoken song, rappers are forcing cultural realities into the public arena. Rap music, therefore, serves not only as a mirror to this problematic community, but as a catalyst for it, providing legitimacy and hope.

Within popular culture, rap music has increased the sense of awareness outside urban black America and interrupted normal flow of the commercialization process with a large dose of substance. Cultural musics, such as rap, often get caught in a repetitive cycle of acculturation, and are gradually absorbed into the pop mode. But, in opposition to pop-crossover rap, cultural rap has somehow managed to maintain elements which lie outside of social control, and escape the oppressive hegemonic forces.

Fiske's (1989) observations about such resistance and popular culture can be applied to the rap phenomenon. "The resistances of popular culture are not just evasive or semiotic; they do have a social dimension at the micro-level. And at this micro-level, they may well act as a constant erosive force upon the macro, weakening the system from within so that it is more amenable to change at the structural level." This is the power and promise of cultural rap.

The negative climate toward rap has been challenged by various scholars as inaccurate and inadequate. Spencer (1991) believes that the current emergence of rap is a by-product of the "emergency of black." He connects rap ideology to the racial concerns of scholar Manning Marable, saying, "This emergency still involves the dilemma of the racial color-line, but it is complicated by the threat of racial genocide, the obliteration of all black institutions, the political separation of the black elite from the black working class, and the benign decimation of the 'ghetto poor,' who are perceived as nonproduction and therefore dispensable."

Dyson (1991) views rap music as a form of profound musical, cultural, and social creativity. He says, "It expresses the desire of young black people to reclaim their history, reactivate forms of black radicalism, and contest the powers of despair, hopelessness, and genocide that presently besiege the black community. . . . It should be promoted as a worthy form of artistic expression and cultural projection, and as an enabling source of community solidarity."

Finally, Stephens (1991) sees rap music as a "crossroad to a new transnational culture." He believes that "by conceptualizing rap as an intercultural communication crossroads located on a racial frontier, we can conceive how rap's non-black constituents use this artform as an interracial bridge, even as many blacks by defining it as 'only black' attempt to use it as a source of power and exclusive identity formation."

In considering such a transnational culture, the source of rap's popularity for white youth is then, less difficult to ascertain. It is obvious, however, that the rebellious nature of rap in many ways parallels the rebellious nature of original rock and roll. Grossberg (1987), in discussing rock and roll today, says that the practice of critical encapsulation divides the cultural world into Us and Them. "While being a rock and roll fan," he goes on to explain, "sometimes does entail having a visible and self-conscious identity (such as punks, hippies, or mods), it more often does not appear visibly, on the surface of a fan's life, or even as a primary way in which most fans would define themselves."

Rap is also seen as an icon of resentment to the white status quo. According to Spencer, as in any situation where an icon such as rap is attacked, there is always the potential that the attention will grant the music even further symbolic potency and, as a result, increase the population of listeners who subscribe to its newly broadened symbolism of protest.

As rock music sinks deeper into the mainstream, cultural rap music has risen as a new rebellious youth movement. Self-understanding and practice are important elements in the cultural mirror of rap music style and it has fostered a liberating transcultural understanding. This rap experience becomes an all-encompassing one, which includes the outward projection and acceptance of rebellious identity and beliefs for all who listen.

I believe that through rap music, low-income black youth are able to develop empowering values and ideologies, strengthen cultural interaction and establish positive identities. Rap music acts as a distinguishing mechanism as well as an informative cultural force for the mainstream system, similar to other cultural musics such as heavy metal and punk. As an integral part of the urban experience, the rap genre serves as a bridge from favorite songs and artists to personal and social realities. It is easy to see why mainstream society would feel uncomfortable with the sudden popularity of traditionally negative images like dope dealers, pimps, and prostitutes in rap music. Yet these are very real images and messages in the everyday world of the rapper and his original fan: the black urban youth.

Rap music offers itself up as a unique and cohesive component of urban black culture and is a positive struggle for black signification within popular culture. While there remain conflicts between negative and positive, right and wrong, good and bad, the rap dynamic is an explicit means of cultural communication fostering a crucial awareness of a reawakening urban reality.

REFERENCES

Adler, Jerry, "The Rap Attitude," *Newsweek,* March 19, 1990, p. 59.

Bernard, James, "Bitches and Money," *The Source.* November 1991, p. 8.

Berry, Venise, "The Complex Relationship between Pop Music and Low-Income Black Adolescents: A Qualitative Approach," Dissertation, The University of Texas at Austin, May 1989.

Chuck D, "Black II Black," *SPIN,* 6, October 1990, pp. 67–68.

Cocks, Jay, "A Nasty Jolt for the Top Pops," *Time,* July 1, 1991, p. 78.

Cone, James, *The Spirituals and the Blues,* New York: Seabury Press, 1972.

Costello, Mark, and David Foster Wallace, *Signifying Rappers: Rap and Race in the Urban Present,* New York: The Ecco Press, 1990.

Dixon, Wheeler, "Urban Black American Music in the Late 1980s: The 'Word' as Cultural Signifier," *The Midwest Quarterly,* 30, Winter 1989, pp. 229–241.

Dougherty, Steve, "Charges of Anti-Semitism Give Public Enemy a Rep That's Tough to Rap Away," *People Weekly,* 33, March 5, 1990, pp. 40–41.

Dyson, Michael, "Performance, Protest and Prophecy in the Culture of Hip Hop," *Black Sacred Music: A Journal of Theomusicology,* 5, Spring 1991, p. 24.

Fiske, John, *Reading the Popular,* Boston: Unwin Hyman, 1989.

Frankel, Martha, "2 Live Doo Doo," *SPIN,* 6, October 1990, p. 62.

Garland, Phyl, *The Sound and Soul: Story of Black Music,* New York: Simon and Schuster, 1971.

Gates, David, "Decoding Rap Music," *Newsweek,* March 19, 1990, pp. 60–63.

Gladwin, Thomas, *Poverty U.S.A.,* Boston: Little, Brown, 1967.

Green, Kim, "Sisters Stompin' in the Tradition," *Young Sisters and Brothers,* November 1991, pp. 51–53.

———, "The Naked Truth," *The Source,* November 1991, pp. 33–36.

Grossberg, Lawrence, "Rock and Roll in Search of an Audience," in *Popular Music and Communication,* Ed. James Lull, Beverly Hills: Sage Publishing, 1987, pp. 175–198.

Gurevitch, Michael, *Culture, Society and the Media,* London: Methuen, 1982.

Haring, Bruce, "Lyric Concerns Escalate," *Billboard,* 101, November 11, 1989, p. 1.

Henderson, Alex, "New Rap Pack: Public Enemy," *Black Beat,* 20, January 1989, p. 44.

———, "2 Live Crew," *Black Beat,* 21, February 1990, p. 15–16.

———, "LA Rap All Stars: We're All in the Same Gang," *Black Beat,* 21, December 1990, p. 16.

Hochman, Steve, "NWA Cops an Attitude," *Rolling Stone*, 555, June 29, 1989, p. 24.

Hulbary, William, "Race, Deprivation and Adolescent Self-Images," *Social Science Quarterly*, 56, June 1975, pp. 105–114.

Kofsky, Frank, *Black Nationalism and the Revolution in Music*, New York: Pathfinder Press, 1970.

Kot, Greg, "Rap Offers a Soundtrack of Afro-American Experience," *Chicago Sunday Times*, February 16, 1992, Section 13, pp. 5, 24–25.

Leland, John, "Cube on Thin Ice," *Newsweek*, December 2, 1991, p. 69.

Levine, David, "Good Business, Bad Messages," *American Health*, May 1991, p. 16.

Logan, Andy, "Around City Hall," *The New Yorker*, January 27, 1992, pp. 64–65.

Lyndah and Michelle (Bytches wit' Problems), "A Bitch is a Badge of Honor for Us," *Rappages*, 1, October 1991, p. 46.

Maultsby, Portia, "Soul Music: Its Sociological and Political Significance in American Popular Culture," *Journal of Popular Culture*, 17, Fall 1983, pp. 51–60.

Miller, Trudy, "'91 Holiday-Week Biz 3.7% Jollier than '90," *Billboard*, February 1, 1992, p. 46.

Mills, David, "The Obscenity Case: Criminalizing Black Culture," *Washington Post*, June 17, 1990, pp. G1, G8–G9.

———, "Five Percent Revolution," *Washington Post*, January 6, 1991, pp. G–1, G–6.

Nelson, Angela, "Theology in the Hip Hop of Public Enemy and Kool Moe Dee," *Black Sacred Music: A Journal of Theomusicology*, 5, Spring 1991, pp. 51–60.

Newman, Melinda, "Public Enemy Ousts Member over Remarks," *Billboard*, 101, July 1, 1989, pp. 1, 87.

"Paralyzed Man Files Suit over Boyz N' the Hood," *Jet*, 18, April 20, 1992, p. 61.

Pareles, Jon, "Fear and Loathing Along Pop's Outlaw Trail," *New York Times*, February 2, 1992, pp. 1, 23.

Perkins, William, "Nation of Islam Ideology in the Rap of Public Enemy," *Black Sacred Music: A Journal of Theomusicology*, 5, Spring, 1991, pp. 41–51.

Peterson-Lewis, Sonja, "A Feminist Analysis of the Defenses of Obscene Rap Lyrics," *Black Sacred Music: A Journal of Theomusicology*, 5, Spring 1991, pp. 68–80.

Poussaint, Alvin, and Carolyn Atkinson, "Black Youth and Motivation," in *Black Self Concept*, Ed. James Banks and Jean Grambs, New York, McGraw-Hill, 1972, pp. 55–69.

Riley, Norman, "Footnotes of a Culture at Risk," *The Crisis*, 93, March 1986, p. 24.

Roberts-Thomas, K., "Say It Loud I'm Pissed and I'm Proud," *Eight Rock*, 1, Summer 1990, pp. 28–31.

Rogers, Charles, "New Age Rappers with a Conscience," *Black Beat*, 20, April 1989, pp. 41, 75.

Royster, Phillip, "The Rapper as Shaman for a Band of Dancers of the Spirit: 'U Can't Touch This'," *Black Sacred Music: A Journal of Theomusicology*, 5, Spring 1991, pp. 60–68.

Samuels, David, "The Rap on Rap," *The New Republic*, 205, November 11, 1991, pp. 24–26.

Shusterman, Richard, "The Fine Art of Rap," *New Literary History*, 22, Summer 1991, pp. 613–632.

Singletary, Sharon, "Livin' in a Hoe House?" *Rappages*, 1, October 1991, p. 60.

Spencer, Jon Michael, "The Emergency of Black and the Emergence of Rap: Preface," *Black Sacred Music: A Journal of Theomusicology*, 5, Spring 1991, pp. v–vii.

Standifer, James, "Music Behavior of Blacks in American Society," *Black Music Research Journal*, 1, 1980, pp. 51–62.

Stephens, Gregory, "Rap Music's Double Voiced Discourse: A Crossroads for Interracial Communication," *Journal of Communication Inquiry*, 15, Summer 1991, p. 72.

Stephens, Ronald, "Three Waves of Contemporary Rap Music," in *Black Sacred Music: A Journal of Theomusicology*, 5, Spring 1991, pp. 25–41.

"Top 200 Albums," *Billboard*, January 18, 1992, p. 86.

Walton, Ortiz, *Music Black, White and Blue*, New York: William Morrow and Co., 1972.

Williams, Juan, "The Real Crime: Making Heroes of Hate Mongers," *Washington Post*, June 17, 1990, pp G–1, G–8.

Speculations

1. According to Berry, what keeps rap music on the "cutting edge" and what conditions have spurred on its "paradoxical position in American popular culture"? How are these two factors related in shaping the influence and appeal of rap music?

2. What distinctions does Berry make between the "youth movement" of popular culture and the experience of black urban youths? Do you agree with the distinctions that Berry makes concerning black urban youths? Explain your response.

3. Why does Berry title her piece "Redeeming the Rap Music Experience"? What perceptions of rap music does her argument try to overturn and how well does she succeed? Support your response with specific examples.

4. Do you agree with Berry's views about sexually explicit and offensive lyrics in rap music? Do you agree with the responses to this issue from black youths in the "Upward Bound" program? Explain your preferences and how you feel about the public broadcasting of such lyrics.

5. Do you agree that people outside the ghetto hate rap music as "a synonym for hating and fearing young black men who are also the stars of rap"? Explain the implications behind this statement and why you agree or disagree.

6. In her conclusion, Berry lists several important effects of rap on the larger culture as well as important ways in which rap works to define black culture. Make a numbered list of these points and, according to your own judgment, order it from most important to least important. Explain your list and its order.

Assignment Sequences

Sequence One: Rap Music—Positive or Negative?

1. Devise a survey of eight to ten questions on the controversies surrounding rap music. Include two parts to your questionnaire: one to determine individuals' familiarity with rap and the other to ask about more specific issues. For example, devise some basic questions about rap in Part I of the survey such as: "How familiar are you with rap music? (Respond on a scale of 1 to 5 where 1 is 'not at all' and 5 is 'extremely familiar.')" and "Is your basic response to rap music negative or positive? (Respond on a scale of 1 to 5, where 1 is 'very negative' and 5 is 'very positive.')." In Part II of the survey, devise open-ended questions which focus on specific controversies (offensive lyrics, sexism, violence, and other issues). Only people who indicate in Part I that they have some familiarity with rap music can fairly respond to Part II. Submit your questionnaire to as many people as you can until you get at least seven or eight who can respond to Part II. Write an essay that analyzes what you've learned from the survey results and whether your findings agree or disagree with what you've learned from reading about rap music in *Speculations.*

2. Jerry Adler's essay on "The Rap Attitude" describes how some rap lyrics express opinions that support violence, sexism, and racism while other rap lyrics are not offensive at all and even support positive anti-drug messages. Adler finally argues that rap's negative "culture of attitude is repulsive" and that this kind of music will lead nowhere. Other authors in *Speculations* either disagree or agree with Adler. Where do you stand on this issue? Do you agree or disagree with Adler? Write a paper that analyzes Adler's arguments and explores your responses using examples from your own experience and your reading.

3. It is often the lyrics of rap music, especially gangsta rap, that incur the most severe criticism of authors such as Jerry Adler and Arthur Cribbs. Do some research on your own to find lyrics from at least two songs by rap groups. You may have albums of your own, borrow some from friends, or go to the library and find articles or

books on rap that reprint such lyrics. In the light of what Adler and Cribbs say, write a paper that closely analyzes the images, diction, symbolism, and message of the lyrics. Do the lyrics tell a story? How is language used—to shock, entertain, or express feelings? What do the lyrics mean to you and how would you judge the social value of these lyrics?

4. One of the arguments made by Ice-T in the quote in the introduction to this section is that rap does not cause violence. He argues that if you removed rap from the ghetto, you will still have violence because violence is a result of economic deprivation. Francis Davis and Venise Berry similarly argue that rap is often an expression of rage and frustration from an oppressed segment of our population. Based on your own experience and your reading in *Speculations*, write an essay exploring the causes of violent rap lyrics and their effects on society. As Francis Davis does at the end of his essay, you might relate rap to violent images in film and video or to violence in urban America.

5. As authors who have lived and worked in black communities, Arthur Cribbs, bell hooks, and Venise Berry have a great deal to say about how rap music affects blacks and how it relates to the concerns of African-Americans. Write an essay in which you present the different views of these three writers on rap music and explain which you find most persuasive.

6. Based on your writing for the essays above and a careful rereading of specific selections on rap music, create a list of negative and positive responses to rap music. Examine your list and form your own opinion on the value of rap music. Do you think rap music has a positive or negative effect on our culture? Or is it possible to argue a position somewhere between these two extremes? You may choose to rewrite Assignment 2 into a longer paper for this assignment in which you begin with a response to Adler and expand into an editorial essay presenting your opinion on rap music and the reasons supporting your opinion.

Sequence Two: Rap Music and Social Change

1. Jerry Adler and Arthur Cribbs argue about rap music along lines very similar to Allan Bloom's argument about rock music: they each feel that these forms of music have no socially redeeming values. In fact, at the beginning of his essay, Adler asks "What ever happened to the idea that rock and roll would make us free?" After examining rap music, he concludes that the one thing we learned from the 1960s is "how *little* power rock and roll has to change the world." Are Adler and Cribbs right about rap music and its lack of

social value? Based on your experience, do you think rap will fail to bring about social change? Why or why not? Write an essay responding to these questions.

2. Francis Davis makes a complex argument about how younger generations will always try to distinguish their values and interests from those of their parents and Venise Berry argues that like rock and roll before it, rap music's rebellious nature helps provide young people with a "visible and self-conscious identity," "self-understanding," and in the case of low-income, black youths, it helps to "develop empowering values and ideologies." Can the social goals of rap music be compared to the goals that Tori Amos pursues for women or to the outlet for self-expression provided by Kurt Cobain's music? Based on your experience of how young people receive and listen to popular music and the readings in *Speculations,* write an essay describing your perspective of the "youth movement." What ideologies or beliefs have you gained from growing up with specific kinds of popular music? How do your parents' musical experiences differ from yours? How is your experience similar to or dissimilar to the culture of rap music?

3. bell hooks argues that "gansta rap" reinforces black males' sexist attitudes toward women, but she also says that this is an expression of black males' "subjugation and humiliation by more powerful, less visible forces of patriarchal gangersterism." Write a paper in which you explain hooks's argument and its implications. Refer to Adler, Cribbs, or Berry for additional examples of sexism.

4. Identify a rap group that you think has a social message, even if it is a message with which you do not completely agree. Select a song that is especially representative of the group's message—you may get it from an album or a video. Type out the lyrics to the song and write an analysis of those lyrics, explaining the message they contain, and why you think the message is important. Refer to selections from *Speculations* to support your argument as needed.

5. Building on Assignment 4, show the rap lyrics you've typed to several people, including friends, relatives, classmates, or teachers—try to get a mixture of men and women as well as older and younger people. If possible, play the recording or the video for these people. Ask them about their responses to the lyrics and what they think of the lyrics? Be sure to ask about negative and positive impressions and the social message of the music. Take careful notes on their responses, and write a paper summarizing and analyzing how people responded to the social message of the music. Explain how and why the responses of others were differ-

ent from, or similar to, your own. Be prepared to share your chosen lyrics and findings in class.

6. One of the pervasive themes throughout this section is how rap music relates to and influences the larger culture in which it exists. Some authors argue that its influence is negative or without lasting merit. Others point to the way that rap music is being absorbed into mainstream culture and changing styles in the youth culture. All seem to agree that it is an index of some kind of change in social behavior. Francis Davis says flatly that rap is "the only thing happening right now" that has larger cultural significance. Venise Berry sums up: "right or wrong, good or bad, the rap dynamic is an explicit means of cultural communication fostering a crucial awareness of a reawakening urban reality." Write an essay in which you discuss the likely future of rap music as a social force. In addition to readings from *Speculations*, go to the library and find out what critics and authors are saying about rap this year. Consult with the reference librarian if you have difficulty finding information. Use these sources to argue whether you think rap will be assimilated into mainstream music, maintain its separate but vital presence as an indicator of social change, or simply fade away. What are the implications of your choice among these three possibilities?

3

CRIME
——— AND ———
PUNISHMENT

America is virtually obsessed with crime—and with punishment. We see a barrage of media reports on teens killing for clothes, children killing children, rampant illegal drug use, robberies, burglaries, assaults, illegal dumping of toxic chemicals, embezzlements, stock frauds, and white-collar corruption. According to some reports, at the current rate of incarceration, 25 years from now half of all Americans will be in prison and the other half will be guarding them.

For black men, the situation is already at crisis stage. According to author Salim Muwakkil writing in a 1993 issue of *In These Times*:

> One out of every two African-American men is likely to be arrested during his lifetime, and a black man is 7.5 times more likely to be incarcerated than a white man. Black men total about 6 percent of the population but 44 percent of prison inmates.

Nor are wealth and fame sufficient deterrents, as the recent cases of Mike Tyson, William Kennedy Smith, and O. J. Simpson remind us. It is also interesting to note that those cases swirl around issues of gender, of male/female relations. Thus two of the crucial subtexts in America's discussion about crime concern those most controversial subjects—race and gender; this is one of the reasons that the debate can heat up to a critical mass so quickly.

Aside from issues of race and gender, almost all of us have a strong interest in the cruelties and complexities of crime. Movies and television shows abound featuring inspirational law enforcement officers, serious and silly superheroes, despicable villains, cops, bad boys, and "America's Most Wanted." Many people in America line up hours before court convenes so that they can sit in the back of the room and observe the trial of a mass murderer or celebrity felon—or they subscribe to Court TV and watch for hours at home as trials tediously unfold. It is as if we hope to glimpse something forbidden or mysterious on the other side of the glass; criminality and its attendant consequences lurk at the edges of our sensibilities—and we flirt with the possibility. Perhaps our interest derives from identification: there but for the grace of God go I.

This section of *Speculations,* however, attempts to move us past prurient and psychoanalytic interests to a consideration of crime and punishment within the larger context of socio-economic, racial, and gender issues. It circles around a series of questions: What factors encourage a person to break the law? Who within our society gets labeled a criminal? What constitutes a crime? What is the relationship between law and justice? What happens to convicted felons once they enter our prison system? What forms of punishment are appropriate—or inappropriate? These and other questions are considered by the writers represented here. They offer a variety of subjects related to crime and punishment, and, I hope, will stimulate you to do additional reading and research, analyzing, and speculating.

If there is one master text that lies behind this entire section it is Michel Foucault's brilliant study *Discipline and Punish*. We were strongly tempted to include an excerpt from that book in this edition, but for a variety of reasons (especially our desire not to include works in translation) we did not. In *Discipline and Punish*, Foucault traces the extraordinary changes that have occurred in the ways society conceives of errant behavior and appropriate punishment. For Foucault, the history of "discipline and punish" is a history of the distribution—and redistribution—of power in society; the ways we punish, for example, have a great deal to do with the ways we define the power of the state in relation to individual autonomy. Anyone interested in reading a challenging and disturbing inquiry into the nature of our prisons and their perverse advocacy of discipline and rehabilitation is urged to read Foucault. We hope the section which follows—though it is much less theoretical than Foucault's analysis—will provide at least a starting point for fruitful discussions about crime and punishment in contemporary society.

THE CRIMINAL TYPE

Jessica Mitford

Jessica Mitford has dedicated much of her professional life to exposing the hypocrisy, venality, and soft underbelly of various American fads and institutions. Her targets include the funeral business (*The American Way of Death*), the American prison system (*Kind and Unusual Punishment: The Prison Business*), and a variety of other subjects including television executives, a "fat farm" for wealthy women, and the Famous Writers School. A collection of her articles can be found in *Poison Penmanship: The Gentle Art of Muckraking*, which has been celebrated as "a virtual textbook on investigative reporting." Most recently she published *The American Way of Birth* (1994).

Mitford was born in England in 1917 but has spent most of her life in the United States. Daughter of a baron and baroness, she found herself the odd woman out politically compared to her sisters. Although her sympathies leaned toward the liberal left (she ran away to Loyalist Spain during the Spanish Civil War and married a communist sympathizer who also happened to be her cousin and Winston Churchill's nephew), two of her sisters were arch-rightists, and they both were on a first-name basis with Adolph Hitler and other German and British fascists. Her first husband was killed in action during

World War II; a few years later she married an American labor lawyer and moved to a racially integrated neighborhood in Oakland, California.

Mitford is best known for her witty and brilliant exposé of the practices of funeral directors, their glorification of dying, and their interest in persuading bereaved families to spend thousands of dollars on exorbitantly outfitted caskets.

Her other work, however, has also hit its target. As *Esquire* put it:

> Her legwork is tireless, her strategies simple but ingenious. . . . Behind these exposés of venal doings, we sense a woman who is jocular, common-sensical, forthright, self-reliant, amused, stout-hearted, opinionated, and utterly intoxicated with the chase.

The excerpt from *Kind and Unusual Punishment* featured here reveals that same sense of character; in it, Mitford examines the ways society perceives and misperceives criminal behavior.

Time was when most crimes were laid at the door of the Devil. The English indictment used in the last century took note of Old Nick's complicity by accusing the defendant not only of breaking the law but of "being prompted and instigated by the Devil," and the Supreme Court of North Carolina declared in 1862: "To know the right and still the wrong pursue proceeds from a perverse will brought about by the seductions of the Evil One."

With the advent of the new science of criminology toward the end of the nineteenth century, the Devil (possibly to his chagrin) was deposed as primary cause of crime by the hand of an Italian criminologist, one of the first of that calling, Cesare Lombroso. Criminals, Lombroso found, are born that way and bear physical stigmata to show it (which presumably saddles God with the responsibility, since He created them). They are "not a variation from a norm but practically a special species, a subspecies, having distinct physical and mental characteristics. In general all criminals have long, large, projecting ears, abundant hair, thin beard, prominent frontal sinuses, protruding chin, large cheekbones." Furthermore, his studies, consisting of exhaustive examination of live prisoners and the skulls of dead ones, enabled him to classify born criminals according to their offense: "Thieves have mobile hands and face; small, mobile, restless, frequently oblique eyes; thick and closely set eyebrows; flat or twisted nose; thin beard; hair frequently thin." Rapists may be distinguished by "brilliant eyes, delicate faces" and murderers by "cold, glassy eyes; nose always large and frequently aquiline; jaws strong; cheekbones large; hair curly, dark and abundant." Which caused a contemporary French savant to remark that Lombroso's portraits were very similar to the photographs of his friends.

A skeptical Englishman named Charles Goring, physician of His Majesty's Prisons, decided to check up on Lombroso's findings.

Around the turn of the century he made a detailed study of the physical characteristics of 3,000 prisoners—but took the precaution of comparing these with a group of English university students, impartially applying his handy measuring tape to noses, ears, eyebrows, chins of convicts and scholars alike over a twelve-year period. His conclusion: "In the present investigation we have exhaustively compared with regard to many physical characteristics different kinds of criminals with each other and criminals as a class with the general population. From these comparisons no evidence has emerged of the existence of a physical criminal type."

As the twentieth century progressed, efforts to pinpoint the criminal type followed the gyrations of scientific fashions of the day with bewildering results. Studies published in the thirties by Gustav Aschaffenburg, a distinguished German criminologist, show that the pyknic type (which means stout, squat, with large abdomen) is more prevalent among occasional offenders, while the asthenic type (of slender build and slight muscular development) is more often found among habitual criminals. In the forties came the gland men, Professor William H. Sheldon of Harvard and his colleagues, who divided the human race into three: endomorphs, soft, round, comfort-loving people; ectomorphs, fragile fellows who complain a lot and shrink from crowds; mesomorphs, muscular types with large trunks who walk assertively, talk noisily, and behave aggressively. Watch out for those.

Yet no sooner were these elaborate findings by top people published than equally illustrious voices were heard in rebuttal. Thus Professor M. F. Ashley Montagu, a noted anthropologist: "I should venture the opinion that not one of the reports on the alleged relationship between glandular dysfunctions and criminality has been carried out in a scientific manner, and that all such reports are glaring examples of the fallacy of *false cause* . . . to resort to that system for an explanation of criminality is merely to attempt to explain the known by the unknown."

Practitioners of the emerging disciplines of psychology and psychiatry turned their attention early on to a study of the causes of criminality. Dr. Henry Goddard, Princeton psychologist, opined in 1920 that "criminals, misdemeanants, delinquents, and other antisocial groups" are in nearly all cases persons of low mentality: "It is no longer to be denied that the greatest single cause of delinquency and crime is low-grade mentality, much of it within the limits of feeble-mindedness." But hard on his heels came the eminent professor Edwin H. Sutherland of Chicago, who in 1934 declared that the test results "are much more likely to reflect the methods of the testers than the intelligence of the criminals" and that "distribution of intelligence scores of delinquents is very similar to the distribution of intelligence scores of the general population. . . . Therefore, this analysis shows that the relationship between crime and feeblemind-edness is, in general, comparatively slight." In *New Horizons in Criminology,* Harry E. Barnes and Negley K. Teeters go further: "Studies made by clinical psychologists of prison populations demonstrate that those behind bars compare favorably with the general population in intelligence. Since we seldom arrest and convict criminals except the poor, inept, and friendless, we can know very little of the intelligence of the bulk of the criminal world. It is quite possible that it is, by and large, superior."

Coexistent with these theories of the criminal type was one that declares the lawbreaker to be a deviant personality, mentally ill, of which more later.

It may be conjectured that prison people were not entirely pleased by the early explanations of criminality; perhaps they welcomed the rebuttals, for if the malfeasant is that way because of the shape of his ears, or because of malfunctioning glands, or because he is dimwitted—none of which he can help—why punish? In this context, George Bernard Shaw points out, "As the obvious conclusion was that criminals were not morally responsible for their actions, and therefore should not be punished for them, the prison authorities saw their occupation threatened, and denied that there was any criminal type. The criminal type was off." The perverse old soul added that he knows what the criminal type is—it is manufactured in prison by the prison system: "If you keep one [man] in penal servitude and another in the House of Lords for ten years, the one will show the stigmata of a typical convict, and the other of a typical peer." Eugene V. Debs expressed the same thought: "I have heard people refer to the 'criminal countenance.' I never saw one. Any man or woman looks like a criminal behind bars."

Skull shape, glands, IQ, and deviant personality aside, to get a more pragmatic view of the criminal type one merely has to look at the composition of the prison population. Today the prisons are filled with the young, the poor white, the black, the Chicano, the Puerto Rican. Yesterday they were filled with the young, the poor native American, the Irish or Italian immigrant.

Discussing the importance of identifying the dangerous classes of 1870, a speaker at the American Prison Congress said: "The quality of being that constitutes a criminal cannot be clearly known, until observed as belonging to the class from which criminals come. . . . A true prison system should take cognizance of criminal classes as such." His examination of 15 prison populations showed that 53,101 were born in foreign countries, 47,957 were native-born, and of these, "full 50 percent were born of foreign parents, making over 76 percent of the whole number whose tastes and habits were those of such foreigners as emigrate to this country."

At the same meeting, J. B. Bittinger of Pennsylvania described the tastes and habits of these dissolute aliens: "First comes *rum,* to keep up spirits and energy for night work; then three fourths of their salaries are spent in *theaters* and *bar-rooms* . . . many go to *low concert saloons* only to kill time . . . they play *billiards* for *drinks,* go to the *opera,* to the *theater, oyster suppers* and *worse* . . . they have their peculiar literature: dime novels, sporting papers, illustrated papers, obscene prints and photographs." Commenting on the large numbers of foreign-born in prison, he added: "The figures here are so startling in their disproportions as to foster, and apparently justify, a strong prejudice against our foreign population."

The criminal type of yesteryear was further elaborated on in 1907 by J. E. Brown, in an article entitled "The Increase of Crime in the United States": "In the poorer quarters of our great cities may be found huddled together the Italian bandit and the bloodthirsty Spaniard, the bad man from Sicily, the Hungarian, Croatian and the Pole, the Chinaman and the Negro, the Cockney Englishman, the Russian and the Jew, with all the centuries of hereditary hate back of them."

In 1970 Edward G. Banfield, chairman of President Nixon's task force on the Model Cities Program, updated these descriptions of the lower-class slum-dweller in his book *The Unheavenly City: The Nature and Future of the Urban Crisis,* an influential book that is required reading in innumerable college courses. Since it is reportedly also recommended reading in the White House, presumably it reflects the Administration's conception of the criminal classes as they exist today.

"A slum is not simply a district of low-quality housing," says Mr. Banfield. "Rather it is one in which the style of life is squalid and vicious." The lower-class individual is "incapable of conceptualizing the future or of controlling his impulses and is therefore obliged to live from moment to moment . . . impulse governs his behavior . . . he is therefore radically improvident; whatever he cannot consume immediately he considers valueless. His bodily needs (especially for sex) and his taste for 'action' take precedence over everything else—and certainly over any work routine." Furthermore he has a "feeble, attenuated sense of self. . . .

"The lower-class individual lives in the slum and sees little or no reason to complain. He does not care how dirty and dilapidated his housing is either inside or out, nor does he mind the inadequacy of such public facilities as schools, parks, and libraries; indeed, where such things exist, he destroys them by acts of vandalism if he can. Features that make the slum repellent to others actually please him."

Most studies of the causes of crime in this decade, whether contained in sociological texts, high-level governmental commission reports, or best-selling books like Ramsey Clark's *Crime in America,* lament the disproportionately high arrest rate for blacks and poor people and assert with wearying monotony that criminality is a product of slums and poverty. Mr. Clark invites the reader to mark on his city map the areas where health and education are poorest, where unemployment and poverty are highest, where blacks are concentrated—and he will find these areas also have the highest crime rate.

Hence the myth that the poor, the young, the black, the Chicano are indeed the criminal type of today is perpetuated, whereas in fact crimes are committed, although not necessarily punished, at all levels of society.

There is evidence that a high proportion of people in all walks of life have at some time or other committed what are conventionally called "serious crimes." A study of 1,700 New Yorkers weighted toward the upper income brackets, who had never been arrested for anything, and who were guaranteed anonymity, revealed that 91 percent had committed at least one felony or serious misdemeanor. The mean number of offenses per person was 18. Sixty-four percent of the men and 27 percent of the women had committed at least one felony, for which they could have been sent to the state penitentiary. Thirteen percent of the men admitted to grand larceny, 26 percent to stealing cars, and 17 percent to burglary.

If crimes are committed by people of all classes, why the near-universal equation of criminal type and slum-dweller, why the vastly unequal representation of poor, black, brown in the nation's jails and prisons? When the "Italian bandit, bloodthirsty Spaniard, bad man from Sicily," and the rest of them climbed their way out of the slums and moved to the suburbs, they ceased to figure as an important factor in crime statistics. Yet as succeeding waves of immigrants, and later blacks, moved into the same slum area the rates of reported crime and delinquency remained high there.

No doubt despair and terrible conditions in the slums give rise to one sort of crime, the only kind available to the very poor: theft, robbery, purse-snatching; whereas crimes committed by the former slum-dweller have moved up the scale with his standard of living to those less likely to be detected and punished: embezzlement, sale of fraudulent stock, price-fixing. After all, the bank president is not likely to become a bank robber; nor does the bank robber have the opportunity to embezzle depositors' funds.

Professor Theodore Sarbin suggests the further explanation that police are conditioned to perceive some classes of persons (formerly immigrants, now blacks and browns) as being actually or potentially "dangerous," and go about their work accordingly: "The belief that some classes of persons were 'dangerous' guided the search for suspects. . . . Laws are broken by many citizens for many reasons: those suspects who fit the concurrent social type of the criminal are most likely to become objects of police suspicion and of judicial decision-making." The President's Crime Commission comments on the same phenomenon: "A policeman in attempting to solve crimes must employ, in the absence of concrete evidence, circumstantial indicators to link specific crimes with specific people. Thus policemen may stop Negro and Mexican youths in white neighborhoods, may suspect juveniles who act in what the policemen consider an impudent or overly casual manner, and may be influenced by such factors as unusual hair styles or clothes uncommon to the wearer's group or area . . . those who act frightened, penitent, and respectful are more likely to be released, while those who assert their autonomy and act indifferent or resistant run a substantially greater risk of being frisked, interrogated, or even taken into custody."

An experiment conducted in the fall of 1970 by a sociology class at the University of California at Los Angeles bears out these observations. The class undertook to study the differential application of police definitions of criminality by varying one aspect of the "identity" of the prospective criminal subject. They selected a dozen students, black, Chicano, and white, who had blameless driving records free of any moving violations, and asked them to drive to and from school as they normally did, with the addition of a "circumstantial indicator" in the shape of a phosphorescent bumper sticker reading "Black Panther Party." In the first 17 days of the study these students amassed 30 driving citations—failure to signal, improper lane changes, and the like. Two students had to withdraw from the experiment after two days because their licenses were suspended; and the project soon had to be abandoned because the $1,000 appropriation for the experiment had been used up in paying bails and fines of the participants.

The President's Crime Commission Report notes that "the criminal justice process may be viewed as a large-scale screening system. At each stage it tries to sort out the better risks to return to the general population," but the report does not elaborate on *how* these better risks are sorted. Professor Sarbin suggests an answer: "To put the conclusion bluntly, membership in the class 'lawbreakers' is *not* distributed according to economic or social status, but membership in the class 'criminals' *is* distributed according to social or economic status. . . . To account for the disproportionate number of lower class and black prisoners, I propose that the agents of law enforcement and justice engage in decision-making against a backcloth of belief that people can be readily classified into two types, criminal and noncriminal."

This point is underlined by Professor Donald Taft: "Negroes are more likely to be suspected of crime than are whites. They are also more likely to be arrested. If the perpetrator of a crime is known to be a Negro the police may arrest all Negroes who were near the scene—a procedure they would rarely dare to follow with whites. After arrest, Negroes are less likely to secure bail, and so are more liable to be counted in jail statistics. They are more liable than whites to be indict-ed and less likely to have their cases *nol prossed* or otherwise dismissed. If tried, Negroes are more likely to be convicted. If convicted, they are less likely to be given probation. For this reason they are more likely to be included in the count of prisoners. Negroes are also more liable than whites to be kept in prison for the full terms of their commitments and correspondingly less likely to be paroled."

As anyone versed in the ways of the criminal justice system will tell you, the screening process begins with the policeman on the beat: the young car thief from a "nice home" will be returned to his family with a warning. If he repeats the offense or gets into more serious trou-ble, the parents may be called in for a conference with the prosecuting authorities. The well-to-do family has a dozen options: they can send their young delinquent to a boarding school, or to stay with relatives in another part of the country, they can hire the professional services of a psychiatrist or counselor—and the authorities will support them in these efforts. The Juvenile Court judge can see at a glance that this boy does not belong in the toils of the criminal justice system, that given a little tolerance and helpful guidance there is every chance he will straighten out by the time he reaches college age.

For the identical crime the ghetto boy will be arrested, imprisoned in the juvenile detention home, and set on the downward path that ends in the penitentiary. The screening process does not end with ar-rest, it obtains at every stage of the criminal justice system.

To cite one example that any observer of the crime scene—and par-ticularly the black observer—will doubtless be able to match from his own experience: a few years ago a local newspaper reported horren-dous goings-on of high school seniors in Piedmont, a wealthy enclave in Alameda County, California, populated by executives, businessmen, rich politicians. The students had gone on a general rampage that in-cluded arson, vandalism, breaking and entering, assault, car theft, rape. Following a conference among parents, their lawyers, and prose-cuting authorities, it was decided that no formal action should be taken against the miscreants; they were all released to the custody of their families, who promised to subject them to appropriate discipline. In the very same week, a lawyer of my acquaintance told me with tight-lipped fury of the case of a nine-year-old black ghetto dweller in the same county, arrested for stealing a nickel from a white classmate, charged with "extortion and robbery," hauled off to juvenile hall, and, despite the urgent pleas of his distraught mother, there imprisoned for six weeks to wait for his court hearing.

Thus it seems safe to assert that there is indeed a criminal type—but he is not a biological, anatomical, phrenological, or anthropological type; rather, he is a social creation, etched by the dominant class and ethnic prejudices of a given society.

The day may not be far off when the horny-handed policeman on the beat may expect an assist in criminal-type-spotting from practitioners of a new witchcraft: behavior prediction. In 1970, Dr. Arnold Hutschnecker, President Nixon's physician, proposed mass psychological testing of six- to eight-year-old children to determine which were criminally inclined, and the establishment of special camps to house those found to have "violent tendencies." Just where the candidates for the mass testing and the special camps would be sought out was made clear when Dr. Hutschnecker let slip the fact he was proposing this program as an alternative to slum reconstruction. It would be, he said, "a direct, immediate, effective way of attacking the problem at its very origin, by focusing on the criminal mind of the child."

The behavior-predictors would catch the violence-prone *before* he springs, would confine him, possibly treat him, but in any event would certainly not let him out to consummate the hideous deeds of which he is so demonstrably capable. Their recurring refrain: "If only the clearly discernible defects in Oswald's psychological makeup had been detected in his childhood—had he been turned over to us, who have the resources to diagnose such deviant personalities—we would have tried to help him. If we decided he was beyond help, we would have locked him up forever and a major tragedy of this generation could have been averted." They refer, of course, to Lee Harvey Oswald, who allegedly gunned down President Kennedy, not to Russell G. Oswald, the New York Commissioner of Corrections who ordered the troops into Attica, as a result of which 43 perished by gunfire.

Speculations

1. Early in this chapter, Jessica Mitford summarizes Cesare Lombroso's study of the physical characteristics of various kinds of criminals. Although she dismisses his findings, do you find Lombroso's conclusions persuasive? Do you believe in a "criminal type"? If so, how would you describe the criminal?
2. Mitford's view is that:

   > Today the prisons are filled with the young, the poor white, the black, the Chicano, the Puerto Rican. Yesterday they were filled with the young, the poor native American, the Irish or Italian immigrant.

   Compare the prison population with society's attitudes toward various socio-economic and ethnic populations.
3. In the opening section of this chapter, Mitford follows a particular rhetorical pattern. How would you describe it? Do you find it effective as a way of presenting the various controversies that have swirled around "the criminal type" during the past several centuries?

4. Have you ever been surprised that someone you thought was a sincere and honest person turned out to be a liar, cheat, or criminal? Conversely, did you view someone as a criminal type who turned out to be a decent, helpful, ethical person? What led you to those false impressions? Would you respond differently now that you are older and wiser? How much difference did certain factors make, such as setting, appearance, clothing, your own fears, the person's demeanor?

5. Mitford wrote *Kind and Unusual Punishment* in the early 1970s. Do you think her analysis of the "criminal type" is dated and invalid? Have the past twenty years seen progress in the ways that the police and society view the criminal? Is her account of class and criminality still relevant?

6. Mitford's tone in this chapter strongly suggests her own attitude toward the variety of opinions that experts hold in regard to criminals and criminality. Describe that tone in relation to: Lombroso, Aschaffenburg, Sheldon, Montagu, and Goddard. What specific words and phrases reveal Mitford's attitude toward the experts she is citing?

LETTER FROM BIRMINGHAM JAIL

Martin Luther King, Jr.

Martin Luther King, Jr., winner of the Nobel Peace Prize and a major contributor to the cause of civil rights, race relations, and social justice in this century, was one of the finest orators this country has ever known. King was for many years the conscience of racist America, the president of the Southern Christian Leadership Conference from its inception in 1957 until his death by assassination in 1968.

Born into the black middle class in Atlanta in 1929, King was the son of a minister and a schoolteacher. Although he lived a fairly comfortable life, he suffered many of the same racist indignities as poorer blacks, something that caused him great anger and grief. According to noted biographer Stephen Oates, King

> had to attend separate, inferior schools, which he sailed through with a modicum of effort, skipping grades as he went. He found out that he—a preacher's boy—could not sit at lunch counters in Atlanta's downtown stores. He had to drink from a "colored" water fountain, relieve himself in a rancid "colored" restroom, and ride a rickety "colored" elevator. If he rode a city bus, he had to sit in the back as though

he were contaminated. If he wanted to see a movie in a downtown theater, he had to enter through a side door and sit in the "colored section in the balcony." He discovered that whites referred to blacks as "boys" and "girls" regardless of age . . . and that he resided in "nigger town."

For King, as for virtually all black Americans, there were two worlds—one desirable and white, the other undesirable and black.

King excelled in school and college, earning a B.A. from Morehouse College. He was one of six black students at Crozer Theological Seminary in Pennsylvania where he was awarded a divinity degree. In 1955 he received a Ph.D. in theology from Boston University, the same year that Rosa Parks refused to give up her seat to a white person on a public bus in Montgomery, Alabama. King returned to the South and ultimately succeeded both his grandfather and his father as pastor of the Ebenezer Baptist Church in Atlanta. But his most significant contribution was dedicated and fearless leadership of the civil rights movement with persistent emphasis on nonviolent civil disobedience. King was reviled in the press, considered a national menace by the FBI, beaten, threatened, imprisoned, and ultimately murdered.

The "Letter from Birmingham Jail" emerged from King's organization of a mass protest on behalf of fair hiring practices in Birmingham, Alabama. Defying a court order barring massive public demonstrations, King was arrested in April, 1963 and jailed. During his confinement, he wrote the now famous Letter which is addressed to the white religious leaders of Birmingham—Catholic, Protestant, and Jewish—who faulted him for his "unwise and untimely" protest.

For more information on the Birmingham boycott, see King's book about the civil rights movement, *Why We Can't Wait* (1964), or consult the excellent biography by Lerone Bennett, Jr., entitled *What Manner of Man* (1964). Additional reading is helpful, particularly to appreciate the eloquence, vision, and rhetorical power which characterize the "Letter."

My Dear Fellow Clergymen:

While confined here in the Birmingham city jail, I came across your recent statement calling my present activities "unwise and untimely." Seldom do I pause to answer criticism of my work and ideas. If I sought to answer all the criticisms that cross my desk, my secretaries would have little time for anything other than such correspondence in the course of the day, and I would have no time for constructive work. But since I feel that you are men of genuine good will and that your criticisms are sincerely set forth, I want to try to answer your statement in what I hope will be patient and reasonable terms.

I think I should indicate why I am here in Birmingham, since you have been influenced by the view which argues against "outsiders coming in." I have the honor of serving as president of the Southern Christian Leadership Conference, an organization operating in every southern state, with headquarters in Atlanta, Georgia. We have some eighty-five affiliated organizations across the South, and one of them is the Alabama Christian Movement for Human Rights. Frequently we share staff, educational, and financial resources with our affiliates. Several months ago the affiliate here in Birmingham asked us to be on call to engage in a nonviolent direct-action program if such were deemed necessary. We readily consented, and when the hour came, we lived up to our promise. So I, along with several members of my staff, am here because I was invited here. I am here because I have organizational ties here.

But more basically, I am in Birmingham because injustice is here. Just as the prophets of the eighth century B.C. left their villages and carried their "thus saith the Lord" far beyond the boundaries of their home towns, and just as the Apostle Paul left his village of Tarsus and carried the gospel of Jesus Christ to the far corners of the Greco-Roman world, so am I compelled to carry the gospel of freedom beyond my own home town. Like Paul, I must constantly respond to the Macedonian call for aid.

Moreover, I am cognizant of the interrelatedness of all communities and states. I cannot sit idly by in Atlanta and not be concerned about what happens in Birmingham. Injustice anywhere is a threat to justice everywhere. We are caught in an inescapable network of mutuality, tied in a single garment of destiny. Whatever affects one directly, affects all indirectly. Never again can we afford to live with the narrow, provincial "outside agitator" idea. Anyone who lives inside the United States can never be considered an outsider anywhere within its bounds.

You deplore the demonstrations taking place in Birmingham. But your statement, I am sorry to say, fails to express a similar concern for the conditions that brought about the demonstrations. I am sure that none of you would want to rest content with the superficial kind of social analysis that deals merely with effects and does not grapple with underlying causes. It is unfortunate that demonstrations are taking place in Birmingham, but it is even more unfortunate that the city's white power structure left the Negro community with no alternative.

In any nonviolent campaign there are four basic steps: collection of the facts to determine whether injustices exist; negotiation; self-purification; and direct action. We have gone through all these steps in Birmingham. There can be no gainsaying the fact that racial injustice engulfs this community. Birmingham is probably the most thoroughly segregated city in the United States. Its ugly record of brutality is widely known. Negroes have experienced grossly unjust treatment in the courts. There have been more unsolved bombings of Negro homes and churches in Birmingham than in any other city in the nation. These are the hard, brutal facts of the case. On the basis of these conditions,

Negro leaders sought to negotiate with the city fathers. But the latter consistently refused to engage in good-faith negotiation.

Then, last September, came the opportunity to talk with leaders of Birmingham's economic community. In the course of the negotiations, certain promises were made by the merchants—for example, to remove the stores' humiliating racial signs. On the basis of these promises, the Reverend Fred Shuttlesworth and the leaders of the Alabama Christian Movement for Human Rights agreed to a moratorium on all demonstrations. As the weeks and months went by, we realized that we were the victims of a broken promise. A few signs, briefly removed, returned; the others remained.

As in so many past experiences, our hopes had been blasted, and the shadow of deep disappointment settled upon us. We had no alternative except to prepare for direct action, whereby we would present our very bodies as a means of laying our case before the conscience of the local and the national community. Mindful of the difficulties involved, we decided to undertake a process of self-purification. We began a series of workshops on nonviolence, and we repeatedly asked ourselves: "Are you able to accept blows without retaliating?" "Are you able to endure the ordeal of jail?" We decided to schedule our direct-action program for the Easter season, realizing that except for Christmas, this is the main shopping period of the year. Knowing that a strong economic-withdrawal program would be the by-product of direct action, we felt that this would be the best time to bring pressure to bear on the merchants for the needed change.

Then it occurred to us that Birmingham's mayoral election was coming up in March, and we speedily decided to postpone action until after election day. When we discovered that the Commissioner of Public Safety, Eugene "Bull" Connor, had piled up enough votes to be in the run-off, we decided again to postpone action until the day after the run-off so that the demonstrations could not be used to cloud the issues. Like many others, we wanted to see Mr. Connor defeated, and to this end we endured postponement after postponement. Having aided in this community need, we felt that our direct-action program could be delayed no longer.

You may well ask, "Why direct action? Why sit-ins, marches, and so forth? Isn't negotiation a better path?" You are quite right in calling for negotiation. Indeed, this is the very purpose of direct action. Nonviolent direct action seeks to create such a crisis and foster such a tension that a community which has constantly refused to negotiate is forced to confront the issue. It seeks so to dramatize the issue that it can no longer be ignored. My citing the creation of tension as part of the work of the nonviolent-resister may sound rather shocking. But I must confess that I am not afraid of the word "tension." I have earnestly opposed violent tension, but there is a type of constructive, nonviolent tension which is necessary for growth. Just as Socrates felt that it was necessary to create a tension in the mind so that individuals could rise from the bondage of myths and half-truths to the unfettered realm of creative analysis and objective appraisal, so must we see the need for nonviolent gadflies to create the kind of tension in society that will help men rise from the dark depths of prejudice and racism to the majestic heights of understanding and brotherhood.

The purpose of our direct-action program is to create a situation so crisis-packed that it will inevitably open the door to negotiation. I therefore concur with you in your call for negotiation. Too long has our beloved Southland been bogged down in a tragic effort to live in monologue rather than dialogue.

One of the basic points in your statement is that the action that I and my associates have taken in Birmingham is untimely. Some have asked: "Why didn't you give the new city administration time to act?" The only answer that I can give to this query is that the new Birmingham administration must be prodded about as much as the outgoing one, before it will act. We are sadly mistaken if we feel that the election of Albert Boutwell as mayor will bring the millennium to Birmingham. While Mr. Boutwell is a much more gentle person than Mr. Connor, they are both segregationists, dedicated to maintenance of the status quo. I have hoped that Mr. Boutwell will be reasonable enough to see the futility of massive resistance to desegregation. But he will not see this without pressure from devotees of civil rights. My friends, I must say to you that we have not made a single gain in civil rights without determined legal and nonviolent pressure. Lamentably, it is an historical fact that privileged groups seldom give up their privileges voluntarily. Individuals may see the moral light and voluntarily give up their unjust posture; but, as Reinhold Niebuhr has reminded us, groups tend to be more immoral than individuals.

We know through painful experience that freedom is never voluntarily given by the oppressor; it must be demanded by the oppressed. Frankly, I have yet to engage in a direct-action campaign that was "well timed" in the view of those who have not suffered unduly from the disease of segregation. For years now I have heard the word "Wait!" It rings in the ear of every Negro with piercing familiarity. This "Wait" has almost always meant "Never." We must come to see, with one of our distinguished jurists, that "justice too long delayed is justice denied."

We have waited for more than 340 years for our constitutional and God-given rights. The nations of Asia and Africa are moving with jet-like speed toward gaining political independence, but we still creep at horse-and-buggy pace toward gaining a cup of coffee at a lunch counter. Perhaps it is easy for those who have never felt the stinging darts of segregation to say, "Wait." But when you have seen vicious mobs lynch your mothers and fathers at will and drown your sisters and brothers at whim; when you have seen hate-filled policemen curse, kick, and even kill your black brothers and sisters; when you see the vast majority of your twenty million Negro brothers smothering in an airtight cage of poverty in the midst of an affluent society; when you suddenly find your tongue twisted and your speech stammering as you seek to explain to your six-year-old daughter why she can't go to the public amusement park that has just been advertised on television, and see tears welling up in her eyes when she is told that Funtown is closed to colored children, and see ominous clouds of inferiority be-ginning to form in her little mental sky, and see her beginning to dis-tort her personality by developing an unconscious bitterness toward white people; when you have to concoct an answer for a five-year-old son who is asking "Daddy, why do white people treat colored people so mean?"; when you take a cross-country drive and find it necessary to sleep night after night in the uncomfortable corners of your auto-mobile because no motel will accept you; when you are humiliated day in and day out by nagging signs reading "white" and "colored"; when your first name becomes "nigger," your middle name becomes "boy" (however old you are) and your last name becomes "John," and your wife and mother are never given the respected title "Mrs."; when you are harried by day and haunted by night by the fact that you are a Negro, living constantly at tiptoe stance, never quite knowing what to expect next, and are plagued with inner fears and outer resentments; when you are forever fighting a degenerating sense of "nobodiness"— then you will understand why we find it difficult to wait. There comes a time when the cup of endurance runs over, and men are no longer willing to be plunged into the abyss of despair. I hope, sirs, you can understand our legitimate and unavoidable impatience.

You express a great deal of anxiety over our willingness to break laws. This is certainly a legitimate concern. Since we so diligently urge people to obey the Supreme Court's decision of 1954 outlawing segre-gation in the public schools, at first glance it may seem rather para-doxical for us consciously to break laws. One may well ask: "How can you advocate breaking some laws and obeying others?" The answer lies in the fact that there are two types of laws: just and unjust. I would be the first to advocate obeying just laws. One has not only a legal but a moral responsibility to obey just laws. Conversely, one has a moral responsibility to disobey unjust laws. I would agree with St. Augustine that "an unjust law is no law at all."

Now, what is the difference between the two? How does one de-termine whether a law is just or unjust? A just law is a man-made code that squares with the moral law or the law of God. An unjust law is a code that is out of harmony with the moral law. To put it in the terms of St. Thomas Aquinas: An unjust law is a human law that is not rooted in eternal law and natural law. Any law that uplifts human personality is just. Any law that degrades human personality is unjust. All segregation statutes are unjust because segregation distorts the soul and damages the personality. It gives the segregator a false sense of superiority and the segregated a false sense of inferiority. Segregation, to use the terminology of the Jewish philosopher Martin Buber, substitutes "I-it" relationship for an "I-thou" relationship and ends up relegating persons to the status of things. Hence segregation is not only politically, economically, and sociologically unsound, it is morally wrong and sinful. Paul Tillich has said that sin is separation. Is not segregation an existential expression of man's tragic separation, his awful estrangement, his terrible sinfulness? Thus it is that I can urge men to obey the 1954 decision of the Supreme Court, for it is morally right; and I can urge them to disobey segregation ordinances, for they are morally wrong.

Let us consider a more concrete example of just and unjust laws. An unjust law is a code that a numerical or power majority group compels a minority group to obey but does not make binding on itself. This is *difference* made legal. By the same token, a just law is a code that a majority compels a minority to follow and that it is willing to follow itself. This is *sameness* made legal.

Let me give another explanation. A law is unjust if it is inflicted on a minority that, as a result of being denied the right to vote, had no part in enacting or devising the law. Who can say that the legislature of Alabama which set up that state's segregation laws was democratically elected? Throughout Alabama all sorts of devious methods are used to prevent Negroes from becoming registered voters, and there are some counties in which, even though Negroes constitute a majority of the population, not a single Negro is registered. Can any law enacted under such circumstances be considered democratically structured?

Sometimes a law is just on its face and unjust in its application. For instance, I have been arrested on a charge of parading without a permit. Now, there is nothing wrong in having an ordinance which requires a permit for a parade. But such an ordinance becomes unjust when it is used to maintain segregation and to deny citizens the First-Amendment privilege of peaceful assembly and protest.

I hope you are able to see the distinction I am trying to point out. In no sense do I advocate evading or defying the law, as would the rabid segregationist. That would lead to anarchy. One who breaks an unjust law must do so openly, lovingly, and with a willingness to accept the penalty. I submit that an individual who breaks a law that conscience tells him is unjust, and who willingly accepts the penalty of imprisonment in order to arouse the conscience of the community over its injustice, is in reality expressing the highest respect for law.

Of course, there is nothing new about this kind of civil disobedience. It was evidenced sublimely in the refusal of Shadrach, Meshach, and Abednego to obey the laws of Nebuchadnezzar, on the ground that a higher moral law was at stake. It was practiced superbly by the early Christians, who were willing to face hungry lions and the excruciating pain of chopping blocks rather than submit to certain unjust laws of the Roman Empire. To a degree, academic freedom is a reality today because Socrates practiced civil disobedience. In our own nation, the Boston Tea Party represented a massive act of civil disobedience.

We should never forget that everything Adolf Hitler did in Germany was "legal" and everything the Hungarian freedom fighters did in Hungary was "illegal." It was "illegal" to aid and comfort a Jew in Hitler's Germany. Even so, I am sure that, had I lived in Germany at the time, I would have aided and comforted my Jewish brothers. If today I lived in a Communist country where certain principles dear to the Christian faith are suppressed, I would openly advocate disobeying that country's anti-religious laws.

I must make two honest confessions to you, my Christian and Jewish brothers. First, I must confess that over the past few years I have been gravely disappointed with the white moderate. I have almost reached the regrettable conclusion that the Negro's great stumbling block in his stride toward freedom is not the White Citizen's Counciler or the Ku Klux Klanner, but the white moderate, who is more devoted to "order" than to justice; who prefers a negative peace which is the absence of tension to a positive peace which is the presence of justice; who constantly says, "I agree with you in the goal you seek, but I cannot agree with your methods of direct action"; who paternalistically believes he can set the timetable for another man's freedom; who lives by a mythical concept of time and who constantly advises the Negro to wait for a "more convenient season." Shallow understanding from people of good will is more frustrating than absolute misunderstanding from people of ill will. Lukewarm acceptance is much more bewildering than outright rejection.

I had hoped that the white moderate would understand that law and order exist for the purpose of establishing justice and that when they fail in this purpose they become the dangerously structured dams that block the flow of social progress. I had hoped that the white moderate would understand that the present tension in the South is a necessary phase of the transition from an obnoxious negative peace, in which the Negro passively accepted his unjust plight, to a substantive and positive peace, in which all men will respect the dignity and worth of human personality. Actually, we who engage in nonviolent direct action are not the creators of tension. We merely bring to the surface the hidden tension that is already alive. We bring it out in the open, where it can be seen and dealt with. Like a boil that can never be cured so long as it is covered up but must be opened with all its ugliness to the natural medicines of air and light, injustice must be exposed, with all the tension its exposure creates, to the light of human conscience and the air of national opinion, before it can be cured.

In your statement you assert that our actions, even though peaceful, must be condemned because they precipitate violence. But is this a logical assertion? Isn't this like condemning a robbed man because his possession of money precipitated the evil act of robbery? Isn't this like condemning Socrates because his unswerving commitment to truth and his philosophical inquiries precipitated the act by the misguided populace in which they made him drink hemlock? Isn't this like condemning Jesus because his unique God-consciousness and never-ceasing devotion to God's will precipitated the evil act of crucifixion? We must come to see that, as the federal courts have consistently affirmed, it is wrong to urge an individual to cease his efforts to gain his basic constitutional rights because the quest may precipitate violence. Society must protect the robbed and punish the robber.

I had also hoped that the white moderate would reject the myth concerning time in relation to the struggle for freedom. I have just received a letter from a white brother in Texas. He writes: "All Christians know that the colored people will receive equal rights eventually, but it is possible that you are in too great a religious hurry. It has taken Christianity almost two thousand years to accomplish what it has. The teachings of Christ take time to come to earth." Such an attitude stems from a tragic misconception of time, from the strangely irrational notion that there is something in the very flow of time that will inevitably cure all ills. Actually, time itself is neutral; it can be used either destructively or constructively. More and more I feel that the people of ill will have used time much more effectively than have the people of good will. We will have to repent in this generation not merely for the hateful words and actions of the bad people, but for the appalling silence of the good people. Human progress never rolls in on wheels of inevitability; it comes through the tireless efforts of men willing to be co-workers with God, and without this hard work, time itself becomes an ally of the forces of social stagnation. We must use time creatively, in the knowledge that the time is always ripe to do right. Now is the time to make real the promise of democracy and transform our pending national elegy into a creative psalm of brotherhood. Now is the time to lift our national policy from the quicksand of racial injustice to the solid rock of human dignity.

You speak of our activity in Birmingham as extreme. At first I was rather disappointed that fellow clergymen would see my nonviolent efforts as those of an extremist. I began thinking about the fact that I stand in the middle of two opposing forces in the Negro community. One is a force of complacency, made up in part of Negroes who, as a result of long years of oppression, are so drained of self-respect and a sense of "somebodiness" that they have adjusted to segregation; and in part of a few middle-class Negroes who, because of a degree of academic and economic security and because in some ways they profit by segregation, have become insensitive to the problems of the masses. The other force is one of bitterness and hatred, and it comes perilously close to advocating violence. It is expressed in the various black nationalist groups that are springing up across the nation, the largest and best-known being Elijah Muhammad's Muslim movement. Nourished by the Negro's frustration over the continued existence of racial discrimination, this movement is made up of people who have lost faith in America, who have absolutely repudiated Christianity, and who have concluded that the white man is an incorrigible "devil."

I have tried to stand between these two forces, saying that we need emulate neither the "do-nothingism" of the complacent nor the hatred and despair of the black nationalist. For there is the more excellent way of love and nonviolent protest. I am grateful to God that, through the influence of the Negro church, the way of nonviolence became an integral part of our struggle.

If this philosophy had not emerged, by now many streets of the South would, I am convinced, be flowing with blood. And I am further convinced that if our white brothers dismiss as "rabblerousers" and "outside agitators" those of us who employ nonviolent direct action, and if they refuse to support our nonviolent efforts, millions of Negroes will, out of frustration and despair, seek solace and security in Black-nationalist ideologies—a development that would inevitably lead to a frightening racial nightmare.

Oppressed people cannot remain oppressed forever. The yearning for freedom eventually manifests itself, and that is what has happened to the American Negro. Something within has reminded him of his birthright of freedom, and something without has reminded him that it can be gained. Consciously or unconsciously, he has been caught up by the *Zeitgeist,* and with his black brothers of Africa and his brown and yellow brothers of Asia, South America, and the Caribbean, the United States Negro is moving with a sense of great urgency toward the promised land of racial justice. If one recognizes this vital urge that has engulfed the Negro community, one should readily understand why public demonstrations are taking place. The Negro has many pent-up resentments and latent frustrations, and he must release them. So let him march; let him make prayer pilgrimages to the city hall; let him go on freedom rides—and try to understand why he must do so. If his repressed emotions are not released in nonviolent ways, they will seek expression through violence; this is not a threat but a fact of history. So I have not said to my people, "Get rid of your discontent." Rather, I have tried to say that this normal and healthy discontent can be channeled into the creative outlet of nonviolent direct action. And now this approach is being termed extremist.

But though I was initially disappointed at being categorized as an extremist, as I continued to think about the matter I gradually gained a measure of satisfaction from the label. Was not Jesus an extremist for love: "Love your enemies, bless them that curse you, do good to them that hate you, and pray for them which despitefully use you, and persecute you." Was not Amos an extremist for justice: "Let justice roll down like waters and righteousness like an everflowing stream." Was not Paul an extremist for the Christian gospel: "I bear in my body the marks of the Lord Jesus." Was not Martin Luther an extremist: "Here I stand; I cannot do otherwise, so help me God." And John Bunyan: "I will stay in jail to the end of my days before I make a butchery of my conscience." And Abraham Lincoln: "This nation cannot survive half slave and half free." And Thomas Jefferson: "We hold these truths to be self-evident, that all men are created equal. . . ." So the question is not whether we will be extremists, but what kind of extremists we will be. Will we be extremists for hate or for love? Will we be extremists for the preservation of injustice or for the extension of justice? In that dramatic scene on Calvary's hill three men were crucified. We must never forget that all three were crucified for the same crime—the crime of extremism. Two were extremists for immorality, and thus fell below their environment. The other, Jesus Christ, was an extremist for love, truth, and goodness, and thereby rose above his environment. Perhaps the South, the nation, and the world are in dire need of creative extremists.

I had hoped that the white moderate would see this need. Perhaps I was too optimistic; perhaps I expected too much. I suppose I should have realized that few members of the oppressor race can understand the deep groans and passionate yearnings of the oppressed race, and still fewer have the vision to see that injustice must be rooted out by strong, persistent, and determined action. I am thankful, however, that some of our white brothers in the South have grasped the meaning of this social revolution and committed themselves to it. They are still all too few in quantity, but they are big in quality. Some—such as Ralph McGill, Lillian Smith, Harry Golden, James McBridge Dabbs, Anne Braden, and Sarah Patton Boyle—have written about our struggle in eloquent and prophetic terms. Others have marched with us down nameless streets of the South. They have languished in filthy, roach-infested jails, suffering the abuse and brutality of policemen who view them as "dirty nigger-lovers." Unlike so many of their moderate brothers and sisters, they have recognized the urgency of the moment and sensed the need for powerful "action" antidotes to combat the disease of segregation.

Let me take note of my other major disappointment. I have been so greatly disappointed with the white church and its leadership. Of course, there are some notable exceptions. I am not unmindful of the fact that each of you has taken some significant stands on this issue. I commend you, Reverend Stallings, for your Christian stand on this past Sunday, in welcoming Negroes to your worship service on a non-segregated basis. I commend the Catholic leaders of this state for integrating Spring Hill College several years ago.

But despite these notable exceptions, I must honestly reiterate that I have been disappointed with the church. I do not say this as one of those negative critics who can always find something wrong with the church. I say this as a minister of the gospel, who loves the church; who was nurtured in its bosom; who has been sustained by its spiritual blessings and who will remain true to it as long as the cord of life shall lengthen.

When I was suddenly catapulted into the leadership of the bus protest in Montgomery, Alabama, a few years ago, I felt we would be supported by the white church. I felt that the white ministers, priests, and rabbis of the South would be among our strongest allies. Instead, some have been outright opponents, refusing to understand the freedom movement and misrepresenting its leaders; all too many others have been more cautious than courageous and have remained silent behind the anesthetizing security of stained glass windows.

In spite of my shattered dreams, I came to Birmingham with the hope that the white religious leadership of this community would see the justice of our cause and, with deep moral concern, would serve as the channel through which our just grievances could reach the power structure. I had hoped that each of you would understand. But again I have been disappointed.

I have heard numerous southern religious leaders admonish their worshipers to comply with a desegregation decision because it is the law, but I have longed to hear white ministers declare: "Follow this decree because integration is morally right and because the Negro is your brother." In the midst of blatant injustices inflicted upon the Negro, I have watched white churchmen stand on the sideline and mouth pious irrelevancies and sanctimonious trivialities. In the midst of a mighty struggle to rid our nation of racial and economic injustice I have heard many ministers say: "Those are social issues, with which the gospel has no real concern." And I have watched many churches commit themselves to a completely otherworldly religion which makes a strange, un-Biblical distinction between body and soul, between the sacred and the secular.

I have traveled the length and breadth of Alabama, Mississippi, and all the other southern states. On sweltering summer days and crisp autumn mornings I have looked at the South's beautiful churches with their lofty spires pointing heavenward. I have beheld the impressive outlines of her massive religious-education buildings. Over and over I have found myself asking: "What kind of people worship here? Who is their God? Where were their voices when the lips of Governor Barnett dripped with words of interposition and nullification? Where were they when Governor Wallace gave a clarion call for defiance and hatred? Where were their voices of support when bruised and weary Negro men and women decided to rise from the dark dungeons of complacency to the bright hills of creative protest?"

Yes, these questions are still in my mind. In deep disappointment I have wept over the laxity of the church. But be assured that my tears have been tears of love. There can be no deep disappointment where there is not deep love. Yes, I love the church. How could I do otherwise? I am in the rather unique position of being the son, the grandson, and the great-grandson of preachers. Yes, I see the church as the body of Christ. But, oh! How we have blemished and scarred that body through social neglect and through fear of being nonconformists.

There was a time when the church was very powerful—in the time when the early Christians rejoiced at being deemed worthy to suffer for what they believed. In those days the church was not merely a thermometer that recorded the ideas and principles of popular opinion; it was a thermostat that transformed the mores of society. Whenever the early Christians entered a town, the people in power became disturbed and immediately sought to convict the Christians for being "disturbers of the peace" and "outside agitators." But the Christians pressed on, in the conviction that they were "a colony of heaven," called to obey God rather than man. Small in number, they were big in commitment. They were too God-intoxicated to be "astronomically intimidated." By their effort and example they brought an end to such ancient evils as infanticide and gladiatorial contests.

Things are different now. So often the contemporary church is a weak, ineffectual voice with an uncertain sound. So often it is an archdefender of the status quo. Far from being disturbed by the presence of the church, the power structure of the average community is consoled by the church's silent—and often even vocal—sanction of things as they are.

But the judgment of God is upon the church as never before. If today's church does not recapture the sacrificial spirit of the early church, it will lose its authenticity, forfeit the loyalty of millions, and be dismissed as an irrelevant social club with no meaning for the twentieth century. Every day I meet young people whose disappointment with the church has turned into outright disgust.

Perhaps I have once again been too optimistic. Is organized religion too inextricably bound to the status quo to save our nation and the world? Perhaps I must turn my faith to the inner spiritual church, the church within the church, as the true *ekklesia*[1] and the hope of the world. But again I am thankful to God that some noble souls from the ranks of organized religion have broken loose from the paralyzing chains of conformity and joined us as active partners in the struggle for freedom. They have left their secure congregations and walked the streets of Albany, Georgia, with us. They have gone down the highways of the South on tortuous rides for freedom. Yes, they have gone to jail with us. Some have been dismissed from their churches, have lost the support of their bishops and fellow ministers. But they have acted in the faith that right defeated is stronger than evil triumphant. Their witness has been the spiritual salt that has preserved the true meaning of the gospel in these troubled times. They have carved a tunnel of hope through the dark mountain of disappointment.

I hope the church as a whole will meet the challenge of this decisive hour. But even if the church does not come to the aid of justice, I have no despair about the future. I have no fear about the outcome of our struggle in Birmingham, even if our motives are at present misunderstood. We will reach the goal of freedom in Birmingham and all over the nation, because the goal of America is freedom. Abused and scorned though we may be, our destiny is tied up with America's destiny. Before the pilgrims landed at Plymouth, we were here. Before the pen of Jefferson etched the majestic words of the Declaration of Independence across the pages of history, we were here. For more than two centuries our forebears labored in this country without wages; they made cotton king; they built the homes of their masters while suffering gross injustice and shameful humiliation—and yet out of a bottomless vitality they continued to thrive and develop. If the inexpressible cruelties of slavery could not stop us, the opposition we now face will surely fail. We will win our freedom because the sacred heritage of our nation and the eternal will of God are embodied in our echoing demands.

Before closing I feel impelled to mention one other point in your statement that has troubled me profoundly. You warmly commended the Birmingham police force for keeping "order" and "preventing violence." I doubt that you would have so warmly commended the police force if you have seen its dogs sinking their teeth into unarmed, nonviolent Negroes. I doubt that you would so quickly commend the policemen if you were to observe their ugly and inhumane treatment of Negroes here in the city jail; if you were to watch them push and curse old Negro women and young Negro girls; if you were to see them slap and kick old Negro men and young boys; if you were to observe them, as they did on two occasions, refuse to give us food because we wanted to sing our grace together. I cannot join you in your praise of the Birmingham police department.

---

[1] A Greek word for the early Christian church. [Eds.]

It is true that the police have exercised a degree of discipline in handling the demonstrators. In this sense they have conducted themselves rather "nonviolently" in public. But for what purpose? To preserve the evil system of segregation. Over the past few years I have consistently preached that nonviolence demands that the means we use must be as pure as the ends we seek. I have tried to make clear that it is wrong to use immoral means to attain moral ends. But now I must affirm that it is just as wrong, or perhaps even more so, to use moral means to preserve immoral ends. Perhaps Mr. Connor and his policemen have been rather nonviolent in public, as was Chief Pritchett in Albany, Georgia, but they have used the moral means of nonviolence to maintain the immoral end of racial injustice. As T. S. Eliot has said, "The last temptation is the greatest treason: To do the right deed for the wrong reason."

I wish you had commended the Negro sit-inners and demonstrators of Birmingham for their sublime courage, their willingness to suffer, and their amazing discipline in the midst of great provocation. One day the South will recognize its real heroes. They will be the James Merediths, with the noble sense of purpose that enables them to face jeering and hostile mobs, and with the agonizing loneliness that characterizes the life of the pioneer. They will be old, oppressed, battered Negro women, symbolized in a seventy-two-year-old woman in Montgomery, Alabama, who rose up with a sense of dignity and with her people decided not to ride segregated buses, and who responded with ungrammatical profundity to one who inquired about her weariness: "My feets is tired, but my soul is at rest." They will be the young high school and college students, the young ministers of the gospel and a host of their elders, courageously and nonviolently sitting in at lunch counters and willingly going to jail for conscience' sake. One day the South will know that when these disinherited children of God sat down at lunch counters, they were in reality standing up for what is best in the American dream and for the most sacred values in our Judaeo-Christian heritage, thereby bringing our nation back to those great wells of democracy which were dug deep by the founding fathers in their formulation of the Constitution and the Declaration of Independence.

Never before have I written so long a letter. I'm afraid it is much too long to take your precious time. I can assure you that it would have been much shorter if I had been writing from a comfortable desk, but what else can one do when he is alone in a narrow jail cell, other than write long letters, think long thoughts, and pray long prayers?

If I have said anything in this letter that overstates the truth and indicates an unreasonable impatience, I beg you to forgive me. If I have said anything that understates the truth and indicates my having a patience that allows me to settle for anything less than brotherhood, I beg God to forgive me.

I hope this letter finds you strong in the faith. I also hope that circumstances will soon make it possible for me to meet each of you, not as an integrationist or a civil-rights leader but as a fellow clergyman and a Christian brother. Let us all hope that the dark clouds of racial prejudice will soon pass away and the deep fog of misunderstanding will be lifted from our fear-drenched communities, and in some not too distant tomorrow the radiant stars of love and brotherhood will shine over our great nation with all their scintillating beauty.

> Yours for the cause of Peace and Brotherhood,
> MARTIN LUTHER KING, JR.

Speculations

1. In this famous letter, King is writing to fellow clergymen who have criticized his actions as president of the Southern Christian Leadership Conference. How do you think his professional relationship with them influenced the writing of this letter? What features does this letter have that indicate that it is a correspondence from one clergyman to another?
2. "Letter from Birmingham Jail" is very long. Why do you think King wrote such a long letter? Would it have been more effective if he had written a more conventional letter of two to three pages? Is this really a letter—and if not, why does King choose to call it one?
3. Summarize three of King's arguments justifying his actions in Birmingham. How are the three arguments you chose persuasive? How do you respond to them on a personal level?
4. King cites a great many thinkers and writers in the Letter. St. Augustine, Paul Tillich, the Bible, John Bunyan, T. S. Eliot, and Socrates are some of the famous individuals to whom King refers. Why does he do so? How do you think King's fellow clergymen and other readers are likely to respond to these citations?
5. King's rich style owes a great deal to both the Bible and to a poetic use of parallel phrasing. Select a short section that you find particularly eloquent, powerful, and stylistically effective. Analyze what King is doing as a stylist to make this passage memorable for you.
6. Have you ever written a letter in which you tried to argue a case or make a sustained plea about something that mattered to you? What kinds of arguments, devices, strategies did you use to make your letter succeed? How successful were you? What would you do differently—if anything—were you to write that letter now?

CRIME AND CRIMINALS: ADDRESS TO THE PRISONERS IN THE COOK COUNTY JAIL

Clarence Darrow

Clarence Darrow is the real-life hero of "Inherit the Wind," a fa-mous play and movie based on the Scopes trial. In this compelling courtroom drama, Darrow defends the right to teach evolution in the Tennessee schools—and although he loses the jury verdict, he suc-ceeds in a greater objective: to ridicule similar discriminatory legisla-tion out of existence in other states. The play is more fact than fiction; Darrow established his reputation as a champion of reason, social jus-tice, and the poor.

Born in Ohio in 1857 to an intellectual and puritanical mother and a free-thinking father, Darrow was self-educated. He attended one year of law school but received most of his law education by read-ing and working for an attorney. He became a well-paid railroad lawyer, but he viewed his own cases unsympathetically, siding more with "the little guy" than with railroads and corporations. Ultimate-ly, he achieved national fame for defending criminals and murderers, including Nathan Leopold and Richard Loeb in the 1920s.

A large and imposing speaker, Darrow knew how to dominate a courtroom. His intellectual and political ideas were well known by many Americans through the end of the last century and the first few decades of this one. His legal writings—forceful, humane, and writ-ten with remarkable clarity—express his judicial philosophy: Poverty is the cause of crime, human beings are often condemned by the law for unconventional behavior rather than for doing evil, and capital punishment is nothing more than "organized, legalized murder." Those views are evident in this address, which offers an analysis that runs counter to a great deal of thinking about crime and punishment in America in the 1990s.

If I looked at jails and crimes and prisoners in the way the ordinary person does, I should not speak on this subject to you. The reason I talk to you on the question of crime, its cause and cure, is that I really do not in the least believe in crime. There is no such thing as a crime as the word is generally understood. I do not believe there is any sort of distinction between the real moral conditions of the people in and out of jail. One is just as good as the other. The people here can no more help being here than the people outside can avoid being outside. I do not believe that people are in jail because they deserve to be. They are in jail simply because they cannot avoid it on account of circumstances which are entirely beyond their control and for which they are in no way responsible.

I suppose a great many people on the outside would say I was doing you harm if they should hear what I say to you this afternoon, but you cannot be hurt a great deal anyway, so it will not matter. Good people outside would say that I was really teaching you things that were calculated to injure society, but it's worthwhile now and then to hear something different from what you ordinarily get from preachers and the like. These will tell you that you should be good and then you will get rich and be happy. Of course we know that people do not get rich by being good, and that is the reason why so many of you people try to get rich some other way, only you do not understand how to do it quite as well as the fellow outside.

There are people who think that everything in this world is an accident. But really there is no such thing as an accident. A great many folks admit that many of the people in jail ought to be there, and many who are outside ought to be in. I think none of them ought to be here. There ought to be no jails; and if it were not for the fact that the people on the outside are so grasping and heartless in their dealings with the people on the inside, there would be no such institution as jails.

I do not want you to believe that I think all you people here are angels. I do not think that. You are people of all kinds, all of you doing the best you can—and that is evidently not very well. You are people of all kinds and conditions and under all circumstances. In one sense everybody is equally good and equally bad. We all do the best we can under the circumstances. But as to the exact things for which you are sent here, some of you are guilty and did the particular act because you needed the money. Some of you did it because you are in the habit of doing it, and some of you because you are born to it, and it comes to be as natural as it does, for instance, for me to be good.

Most of you probably have nothing against me, and most of you would treat me the same as any other person would, probably better than some of the people on the outside would treat me, because you think I believe in you and they know I do not believe in them. While you would not have the least thing against me in the world, you might pick my pockets. I do not think all of you would, but I think some of you would. You would not have anything against me, but that's your profession, a few of you. Some of the rest of you, if my doors were unlocked, might come in if you saw anything you wanted—not out of any malice to me, but because that is your trade. There is no doubt there are quite a number of people in this jail who would pick my pockets. And still I know this—that when I get outside pretty nearly everybody picks my pocket. There may be some of you who would hold up a man on the street, if you did not happen to have something else to do, and needed the money; but when I want to light my house or my office the gas company holds me up. They charge me one dollar for something that is worth twenty-five cents. Still all these people are good people; they are pillars of society and support the churches, and they are respectable.

When I ride on the streetcars I am held up—I pay five cents for a ride that is worth two and a half cents, simply because a body of men have bribed the city council and the legislature, so that all the rest of us have to pay tribute to them.

If I do not want to fall into the clutches of the gas trust and choose to burn oil instead of gas, then good Mr. Rockefeller holds me up, and he uses a certain portion of his money to build universities and support churches which are engaged in telling us how to be good.

Some of you are here for obtaining property under false pretenses—yet I pick up a great Sunday paper and read the advertisements of a merchant prince—"Shirtwaists for 39 cents, marked down from $3.00."

When I read the advertisements in the paper I see they are all lies. When I want to get out and find a place to stand anywhere on the face of the earth, I find that it has been taken up long ago before I came here, and before you came here, and somebody says, "Get off, swim into the lake, fly into the air; go anywhere, but get off." That is because these people have the police and they have the jails and the judges and the lawyers and the soldiers and all the rest of them to take care of the earth and drive everybody off that comes in their way.

A great many people will tell you that all this is true, but that it does not excuse you. These facts do not excuse some fellow who reaches into my pocket and takes out a five-dollar bill. The fact that the gas company bribes the members of the legislature from year to year, and fixes the law, so that all you people are compelled to be "fleeced" whenever you deal with them; the fact that the streetcar companies and the gas companies have control of the streets; and the fact that the landlords own all the earth—this, they say, has nothing to do with you.

Let us see whether there is any connection between the crimes of the respectable classes and your presence in the jail. Many of you people are in jail because you have really committed burglary; many of you, because you have stolen something. In the meaning of the law, you have taken some other person's property. Some of you have entered a store and carried off a pair of shoes because you did not have the price. Possibly some of you have committed murder. I cannot tell what all of you did. There are a great many people here who have done some of these things who really do not know themselves why they did them. I think I know why you did them—every one of you; you did these things because you were bound to do them. It looked to you at the time as if you had a chance to do them or not, as you saw fit; but still, after all, you had no choice. There may be people here who had some money in their pockets and who still went out and got some more money in a way society forbids. Now, you may not yourselves see exactly why it was you did this thing, but if you look at the question deeply enough and carefully enough you will see that there were circumstances that drove you to do exactly the thing which you did. You could not help it any more than we outside can help taking the positions that we take. The reformers who tell you to be good and you will be happy, and the people on the outside who have property to protect—they think that the only way to do it is by building jails and locking you up in cells on weekdays and praying for you Sundays.

I think that all of this has nothing whatever to do with right conduct. I think it is very easily seen what has to do with right conduct. Some so-called criminals—and I will use this word because it is handy, it means nothing to me—I speak of the criminals who get caught as distinguished from the criminals who catch them—some of these so-called criminals are in jail for their first offenses, but nine tenths of you are in jail because you did not have a good lawyer and, of course, you did not have a good lawyer because you did not have enough money to pay a good lawyer. There is no very great danger of a rich man going to jail.

Some of you may be here for the first time. If we would open the doors and let you out, and leave the laws as they are today, some of you would be back tomorrow. This is about as good a place as you can get anyway. There are many people here who are so in the habit of coming that they would not know where else to go. There are people who are born with the tendency to break into jail every chance they get, and they cannot avoid it. You cannot figure out your life and see why it was, but still there is a reason for it; and if we were all wise and knew all the facts, we could figure it out.

In the first place, there are a good many more people who go to jail in the wintertime than in summer. Why is this? Is it because people are more wicked in winter? No, it is because the coal trust begins to get in its grip in the winter. A few gentlemen take possession of the coal, and unless the people will pay seven or eight dollars a ton for something that is worth three dollars, they will have to freeze. Then there is nothing to do but to break into jail, and so there are many more in jail in the winter than in summer. It costs more for gas in the winter because the nights are longer, and people go to jail to save gas bills. The jails are electric-lighted. You may not know it, but these economic laws are working all the time, whether we know it or do not know it.

There are more people who go to jail in hard times than in good times—few people, comparatively, go to jail except when they are hard up. They go to jail because they have no other place to go. They may not know why, but it is true all the same. People are not more wicked in hard times. That is not the reason. The fact is true all over the world that in hard times more people go to jail than in good times, and in winter more people go to jail than in summer. Of course it is pretty hard times for people who go to jail at any time. The people who go to jail are almost always poor people—people who have no other place to live, first and last. When times are hard, then you find large numbers of people who go to jail who would not otherwise be in jail.

Long ago, Mr. Buckle, who was a great philosopher and historian, collected facts, and he showed that the number of people who are arrested increased just as the price of food increased. When they put up the price of gas ten cents a thousand, I do not know who will go to jail, but I do know that a certain number of people will go. When the meat combine raises the price of beef, I do not know who is going to jail, but I know that a large number of people are bound to go. Whenever the Standard Oil Company raises the price of oil, I know that a certain number of girls who are seamstresses, and who work night after night long hours for somebody else, will be compelled to go out on the streets and ply another trade, and I know that Mr. Rockefeller and his associates are responsible and not the poor girls in the jails.

First and last, people are sent to jail because they are poor. Sometimes, as I say, you may not need money at the particular time, but you wish to have thrifty forehanded habits, and do not always wait until you are in absolute want. Some of you people are perhaps plying the trade, the profession, which is called burglary. No man in his right senses will go into a strange house in the dead of night and prowl around with a dark lantern through unfamiliar rooms and take chances of his life, if he has plenty of the good things of the world in his own home. You would not take any such chances as that. If a man had clothes in his clothes-press and beefsteak in his pantry and money in the bank, he would not navigate around nights in houses where he knows nothing about the premises whatever. It always requires experience and education for this profession, and people who fit themselves for it are no more to blame than I am for being a lawyer. A man would not hold up another man on the street if he had plenty of money in his own pocket. He might do it if he had one dollar or two dollars, but he wouldn't if he had as much money as Mr. Rockefeller has. Mr. Rockefeller has a great deal better hold-up game than that.

The more that is taken from the poor by the rich, who have the chance to take it, the more poor people there are who are compelled to resort to these means for a livelihood. They may not understand it, they may not think so at once, but after all they are driven into that line of employment.

There is a bill before the legislature of this state to punish kidnapping children with death. We have wise members of the legislature. They know the gas trust when they see it and they always see it—they can furnish light enough to be seen; and this legislature thinks it is going to stop kidnapping children by making a law punishing kidnappers of children with death. I don't believe in kidnapping children, but the legislature is all wrong. Kidnapping children is not a crime, it is a profession. It has been developed with the times. It has been developed with our modern industrial conditions. There are many ways of making money—many new ways that our ancestors knew nothing about. Our ancestors knew nothing about a billion-dollar trust; and here comes some poor fellow who has no other trade and he discovers the profession of kidnapping children.

This crime is born, not because people are bad; people don't kidnap other people's children because they want the children or because they are devilish, but because they see a chance to get some money out of it. You cannot cure this crime by passing a law punishing by death kidnappers of children. There is one way to cure it. There is one way to cure all these offenses, and that is to give the people a chance to live. There is no other way, and there never was any other way since the world began; and the world is so blind and stupid that it will not see. If every man and woman and child in the world had a chance to make a decent, fair, honest living, there would be no jails and no lawyers and no courts. There might be some persons here or there with some peculiar formation of their brain, like Rockefeller, who would do these things simply to be doing them; but they would be very, very few, and those should be sent to a hospital and treated, and not sent to jail; and they would entirely disappear in the second generation, or at least in the third generation.

I am not talking pure theory. I will just give you two or three illustrations.

The English people once punished criminals by sending them away. They would load them on a ship and export them to Australia. England was owned by lords and nobles and rich people. They owned the whole earth over there, and the other people had to stay in the streets. They could not get a decent living. They used to take their criminals and send them to Australia—I mean the class of criminals who got caught. When these criminals got over there, and nobody else had come, they had the whole continent to run over, and so they could raise sheep and furnish their own meat, which is easier than stealing it. These criminals then became decent, respectable people because they had a chance to live. They did not commit any crimes. They were just like the English people who sent them there, only better. And in the second generation the descendants of those criminals were as good and respectable a class of people as there were on the face of the earth, and then they began building churches and jails themselves.

A portion of this country was settled in the same way, landing prisoners down on the southern coast; but when they got here and had a whole continent to run over and plenty of chances to make a living, they became respectable citizens, making their own living just like any other citizen in the world. But finally the descendants of the English aristocracy who sent the people to Australia found out they were getting rich, and so they went over to get possession of the earth as they always do, and they organized land syndicates and got control of the land and ores, and then they had just as many criminals in Australia as they did in England. It was not because the world had grown bad; it was because the earth had been taken away from the people.

Some of you people have lived in the country. It's prettier than it is here. And if you have ever lived on a farm you understand that if you put a lot of cattle in a field, when the pasture is short they will jump over the fence; but put them in a good field where there is plenty of pasture, and they will be law-abiding cattle to the end of time. The human animal is just like the rest of the animals, only a little more so. The same thing that governs in the one governs in the other.

Everybody makes his living along the lines of least resistance. A wise man who comes into a country early sees a great undeveloped land. For instance, our rich men twenty-five years ago saw that Chicago was small and knew a lot of people would come here and settle, and they readily saw that if they had all the land around here it would be worth a good deal, so they grabbed the land. You cannot be a landlord because somebody has got it all. You must find some other calling. In England and Ireland and Scotland less than five percent own all the land there is, and the people are bound to stay there on any kind of terms the landlords give. They must live the best they can, so they develop all these various professions—burglary, picking pockets and the like.

Again, people find all sorts of ways of getting rich. These are diseases like everything else. You look at people getting rich, organizing trusts and making a million dollars, and somebody gets the disease and he starts out. He catches it just as a man catches the mumps or the measles; he is not to blame, it is in the air. You will find men speculating beyond their means, because the mania of money-getting is taking possession of them. It is simply a disease—nothing more, nothing less. You cannot avoid catching it; but the fellows who have control of the earth have the advantage of you. See what the law is: when these men get control of things, they make the laws. They do not make the laws to protect anybody; courts are not instruments of justice. When your case gets into court it will make little difference whether you are guilty or innocent, but it's better you have a smart lawyer. And you cannot have a smart lawyer unless you have money. First and last it's a question of money. Those men who own the earth make the laws to protect what they have. They fix up a sort of fence or pen around what they have, and they fix the law so the fellow on the outside cannot get in. The laws are really organized for the protection of the men who rule the world. They were never organized or enforced to do justice. We have no system for doing justice, not the slightest in the world.

Let me illustrate: Take the poorest person in this room. If the community had provided a system of doing justice, the poorest person in this room would have as good a lawyer as the richest, would he not? When you went into court you would have just as long a trial and just as fair a trial as the richest person in Chicago. Your case would not be tried in fifteen or twenty minutes, whereas it would take fifteen days to get through with a rich man's case.

Then if you were rich and were beaten, your case would be taken to the Appellate Court. A poor man cannot take his case to the Appellate Court; he has not the price. And then to the Supreme Court. And if he were beaten there he might perhaps go to the United States Supreme Court. And he might die of old age before he got into jail. If you are poor, it's a quick job. You are almost known to be guilty, else you would not be there. Why should anyone be in the criminal court if he were not guilty? He would not be there if he could be anywhere else. The officials have no time to look after all these cases. The people who are on the outside, who are running banks and building churches and making jails, they have no time to examine 600 or 700 prisoners each year to see whether they are guilty or innocent. If the courts were organized to promote justice, the people would elect somebody to defend all these criminals, somebody as smart as the prosecutor—and give him as many detectives and as many assistants to help, and pay as much money to defend you as to prosecute you. We have a very able man for state's attorney, and he has many assistants, detectives and policemen without end, and judges to hear the cases—everything handy.

Most all of our criminal code consists in offenses against property. People are sent to jail because they have committed a crime against property. It is of very little consequence whether one hundred people more or less go to jail who ought not to go—you must protect property, because in this world property is of more importance than anything else.

How is it done? These people who have property fix it so they can protect what they have. When somebody commits a crime it does not follow that he has done something that is morally wrong. The man on the outside who has committed no crime may have done something. For instance: to take all the coal in the United States and raise the price two dollars or three dollars when there is no need of it, and thus kill thousands of babies and send thousands of people to the poorhouse and tens of thousands to jail, as is done every year in the United States—this is a greater crime than all the people in our jails ever committed; but the law does not punish it. Why? Because the fellows who control the earth make the laws. If you and I had the making of the laws, the first thing we would do would be to punish the fellow who gets control of the earth. Nature put this coal in the ground for me as well as for them and nature made the prairies up here to raise wheat for me as well as for them, and then the great railroad companies came along and fenced it up.

Most all of the crimes for which we are punished are property crimes. There are a few personal crimes, like murder—but they are very few. The crimes committed are mostly those against property. If this punishment is right the criminals must have a lot of property. How much money is there in this crowd? And yet you are all here for crimes against property. The people up and down the Lake Shore have not committed crime; still they have so much property they don't know what to do with it. It is perfectly plain why these people have not committed crimes against property; they make the laws and therefore do not need to break them. And in order for you to get some property you are obliged to break the rules of the game. I don't know but what some of you may have had a very nice chance to get rich by carrying a hod for one dollar a day, twelve hours. Instead of taking that nice, easy profession, you are a burglar. If you had been given a chance to be a banker you would rather follow that. Some of you may have had a chance to work as a switchman on a railroad where you know, according to statistics, that you cannot live and keep all your limbs more than seven years, and you can get fifty dollars or seventy-five dollars a month for taking your lives in your hands; and instead of taking that lucrative position you chose to be a sneak thief, or something like that. Some of you made that sort of choice. I don't know which I would take if I was reduced to this choice. I have an easier choice.

I will guarantee to take from this jail, or any jail in the world, five hundred men who have been the worst criminals and law-breakers who ever got into jail, and I will go down to our lowest streets and take five hundred of the most abandoned prostitutes, and go out somewhere where there is plenty of land, and will give them a chance to make a living, and they will be as good people as the average in the community.

There is a remedy for the sort of condition we see here. The world never finds it out, or when it does find it out it does not enforce it. You may pass a law punishing every person with death for burglary, and it will make no difference. Men will commit it just the same. In England there was a time when one hundred different offenses were punishable with death, and it made no difference. The English people strangely found out that so fast as they repealed the severe penalties and so fast as they did away with punishing men by death, crime decreased instead of increased; that the smaller the penalty the fewer the crimes.

Hanging men in our county jails does not prevent murder. It makes murderers.

And this has been the history of the world. It's easy to see how to do away with what we call crime. It is not so easy to do it. I will tell you how to do it. It can be done by giving the people a chance to live—by destroying special privileges. So long as big criminals can get the coal fields, so long as the big criminals have control of the city council and get the public streets for streetcars and gas rights—this is bound to send thousands of poor people to jail. So long as men are allowed to monopolize all the earth, and compel others to live on such terms as these men see fit to make, then you are bound to get into jail.

The only way in the world to abolish crime and criminals is to abolish the big ones and the little ones together. Make fair conditions of life. Give men a chance to live. Abolish the right of private ownership of land, abolish monopoly, make the world partners in production, partners in the good things of life. Nobody would steal if he could get something of his own some easier way. Nobody will commit burglary when he has a house full. No girl will go out on the streets when she has a comfortable place at home. The man who owns a sweatshop or a department store may not be to blame himself for the condition of his girls, but when he pays them five dollars, three dollars, and two dollars a week, I wonder where he thinks they will get the rest of their money to live. The only way to cure these conditions is by equality. There should be no jails. They do not accomplish what they pretend to accomplish. If you would wipe them out there would be no more criminals than now. They terrorize nobody. They are a blot upon any civilization, and a jail is an evidence of the lack of charity of the people on the outside who make the jails and fill them with the victims of their greed.

Speculations

1. Assess the rhetorical dimension of this speech—that is, a famous lawyer delivering a talk to the inmates of the Cook County Jail. Was Darrow serious? Was he trying to be outrageous just to shock the authorities? Was it appropriate for Darrow to give such a speech? Explain your answer.
2. Darrow attempts to collapse the distinction between those in jail and those out of jail, ultimately claiming that they are all criminals. How does he make this argument? Are you convinced?
3. Darrow states that "If the community had provided a system of doing justice, the poorest person in this room would have as good a lawyer as the richest, would he not?" Does Darrow's criticism have merit? Should the criminal justice system be "dollar neutral"?
4. Darrow considers the different legal treatments accorded the rich as opposed to the poor. But what differences in treatment do we

see also between the young and the old? Given your own experience, do young people get better or worse treatment from authorities than older people? You might want to consider this question in light of some specific incident in your own life—say, being falsely accused of cheating, shoplifting, lying, or the like.

5. Do you agree with Darrow that if he took five hundred male criminals and five hundred "of the most abandoned prostitutes" and gave them land and "a chance to make a living," that they would be "as good people as the average in the community"? Discuss, if you wish, the example of settlement in Australia to support your argument.

HUSTLER

Malcolm X

In a sense, Malcolm X was born into a life of violence, disruption, and despair—and it took him most of his life and a trip to Mecca to discover the possibilities of hope and brotherhood. Tragically, for Malcolm X, his followers, and America, the great black leader was never able to translate his vision into political and social gains: He was assassinated in 1965 by three men—reputedly followers of the rival black leader, Elijah Muhammad of the Black Muslims—as he addressed a group of supporters in a Harlem ballroom.

Malcolm X was born in Omaha in 1925, one of eight children of Reverend Earl Little, a Baptist minister, and Louise Little. His father was a physically powerful man who could behead chickens or rabbits "with one twist of his big black hands." Earl Little preached a form of black nationalism, was driven out of Nebraska by the Ku Klux Klan, and settled in Lansing, Michigan. There too he was called an "uppity nigger" and his home was torched by a band of white supremacists; after one of many frequent battles with his wife, Earl Little stalked out of the house and was later found mutilated and murdered. Malcolm Little was six. His mother, forced to accept welfare and do odd jobs within the same society that had murdered her husband, succumbed to mental illness; the children were sent to a succession of foster homes. In spite of this difficult life, Malcolm Little succeeded in school and aspired to become a lawyer. His high school English teacher, however, told him it was just a pipe dream and that he should be "realistic about being a nigger."

Malcolm X quit school and turned to serious criminal activities. "Hustler," a chapter from his *Autobiography*, recounts part of this experience. Malcolm Little was eventually caught, convicted, and imprisoned. He educated himself in the prison library and became a follower of Elijah Muhammad, who urged his followers to renounce white America in favor of an autonomous black society. Malcolm became a convert and changed his name to Malcolm X.

Upon release from prison in 1952, Malcolm X assumed an increasingly powerful and influential ministerial role within the Black Muslim movement. He grew disillusioned with Elijah Muhammad, who became jealous of his greatest disciple. Concerned that he would be assassinated, Malcolm X left America and toured Mecca, birthplace of the Muslim prophet Mohammed, thereupon renaming himself El-Hajj Mahlik El-Shabazz and rededicating himself to promote harmony among all blacks throughout the world. Within a year he lay dead on a Harlem stage.

Malcolm X was also a man, a husband, and a father; he and his wife Betty Shabazz married in 1958 and had six daughters. According to George Metcalf:

> During brief visits home, Malcolm never lost a chance to romp with his children, and filled the free time with voracious reading. Betty marveled at his concentration. He picked up the classics, anthropology, African history, delved into the origins of religion and would tackle anything by or about black people. His capacity for speed reading was now so acute he could devour a difficult book "in three hours and easier ones in one to two hours."

A reading of the entire *Autobiography* (and other published work) reveals Malcolm X's genius, erudition, and vision. His power and charisma were translated to the screen by Denzel Washington in Spike Lee's masterful film biography. This selection offers a more particular view of the whys and wherefores of criminal life for a black man as well as his observations about the class response to crime and punishment.

I can't remember all the hustles I had during the next two years in Harlem, after the abrupt end of my riding the trains and peddling reefers to the touring bands.

Negro railroad men waited for their trains in their big locker room on the lower level of Grand Central Station. Big blackjack and poker games went on in there around the clock. Sometimes five hundred dollars would be on the table. One day, in a blackjack game, an old cook who was dealing the cards tried to be slick, and I had to drop my pistol in his face.

The next time I went into one of those games, intuition told me to stick my gun under my belt right down the middle of my back. Sure enough, someone had squealed. Two big, beefy-faced Irish cops came in. They frisked me—and they missed my gun where they hadn't expected one.

The cops told me never again to be caught in Grand Central Station unless I had a ticket to ride somewhere. And I knew that by the next day, every railroad's personnel office would have a blackball on me, so I never tried to get another railroad job.

There I was back in Harlem's streets among all the rest of the hustlers. I couldn't sell reefers; the dope squad detectives were too familiar with me. I was a true hustler—uneducated, unskilled at anything honorable, and I considered myself nervy and cunning enough to live by my wits, exploiting any prey that presented itself. I would risk just about anything.

Right now, in every big city ghetto, tens of thousands of yesterday's and today's school drop-outs are keeping body and soul together by some form of hustling in the same way I did. And they inevitably move into more and more, worse and worse, illegality and immorality. Full-time hustlers never can relax to appraise what they are doing and where they are bound. As is the case in any jungle, the hustler's every waking hour is lived with both the practical and the subconscious knowledge that if he ever relaxes, if he ever slows down, the other hungry, restless foxes, ferrets, wolves, and vultures out there with him won't hesitate to make him their prey.

During the next six to eight months, I pulled my first robberies and stick-ups. Only small ones. Always in other, nearby cities. And I got away. As the pros did, I too would key myself to pull these jobs by my first use of hard dope. I began with Sammy's recommendation—sniffing cocaine.

Normally now, for street wear, I might call it, I carried a hardly noticeable little flat, blue-steel .25 automatic. But for working, I carried a .32, a .38 or a .45. I saw how when the eyes stared at the big black hole, the faces fell slack and the mouths sagged open. And when I spoke, the people seemed to hear as though they were far away, and they would do whatever I asked.

Between jobs, staying high on narcotics kept me from getting nervous. Still, upon sudden impulses, just to play safe, I would abruptly move from one to another fifteen- to twenty-dollars-a-week room, always in my favorite 147th–150th Street area, just flanking Sugar Hill.

Once on a job with Sammy, we had a pretty close call. Someone must have seen us. We were making our getaway, running, when we heard the sirens. Instantly, we slowed to walking. As a police car screeched to a stop, we stepped out into the street, meeting it, hailing it to ask for directions. They must have thought we were about to give them some information. They just cursed us and raced on. Again, it didn't cross the white men's minds that a trick like that might be pulled on them by Negroes.

The suits that I wore, the finest, I bought hot for about thirty-five to fifty dollars. I made it my rule never to go after more than I needed to live on. Any experienced hustler will tell you that getting greedy is the quickest road to prison. I kept "cased" in my head vulnerable places and situations and I would perform the next job only when my bankroll in my pocket began to get too low.

Some weeks, I bet large amounts on the numbers. I still played with the same runner with whom I'd started in Small's Paradise. Playing my hunches, many a day I'd have up to forty dollars on two numbers, hoping for that fabulous six hundred-to-one payoff. But I never did hit a big number full force. There's no telling what I would have done if ever I'd landed $10,000 or $12,000 at one time. Of course, once in a while I'd hit a small combination figure. Sometimes, flush like that, I'd telephone Sophia to come over from Boston for a couple of days.

I went to the movies a lot again. And I never missed my musician friends whenever they were playing, either in Harlem, downtown at the big theaters, or on 52nd Street.

Reginald and I got very close the next time his ship came back into New York. We discussed our family, and what a shame it was that our book-loving oldest brother Wilfred had never had the chance to go to some of those big universities where he would have gone far. And we exchanged thoughts we had never shared with anyone.

Reginald, in his quiet way, was a mad fan of musicians and music. When his ship sailed one morning without him, a principal reason was that I had thoroughly exposed him to the exciting musical world. We had wild times backstage with the musicians when they were playing the Roxy, or the Paramount. After selling reefers with the bands as they traveled, I was known to almost every popular Negro musician around New York in 1944–1945.

Reginald and I went the Savoy Ballroom, the Apollo Theater, the Braddock Hotel bar, the nightclubs and speak-easies, wherever Negroes played music. The great Lady Day, Billie Holiday, hugged him and called him "baby brother." Reginald shared tens of thousands of Negroes' feelings that the living end of the big bands was Lionel Hampton's. I was very close to many of the men in Hamp's band; I introduced Reginald to them, and also to Hamp himself, and Hamp's wife and business manager, Gladys Hampton. One of this world's sweetest people is Hamp. Anyone who knows him will tell you that he'd often do the most generous things for people he barely knew. As much money as Hamp has made, and still makes, he would be broke today if his money and his business weren't handled by Gladys, who is one of the brainiest women I ever met. The Apollo Theater's owner, Frank Schiffman, could tell you. He generally signed bands to play for a set weekly amount, but I know that once during those days Gladys Hampton instead arranged a deal for Hamp's band to play for a cut of the gate. Then the usual number of shows was doubled up—if I'm not mistaken, eight shows a day, instead of the usual four—and Hamp's pulling power cleaned up. Gladys Hampton used to talk to me a lot, and she tried to give me good advice: "Calm down, Red." Gladys saw how wild I was. She saw me headed toward a bad end.

One of the things I liked about Reginald was that when I left him to go away "working," Reginald asked me no questions. After he came to Harlem, I went on more jobs than usual. I guess that what influenced me to get my first actual apartment was my not wanting Reginald to be knocking around Harlem without anywhere to call "home." That first apartment was three rooms, for a hundred dollars a month, I think, in the front basement of a house on 147th Street between Convent and St. Nicholas Avenues. Living in the rear basement apartment, right behind Reginald and me, was one of Harlem's most successful narcotics dealers.

With the apartment as our headquarters, I gradually got Reginald introduced around to Creole Bill's, and other Harlem after-hours spots. About two o'clock every morning, as the downtown white nightclubs closed, Reginald and I would stand around in front of this or that Harlem after-hours place, and I'd school him to what was happening.

Especially after the nightclubs downtown closed, the taxis and black limousines would be driving uptown, bringing those white people who never could get enough of Negro *soul*. The places popular with these whites ranged all the way from the big locally famous ones such as Jimmy's Chicken Shack, and Dickie Wells', to the little here-tonight-gone-tomorrow-night private clubs, so-called, where a dollar was collected at the door for "membership."

Inside every after-hours spot, the smoke would hurt your eyes. Four white people to every Negro would be in there drinking whisky from coffee cups and eating fried chicken. The generally flush-faced white men and their makeup-masked, glittery-eyed women would be pounding each other's backs and uproariously laughing and applauding the music. A lot of whites, drunk, would go staggering up to Negroes, the waiters, the owners, or Negroes at tables, wringing their hands, even trying to hug them, "You're just as good as I am— I want you to know that!" The most famous places drew both Negro and white celebrities who enjoyed each other. A jam-packed four-thirty A.M. crowd at Jimmie's Chicken Shack or Dickie Wells' might have such jam-session entertainment as Hazel Scott playing the piano for Billie Holiday singing the blues. Jimmy's Chicken Shack, incidentally, was where once, later on, I worked briefly as a waiter. That's where Redd Foxx was the dishwasher who kept the kitchen crew in stitches.

After a while, my brother Reginald had to have a hustle, and I gave much thought to what would be, for him, a good, safe hustle. After he'd learned his own way around, it would be up to him to take risks for himself—if he wanted to make more and quicker money.

The hustle I got Reginald into really was very simple. It utilized the psychology of the ghetto jungle. Downtown, he paid the two dollars, or whatever it was, for a regular city peddler's license. Then I took him to a manufacturers' outlet where we bought a supply of cheap imperfect "seconds"—shirts, underwear, cheap rings, watches, all kinds of quick-sale items.

Watching me work this hustle back in Harlem, Reginald quickly caught on to how to go into barbershops, beauty parlors, and bars acting very nervous as he let the customers peep into his small valise of "loot." With so many thieves around anxious to get rid of stolen good-quality merchandise cheaply, many Harlemites, purely because of this conditioning, jumped to pay hot prices for inferior goods whose sale was perfectly legitimate. It never took long to get rid of a valiseful for at least twice what it had cost. And if any cop stopped Reginald, he had in his pocket both the peddler's license and the manufacturers' outlet bills of sale. Reginald only had to be certain that none of the customers to whom he sold ever saw that he was legitimate.

I assumed that Reginald, like most of the Negroes I knew, would go for a white woman. I'd point out Negro-happy white women to him, and explain that a Negro with any brains could wrap these women around his fingers. But I have to say this for Reginald: he never liked white women. I remember the one time he met Sophia; he was so cool it upset Sophia, and it tickled me.

Reginald got himself a black woman. I'd guess she was pushing thirty; an "old settler," as we called them back in those days. She was a waitress in an exclusive restaurant downtown. She lavished on Reginald everything she had, she was so happy to get a young man. I mean she bought his clothes, cooked and washed for him, and everything, as though he were a baby.

That was just another example of why my respect for my younger brother kept increasing. Reginald showed, in often surprising ways, more sense than a lot of working hustlers twice his age. Reginald then was only sixteen, but, a six-footer, he looked and acted much older than his years.

All through the war, the Harlem racial picture never was too bright. Tension built to a pretty high pitch. Old-timers told me that Harlem had never been the same since the 1935 riot, when millions of dollars worth of damage was done by thousands of Negroes, infuriated chiefly by the white merchants in Harlem refusing to hire a Negro even as their stores raked in Harlem's money.

During World War II, Mayor LaGuardia officially closed the Savoy Ballroom. Harlem said the real reason was to stop Negroes from dancing with white women. Harlem said that no one dragged the white women in there. Adam Clayton Powell made it a big fight. He had successfully fought Consolidated Edison and the New York Telephone Company until they had hired Negroes. Then he had helped to battle the U.S. Navy and the U.S. Army about their segregating of uniformed Negroes. But Powell couldn't win this battle. City Hall kept the Savoy closed for a long time. It was just another one of the "liberal North" actions that didn't help Harlem to love the white man any.

Finally, rumor flashed that in the Braddock Hotel, white cops had shot a Negro soldier. I was walking down St. Nicholas Avenue; I saw all of these Negroes hollering and running north from 125th Street. Some of them were loaded down with armfuls of stuff. I remember it was the band-leader Fletcher Henderson's nephew "Shorty" Henderson who told me what had happened. Negroes were smashing store windows, and taking everything they could grab and carry—furniture, food, jewelry, clothes, whisky. Within an hour, every New York City cop seemed to be in Harlem. Mayor LaGuardia and the NAACP's then-Secretary, the famed late Walter White, were in a red firecar, riding around pleading over a loudspeaker to all of those shouting, milling, angry Negroes to please go home and stay inside.

Just recently I ran into Shorty Henderson on Seventh Avenue. We were laughing about a fellow whom the riot had left with the nickname of "Left Feet." In a scramble in a women's shoe store, somehow he'd grabbed five shoes, all of them for left feet! And we laughed about the scared little Chinese whose restaurant didn't have a hand laid on it, because rioters just about convulsed laughing when they saw the sign the Chinese had hastily stuck on his front door: "Me Colored Too."

After the riot, things got very tight in Harlem. It was terrible for the night-life people, and for those hustlers whose main income had been the white man's money. The 1935 riot had left only a relative trickle of the money which had poured into Harlem during the 1920s. And now this new riot ended even that trickle.

Today the white people who visit Harlem, and this mostly on weekend nights, are hardly more than a few dozen who do the twist, the frug, the Watusi, and all the rest of the current dance crazes in Small's Paradise, owned now by the great basketball champion "Wilt the Stilt" Chamberlain, who draws crowds with his big, clean, All-American-athlete image. Most white people today are physically afraid to come to Harlem—and it's for good reasons, too. Even for Negroes, Harlem night life is about finished. Most of the Negroes who have money to spend are spending it downtown somewhere in this hypocritical "integration," in places where previously the police would have been called to haul off any Negro insane enough to try and get in. The already Croesus-rich white man can't get another skyscraper hotel finished and opened before all these integration-mad Negroes, who themselves don't own a tool shed, are booking the swanky new hotel for "cotillions" and "conventions." Those rich whites could afford it when they used to throw away their money in Harlem. But Negroes can't afford to be taking their money downtown to the white man.

Sammy and I, on a robbery job, got a bad scare, a very close call.

Things had grown so tight in Harlem that some hustlers had been forced to go to work. Even some prostitutes had gotten jobs as domestics, and cleaning office buildings at night. The pimping was so poor, Sammy had gone on the job with me. We had selected one of those situations considered "impossible." But wherever people think that, the guards will unconsciously grow gradually more relaxed, until sometimes those can be the easiest jobs of all.

But right in the middle of the act, we had some bad luck. A bullet grazed Sammy. We just barely escaped.

Sammy fortunately wasn't really hurt. We split up, which was always wise to do.

Just before daybreak, I went to Sammy's apartment. His newest woman, one of those beautiful but hot-headed Spanish Negroes, was in there crying and carrying on over Sammy. She went for me, screaming and clawing; she knew I'd been in on it with him. I fended her off. Not able to figure out why Sammy didn't shut her up, I did . . . and from the corner of my eye, I saw Sammy going for his gun.

Sammy's reaction that way to my hitting his woman—close as he and I were—was the only weak spot I'd ever glimpsed. The woman screamed and dove for him. She knew as I did that when your best friend draws a gun on you, he usually has lost all control of his emotions, and he intends to shoot. She distracted Sammy long enough for me to bolt through the door. Sammy chased me, about a block.

We soon made up—on the surface. But things never are fully right again with anyone you have seen trying to kill you.

Intuition told us that we had better lay low for a good while. The worst thing was that we'd been seen. The police in that nearby town had surely circulated our general descriptions.

I just couldn't forget that incident over Sammy's woman. I came to rely more and more upon my brother Reginald as the only one in my world I could completely trust.

Reginald was lazy, I'd discovered that. He had quit his hustle altogether. But I didn't mind that, really, because one could be as lazy as he wanted, if he would only use his head, as Reginald was doing. He had left my apartment by now. He was living off his "old settler" woman—when he was in town. I had also taught Reginald how he could work for a little while for a railroad, then use his identification card to travel for nothing—and Reginald loved to travel. Several times, he had gone visiting all around, among our brothers and sisters. They had now begun to scatter to different cities. In Boston, Reginald was closer to our sister Mary than to Ella, who had been my favorite. Both Reginald and Mary were quiet types, and Ella and I were extroverts. And Shorty in Boston had given my brother a royal time.

Because of my reputation, it was easy for me to get into the numbers racket. That was probably Harlem's only hustle which hadn't slumped in business. In return for a favor to some white mobster, my new boss and his wife had just been given a six-months numbers banking privilege for the Bronx railroad area called Motthaven Yards. The white mobsters had the numbers racket split into specific areas. A designated area would be assigned to someone for a specified period of time. My boss's wife had been Dutch Schultz's secretary in the 1930s, during the time when Schultz had strong-armed his way into control of the Harlem numbers business.

My job now was to ride a bus across the George Washington Bridge where a fellow was waiting for me to hand him a bag of numbers betting slips. We never spoke. I'd cross the street and catch the next bus back to Harlem. I never knew who that fellow was. I never knew who picked up the betting money for the slips that I handled. You didn't ask questions in the rackets.

My boss's wife and Gladys Hampton were the only two women I ever met in Harlem whose business ability I really respected. My boss's wife, when she had the time and the inclination to talk, would tell me many interesting things. She would talk to me about the Dutch Schultz days—about deals that she had known, about graft paid to officials—rookie cops and shyster lawyers right on up into the top levels of police and politics. She knew from personal experience how crime existed only to the degree that the law cooperated with it. She showed me how, in the country's entire social, political and economic structure, the criminal, the law, and the politicians were actually inseparable partners.

It was at this time that I changed from my old numbers man, the one I'd used since I first worked in Small's Paradise. He hated to lose a heavy player, but he readily understood why I would now want to play with a runner of my own outfit. That was how I began placing my bets with West Indian Archie. I've mentioned him before—one of Harlem's really *bad* Negroes; one of those former Dutch Schultz strong-arm men around Harlem.

West Indian Archie had finished time in Sing Sing not long before I came to Harlem. But my boss's wife had hired him not just because she knew him from the old days. West Indian Archie had the kind of photographic memory that put him among the elite of numbers runners. He never wrote down your number; even in the case of combination plays, he would just nod. He was able to file all the numbers in his head, and write them down for the banker only when he turned in his money. This made him the ideal runner because cops could never catch him with any betting slips.

I've often reflected upon such black veteran numbers men as West Indian Archie. If they had lived in another kind of society, their exceptional mathematical talents might have been better used. But they were black.

Anyway, it was status just to be known as a client of West Indian Archie's, because he handled only sizable bettors. He also required integrity and sound credit: it wasn't necessary that you pay as you played; you could pay West Indian Archie by the week. He always carried a couple of thousand dollars on him, his own money. If a client came up to him and said he'd hit for some moderate amount, say a fifty-cent or one dollar combination, West Indian Archie would peel off the three or six hundred dollars, and later get his money back from the banker.

Every weekend, I'd pay my bill—anywhere from fifty to even one hundred dollars, if I had really plunged on some hunch. And when, once or twice, I did hit, always just some combination, as I've described, West Indian Archie paid me off from his own roll.

The six months finally ended for my boss and his wife. They had done well. Their runners got nice tips, and promptly were snatched by other bankers. I continued working for my boss and his wife in a gambling house they opened.

A Harlem madam I'd come to know—through having done a friend of hers a favor—introduced me to a special facet of the Harlem night world, something which the riot had only interrupted. It was the world where, behind locked doors, Negroes catered to monied white people's weird sexual tastes.

The whites I'd known loved to rub shoulders publicly with black folks in the after-hours clubs and speakeasies. These, on the other hand, were whites who did not want it known that they had been anywhere near Harlem. The riot had made these exclusive white customers nervous. Their slipping into and about Harlem hadn't been so noticeable when other whites were also around. But now they would be conspicuous; they also feared the recently aroused anger of Harlem Negroes. So the madam was safeguarding her growing operation by offering me a steerer's job.

During the war, it was extremely difficult to get a telephone. One day the madam told me to stay at my apartment the next morning. She talked to somebody. I don't know who it was, but before the next noon, I dialed the madam from my own telephone—unlisted.

This madam was a specialist in her field. If her own girls could not—or would not—accommodate a customer, she would send me to another place, usually an apartment somewhere else in Harlem, where the requested "specialty" was done.

My post for picking up the customers was right outside the Astor Hotel, that always-busy northwest corner of 45th Street and Broadway. Watching the moving traffic, I was soon able to spot the taxi, car, or limousine—even before it slowed down—with the anxious white faces peering out for the tall, reddish-brown-complexioned Negro wearing a dark suit, or raincoat, with a white flower in his lapel.

If they were in a private car, unless it was chauffeured, I would take the wheel and drive where we were going. But if they were in a taxi, I would always tell the cabbie, "The Apollo Theater in Harlem, please," since among New York City taxis a certain percentage are driven by cops. We would get another cab—driven by a black man—and I'd give him the right address.

As soon as I got that party settled, I'd telephone the madam. She would generally have me rush by taxi right back downtown to be on the 45th Street and Broadway corner at a specified time. Appointments were strictly punctual; rarely was I on the corner as much as five minutes. And I knew how to keep moving about so as not to attract the attention of any vice squad plainclothes men or uniformed cops.

With tips, which were often heavy, sometimes I would make over a hundred dollars a night steering up to ten customers in a party—to see anything, to do anything, to have anything done to them, that they wanted. I hardly ever knew the identities of my customers, but the few I did recognize, or whose names I happened to hear, remind me now of the Profumo case in England. The English are not far ahead of rich and influential Americans when it comes to seeking rarities and oddities.

Rich men, middle-aged and beyond, men well past their prime: these weren't college boys, these were their Ivy League fathers. Even grandfathers, I guess. Society leaders. Big politicians. Tycoons. Important friends from out of town. City government big shots. All kinds of professional people. Star performing artists. Theatrical and Hollywood celebrities. And, of course, racketeers.

Harlem was their sin-den, their fleshpot. They stole off among taboo black people, and took off whatever antiseptic important, dignified masks they wore in their white world. These were men who could afford to spend large amounts of money for two, three, or four hours indulging their strange appetites.

But in this black–white nether world, nobody judged the customers. Anything they could name, anything they could imagine, anything they could describe, they could do, or could have done to them, just as long as they paid.

In the Profumo case in England, Christine Keeler's friend testified that some of her customers wanted to be whipped. One of my main steers to one specialty address away from the madam's house was the apartment of a big, coal-black girl, strong as an ox, with muscles like a dockworker's. A funny thing, it generally was the oldest of these white men—in their sixties, I know, some maybe in their seventies—they couldn't seem to recover quickly enough from their last whipping so they could have me meet them again at 45th and Broadway to take them back to that apartment, to cringe on their knees and beg and cry out for mercy under that black girl's whip. Some of them would pay me extra to come and watch them being beaten. That girl greased her big Amazon body all over to look shinier and blacker. She used small, plaited whips, she would draw blood, and she was making herself a small fortune off those old white men.

I wouldn't tell all the things I've seen. I used to wonder, later on, when I was in prison, what a psychiatrist would make of it all. And so many of these men held responsible positions; they exercised guidance, influence, and authority over others.

In prison later, I'd think, too, about another thing. Just about all of those whites specifically expressed as their preference black, *black*, "the blacker the better!" The madam, having long since learned this, had in her house nothing but the blackest accommodating women she could find.

In all of my time in Harlem, I never saw a white prostitute touched by a white man. White girls were in some of the various Harlem specialty places. They would participate in customers' most frequent exhibition requests—a sleek, black Negro male having a white woman. Was this the white man wanting to witness his deepest sexual fear? A few times, I even had parties that included white women whom the men had brought with them to watch this. I never steered any white women other than in these instances, brought by their own men, or who had been put into contact with me by a white Lesbian whom I knew, who was another variety of specialty madam.

This Lesbian, a beautiful white woman, had a male Negro stable. Her vocabulary was all profanity. She supplied Negro males, on order, to well-to-do white women.

I'd seen this Lesbian and her blonde girl friend around Harlem, drinking and talking at bars, always with young Negroes. No one who didn't know would ever guess that the Lesbian was recruiting. But one night I gave her and her girl friend some reefers which they said were the best they'd ever smoked. They lived in a hotel downtown, and after that, now and then, they would call me, and I would bring them some reefers, and we'd talk.

She told me how she had accidentally gotten started in her specialty. As a Harlem habitué, she had known Harlem Negroes who liked white women. Her role developed from a pattern of talk she often heard from bored, well-to-do white women where she worked, in an East Side beauty salon. Hearing the women complain about sexually inadequate mates, she would tell what she'd "heard" about Negro men. Observing how excited some of the women seemed to become, she finally arranged some dates with some of the Harlem Negroes she knew at her own apartment.

Eventually, she rented three midtown apartments where a woman customer could meet a Negro by appointment. Her customers recommended her service to their friends. She quit the beauty salon, set up a messenger service as an operating front, and ran all of her business by telephone.

She had also noticed the color preference. I never could substitute in an emergency, she would tell me with a laugh, because I was too light. She told me that nearly every white woman in her clientele would specify "a black one"; sometimes they would say "a *real* one," meaning black, no brown Negroes, no red Negroes.

The Lesbian thought up her messenger service idea because some of her trade wanted the Negroes to come to their homes, at times carefully arranged by telephone. These women lived in neighborhoods of swank brownstones and exclusive apartment houses, with doormen dressed like admirals. But white society never thinks about challenging any Negro in a servant role. Doormen would telephone up and hear "Oh, yes, send him right up, James"; service elevators would speed those neatly dressed Negro messenger boys right up—so that they could "deliver" what had been ordered by some of the most privileged white women in Manhattan.

The irony is that those white women had no more respect for those Negroes than white men have had for the Negro women they have been "using" since slavery times. And, in turn, Negroes have no respect for the whites they get into bed with. I know the way I felt about Sophia, who still came to New York whenever I called her.

The West Indian boyfriend of the Profumo scandal's Christine Keeler, Lucky Gordon, and his friends must have felt the same way. After England's leaders had been with those white girls, those girls, for their satisfaction, went to Negroes, to smoke reefers and make fun of some of England's greatest peers as cuckolds and fools. I don't doubt that Lucky Gordon knows the identity of "the man in the mask" and much more. If Gordon told everything those white girls told him, he would give England a new scandal.

It's no different from what happens in some of America's topmost white circles. Twenty years ago, I saw them nightly, with my own eyes. I heard them with my own ears.

The hypocritical white man will talk about the Negro's "low morals." But who has the world's lowest morals if not whites? And not only that, but the "upper-class" whites! Recently, details were published about a group of suburban New York City white housewives and mothers operating as a professional call-girl ring. In some cases, these wives were out prostituting with the agreement, even the cooperation of husbands, some of whom even waited at home, attending the children. And the customers—to quote a major New York City morning newspaper: "Some 16 ledgers and books with names of 200 Johns, many important social, financial and political figures, were seized in the raid Friday night."

I have also read recently about groups of young white couples who get together, the husbands throw their house keys into a hat, then, blindfolded, the husbands draw out a key and spend the night with the wife that the house key matches. I have never heard of anything like that being done by Negroes, even Negroes who live in the worst ghettoes and alleys and gutters.

Early one morning in Harlem, a tall, light Negro wearing a hat and with a woman's stocking drawn down over his face held up a Negro bartender and manager who were counting up the night's receipts. Like most bars in Harlem, Negroes fronted, and a Jew really owned the place. To get a license, one had to know somebody in the State Liquor Authority, and Jews working with Jews seemed to have the best S.L.A. contacts. The black manager hired some Negro hoodlums to go hunting for the hold-up man. And the man's description caused them to include me among their suspects. About daybreak that same morning, they kicked in the door of my apartment.

I told them I didn't know a thing about it, that I hadn't had a thing to do with whatever they were talking about. I told them I had been out on my hustle, steering, until maybe four in the morning, and then I had come straight to my apartment and gone to bed.

The strong-arm thugs were bluffing. They were trying to flush out the man who had done it. They still had other suspects to check out— that's all that saved me.

I put on my clothes and took a taxi and I woke up two people, the madam, then Sammy. I had some money, but the madam gave me some more, and I told Sammy I was going to see my brother Philbert in Michigan. I gave Sammy the address, so that he could let me know when things got straightened out.

This was the trip to Michigan in the wintertime when I put congolene on my head, then discovered that the bathroom sink's pipes were frozen. To keep the lye from burning up my scalp, I had to stick my head in the stool and flush and flush to rinse out the stuff.

A week passed in frigid Michigan before Sammy's telegram came. Another red Negro had confessed, which enabled me to live in Harlem again.

But I didn't go back into steering. I can't remember why I didn't. I imagine I must have felt like staying away from hustling for a while, going to some of the clubs at night, and narcotizing with my friends. Anyway, I just never went back to the madam's job.

It was at about this time, too, I remember, that I began to be sick. I had colds all the time. It got to be a steady irritation, always sniffling and wiping my nose, all day, all night. I stayed so high that I was in a dream world. Now, sometimes, I smoked opium with some white friends, actors who lived downtown. And I smoked more reefers than ever before. I didn't smoke the usual wooden-match-sized sticks of marijuana. I was so far gone by now that I smoked it almost by the ounce.

After awhile, I worked downtown for a Jew. He liked me because of something I had managed to do for him. He bought rundown restaurants and bars. Hymie was his name. He would remodel these places, then stage a big, gala reopening, with banners and a spotlight outside. The jam-packed, busy place with the big "Under New Management" sign in the window would attract speculators, usually other Jews who were around looking for something to invest money in. Sometimes even in the week of the new opening, Hymie would resell at a good profit.

Hymie really liked me, and I liked him. He loved to talk. I loved to listen. Half his talk was about Jews and Negroes. Jews who had anglicized their names were Hymie's favorite hate. Spitting and curling his mouth in scorn, he would reel off names of people he said had done this. Some of them were famous names whom most people never thought of as Jews.

"Red, I'm a Jew and you're black," he would say. "These Gentiles don't like either one of us. If the Jew wasn't smarter than the Gentile, he'd get treated worse than your people."

Hymie paid me good money while I was with him, sometimes two hundred and three hundred dollars a week. I would have done anything for Hymie. I did do all kinds of things. But my main job was transporting bootleg liquor that Hymie supplied, usually to those spruced-up bars which he had sold to someone.

Another fellow and I would drive out to Long Island where a big bootleg whiskey outfit operated. We'd take with us cartons of empty bonded whiskey bottles that were saved illegally by bars we supplied. We would buy five-gallon containers of bootleg, funnel it into the bottles, then deliver, according to Hymie's instructions, this or that many crates back to the bars.

Many people claiming they drank only such-and-such a brand couldn't tell their only brand from pure week-old Long Island bootleg. Most ordinary whiskey drinkers are "brand" chumps like this. On the side, with Hymie's approval, I was myself at that time supplying some lesser quantities of bootleg to reputable Harlem bars, as well as to some of the few speakeasies still in Harlem.

But one weekend on Long Island, something happened involving the State Liquor Authority. One of New York State's biggest recent scandals has been the exposure of wholesale S.L.A. graft and corruption. In the bootleg racket I was involved in, someone high up must have been taken for a real pile. A rumor about some "inside" tipster spread among Hymie and the others. One day Hymie didn't show up where he had told me to meet him. I never heard from him again . . . but I did hear that he was put in the ocean, and I knew he couldn't swim.

Up in the Bronx, a Negro held up some Italian racketeers in a floating crap game. I heard about it on the wire. Whoever did it, aside from being a fool, was said to be a "tall, light-skinned" Negro, masked with a woman's stocking. It has always made me wonder if that bar stickup had really been solved, or if the wrong man had confessed under beatings. But, anyway, the past suspicion of me helped to revive suspicion of me again.

Up in Fat Man's Bar on the hill overlooking the Polo Grounds, I had just gone into a telephone booth. Everyone in the bar—all over Harlem, in fact—was drinking up, excited about the news that Branch Rickey, the Brooklyn Dodgers' owner, had just signed Jackie Robinson to play in major league baseball, with the Dodgers' farm team in Montreal—which would place the time in the fall of 1945.

Earlier in the afternoon, I had collected from West Indian Archie for a fifty-cent combination bet; he had paid me three hundred dollars right out of his pocket. I was telephoning Jean Parks. Jean was one of the most beautiful women who ever lived in Harlem. She once sang with Sarah Vaughan in the Bluebonnets, a quartet that sang with Earl Hines. For a long time, Jean and I had enjoyed a standing, friendly deal that we'd go out and celebrate when either of us hit the numbers. Since my last hit, Jean had treated me twice, and we laughed on the phone, glad that now I'd treat her to a night out. We arranged to go to a 52nd Street night club to hear Billie Holiday, who had been on the road and was just back in New York.

As I hung up, I spotted the two lean, tough-looking *paisanos* gazing in at me cooped in the booth.

I didn't need any intuition. And I had no gun. A cigarette case was the only thing in my pocket. I started easing my hand down into my pocket, to try bluffing . . . and one of them snatched open the door. They were dark-olive, swarthy-featured Italians. I had my hand down into my pocket.

"Come on outside, we'll hold court," one said.

At that moment, a cop walked through the front door. The two thugs slipped out. I never in my life have been so glad to see a cop.

I was still shaking when I got to the apartment of my friend, Sammy the Pimp. He told me that not long before, West Indian Archie had been there looking for me.

Sometimes, recalling all of this, I don't know, to tell the truth, how I am alive to tell it today. They say God takes care of fools and babies. I've so often thought that Allah was watching over me. Through all of this time in my life, I really *was* dead—mentally dead. I just didn't know that I was.

Anyway, to kill time, Sammy and I sniffed some of his cocaine, until the time came to pick up Jean Parks, to go down and hear Lady Day. Sammy's having told me about West Indian Archie looking for me didn't mean a thing . . . not right then.

Speculations

1. In this chapter, Malcolm X aptly describes the life of the hustler. How would you characterize that life? What are its values? What are the central principles by which Malcolm X lived during this time?

2. The white/black racial tensions that ripple throughout this chapter are still prevalent in America. What are Malcolm X's attitudes toward whites as revealed by this chapter? Upon what facts, prejudices, assumptions are these attitudes based?

3. The *Autobiography* is not written by Malcolm X; it is a series of oral interviews that Malcolm X did with the late Alex Haley, author of *Roots.* Do you think this chapter has an oral quality to it? How so? How would you describe the organization of this chapter? Would you describe the overall structure as more characteristic of a written or an oral discourse?

4. Early in this chapter, Malcolm X says:

   > Full-time hustlers never can relax to appraise what they are doing and where they are bound. As is the case in any jungle, the hustler's every waking hour is lived with both the practical and the subconscious knowledge that if he ever relaxes, if he ever slows down, the other hungry, restless foxes, ferrets, wolves, and vultures out there with him won't hesitate to make him their prey.

   Is this true of Malcolm X's own experience as revealed by this chapter? What allows him to survive the "hustler business?" How appropriate is this Darwinian metaphor to any business or professional person in America?

5. There is an edge of anger throughout much of the *Autobiography*, and certainly one can feel that edge of anger in this chapter. Can you locate specific instances where you feel Malcolm X's anger— at whites, at police, at the value system of 1960s America? How do you respond to Malcolm X's anger and his charges about racist individuals and a racist society? Is Malcolm X himself vulnerable to the same charges, at least as represented in this one chapter? Do you feel at least some of the same anger?

6. Throughout this chapter, Malcolm X refers to people specifically by name—and often those names are of famous Harlem personalities. How does this recitation of names affect you? Does it make this account more or less pleasureable to read? Does it add or detract from Malcolm X's authority or veracity? Do you recognize any of the names, especially those from the Harlem music scene? Why do you think Malcolm X includes those in particular?

SENSELESS CRIMES

Rick Telander

Having worked as a gravedigger, a farmer, a merchant seaman, an insurance salesman, a rock-and-roll guitarist (for the Del-Crustaceans), and a dog breeder, Rick Telander has now settled firmly upon the career of writer. A frequent contributor to *Sports Illustrated*, the now defunct *Sport*, and other magazines, he is also the author of *Heaven Is a Playground* (1976), *Joe Namath and the Other Guys* (1976), and *The Hundred Yard Lie: College Football and What We Can Do to Stop It* (1989). An ex-professional football player, Telander says he began writing

> . . . after my leg was crushed in a pileup while playing for the Kansas City Chiefs. While recovering for 6 months in the hospital I wrote a five hundred-page autobiography (unpublished). . . . Encouraged by the response from those who read the book, I wrote several short stories, another novel and a rock opera (music included). None of these ever appeared in print but, undaunted, I continued my career in earnest. After two short articles appeared in *Dog World* magazine I finally published in *Sports Illustrated*. Today, after some success, I write at least ten hours every day.

His writing history is typical; most professional writers spend years learning their craft without a word getting published.

Telander was born in 1948 in Peoria, Illinois. His father was an oilman, his mother a poet. Telander has a B.A. from Northwestern University in Illinois, and currently makes Chicago his home.

In "Senseless Crimes," Telander combines his understanding of sports with his interest in social justice. His essay delineates that blurred line between adoration and idolatry, commercialism and exploitation.

Is it the shoes? . . .
Money, it's gotta
be the shoes!

MARS BLACKMON, TO MICHAEL JORDAN, IN A NIKE COMMERCIAL

For 15-year-old Michael Eugene Thomas, it definitely was the shoes. A ninth-grader at Meade Senior High School in Anne Arundel County, Md., Thomas was found strangled on May 2, 1989. Charged with first-degree murder was James David Martin, 17, a basketball buddy who allegedly took Thomas's two-week-old Air Jordan basketball shoes and left Thomas's barefoot body in the woods near school.

Thomas loved Michael Jordan, as well as the shoes Jordan endorses, and he cleaned his own pair each evening. He kept the cardboard shoe box with Jordan's silhouette on it in a place of honor in his room. Inside the box was the sales ticket for the shoes. It showed he paid $115.50, the price of a product touched by deity.

"We told him not to wear the shoes to school," said Michael's grandmother, Birdie Thomas. "We said somebody might like them, and he said, 'Granny, before I let anyone take those shoes, they'll have to kill me.'"

Michael Jordan sits in the locked press room before a workout at the Chicago Bulls' practice facility in suburban Deerfield, Ill. He is wearing his practice uniform and a pair of black Air Jordans similar to the ones young Thomas wore, except that these have Jordan's number, 23, stitched on the sides. On the shoelaces Jordan wears plastic toggles to prevent the shoes from loosening if the laces should come untied. Two toggles come in each box of Air Jordans, and if kids knew that Jordan actually wears them, they would never step out the door without their own toggles securely in place. The door is locked to keep out the horde of fans, journalists and favor seekers who dog Jordan wherever he goes. Jordan needs a quiet moment. He is reading an account of Thomas's death that a reporter has shown him.

For just an instant it looks as though Jordan might cry. He has so carefully nurtured his image as the all-American role model that he refuses to go anywhere, get into any situation, that might detract from that image. He moves swiftly and smoothly from the court to home to charity events to the golf course, all in an aura of untarnished integrity. "I can't believe it," Jordan says in a low voice.

"Choked to death. By his friend." He sighs deeply. Sweat trickles down one temple.

He asks if there have been other such crimes. Yes, he is told. Plenty, unfortunately. Not only for Air Jordans, but also for other brands of athletic shoes, as well as for jackets and caps bearing sports insignia—apparel that Jordan and other athlete endorsers have encouraged American youth to buy.

The killings aren't new. In 1983, 14-year-old Dewitt Duckett was shot to death in the hallway of Harlem Park Junior High in Baltimore by someone who apparently wanted Duckett's silky blue Georgetown jacket. In 1985, 13-year-old Shawn Jones was shot in Detroit after five youths took his Fila sneakers. But lately the pace of the carnage has quickened. In January 1988, an unidentified 14-year-old Houston boy, a star athlete in various sports, allegedly stabbed and killed 22-year-old Eric Allen with a butcher knife after the two argued over a pair of tennis shoes in the home the youths shared with their mothers. Seven months later a gunman in Atlanta allegedly robbed an unnamed 17-year-old of his Mercedes-Benz hat and Avia hightops after shooting to death the boy's 25-year-old friend, Carl Middlebrooks, as Middlebrooks pedaled away on his bike. Last November, Raheem Wells, the quarterback for Detroit Kettering High, was murdered, allegedly by six teenagers who swiped his Nike sneakers. A month later, 17-year-old Tyrone Brown of Hapeville, Ga., was fatally shot in the head, allegedly by two acquaintances who robbed him of money, cocaine and his sneakers. In Baltimore last summer 18-year-old Ronnell Ridgeway was robbed of his $40 sweatpants and then shot and killed. In March, Chris Demby, a 10th-grader at Franklin Learning Center in West Philadelphia, was shot and killed for his new Nikes.

In April 1989, 16-year-old Johnny Bates was shot to death in Houston by 17-year-old Demetrick Walker after Johnny refused to turn over his Air Jordan hightops. In March, Demetrick was sentenced to life in prison. Said prosecutor Mark Vinson, "It's bad when we create an image of luxury about athletic gear that it forces people to kill over it."

Jordan shakes his head.

"I thought I'd be helping out others and everything would be positive," he says. "I thought people would try to emulate the good things I do, they'd try to achieve, to be better. Nothing bad. I never thought because of my endorsement of a shoe, or any product, that people would harm each other. Everyone likes to be admired, but when it comes to kids actually killing each other"—he pauses—"then you have to reevaluate things."

We certainly do. In a country that has long been hung up on style over substance, flash over depth, the athletic shoe and sportswear industries (a projected $5.5 billion in domestic sales of name-brand shoes in 1990; more than $2 billion in sweatpants, sweatshirts and warmup suits) suddenly have come to represent the pinnacle of consumer exploitation. In recent months the industries, which include heavyweights Nike and Reebok as well as smaller players Adidas, Asics, British Knights, Brooks, Converse, Ellesse, Etonic, Fila, L.A. Gear, New Balance, Pony, Puma, Starter and numerous other makers of sports shoes, caps and jackets, have been accused of creating a fantasy-fueled market for luxury items in the economically blasted inner cities and willingly tapping into the flow of drug and gang money. This has led to a frightening outbreak of crimes among poor black kids trying to make their mark by "busting fresh," or dressing at the height of fashion.

In some cities muggings for sportswear are commonplace—Atlanta police, for instance, estimate they have handled more than 50 such robberies in the last four months. Yet it is not only the number of violent acts but also the seeming triviality of the booty that has stunned the public. In February, 19-year-old Calvin Wash was about to cross Central Park Avenue on Chicago's West Side when, according to police, two youths drove up in a van and demanded that he give them the Cincinnati Bengal jacket he was wearing. When Wash resisted, one of the youths is alleged to have fatally shot him in the back—through the A in BENGALS.

Chicago police sergeant Michael Chasen, who works in the violent crimes division in Area Four, which covers four of Chicago's 25 police districts, says his districts have about 50 reported incidents involving jackets and about a dozen involving gym shoes each month. "When you really think about the crime itself—taking someone's clothes off their body—you can't get much more basic," he says.

But, of course, these assailants aren't simply taking clothes from their victims. They're taking status. Something is very wrong with a society that has created an underclass that is slipping into economic and moral oblivion, an underclass in which pieces of rubber and plastic held together by shoelaces are sometimes worth more than a human life. The shoe companies have played a direct role in this. With their million-dollar advertising campaigns, superstar spokesmen and over-designed, high-priced products aimed at impressionable young people, they are creating status from thin air to feed those who are starving for self-esteem. "No one person is responsible for this type of violence," says Patricia Graham, principal of Chicago's Simeon High, one of the city's perennial basketball powers. "It's a combination of circumstances. It's about values and training. Society's values are out of sync, which is why these things have become important."

"The classic explanation in sociology is that these people are driven by peer pressure," says Mervin Daniel, a sociology professor at Morgan State. "What is advertised on TV and whatever your peers are doing, you do it too." Most assuredly, the shoe industry relies heavily on advertising; it spends more than $200 million annually to promote and advertise its products, churning out a blizzard of images and words that make its shoes seem preternaturally hip, cool and necessary. Nike alone will spend $60 million in 1990 on TV and print ads that have built such slogans as "Bo knows," and "Just do it," and "Do you know? Do you know? Do you know?" into mantras of consumerism.

What is baffling, however, is the strength of certain sporting products as icons for drug dealers and gangs. In Boston the Greenwood Street gang wears Green Bay Packers garb, the Vamp Hill Kings wear Los Angeles Kings and Raider gear, and the Castlegate gang wears Cincinnati Reds clothes. "The Intervale gang uses all Adidas stuff exclusively—hats, jackets, sweatpants, shoes," says Bill Stewart III, the probation officer at the Dorchester District Court in Boston, one of the busiest criminal courts in the nation. "They even have an Adidas handshake, copying the three stripes on the product. They extend three fingers when they shake hands."

Stewart knows how certain young drug dealers feverishly load up on the latest models of sneakers, tossing out any old ones that are scuffed or even slightly worn and replacing them with new pairs. "I was in a kid's apartment recently and there were about 50 pairs of brand-new sneakers, all top-of-the-line stuff—Adidas, Reebok and so forth," he says. "I asked the kid's mother how he came into all this stuff. She said she didn't know."

The use of Major League Baseball hats by gangs has prompted some high schools around the nation to ban them from school grounds, and expensive gold chains, major league or major college team jackets and other ostentatious, potentially troublesome items have also been prohibited. "When I look around sometimes, I think I'm in spring training in Florida," says Stewart.

When informed that baseball caps are being used by gangs as part of their uniforms, Major League Baseball public relations director Richard Levin seemed shocked. "I'm not aware of it at all, nor would I understand why," he said. "Obviously, we don't support it in any way."

Could any respectable U.S. corporation support the use of its products in this way? Absolutely not, said most shoe company executives contacted for this article. You better believe it, said a number of sports apparel retailers, as well as some of the more candid shoe execs.

Among the retailers is Wally Grigo, the owner of three sportswear shops in and near New Haven, Connecticut. Last August, Grigo put a sign in the front window of his inner city store that reads, IF YOU DEAL DRUGS, WE DON'T WANT YOUR BUSINESS. SPEND YOUR MONEY SOMEWHERE ELSE. "Unfortunately, it'll probably have to stay up forever," says

Grigo. "I was doing, I'd say $2,000 a week in drug money sales that disappeared after the sign went up. Our industry is sick, addicted to drug money. We're going through the first phase of addiction, which is total denial."

Before he put up the sign, Grigo had been told by sales reps from two sportswear companies that he should "hook up" the local drug dealers to expose the companies' new products to the neighborhood clientele. After the sign went up, Grigo says, the rep from the smaller company returned and said, "Wally, we're thinking about giving you the line. But, you know, I can't do anything until you cut out the crap and take that sign out of your window. The bulk of our business is done with drug dealers. Wake up!"

Grigo was so stunned that he thought of wearing a wire to record the rep making similar statements. He didn't do so, though, figuring the company's officials would dismiss any evidence by saying the rep was a loose cannon. But Grigo says the companies know what's going on, because the reps are "in the trenches, and they go back and report."

Grigo doesn't want to publicly state the names of the suppliers, for economic reasons. "I'm not afraid of the drug dealers," he says. "But the shoe companies could put me out of business anytime, just by canceling my credit."

One obvious question: How does Grigo, or anyone, know when a drug dealer and not a law-abiding citizen is making a buy? "Hey, spend 10 minutes in any city store," says Grigo. "When an 18-year-old kid pulls up in a BMW, walks down the aisle saying, 'I want this, this, this and this,' then peels off 50's from a stack of bills three inches thick, maybe doesn't even wait for change, then comes back a couple weeks later and does the same thing, hey . . . you know what I'm saying?"

And what about all those good guys advertising the shoes? What about Nike's Jordan and Spike Lee, the gifted film-maker and actor who portrays Mars Blackmon, the hero-worshipping nerd in the company's Air Jordan ads? Are they and other pitchmen at fault, too?

"Maybe the problem is those guys don't know what's going on," says Grigo. "There are stores doing $5,000 to $10,000 a week in drug money, all over. Drug money is part of the economic landscape these days. Even if the companies don't consciously go after the money, they're still getting it. Hey, all inner-city kids aren't drug dealers. Most of them are good, honest kids. Drug dealers are a very small percent. But the drug dealers, man, they set fashion trends."

Liz Dolan, director of public relations for Nike, hits the ceiling when she hears such talk. "Our commercials are about sport, they're not about fashion," she says.

But the industry's own figures make that assertion extremely questionable. At least 80% of the athletic shoes sold in the U.S. are not used for their avowed purpose—that is, playing sports.

Dolan sighs. She says that all of Nike's athlete-endorsers are quality citizens as well as superjocks. "We're not putting Leon Spinks in the commercials," she says. Then she says that the people who raise the alarm that Nike, as well as other sports apparel companies, is exploiting the poor and creating crime just to make money, are bizarre and openly racist. "What's baffling to us is how easily people accept the assumption that black youth is an unruly mob that will do anything to get its hands on what it wants," she says, excitedly. "They'll say, 'Show a black kid something he wants, and he'll kill for it.' I think it's racist hysteria, just like the Charles Stuart case in Boston or the way the Bush campaign used Willie Horton."

Lee also says he has heard such panic before. "Everybody says last summer that my movie *Do the Right Thing* was going to cause 30 million black people to riot," he says angrily. "But I haven't heard of one garbage can being thrown through a pizzeria window, have you? I want to work with Nike to address the special problems of inner-city black youths, but the problem is not shoes."

Lee is particularly irate because he has been singled out by *New York Post* sports columnist Phil Mushnick as being untrue to the very people Lee champions in his films. In Mushnick's April 6 [1990] column headlined, SHADDUP, I'M SELLIN' OUT . . . SHADDUP, he sharply criticized Lee for leading the hype. The caption under four photos—one of Lee; the others of soaring pairs of Air Jordans—said, "While Spike Lee watches Michael Jordan (or at least his shoes) dunk all over the world, parents around the country are watching their kids get mugged, or even killed, over the same sneakers Lee and Jordan are promoting." In his column Mushnick said, "It's murder, gentlemen. No rhyme, no reason, just murder. For sneakers. For jackets. Get it, Spike? Murder."

Lee wrote a response in *The National*, the daily sports newspaper, in which he angrily accused Mushnick of "thinly veiled racism" for going after him and other high-profile black endorsers and not white endorsers like Larry Bird or Joe Montana. Lee also questioned Mushnick's sudden "great outpouring of concern for Afro-American youths." Lee wrote, "The Nike commercials Michael Jordan and I do have never gotten anyone killed. . . . The deal is this: Let's try to effectively deal with the conditions that make a kid put so much importance on a pair of sneakers, a jacket and gold. These kids feel they have no options, no opportunities."

Certainly Lee is right about that. Elijah Anderson, a University of Pennsylvania sociologist who specializes in ethnography, the study of individual cultures, links the scourge of apparel-related crimes among young black males to "inequality in race and class. The uneducated, inner-city kids don't have a sense of opportunity. They feel the system is closed off to them. And yet they're bombarded with the same cultural apparatus that the white middle class is. They don't have the means to attain the things offered, and yet they have the same desire. So they value these 'emblems,' these symbols of supposed success. The gold, the shoes, the drug dealer's outfit—those things all belie the real situation, but it's a symbolic display that seems to say that things are all right.

"Advertising fans this whole process by presenting the images that appeal to the kids, and the shoe companies capitalize on the situation, because it exists. Are the companies abdicating responsibility by doing this? That's a hard one to speak to. This is, after all, a free market."

But what about social responsibility? One particularly important issue is the high price of the shoes—many companies have models retailing for considerably more than $100, with the Reebok Pump leading the parade at $170. There is also the specific targeting of young black males as buyers, through the use of seductive, macho-loaded sales pitches presented by black stars.

"You can quibble about our tactics, but we don't stand for the drug trade," says Dolan. She points out that Nike's fall promotion campaign will include $5 million worth of "strictly pro-education, stay-in-school" public service commercials that will "not run late at night, but on the same major sporting events as the prime-time ads." Nike is not alone in playing the good corporate citizen. Reebok recently gave $750,000 to fund Project Teamwork, a program designed to combat racism that is administered by the Center for the Study of Sport in Society at Northeastern University.

Nevertheless, certain products wind up having dubious associations—some products more than others. John Hazard, the head buyer for the chain of City Sports stores in Boston, says, "We used to have brawls in here, robberies, a tremendous amount of stealing. But we cut back on 90 percent of it by getting rid of certain products. We don't carry Adidas, Fila, British Knights. Those things bring in the gangs.

"There's a store not far away that carries all that stuff. They have after-hours sales to show the new lines to big drug dealers. They even have guys on beepers, to let them know when the latest shoes have come in. It would be nothing for those guys to buy 20, 30 pair of shoes to give to their 12-year-old runners."

He thinks for a moment. "I don't know if you can really blame the shoe companies for what happens. Not long ago there was a murder, a gang deal, here in Boston. The cops had the murderer, and they were walking him somewhere. It was on TV. The murderer was bent over at first, and then the cops stood him up, and—I couldn't believe it—all of a sudden you could see he was wearing a City Sports T-shirt. There's no way you can control what people wear."

John Donahoe, manager of a Foot Locker in Chicago's Loop, agrees. "Right now, this is the hottest thing we've got," he says, holding up a simple, ugly, blue nylon running shoe. Behind him are shelves filled with more than 100 different model or color variations. "Nike Cortez: $39," he says. "Been around for 20 years. Why is it hot now?" He shrugs, "I don't know."

Assistant manager James Crowder chimes in helpfully. "It's not the price, or who's endorsing it. It's just . . . what's happening."

Keeping up with what's happening has shoe manufacturers scrambling these days. "It used to be you could have a product out and fiddle with it for years, to get it just right," says Roger Morningstar, the assistant vice-president of promotions at Converse. "Now, if you don't come out with two or three new models every month, you're dead."

At home I go to my closet and pull out my own meager assortment of sports shoes—nine pairs, all told. A pair of ancient turf football shoes; some nubbed softball shoes; a pair of old running shoes; a pair of original, hideous red-and-black Air Jordans, kept for historical reasons; a pair of Avia volleyball shoes, worn-out, though they were never used for their intended purpose; two pairs of low-cut tennis shoes (or are they walking shoes?); a pair of Nike cross-training shoes (though I don't cross-train or even know what it means) in bad shape; a pair of sweat-stained, yet still awe-inspiring hightop basketball Reebok Pumps, a Christmas gift from my sister and brother-in-law. I pick these up. They are happening.

There are three colors on them, and the words REEBOK BASKETBALL are stitched in the tongue, right below the wondrous pump itself, colored orange and pebbled to resemble a basketball. On the bottom of the shoes are three colors of textured rubber. And there is an indented section in the heel with clear plastic laid over four orange tubes, and embossed with the words REEBOK ENERGY RETURN SYSTEM. On the back of the hightops there is the orange release valve that, when touched, decompresses the whole shebang.

The shoes haven't changed my hoops game at all, though they are comfortable, unless I pump them up too much and my toes slowly go numb. While I could never bring myself to pay for a pair out of my own pocket, I will admit that when I opened the shoe box on Christmas Day, I was thrilled by the sheer techno-glitz of the things. It was identical to the way I felt when, at the age of eight, I received a Robert-the-Robot.

But can promoting athletic shoes possibly be wrong in a capitalist society? Reebok chairman Paul Fireman was recently quoted as describing the Pump as "a product that's aspirational to a young person"—that is, something to be desired. He added, if prospective buyers couldn't afford the shoes, "that's the place for a kid to get a job after school." What, indeed, is the point of ads if not to inform the public of products that it may or may not need, but that it may wish to buy? Should we demand that the sports shoe industry be held to a higher standard than, say, the junk food industry? The advertising community itself thought so highly of Nike's "Bo knows" spot with Bo Jackson and Bo Diddley that *Advertising Age* named Jackson its Star Presenter of 1989.

What are we looking for here, anyway?

"Responsibility," says Grigo, the New Haven store owner. "Have Spike Lee and Michael Jordan look at the camera and say, 'Drug dealers, don't you dare wear my shoes!' Put antidrug labels on the box. I already do at my stores."

"Everybody wants to do everything," says Nike's Dolan. "It's naïve to think an antidrug message on the shoe box is going to change anyone's behavior. Our theme is 'Just do it!' because we want people playing sports, because they'll need more shoes. The healthier people are, the more shoes we'll sell."

Trouble is, young black males—a significant portion of the market—are not healthy right now. In fact, 23% of black males between the ages of 20 and 29 are under the supervision of the criminal justice system—incarcerated, paroled or on probation. According to a 1989 study in the *Journal of the American Medical Association*, a black male is six times more likely to be a homicide victim than a white male. Writes *Washington Post* columnist William Raspberry: "The inability of so many young black men to see themselves as providers, or even as necessary to their families, may be one explanation for their irresponsible behavior." Marc Mauer, of the Sentencing Project, a non-profit group concerned with disparities in the administration of criminal justice, says, "We now risk the possibility of writing off an entire generation of black men."

Obviously we are talking about something bigger than shoes here. Jordan sits up straight in his chair. It's time for practice to start. "I'd rather eliminate the product [the shoes] than know drug dealers are providing the funds that pay me," he says.

Of course drug money is, to a troubling extent, supporting the product, as well as other brands of sneakers and sports apparel. And kids are being killed for them. So what should the shoe companies, the schools, the advertising industry, the endorsers, the media, parents— all of us—do about it?

Do you know? Do you know? Do you know?

Speculations

1. Telander writes:

> Something is very wrong with a society that has created an underclass that is slipping into economic and moral oblivion, an underclass in which pieces of rubber and plastic held together by shoelaces are sometimes worth more than a human life.

What are the causes for such an attitude among poor youths? Are kids who kill over sports clothes really engaging in "senseless" acts? Explain your answer.

2. Like many essayists, Telander opens with an anecdote—a short narrative that pinpoints the central theme. Why do you think he chose to write about the murder of Michael Thomas? Why do you think he described the scene with Michael Jordan in the locker room, a scene he alternates with other accounts of clothes killings?

3. Telander's essay invites a consideration of fashion—of the importance people attach to wearing "the right" clothes. How do you define the term "fashion"? What is fashionable and why? How important is it to be fashionable? Explain your answer.

4. Telander's method of reporting of these "senseless" crimes is to give one point of view, then its counterpoint. For example, he gives us the account of Grigo, the New Haven shoe store owner; then the shoe salesman; then the Nike director of public relations; then Spike Lee responding to Phil Mushnick; etc. Is this form of presentation effective? Who is right? Who is responsible?

5. What is your attitude toward clothing and personal possessions? Are there things you want so bad that you have—however briefly—contemplated doing almost anything to get them? If you lacked the money to buy something you really wanted or needed, would you under some circumstances steal to get it? If not, what would prevent you from engaging in an "immoral" act?

NOTES FROM THE COUNTRY CLUB

Kimberly Wozencraft

"I have no misgivings about why I went to prison," Kimberly Wozencraft writes in this essay. "I deserved it. I was a cop, I got strung out on cocaine, I violated the rights of a pornographer. My own drug use as an undercover narcotics agent was a significant factor in my crime. But I did it and I deserved to be punished."

Such candor is typical of Wozencraft whose novel, *Rush* (1991), has been made into a film that brings viewers inside the world of America's addicts.

Kimberly Wozencraft was born in Dallas, Texas, in 1954, and dropped out of college to join the police force. She began her work as a narcotics agent and, as she confesses, became an addict and ultimately a felon. She was convicted in 1981 of violating the rights of an accused child pornographer and served eighteen months in the Federal Correctional Institute in Lexington, Kentucky. "Notes from the Country Club" is drawn largely from that experience.

Since her release, she has lived in New York City. She earned a Master of Fine Arts degree from Columbia University, and has published essays, poems, and stories in many literary magazines including *Northwest Review* and *Quarto*. Her work has been very well received. A critic commenting recently on *Rush* in the *National Review* wrote:

> Miss Wozencraft also has down cold something normal people don't often consider: that an addict's life is boring. Addicts are boring, drugs become boring, everything that isn't drugs even more boring. To convey this numbing triviality without exemplifying it is no mean feat. In this regard, it may help to read *Rush* as both Miss Wozencraft's agent and I first read it: with a case of flu. The enforced immobility of illness and the narrowed mental horizons of addiction make a good fit.

That same sense of enforced immobility and enforced meaninglessness is carefully etched by Wozencraft in the following essay, which offers an insider's view of punishment—and complements the selection by Jessica Mitford that began this section.

They had the Haitians up the hill, in the "camp" section where they used to keep the minimum security cases. The authorities were concerned that some of the Haitians might be diseased, so they kept them isolated from the main coed prison population by lodging them in the big square brick building surrounded by eight-foot chain-link with concertina wire on top. We were not yet familiar with the acronym AIDS.

One or two of the Haitians had drums, and in the evenings when the rest of us were in the Big Yard, the drum rhythms carried over the bluegrass to where we were playing gin or tennis or softball or just hanging out waiting for dark. When they really got going some of them would dance and sing. Their music was rhythmic and beautiful, and it made me think of freedom.

There were Cubans loose in the population, spattering their guttural Spanish in streams around the rectangular courtyard, called Central Park, at the center of the prison compound. These were Castro's Boat People, guilty of no crime in this country, but requiring sponsors before they could walk the streets as free people.

Walking around the perimeter of Central Park was like taking a trip in microcosm across the United States. Moving leftward from the main entrance, strolling along under the archway that covers the wide sidewalk, you passed the doorway to the Women's Unit, where I lived, and it was how I imagined Harlem to be. There was a white face here and there, but by far most of them were black. Ghetto blasters thunked out rhythms in the sticky evening air, and folks leaned against the window sills, smoking, drinking Cokes, slinking and nodding. Every once in a while a joint was passed around, and always there was somebody pinning, checking for hacks on patrol.

Past Women's Unit was the metal door to the Big Yard, the main recreation area of three or four acres, two sides blocked by the building, two sides fenced in the usual way—chain-link and concertina wire.

Past the Big Yard you entered the Blue Ridge Mountains, a sloping grassy area on the edge of Central Park, where the locals, people from Kentucky, Tennessee, and the surrounding environs, sat around playing guitars and singing, and every once in a while passing around a quart of hooch. They make it from grapefruit juice and a bit of yeast smuggled out of the kitchen. Some of the inmates who worked in Cable would bring out pieces of a black foam rubber substance and wrap it around empty Cremora jars to make thermos jugs of sorts. They would mix the grapefruit juice and yeast in the containers and stash them in some out-of-the-way spot for a few weeks until presto! you had hooch, bitter and tart and sweet all at once, only mildly alcoholic, but entirely suitable for evening cocktails in Central Park.

Next, at the corner, was the Commissary, a tiny store tucked inside the entrance to Veritas, the second women's unit. It wasn't much more than a few shelves behind a wall of Plexiglas, with a constant line of inmates spilling out of the doorway. They sold packaged chips, cookies, pens and writing paper, toiletries, some fresh fruit, and the ever-popular ice cream, sold only in pints. You had to eat the entire pint as soon as you bought it, or else watch it melt, because there weren't any refrigerators. Inmates were assigned one shopping night per week, allowed to buy no more than seventy-five dollars' worth of goods per month, and were permitted to pick up a ten-dollar roll of quarters if they had enough money in their prison account. Quarters were the basic spending unit in the prison; possession of paper money was a shippable offense. There were vending machines stocked with junk food and soda, and they were supposedly what the quarters were to be used for. But we gambled, we bought salami or fried chicken sneaked out by the food service workers, and of course people sold booze and drugs. The beggars stood just outside the Commissary door. Mostly they were Cubans, saying "Oyez! Mira! Mira! Hey, Poppy, one quarter for me. One cigarette for me, Poppy?"

There was one Cuban whom I was specially fond of. His name was Shorty. The name said it, he was only about five-two, and he looked just like Mick Jagger. I met him in Segregation, an isolated section of tiny cells where prisoners were locked up for having violated some institutional rule or another. They tossed me in there the day I arrived; again the authorities were concerned, supposedly for my safety. I was a police woman before I became a convict, and they weren't too sure that the other inmates would like that. Shorty saved me a lot of grief when I went into Seg. It didn't matter if you were male or female there, you got stripped and handed a tee shirt, a pair of boxer shorts and a set of Peter Pans—green canvas shoes with thin rubber soles designed to prevent you from running away. As if you could get past three steel doors and a couple of hacks just to start with. When I was marched down the hall between the cells the guys started whistling and hooting and they didn't shut up even after I was locked down. They kept right on screaming until finally I yelled out, "Yo no comprendo!" and then they all moaned and said, "Another . . . Cuban," and finally got quiet. Shorty was directly across from me, I could see his eyes through the rectangular slot in my cell door. He rattled off a paragraph or two of Spanish, all of which was lost on me, and I said quietly, "Yo no comprendo bien español. Yo soy de Texas, yo hablo inglés?" I could tell he was smiling by the squint of his eyes, and he just said, "Bueno." When the hacks came around to take us out for our mandatory hour of recreation, which consisted of standing around in the Rec area while two guys shot a game of pool on the balcony above the gym, Shorty slipped his hand into mine and smiled up at me until the hack told him to cut it out. He knew enough English to tell the others in Seg that I was not really Spanish, but he kept quiet about it, and they left me alone.

Beyond the Commissary, near the door to the dining hall, was East St. Louis. The prison had a big portable stereo system which they rolled out a few times a week so that an inmate could play at being a disc jockey. They had a good-sized collection of albums and there was usually some decent jazz blasting out of there. Sometimes people danced, unless there were uptight hacks on duty to tell them not to.

California was next. It was a laid back kind of corner near the doors to two of the men's units. People stood around and smoked hash or grass or did whatever drugs happened to be available and there was sometimes a sort of slow-motion game of handball going on. If you wanted drugs, this was the place to come.

If you kept walking, you would arrive at the Power Station, the other southern corner where the politicos-gone-wrong congregated. It might seem odd at first to see these middle-aged government mavens standing around in their Lacoste sport shirts and Sans-a-belt slacks, smoking pipes or cigars and waving their arms to emphasize some point or other. They kept pretty much to themselves and ate together at the big round tables in the cafeteria, sipping cherry Kool-Aid and pretending it was Cabernet Sauvignon.

That's something else you had to deal with—the food. It was worse than elementary school steam table fare. By the time they finished cooking it, it was tasteless, colorless, and nutritionless. The first meal I took in the dining room was lunch. As I walked toward the entry, a tubby fellow was walking out, staggering really, rolling his eyes as though he were dizzy. He stopped and leaned over, and I heard someone yell, "Watch out, he's gonna puke!" I ducked inside so as to miss the spectacle. They were serving some rubbery, faint pink slabs that were supposed to be ham, but I didn't even bother to taste mine. I just slapped at it a few times to watch the fork bounce off and then ate my potatoes and went back to the unit.

Shortly after that I claimed that I was Jewish, having gotten the word from a friendly New York lawyer who was in for faking some of his clients' immigration papers. The kosher line was the only way to get a decent meal in there. In fact, for a long time they had a Jewish baker from Philadelphia locked up, and he made some truly delicious cream puffs for dessert. They sold for seventy-five cents on the black market, but once I had established myself in the Jewish community I got them as part of my regular fare. They fed us a great deal of peanut butter on the kosher line; every time the "goyim" got meat, we got peanut butter, but that was all right with me. Eventually I was asked to light the candles at the Friday evening services, since none of the real Jewish women bothered to attend. I have to admit that most of the members of our little prison congregation were genuine *alter kokers,* but some of them were amusing. And I enjoyed learning first hand about Judaism. The services were usually very quiet, and the music, the ancient intoning songs, fortified me against the screeching, pop-rock vocal assaults that were a constant in the Women's Unit. I learned to think of myself as the *shabot shiksa,* and before my time was up, even the rabbi seemed to accept me.

I suppose it was quite natural that the Italians assembled just "down the street" from the offending ex-senators, judges, and power brokers. Just to the left of the main entrance. The first night I made the tour, a guy came out of the shadows near the building and whispered to me, "What do you need, sweetheart? What do you want, I can get it. My friend Ahmad over there, he's very rich, and he wants to buy you things. What'll it be, you want some smoke, a few ludes, vodka, cigarettes, maybe some kosher salami fresh from the kitchen? What would you like?" I just stared at him. The only thing I wanted at that moment was out, and even Ahmad's millions, if they existed at all, couldn't do that. The truth is, every guy I met in there claimed to be wealthy, to have been locked up for some major financial crime. Had I taken all of them up on their offers of limousines to pick me up at the front gate when I was released and take me to the airport for a ride home in a private Lear jet, I would have needed my own personal cop out front just to direct traffic.

Ahmad's Italian promoter eventually got popped for zinging the cooking teacher one afternoon on the counter in the home economics classroom, right next to the new Cuisinart. The assistant warden walked in on the young lovebirds, and before the week was up, even the Cubans were walking around singing about it. They had a whole song down, to the tune of "Borracho Me Acosté a Noche."

At the end of the tour, you would find the jaded New Yorkers, sitting at a picnic table or two in the middle of the park, playing gin or poker and bragging about their days on Madison Avenue and Wall Street, lamenting the scarcity of good deli, even on the kosher line, and planning where they would take their first real meal upon release.

If you think federal correctional institutions are about the business of rehabilitation, drop by for an orientation session one day. There at the front of the classroom, confronting rows of mostly black faces, will be the warden, or the assistant warden, or the prison shrink, pacing back and forth in front of the blackboard and asking the class, "Why do you think you're here?" This gets a general grumble, a few short, choked laughs. Some well-meaning soul always says it—rehabilitation.

"Nonsense!" the lecturer will say. "There are several reasons for locking people up. Number one is incapacitation. If you're in here, you can't be out there doing crime. Secondly, there is deterrence. Other people who are thinking about doing crime see that we lock people up for it and maybe they think twice. But the real reason you are here is to be punished. Plain and simple. You done wrong, now you got to pay for it. Rehabilitation ain't even part of the picture. So don't be looking to us to rehabilitate you. Only person can rehabilitate you is you. If you feel like it, go for it, but leave us out. We don't want to play that game."

So that's it. You're there to do time. I have no misgivings about why I went to prison. I deserved it. I was a cop, I got strung out on cocaine, I violated the rights of a pornographer. My own drug use as an undercover narcotics agent was a significant factor in my crime. But I did it and I deserved to be punished. Most of the people I met in Lexington, though, were in for drugs, and the majority of them hadn't done anything more than sell an ounce of cocaine or a pound of pot to some apostle of the law.

It seems lately that almost every time I look at the *New York Times* op-ed page, there is something about the drug problem. I have arrested people for drugs, and I have had a drug problem myself. I have seen how at least one federal correctional institution functions. It does not appear that the practice of locking people up for possession or distribution of an insignificant quantity of a controlled substance makes any difference at all in the amount of drug use that occurs in the United States. The drug laws are merely another convenient source of political rhetoric for aspiring officeholders. Politicians know that an antidrug stance is an easy way to get votes from parents who are terrified that their children might wind up as addicts. I do not advocate drug use. Yet, having seen the criminal justice system from several angles, as a police officer, a court bailiff, a defendant, and a prisoner, I am convinced that prison is not the answer to the drug problem, or for that matter to many other white-collar crimes. If the taxpayers knew how their dollars were being spent inside some prisons, they might actually scream out loud.

There were roughly 1,800 men and women locked up in Lex, at a ratio of approximately three men to every woman, and it did get warm in the summertime. To keep us tranquil they devised some rather peculiar little amusements. One evening I heard a commotion on the steps at the edge of Central Park and looked over to see a rec specialist with three big cardboard boxes set up on the plaza, marked 1, 2, and 3. There were a couple of hundred inmates sitting at the bottom of the steps. Dennis, the rec specialist, was conducting his own version of the television game show "Let's Make a Deal!" Under one of the boxes was a case of soda, under another was a racquetball glove, and under a third was a fly swatter. The captive contestant picked door number 2, which turned out to contain the fly swatter, to my way of thinking the best prize there. Fly swatters were virtually impossible to get through approved channels, and therefore cost as much as two packs of cigarettes on the black market.

Then there was the Annual Fashion Show, where ten or twenty inmates had special packages of clothing sent in, only for the one evening, and modeled them on stage while the baddest drag queen in the compound moderated and everyone else ooohed and aahhed. They looked good up there on stage in Christian Dior and Ralph Lauren instead of the usual fatigue pants and white tee shirts. And if such activities did little to prepare inmates for a productive return to society, well, at least they contributed to the fantasyland aura that made Lexington such an unusual place.

I worked in Landscape, exiting the rear gate of the compound each weekday morning at about nine after getting a half-hearted frisk from one of the hacks on duty. I would climb on my tractor to drive to the staff apartment complex and pull weeds or mow the lawn. Landscape had its prerogatives. We raided the gardens regularly and at least got to taste fresh vegetables from time to time. I had never eaten raw corn before, but it could not have tasted better. We also brought in a goodly supply of real vodka, and a bit of hash now and then, for parties in our rooms after lights out. One guy strapped a six-pack of Budweiser to his arms with masking tape and then put on his prison-issue Army field jacket. When he got to the rear gate, he raised his arms straight out at shoulder level, per instructions, and the hack patted down his torso and legs, never bothering to check his arms. The inmate had been counting on that. He smiled at the hack and walked back to his room, a six-pack richer.

I was fortunate to be working Landscape at the same time as Horace, a fellow who had actually lived in the city of Lexington before he was locked up. His friends made regular deliveries of assorted contraband, which they would stash near a huge elm tree near the outer stone fence of the reservation. Horace would drive his tractor over, make the pickup, and the rest of us would carry it, concealed, through the back gate when we went back inside for lunch or at the end of the day. "Contraband" included everything from drugs to blue eye shadow. The assistant warden believed that female inmates should wear no cosmetics other than what she herself used—a bit of mascara and a light shade of lipstick. I have never been a plaything of Fashion, but I did what I could to help the other women prisoners in their never-ending quest for that Cover Girl look.

You could depend on the fact that most of the hacks would rather have been somewhere else, and most of them really didn't care *what* the inmates did, as long as it didn't cause any commotion. Of course, there were a few you had to look out for. The captain in charge of security was one of them. We tried a little experiment once, after having observed that any time he saw someone laughing, he took immediate steps to make the inmate and everyone around him acutely miserable. Whenever we saw him in the area, we immediately assumed expressions of intense unhappiness, even of despair. Seeing no chance to make anyone more miserable than they already appeared to be, the captain left us alone.

Almost all of the female hacks, and a good number of the males, had outrageously large derrières, a condition we inmates referred to as "the federal ass." This condition may have resulted from the fact that most of them appeared, as one inmate succinctly described it, simply to be "putting in their forty a week to stay on the government teat." Employment was not an easy thing to find in Kentucky.

Despite the fact that Lexington is known as a "country club" prison, I must admit that I counted days. From the first moment that I was in, I kept track of how many more times I would have to watch the sun sink behind eight feet of chain-link, of how many more days I would have to spend eating, working, playing and sleeping according to the dictates of a "higher authority." I don't think I can claim that I was rehabilitated. If anything I underwent a process of dehabilitation. What I learned was what Jessica Mitford tried to tell people many years ago in her book *Kind and Usual Punishment.* Prison is a business, no different from manufacturing tires or selling real estate. It keeps people employed and it provides cheap labor for NASA, the U.S. Postal Service, and other governmental or quasi-governmental agencies. For a short time, before I was employed in Landscape, I worked as a finisher of canvas mailbags, lacing white ropes through metal eyelets around the top of the bags and attaching clamps to the ropes. I made one dollar and fourteen cents for every one hundred that I did. If I worked very hard, I could do almost two hundred a day.

It's not about justice. If you think it's about justice, look at the newspapers and notice who walks. Not the little guys, the guys doing a tiny bit of dealing, or sniggling a little on their income tax, or the woman who pulls a stunt with welfare checks because her husband has skipped out and she has no other way to feed her kids. I do not say that these things are right. But the process of selective prosecution, the "making" of cases by D.A.s and police departments, and the presence of some largely unenforceable statutes currently on the books (it is the reality of "compliance": no law can be forced on a public which chooses to ignore it, hence, selective prosecution) make for a criminal justice system which cannot realistically function in a fair and equitable manner. Criminal justice—I cannot decide if it is the ultimate oxymoron or a truly accurate description of the law enforcement process in America.

In my police undercover capacity, I have sat across the table from an armed robber who said, "My philosophy of life is slit thy neighbor's throat and pimp his kids." I believe that the human animals who maim and kill people should be dealt with, as they say, swiftly and surely. But this business of locking people up, at enormous cost, for minor, nonviolent offenses does not truly or effectively serve the interest of the people. It serves only to promote the wasteful aspects of the federal prison system, a system that gulps down tax dollars and spews up "Let's Make a Deal!"

I think about Lexington almost daily. I will be walking up Broadway to shop for groceries, or maybe riding my bike in the original Central Park and suddenly I'm wondering who's in there now, at this very moment, and for what inane violations, and what they are doing. Is it chow time, is the Big Yard open, is some inmate on stage in the auditorium singing "As Time Goes By" in a talent show? It is not a fond reminiscence, or a desire to be back in the Land of No Decisions. It is an awareness of the waste. The waste of tax dollars, yes, but taxpayers are used to that. It is the unnecessary trashing of lives that leaves me uneasy. The splitting of families, the enforced monotony, the programs which purport to prepare an inmate for re-entry into society but which actually succeed only in occupying a few more hours of the inmate's time behind the walls. The nonviolent offenders, such as small-time drug dealers and the economically deprived who were driven to crime out of desperation, could remain in society under less costly supervision, still undergoing "punishment" for their crime, but at least contributing to rather than draining the resources of society.

Horace, who was not a subtle sort of fellow, had some tee shirts made up. They were delivered by our usual supplier out in Landscape, and we wore them back in over our regular clothes. The hacks tilted their heads when they noticed, but said nothing. On the front of each shirt was an outline of the state of Kentucky, and above the northwest corner of the state were the words "Visit Beautiful Kentucky!" Inside the state boundary were:

- Free Accommodations
- Complimentary Meals
- Management Holds Calls
- Recreational Exercise

In small letters just outside the southwest corner of the state was: "Length of Stay Requirement." And in big letters across the bottom:

Take Time to Do Time
F.C.I. Lexington

I gave mine away on the day I finished my sentence. It is a time-honored tradition to leave some of your belongings to friends who have to stay behind when you are released. But you must never leave shoes. Legend has it that if you do, you will come back to wear them again.

Speculations

1. A common technique for opening a narrative is to begin *in medias res,* which is Latin for "in the middle of things." How does Wozencraft use that strategy here? Why do you think she starts the reader off right in the middle of things?

2. Wozencraft describes everyday life inside the prison. How would you describe the life and culture of the Federal Correctional Institute at Lexington, Kentucky? What are its rewards and punishments? How does the illegal "contraband" affect the prisoner's life?

3. Wozencraft chooses to use quite a bit of prison slang in writing this essay. Select three to five words or phrases that you think contribute to the meaning and intent of "Notes from the Country Club." Define them, using everyday English, and discuss why and how they add to your enjoyment and understanding of the selection.

4. Wozencraft admits that she is in prison because she has violated a law. What laws have you ever wanted to violate? Any that might have caused you to be arrested and possibly imprisoned?

How did the fear of consequences inhibit you? What laws do you think are worth breaking, even if the consequences are severe?

5. At various points in this essay, Wozencraft says:

> If the taxpayers knew how their dollars were being spent inside some prisons, they might actually scream out loud.

> Prison is a business, no different from manufacturing tires or selling real estate.

> . . . the process of selective prosecution, the "making" of cases by D.A.s and police departments, and the presence of some largely unenforceable statutes currently on the books . . . make for a criminal justice system which cannot realistically function in a fair and equitable manner.

How does her essay support these assertions? How do you assess those claims? In what ways is Wozencraft a credible spokesperson for these views? In what ways is she not?

————— ASSIGNMENT SEQUENCES —————

Sequence One: Defining the Terms

1. Although the terms "crime," "criminal" and "victim" may seem obvious, they are not always so easy to define. Write an essay in which you define these three terms. Do not go to a dictionary; instead, consider what they mean to you and what their relationship is to each other beyond the very simple and obvious statement that a criminal commits a crime upon a victim. You might want to write about the impressions that occur to you when you hear or read the term "criminal," what you think when you hear that a "crime" has been committed, what images and associations come to mind when you hear the word "victim." For example, what about drug addicts who have the financial means to support their habit? Are they committing a crime? Are they criminals? Who is the victim? Kimberly Wozencraft's essay might be particularly useful here.

2. As a follow-up, analyze in an essay why you created those particular definitions of "crime," "criminal" and "victim." To what extent is your account based on personal experience? To what extent is it based on books, newspaper accounts, television news shows, television crime shows, movies, conversations with friends and family? As part of your analysis, consider how your views and attitudes have been shaped by the culture of images and values that surrounds you.

3. In "The Criminal Type," Jessica Mitford makes the following argument in the form of an assertion:

> Thus it seems safe to assert that there is indeed a criminal type—
> but he is not a biological, anatomical, phrenological, or anthro-
> pological type; rather, he is a social creation, etched by the dom-
> inant class and ethnic prejudices of a given society.

In an essay that draws upon Mitford, Darrow, Wozencraft, other essays, or personal experience, offer your own view of what a "criminal type" looks and acts like. What image is conjured up in your imagination when you hear or read of a criminal? Does your criminal have a specific gender, color, appearance, height, accent, neighborhood? Support your views with facts, readings, observations, and so on.

4. Occasionally people talk about a "victimless crime." Can there be such a thing as a victimless crime? Returning to the definitions you wrote in essay one, argue whether you think this category exists. Feel free to do some library research on this subject to support your position.

5. In general, the legal system spends a lot of time on crime and criminals, but relatively little time on victims. Do you believe that victims should have certain rights? What should they be? Should government or social agencies be required to help victims? What kinds of responsibilities—if any—does society have to the victims of crime?

6. What kinds of restitution to the victim—if any—should be required of a criminal? What about crimes committed by corporations that overcharge the government, governmental bureaucracies that endanger or directly cause harm to American citizens; citizens who cheat the government out of taxes? Offer your views on the nature of punishment and what should be done to redress the wrongs done to victims. You will likely want to focus on just one or two significant issues. Kimberly Wozencraft's essay might be useful here.

7. As a follow-up, write an editorial for a local, regional, or national newspaper on some aspect of the criminal justice system that you have read and thought about. Does the system work? Are reforms needed—and if so, what kinds? Do we need more police, prisons, midnight basketball, social programs for the poor, death penalties, high-paying jobs, mandatory sentences? Do we need more judges or fewer lawyers? Focus on just one or two closely related issues and offer an argument that is full of specifics, details, and persuasive evidence.

Sequence Two: Just and Unjust

1. In "The Criminal Type," Jessica Mitford writes that the criminal type is a social creation, that it is a projection of class and ethnic prejudices. According to Mitford:

> No doubt despair and terrible conditions in the slums give rise to one sort of crime, the only kind available to the very poor: theft, robbery, purse-snatching; whereas crimes committed by the former slum-dweller have moved up the scale with his standard of living to those less likely to be detected and punished: embezzlement, sale of fraudulent stock, price-fixing. After all, the bank president is not likely to become a bank robber; nor does the bank robber have the opportunity to embezzle depositors' funds.

Offer a response to Mitford, taking into account her view of the criminal. If you agree with Mitford, offer your explanation concerning society's preoccupation with the crimes of the poor.

2. In "Hustler," Malcolm X writes:

> The hypocritical white man will talk about the Negro's low morals. But who has the world's lowest morals if not whites? And not only that, but the "upper-class" whites!

Malcolm X is combining an attack on both whites and upper class individuals. He provides some evidence to support his view, which can be interpreted as an attempt to turn the tables on the white establishment of the 1960s which was always blaming "the Negro" for having low morals and committing crimes.

Your job is to find your own evidence. For one week, read your daily newspaper and cut out articles related to crime. Assemble them in different categories according to who perpetrated the crime; those categories might include gender, age, race, neighborhood, presumed economic status, and so on. Share your evidence with your classmates, seeing if your evidence agrees with theirs. Then write an essay that considers the reported crimes that you have collected.

3. Your college or university may produce a monthly report from the campus police; even if the campus police office does not issue such a report, it is likely to be willing to share its statistical information with you.

Examine a month's worth of criminal activity on your campus. What conclusions do you draw about who is committing crimes and for what purposes? Are the categories fair? Are there "crimes" that never get reported—either because they are hidden or because they are not considered crimes by law? As you analyze the report, you might want to interview a campus police officer concerning crime (and punishment). Compare your findings to those of Jessica Mitford.

4. Martin Luther King, Jr. focuses considerable attention on the differences between just and unjust laws, in part resting his justification for engaging in civil disobedience on God's law and natural law. Assess his argument. Discuss whether you agree with King that "an individual who breaks a law that conscience tells him is unjust, and who willingly accepts the penalty of imprisonment in order to arouse the conscience of the community over its injustice, is in reality expressing the highest respect for law."

5. Consider that Martin Luther King, Jr. has just been tried for refusing to respond to the orders of the police in Birmingham, Alabama. Based on "Letter from Birmingham Jail," offer a speculative account of the debate that you think must have ensued in the jury room. What arguments would jurors have to consider as they decide whether to find Reverend King "guilty" or "not guilty." That he violated the law is not the issue—or is it? As you write up your account of the discussion, remember that jurors have considerable latitude in deciding cases and can consider motive and extenuating circumstances—but they also are responsible for upholding the law.

Sequence Three: Guilty or Innocent

1. Imagine that you are asked to defend a 15-year-old youth accused of killing for clothes, the kind of "senseless" crime that Rick Telander analyzes in his essay. Write the specific argument that you would make to the jury. That the defendant actually committed the killing is not the issue: eyewitnesses and the defendant do not deny the crime. Your job as defense attorney is to make the best case, provide the most compelling argument for the defendant. You can do some research on how these kinds of summations are put together by observing actual court sessions (on TV or in person) or finding appropriate research materials in the library.

2. Now imagine that you are the judge who is presiding over the case described in Assignment 1. The defendant has been found guilty; it is up to you to determine an appropriate punishment and then justify your sentence. Write that statement. In your statement,

make use of statements and arguments that you find in the essays by Telander, Darrow, or Wozencraft.

3. Kimberly Wozencraft speculates as to what prison is all about—its ostensible goal of rehabilitation, its philosophy of punishment, its usefulness as a place of quarantine. In an essay that takes into account Wozencraft's perspective, as well as others expressed in this section, develop your own philosophy about appropriate consequences for the criminal. Think of specific crimes: burglary, robbery, rape, extortion, assault, child abuse, neglect, white collar crime, and so on. Is prison the appropriate response to these various crimes? Should we treat one class of criminal different from another? Is there a better alternative than prison? Do prisons rehabilitate? Should they? As you work on this essay, you might well want to do additional research, including interviews of community experts.

4. Here are five different situations in which at least one victim ends up dead:

   a. a young woman kills a rival in a fit of jealous rage in the victim's apartment after a loud, verbal confrontation;

   b. a young man, driving home after spending two hours in a tavern, kills an elderly woman in a car accident; evaluated on the scene, the young man tests above the blood alcohol limit;

   c. a doctor administers a lethal dose of morphine to a terminally ill patient who wants to die;

   d. the owner of an apartment building refuses to correct safety violations or to install smoke alarms; an electrical fire results, killing a family of seven;

   e. the president of a corporation knowingly markets a product that is unsafe; 14 individuals die.

   In an essay that analyzes these five cases and which draws upon the readings you have done in this section, offer your views about these "crimes" and what kinds of "punishments" you think would be most appropriate.

5. In his address to the prisoners of the Cook County Jail, Clarence Darrow analyzes the proposed Illinois law (in 1902) which would make kidnapping a crime punishable by death. He thinks the proposed legislation is "all wrong" because:

   > You cannot cure this crime by passing a law punishing by death kidnappers of children. There is one way to cure it. There is one

way to cure all these offenses, and that is to give the people a chance to live.... If every man and woman and child in the world had a chance to make a decent, fair, honest living, there would be no jails and no lawyers and no courts.

Do you agree? Do you believe that criminal laws are effective deterrents? Does Darrow make a good case, or do you find his argument inadequate? Basing your argument on selections by Telander and Malcolm X, offer your own views on Darrow's position.

6. Whatever your view of O.J. Simpson's innocence or guilt, his murder trial raises fundamental questions about crime and punishment, law and order, particularly in relation to celebrities and the justice system. Examine several commentaries on the trial and offer your judgment as to whether Simpson received a fair trial. To what degree, if any, do you think money and fame made a difference—to the prosecution, the defense, the jury?

FOCUS ON

Date Rape

Susan Estrich, a professor at Harvard Law School, opens the second chapter in her book *Real Rape*, with the following statement:

> A man commits rape when he engages in intercourse (in the old statutes, carnal knowledge) with a woman not his wife; by force or threat of force; against her will and without her consent. That is the traditional, common law definition of rape, and it remains the essence of even the most radical reform statutes.

Even with this relatively clear cut definition, the subject of date rape or acquaintance rape is hotly debated on college campuses, as the following selections attest. The problem is that date rape is rarely an act of violence committed by a stranger but rather by a friend, an acquaintance, someone whom the victim knows and frequently trusts. According to Estrich, for example, "the overwhelming majority of women who contacted rape centers [in Massachusetts and Seattle] had been attacked by men they knew." Similarly, a survey of 930 adult women in San Francisco concluded that 82 percent of rape victims "involved non-strangers—and less than 10 percent of them were reported to the police."

Even if we agree that there is a problem—and not everyone does—the subject of date rape raises significant questions. Who is responsible for the crime of rape? Do particular behaviors by men and women contribute to date rape? What, if anything, should campuses do to prevent date rape? How are police, prosecutors, and jurors to determine if a real crime was committed, particularly in the absence of physical evidence? Should students create their own "dating code of conduct" to prevent acquaintance rape? These are the kinds of questions and concerns we encourage you to consider as you read, think, and write about the Focus on Date Rape that follows.

DATE RAPE: THE STORY OF AN EPIDEMIC AND THOSE WHO DENY IT

Ellen Sweet

Very little is known about Ellen Sweet except that she published "Date Rape: The Story of an Epidemic and Those Who Deny It" in the

October 1985 issue of *Ms.* magazine as part of the "campus times" feature. According to the byline of that article, Ellen Sweet was the *Ms.* editor who coordinated the *Ms.* Magazine Campus Project on Sexual Assault.

The project to which Sweet refers was a groundbreaking study on date rape (or "campus rape" or "acquaintance rape") researched by Dr. Mary Koss of Kent State University in Ohio. Koss's study consists of a careful compilation of data which paints a frightening picture about the incidence of date rape on college campuses. This report became the foundation of a book entitled *I Never Called It Rape: The* Ms. *Report on Recognizing, Fighting, and Surviving Date and Acquaintance Rape* (1986) by Robin Warshaw. Ellen Sweet served as a consulting editor on that project, which describes case studies of acquaintance rape along with a barrage of stunning statistics, such as:

Of 3,187 female college students questioned:

15.3% had been raped.

11.8% were victims of attempted rape.

11.2% had experienced sexual coercion.

14.5% had been touched sexually against their will.

42% of the rape victims told no one about their assaults.

55% of the men who raped said they had sex again with their victims.

41% of the raped women said they expect to be raped again.

Such statistics—and the case studies that go along with them—suggest the widespread nature of this particular kind of violent crime—and the social and cultural confusion that often clouds the issue, excusing the perpetrator and blaming the victim. These are the kinds of issues that Sweet analyzes in the following essay.

It was the beginning of spring break when I was a junior. I was in good spirits and had been out to dinner with an old friend. We returned to his college (dorm). There were some seniors on the ground floor, drinking beer, playing bridge. I'm an avid player, so we joined them, joked around a lot. One of them, John, wasn't playing, but he was interested in the game. I found him attractive. We talked, and it turned out we had a mutual friend, shared experiences. It was getting late, and my friend had gone to bed, so John offered to see me safely home. We took our time, sat outside talking for a while. Then he said we could get inside one of the most beautiful campus buildings, which was usually locked at night. I went with him. Once we were inside, he kissed me. I didn't resist, I was excited. He kissed me again. But when he tried for more, I said no. He just grew completely silent. I couldn't get him to talk to me any more. He pinned me down and ripped off my pants. I couldn't believe it was happening to me . . .

Let's call this Yale graduate Judy. Her experience and her disbelief, as she describes them, are not unique. Gretchen, another student victim of date rape (or acquaintance rape, as it is also called), had known for five years the man who invited her to an isolated vacation cabin and then raped her. "I considered him my best friend," she says on a Stanford University videotape used in discussions of the problem. "I couldn't believe it. *I couldn't believe it was actually happening to me.*"

Such denial, the inability to believe that someone they know could have raped them, is a common reaction of victims of date rape, say psychologists and counselors who have researched the topic and treated these women. In fact, so much silence surrounds this kind of crime that many women are not even aware that they have been raped. In one study, Mary P. Koss, a psychology professor at Kent State University, Ohio, asked female students if they had had sexual intercourse against their will through use of or threat of force (the minimal legal definition of rape). Of those who answered yes, only 57 percent went on to identify their experience as rape. Koss also identified the other group (43 percent) as those who hadn't even acknowledged the rape to themselves.

"I can't believe it's happening on our campus," is usually the initial response to reports such as Koss's. She also found that one in eight women students had been raped, and another one in four were victims of attempted rape. Since only 4 percent of all those reported the attack, Koss concluded that "at least ten times more rapes occur among college students than are reflected in official crime statistics." (Rape is recognized to be the most underreported of all crimes, and date rape is among the least reported, least believed, and most difficult to prosecute, second only to spouse rape.)

Working independently of Koss, researchers at Auburn University, Alabama, and more recently, University of South Dakota and St. Cloud State University, Minnesota, all have found that 1 in 5 women students were raped by men they knew.

Koss also found a core group of highly sexually aggressive men (4.3 percent) who use physical force to compel women to have intercourse but who are unlikely to see their act as rape. These "hidden rapists" have "oversubscribed" to traditional male roles, she says. They believe that aggression is normal and that women don't really mean it when they say no to sexual advances. Such men answer "True" to statements like "most women are sly and manipulating when they want to attract a man," "a woman will only respect a man who will lay down the law to her," and "a man's got to show the woman who's boss right from the start or he'll end up hen-pecked."

In Koss's current study, one respondent who answered yes to a question about obtaining intercourse through physical force, wrote in the comment, "I didn't rape the chick, she was enjoying it and responding," and later, "I feel that sex is a very pleasant way to relieve stress. Especially when there are no strings attached."

"He acted like he had a right, like he *didn't believe me*," says a coed from Auburn University on a videotaped dramatization of date rape experiences. And several weeks later, when she confronts him, saying he forced her, he says no, she wanted it. "You raped me," she finally tells him. And the picture freezes on his look of incredulity.

Barry Burkhart, a professor of psychology at Auburn, who has also studied sexual aggression among college men, found that 10 percent had used physical force to have intercourse with a woman against her will, and a large majority admitted to various other kinds of aggression. "These are ordinary males operating in an ordinary social context," he says. "So what we conclude is that there's something wrong with that social context."

The something wrong is that our culture fosters a "rape supportive belief system," according to social psychologist Martha Burt. She thinks that "there's a large category of 'real' rapes, and a much smaller category of what our culture is willing to call a 'real' rape. The question is, how does the culture manage to write off all those other rapes?" The way it's done, says Burt, currently director of the Social Services Research Center at the Urban Institute in Washington, D.C., is by believing in a series of myths about rape, including:

> It didn't really happen (the woman was lying);
> Women like rape (so there's no such thing as rape);
> Yes, it happened, but no harm was done (she wasn't a virgin; she wasn't white);
> Women provoke it (men can't control themselves);
> Women deserve it anyway.

It's easy to write off date rapes with such myths, coupled with what Burt calls our culture's "adversarial sexual beliefs": the gamesmanship theory that everybody is out for what they can get, and that all sexual relationships are basically exploitive and predatory. In fact, most victims of date rape initially blame themselves for what happened, and almost none report it to campus authorities. And most academic institutions prefer to keep it that way, judging from the lack of surveys on date rape—all of which makes one wonder if they don't actually blame the victim, too.

As long as such attacks continue to be a "hidden" campus phenomenon, unreported and unacknowledged by many college administrators, law enforcement personnel, and students, the problem will persist. Of course, the term has become much better known in the three years since *Ms.* reported on the prevalence of experiences such as Judy's and Gretchen's. (See "Date Rape: A Campus Epidemic?" September, 1982.) It has been the subject of talk shows such as "The Donahue Show" and TV dramas ("Cagney and Lacey"). But for most people it remains a contradiction in terms. "Everybody has a stake in denying that it's happening so often," says Martha Burt. "For women, it's self-protective . . . if only bad girls get raped, then I'm personally safe. For men, it's the denial that 'nice' people like them do it."

The fault has not entirely been that of the institutions. "Ten years ago, we were telling women to look over your shoulder when you go out at night and lock your doors," says Py Bateman, director of a nationally known rape education program in Seattle, Alternatives to Fear. The prevailing myth was that most rapes were committed by strangers in dark alleys.

"If you have to think that sixty to eighty percent of rape is by people you know—that's hard to deal with," says Sylvia Callaway, who directed the Austin, Texas, Rape Crisis Center for more than eight years before leaving last July. "No rape center in a university community would be surprised that the university is not willing to deal with the problem."

Statistics alone will not solve the problem of date rape, but they could help bring it out into the open. Which is why *Ms.* undertook the first nationwide survey on college campuses. The *Ms.* Magazine Campus Project on Sexual Assault, directed by Mary P. Koss at Kent State and funded by the National Center for the Prevention and Control of Rape, reached more than 7,000 students at a nationally representative sample of 35 schools, to find out how often, under what circumstances, and with what aftereffects a wide range of sexual assaults, including date rape, took place.

Preliminary results are now ready, and the information is no surprise. (See page 298.) Participating schools were promised anonymity, but each will receive the results applying to its student body. Our hope is that the reaction of "we can't believe it's happening on our campus" will be followed by "what can we do about it—now."

Just how entrenched is denial of this problem today? One gauge might be the difficulty our own researchers had in persuading schools to let us on campus. For every college that approved our study, two others rejected it. Their reasons (in writing and in telephone conversations) were themselves instructive: "we don't want to get involved," "limited foreseeable benefit," "too volatile a topic," "have not had any problems in this area," "worried about publicity," "can't allow surveys in classroom," "just can't invest the time now," "would be overintrusive," "don't want to be left holding the bag if something goes wrong."

Several schools rejected the study on the basis that filling out the questionnaire might upset some students, and that we were not providing adequate follow-up counseling. (Researchers stayed on campus for at least a day after the distribution of the questionnaire, gave the students listings of counselors or rape crisis centers to consult if anything upset them, and offered to meet with school personnel to brief them.) But isn't it less upsetting for a student to recognize and admit that she has been the victim of an acquaintance rape than to have buried the trauma of that rape deep inside herself?

"It's a Catch-22 situation. You want a survey to publicize a problem that has tremendous psychological implications. And the school says, 'Don't do it, because it will get people psychologically upset'," admits John Jung, who heads the human subjects review committee at California State University/Long Beach (a school that declined our study).

One wonders just who are the "people" who will get most psychologically upset: the students, or their parents who pay for their educations, or the administrators who are concerned about the school's image. "There may have been an episode here," said John Hose, executive assistant to the president of Brandeis University, "but there is no cause célèbre surrounding the issue. In such cases, the reaction of Student Affairs is to encourage the student to be in touch with her parents and to take legal action."

"Student Affairs" at Brandeis is headed by Rodger Crafts, who moved to this post about a year ago from the University of Rhode Island. "I don't think we have a significant problem here because we have a sophisticated and intelligent group of students," said Dean Crafts. As for the University of Rhode Island, more students there are "first generation college attenders," as he put it, and therefore have "less respect" for other people. Vandalism and physical harm are more likely to occur with "lower educational levels." Respect for other people goes along with "intelligence level."

Back at the University of Rhode Island, the counseling center is sponsoring a 12-week support and therapy group this fall for male students who are coercive and abusive in their relationships with women. Even though Nancy Carlson, director of Counseling and Career Services, is enthusiastic about such programs and workshops she notes, "the awareness about date rape has been a long time coming."

Another school where administrators were the last to confront the challenge to their school's self-image is Yale. Last year, two student publications reported instances of date rape on campus that surprised students, faculty, and administration. "There are no full statistics available on rape between the students at Yale anywhere. . . . There is no mention of rape in the 1983–1984 Undergraduate Regulations. There is no procedure for a victim to file a formal complaint of rape with the university. But there is rape between students at Yale," wrote Sarah Oates in the *Yale Daily News*. Partly in response to such charges, current Yale undergraduate regulations now list "sexual harassment" under "offenses that are subject to disciplinary action"—but still no mention of rape.

Yale students brave enough to bring a charge of sexual harassment may go before the Yale College Executive Committee, a specially convened group of faculty, administrators, and students that can impose a series of penalties, graduated in severity, culminating in expulsion. All its hearings and decisions are kept secret (but can in theory be subpoenaed in a court of law). But Michael McBride, current chair of the committee, told me that cases of date rape have come up during the past year, leading in one instance to a student being asked to "resign" from the university, and in another, the conclusion that there was not "sufficient evidence." (In Judy's case, described at the beginning of this article, the senior she charged was penalized by being denied the privilege of graduating with his class. But she claims that after he demanded that the case be reconsidered, he was fully exonerated.) Said McBride, "What surprised me the most was how complicated these cases are. It's only one person's word against another's. It's amazing how different their perceptions can be."

Judy chose to take her case before the Executive Committee rather than report it to the local police, because she felt she would have complete confidentiality and quick action. Actually, there were many delays. And then, because the man she accused hired a lawyer, she was forced to hire one too. As a result, the meeting felt very much like a jury trial to her, complete with cross-examinations that challenged her truthfulness and raised excruciatingly embarrassing questions.

Judy's lawyer felt that such painful questions were necessary. But it seems as if the lesson feminists in the sixties and seventies worked so hard and successfully to make understood—not to blame the victim for stranger rape—is one that will have to be learned all over again in the case of acquaintance rape. Only this time, the woman who reports the rape suffers a triple victimization. Not only is she attacked and then not believed, but she carries the added burden of losing faith in her own judgment and trust in other people.

In a recently published study of jurors in rape trials, University of Illinois sociologist Barbara Reskin found that jurors were less likely to convict a man if the victim knew him. "Consent is the preferred rape defense and gets the highest acquittal rates," Reskin observes. "In a date rape situation, I would think the jury would assume that the woman had already accepted his invitation in a romantic sense. It would be a matter of how *much* did she consent to."

Personal characteristics also influence jurors, Reskin says. Those she studied couldn't imagine that certain men would commit rape: if they were attractive, had access to sexual partners such as a girlfriend or a wife. More often than not, they'd say, "But he doesn't look like a rapist." Reskin imagines that this pattern would be "magnified in date rape, because these are men who could get a date, they're not complete losers."

It may turn out that solutions to the problem will turn up at places with a less genteel image to protect. Jan Strout, director of Montana State Women's Resource Center, wonders if schools such as hers, which recognize that they are dealing with a more conservative student body and a "macho cowboy image," aren't more willing to take the first step toward acknowledging the problem. A group called Students Against Sexual Assault was formed there two-and-a-half years ago after several students who were raped or resisted an attempted rape "went public." With men and women sharing leadership, this group is cosponsored by the Women's Resource Center and the student government.

Admitting to the problem isn't easy even when data is available, as doctoral student Genny Sandberg found at University of South Dakota. Last spring, she announced the results of a dating survey she coauthored with psychologists Tom Jackson and Patricia Petretic-Jackson. The most shocking statistic: 20 percent of the students (most from rural backgrounds and living in a rural campus setting) had been raped in a dating situation. The state board of regents couldn't believe it. "I just think that that's absolutely ridiculous," former regent Michael Rost said, according to the Brookings *Daily Register*, "I can't believe we would allow that to occur. If it is true, it's a very serious problem." Regent William Srstka agreed, "If this is true it's absolutely intolerable."

Following testimony by one of the researchers, the board changed its tune. Members are now discussing how to begin a statewide education and prevention program.

An inspiring example of how an administration can be led to new levels of consciousness took place at the University of Michigan earlier this year. Spurred by an article in *Metropolitan Detroit* magazine, a group of students staged a sit-in at the office of a university vice-president who had been quoted as saying that "Rape is a red flag word. . . . [The university] wants to present an image that is receptive and palatable to the potential student cohort," and also that "Rape is an issue like Alzheimer's disease or mental retardation [which] impacts on a small but sizable part of the population. . . . Perhaps it has to become a crisis that is commonly shared in order to get things done."

The students who spent the entire day in Vice President Henry Johnson's office claimed that rape had already become a crisis on their campus. They presented a list of 12 demands, ranging from a rape crisis center on campus to better lighting and installation of outdoor emergency phones. By the end of the day, Johnson had started to change his mind. Although he insisted that he had been misquoted and quoted out of context in the press, he told me that "I did not realize [before that] acquaintance rape was so much of a problem, that it was the most prevalent type of rape. There is a heightened awareness now on this campus. Whether we as a faculty and administration are as sensitive as we should be is another issue—and that will take some time."

In the meantime, members of the Michigan Student Assembly Women's Issues Committee (one of the groups active in organizing the protest) took their demands before the school's board of regents. The result: a $75,000 program for rape prevention and education on campus, directly reporting to Johnson's office. "We'll now be in a position to document the problem and to be proactive," says Johnson. Jennifer Faigel, an organizer of the protest, acknowledges a change in the administration's awareness but says the students themselves, disappointed in the amount of funding promised for the program, have already formed a group (Students Organized Against Rape) to develop programs in the dorms.

In just the three years since *Ms.* first reported on date rape, several new campus organizations have sprung up and other ongoing programs have surfaced.

But the real measure of a school's commitment to dealing with this problem is the range of services it provides, says Mary Harvey, who did a nationwide study of exemplary rape programs for the National Center for the Prevention and Control of Rape. "It should have preventive services, crisis intervention, possibilities for long-term treatment, advocacy, and women's studies programs that educate about violence. The quality of a university's services to rape victims can be measured by the degree to which these other things are in place."

Minimally, rape counselors and educators feel, students need to be exposed to information about date rape as soon as they enter college. Studies show that the group most vulnerable to acquaintance rape are college freshmen, followed by high school seniors. In Koss's original survey, for example, the average age of the victim was 18.

"I'd like a program where no first-year students could finish their starting week at college without being informed about the problem of acquaintance rape," says Andrea Parrot, a lecturer in human service studies at Cornell University, who is developing a program to train students and dorm resident advisers as date rape awareness counselors. Parrot and others admit that this would be a bare minimum. Handing out a brochure to read, even conducting a workshop on the subject during the busy orientation week and counting on students voluntarily attending, needs to be followed up with sessions in dormitories or other living units. These are the most common settings for date rapes, according to a study by Parrot and Robin Lynk.

So how do we go about changing attitudes? And how do we do it without "setting student against student?" asks Gretchen Mieszkowski, chair of the Sexual Assault Prevention Committee at the University of Houston/Clear Lake. Chiefly a commuter campus, with a majority of married women students, Clear Lake nevertheless had 17 acquaintance rapes reported to the local crisis hot line last year. "We had always focused on traditional solutions like lighting and escort services at night," Mieszkowski says. "But changing lighting in the parking lot is easy; it's only money."

Many who have studied the problem of rape education believe it has to begin with college-age women and men talking to each other more frankly about their beliefs and expectations about sex. Py Bateman of Alternatives to Fear thinks it has to start earlier, among teenagers, by developing rudimentary dating skills at the lower end of the sexual activity scale. "We need to learn more about holding hands than about sexual intercourse."

Bateman continues: "We've got to work on both sides. Boys don't know what they want any more than girls do. The way our sexual interaction is set up is that boys are supposed to push. Their peers tell them that scoring is what counts. They're as divorced from intimacy as girls."

Gail Abarbanel of the Rape Treatment Center at Santa Monica Hospital agrees. Her Center conducts educational programs for schools in Los Angeles County. In a recent survey of more than 5,000 teenagers, she found a high degree of misconception and lack of information about rape: "Most boys say yes to the question, 'If a girl goes back to a guy's house when she knows no one is home, is she consenting to sex?' And most boys believe that girls don't mean no when they say it."

Women clearly need to get more convincing, and men clearly need to believe them more. But until that ideal time, Montana State's Jan Strout warns, "Because men have been socialized to hear yes when women say no, we have to scream it."

Results of Ms. Study

One quarter of women in college today have been the victims of rape or attempted rape, and almost 90 percent of them knew their assailants. These are two of the more startling statistics to emerge from the Ms. Magazine Campus Project on Sexual Assault, the most far-reaching study to date on patterns of sexual aggression at America's institutions of higher learning. Funded by a grant from the National Center for the Prevention and Control of Rape, and under the direction of Kent State University psychologist Mary P. Koss, the survey reached more than 7,000 students at 35 schools. Preliminary results of the three-year study show:

- Fifty-two percent of all the women surveyed have experienced some form of sexual victimization.

- One in every eight women were the victims of rape, according to the prevailing legal definition.
- One in every 12 men admitted to having fulfilled the prevailing definition of rape or attempted rape, yet virtually none of those men identified themselves as rapists.
- Of the women who were raped, almost three quarters did not identify their experience as rape.
- Forty-seven percent of the rapes were by first or casual dates, or by romantic acquaintances.
- Three quarters of the women raped were between ages 15 and 21; the average age at the time of the rape was 18.
- More than 80 percent of the rapes occurred off-campus, with more than 50 percent on the man's turf: home, car, or other.
- More than one third of the women raped did not discuss their experience with anyone; more than 90 percent did not tell the police.

The full report will be ready later this year. It will include valuable information on the aftermath of date rape, sex-role expectations that may foster such rapes, and details about the circumstances of date rape—all of which will help in developing preventive and educational programs.

Speculations

1. Ellen Sweet emphasizes statements of denial and disbelief—"I couldn't believe that it was happening to me" or "date rape is not a significant problem on this campus." Why does she do this? What is her point?
2. What is the legal definition of rape? Is that definition meaningful and appropriate in the case of date rape?
3. Ellen Sweet says that "most victims of date rape initially blame themselves for what happened, and almost none report it to campus authorities." Why do you think that is the case? Is it still the case now, more than ten years after Sweet published this essay in *Ms.?*
4. What cultural myths perpetuate the tendency toward date rape among American men? Can you come up with other myths in addition to those cited by Sweet?
5. Have you ever been in a situation where someone you knew used force to make you do something that you did not want to do? How did you feel? What effects did being victimized by violence—even minor violence—have on you?

6. Do you agree with Jan Strout that "because men have been so-
cialized to hear yes when women say no, we have to scream it"?
What evidence do you see, either supporting or contradicting
Strout's assertion, in television shows, movies, music lyrics?

RAPE AND MODERN SEX WAR

Camille Paglia

"Hurricane Camille," "Feminism's Material Girl," "the avenging
angel of the sixties"—Camille Paglia delights in outraging the sensibilities of virtually everyone, but particularly contemporary feminists,
those who advocate censorship, homophobes, upholders of middle
class moral pieties, and conventional thinkers of every size and stripe.
A strong believer in classical education, rigorous academic standards,
and intellectual discipline, Paglia also loves pop culture, contending
that film and rock music stand at the apex of twentieth-century civilization. Two of her idols are Madonna and Keith Richards; her feminist heroes include Amelia Earhart, Katharine Hepburn, and Simone
de Beauvoir, author of *Second Sex.*

Born in 1947 in Endicott, New York, Camille Paglia attended the
State University of New York at Binghamton for her B.A. and then
completed her Ph.D. at Yale in 1974. She has taught at Bennington College, Wesleyan, Yale, and is now a professor of humanities at the University of the Arts in Philadelphia. For Paglia, the relative obscurity of
her home institution is a plus: "I'm totally outside the establishment,"
she has stated. "That's why I am free to rock the boat. I am attacked,
assailed, and reviled. And that's *wonderful!* I say, 'go ahead, hit me
with your best shot.' That's the price you pay for speaking out."

Paglia delights in fierce, bare-knuckled debate on significant issues, something she has done in all three of her books: *Sexual Personae: Art and Decadence from Nefertiti to Emily Dickinson* (1990), *Sex, Art,
and American Culture: Essays* (1992), and the recent *Vamps and Tramps*
(1994), a collection of essays, reviews, and commentary that includes
a loving account of four homosexual friends and a long essay on rape,
harassment, and pornography.

Paglia's central argument in *Sexual Personae* is that men create
music, art, and other forms of culture as a defense against women's
all-consuming sexual and procreative powers: "Male aggressions and
lust are the energizing factors in culture. They are men's tools of survival in the pagan vastness of female nature ... If civilization had
been left in female hands, we would still be living in grass huts." Although accused of celebrating sexual stereotypes, Paglia has stated

that she celebrates "woman's ancient mystery and glamour. I see the mother as an overwhelming force who condemns men to lifelong sexual anxiety, from which they escape through rationalism and physical achievement." In the following essay from *Sex, Art, and American Culture,* Paglia demands that women wake up to the differing sexualities of men and women—and argues that it is women who must take responsibility for the "sizzle of sexual passion" (her own phrase from another essay) because men too often lose control.

Rape is an outrage that cannot be tolerated in civilized society. Yet feminism, which has waged a crusade for rape to be taken more seriously, has put young women in danger by hiding the truth about sex from them.

In dramatizing the pervasiveness of rape, feminists have told young women that before they have sex with a man, they must give consent as explicit as a legal contract's. In this way, young women have been convinced that they have been the victims of rape. On elite campuses in the Northeast and on the West Coast, they have held consciousness-raising sessions, petitioned administrations, demanded inquests. At Brown University, outraged, panicky "victims" have scrawled the names of alleged attackers on the walls of women's rest rooms. What marital rape was to the Seventies, "date rape" is to the Nineties.

The incidence and seriousness of rape do not require this kind of exaggeration. Real acquaintance rape is nothing new. It has been a horrible problem for women for all of recorded history. Once fathers and brothers protected women from rape. Once the penalty for rape was death. I come from a fierce Italian tradition where, not so long ago in the motherland, a rapist would end up knifed, castrated, and hung out to dry.

But the old clans and small rural communities have broken down. In our cities, on our campuses far from home, young women are vulnerable and defenseless. Feminism has not prepared them for this. Feminism keeps saying the sexes are the same. It keeps telling women they can do anything, go anywhere, say anything, wear anything. No, they can't. Women will always be in sexual danger.

One of my male students recently slept overnight with a friend in a passageway of the Great Pyramid in Egypt. He described the moon and sand, the ancient silence and eerie echoes. I will never experience that. I am a woman. I am not stupid enough to believe I could ever be safe there. There is a world of solitary adventure I will never have. Women have always known these somber truths. But feminism, with its pie-in-the-sky fantasies about the perfect world, keeps young women from seeing life as it is.

We must remedy social injustice whenever we can. But there are some things we cannot change. There are sexual differences that are based in biology. Academic feminism is lost in a fog of social construc-tionism. It believes we are totally the product of our environment. This idea was invented by Rousseau. He was wrong. Emboldened by dumb French language theory, academic feminists repeat the same hollow slogans over and over to each other. Their view of sex is naïve and prudish. Leaving sex to the feminists is like letting your dog vacation at the taxidermist's.

The sexes are at war. Men must struggle for identity against the overwhelming power of their mothers. Women have menstruation to tell them they are women. Men must do or risk something to be men. Men become masculine only when other men say they are. Having sex with a woman is one way a boy becomes a man.

College men are at their hormonal peak. They have just left their mothers and are questing for their male identity. In groups, they are dangerous. A woman going to a fraternity party is walking into Testos-terone Flats, full of prickly cacti and blazing guns. If she goes, she should be armed with resolute alertness. She should arrive with girl-friends and leave with them. A girl who lets herself get dead drunk at a fraternity party is a fool. A girl who goes upstairs alone with a broth-er at a fraternity party is an idiot. Feminists call this "blaming the vic-tim." I call it common sense.

For a decade, feminists have drilled their disciples to say, "Rape is a crime of violence but not of sex." This sugar-coated Shirley Temple nonsense has exposed young women to disaster. Misled by feminism, they do not expect rape from the nice boys from good homes who sit next to them in class.

Aggression and eroticism are deeply intertwined. Hunt, pursuit, and capture are biologically programmed into male sexuality. Genera-tion after generation, men must be educated, refined, and ethically per-suaded away from their tendency toward anarchy and brutishness. So-ciety is not the enemy, as feminism ignorantly claims. Society is woman's protection against rape. Feminism, with its solemn Carry Na-tion repressiveness, does not see what is for men the eroticism or fun element in rape, especially the wild, infectious delirium of gang rape. Women who do not understand rape cannot defend themselves against it.

The date-rape controversy shows feminism hitting the wall of its own broken promises. The women of my Sixties generation were the first respectable girls in history to swear like sailors, get drunk, stay out all night—in short, to act like men. We sought total sexual freedom and equality. But as time passed, we woke up to cold reality. The old dou-ble standard protected women. When anything goes, it's women who lose.

Today's young women don't know what they want. They see that feminism has not brought sexual happiness. The theatrics of public rage over date rape are their way of restoring the old sexual rules that were shattered by my generation. Because nothing about the sexes has really changed. The comic film *Where the Boys Are* (1960), the ultimate expression of Fifties man-chasing, still speaks directly to our time. It shows smart, lively women skillfully anticipating and fending off the dozens of strategies with which horny men try to get them into bed. The agonizing date-rape subplot and climax are brilliantly done. The victim, Yvette Mimieux, makes mistake after mistake, obvious to the other girls. She allows herself to be lured away from her girlfriends and into isolation with boys whose character and intentions she misreads. *Where the Boys Are* tells the truth. It shows courtship as a dangerous game in which the signals are not verbal but subliminal.

Neither militant feminism, which is obsessed with politically correct language, nor academic feminism, which believes that knowledge and experience are "constituted by" language, can understand preverbal or nonverbal communication. Feminism, focusing on sexual politics, cannot see that sex exists in and through the body. Sexual desire and arousal cannot be fully translated into verbal terms. This is why men and women misunderstand each other.

Trying to remake the future, feminism cut itself off from sexual history. It discarded and suppressed the sexual myths of literature, art, and religion. Those myths show us the turbulence, the mysteries and passions of sex. In mythology we see men's sexual anxiety, their fear of woman's dominance. Much sexual violence is rooted in men's sense of psychological weakness toward women. It takes many men to deal with one woman. Woman's voracity is a persistent motif. Clara Bow, it was rumored, took on the USC football team on weekends. Marilyn Monroe, singing "Diamonds Are a Girl's Best Friend," rules a conga line of men in tuxes. Half-clad Cher, in the video for "If I Could Turn Back Time," deranges a battleship of screaming sailors and straddles a pink-lit cannon. Feminism, coveting social power, is blind to woman's cosmic sexual power.

To understand rape, you must study the past. There never was and never will be sexual harmony. Every woman must take personal responsibility for her sexuality, which is nature's red flame. She must be prudent and cautious about where she goes and with whom. When she makes a mistake, she must accept the consequences and, through self-criticism, resolve never to make that mistake again. Running to Mommy and Daddy on the campus grievance committee is unworthy of strong women. Posting lists of guilty men in the toilet is cowardly, infantile stuff.

The Italian philosophy of life espouses high-energy confrontation. A male student makes a vulgar remark about your breasts? Don't slink off to whimper and simper with the campus shrinking violets. Deal with it. On the spot. Say, "Shut up, you jerk! And crawl back to the barnyard where you belong!" In general, women who project this take-charge attitude toward life get harassed less often. I see too many dopey, immature, self-pitying women walking around like melting sticks of butter. It's the Yvette Mimieux syndrome: make me happy. And listen to me weep when I'm not.

The date-rape debate is already smothering in propaganda churned out by the expensive Northeastern colleges and universities, with their overconcentration of boring, uptight academic feminists and spoiled, affluent students. Beware of the deep manipulativeness of rich students who were neglected by their parents. They love to turn the campus into hysterical psychodramas of sexual transgression, followed by assertions of parental authority and concern. And don't look for sexual enlightenment from academe, which spews out mountains of books but never looks at life directly.

As a fan of football and rock music, I see in the simple, swaggering masculinity of the jock and in the noisy posturing of the heavy-metal guitarist certain fundamental, unchanging truths about sex. Masculinity is aggressive, unstable, combustible. It is also the most creative cultural force in history. Women must reorient themselves toward the elemental powers of sex, which can strengthen or destroy.

The only solution to date rape is female self-awareness and self-control. A woman's number one line of defense is herself. When a real rape occurs, she should report it to the police. Complaining to college committees because the courts "take too long" is ridiculous. College administrations are not a branch of the judiciary. They are not equipped or trained for legal inquiry. Colleges must alert incoming students to the problems and dangers of adulthood. Then colleges must stand back and get out of the sex game.

Speculations

1. In her opening paragraph, Paglia states a seeming paradox: feminism has "waged a crusade for rape to be taken more seriously," and yet this crusade has "put young women in danger." How can this be so? Do you agree that the crusade about date rape has been counter-productive? Offer at least two reasons to support your thinking.

2. Paglia states: "Masculinity is aggressive, unstable, combustible. It is also the most creative cultural force in history. Women must reorient themselves toward the elemental powers of sex, which can strengthen or destroy." What conclusions do you draw from this statement concerning male and female sex roles? Is Paglia implying that women are inferior? Do you agree that masculinity is "aggressive, unstable, combustible," and if so, how would you characterize femininity?

3. Paglia is very effective at tossing verbal hand grenades, explosive statements that stay in the reader's mind. Select three such statements from this essay and write a short response to each. Be ready to share these in class.

4. How would you characterize Paglia's depiction of men and women? Write a brief account in your own words that summarizes Paglia's views. In what ways are men and women alike? In what ways are they dissimilar? In what ways are they necessarily in conflict?

5. Paglia is contemptuous of expensive Northeastern colleges and of women putting their trust in college administrations to solve the problem. Do you agree? Why do you think Paglia attacks these targets?

6. Why do you think Paglia begins her essay as she does? Is her opening sentence effective? Given what she says later in the essay, how do you think Paglia defines "rape"? Do you agree? Does Paglia's opening sentence encourage you to keep reading? Why or why not?

DATE RAPE'S OTHER VICTIM

Katie Roiphe

"When I was young," Katie Roiphe has stated, "I thought of feminism as something like a train you could catch and ride to someplace better." Right now, many feminists would like to throw her right off the train without even slowing down to say good-bye.

Katie Roiphe (pronounced ROY-fee) was born in July, 1968, the daughter of well-known feminist author and journalist Anne Roiphe and a psychoanalyst father. Raised on the Upper West Side of New York City, Roiphe graduated from an exclusive private high school and then went on to Harvard, and graduated from Princeton University with a Ph.D. in English.

Roiphe wrote "Date Rape's Other Victim" (it appeared as the feature essay in *The New York Times Magazine,* 1993) as a response to her view that contemporary feminism was ill-serving women, particularly in relation to dating, sex, romance, sexual harassment, and definitions of feminism. The reaction was stunning: Roiphe received truckloads of letters, many of them vitriolic and condemnatory; some friends at Princeton stopped speaking to her; other students formed protest marches. Undaunted, Roiphe wrote a series of essays which she published as *The Morning After: Sex, Fear, and Feminism on Campus* (Little-Brown, 1993). In this collection of essays, Roiphe attacks the hypocrisy within society that idealizes the freedom to speak and act but practices a variety of forms of intolerance, bigotry, victimology, and sexual prudery. Like her essay, Roiphe's book kindled a firestorm of response, including more than 300 magazine and newspaper articles.

Roiphe does not consider her work an attack on women, women's rights, or feminism; rather, Roiphe wants to take to task those who apply the word "rape" to everything from job discrimination to fraternity ogling—and she hopes to establish meaningful terms for social relationships between men and women, particularly college-age students. "There are all these pressures that we should go out and have sex, and there are all these pressures that we shouldn't, that it's dangerous, in all kinds of ways—we might get AIDS, we might be raped. We're getting very powerful mixed messages, and it's a difficult backdrop for conducting one's youth," Roiphe told Art Carey of the *Philadelphia Inquirer*. Feminism, she says, encourages people to identify themselves as oppressed: "This is the way you get a certain kind of authority right now—by saying, 'I am a victim.' My argument in the book is that, at this point, this is bad for feminism and bad for women."

The essay that follows, "Date Rape's Other Victim," is the one that started it all. In it, Roiphe argues that women must renounce the passive role into which they are placed by both their "enemies" and their "friends." For Roiphe, social activism begins with a casting off of traditional attitudes and alliances, with a reassessment of what it means to be a feminist.

One in four college women has been the victim of rape or attempted rape. One in four. I remember standing outside the dining hall in college, looking at a purple poster with this statistic written in bold letters. It didn't seem right. If sexual assault was really so pervasive, it seemed strange that the intricate gossip networks hadn't picked up more than one or two shadowy instances of rape. If I was really standing in the middle of an "epidemic," a "crisis"—if 25 percent of my women friends were really being raped—wouldn't I know it?

These posters were not presenting facts. They were advertising a mood. Preoccupied with issues like date rape and sexual harassment, campus feminists produce endless images of women as victims—women offended by a professor's dirty joke, women pressured into sex by peers, women trying to say no but not managing to get it across.

This portrait of the delicate female bears a striking resemblance to that 50's ideal my mother and other women of her generation fought so hard to leave behind. They didn't like her passivity, her wide-eyed innocence. They didn't like the fact that she was perpetually offended by sexual innuendo. They didn't like her excessive need for protection. She represented personal, social and intellectual possibilities collapsed, and they worked and marched, shouted and wrote to make her irrelevant for their daughters. But here she is again, with her pure intentions and her wide eyes. Only this time it is the feminists themselves who are breathing new life into her.

Is there a rape crisis on campus? Measuring rape is not as straightforward as it might seem. Neil Gilbert, a professor of social welfare at the University of California at Berkeley, questions the validity of the one-in-four statistic. Gilbert points out that in a 1985 survey undertaken by *Ms.* magazine and financed by the National Institute of Mental Health, 73 percent of the women categorized as rape victims did not initially define their experience as rape; it was Mary Koss, the psychologist conducting the study, who did.

One of the questions used to define rape was: "Have you had sexual intercourse when you didn't want to because a man gave you alcohol or drugs?" The phrasing raises the issue of agency. Why aren't college women responsible for their own intake of alcohol or drugs? A man may give her drugs, but she herself decides to take them. If we assume that women are not all helpless and naive, then they should be held responsible for their choice to drink or take drugs. If a woman's "judgment is impaired" and she has sex, it isn't necessarily always the man's fault; it isn't necessarily always rape.

As Gilbert delves further into the numbers, he does not necessarily disprove the one-in-four statistic, but he does clarify what it means—the so-called rape epidemic on campuses is more a way of interpreting, a way of seeing, than a physical phenomenon. It is more about a change in sexual politics than a change in sexual behavior. Whether or not one in four college women has been raped, then, is a matter of opinion, not a matter of mathematical fact.

That rape is a fact in some women's lives is not in question. It's hard to watch the solemn faces of young Bosnian girls, their words haltingly translated, as they tell of brutal rapes; or to read accounts of a suburban teen-ager raped and beaten while walking home from a shopping mall. We all agree that rape is a terrible thing, but we no longer agree on what rape is. Today's definition has stretched beyond bruises and knives, threats of death or violence to include emotional pressure and the influence of alcohol. The lines between rape and sex begin to blur. The one-in-four statistic on those purple posters is measuring something elusive. It is measuring her word against his in a realm where words barely exist. There is a gray area in which one person's rape may be another's bad night. Definitions become entangled in passionate ideological battles. There hasn't been a remarkable change in the number of women being raped; just a change in how receptive the political climate is to those numbers.

The next question, then, is who is identifying this epidemic and why. Somebody is "finding" this rape crisis, and finding it for a reason.

Asserting the prevalence of rape lends urgency, authority to a broader critique of culture.

In a dramatic description of the rape crisis, Naomi Wolf writes in "The Beauty Myth" that "Cultural representation of glamorized degradation has created a situation among the young in which boys rape and girls get raped *as a normal course of events.*" The italics are hers. Whether or not Wolf really believes rape is part of the "normal course of events" these days, she is making a larger point. Wolf's rhetorical excess serves her larger polemic about sexual politics. Her dramatic prose is a call to arms. She is trying to rally the feminist troops. Wolf uses rape as a red flag, an undeniable sign that things are falling apart.

From Susan Brownmiller—who brought the politics of rape into the mainstream with her 1975 best seller, "Against Our Will: Men, Women and Rape"—to Naomi Wolf, feminist prophets of the rape crisis are talking about something more than forced penetration. They are talking about what they define as a "rape culture." Rape is a natural trump card for feminism. Arguments about rape can be used to sequester feminism in the teary province of trauma and crisis. By blocking analysis with its claims to unique pandemic suffering, the rape crisis becomes a powerful source of authority.

Dead serious, eyes wide with concern, a college senior tells me that she believes one in four is too conservative an estimate. This is not the first time I've heard this. She tells me the right statistic is closer to one in two. That means one in two women are raped. It's amazing, she says, amazing that so many of us are sexually assaulted every day.

What is amazing is that this student actually believes that 50 percent of women are raped. This is the true crisis. Some substantial number of young women are walking around with this alarming belief: a hyperbole containing within it a state of perpetual fear.

"Acquaintance Rape: Is Dating Dangerous?" is a pamphlet commonly found at counseling centers. The cover title rises from the shards of a shattered photograph of a boy and girl dancing. Inside, the pamphlet offers a sample date-rape scenario. She thinks:

"He was really good looking and he had a great smile.... We talked and found we had a lot in common. I really liked him. When he asked me over to his place for a drink I thought it would be O.K. He was such a good listener and I wanted him to ask me out again."

She's just looking for a sensitive boy, a good listener with a nice smile, but unfortunately his intentions are not as pure as hers. Beneath that nice smile, he thinks:

"She looked really hot, wearing a sexy dress that showed off her great body. We started talking right away. I knew that she liked me by the way she kept smiling and touching my arm while she was speaking. She seemed pretty relaxed so I asked her back to my place for a drink. . . . When she said 'Yes' I knew that I was going to be lucky!"

These cardboard stereotypes don't just educate freshmen about rape. They also educate them about "dates" and about sexual desire. With titles like "Friends Raping Friends: Could It Happen to You?" date-rape pamphlets call into question all relationships between men and women. Beyond warning students about rape, the rape-crisis movement produces its own images of sexual behavior, in which men exert pressure and women resist. By defining the dangerous date in these terms—with this type of male and this type of female, and their different expectations—these pamphlets promote their own perspective on how men and women feel about sex: men are lascivious, women are innocent.

The sleek images of pressure and resistance projected in rape education movies, videotapes, pamphlets and speeches create a model of acceptable sexual behavior. The don'ts imply their own set of do's. The movement against rape, then, not only dictates the way sex *shouldn't be* but also the way it *should be.* Sex should be gentle, it should not be aggressive; it should be absolutely equal, it should not involve domination and submission; it should be tender, not ambivalent; it should communicate respect, it shouldn't communicate consuming desire.

In "Real Rape," Susan Estrich, a professor of law at the University of Southern California Law Center, slips her ideas about the nature of sexual encounters into her legal analysis of the problem of rape. She writes: "Many feminists would argue that so long as women are powerless relative to men, viewing a 'yes' as a sign of true consent is misguided. . . . Many women who say yes to men they know, whether on dates or on the job, would say no if they could. . . . Women's silence sometimes is the product not of passion and desire but of pressure and fear."

Like Estrich, most rape-crisis feminists claim they are not talking about sex; they're talking about violence. But, like Estrich, they are also talking about sex. With their advice, their scenarios, their sample aggressive male, the message projects a clear comment on the nature of sexuality: women are often unwilling participants. They say yes because they feel they have to, because they are intimidated by male power.

The idea of "consent" has been redefined beyond the simple assertion that "no means no." Politically correct sex involves a yes, and a specific yes at that. According to the premise of "active consent," we can no longer afford ambiguity. We can no longer afford the dangers of unspoken consent. A former director of Columbia's date-rape education program told *New York* magazine, "Stone silence throughout an entire physical encounter with someone is not explicit consent."

This apparently practical, apparently clinical proscription cloaks retrograde assumptions about the way men and women experience sex. The idea that only an explicit yes means yes proposes that, like children, women have trouble communicating what they want. Beyond its dubious premise about the limits of female communication, the idea of active consent bolsters stereotypes of men just out to "get some" and women who don't really want any.

Rape-crisis feminists express nostalgia for the days of greater social control, when the university acted in loco parentis and women were protected from the insatiable force of male desire. The rhetoric of feminists and conservatives blurs and overlaps in this desire to keep our youth safe and pure.

By viewing rape as encompassing more than the use or threat of physical violence to coerce someone into sex, rape-crisis feminists reinforce traditional views about the fragility of the female body and will. According to common definitions of date rape, even "verbal coercion" or "manipulation" constitute rape. Verbal coercion is defined as "a woman's consenting to unwanted sexual activity because of a man's verbal arguments not including verbal threats of force." The belief that "verbal coercion" is rape pervades workshops, counseling sessions and student opinion pieces. The suggestion lurking beneath this definition of rape is that men are not just physically but also intellectually and emotionally more powerful than women.

Imagine men sitting around in a circle talking about how she called him impotent and how she manipulated him into sex, how violated and dirty he felt afterward, how coercive she was, how she got him drunk first, how he hated his body and he couldn't eat for three weeks afterward. Imagine him calling this rape. Everyone feels the weight of emotional pressure at one time or another. The question is not whether people pressure each other but how our minds and our culture transform that pressure into full-blown assault. There would never be a rule or a law or even a pamphlet or peer counseling group for men who claimed to have been emotionally raped or verbally pressured into sex. And for the same reasons—assumption of basic competence, free will and strength of character—there should be no such rules or groups or pamphlets about women.

In discussing rape, campus feminists often slip into an outdated sexist vocabulary. But we have to be careful about using rape as metaphor. The sheer physical fact of rape has always been loaded with cultural meaning. Throughout history, women's bodies have been seen as property, as chaste objects, as virtuous vessels to be "dishonored," "ruined," "defiled." Their purity or lack of purity has been a measure of value for the men to whom they belonged.

"Politically, I call it rape whenever a woman has sex and feels violated," writes Catharine MacKinnon, a law professor and feminist legal scholar best known for her crusade against pornography. The language of virtue and violation reinforces retrograde stereotypes. It backs women into old corners. Younger feminists share MacKinnon's vocabulary and the accompanying assumptions about women's bodies. In one student's account of date rape in the Rag, a feminist magazine at Harvard, she talks about the anguish of being "defiled." Another writes, "I long to be innocent again." With such anachronistic constructions of the female body, with all their assumptions about female purity, these young women frame their experience of rape in archaic, sexist terms. Of course, sophisticated modern-day feminists don't use words like honor or virtue anymore. They know better than to say date-rape victims have been "defiled." Instead, they call it "post-traumatic stress syndrome." They tell the victim she should not feel "shame," she should feel "traumatized." Within their overtly political psychology, forced penetration takes on a level of metaphysical significance: date rape resonates through a woman's entire life.

Combating myths about rape is one of the central missions of the rape-crisis movement. They spend money and energy trying to break down myths like "She asked for it." But with all their noise about rape myths, rape-crisis feminists are generating their own. The plays, the poems, the pamphlets, the Take Back the Night speakouts, are propelled by the myth of innocence lost.

All the talk about empowering the voiceless dissolves into the image of the naïve girl child who trusts the rakish man. This plot reaches back centuries. It propels Samuel Richardson's 18th-century epistolary novel, "Clarissa": after hundreds of pages chronicling the minute details of her plight, her seduction and resistance, her break from her family, Clarissa is raped by the duplicitous Robert Lovelace. Afterward, she refuses to eat and fades toward a very virtuous, very religious death. Over a thousand pages are devoted to the story of her fall from innocence, a weighty event by 18th-century standards. But did these 20th-century girls, raised on Madonna videos and the 6 o'clock news, really trust that people were good until they themselves were raped? Maybe. Were these girls, raised on horror movies and glossy Hollywood sex scenes, really as innocent as all that? Maybe. But maybe the myth of lost innocence is a trope—convenient, appealing, politically effective.

As long as we're taking back the night, we might as well take back our own purity. Sure, we were all kind of innocent, playing in the sandbox with bright red shovels—boys, too. We can all look back through the tumultuous tunnel of adolescence on a honey-glazed childhood, with simple rules and early bedtimes. We don't have to look at parents fighting, at sibling struggles, at casting out one best friend for another in the Darwinian playground. This is not the innocence lost; this is the innocence we never had.

The idea of a fall from childhood grace, pinned on one particular moment, a moment over which we had no control, much lamented, gives our lives a compelling narrative structure. It's easy to see why the

17-year-old likes it; it's easy to see why the rape-crisis feminist likes it. It's a natural human impulse put to political purpose. But in generating and perpetuating such myths, we should keep in mind that myths about innocence have been used to keep women inside and behind veils. They have been used to keep them out of work and in labor.

It's not hard to imagine Clarissa, in jeans and a sweatshirt, transported into the 20th century, at a Take Back the Night march. She would speak for a long time about her deception and rape, about verbal coercion and anorexia, about her ensuing post-traumatic stress syndrome. Latter-day Clarissas may worry more about their "self-esteem" than their virtue, but they are still attaching the same quasi-religious value to the physical act.

"Calling it Rape," a play by Sonya Rasminsky, a recent Harvard graduate, is based on interviews with date-rape victims. The play, which has been performed at Harvard and may be taken into Boston-area high schools, begins with "To His Coy Mistress," by the 17th-century poet Andrew Marvell. Although generations of high-school and college students have read this as a romantic poem, a poem about desire and the struggle against mortality, Rasminsky has reinterpreted it as a poem about rape. "Had we but world enough, and time, this coyness, lady, were no crime." But what Andrew Marvell didn't know then, and we know now, is that the real crime is not her coyness but his verbal coercion.

Farther along, the actors recount a rape that hinges on misunderstanding. A boy and girl are watching videos and he starts to come on to her. She does not want to have sex. As the situation progresses, she says, in an oblique effort to communicate her lack of enthusiasm, "If you're going to [expletive] me, use a condom." He interprets that as a yes, but it's really a no. And, according to this play, what happens next, condom or no condom, is rape.

This is a central idea of the rape-crisis movement: that sex has become our tower of Babel. He doesn't know what she wants (not to have sex) and she doesn't know what he wants (to have sex)—until it's too late. He speaks boyspeak and she speaks girlspeak and what comes out of all this verbal chaos is a lot of rapes. The theory of mixed signals and crossed stars has to do with more than gender politics. It comes in part, from the much-discussed diversity that has so radically shifted the social composition of the college class since the 50's.

Take my own Harvard dorm: the Adams House dining hall is large, with high ceilings and dark paneling. It hasn't changed much for generations. As soon as the students start milling around gathering salads, ice cream and coffee onto green trays, there are signs of change. There are students in jeans, flannel shirts, short skirts, girls in jackets, boys in bracelets, two pierced noses and lots of secondhand clothes.

Not so many years ago, this room was filled with boys in jackets and ties. Most of them were white, Christian and what we now call privileged. Students came from the same social milieu with the same social rules and it was assumed that everyone knew more or less how they were expected to behave with everyone else. Diversity and multiculturalism were unheard of, and if they had been, they would have been dirty words. With the shift in college environments, with the introduction of black kids, Asian kids, Jewish kids, kids from the wrong side of the tracks of nearly every railroad in the country, there was an accompanying anxiety about how people behave. When ivory tower meets melting pot, it causes tension, some confusion, some need for readjustment. In explaining the need for intensive "orientation" programs, including workshops on date rape, Columbia's assistant dean for freshmen stated in an interview in the *New York Times*: "You can't bring all these people together and say, 'Now be one big happy community,' without some sort of training. You can't just throw together somebody from a small town in Texas and someone from New York City and someone from a conservative fundamentalist home in the Midwest and say, 'Now without any sort of conversation, be best friends and get along and respect one another.'"

Catharine Stimpson, a University Professor at Rutgers and long-time advocate of women's studies programs, once pointed out that it's sometimes easier for people to talk about gender than to talk about class. "Miscommunication" is in some sense a word for the friction between the way we were and the way we are. Just as the idea that we speak different languages is connected to gender—the arrival of women in classrooms, in dorms and in offices—it is also connected to class.

When the Southern heiress goes out with the plumber's son from the Bronx, when the kid from rural Arkansas goes out with a boy from Exeter, the anxiety is that they have different expectations. The dangerous "miscommunication" that recurs through the literature on date rape is a code word for difference in background. The rhetoric surrounding date rape and sexual harassment is in part a response to cultural mixing. The idea that men don't know what women mean when women say no stems from something deeper and more complicated than feminist concerns with rape.

People have asked me if I have ever been date-raped. And thinking back on complicated nights, on too many glasses of wine, on strange and familiar beds, I would have to say yes. With such a sweeping definition of rape, I wonder how many people there are, male or female, who haven't been date-raped at one point or another. People pressure and manipulate and cajole each other into all sorts of things all of the time. As Susan Sontag wrote, "Since Christianity upped the ante and concentrated on sexual behavior as the root of virtue, everything pertaining to sex has been a 'special case' in our culture, evoking peculiarly inconsistent attitudes." No human interactions are free from pressure, and the idea that sex is, or can be, makes it what Sontag calls a "special case," vulnerable to the inconsistent expectations of double standard.

With their expansive version of rape, rape-crisis feminists are inventing a kinder, gentler sexuality. Beneath the broad definition of rape, these feminists are endorsing their own utopian vision of sexual relations: sex without struggle, sex without power, sex without persuasion, sex without pursuit. If verbal coercion constitutes rape, then the word rape itself expands to include any kind of sex a woman experiences as negative.

When Martin Amis spoke at Princeton, he included a controversial joke: "As far as I'm concerned, you can change your mind before, even during, but just not after sex." The reason this joke is funny, and the reason it's also too serious to be funny, is that in the current atmosphere you *can* change your mind afterward. Regret can signify rape. A night that was a blur, a night you wish hadn't happened, can be rape. Since "verbal coercion" and "manipulation" are ambiguous, it's easy to decide afterwards that he manipulated you. You can realize it weeks or even years later. This is a movement that deals in retrospective trauma.

Rape has become a catch-all expression, a word used to define everything that is unpleasant and disturbing about relations between the sexes. Students say things like "I realize that sexual harassment is a kind of rape." If we refer to a whole range of behavior from emotional pressure to sexual harassment as "rape," then the idea itself gets diluted. It ceases to be powerful as either description or accusation.

Some feminists actually collapse the distinction between rape and sex. Catharine MacKinnon writes: "Compare victims' reports of rape with women's reports of sex. They look a lot alike. . . . In this light, the major distinction between intercourse (normal) and rape (abnormal) is that the normal happens so often that one cannot get anyone to see anything wrong with it."

There are a few feminists involved in rape education who object to the current expanding definitions of sexual assault. Gillian Greensite, founder of the rape prevention education program at the University of California at Santa Cruz, writes that the seriousness of the crime "is being undermined by the growing tendency of some feminists to label all heterosexual miscommunication and insensitivity as acquaintance rape." From within the rape-crisis movement, Greensite's dissent makes an important point. If we are going to maintain an *idea* of rape, then we need to reserve it for instances of physical violence, or the threat of physical violence.

But some people want the melodrama. They want the absolute value placed on experience by absolute words. Words like "rape" and "verbal coercion" channel the confusing flow of experience into something easy to understand. The idea of date rape comes at us fast and coherent. It comes at us when we've just left home and haven't yet figured out where to put our new futons or how to organize our new social lives. The rhetoric about date rape defines the terms, gives names to nameless confusions and sorts through mixed feelings with a sort of insistent consistency. In the first rush of sexual experience, the fear of date rape offers a tangible framework to locate fears that are essentially abstract.

When my 55-year-old mother was young, navigating her way through dates, there was a definite social compass. There were places not to let him put his hands. There were invisible lines. The pill wasn't available. Abortion wasn't legal. And sex was just wrong. Her mother gave her "mad money" to take out on dates in case her date got drunk and she needed to escape. She had to go far enough to hold his interest and not far enough to endanger her reputation.

Now the rape-crisis feminists are offering new rules. They are giving a new political weight to the same old no. My mother's mother told her to drink sloe gin fizzes so she wouldn't drink too much and get too drunk and go too far. Now the date rape pamphlets tell us: "Avoid excessive use of alcohol and drugs. Alcohol and drugs interfere with clear thinking and effective communication." My mother's mother told her to stay away from empty rooms and dimly lighted streets. In "I Never Called It Rape," Robin Warshaw writes, "Especially with recent acquaintances, women should insist on going only to public places such as restaurants and movie theaters."

There is a danger in these new rules. We shouldn't need to be reminded that the rigidly conformist 50's were not the heyday of women's power. Barbara Ehrenreich writes of "re-making love," but there is a danger in re-making love in its old image. The terms may have changed, but attitudes about sex and women's bodies have not. Rape-crisis feminists threaten the progress that's been made. They are chasing the same stereotypes our mothers spent so much energy escaping.

One day I was looking through my mother's bookshelves and I found her old battered copy of Germaine Greer's feminist classic, "The Female Eunuch." The pages were dogeared and whole passages marked with penciled notes. It was 1971 when Germaine Greer fanned the fires with "The Female Eunuch" and it was 1971 when my mother read it, brand new, explosive, a tough and sexy terrorism for the early stirrings of the feminist movement.

Today's rape-crisis feminists threaten to create their own version of the desexualized woman Greer complained of 20 years ago. Her comments need to be recycled for present-day feminism. "It is often falsely assumed," Greer writes, "even by feminists, that sexuality is the enemy of the female who really wants to develop these aspects of her personality. . . . It was not the insistence upon her sex that weakened the American woman student's desire to make something of her education, but the insistence upon a *passive* sexual *role* [Greer's italics]. In fact, the chief instrument in the deflection and perversion of female energy is the denial of female sexuality for the substitution of femininity or sexlessness."

It is the passive sexual role that threatens us still, and it is the denial of female sexual agency that threatens to propel us backward.

Speculations

1. Katie Roiphe's title is a bit enigmatic. Who is "date rape's other victim"? Why do you think Roiphe entitled her essay this way? Is it effective in inviting the reader into the essay and establishing Roiphe's point of view?

2. Roiphe claims that in a number of ways, perception does not match reality when it comes to rape and date rape. Write down two or three such instances described by Roiphe. To what (or whom) does Roiphe attribute this discrepancy between claims that people make and the real state of affairs? Do you agree with her?

3. According to Roiphe, what is "politically correct sex?" Do you agree with her view that Susan Estrich (see the introduction to this section) and other rape-crisis feminists distort and conceal "the way men and women experience sex"?

4. Why do you think Roiphe includes the example of the "wide-eyed senior coed" who believes that half of all women have been raped? How does Roiphe communicate her disbelief and disagreement? Here and elsewhere, does Roiphe consider fairly the views and arguments of those who argue that date rape is a serious problem?

5. In attacking those who advocate that women abstain from alcohol and stay in brightly lit, well-populated rooms when they go out on dates, Roiphe claims that feminists are pushing women back into the gendered, conservative, powerless role of 1950s women—the precise role Roiphe's mother fought so hard to escape. Do you agree? What advice would you offer to women about dating?

6. "It is the passive sexual role that threatens us still," Roiphe concludes, "and it is the denial of female sexual agency that threatens to propel us backward." Do you agree? In what ways can or

should women alter societal expectations when it comes to sex roles and power?

VICTOR FEMINISM

Katherine Greider

A freelance writer based in New York, Katharine Greider started her career at *In These Times,* a monthly magazine of fact and opinion. As a journalist and a reporter, Greider worked for the *Columbia Basin Herald* in Washington State for almost three years covering health care, education, and local government issues. She has published essays and articles in a variety of magazines including *Self, City Limits,* and most recently *Mother Jones.*

Born in 1966 in Louisville, Kentucky, Greider grew up in Washington, D.C., and graduated in 1988 from Princeton University, an East Coast private university similar to Harvard, Katie Roiphe's alma mater. "I was really infuriated by Roiphe's book," she told us, "but I wasn't sure if it was best to ignore it because it was so poorly documented. I obviously didn't attend the 'Take Back the Night' marches she especially describes, but I did attend the ones held three or four years earlier, which I would think would be fairly similar and, in my recollection, they were really very serious events—not just for the core group of feminists Roiphe describes but for the whole university community."

Greider believes that she has found a niche, as a professional writer, focusing on medical and political issues. As the following short response to Roiphe's book suggests, Greider can write eloquently and passionately, particularly when it comes to altering women's self-images from victim to victor.

To read *The Morning After,* you'd think that nothing really bad ever happens to women on campus. Campus feminists, Katie Roiphe says, are obsessed with issues like date rape, sexual harassment and pornography because they long to regulate social behavior and to gain power by exaggerating their own victimization, by projecting their own fear and sexual confusion onto a largely benign environment.

What we have in Roiphe is a "feminist" who attributes the current concern with date rape to a "crisis in sexual identity," who claims that even to talk of sexual harassment is a way of "displac[ing] adolescent uneasiness onto the environment, onto professors, onto older men." Roiphe argues that campus feminists are so wrapped up in playing the victim that they end up encouraging women to see themselves as absurdly delicate. We should be able to censure offending men, she insists, without "crying into our pillow [sic] or screaming for help or counseling."

Life on campus is not always quite as gentle as Roiphe describes it. During my first week at college—I was an undergraduate at Princeton at roughly the same time as Roiphe was an undergraduate at Harvard—a man hoisted me over his shoulder and his friend bit me on the behind, leaving a nasty bruise. This apparently was a game of theirs, and I was not its only prop. I did not cry into my pillow or seek counseling, nor did I report anyone. I kicked and swung. But they only laughed.

Other women faced similar harassment. Some of the intimidation was devastatingly personal—like when the boyfriend of a friend of mine came into her room drunk one night and called her a slut and said he'd like to smash her head against a wall. And there were the impersonal, institutional threats: like "Rape and Pillage Night" at one of the all-male eating clubs.

We fought back against this kind of intimidation with Take Back the Night marches (which Roiphe describes as grotesque festivals of victimization). During a march one spring, a few hundred of us wound our way through campus. When we reached Prospect Street, we were greeted by a banner that read: "The night belongs to Michelob—and men"; by shouts of "Get raped," "Fuck the women's center," and sundry other obscenities.

This reaction was startling, and scary. But we didn't give up; the last thing we wanted was to be victims—we wanted to be victors. The goal of feminism is not simply to identify oppression and leave it at that—to find oneself defeated and cry, aha!—but to *end* it. The women and men who marched that spring night in Princeton planned a second march, which drew hundreds more than the first, including prominent figures in the town and the university. That night we made clear that we the marchers were in the mainstream—and that the relatively few warped young men who had opposed the first march were on the fringe. They had expected the community to support them; instead, the community was telling *them* to change.

Roiphe misses the point, and I think she misses it on purpose. She explains that she wrote her book because she believes that "some feminisms are better than others." But the only good feminism she mentions is that of an older generation. Her mother—feminist writer Anne Roiphe—taught her to stand up for herself, to refuse to be deferential to men. Looking back on my own childhood, I share Roiphe's nostalgia for our mothers' ground-breaking, gutsy early feminism. But to embrace today the principles they fought for two and three decades ago does not require any particular courage.

Feminism doesn't stand still; in many ways it is today as Roiphe herself perceived it as a little girl, "something like a train you could catch and ride to someplace better." We've gotten into universities, clubs and workplaces. Now we need to rid them of acquaintance rape, sexual harassment and other forms of sexual bullying.

Roiphe speaks for those who want that train to stop where it is, who honor the achievements of their mothers but attack the feminism of their peers. She adds a new twist to what Betty Friedan has called the "I'm-not-a-feminist-but generation," referring to those young women who generally agree with the feminist agenda, but decline to wear its label. Roiphe wears the label, but she strips it of its meaning.

She has a right to her opinions about feminism on campus. But I too am entitled to call it like I see it. Roiphe, whatever she chooses to call herself, is no friend of feminism. And it is for precisely this reason that her ideas will be wildly popular.

Speculations

1. Greider thinks Roiphe is wrong about campus life for women; she cites her own experience during her first week at Princeton as one instance. Do you think Greider is right (and Roiphe wrong)? Is life on campus safe, assaultive, both, neither?
2. What does Greider think the best response to sexism is on the part of women? Do you agree? Are some "feminisms" better than others?
3. Greider concludes: "Roiphe, whatever she chooses to call herself, is no friend of feminism. And it is for precisely this reason that her ideas will be wildly popular." What does Greider mean? Is she right?

ON NOT BEING A VICTIM

Mary Gaitskill

Short story writer, essayist, and novelist, Mary Gaitskill, focuses much of her work on issues arising from sexual relationships, including incest and rape. Her work has been published in *Harper's* and *Mirabella,* and she is the author of a collection of stories, *Bad Behavior* (1988), and a novel, *Two Girls, Fat and Thin* (1991). Her story

"The Girl on the Plane" appears in *The Best American Short Stories 1993* and is a disturbing account of a man who confesses a gang rape to the female passenger sitting next to him on a plane trip. Concerning that story and the varied responses she received to it, Gaitskill writes:

> I don't see how people can be responsible for their behavior if they are not responsible for their own thoughts and feelings. In my opinion, most of us have not been taught how to be responsible for our thoughts and feelings. . . . I'm not talking wacky political correctness, I'm talking mainstream. . . . Ladies and Gentlemen, please. Stop asking 'What am I supposed to feel?' Why would an adult look to me or to any other writer to tell him or her what to feel? You're not *supposed* to feel anything. You feel what you feel. Where you go with it is your responsibility. (*The Best American Short Stories 1993*, 367).

Clearly Gaitskill wants to distinguish between the responsibility of the artist and the responsibility of the reader.

Born in 1954 in Lexington, Kentucky, Gaitskill had a turbulent childhood. In her own words, she did not have an easy time as a teenager. "Many articles have, in various tones of voice, chronicled my 'troubled' adolescence, the time spent in mental institutions, the fact that I ran away from home at age sixteen and became a stripper, and so on." Ultimately, she earned a B.A. from the University of Michigan in 1981, moved to New York, and began writing for a living.

Critics have praised her work as honest, memorable, and original. *New York Times* critic Michiko Kakutani states that "Gaitskill writes with such authority, such radar-perfect detail, that she is able to make even the most extreme situations seem real." Other critics have praised her as a "gifted writer whose prose sparkles with wit and surprises" and as "wise beyond her years, utterly unsentimental . . . at once ruthlessly objective and sympathetic."

In the essay included here, Gaitskill writes in an objectively ruthless, unsentimental fashion, but with great sympathy, about the complex relations between men and women, about sexual desire, victimization, and individual responsibility.

In the early 1970s, I had an experience that could be described as acquaintance rape. Actually, I have had two or three such experiences, but this one most dramatically fits the profile. I was sixteen and staying in the apartment of a slightly older girl I'd just met in a seedy community center in Detroit. I'd been in her apartment for a few days when an older guy she knew came over and asked us if we wanted to drop some acid. In those years, doing acid with complete strangers was consistent with my idea of a possible good time, so I said yes. When I started peaking, my hostess decided she had to go see her boyfriend, and there I was, alone with this guy, who, suddenly, was in my face.

He seemed to be coming on to me, but I wasn't sure. My perception was quite loopy, and on top of that he was black and urban-poor, which meant mean that I, being very inexperienced and suburban-white, did not know how to read him the way I might have read another white kid. I tried to distract him with conversation, but it was hard, considering that I was having trouble with logical sentences, let alone repartee. During one long silence, I asked him what he was thinking. Avoiding my eyes, he answered, "That if I wasn't such a nice guy you could really be getting screwed." The remark sounded to me like a threat, albeit a low-key one. But instead of asking him to explain himself or to leave, I changed the subject. Some moments later, when he put his hand on my leg, I let myself be drawn into sex because I could not face the idea that if I said no, things might get ugly. I don't think he had any idea how unwilling I was—the cultural unfamiliarity cut both ways—and I suppose he may have thought that all white girls just kind of lie there and don't do or say much. My bad time was made worse by his extreme gentleness; he was obviously trying very hard to please me, which, for reasons I didn't understand, broke my heart. Even as inexperienced as I was, I sensed that in his own way he intended a romantic encounter.

For some time afterward I described this event as "the time I was raped." I knew when I said it that the statement wasn't quite accurate, that I hadn't, after all, said no. Yet it *felt* accurate to me. In spite of my ambiguous, even empathic feelings for my unchosen partner, unwanted sex on acid is a nightmare, and I did feel violated by the experience. At times I even flat-out lied about what had happened, grossly exaggerating the violence and the threat—not out of shame or guilt, but because the pumped-up version was more congruent with my feelings of violation than the confusing facts. Every now and then, in the middle of telling an exaggerated version of the story, I would remember the actual man and internally pause, uncertain of how the memory squared with what I was saying or where my sense of violation was coming from—and then I would continue with my story. I am ashamed to admit this, both because it is embarrassing to me and because I am afraid the admission could be taken as evidence that women lie "to get revenge." I want to stress that I would not have lied that way in court or in any other context that might have had practical consequences; it didn't even occur to me to take my case to court. My lies were told not for revenge but in service of what I felt to be the metaphorical truth.

I remember my experience in Detroit, including its aftermath, every time I hear or read yet another discussion of what constitutes "date rape." I remember it when yet another critic castigates "victimism" and complains that everyone imagines himself or herself to be a victim and that no one accepts responsibility anymore. I could imagine telling my story as a verification that rape occurs by subtle threat as well as by overt force. I could also imagine telling it as if I were one of those cry-babies who want to feel like victims. Both stories would be true and not true. The complete truth is more complicated than most of the intellectuals who have written scolding essays on victimism seem willing to accept. I didn't understand my own story fully until I described it to an older woman many years later, as a proof of the unreliability of feelings. "Oh, I think your feelings were reliable," she returned. "It sounds like you were raped. It sounds like you raped yourself." I immediately knew that what she said was true, that in failing even to try to speak up for myself, I had, in a sense, raped myself.

I don't say this in a tone of self-recrimination. I was in a difficult situation: I was very young, and he was aggressive. But my inability to speak for myself—to *stand up* for myself—had little to do with those facts. I was unable to stand up for myself because I had never been taught how.

When I was growing up in the 1960s, I was taught by the adult world that good girls never had sex and bad girls did. This rule had clarity going for it but little else; as it was presented to me, it allowed no room for what I actually might feel, what I might want or not want. Within the confines of this rule, I didn't count for much, and I quite vigorously rejected it. Then came the less clear "rules" of cultural trend and peer example that said that if you were cool you wanted to have sex as much as possible with as many people as possible. This message was never stated as a rule, but, considering how absolutely it was woven into the social etiquette of the day (at least in the circles I cared about), it may as well have been. It suited me better than the adults' rule—it allowed me my sexuality, at least—but again it didn't take into account what I might actually want or not want.

The encounter in Detroit, however, had nothing to do with being good or bad, cool or uncool. It was about someone wanting something I didn't want. Since I had been taught only how to follow rules that were somehow more important than I was, I didn't know what to do in a situation where no rules obtained and that required me to speak up on my own behalf. I had never been taught that my behalf mattered. And so I felt helpless, even victimized, without really knowing why.

My parents and my teachers believed that social rules existed to protect me and that adhering to these rules constituted social responsibility. Ironically, my parents did exactly what many commentators recommend as a remedy for victimism. They told me they loved me and that I mattered a lot, but this was not the message I got from the way they conducted themselves in relation to authority and social convention—which was not only that I didn't matter but that *they* didn't matter. In this, they were typical of other adults I knew as well as of the culture around them. When I began to have trouble in school, both socially and academically, a counselor exhorted me to "just play the game"—meaning to go along with everything from school policy to the adolescent pecking order—regardless of what I thought of "the game." My aunt, with whom I lived for a short while, actually burned my jeans and T-shirts because they violated what she understood to be the standards of decorum. A close friend of mine lived in a state of war with her father because of her hippie clothes and hair—which were, of course, de rigueur among her peers. Upon discovering that she was smoking pot, he had her institutionalized.

Many middle-class people—both men and women—were brought up, like I was, to equate responsibility with obeying external rules. And when the rules no longer work, they don't know what to do—much like the enraged, gun-wielding protagonist of the movie *Falling Down,* played by Michael Douglas, who ends his ridiculous trajectory by helplessly declaring, "I did everything they told me to." If I had been brought up to reach my own conclusions about which rules were congruent with my internal experience of the world, those rules would have had more meaning for me. Instead, I was usually given a series of static pronouncements. For example, when I was thirteen, I was told by my mother that I couldn't wear a short skirt because "nice girls don't wear skirts above the knee." I countered, of course, by saying that my friend Patty wore skirts above the knee. "Patty is not a nice girl," returned my mother. But Patty *was* nice. My mother is a very intelligent and sensitive person, but it didn't occur to her to define for me what she meant by "nice," what "nice" had to do with skirt length, and how the two definitions might relate to what I had observed to be nice or not nice—and then let me decide for myself. It's true that most thirteen-year-olds aren't interested in, or much capable of, philosophical discourse, but that doesn't mean that adults can't explain themselves more completely to children. Part of becoming responsible is learning how to make a choice about where you stand in respect to the social code and then holding yourself accountable for your choice. In contrast, many children who grew up in my milieu were given abstract absolutes that were placed before us as if our thoughts, feelings, and observations were irrelevant.

Recently I heard a panel of feminists on talk radio advocating that laws be passed prohibiting men from touching or making sexual comments to women on the street. Listeners called in to express reactions both pro and con, but the one I remember was a woman who said, "If a man touches me and I don't want it, I don't need a law. I'm gonna beat the hell out of him." The panelists were silent. Then one of them responded in an uncertain voice, "I guess I just never learned how to do that." I understood that the feminist might not want to get into a fistfight with a man likely to be a lot bigger than she, but if her self-respect was so easily shaken by an obscene comment made by some slob on the street, I wondered, how did she expect to get through life? She was exactly the kind of woman whom the cultural critics Camille Paglia and Katie Roiphe have derided as a "rape-crisis feminist"—puritans, sissies, closet-Victorian ladies who want to legislate the ambiguity out of sex. It was very easy for me to feel self-righteous, and I muttered sarcastically at my radio as the panel yammered about self-esteem.

I was conflicted, however. If there had been a time in my own life when I couldn't stand up for myself, how could I expect other people to do it? It could be argued that the grown women on the panel should be more capable than a sixteen-year-old girl whacked out on acid. But such a notion presupposes that people develop at a predictable rate or react to circumstances by coming to universally agreed-upon conclusions. This is the crucial unspoken presumption at the center of the date-rape debate as well as of the larger discourse on victimism. It is a presumption that in a broad but potent sense reminds me of a rule.

Feminists who postulate that boys must obtain a spelled-out "yes" before having sex are trying to establish rules, cut in stone, that will apply to any and every encounter and that every responsible person must obey. The new rule resembles the old good girl/bad girl rule not only because of its implicit suggestion that girls have to be protected but also because of its absolute nature, its iron-fisted denial of complexity and ambiguity. I bristle at such a rule and so do a lot of other people. But should we really be so puzzled and indignant that another rule has been presented? If people have been brought up believing that to be responsible is to obey certain rules, what are they going to do with a can of worms like "date rape" except try to make new rules that they see as more fair or useful than the old ones?

But the "rape-crisis feminists" are not the only absolutists here; their critics play the same game. Camille Paglia, author of *Sexual Personae,* has stated repeatedly that any girl who goes alone into a frat house and proceeds to tank up is cruising for a gang bang, and if she doesn't know that, well, then she's "an idiot." The remark is most striking not for its crude unkindness but for its reductive solipsism. It assumes that all college girls have had the same life experiences as Paglia, and have come to the same conclusions about them. By the time I got to college, I'd been living away from home for years and had been around the block several times. I never went to a frat house, but I got involved with men who lived in rowdy "boy houses" reeking of dirty socks and rock and roll. I would go over, drink, and spend the night with my lover of the moment; it never occurred to me that I was in danger of being gang-raped, and if I had been, I would have been shocked and badly hurt. My experience, though some of it had been bad, hadn't led me to conclude that boys plus alcohol equals gang bang, and I was not naive or idiotic. Katie Roiphe, author of *The Morning After: Fear, Sex, and Feminism on Campus,* criticizes girls who, in her view, create a myth of false innocence: "But did these twentieth-century girls, raised on Madonna videos and the six o'clock news, really trust that people were good until they themselves were raped? Maybe. Were these girls, raised on horror movies and glossy Hollywood sex scenes, really as innocent as all that?" I am sympathetic to Roiphe's annoyance, but I'm surprised that a smart chick like her apparently doesn't know that people process information and imagery (like Madonna videos and the news) with a complex subjectivity that doesn't in any predictable way alter their ideas about what they can expect from life.

Roiphe and Paglia are not exactly invoking rules, but their comments seem to derive from a belief that everyone except idiots interprets information and experience in the same way. In that sense, they are not so different in attitude from those ladies dedicated to establishing feminist-based rules and regulations for sex. Such rules, just like the old rules, assume a certain psychological uniformity of experience, a right way.

The accusatory and sometimes painfully emotional rhetoric conceals an attempt not only to make new rules but also to codify experience. The "rape-crisis feminists" obviously speak for many women and girls who have been raped or have *felt* raped in a wide variety of circumstances. They would not get so much play if they were not addressing a widespread and real experience of violation and hurt. By asking, "Were they really so innocent?" Roiphe doubts the veracity of the experience she presumes to address because it doesn't square with hers or with that of her friends. Having not felt violated herself—even though she says she has had an experience that many would now call date rape—she cannot understand, or even quite believe, that anyone else would feel violated in similar circumstances. She therefore believes all the fuss to be a political ploy or, worse, a retrograde desire to return to crippling ideals of helpless femininity. In turn, Roiphe's detractors, who have not had her more sanguine "morning after" experience, believe her to be ignorant and callous, or a secret rape victim in deep denial. Both camps, believing their own experience to be the truth, seem unwilling to acknowledge the emotional truth on the other side.

It is at this point that the "date-rape debate" resembles the bigger debate about how and why Americans seem so eager to identify themselves and be identified by others as victims. Book after article has appeared, written in baffled yet hectoring language, deriding the P.C. goody-goodies who want to play victim and the spoiled, self-centered fools who attend twelve-step programs, meditate on their inner child, and study pious self-help books. The revisionist critics have all had a lot of fun with the recovery movement, getting into high dudgeon over those materially well-off people who describe their childhoods as "holocausts" and winding up with a fierce exhortation to return to rationality. Rarely do such critics make any but the most superficial attempt to understand why the population might behave thus.

In a fussing, fuming essay that has almost become a prototype of the genre, David Rieff expressed his outrage and bewilderment that affluent people would feel hurt and disappointed by life. He angrily contrasted rich Americans obsessed with their inner children to Third World parents concerned with feeding their actual children. On the most obvious level, the contrast is one that needs to be made, but I question Rieff's idea that suffering is one definable thing, that he knows what it is, and that since certain kinds of emotional pain don't fit this definition they can't really exist. This idea doesn't allow him to have much respect for other people's experience—or even to see it. It may be ridiculous and perversely self-aggrandizing for most people to describe whatever was bad about their childhood as a "holocaust," but I suspect that when people talk like that they are saying that as children they were not given enough of what they would later need in order to know who they are or to live truly responsible lives. Thus they find themselves in a state of bewildering loss that they can't articulate, except by wild exaggeration—much like I defined my inexplicable feelings after my Detroit episode. "Holocaust" may be a grossly inappropriate exaggeration. But to speak in exaggerated metaphors about psychic injury is not so much the act of a crybaby as it is a distorted attempt to explain one's own experience. I think the distortion comes from a desperate desire to make one's experience have consequence in the eyes of others, and that such desperation comes from a crushing doubt that one's own experience counts at all.

In her book *I'm Dysfunctional, You're Dysfunctional*, Wendy Kaminer speaks harshly of women in some twelve-step programs who talk about being metaphorically raped. "It is an article of faith here that suffering is relative; no one says she'd rather be raped metaphorically than in fact," she writes, as if not even a crazy person would prefer a literal rape to a metaphorical one. But actually, I might. About two years after my "rape" in Detroit, I was raped for real. The experience was terrifying: my attacker repeatedly said he was going to kill me, and I thought he might. The terror was acute, but after it was over it actually affected me less than many other mundane instances of emotional brutality I've suffered or seen other people suffer. Frankly, I've been scarred more by experiences I had on the playground in elementary school. I realize that the observation may seem bizarre, but for me the rape was a clearly defined act, perpetrated upon me by a crazy asshole whom I didn't know or trust; it had nothing to do with me or who I was, and so, when it was over, it was relatively easy to dismiss. Emotional cruelty is more complicated. Its motives are often impossible to understand, and it is sometimes committed by people who say they like or even love you. Nearly always it's hard to know whether you played a role in what happened, and, if so, what the role was. The experience *sticks* to you. By the time I was raped I had seen enough emotional cruelty to feel that the rape, although bad, was not especially traumatic.

My response may seem strange to some, but my point is that pain can be an experience that defies codification. If thousands of Americans say that they are in psychic pain, I would not be so quick to write them off as self-indulgent fools. A metaphor like "the inner child" may be silly and schematic, but it has a fluid subjectivity, especially when projected out into the world by such a populist notion as "recovery." Ubiquitous recovery-movement phrases like "We're all victims" and "We're all co-dependent" may not seem to leave a lot of room for interpretation, but they are actually so vague that they beg for interpretation and projection. Such phrases may be fair game for ridicule, but it is shallow to judge them on their face value, as if they hold the same meaning for everyone. What is meant by an "inner child" depends on the person speaking, and not everyone will see it as a metaphor for helplessness. I suspect that most inner-child enthusiasts use the image of themselves as children not so that they can *avoid* being responsible but to learn responsibility by going back to the point in time when they *should* have been taught responsibility—the ability to think, choose, and stand up for themselves—and were not. As I understand it, the point of identifying an "inner child" is to locate the part of yourself that didn't develop into adulthood and then to develop it yourself. Whether or not this works is an open question, but it is an attempt to accept responsibility, not to flee it.

When I was in my late teens and early twenties, I could not bear to watch movies or read books that I considered demeaning to women in any way; I evaluated everything I saw or read in terms of whether it expressed a "positive image" of women. I was a very P.C. feminist before the term existed, and, by the measure of my current understanding, my critical rigidity followed from my inability to be responsible for my own feelings. In this context, being responsible would have meant that I let myself feel whatever discomfort, indignation, or disgust I experienced without allowing those feelings to determine my entire reaction to a given piece of work. In other words, it would have meant dealing with my feelings and what had caused them, rather than expecting the outside world to assuage them. I could have chosen not to see the world through the lens of my personal unhappiness and yet maintained a kind of respect for my unhappiness. For example, I could have decided to avoid certain films or books because of my feelings without blaming the film or book for making me feel the way I did.

My emotional irresponsibility did not spring from a need to feel victimized, although it may have looked that way to somebody else. I essentially was doing what I had seen most mainstream cultural critics do—it was from them that I learned to view works of art in terms of the message they imparted and, further, that the message could be judged on the basis of consensual ideas about what life is, and how it can and should be seen. My ideas, like most P.C. ideas, were extreme, but they were consistent with more mainstream thought—they just shifted the parameters of acceptability a bit.

Things haven't changed much: at least half the book and film reviews that I read praise or condemn a work on the basis of the likability of the characters (as if there is a standard idea of what is likable) or because the author's point of view is or is not "life-affirming"—or whatever the critic believes the correct attitude toward life to be. The lengthy and rather hysterical debate about the film *Thelma and Louise,* in which two ordinary women become outlaws after one of them shoots the other's rapist, was predicated on the idea that stories are supposed to function as instruction manuals, and that whether the film was good or bad depended on whether the instructions were correct. Such criticism assumes that viewers or readers need to see a certain type of moral universe reflected back at them or, empty vessels that they are, they might get confused or depressed or something. A respected mainstream essayist writing for *Time* faulted my novel *Two Girls, Fat and Thin* for its nasty male characters, which he took to be a moral statement about males generally. He ended his piece with the fervent wish that fiction not "diminish" men or women but rather seek to "raise our vision of" both—in other words, that it should present the "right" way to the reader, who is apparently not responsible enough to figure it out alone.

I have changed a lot from the P.C. teenager who walked out of movies that portrayed women in a demeaning light. As I've grown older, I've become more confident of myself and my ability to determine what happens to me, and, as a result, those images no longer have such a strong emotional charge. I don't believe they will affect my life in any practical sense unless I allow them to do so. I no longer feel that misogynistic stories are about me or even about women (whether they purport to be or not) but rather are about the kinds of experience the authors wish to render—and therefore are not my problem. I consider my current view more balanced, but that doesn't mean my earlier feelings were wrong. The reason I couldn't watch "disrespect to women" at that time was that such depictions were too close to my own experience (most of which was not unusual), and I found them painful. I was displaying a simplistic self-respect by not subjecting myself to something I was not ready to face. Being unable to separate my personal experience from what I saw on the screen, I was not dealing with my own particular experience—I think, paradoxically, because I hadn't yet learned to value it. It's hard to be responsible for something that isn't valuable. Someone criticizing me as dogmatic and narrow-minded would have had a point, but the point would have ignored the truth of my unacknowledged experience, and thus ignored me.

Many critics of the self-help culture argue against treating emotional or metaphoric reality as if it were equivalent to objective reality. I agree that they are not the same. But emotional truth is often bound up with truth of a more objective kind and must be taken into account. This is especially true of conundrums such as date rape and victimism, both of which often are discussed in terms of unspoken assumptions about emotional truth anyway. Sarah Crichton, in a cover story for *Newsweek* on "Sexual Correctness," described the "strange detour" taken by some feminists and suggested that "we're not creating a society of Angry Young Women. These are Scared Little Girls." The comment is both contemptuous and superficial; it shows no interest in *why* girls might be scared. By such logic, anger implicitly is deemed to be the more desirable emotional state because it appears more potent, and "scared" is used as a pejorative. It's possible to shame a person into hiding his or her fear, but if you don't address the cause of the fear, it won't go away. Crichton ends her piece by saying, "Those who are growing up in environments where they don't have to figure out what the rules should be, but need only follow what's been prescribed, are being robbed of the most important lesson there is to learn. And that's how to live." I couldn't agree more. But unless you've been taught how to think for yourself, you'll have a hard time figuring out your own rules, and you'll feel scared—especially when there is real danger of sexual assault.

One reason I had sex with strangers when I didn't really want to was that part of me wanted the adventure, and that tougher part ran roughshod over the part of me that was scared and uncertain. I'll bet the same thing happened to many of the boys with whom I had these experiences. All people have their tough, aggressive selves as well as their more delicate selves. If you haven't developed these characteristics in ways that are respectful of yourself and others, you will find it hard to be responsible for them. I don't think it's possible to develop yourself in such ways if you are attuned to following rules and codes that don't give your inner world enough importance. I was a strong-willed child with a lot of aggressive impulses, which, for various reasons, I was actively discouraged from developing. They stayed hidden under a surface of extreme passivity, and when they did appear it was often in a wildly irresponsible, almost crazy way. My early attraction to aggressive boys and men was in part a need to see *somebody* act out the distorted feelings I didn't know what to do with, whether it was destructive or not. I suspect that boys who treat girls with disrespectful aggression have failed to develop their more tender, sensitive side and futilely try to regain it by "possessing" a woman. Lists of instructions about what's nice and what isn't will not help people in such a muddled state, and it's my observation that many people are in such a state to a greater or lesser degree.

I am not idealistic enough to hope that we will ever live in a world without rape and other forms of sexual cruelty; I think men and women will always have to struggle to behave responsibly. But I think we could make the struggle less difficult by changing the way we teach responsibility and social conduct. To teach a boy that rape is "bad" is not as effective as making him see that rape is a violation of his own masculine dignity as well as a violation of the raped woman. It's true that children don't know big words and that teenage boys aren't all that interested in their own dignity. But these are things that children learn more easily by example than by words, and learning by example runs deep.

A few years ago I invited to dinner at my home a man I'd known casually for two years. We'd had dinner and comradely drinks a few times. I didn't have any intention of becoming sexual with him, but after dinner we slowly got drunk and were soon floundering on the couch. I was ambivalent not only because I was drunk but because I realized that although part of me was up for it, the rest of me was not. So I began to say no. He parried each "no" with charming banter and became more aggressive. I went along with it for a time because I was amused and even somewhat seduced by the sweet, junior-high spirit of his manner. But at some point I began to be alarmed, and then he did and said some things that turned my alarm into fright. I don't remember the exact sequence of words or events, but I do remember taking one of his hands in both of mine, looking him in the eyes, and saying, "If this comes to a fight you would win, but it would be very ugly for both of us. Is that really what you want?"

His expression changed and he dropped his eyes; shortly afterward he left.

I consider that small decision to have been a responsible one because it was made by taking both my vulnerable feelings and my carnal impulses into account. When I spoke, my words came from my feeling of delicacy as well as from my capacity for aggression. And I respected my friend as well by addressing both sides of his nature. It is not hard for me to make such decisions now, but it took me a long time to get to this point. I only regret that it took so long, both for my young self and for the boys I was with, under circumstances that I now consider disrespectful to all concerned.

Speculations

1. In trying to explain why she fabricated a version of her "date rape" encounter in Detroit, Gaitskill writes: "My lies were told not for revenge but in service of what I felt to be the metaphorical truth." What do you think Gaitskill means by "metaphorical truth"? How does this kind of truth differ from real truth? Do you think Gaitskill's explanation is the right one?

2. Gaitskill tells us that an older woman responded to her account of the Detroit incident by saying "you raped yourself." Is this true? Do you think that the older woman (and Gaitskill, who agrees with this pronouncement) are being accurate, or is this another instance of "metaphorical truth"?

3. Much of Gaitskill's commentary focuses on rules: rules that are clear but insufficiently explained, rules that make no sense, rules that replace other rules, rules that seem to apply to some people and not to others. Offer your analysis of Gaitskill's perspective on rules, particularly relating to date rape.

4. One recurrent strategy Gaitskill uses in this essay is to critique the work of other essayists and commentators: Paglia, Roiphe, a panel of feminists, David Rieff, and Sarah Crichton. Why do you think she does this? Do you find it informative, useful, distracting, confusing? Does this strategy help her make her arguments?

5. Toward the end of her essay, Gaitskill announces that about "two years after my 'rape' in Detroit, I was raped for real." She describes, briefly, the brutality of this incident and then states, rather surprisingly:

   > The terror was acute, but after it was over it actually affected me less than many other mundane instances of emotional brutality I've suffered or seen other people suffer. Frankly, I've been scarred more by experiences I had on the playground in elementary school.

   How do you respond to this statement? Is Gaitskill diminishing the trauma of rape? How does her admission relate to her statements about the "inner child" and the recovery movement?

6. Gaitskill writes a largely narrative essay. What is gained and what is lost by Gaitskill's decision to write a narrative rather than an expository essay? Does it make her essay easier or harder to respond to in terms of the issues she raises? Explain your answer.

ASSIGNMENT SEQUENCES

Sequence One: A Case Study Approach to Date Rape

1. Let's begin with an attempt at definition. How would you define date rape or acquaintance rape? In an essay, explore and explain

what you think this term means. Is date rape different from rape? Is date rape different from acquaintance rape? Does it necessarily involve dating? What distinguishes this action from other kinds of sexual assault? Is it a crime? Should it be a crime? Do not feel that you must answer all of these questions or follow the order in which they are presented in your essay; rather, use them as possible issues to consider as you think about defining date rape.

2. The perspectives that are offered about date rape in this book reveal some basic differences about women, crime, date rape on campus, and so on. In an essay, state your own view concerning date rape. Do you agree with Roiphe and Paglia that current definitions of date rape presume that women are helpless, immature, weak, and unable to make thoughtful decisions? Do you agree with Sweet and Greider that date rape is a serious problem, particularly on college campuses where it is often ignored, and that women are its particular victims? Do you agree with Gaitskill that it is impossible to generalize about women and date rape? In your essay, draw upon the readings to support your argument.

3. Here is a scenario: Two students go out on a date. They see a movie, then go to a bar for a few drinks. After returning to Student A's apartment, things start getting out of hand. Student A gets passionate and wants to engage in sex. Student B says no, but they have already been engaging in lots of kissing and touching and ultimately Student B submits. Is this date rape? Who is responsible? Has a crime been committed? Write an essay in which you consider what facts, contexts, and evidence you would need to know in order to make a considered decision about what has happened here.

4. Assume for the moment that Student B pressed charges against Student A in the above scenario and that Student A is arrested and convicted of rape. Discuss whether you think Student A should be treated by the justice system precisely the same as any other convicted rapist. In your essay, be sure to include justifications for your position—and a careful analysis of other possible perspectives as well.

5. Here is another case, this one factual. We have changed the name of the student and the university to protect identities. As reported by press accounts:

> Roman Gort, a junior at Aesop State University, posted fantasies of rape and torture about a fellow student on the Internet. The Internet story describes the torture, sodomy, and mutilation of a woman whom Gort encountered in a class but never actually met. However, the woman was named in the story, and her last name

served as the story's title. Gort signed his real name to the story before posting it in an area on the Internet reserved for sex stories. The story was available to be read by millions of Internet users. Gort has subsequently publicly apologized for writing this story.

Did Roman Gort commit a crime? Did he engage in a form of date rape? What punishment, if any, is appropriate?

6. Let's follow up the previous assignment with another factual event. (Again, the names have been changed to protect identities.) After hearing about Roman Gort, Artemis Gronk, a female student, writes her own "fantasy" which she signs and posts on Internet. Gronk's fantasy describes the torture of Roman Gort, whom she names. Did Artemis Gronk commit a crime? Did she engage in a form of date rape? What punishment, if any, is appropriate?

Sequence Two: Rules and Victims

1. In 1993, the students at Antioch College in Ohio developed a set of guidelines about appropriate activities on campus. One part of their guidelines became known as the "May-I-kiss-you-on-the-lips-now" clause. It requires that students obtain "verbal consent . . . with each new level of physical and or sexual contact/conduct in any given interaction regardless of who initiates it." The "verbal consent" clause was put into place by the students because they thought it would solve problems related to unwanted sexual advances, date rape, and other sexual behavior. During the past several years, this policy has been publicized throughout the world; it has been both defended as a useful and fair set of rules for dating students, and attacked for being foolish and unenforceable.

Do you think this policy is a good one for college students? In offering your view as to whether you think such a policy is worth imitating on other college campuses, be sure to present your own arguments and analysis. You should include as well appropriate supporting material from the essays by Sweet, Roiphe, Greider, Gaitskill, and Paglia. You may also use examples from other reading you have done and/or personal experience, etc.

2. Assume that the Dean of Students at your school has decided that some specific guidelines and warnings concerning date rape are necessary—and that these guidelines and warnings are to be distributed to all students on campus. The Dean has asked you to draw up this document. In the form of an essay that includes suggestions and guidelines, draw up a date rape policy and procedures statement. If you feel that such a statement is a bad idea,

write an essay to the Dean in which you argue your position close-ly and carefully. In either case, feel free to draw on the readings in this section.

3. Much of the debate about date rape circles around one issue: vic-timization. Write an essay in which you make clear your position about who is really being victimized in date rape cases—and how best to prepare both women and men not to be victims of this crime. In your essay, draw as much as you can upon the arguments and statements made about date rape and victimization by Roiphe, Greider, Paglia, and Gaitskill.

4. Gaitskill as well as other commentators about date rape believe that women often get into trouble because they are taught to follow the rules, to behave in accepted ways, not to make waves, to please men even at the cost of their self-esteem. In an essay, offer your own perspective about men, women, and rules—and then apply your views to the issue of date rape. Are men and women taught rules differently? Do those differences, if they exist, contribute to the problem of date rape?

5. Clarence Darrow does not consider the crime of date rape. Assume for this assignment that you are Clarence Darrow and that you have been asked to write a follow-up article to Ellen Sweet's essay. Write that essay. Try to capture some of the substance and the style of Darrow in your essay.

4

GENDER

MATTERS

It is usually the first question we ask upon hearing that someone has had a baby: "Is it a boy or a girl?" Whether we know it consciously, we ask the question because the answer will shape how that baby is treated by parents, siblings, friends, school, culture, and government. Hence our title for this section of *Speculations:* Gender Matters. The ambiguity is intentional. We wanted this title to convey both a declaration and a description of the fundamental importance of this subject: we discuss gender matters because gender matters.

Indeed, other than race, gender is probably the single greatest factor in determining who we become and how we relate to others—and it is never completely within our control. Kobena Mercer states the case strongly in her essay, "'1968': Periodizing Politics and Identity": "identities are not found but *made;* they are not just there, waiting to be discovered in the vocabulary of Nature . . . they have to be culturally and politically *constructed* through political antagonism and cultural struggle." Although we might temper her claim by stating that biological and physiological attributes also play a role, we agree with the general thrust of her argument: identity is not a given. We are prominent players in the unfolding drama of identity formation; we make our gender just as our gender makes us.

Often confused with sex or biology, gender is something significantly different. A person's biological sex is "male" or "female"; by that designation, we mean that a person is anatomically male, female, or in rare instances hermaphroditic. Given the indisputable physical evidence, there can be no debate about how to categorize someone biologically. Gender is a whole other matter. Socially constructed, gender is comprised of the values, behaviors, and social roles that we expect human beings to enact within culture. Thus, although there are basically only two sexes, we find a range of genders within society. In the United States, these include heterosexual male, gay male, lesbian female, bisexual male or female, and heterosexual female. Some societies, according to Judith Lorber, author of *Paradoxes of Gender,* recognize additional categories: "biological males who behave, dress, work, and are treated in most respects as social women" or "*manly hearted women*—biological females who work, marry, and parent as men." Whatever the range or emphasis, gender is a learned behavior: we may be born male or female, but we learn how to act like men and women.

We offer this thumbnail sketch of gender to introduce complexity to the debate about what it means to be straight, gay, lesbian, or bisexual. After all, I can be "female" but I can be gendered "male" by my clothes, behavior, job, sexual orientation, physical appearance, and more. Perhaps even more surprising, I can gender myself as a lesbian female at one time and a heterosexual female at another—or as a "man" during the day and as a "woman" during the evening. The questions raised by the authors in the following selections focus on both the causes and effects of societal gender roles. In what ways do gender roles limit us? How can we reshape gender—or should we do so? What can we learn from the current debate over gay/lesbian identity, particularly in relation to civil and legal rights? These are the kinds of issues and questions that this section invites you to consider.

NO NAME WOMAN

Maxine Hong Kingston

What does it mean to grow up female and Chinese in America? This question lies at the heart of *The Woman Warrior*, Maxine Hong Kingston's lyrical, intense, poetic autobiography that combines the magic of remembrance with the ghostly evocation of a world that lies just beyond understanding. For Kingston, *The Woman Warrior* not only offered the possibility to construct a self through writing but also to define herself as an American. Interviewed in 1976 by the *New York Times Book Review*, she said, "What I am doing in this book is claiming America." America now also gladly claims her.

Born in Stockton, California, in 1940 to Chinese immigrants, Maxine Hong Kingston grew up listening to her mother's "talk-stories" of Chinese myths, legends, and family history. Her family ran the New Port Laundry, where many immigrants from her parents' Cantonese village met to speak Say Yup and tell stories. These tales, told in the singsong cadence of Say Yup, became the basis for her autobiographical works: *The Woman Warrior*, which won the 1976 National Book Critics Circle Award; *China Men*; and *Tripmaster Monkey*. She views her narratives about the coming of the Chinese to America and their contribution to the growth of the country as thematically linked to other American writers, notably William Carlos Williams.

In a 1976 *People* magazine interview, Kingston described how the cadence of the "talk-story" imbued her writing with poetic force and originality: "I wanted to get a Chinese rhythm in my voice. I tried to make [*The Woman Warrior*] typical of Chinese-American speech, rich with images." In a 1980 interview with Peter Grier of the *Christian Science Monitor*, she explained, "Each story changes from day to day, in the telling. The listener changes and the speaker changes and the situation changes. I want to capture that changeable quality in writing."

In *The Woman Warrior*, Kingston writes:

> There is a Chinese word for the female I—which is "slave." Break the women with their own tongues. . . . Even now China wraps double binds around my feet.

Woman, wife, slave, victim—these are the associations that Kingston evokes in the selection that follows, the opening chapter of *The Woman Warrior*. In it, Kingston recreates the history of her aunt's difficult life and troubling death.

"You must not tell anyone," my mother said, "what I am about to tell you. In China your father had a sister who killed herself. She jumped into the family well. We say that your father has all brothers because it is as if she had never been born.

"In 1924 just a few days after our village celebrated seventeen hurry-up weddings—to make sure that every young man who went 'out on the road' would responsibly come home—your father and his brothers and your grandfather and his brothers and your aunt's new husband sailed for America, the Gold Mountain. It was your grandfather's last trip. Those lucky enough to get contracts waved goodbye from the decks. They fed and guarded the stowaways and helped them off in Cuba, New York, Bali, Hawaii. 'We'll meet in California next year,' they said. All of them sent money home.

"I remember looking at your aunt one day when she and I were dressing; I had not noticed before that she had such a protruding melon of a stomach. But I did not think, 'She's pregnant,' until she began to look like other pregnant women, her shirt pulling and the white tops of her black pants showing. She could not have been pregnant, you see, because her husband had been gone for years. No one said anything. We did not discuss it. In early summer she was ready to have the child, long after the time when it could have been possible.

"The village had also been counting. On the night the baby was to be born the villagers raided our house. Some were crying. Like a great saw, teeth strung with lights, files of people walked zigzag across our land, tearing the rice. Their lanterns doubled in the disturbed black water, which drained away through the broken bunds. As the villagers closed in, we could see that some of them, probably men and women we knew well, wore white masks. The people with long hair hung it over their faces. Women with short hair made it stand up on end. Some had tied white bands around their foreheads, arms, and legs.

"At first they threw mud and rocks at the house. Then they threw eggs and began slaughtering our stock. We could hear the animals scream their deaths—the roosters, the pigs, a last great roar from the ox. Familiar wild heads flared in our night windows; the villagers encircled us. Some of the faces stopped to peer at us, their eyes rushing like searchlights. The hands flattened against the panes, framed heads, and left red prints.

"The villagers broke in the front and the back doors at the same time, even though we had not locked the doors against them. Their knives dripped with the blood of our animals. They smeared blood on the doors and walls. One woman swung a chicken, whose throat she had slit, splattering blood in red arcs about her. We stood together in the middle of our house, in the family hall with the pictures and tables of the ancestors around us, and looked straight ahead.

"At that time the house had only two wings. When the men came back, we would build two more to enclose our courtyard and a third one to begin a second courtyard. The villagers pushed through both wings, even your grandparents' rooms, to find your aunt's, which was also mine until the men returned. From this room a new wing for one of the younger families would grow. They ripped up her clothes and shoes and broke her combs, grinding them underfoot. They tore her work from the loom. They scattered the cooking fire and rolled the new weaving in it. We could hear them in the kitchen breaking our bowls and banging the pots. They overturned the great waist-high earthenware jugs; duck eggs, pickled fruits, vegetables burst out and mixed in acrid torrents. The old woman from the next field swept a broom through the air and loosed the spirits-of-the-broom over our heads. 'Pig.' 'Ghost.' 'Pig,' they sobbed and scolded while they ruined our house.

"When they left, they took sugar and oranges to bless themselves. They cut pieces from the dead animals. Some of them took bowls that were not broken and clothes that were not torn. Afterward we swept up the rice and sewed it back up into sacks. But the smells from the spilled preserves lasted. Your aunt gave birth in the pigsty that night. The next morning when I went for the water, I found her and the baby plugging up the family well.

"Don't let your father know that I told you. He denies her. Now that you have started to menstruate, what happened to her could happen to you. Don't humiliate us. You wouldn't like to be forgotten as if you had never been born. The villagers are watchful."

Whenever she had to warn us about life, my mother told stories that ran like this one, a story to grow up on. She tested our strength to establish realities. Those in the emigrant generations who could not reassert brute survival died young and far from home. Those of us in the first American generations have had to figure out how the invisible world the emigrants built around our childhoods fits in solid America.

The emigrants confused the gods by diverting their curses, misleading them with crooked streets and false names. They must try to confuse their offspring as well, who, I suppose, threaten them in similar ways—always trying to get things straight, always trying to name the unspeakable. The Chinese I know hide their names; sojourners take new names when their lives change and guard their real names with silence.

Chinese-Americans, when you try to understand what things in you are Chinese, how do you separate what is peculiar to childhood, to poverty, insanities, one family, your mother who marked your growing with stories, from what is Chinese? What is Chinese tradition and what is the movies?

If I want to learn what clothes my aunt wore, whether flashy or ordinary, I would have to begin, "Remember Father's drowned-in-the-well sister?" I cannot ask that. My mother has told me once and for all the useful parts. She will add nothing unless powered by Necessity, a riverbank that guides her life. She plants vegetable gardens rather than lawns; she carries the odd-shaped tomatoes home from the fields and eats food left for the gods.

Whenever we did frivolous things, we used up energy; we flew high kites. We children came up off the ground over the melting cones our parents brought home from work and the American movie on New Year's Day—*Oh, You Beautiful Doll* with Betty Grable one year, and *She Wore a Yellow Ribbon* with John Wayne another year. After the one carnival ride each, we paid in guilt; our tired father counted his change on the dark walk home.

Adultery is extravagance. Could people who hatch their own chicks and eat the embryos and the heads for delicacies and boil the feet in vinegar for party food, leaving only the gravel, eating even the gizzard lining—could such people engender a prodigal aunt? To be a woman, to have a daughter in starvation time was a waste enough. My aunt could not have been the lone romantic who gave up everything for sex. Women in the old China did not choose. Some man had commanded her to lie with him and be his secret evil. I wonder whether he masked himself when he joined the raid on her family.

Perhaps she had encountered him in the fields or on the mountain where the daughters-in-law collected fuel. Or perhaps he first noticed her in the marketplace. He was not a stranger because the village housed no strangers. She had to have dealings with him other than sex. Perhaps he worked an adjoining field, or he sold her the cloth for the dress she sewed and wore. His demand must have surprised, then terrified her. She obeyed him; she always did as she was told.

When the family found a young man in the next village to be her husband, she had stood tractably beside the best rooster, his proxy, and promised before they met that she would be his forever. She was lucky that he was her age and she would be the first wife, an advantage secure now. The night she first saw him, he had sex with her. Then he left for America. She had almost forgotten what he looked like. When she tried to envision him, she only saw the black and white face in the group photograph the men had had taken before leaving.

The other man was not, after all, much different from her husband. They both gave orders: she followed. "If you tell your family, I'll beat you. I'll kill you. Be here again next week." No one talked sex, ever. And she might have separated the rapes from the rest of living if only she did not have to buy her oil from him or gather wood in the same forest. I want her fear to have lasted just as long as rape lasted so that the fear could have been contained. No drawn-out fear. But women at sex hazarded birth and hence lifetimes. The fear did not stop but permeated everywhere. She told the man, "I think I'm pregnant." He organized the raid against her.

On nights when my mother and father talked about their life back home, sometimes they mentioned an "outcast table" whose business they still seemed to be settling, their voices tight. In a commensal tradition, where food is precious, the powerful older people made wrong-doers eat alone. Instead of letting them start separate new lives like the Japanese, who could become samurais and geishas, the Chinese family, faces averted but eyes glowering sideways, hung on to the offenders and fed them leftovers. My aunt must have lived in the same house as my parents and eaten at an outcast table. My mother spoke about the raid as if she had seen it, when she and my aunt, a daughter-in-law to a different household, should not have been living together at all. Daughters-in-law lived with their husbands' parents, not their own; a synonym for marriage in Chinese is "taking a daughter-in-law." Her husband's parents could have sold her, mortgaged her, stoned her. But they had sent her back to her own mother and father, a mysterious act hinting at disgraces not told me. Perhaps they had thrown her out to deflect the avengers.

She was the only daughter; her four brothers went with her father, husband, and uncles "out on the road" and for some years became western men. When the goods were divided among the family, three of the brothers took land, and the youngest, my father, chose an education. After my grandparents gave their daughter away to her husband's family, they had dispensed all the adventure and all the property. They expected her alone to keep the traditional ways, which her brothers, now among the barbarians, could fumble without detection. The heavy, deep-rooted women were to maintain the past against the flood, safe for returning. But the rare urge west had fixed upon our family, and so my aunt crossed boundaries not delineated in space.

The work of preservation demands that the feelings playing about in one's guts not be turned into action. Just watch their passing like cherry blossoms. But perhaps my aunt, my forerunner, caught in a slow life, let dreams grow and fade and after some months or years went toward what persisted. Fear at the enormities of the forbidden kept her desires delicate, wire and bone. She looked at a man because she liked the way the hair was tucked behind his ears, or she liked the question-mark line of a long torso curving at the shoulder and straight at the hip. For warm eyes or a soft voice or a slow walk—that's all—a few hairs, a line, a brightness, a sound, a pace, she gave up family. She offered us up for a charm that vanished with tiredness, a pigtail that didn't toss when the wind died. Why, the wrong lighting could erase the dearest thing about him.

It could very well have been, however, that my aunt did not take subtle enjoyment of her friend, but, a wild woman, kept rollicking company. Imagining her free with sex doesn't fit, though. I don't know any women like that, or men either. Unless I see her life branching into mine, she gives me no ancestral help.

To sustain her being in love, she often worked at herself in the mirror, guessing at the colors and shapes that would interest him, changing them frequently in order to hit on the right combination. She wanted him to look back.

On a farm near the sea, a woman who tended her appearance reaped a reputation for eccentricity. All the married women blunt-cut their hair in flaps about their ears or pulled it back in tight buns. No nonsense. Neither style blew easily into heart-catching tangles. And at their weddings they displayed themselves in their long hair for the last time. "It brushed the backs of my knees," my mother tells me. "It was braided, and even so, it brushed the backs of my knees."

At the mirror my aunt combed individuality into her bob. A bun could have been contrived to escape into black streamers blowing in the wind or in quiet wisps about her face, but only the older women in our picture album wear buns. She brushed her hair back from her forehead, tucking the flaps behind her ears. She looped a piece of thread, knotted into a circle between her index fingers and thumbs, and ran the double strand across her forehead. When she closed her fingers as if she were making a pair of shadow geese bite, the string twisted together catching the little hairs. Then she pulled the thread away from her skin, ripping the hairs out neatly, her eyes watering from the needles of pain. Opening her fingers, she cleaned the thread, then rolled it along her hairline and the tops of her eyebrows. My mother did the same to me and my sisters and herself. I used to believe that the expression "caught by the short hairs" meant a captive held with a depilatory string. It especially hurt at the temples, but my mother said we were lucky we didn't have to have our feet bound when we were seven. Sisters used to sit on their beds and cry together, she said, as their mothers or their slave removed the bandages for a few minutes each night and let the blood gush back into their veins. I hope that the man my aunt loved appreciated a smooth brow, that he wasn't just a tits-and-ass man.

Once my aunt found a freckle on her chin, at a spot that the almanac said predestined her for unhappiness. She dug it out with a hot needle and washed the wound with peroxide.

More attention to her looks than these pullings of hairs and pickings at spots would have caused gossip among the villagers. They owned work clothes and good clothes, and they wore good clothes for feasting the new seasons. But since a woman combing her hair hexes beginnings, my aunt rarely found an occasion to look her best. Women looked like great sea snails—the corded wood, babies, and laundry they carried were the whorls on their backs. The Chinese did not admire a bent back; goddesses and warriors stood straight. Still there must have been a marvelous freeing of beauty when a worker laid down her burden and stretched and arched.

Such commonplace loveliness, however, was not enough for my aunt. She dreamed of a lover for the fifteen days of New Year's, the time for families to exchange visits, money, and food. She plied her secret comb. And sure enough she cursed the year, the family, the village, and herself.

Even as her hair lured her imminent lover, many other men looked at her. Uncles, cousins, nephews, brothers would have looked, too, had they been home between journeys. Perhaps they had already been restraining their curiosity, and they left, fearful that their glances, like a field of nesting birds, might be startled and caught. Poverty hurt, and that was their first reason for leaving. But another, final reason for leaving the crowded house was the never-said.

She may have been unusually beloved, the precious only daughter, spoiled and mirror gazing because of the affection the family lavished on her. When her husband left, they welcomed the chance to take her back from the in-laws; she could live like the little daughter for just a while longer. There are stories that my grandfather was different from other people, "crazy ever since the little Jap bayoneted him in the head." He used to put his naked penis on the dinner table, laughing. And one day he brought home a baby girl, wrapped up inside his brown western-style greatcoat. He had traded one of his sons, probably my father, the youngest, for her. My grandmother made him trade back. When he finally got a daughter of his own, he doted on her. They must have all loved her, except perhaps my father, the only brother who never went back to China, having once been traded for a girl.

Brothers and sisters, newly men and women, had to efface their sexual color and present plain miens. Disturbing hair and eyes, a smile like no other, threatened the ideal of five generations living under one roof. To focus blurs, people shouted face to face and yelled from room to room. The immigrants I know have loud voices, unmodulated to American tones even after years away from the village where they called their friendships out across the fields. I have not been able to stop my mother's screams in public libraries or over telephones. Walking erect (knees straight, toes pointed forward, not pigeon-toed, which is Chinese-feminine) and speaking in an inaudible voice, I have tried to turn myself American-feminine. Chinese communication was loud, public. Only sick people had to whisper. But at the dinner table, where the family members came nearest one another, no one could talk, not the outcasts nor any eaters. Every word that falls from the mouth is a coin lost. Silently they gave and accepted food with both hands. A preoccupied child who took his bowl with one hand got a sideways glare. A complete moment of total attention is due everyone alike. Children and lovers have no singularity here, but my aunt used a secret voice, a separate attentiveness.

She kept the man's name to herself throughout her labor and dying; she did not accuse him that he be punished with her. To save her inseminator's name she gave silent birth.

He may have been somebody in her own household, but intercourse with a man outside the family would have been no less abhorrent. All the village were kinsmen, and the titles shouted in loud country voices never let kinship be forgotten. Any man within visiting distance would have been neutralized as a lover—"brother," "younger brother," "older brother"—one hundred and fifteen relationship titles. Parents researched birth charts probably not so much to assure good fortune as to circumvent incest in a population that has but one hundred surnames. Everybody has eight million relatives. How useless then sexual mannerisms, how dangerous.

As if it came from an atavism deeper than fear, I used to add "brother" silently to boys' names. It hexed the boys, who would or would not ask me to dance and made them less scary and as familiar and deserving of benevolence as girls.

But, of course, I hexed myself also—no dates. I should have stood up, both arms waving, and shouted out across libraries, "Hey, you! Love me back." I had no idea, though, how to make attraction selective, how to control its direction and magnitude. If I made myself American-pretty so that the five or six Chinese boys in the class fell in love with me, everyone else—the Caucasian, Negro, and Japanese boys—would too. Sisterliness, dignified and honorable, made much more sense.

Attraction eludes control so stubbornly that whole societies designed to organize relationships among people cannot keep order, not even when they bind people to one another from childhood and raise them together. Among the very poor and the wealthy, brothers married their adopted sisters, like doves. Our family allowed some romance, paying adult brides' prices and providing dowries so that their sons and daughters could marry strangers. Marriage promises to turn strangers into friendly relatives—a nation of siblings.

In the village structure, spirits shimmered among the live creatures, balanced and held in equilibrium by time and land. But one human being flaring up into violence could open up a black hole, a maelstrom that pulled in the sky. The frightened villagers, who depended on one another to maintain the real, went to my aunt to show her a personal, physical representation of the break she had made in the "roundness." Misallying couples snapped off the future, which was to be embodied in true offspring. The villagers punished her for acting as if she could have a private life, secret and apart from them.

If my aunt had betrayed the family at a time of large grain yields and peace, when many boys were born, and wings were being built on many houses, perhaps she might have escaped such severe punishment. But the men—hungry, greedy, tired of planting in dry soil—had been forced to leave the village in order to send food-money home. There were ghost plagues, bandit plagues, wars with the Japanese, floods. My Chinese brother and sister had died of an unknown sickness. Adultery, perhaps only a mistake during good times, became a crime when the village needed food.

The round moon cakes and round doorways, the round tables of graduated size that fit one roundness inside another, round windows and rice bowls—these talismans had lost their power to warn this family of the law: a family must be whole, faithfully keeping the descent line by having sons to feed the old and the dead, who in turn look after the family. The villagers came to show my aunt and her lover-in-hiding a broken house. The villagers were speeding up the circling of events because she was too shortsighted to see that her infidelity had already harmed the village, that waves of consequences would return unpredictably, sometimes in disguise, as now, to hurt her. This roundness had to be made coin-sized so that she would see its circumference: punish her at the birth of her baby. Awaken her to the inexorable. People who refused fatalism because they could invent small resources insisted on culpability. Deny accidents and wrest fault from the stars.

After the villagers left, their lanterns now scattering in various directions toward home, the family broke their silence and cursed her. "Aiaa, we're going to die. Death is coming. Death is coming. Look what you've done. You've killed us. Ghost! Dead ghost! Ghost! You've never been born." She ran out into the fields, far enough from the house so that she could no longer hear their voices, and pressed herself against the earth, her own land no more. When she felt the birth coming, she thought that she had been hurt. Her body seized together. "They've hurt me too much," she thought. "This is gall, and it will kill me." With forehead and knees against the earth, her body convulsed and then relaxed. She turned on her back, lay on the ground. The black well of sky and stars went out and out and out forever; her body and her complexity seemed to disappear. She was one of the stars, a bright dot in blackness, without home, without a companion, in eternal cold and silence. An agoraphobia rose in her, speeding higher and higher, bigger and bigger; she would not be able to contain it; there would be no end to fear.

Flayed, unprotected against space, she felt pain return, focusing her body. This pain chilled her—a cold, steady kind of surface pain. Inside, spasmodically, the other pain, the pain of the child, heated her. For hours she lay on the ground, alternately body and space. Sometimes a vision of normal comfort obliterated reality: she saw the family in the evening gambling at the dinner table, the young people massaging their elders' backs. She saw them congratulating one another, high joy on the mornings the rice shoots came up. When these pictures burst, the stars drew yet further apart. Black space opened.

She got to her feet to fight better and remembered that old-fashioned women gave birth in their pigsties to fool the jealous, pain-dealing gods, who do not snatch piglets. Before the next spasms could stop her, she ran to the pigsty, each step a rushing out into emptiness. She climbed over the fence and knelt in the dirt. It was good to have a fence enclosing her, a tribal person alone.

Laboring, this woman who had carried her child as a foreign growth that sickened her every day, expelled it at last. She reached down to touch the hot, wet, moving mass, surely smaller than anything human, and could feel that it was human after all—fingers, toes, nails, nose. She pulled it up on to her belly, and it lay curled there, butt in the air, feet precisely tucked one under the other. She opened her loose shirt and buttoned the child inside. After resting, it squirmed and thrashed and she pushed it up to her breast. It turned its head this way and that until it found her nipple. There, it made little snuffling noises. She clenched her teeth at its preciousness, lovely as a young calf, a piglet, a little dog.

She may have gone to the pigsty as a last act of responsibility: she would protect this child as she had protected its father. It would look after her soul, leaving supplies on her grave. But how would this tiny child without family find her grave when there would be no marker for her anywhere, neither in the earth nor the family hall? No one would give her a family hall name. She had taken the child with her into the wastes. At its birth the two of them had felt the same raw pain of separation, a wound that only the family pressing tight could close. A child with no descent line would not soften her life but only trail after her, ghost-like, begging her to give it purpose. At dawn the villagers on their way to the fields would stand around the fence and look.

Full of milk, the little ghost slept. When it awoke, she hardened her breasts against the milk that crying loosens. Toward morning she picked up the baby and walked to the well.

Carrying the baby to the well shows loving. Otherwise abandon it. Turn its face into the mud. Mothers who love their children take them along. It was probably a girl; there is some hope of forgiveness for boys.

"Don't tell anyone you had an aunt. Your father does not want to hear her name. She has never been born." I have believed that sex was unspeakable and words so strong and fathers so frail that "aunt" would do my father mysterious harm. I have thought that my family, having settled among immigrants who had also been their neighbors in the ancestral land, needed to clean their name, and a wrong word would incite the kinspeople even here. But there is more to this silence: they want me to participate in her punishment. And I have.

In the twenty years since I heard this story I have not asked for details nor said my aunt's name; I do not know it. People who can comfort the dead can also chase after them to hurt them further—a reverse ancestor worship. The real punishment was not the raid swiftly inflicted by the villagers, but the family's deliberately forgetting her. Her betrayal so maddened them, they saw to it that she would suffer forever, even after death. Always hungry, always needing, she would have to beg food from other ghosts, snatch and steal it from those whose living descendants give them gifts. She would have to fight the ghosts massed at crossroads for the buns a few thoughtful citizens leave to decoy her away from village and home so that the ancestral spirits could feast unharassed. At peace, they could act like gods, not ghosts, their descent lines providing them with paper suits and dresses, spirit money, paper houses, paper automobiles, chicken, meat, and rice into eternity—essences delivered up in smoke and flames, steam and incense rising from each rice bowl. In an attempt to make the Chinese care for people outside the family, Chairman Mao encourages us now to give our paper replicas to the spirits of outstanding soldiers and workers, no matter whose ancestors they may be. My aunt remains forever hungry. Goods are not distributed evenly among the dead.

My aunt haunts me—her ghost drawn to me because now, after fifty years of neglect, I alone devote pages of paper to her, though not origamied into houses and clothes. I do not think she always means me well. I am telling on her, and she was a spite suicide, drowning herself in the drinking water. The Chinese are always very frightened of the drowned one, whose weeping ghost, wet hair hanging and skin bloated, waits silently by the water to pull down a substitute.

Speculations

1. What is the significance of the title, "No Name Woman"? Compare what it would mean to be a person without a name in Chinese society to what it would mean to be a person without a name in the United States. Use examples from this excerpt of how the Chinese treat their names.

2. Kingston uses the "talk-story" method of retelling in different ways to describe who her aunt was and what she was like. What is significant about this method of storytelling? Compared to traditional storytelling, how does the talk-story develop a picture of the aunt? Kingston? Chinese values?

3. After looking closely at Kingston's descriptions of her aunt, her mother, and other women, how would you describe women's

position in Chinese society? How is the "place" of women bound up in silence and having no name?

4. Why do you think the villagers' collective punishment of the aunt and her family was so extreme? What rationale do you think the villagers might offer for inflicting this punishment? What does Kingston mean when she says the villagers wanted to show the aunt "a personal, physical representation of the break she had made in the 'roundness'" of their society?

5. How would you describe the strengths and weaknesses of the aunt's character? Why is she alone punished and not her secret lover? Why is Kingston "haunted" by her?

DISAPPEARING ACTS

Nina Berman

A photograph may not always be worth a thousand words, but image and text together can create a powerful statement. In the tradition of James Agee and Walker Evans, whose depiction of southern rural poverty in the classic *Let Us Now Praise Famous Men* altered America's moral landscape, Nina Berman also combines photograph and textual analysis.

"I'm primarily a photographer now," Berman told *Speculations*. "I used to be a writer, and I still write the texts for certain projects like I did with 'Disappearing Acts.' But now I'm a magazine photographer. I work for a picture agency called SIPA Press, and my work has appeared in *Time, Newsweek, New York Magazine, Fortune,* and *People.*"

Nina Berman was born in New York City in 1960 and grew up in New York and New Jersey. After earning a B.A. in English at the University of Chicago and a M.A. in journalism at Columbia University, she began her career as a reporter for the *Bergen Record,* a New Jersey newspaper. Over the years, however, she gravitated slowly from writing to photography.

For several years she has been working on a photography project concerning woman and gender roles in sociocultural terms. "'Disappearing Acts' is actually part of this photography project," she told us. "It is a study of 'the beauty myth' revealed in pictures." In addition to this feature on anorexia which appeared in *Ms.,* Berman has published a photo feature on Mary Kay cosmetics in *Fortune.* "I'm focusing on things like Miss America, silicone breast implants, face lifts, and nose jobs—which are really amazing to me. And I am interested in street stuff—like the Macy's Department Store window, when they do make-overs." Berman's interviews—done in the style of Studs Terkel—resonate powerfully with the Naomi Wolf essay that follows.

Cindy, age 42

I have an older sister who was really thin and pretty and I always wanted to look like her, and I thought, Gee, everybody always notices her, O.K., I can be thinner than her. I became obsessed with weight and exercising. It started out with a diet, cut the calories. All through high school, no fat, no chocolate. I remember going out with girls in the summertime and they would have ice cream and I wouldn't. I didn't need it. It made me feel good, that control. I was starving, but I stuck to it. It was the one thing I could do. And it was, like, such an admirable thing. And they noticed. Finally they noticed me. I would be with my sister, and people would say, "You're even thinner than she is," and I thought finally I made it.

The bulimia started in college. I went to Madison. When I think about it, it seems so weird. With everything going on, all the people being killed each day, they're napalming, they're demonstrating, the National Guard was outside the door, and I was worrying about how many calories I was eating. That was the focus. Other girls too. It's funny. We thought everything was bad. The establishment. But everyone accepted the fashion line that you had to be thin and look like a model.

It certainly starts out with wanting to be thin and wanting to look good. You know, women operate in a man's world and no matter how accomplished you are, or how good you are at anything, you have to look the part of the beautiful woman, the model thin woman. You have to be perfect-looking. Perfect in every way. But then it becomes a way of not thinking about your life because you're always thinking about food, and physically it has a kind of calming effect, of getting rid of it.

I go out to exercise to try to get rid of it, and to some extent the exercise replaces the bingeing and the purging, but then the end of the day comes, or the middle of the day, and I'll constantly be thinking about how bad my marriage is, and I get really upset, and then something happens, and I always feel like I have to get rid of it. I don't binge, like eating tons of food. I'll try to eat a meal, and then a little while later I have to get rid of it.

My marriage really has contributed to my eating disorder. He can tear me apart with name-calling, and I can never say anything back. That's just never allowed. I can't express myself. I feel like I have no right to say anything. I get real depressed. I don't know what to do with the anger. I blame myself for everything: if only I could do something right.

I grew up in a family where we all had to look like the perfect middle-American family. Norman Rockwell. Women are kind of second-class. Women are weak. You couldn't show any emotion. I learned early not to cry. I never cried. You grow up to get married and have someone to take care of you.

I can't go on with this. I'm getting too old. I'm not a kid anymore. When I go to family meetings and I see the kids, I think they could be mine. I'm older than some of the parents. I've spent my whole life wanting to avoid thinking about what I should really do with my life.

Jane, age 27

I didn't start with my bulimia until my junior or senior year in high school, but I remember being in fourth grade and worrying about my weight. I had a friend who went to the same doctor as me. She was one of those gangly kids, and I was always a skinny kid anyway—my dad used to call me "bones"—and I remember she was smaller than me, and I asked her how much she weighed and she weighed less, and I remember I asked the doctor if I weighed too much. I don't know why, I felt bad, I thought that I should be thinner.

I remember being in day camp and eating a hamburger without bread and thinking that I shouldn't eat bread because it was bad. There was certain pop I wouldn't drink because it had four calories instead of two. I've gotten better. Now I just mostly drink water. Eighty ounces a day.

My grandma has a lot to do with this because she's, like, obsessed with her weight. Since I can remember there was dieting. I'll call her and she'll tell me what she ate. I'm named after her mother so she lives kind of through me. In her eyes, I always had to be perfect. She told me that I needed a nose job when I was 12. We were having some sort of party at the house, and there were people over, and I remember her saying, "Well, you'll have a nose job when you're 16." Of course, I had one after that.

In high school, I was more toward the anorexic side. I did my junior theme on it while I wasn't eating. I was just real interested in it. Anorexia was something I wanted to have. I remember thinking in high school that if I was thinner, everything would be O.K. I had a diary and I remember writing in it that I weighed this much and if I didn't weigh that much, everything would be O.K. I don't know how I got it into my mind. Some of it probably came from my grandma: you know, I'm supposed to look good. I'm supposed to be this beautiful, cute thing.

In college I threw up occasionally. My first year out of graduate school, I would throw up two to three times a day. Usually I felt relieved, that I just got rid of the food, that maybe I wouldn't gain weight from what I ate.

I eat instead of feel. If I eat, I don't feel anything, which is a lot easier. For so many years my emotional needs weren't met. I was doing all these things and I wasn't getting any attention. In college, I tried to kill myself. Nobody cared. No one came to visit me. My family kind of brushed everything under the rug. We won't talk about that.

I hate it. I'm always thinking about it. When will I eat lunch? Will I eat lunch? Where will I get it? I'll drive by McDonald's and smell it. I just wish I could eat normal and not think about it. I think about it all the time. If I'm out with other girls, I notice what they eat. It's obnoxious. It's sick.

I weigh about 115 pounds. I would like to weigh 100. If I weighed 100, I would probably want to weigh 90. I look at the girls in the hospital, the anorexics, the real skinny ones, and I think: I would like to look like that. I still think that way. I know it isn't good, but I think they look good. I don't know why. I know a girl who's in fifth grade and she thinks she's fat. I'm just watching her. She's a prime candidate for an eating disorder.

Cait, age 17

I was going to make myself be perfect. I thought I had control of it. I didn't think I had a problem. I thought I was happy, but I can't really figure out what happy is.

I ate every couple of days. Or I would have a rice cake. I was convinced that an orange was too much. I got to the point where everything was too much. I restricted everything. After a while you don't feel the hunger pains anymore. And you don't know when you're hungry. I started restricting more and more, and then after a while I was craving food and that's when the bingeing started.

In the beginning I was throwing up healthy food, broccoli, carrots, apples. And then I thought, If I'm going to do this, I might as well binge on what I like. I left a party early because I had to have a binge. I told my boyfriend I was tired, got in my car, and went to McDonald's. God, it was scary while I was doing it. I ate a Big Mac, a large fries, an apple pie, a hot fudge sundae with nuts, and I wasn't done. There was a grocery store right there. I got, like, a thing of Ben & Jerry's ice cream, a couple of candy bars, a big, like, two-pound bag of Peanut M&Ms. I ate at McDonald's, I ate in my car, and then I ate the rest of it at home.

I felt good after because it was gone. But in the end it was not so much the bingeing, it was not eating at all. I wouldn't drink pop, not even diet pop. My logic was: why? I don't need it. It was something extra. I knew there were no calories, but I thought there had to be something in the pop.

I didn't want anybody to find out. I would make food, Spaghet-tiOs, and give it to my dog. My boyfriend has never seen me eat. I would say, "Oh, I just ate," or "I'm not hungry." I didn't want him to think that I was a cow or a pig or something. Like, if we were out and other girls were eating, I would get satisfaction out of the fact that I wasn't. It made me feel better than them.

I make people tired. I'm constantly on the go. I was doing a thousand and one things. It was easier to go a thousand miles an hour than to deal with anything. I think I wasn't really happy with the image I was living, but I didn't know what to do.

I practice being gentle. I practice in front of the mirror saying hello. I want to present myself in the best possible way, and if I can present myself better, as happier, as more energetic, then I want to know how to do it.

I want so badly to just be me. I want to get out of this person, this perfectionist that everyone admires.

Nicole, age 16

It's like a huge feeling that I'm not right. That I could be better. I feel like I am a heavy person. You know how really, really fat people must feel? That's how I feel. I could not tell you how I look in jeans. I always had to go shopping with my mom so she could tell me how they looked. I honestly don't know what I'm supposed to look like.

It started the spring of sophomore year. People said I had a good body all the time, a nice butt. I would turn my head away and blush. I got compliments up until the time I came into the hospital. Guys said I looked hot and I was wearing children's size 14 jeans.

I hate the curves. I've got to get rid of the curves. I think my legs are fat. And this muscle here. I never sit with my legs crossed. I always look in the mirror sideways.

I used to spit out my food instead of throwing up. Tootsie Rolls, peanut butter, M&Ms, Starburst. I had *Jane Fonda's Workout, Kathy Smith's Fat Burning Workout*. They're addicting. I watched them in the basement. I did butt exercises, sit-ups, stretches. I was never too thin. I never had a goal weight; it was always just not yet.

My boyfriend couldn't bear to touch me. He stopped sleeping with me because he said I was just bones. I tried to get thinner to look better and win him back, but it just repulsed him. I thought I could be more appealing to him because all of the most beautiful women, the sexiest, are the thinnest. All the women men desire are thin. In the movies, the desired women are thin. Magazines. I would look through them at night: *Vogue, Mademoiselle, Seventeen, Cosmopolitan, Elle, Harper's Bazaar.*

I based how I felt about myself on the way a guy felt about me. I would try to be a good girlfriend and when I did get hurt, it was a big blow.

I was readmitted because I tried to kill myself. In my car, in the garage. It was the most real attempt. Everyone said I was doing so good, and then when I wasn't, when they build it up, I get sick.

A lot of it has to do with my relationship with my father. I was taught to be quiet. Girls should be quiet. I should not express myself. I've always wanted a father that I know I can never have. For 16 years, I've wanted a father that I can never have.

Sometimes I still wish I could fit into my old jeans. And that empty feeling—on top of the world, like you could conquer anything. I loved it.

Speculations

1. Cindy tells Nina Berman that "women operate in a man's world and no matter how accomplished you are, or how good you are at anything, you have to look the part of the beautiful woman, the model thin woman." Do you agree? Does Cindy's analysis help explain the cause of eating disorders or is it just an excuse? Support your view.

2. Jane views her bulimia as an emotional disorder. She says, "I eat instead of feel. If I eat, I don't feel anything, which is a lot easier." Can food be a substitute for emotion? Offer an explanation of how food is valued in our society. Consider the emotional and personal associations people generally have with foods like chocolate, apple pie, fried chicken, and Thanksgiving dinner.

3. Berman chose to have these women express their views in the first person, as if they are giving dramatic monologues. Why do you think she made this choice? Is it the most effective way to present this information? Would this piece be stronger if Berman had written it from her point of view? Support your views.

4. Cait states that she wants "so badly to just be me. I want to get out of this person, this perfectionist that everyone admires." What do you think she means by this? Shouldn't all of us strive for perfection? Does striving for perfection necessarily lead toward a serious eating disorder? Offer your own views about this complicated problem.

5. Berman's title for this essay is at least to some degree humorous, facetious, tongue-in-cheek. Do you think this tone is appropriate for this serious subject? Is Berman making light of eating disorders and the women she is featuring?

HUNGER: A FEMINIST CRITIQUE

Naomi Wolf

In *People* magazine, Naomi Wolf states that she is "trying to seize this culture by its collar and say 'Stop! Look what you're doing!' To the extent that people get angry, I know I've done a good job." This is exactly what she does in *The Beauty Myth*, a scorching attack on popular conceptions of beauty and the feminine. Wolf argues in *The Beauty Myth* that society imposes an idealistic, unreasonable standard of beauty on all women, a standard that leads women to starve themselves, wear unhealthy shoes and impractical clothing, buy millions of dollars of cosmetics, and even submit to unnecessary plastic surgery, including sometimes fatal surgery such as breast implants. "Over and over in the course of women's history," Wolf stated in *People*, "the female ideals that form just happen to be ones that serve what the economy needs at the moment. There's no male conspiracy. There doesn't need to be."

In her preface to the paperback edition of *The Beauty Myth*, Wolf writes:

> As my feminist foremothers taught me, naming a problem has power. Many young women tell me that the connections they were able to make between the beauty myth with its stereotype of "the ugly feminist" and their own fears about calling themselves feminists, allowed them to speak up at last on their own behalf as women. The turbulence of the past year is worth it a thousand times over, when I see it in the light of that gift.

Naomi Wolf wrote *The Beauty Myth* (1990) while still in her twenties. Born in San Francisco in 1962, she earned a B.A. from Yale University and attended New College, Oxford. She currently lives in New York and writes essays and articles for a range of periodicals including the *New Republic*, the *New York Times*, and the *Wall Street Journal*. In 1993, she published a second book on women's issues, *Fire with Fire: The New Female Power and How It will Change the Twenty-First Century*.

In the following edited selection from *The Beauty Myth*, Wolf specifically attacks those conceptions of beauty that compel women to starve themselves into a socially accepted thinness. For many women, Wolf argues, hunger and starvation have nothing to do with poverty or physical illness; they are a necessary condition for being "beautiful." And, according to Wolf, they are one powerful and indirect way to erode women's confidence, power, and potential for success.

How would America react to the mass self-immolation by hunger of its favorite sons? How would Western Europe absorb the export of such a disease? One would expect an emergency response: crisis task forces convened in congressional hearing rooms, unscheduled alumni meetings, the best experts money can hire, cover stories in newsmagazines, a flurry of editorials, blame and counterblame, bulletins, warnings, symptoms, updates; an epidemic blazoned in boldface red. The sons of privilege *are* the future; the future is committing suicide.

Of course, this is actually happening right now, only with a gender difference. The institutions that shelter and promote these diseases are hibernating. The public conscience is fast asleep. Young women are dying from institutional catatonia: four hundred dollars a term from the college endowment for the women's center to teach "self-help"; fifty to buy a noontime talk from a visiting clinician. The world is not coming to an end because the cherished child in five who "chooses" to die slowly is a girl. And she is merely doing too well what she is expected to do very well in the best of times.

Up to one-tenth of all young American women, up to one-fifth of women students in the United States, are locked into one-woman hunger camps. When they fall, there are no memorial services, no intervention through awareness programs, no formal message from their schools and colleges that the society prefers its young women to eat and thrive rather than sicken and die. Flags are not lowered in recognition of the fact that in every black-robed ceremonial marches a fifth column of death's-heads. . .

There are no reliable statistics about death rates from anorexia, but a disease that strikes between 5 and 10 percent of American women, and has one of the highest fatality rates for a mental illness, deserves the kind of media investigation that is devoted to serious and potentially fatal epidemics. This killer epidemic, however, has never made the cover of *Time;* it is relegated to the "Style" sections. The National Institutes of Health has, to date, no education and prevention program whatsoever. So it appears that the bedrock question—why must Western women go hungry—is one too dangerous to ask even in the face of a death toll such as this. . .

Some women's magazines report that 60 percent of American women have serious trouble eating. The majority of middle-class women in the United States, it appears, suffer a version of anorexia or bulimia; but if anorexia is defined as a compulsive fear of and fixation upon food, perhaps most Western women can be called, twenty years into the backlash, mental anorexics.

What happened? Why now? The first obvious clue is the progressive chiseling away of the Iron Maiden's body over this century of female emancipation, in reaction to it. Until seventy-five years ago in the male artistic tradition of the West, women's natural amplitude was their beauty; representations of the female nude reveled in women's lush fertility. Various distributions of sexual fat were emphasized according to fashion—big, ripe bellies from the fifteenth to the seventeenth centuries, plump faces and shoulders in the early nineteenth, progressively generous dimpled buttocks and thighs until the twentieth—but never, until women's emancipation entered law, this absolute negation of the female state that fashion historian Ann Hollander in *Seeing Through Clothes* characterizes, from the point of view of any age but our own, as "the look of sickness, the look of poverty, and the look of nervous exhaustion."

Dieting and thinness began to be female preoccupations when Western women received the vote around 1920; between 1918 and 1925, "the rapidity with which the new, linear form replaced the more curvaceous one is startling." In the regressive 1950s, women's natural fullness could be briefly enjoyed once more because their minds were occupied in domestic seclusion. But when women came en masse into male spheres, that pleasure had to be overridden by an urgent social expedient that would make women's bodies into the prisons that their homes no longer were.

A generation ago, the average model weighed 8 percent less than the average American woman, whereas today she weighs 23 percent less. Twiggy appeared in the pages of *Vogue* in 1965, simultaneous with the advent of the Pill, to cancel out its most radical implications. Like many beauty-myth symbols, she was double-edged, suggesting to women the freedom from the constraint of reproduction of earlier generations (since female fat is categorically understood by the subconscious as fertile sexuality), while reassuring men with her suggestion of female weakness, asexuality, and hunger. Her thinness, now commonplace, was shocking at the time; even *Vogue* introduced the model with anxiety: "'Twiggy' is called Twiggy because she looks as though a strong gale would snap her in two and dash her to the ground . . . Twiggy is of such a meagre constitution that other models stare at her. Her legs look as though she has not had enough milk as a baby and her face has that expression one feels Londoners wore in the blitz." The fashion writer's language is revealing: Undernurtured, subject to being overpowered by a strong wind, her expression the daze of the besieged, what better symbol to reassure an establishment faced with women who were soon to march tens of thousands strong down Fifth Avenue?

In the twenty years after the start of the second wave of the women's movement, the weight of Miss Americas plummeted, and the average weight of Playboy Playmates dropped from 11 percent below the national average in 1970 to 17 percent below it in eight years. Model Aimee Liu in her autobiography claims that many models are anorexic; she herself continued to model as an anorexic. Of dancers, 38 percent show anorexic behavior. The average model, dancer, or actress is thinner than 95 percent of the female population. The Iron Maiden put the shape of a near skeleton and the texture of men's musculature where the shape and feel of a woman used to be, and the small elite corps of women whose bodies are used to reproduce the Iron Maiden often become diseased themselves in order to do so.

As a result, a 1985 survey says, 90 percent of respondents think they weigh too much. On any day, 25 percent of women are on diets, with 50 percent finishing, breaking, or starting one. This self-hatred was generated rapidly, coinciding with the women's movement: Between 1966 and 1969, two studies showed, the number of high school girls who thought they were too fat had risen from 50 to 80 percent. Though heiresses to the gains of the women's movement, their daughters are, in terms of this distress, no better off: In a recent study of high school girls, 53 percent were unhappy with their bodies by age thirteen; by age eighteen and over, 78 percent were dissatisfied. The hunger cult has been a major victory against women's fight for equality if the evidence of the 1984 *Glamour* survey of thirty-three thousand women is representative: 75 percent of those aged eighteen to thirty-five believed they were fat, while only 25 percent were medically overweight (the same percentage as men); 45 percent of the *underweight* women thought they were too fat. But more heart-breaking in terms of the way in which the myth is running to ground hopes for women's advancement and gratification, the *Glamour* respondents chose losing ten to fifteen pounds above success in work or in love as their most desired goal.

Those ten to fifteen pounds, which have become a fulcrum, if these figures are indicative, of most Western women's sense of self, are the medium of what I call the One Stone Solution. One stone, the British measurement of fourteen pounds, is roughly what stands between the 50 percent of women who are not overweight who believe they are and their ideal self. That one stone, once lost, puts these women well below the weight that is natural to them, and beautiful, if we saw with eyes unconstrained by the Iron Maiden. But the body quickly restores itself, and the cycle of gain and loss begins, with its train of torment and its risk of disease, becoming a fixation of the woman's consciousness. The inevitable cycles of failure ensured by the One Stone Solution create and continually reinforce in women our uniquely modern neurosis. This great weight-shift bestowed on women, just when we were free to begin to forget them, new versions of low self-esteem, loss of control, and sexual shame. It is a genuine-ly elegant fulfillment of a collective wish: By simply dropping the of-ficial weight one stone below most women's natural level, and re-defining a woman's womanly shape as by definition "too fat," a wave of self-hatred swept over First World women, a reactionary psychol-ogy was perfected, and a major industry was born. It suavely coun-tered the historical groundswell of female success with a mass con-viction of female failure, a failure defined as implicit in womanhood itself.

The proof that the One Stone Solution is political lies in what women feel when they eat "too much": guilt. Why should guilt be the operative emotion, and female fat be a moral issue articulated with words like good and bad? If our culture's fixation on female fatness or thinness were about sex, it would be a private issue be-tween a woman and her lover; if it were about health, between a woman and herself. Public debate would be far more hysterically fo-cused on male fat than on female, since more men (40 percent) are medically overweight than women (32 percent) and too much fat is far more dangerous for men than for women. In fact, "there is very little evidence to support the claim that fatness causes poor health among women. . . . The results of recent studies have suggested that women may in fact live longer and be generally healthier if they weigh ten to fifteen percent *above* the life-insurance figures *and* they refrain from dieting," asserts *Radiance;* when poor health is correlat-ed to fatness in women, it is due to chronic dieting and the emotion-al stress of self-hatred. The National Institutes of Health studies that linked obesity to heart disease and stroke were based on male sub-jects; when a study of females was finally published in 1990, it showed that weight made only a fraction of the difference for women that it made for men. The film *The Famine Within* cites a six-teen-country study that fails to correlate fatness to ill health. Female fat is not in itself unhealthy.

But female fat is the subject of public passion, and women feel guilty about female fat, because we implicitly recognize that under the myth, women's bodies are not our own but society's, and that thinness is not a private aesthetic, but hunger a social concession exacted by the community. A cultural fixation on female thinness is not an obsession about female beauty but an obsession about female obedience. Women's dieting has become what Yale psychologist Judith Rodin calls a "normative obsession," a never-ending passion play given in-ternational coverage out of all proportion to the health risks associated with obesity, and using emotive language that does not figure even in discussions of alcohol or tobacco abuse. The nations seize with com-pulsive attention on this melodrama because women and men understand that it is not about cholesterol or heart rate or the disruption of a line of tailoring, but about how much social freedom women are going to get away with or concede. The media's convulsive analysis of the endless saga of female fat and the battle to vanquish it are actually bulletins of the sex war: what women are gaining or losing in it, and how fast.

The great weight shift must be understood as one of the major historical developments of the century, a direct solution to the dangers posed by the women's movement and economic and reproductive freedom. Dieting is the most potent political sedative in women's history; a quietly mad population is a tractable one. Researchers S. C. Wooley and O. W. Wooley confirmed what most women know too well—that concern with weight leads to "a virtual collapse of self-esteem and sense of effectiveness." Researchers J. Polivy and C. P. Herman found that "prolonged and periodic caloric restriction" resulted in a distinctive personality whose traits are "passivity, anxiety and emotionality."

It is those traits, and not thinness for its own sake, that the dominant culture wants to create in the private sense of self of recently liberated women in order to cancel out the dangers of their liberation.

Women's advances had begun to give them the opposite traits—high self-esteem, a sense of effectiveness, activity, courage, and clarity of mind. "Prolonged and periodic caloric restriction" is a means to take the teeth out of this revolution. The great weight shift and its One Stone Solution followed the rebirth of feminism so that women just reaching for power would become weak, preoccupied, and, as it evolved, mentally ill in useful ways and in astonishing proportions. To understand how the gaunt toughness of the Iron Maiden has managed spectacularly to roll back women's advances toward equality, we have to see that what is really at stake is not fashion or beauty or sex, but a struggle over political hegemony that has become—for women, who are often unaware of the real issues behind our predicament—one of life and death. . . .

We need to reexamine all the terms, then, in the light of a public agenda. What, first, is food? Certainly, within the context of the intimate family, food is love, and memory, and language. But in the public realm, food is status and honor.

Food is the primal symbol of social worth. Whom a society values, it feeds well. The piled plate, the choicest cut, say: We think you're worth this much of the tribe's resources. Samoan women, who are held in high esteem, exaggerate how much they eat on feast days. Publicly apportioning food is about determining power relations, and sharing it is about cementing social equality: When men break bread together, or toast the queen, or slaughter for one another the fatted calf, they've become equals and then allies. The word *companion* comes from the Latin for "with" and "bread"—those who break bread together.

But under the beauty myth, now that all women's eating is a public issue, our portions testify to and reinforce our sense of social inferiority. If women cannot eat the same food as men, we cannot experience equal status in the community. As long as women are asked to bring a self-denying mentality to the communal table, it will never be round, men and women seated together; but the same traditional hierarchical dais, with a folding table for women at the foot.

In the current epidemic of rich Western women who cannot "choose" to eat, we see the continuation of an older, poorer tradition of women's relation to food. Modern Western female dieting descends from a long history. Women have always had to eat differently from men: less and worse. In Hellenistic Rome, reports classicist Sarah B. Pomeroy, boys were rationed sixteen measures of meal to twelve measures allotted to girls. In medieval France, according to historian John Boswell, women received two thirds of the grain allocated to men. Throughout history, when there is only so much to eat, women get little, or none: A common explanation among anthropologists for female infanticide is that food shortage provokes it. According to UN publications, where hunger goes, women meet it first: In Bangladesh and Botswana, female infants die more frequently than male, and girls are more often malnourished, because they are given smaller portions. In Turkey, India, Pakistan, North Africa, and the Middle East, men get the lion's share of what food there is, regardless of women's caloric needs. "It is not the caloric value of work which is represented in the patterns of food consumption" of men in relation to women in North Africa, "nor is it a question of physiological needs. . . . Rather these patterns tend to guarantee priority rights to the 'important' members of society, that is, adult men." In Morocco, if women are guests, "they will swear they have eaten already" or that they are not hungry. "Small girls soon learn to offer their share to visitors, to refuse meat and deny hunger." A North African woman described by anthropologist Vanessa Mahler assured her fellow diners that "she preferred bones to meat." Men, however, Mahler reports, "are supposed to be exempt from facing scarcity which is shared out among women and children."

"Third World countries provide examples of undernourished female and well-nourished male children, where what food there is goes to the boys of the family," a UN report testifies. Two thirds of women in Asia, half of all women in Africa, and a sixth of Latin American women are anemic—through lack of food. Fifty percent more Nepali women than men go blind from lack of food. Cross-culturally, men receive hot meals, more protein, and the first helpings of a dish, while women eat the cooling leftovers, often having to use deceit and cunning to get enough to eat. "Moreover, what food they do receive is consistently less nutritious."

This pattern is not restricted to the Third World: Most Western women alive today can recall versions of it at their mothers' or grandmothers' table: British miners' wives eating the grease-soaked bread left over after their husbands had eaten the meat; Italian and Jewish wives taking the part of the bird no one else would want.

These patterns of behavior are standard in the affluent West today, perpetuated by the culture of female caloric self-deprivation. A generation ago, the justification for this traditional apportioning shifted: Women still went without, ate leftovers, hoarded food, used deceit to get it—but blamed themselves. Our mothers still exiled themselves from the family circle that was eating cake with silver cutlery off Wedgwood china, and we would come upon them in the kitchen, furtively devouring the remains. The traditional pattern was cloaked in modern shame, but otherwise changed little. Weight control became its rationale once natural inferiority went out of fashion.

The affluent West is merely carrying on this traditional apportioning. Researchers found that parents in the United States urged boys to eat, regardless of their weight, while they did so with daughters only if they were relatively thin. In a sample of babies of both sexes, 99 percent of the boys were breast-fed, but only 66 percent of the girls, who were given 50 percent less time to feed. "Thus," writes Susie Orbach, "daughters are often fed less well, less attentively and less sensitively than they need." Women do not feel entitled to enough food because they have been taught to go with less than they need since birth, in a tradition passed down through an endless line of mothers; the public role of "honored guest" is new to us, and the culture is telling us through the ideology of caloric restriction that we are not welcome finally to occupy it.

What, then, is fat? Fat is portrayed in the literature of the myth as expendable female filth; virtually cancerous matter, an inert or treacherous infiltration into the body of nauseating bulk waste. The demonic characterizations of a simple body substance do not arise from its physical properties but from old-fashioned misogyny, for above all fat is female; it is the medium and regulator of female sexual characteristics.

Cross-culturally, from birth, girls have 10–15 percent more fat than boys. At puberty, male fat-to-muscle ratio decreases as the female ratio increases. The increased fat ratio in adolescent girls is the medium for sexual maturation and fertility. The average healthy twenty-year-old female is made of 28.7 percent body fat. By middle age, women cross-culturally are 38 percent body fat: This is, contrary to the rhetoric of the myth, "not unique to the industrialized advanced Western nations. They are norms characteristic of the female of the species." A moderately active woman's caloric needs, again in contradiction to a central tenet of the myth, are only 250 calories less than a moderately active man's (2,250 to 2,500), or two ounces of cheese. Weight gain with age is also normal cross-culturally for both sexes. The body is evidently programmed to weigh a certain amount, which weight the body defends.

Fat is sexual in women; Victorians called it affectionately their "silken layer." The leanness of the Iron Maiden impairs female sexuality. One fifth of women who exercise to shape their bodies have menstrual irregularities and diminished fertility. The body of the model, remember, is 22 to 23 percent leaner than that of the average woman; the average woman wants to be as lean as the model; infertility and hormone imbalance are common among women whose fat-to-lean ratio falls below 22 percent. Hormonal imbalances promote ovarian and endometrial cancer and osteoporosis. Fat tissues store sex hormones, so low fat reserves are linked with weak estrogens and low levels of all the other important sex hormones, as well as with inactive ovaries. Rose E. Frisch in *Scientific American* refers to the fatness of Stone Age fertility figures, saying that "this historical linking of fatness and fertility actually makes biological sense" since fat regulates reproduction. Underweight women double their risk of low-birth-weight babies.

Fat is not just fertility in women, but desire. Researchers at Michael Reese Hospital in Chicago found that plumper women desired sex more often than thinner women. On scales of erotic excitability and readiness, they outscored thin women by a factor of almost two to one. To ask women to become unnaturally thin is to ask them to relinquish their sexuality: "Studies consistently show that with dietary deprivation, sexual interests dissipate." Subjects of one experiment stopped masturbating or having sexual fantasies at 1,700 calories a day, 500 more than the Beverly Hills Diet. Starvation affects the endocrine glands; amenorrhea and delayed puberty are common features in starving women and girls; starved men lose their libido and become impotent, sometimes developing breasts. Loyola University's Sexual Dysfunction Clinic reports that weight-loss disorders have a far worse effect on female sexuality than do weight-gaining disorders; the heavier women were eager for courtship and sex, while anorexics "were so concerned with their bodies that they had fewer sexual fantasies, fewer dates, and less desire for sex." The *New England Journal of Medicine* reports that intense exercisers lose interest in sex. Joan Jacobs Brumberg agrees that "clinical materials suggest an absence of sexual activity on the part of anorexics." Pleasure in sex, Mette Bergstrom writes, "is rare for a bulimic because of a strong body hatred." "The evidence seems to suggest," writes Roberta Pollack Seid, "and common sense would confirm, that a hungry, undernourished animal is less, not more, interested in the pleasures of the flesh."

What, finally, is dieting? "Dieting," and, in Great Britain, "slimming," are trivializing words for what is in fact self-inflicted semistarvation. In India, one of the poorest countries in the world, the very poorest women eat 1,400 calories a day, or 600 more than a Western woman on the Hilton Head Diet. "Quite simply," writes Seid, dieters "are reacting the way victims of semi-starvation react . . . semi-starvation, even if caused by self-imposed diets, produces startlingly similar effects on all human beings."

The range of repulsive and pathetic behaviors exhibited by women touched by food diseases is portrayed as quintessentially feminine, proof positive of women's irrationality (replacing the conviction of menstrual irrationality that had to be abandoned when women were needed for the full-time work force). In a classic study done at the University of Minnesota, thirty-six volunteers were placed on an extended low-calorie diet and "the psychological, behavioral and physical effects were carefully documented." The subjects were young and healthy, showing "high levels of ego strength, emotional stability, and good intellectual ability." They "began a six-month period . . . in which their food intake was reduced by half—a typical weight reduction technique for women.

"After losing approximately 25% of their original body weight, pervasive effects of semistarvation were seen." The subjects "became increasingly preoccupied with food and eating, to the extent that they ruminated obsessively about meals and food, collected recipes and cookbooks, and showed abnormal food rituals, such as excessively slow eating and hoarding of food related objects." Then, the majority "suffered some form of emotional disturbance as a result of semistarvation, including depression, hypochondriasis, hysteria, angry outbursts, and, in some cases, psychotic levels of disorganization." Then, they "lost their ability to function in work and social contexts, due to apathy, reduced energy and alertness, social isolation, and decreased sexual interest." Finally, "within weeks of reducing their food intake," they "reported relentless hunger, as well as powerful urges to break dietary rules. Some succumbed to eating binges, followed by vomiting and feelings of self-reproach. Ravenous hunger persisted, even following large meals during refeeding." Some of the subjects "found themselves eating continuously, while others engaged in uncontrollable cycles of gorging and vomiting." The volunteers "became terrified of going outside the experiment environment where they would be tempted by the foods they had agreed not to eat . . . when they did succumb, they made hysterical, half-crazed confessions." They became irritable, tense, fatigued, and full of vague complaints. "Like fugitives, [they] could not shed the feeling they were being shadowed by a sinister force." For some, doctors eventually had to prescribe tranquilizers.

The subjects were a group of completely normal healthy college men.

During the great famine that began in May 1940 during the German occupation of the Netherlands, the Dutch authorities maintained rations at between 600 and 1,600 calories a day, or what they characterized as the level of semistarvation. The worst sufferers were defined as starving when they had lost 25 percent of their body weight, and were given precious supplements. Photos taken of clothed starving Dutch women are striking for how preternaturally modern they look.

At 600–1,600 calories daily, the Dutch suffered semistarvation; the Diet Centers' diet is fixed at 1,600 calories. When they had lost 25 percent of their body weight, the Dutch were given crisis food supplementation. The average healthy woman has to lose almost exactly as much to fit the Iron Maiden. In the Lodz Ghetto in 1941, besieged Jews were allotted starvation rations of 500–1200 calories a day. At Treblinka, 900 calories was scientifically determined to be the minimum necessary to sustain human functioning. At "the nation's top weight-loss clinics," where "patients" are treated for up to a year, the rations are the same. . . .

Authoritative evidence is mounting that eating diseases are caused mainly by dieting. Ilana Attie and J. Brooks-Gunn quote investigators who found "chronic, restrained eating" to "constitute a cumulative stress of such magnitude that dieting itself may be 'a sufficient condition for the development of anorexia nervosa or bulimia.'" Roberta Pollack Seid reaches the same conclusion. "Ironically, dieting . . . itself may provoke obsessive behavior and binge-eating. It may indeed *cause* both eating disorders and obesity itself." Sustained caloric deprivation appears to be a severe shock to the body that it remembers with destructive consequences. Seid writes that "women's problems with food seem to stem . . . from their effort to get an ultra-lean body. . . . The only way 95% can get it is by putting themselves on deprivatory diets." Attie and Brooks-Gunn concur: "Much of the behavior thought to cause anorexia nervosa and bulimia may actually be a consequence of starvation. . . . The normal weight dieter who diets to look and feel thin also is vulnerable to disturbed emotional, cognitive and behavioral patterns by virtue of the constant stress of trying to stay below the body's 'natural' or biologically regulated weight." Dieting and fashionable thinness make women seriously unwell.

Now, if female fat is sexuality and reproductive power; if food is honor; if dieting is semistarvation; if women have to lose 23 percent of their body weight to fit the Iron Maiden and chronic psychological disruption sets in at a body weight loss of 25 percent; if semistarvation is physically and psychologically debilitating, and female strength, sexuality, and self-respect pose the threats explored earlier against the vested interests of society; if women's journalism is sponsored by a $33-billion industry whose capital is made out of the political fear of women; then we can understand why the Iron Maiden is so thin. The thin "ideal" is not beautiful aesthetically; she is beautiful as a political solution. . . .

Hunger makes women feel poor and think poor. A wealthy woman on a diet feels physically at the mercy of a scarcity economy; the rare woman who makes $100,000 a year has a bodily income of 1,000 calories a day. Hunger makes successful women feel like failures: An architect learns that her work crumbles; a politician who oversees a long-range vision is returned to the details, to add up every bite; a woman who can afford to travel can't "afford" rich foreign foods. It undermines each experience of control, economic security, and leadership that women have had only a generation to learn to enjoy. Those who were so recently freed to think beyond the basics are driven, with this psychology, back to the feminine mental yoke of economic dependence: fixation on getting sustenance and safety. . . .

Anorexia is spreading because it works. Not only does it solve the dilemma of the young woman faced with the hunger cult, it also protects her from street harassment and sexual coercion; construction workers leave walking skeletons alone. Having no fat means having no breasts, thighs, hips, or ass, which for once means not having asked for it. Women's magazines tell women they *can* control their bodies; but women's experiences of sexual harassment make them feel they *cannot* control what their bodies are said to provoke. Our culture gives a young woman only two dreams in which to imagine her body, like a coin with two faces: one pornographic, the other anorexic; the first for nighttime, the second for day—the one, supposedly, for men and the other for other women. She does not have the choice to refuse to toss it—nor, yet, to demand a better dream. The anorexic body is sexually safer to inhabit than the pornographic. . . .

Sex, food, and flesh; it is only political ideology—not health, not men's desires, not any law of loveliness—that keeps women from believing we can have all three. Young women believe what they have no memory to question, that they may not have sex, food, and flesh in any abundance; that those three terms cancel each other out.

Dead Easy

It is dead easy to become an anorexic. When I was twelve I went to visit an older, voluptuous cousin. "I try," she said, to explain the deep-breathing exercises she did before bedtime, "to visualize my belly as something I can love and accept and live with." Still compact in a one-piece kid's body, I was alarmed to think that womanhood involved breaking apart into pieces that floated around, since my cousin seemed to be trying to hold herself together by a feat of concentration. It was not a comforting thought. The buds of my breasts hurt already. As she did her exercises, I leafed through a copy of *Cosmopolitan,* which had an article demonstrating to women how to undress and pose and move in bed with their partners so as to disguise their fatness.

My cousin looked me over. "Do you know how much you weigh?" No, I told her. "Why don't you just hop on the scale?" I could feel how much my cousin wished to inhabit a simple, slight twelve-year-old body. That could only mean, I thought, that when I was a woman, I would want to get out of my own body into some little kid's.

A year later, while bent over the drinking fountain in the hall of my junior high school, Bobby Werner, whom I hardly knew, gave me a hard poke in the soft part of my stomach, just below the navel. It would be a decade before I would remember that he was the class fat boy.

That evening I let the juice of the lamb chop congeal on my plate. I could see viscous nodules of fat, a charred outer edge of yellow matter, cooling from liquid to solid, marked USDA CHOICE in edible blue dye. The center bone, serrated, had been cloven with a powerful rotary blade. I felt a new feeling, a nausea wicked with the pleasure of loathing. Rising hungry from the table, a jet of self-righteousness lit up under my esophagus, intoxicating me. All night long I inhaled it.

The next day I passed the small notepad kept by the dishwasher. I knew what it said, though it was my mother's and private: "1/2 grpfruit. Blk. coff. 4 Wheat Thins. 1 Popsicle." A black scrawl: "*binge.*" I wanted to tear it up. Some memoir.

I had no more patience for the trivial confessions of women. I could taste from my mouth that my body had entered ketosis, imbalanced electrolytes—good. The girl stood on the burning deck. I put the dishes in the sink with a crash of declaration.

At thirteen, I was taking in the caloric equivalent of the food energy available to the famine victims of the siege of Paris. I did my schoolwork diligently and kept quiet in the classroom. I was a wind-up obedience toy. Not a teacher or principal or guidance counselor confronted me with an objection to my evident deportation in stages from the land of the living.

There were many starving girls in my junior high school, and every one was a teacher's paragon. We were allowed to come and go, racking up gold stars, as our hair fell out in fistfuls and the pads flattened behind the sockets of our eyes. When our eyeballs moved, we felt the resistance. They allowed us to haul our bones around the swinging rope in gym class, where nothing but the force of an exhausted will stood between the ceiling, to which we clung with hands so wasted the jute seemed to abrade the cartilage itself, and the polished wooden floor thirty-five feet below.

An alien voice took mine over. I have never been so soft-spoken. It lost expression and timbre and sank to a monotone, a dull murmur the opposite of strident. My teachers approved of me. They saw nothing wrong with what I was doing, and I could swear they looked straight at me. My school had stopped dissecting alleycats, since it was considered inhumane. There was no interference in my self-directed science experiment: to find out just how little food could keep a human body alive.

The dreams I could muster were none of the adolescent visions that boys have, or free and healthy girls; no fantasies of sex or escape, rebellion or future success. All the space I had for dreaming was taken up by food. When I lay on my bed, in that posture of adolescent reverie, I could find no comfort. My bones pressed sharply into the mattress. My ribs were hooks and my spine a dull blade and my hunger a heavy shield, all I had to stave off the trivialities that would attach themselves like parasites to my body the minute it made a misstep into the world of women. My doctor put his hand on my stomach and said he could feel my spine. I turned an eye cold with loathing on women who evidently lacked the mettle to suffer as I was suffering. . . .

Anorexia was the only way I could see to keep the dignity in my body that I had had as a kid, and that I would lose as a woman. It was the only choice that really looked like one: By refusing to put on a woman's body and receive a rating, I chose not to have all my future choices confined to little things, and not to have the choices made for me, on the basis of something meaningless to me, in the larger things. But as time went on, my choices grew smaller and smaller. Beef bouillon or hot water with lemon? The bouillion had twenty calories—I'd take the water. The lemon had four; I could live without it. Just. . . .

The larger world never gives girls the message that their bodies are valuable simply because they are inside them. Until our culture tells young girls that they are welcome in any shape—that women are valuable to it with or without the excuse of "beauty"—girls will continue to starve. And institutional messages then reward young women's education in hunger. But when the lesson has been taken too dangerously to heart, they ignore the consequences, reinforcing the disease. Anorexics want to be saved; but they cannot trust individual counselors, family members, or friends; that is too uncertain. They are walking question marks challenging—pleading—with schools, universities, and the other mouthpieces that transmit what is culturally acceptable in women, to tell them unequivocally: This is intolerable. This is unacceptable. We don't starve women here. We value women. By turning an indifferent eye to the ravages of the backlash among their young women, schools and universities are killing off America's daughters; and Europe is learning to do the same to its own. You don't need to die to count as a casualty. An anorexic cannot properly be called alive. To be anorexic is to keep a close daily tally of a slow death; to be a member of the walking undead. . . .

In college, we never had a chance to mourn for Sally. Dressed like a tatty rag doll, in faded ginghams and eyelet lace, she wore a peacock feather in an old hat. She kept her round kwashiorkor belly politely hidden and her vicious intelligence sheathed, but she was able to shred an argument into so much cotton wool and negligently hold up a conclusion sharp as quartz. Her small voice would come to a flat halt and her lips press whitely together. At parties she'd lean back her flossy head, so much too big for her body, to get the leverage to bang it again and again into the nearest wall; her brain loosened for comfort, she would dance like a Halloween creepie, waving her disjointed limbs. It was a campus set piece: "Play something good for Sally to dance to."

She left suddenly. Her roommates had to pack her things up after her: the postage scales for weighing the day's half bread roll; the fifteen-pound hand weights; the essay of devastating clarity left on her desk half-finished.

When I was told her strength had run out, I remembered one bright blue afternoon in autumn, when a group of students came out of a classroom, arguing, high on words. She dropped her books with a crash. Flinging back her shoulders, from which her sweater hung letting in great pockets of icy air, she turned in a slow pirouette, and leaped right up into the knot of the group. A boy caught her before she fell, and offered her to me, wriggling like a troublesome baby.

I held her between my forearms without strain. She'd made it. She had escaped gravity. Her limbs were as light as hollow birch branches, the scrolls of their bark whole, but the marrow crumbled, the sap gone brittle. I folded her up easily, because there was nothing to her.

Bundles of twigs, bones in worn-soled Nikes, slapping forward into a relentless weather; the young women cast shadows of Javanese stick-puppets, huge-headed, disappearing in a sideways light. Dry-mouthed like the old, unsteady, they head home on swollen knees while it is still morning.

Nothing justifies comparison with the Holocaust; but when confronted with a vast number of emaciated bodies starved not by nature but by men, one must notice a certain resemblance. The starving body cannot know it is middle-class. The imprisoned body cannot tell that it is considered free. The experience of living in a severely anorexic body, even if that body is housed in an affluent suburb, is the experience of a body living in Bergen-Belsen—if we imagine for the Belsen inmate a 40-percent chance of imprisonment forever and a 15-percent chance of death. These experiences are closer to one another than either is to that of a middle-class body that is not in prison in the affluent First World. Though I am trying to avoid the imagery of death camps, it returns. These young women weigh no more than the bodies documented in the archives of what is legitimately called Hell. They have, at their sickest, no more to eat; and they have no choice. For an unknown reason that must be physiological, at a certain point in their starvation they lose the ability to stop starving, the choice to eat. Finally—as is seldom acknowledged—they are hungry; I was hungry every conscious moment; I was hungry in my sleep.

Women must claim anorexia as political damage done to us by a social order that considers our destruction insignificant because of what we are—less. We should identify it as Jews identify the death camps, as homosexuals identify AIDS: as a disgrace that is not our own, but that of an inhumane social order.

Anorexia is a prison camp. One fifth of well-educated American young women are inmates. Susie Orbach compared anorexia to the hunger strikes of political prisoners, particularly the suffragists. But the time for metaphors is behind us. To be anorexic or bulimic *is* to be a political prisoner. . . .

Speculations

1. Naomi Wolf argues that "America" ignores the problem of women who starve themselves because the victims are women. Do you agree? Offer evidence from this essay and from other reading to substantiate your view as to whether women are valued as much as men in our society.

2. According to Wolf, it was only when "women's emancipation entered law" that the western, male, artistic tradition altered its view of women. What change occurred? Did it occur as a result of male backlash? What evidence does Wolf provide to support her argument? Is her evidence persuasive? Explain your answer.

3. When Naomi Wolf argues that the "One Stone Solution is political," what does she mean? Are women's eating habits bound up in notions of guilt, morality, and self-loathing? Explain your views fully, making appropriate use of quotations from Naomi Wolf and Nina Berman.

4. Wolf argues that "The ideology of semistarvation undoes feminism; what happens to women's bodies happens to our minds. If women's bodies are and have always been wrong whereas men's are right, then women are wrong and men are right." Do you

agree with this statement? Are anorexia and bulimia indirect expressions of male control over women? Support your views with evidence.

5. Wolf offers an extended autobiographical description of her own experience with anorexia. Is this confessional account persuasive? Why do you think Wolf chooses to reveal herself in this way? In what ways does this narrative either strengthen or weaken Wolf's arguments?

6. Toward the end of her essay, Wolf writes: "Nothing justifies comparison with the Holocaust; but when confronted with a vast number of emaciated bodies starved not by nature but by men, one must notice a certain resemblance." Is Wolf exaggerating here, or is the implied comparison between the Holocaust and anorexia justified? Throughout the essay, do you think Wolf's style—her use of images, her expressions of outrage and anger—are effective? Cite several examples and offer a short commentary.

LEARNING TO BE SUPERIOR

Ben Greenstein

Although it has received little media attention, Ben Greenstein's *The Fragile Male* raises the simple but significant and disturbing question: what does it mean to be "a man?" Greenstein admits in his Preface that he was ultimately "unable to answer it." Moreover, his investigation into what it means to be male made him:

> . . . infinitely more uneasy than when I started. I discovered that the human male is far more dangerous than I could ever have imagined, mainly because he does not understand just how dangerous he is. And there is no telling how much more dangerous he will become as women increasingly take over most of his natural male functions.

Greenstein in many ways seems an unlikely candidate to write such a book. Born in South Africa, Greenstein married and moved to Britain in 1966 where he lives with his wife and two sons. A biologist who has spent over twenty years studying hormones and brain differences in men and women, Greenstein has taught and conducted research focusing on endocrine-related diseases at both Oxford and London Universities. He currently heads a team at a London teaching hospital that is researching the causes of rheumatoid arthritis and systemic lupus erythematosus. The author of *Endocrinology at a Glance* and coeditor of the international scientific journal, *Endocrine*, Greenstein has published highly technical scientific essays such as "Effects of rat alfafetoprotein administration on estradiol free fraction, on the onset of puberty and on neural and uterine estrogen receptors."

Greenstein deserves serious consideration not only for raising troubling issues about maleness, but also for bringing scientific evidence to bear on social and cultural issues. As he states, most such information is buried in "abstruse" scientific language and is thus "unavailable to the general public." Greenstein's intent is to "transmit a small amount of that information" for he believes that scientists "should think seriously about filling an enormous gap in their publishing repertoire, and [should] widen the audience for their often intriguing and controversial data." The following chapter from Greenstein's book represents his effort to do just that; it offers strong evidence that gender roles are shaped less by genetics than by peers and parents.

A teacher in a London primary school asked her class of 11-year-olds to write an essay. She gave them a choice between two titles: "A visit to my Granny", or "The Leader". All the boys chose the latter topic, and all the girls chose the former. The teacher made no suggestions and the children did not discuss their choice of essay title before they started writing. This modest experiment produced a result which shows that little boys and girls think very differently about certain aspects of life.

That statement might be inflammatory to many people, but it is true nonetheless, and in this chapter many examples will bear out its validity. What is *not* claimed here, however, is that this sex difference in thought and attitude is genetically determined. Even so, that possibility exists, and is fiercely debated. There is a great deal of evidence that children are taught at home, at school, at play and at university to think according to their genetic sex, and there is no evidence that this master plan for producing adult men and women has changed to any significant extent, despite the efforts of the Women's Movement. Nature or nurture; which is it, and can anything be done to change attitudes? More importantly, is there a will?

The nature versus nurture theory takes up a lot of paper and time, and people can't agree about the relative importance of genetic imprinting and learning. With regard to the development of gender identity, the controversy is particularly confusing. There are those who swear blind that males are born to pin-striped suits and the boardroom, while females are doomed by their chromosomes to a life in the scullery. This assertion is based mainly on observations of other species, and of men and women's behavior through history. But those who have actually gone into the home, nursery and classroom have come away with evidence that from a very early age boys are groomed to think they are the superior sex. How did they learn this?

One might be forgiven for thinking their teachers are other males. After all, men have a vested interest in perpetuating the myth. Fathers who have sweated away their lives building up a small, medium or large material empire want to think it will be left in safe, strong hands, hopefully those of a worthy son and heir. Therefore they will be anxious to ensure that from an early age their sons are taught how to be tough, decisive and unafraid.

Successful modern men are no less concerned than were their forefathers that their sons should grow into warriors and hunters. But they are too busy to attend personally to the inculcation of their boys with the necessary predatory qualities. So they look to educational institutions to provide the right milieu in which a steady, reliable pool of young bulls can be nurtured. Who better to teach these qualities, or help to bring them out but other men. And indeed in some societies, particularly primitive ones, boys are removed from their homes at a certain age and handed over to men of the tribe who will teach them how to be men. This sexual difference in nurturing was practiced in relatively sophisticated cultures from way back, for example in ancient Sparta. In Britain there is an attenuated example of this primitive practice in the form of the elitist boys' and girls' public schools in which boys are taught mainly by men and girls are taught by women. But in most western societies boys and girls sit side by side in class. And if we look at the sex of the teachers whose influence will be greatest in determining gender identity, we find that in the main they are female. And this doesn't apply only to humans. How much time do males spend with their young? Let's have a quick look at some other species.

Among certain forms of life, parental care is minimal or non-existent. Many parents will never know their young at all. It is unlikely that most species of fish, snakes, turtles and aphids would recognize their own offspring if they bumped into each other in bright sunlight. It has to be concluded, therefore, that the males of those species are not taught to behave like males. Yet they grow up to behave and possibly think like males. It's all enshrined in the genes. They are tightly locked into maleness, and there seems to be no possibility that they have any choice. They do not deviate from their chromosomally determined sex. We cannot say anything about their attitude to the female, assuming they have one.

Certain males will never look after their young. The male Canadian salmon dies, exhausted, after fertilizing the 3000–5000 eggs his mate has laid. She, too, is killed by her reproductive effort. Neither fish was in good condition anyway, having battled miles upstream to their spawning ground. This is semelparity, or self-destruct reproduction. The male salmon isn't the only species to die of parenthood.

In Australia there lives the small nocturnal marsupial, *Antichinus stuartii*. The males of this species copulate with the females, and when the females fall pregnant the males all die within three weeks of mating. Since pregnancy lasts around four weeks, the males never see their offspring. Females, on the other hand, live to breed again.

Many species of father, however, are involved to a greater or lesser extent in the raising of their young. This can last a few days, as we have already seen in the case of the fighting fish, or for many years, as in the case of the human. And the degree of commitment can be quite awesome, even if short-lived.

The male grey-faced petrel will sit on a single egg for seventeen days while his mate flies over 600 km to the nearest fishing grounds. When she returns, she sits while he flies off for a meal. Thus they alternate until the chick hatches out after an incubation period of fifty-five days. They time things pretty well too; the female arrives back just in time for the hatching. She regurgitates food for the chick, who might otherwise have had to wait days for its first meal. Both male and female rear the chick for four months until it takes off on its own. This is a good example of devoted synchronized cooperation between male and female parents to maximize the chances of successfully raising a single offspring.

Examples of what we call biparental care are far less common among mammals. It is rare to find a male who shares in his mate's maternal duties. More commonly, males and females have different parental roles. The female is more likely to be the direct carer, nursing, holding, feeding and grooming her young. The male is the indirect carer. He finds shelter, roams far afield to obtain food, protects his family, and may assist his male offspring to obtain a mate.

The female invests much more time and energy in infant care than does the male. The male is usually too far away to be of much help, especially if he is a wild carnivore. But even if the male stays close to home he may still pay little attention to the rearing of his young. Witness, for example, the lumbering male elephant seal who will squash to death one or more of his young in his eagerness to mount the female. One supposes that he doesn't care, even though he is certain the young are his.

After studying the behavior of many male mammals, one is forced to conclude that their young offspring do not get much attention from them. So it is unlikely that the fathers teach them how to be a male or how to behave towards the female. So who does? Of course we know very little about how animals of other species communicate with each other, and it is possible that a great deal of teaching and learning does go on in these families. But if the young, for example ducklings or cygnets, are learning gender identity from their parents, they must surely be primed genetically at a very fundamental level to absorb and reproduce appropriate behavior patterns, a situation vastly different from the complex discriminatory learning abilities of the primates, especially those of the human child.

In the case of the other primates we have no idea how the male views the female. We shall probably never know if he worships the ground she walks on, is tortured with homicidal jealousy or regards her as inferior in any way. There is very little doubt, however, that the human male has definite views about the role of the female. Most importantly, he views her role biologically and socially as different from his own. Here is a list of statements made by men, women, girls and boys who were asked what they thought about sharing role-duties and play, and about prospects:

A construction worker: "Ain't natural. If God had wanted women to make buildings he'd have given 'em muscles, wouldn't he?"

Boy of ten: "Girls can't do what we do. They don't have the brains. Anyway, they're silly and just giggle."

Housewife: "Personally, I'm glad to let them go out there and tear each other to pieces, dear. It's much safer at home."

Male doctor: "We've opened Pandora's box, mate."

Girl of fifteen: "My mum ended up in the kitchen all her life, and I expect I'll end up there too. Like she says, men have got it all, haven't they?"

Sixteen-year-old boy: "Thank God I'm not a girl, having to worry about rape and all that shit. I feel really sorry for them. But that's life, isn't it. I mean, women make babies, don't they? How can they expect anything else."

Eighteen-year-old girl: "I don't go round feeling their bums at work. I wish they'd keep their hands to themselves."

Playschool teacher: "By the time they get here they know what's expected of them. They already know how to be boys and girls."

Indeed they do. Boys, particularly, have very strong ideas about the image they are meant to project. They also know, or think they know, how to view girls.

Humans are one of the few species to nurse their offspring all the way up to adulthood. And there is a great deal of evidence to show that it is during this period that the male learns to be superior and girls are taught to be mere females. A boy's initial schooling is at home, and what he learns there is reinforced when he goes to school and at other centers of socialization within the male child's cultural environment. Let's look more closely at the parents themselves, especially the father.

From birth onwards, from the point when parents first learn the sex of their offspring, their behavior towards their child is dictated by its sex. Boys will be given boys' toys and girls will get dolls, dollhouses and pink wallpaper. From the word go, boys are shown how to behave differently from girls. As they grow older, they will receive parental rewards for behavior appropriate to their gender, and they will be punished for aberrant behavior. Parents unwittingly initiate sex typing of their babies. They have strong ideas about gender and appearance. Both men and women will describe newborn girls as "softer," having finer features, and being less attentive than baby boys, despite studies which do not find these physical sex differences between infant boys and girls. Women with babies of their own have been presented with six-month-old baby boys dressed as girls and vice versa. When they thought the babies were boys they reacted to them with physical play, whereas those they assumed to be girls were soothed and comforted in an entirely different way. Fathers, too, respond differently according to perceived sex. In fact, fathers will play preferentially with sons rather than with daughters. And this parental preference for a male offspring probably manifests itself as soon as the father learns the sex of his new baby. Thus from a very early point there is pressure on the child to fulfil the gender identity demands made by others.

There is more pressure on boys to conform than there is on girls. This is an important point; it may help in understanding why boys consider that they have to dominate girls. The fact is that there is more pressure on boys to behave like boys than there is on girls to behave like girls. The daughter who enjoys boys' rough-and-tumble play is labeled a tom-boy and nobody minds very much. She'll grow out of it, they say fondly. But a boy who likes to play with dolls, who behaves like a girl and becomes labeled a sissie is likely to be punished by a father who fears he has spawned a homosexual. The father feels that his son will lack power and status in a tough man's world. Thus boys tend to suffer more punishment than do girls. Also, fathers, particularly those who have not come up to their own expectations in life, may transfer those ambitions to their sons. Very rarely, however, do they so burden their daughters. Their son will be rich, rise to the top of their profession, win the Nobel Prize or even become prime minister or president. Not only do fathers transfer these dreams, they make them known to the children, sometimes in subtle, but nonetheless, unmistakable ways. This tactic places heavy pressure on sons to fulfill their father's expectations. Young boys worship their fathers, and it is usually during this period of uncritical adulation that fathers strike. Boys therefore walk around from a relatively early age carrying a burden of responsibility, real or imagined, towards their fathers.

Girls, on the other hand, often have a different battle on their hands. Their fathers may want the exact opposite for them. We have already seen that in primitive (and not so primitive) societies, men view their women as property, and guard them jealously. Daughters in these societies are constrained from a very early age. They may never have the company of a boy until they are introduced by their parents to the man they are going to marry. Fathers ensure that their daughters are hidden away, but they leave their education to the women.

In western societies this rigid educational stricture has all but disappeared. Daughters are free to go to school, play with boys and girls, and are free to choose their own profession. But until their late teens they are still under the influence of a less overtly jealous male parent, but a jealous male nevertheless. Many fathers secretly disapprove of their independent, at times pushy daughters who seem to have picked up many of the ways and ideas of their brothers. Modern western fathers have backed away from confrontation with their daughters, but they have not given up the fight.

This stereotyping of gender is reinforced by the children themselves within their own peer groups. A three-year-old boy who expressed a desire to make a meal was told by a little girl that "daddies don't cook." Three to four-year-old children are unlikely to initiate play with other children if the game involves opposite gender activity. We have to ask whether this comes naturally or whether their play is basically in imitation of their parents. Girls tend to play in small groups, often in pairs; girls place very high value on "best friends." Their play is non-competitive and cooperative. They don't cope well with quarrels, which easily break up the group. As if to steer clear of this danger, girls at play criticize carefully and subtly. They listen carefully, confide willingly and interpret correctly.

Boys play together very differently. They organize their play, but in larger groups. Not for them the cosy intimacy of a confidence, but the loud proclamation of self, the young male rampant. They will be loud and individualistic, full of posture and bombast. The aim is not to share but to take; to take the respect of the other boys if they can: to take leadership; to rule. Speech is directed to these ends.

Boys don't like naked aggression which could result in injury, and differences are quickly patched up. The threat is generally considered enough. Physical aggression for its own sake is feared and the bully is avoided and shunned. Boys establish hierarchies within their peer groups. Leaders do emerge, and they dictate the type and duration of play. The subordinate boys in the group fall into their tiers enthusiastically and willingly. They seem instinctively to know how to make submissive gestures towards the leaders, although it is possible that they have learned these at home. Subordinate boys work hard to maintain the hierarchy, and will turn on those lower in the hierarchy who attempt to promote another male to a position of dominance.

This is all recognizably male-type play, and similar behavior can be observed among adult primates. It could be hypothesized that instinctive (and some learned) behavior in boys is generated by an accumulation of limited experience, immaturity and a developing IQ which puts them temporarily on a par with other primates. Much human juvenile male play is directed towards the establishment and maintenance of superiority over other males.

It is unlikely, however, that pre-adolescent boys fear girls enough to attempt to exert superiority over them. Boys and girls rarely play together, and pair playing with the cautious exploration of sex differences is unlikely to propagate the attitudes that result in the adult male's view of the female.

The lessons don't end at home or in the street. The differences are reinforced at school, especially up to the age of five. In a class of pre-primary school children, it has been noticed that the teachers are more attentive to boys than they are to girls. Furthermore, the help they give to boys is more likely to lead to independence. Girls are taught to be more dependent. Nursery school teachers (women) have been observed to encourage girls to touch each other freely, while boys were discouraged from doing so. Boys were actively encouraged to play "male" games and girls were steered towards the dolls and the wendy house. And if there was any tendency to cross the gender line, teachers swiftly moved in to put in a stop to such "aberrant" behavior.

Are teachers aware that they are doing this? It is sobering to ponder that in these classes the teachers are almost always women. Even in schools where a stated aim was to avoid sex typing, stereotypes were being unconsciously perpetuated. Girls were complimented for wearing pretty dresses but not when they wore pretty trousers. Boys got no compliments for nice clothes. When boys fought, they received praise.

Why should teachers, particularly female ones, unconsciously want to help create the dominant male? Are they merely looking after their jobs? It is just possible that a father who hears that his young son and heir fools around with dolls at kindergarten is going to see to it that someone gets the sack. But the reasons may be far deeper than the fear of losing a job. The teacher may be driven by forces well outside her own control. Her ancestor created man to protect and provide for her, and it is therefore in her own interests to do all she can to help to release into the world as perfect a specimen of the aggressive, independent and dominant male as she can. It matters not that she may have read books pointing out the injustices embedded in a gender-oriented society. Despite the exhortations of friends and newspaper articles she knows, really knows, how the males out there feel about competition from women. Far safer to stick to rules laid down many thousands of years ago. By the same token she will teach little girls the way she herself was taught as a child.

The problem doesn't stop in nursery school. As children grow older they continue to get powerful messages, particularly in mixed sex schools, which reinforce fixed ideas about male dominance and female passivity. It is evident that in the classroom boys get more publicity for bad behavior. Cause trouble and you're sure to be noticed, not only by the teacher, but also by the rest of the class. Boys will also get punished for violent and aggressive behavior, the punishment itself often violent and aggressive. Boys notice that girls receive less harsh punishments and conclude that girls must be a weaker sex. Boys also learn early on that rough behavior gets them into the limelight. They do not fail to notice dad's covert approval when they are punished for fighting.

And it isn't only during social interactions that boys are taught to view themselves as superior to girls. They are encouraged to take academic subjects that have been considered for many years to be "too difficult" for girls.

One of the more sexually slanted subjects at school is undoubtedly mathematics. Traditionally, boys are encouraged to study math, which is a subject associated with prestigious and high status jobs. Teachers of math are more likely to be men. In some schools girls are actively discouraged from studying math. Yet there is no evidence that boys are better at the subject than are girls. This doesn't stop teachers and parents from encouraging boys to do the subject both at school and afterwards at university, and discouraging girls. It follows from this that teachers of math are more likely to be men than women, and one is tempted to feel that this is yet another example of the male protection racket. There is little doubt that if teachers encouraged girls to do math, more girls would, and do well in the subject, as has been happening in Britain. Statistics from the British Department of Education show that girls' performance in GCSE mathematics examinations improved dramatically from 1991 to 1992.

Some educationalists would argue that boys and girls (and men and women) show clear-cut differences in the types of mental skills they have, and that these are not learned, but inherent. They will point to several tests which prove that men have better spatial skills than do women. They are better at map-reading, maze problem solving, and at recognizing specified shapes when these are imbedded in complex designs. But where girls and boys are being given equal attention in the classroom, it turns out that girls are performing as well as, and in some cases better than, the boys in many spheres.

The gospel of male superiority continues to be preached, however, by the media.

Would Batwoman have been as successful a film as was Batman? Why wasn't Tarzan a woman? The answer, quite simply, lies in the box office receipts. They just wouldn't pull in the customers. Any boy who takes his movies seriously has no doubt that you need a Rambo or Schwarzenegger to get things done, and a woman would only get in the way. If she is involved in the action, she's usually in trouble and threatened with death or worse, and, ironically enough, it is only the raging, glistening, muscle-rippling male who can help. His reward is of course her body.

Women make lousy screen heroes for the male viewer. They just aren't believable in the macho theme park of artificial violence. They don't do it in real life so why should they do it on the big screen. A man walks out of the cinema shaken and stirred after a dose of Robert De Niro as *Raging Bull*, and sits hypnotized through Coppola's *Apocalypse Now*. He can even identify with male American Indian heroes in Costner's film *Dances with Wolves*. But the same guy slouches out of Woody Allen's *Hannah and Her Sisters* feeling vaguely cheated.

Similarly, television advertisements leave us in no doubt as to the natural superiority and importance of the male. He is out there ruling big business, driving superb motor cars or jetting in to a golden beach where a stunning blonde in a transparent pink dress stands barefoot waiting to run (in slow motion) to her man. Her sister might stand flustered before a washing machine while the visiting engineer subliminally seduces her with the potency of his washing powder and his masculinity.

The advertisers know what they're doing. They appreciate the thinness of the veneer. They can peel it away more easily than you can peel a banana. And in a boy or girl that veneer is exceedingly thin. The developing mind is very close to its ancestry. The lines are open and reinforcement of the message is going on all the time.

It is not surprising, therefore, to learn that boys would hate to be girls, and many girls would much rather be boys. American boys who were asked how they would see themselves as girls answered that they would have to spend more time at home helping mother, be more concerned about appearance and worry about being raped. They felt that they would be much more restricted. Girls felt that as boys they would have far more freedom, be liberated from a sex-object status and, poignantly, get more time with their father. In view of this, it is worth trying to find out in more depth how the father, or his absence, affects the home and the child.

There is plenty of evidence that by the second half of an infant's first year, an emotional bond is formed between the infant and one or both of its parents. Between the ages of nine to twenty-four months, infants direct attachment and affiliative responses to parents and strangers. However, babies do not show clear-cut differences in preference for mothers or fathers if both are available. If preferences are shown, it is all from the parental side. In other words, favoritism stems from parents and not from their children.

As far as play is concerned, the influence of the father over his child is far more powerful than that of the mother. Mothers tend to engage in more dainty and conventional games such as pat-a-cake, while fathers like more rough-and-tumble play. By the time an infant reaches its second year, it will initiate physical games with a father, and as the infant gets older, the frequency of physical play increases. In a laboratory test, two-thirds of children aged two and a half preferred to play with their father rather than with their mother. The influence of the father on the developing child cannot be underestimated. He is in a unique position to imprint attitudes in the minds of the children of either sex.

Parents, especially mothers and young first-timers, when alerted to the problem of stereotyping react with some fear and apprehension. What ought they to do? What is best for the child? If the parental behavioral input is so influential in determining gender regardless of sex, how is a parent to behave? Is it better to stand back and allow gender to develop from within the very young child, and to try to counter the peer group pressures that will inevitably come the child's way? Or should one consciously accept the way things are and adopt the pink for girls and blue for boys philosophy?

If nature dictates gender as rigidly as it dictates sex, then attempts to distort the self-image could be very damaging, creating strains within the developing child that would present as neuroses or worse later in life. A parent or parents who deliberately coach their son to believe that non-violent, non-competitive play is good and preferable to violent tumbling and fighting may not be doing him any favors. Those who send a crying son back into the boyhood jungle to turn the other cheek instead of striking back may turn a future success story into one of failure. A mild-mannered, yielding boy with soaring poetic vision is not going to be suitable material for a father with hopes of creating a shipping magnate or heavyweight boxer.

On the other hand, it might be argued that without parental intervention a potentially wonderful, well-focused and gender-normal future adult may never happen because the child was allowed to wander unguided. If the boy was not fondled and tossed often into the air as a baby, if he was not tumbled in play-fights with his dad, and if he was not dissuaded from playing with his mum's bra, stockings and lipstick, is it possible that he might grow up to be unsure of his gender?

No answers to those questions are available. But through observing parents at play in a wide range of cultures, some common patterns emerge. It appears that no matter where in the world one looks, fathers are rougher with sons than they are with daughters. They are not generally brutal or cruel, just rough, and one wonders whether there isn't a genetic component to gender-directed behavior after all, and that attempting to modify or interfere with it could be damaging to the father as well as the son. Learning and pattern imprinting is a two-way process, and it is possible that by allowing his instincts to govern the nature of his play and other activities with his son, that a father is giving expression to his own masculinity. If fathers consciously suppress this expression, they too may become stressed.

The human father, no less than the lion, wants to nurture and grow more males, to ensure the survival of his genes. He is primarily concerned to protect his own offspring and cares little, if anything, for the genes of another male. Human societies ensure that the male's role development and ultimate self-image are reinforced both inside and outside the home.

By the time a boy gets to being a man he is primed and ready to be one. And at this point he discovers that he is going out of fashion, especially at work.

Speculations

1. Nature vs. Nurture? In the beginning of this selection, Greenstein stakes out his position: "What is not claimed here, however, is that this sex difference in thought and attitude is genetically determined." Instead, Greenstein believes that sex differences are primarily caused by human actions and behaviors. Does Greenstein make a good case? Why do you think he begins his argument by focusing on this issue?

2. Greenstein looks to scientific studies to answer the question, "How much time do males spend with their young?" Is this rhetorical strategy effective? What is Greenstein's point? What larger argument is he trying to make about how children learn appropriate behaviors?

3. "There is more pressure on boys to conform than there is on girls," writes Greenstein. He then offers evidence for this proposition. Drawing from your own experience, agree or disagree with Greenstein. If you agree, what do you think causes these differences in conformity between boys and girls?

4. Why do teachers, according to Greenstein, reinforce gender stereotypes in the ways they treat children? Are his explanations persuasive? Is he right when he states that the teaching of mathematics is gendered toward boys? Agree or disagree, supporting your view with examples.

5. Greenstein attacks film and advertising for their reductive images of men and women. Are his arguments compelling? Do these two media create these images or are they merely responding to social preferences, the desires of American audiences?

6. How would you characterize Greenstein's tone in this essay? Is he reasonable? witty? compassionate? friendly? objective? angry? Choose three or four phrases to illustrate each of the various tones that you find in this essay.

JUST WALK ON BY: A BLACK MAN PONDERS HIS POWER TO ALTER PUBLIC SPACE

Brent Staples

Brent Staples was born in Chester, Pennsylvania, in 1951. In this selection, he describes Chester as a "small, angry industrial town" that provided an unnerving backdrop of "gang warfare, street knifings, and murders." Familiar with street violence and sensitive to the vulnerability we all sometimes feel in public spaces, Staples describes himself as shy and "one of the good boys" who had only a few fist fights when he was growing up. As an adult he learned to smother his own anger at being taken for a criminal and to whistle cheerful tunes on dark streets so his own large frame would not frighten others passing by.

Staples earned a Ph.D. in psychology from the University of Chicago and is a member of the editorial board of the *New York Times,* where he writes on politics and culture. He has published articles in many magazines and newspapers, and has been a staff reporter for the *Chicago Sun Times.* His autobiography, *Parallel Time: Growing Up in Black and White* was published in 1994 to enthusiastic reviews.

My first victim was a woman—white, well dressed, probably in her early twenties. I came upon her late one evening on a deserted street in Hyde Park, a relatively affluent neighborhood in an otherwise mean, impoverished section of Chicago. As I swung onto the avenue behind her, there seemed to be a discreet, uninflammatory distance between us. Not so. She cast back a worried glance. To her, the youngish black man—a broad six feet two inches with a beard and billowing hair, both hands shoved into the pockets of a bulky military jacket— seemed menacingly close. After a few more quick glimpses, she picked up her pace and was soon running in earnest. Within seconds she disappeared into a cross street.

That was more than a decade ago. I was twenty-two years old, a graduate student newly arrived at the University of Chicago. It was in the echo of that terrified woman's footfalls that I first began to know the unwieldy inheritance I'd come into—the ability to alter public space in ugly ways. It was clear that she thought herself the quarry of a mugger, a rapist, or worse. Suffering a bout of insomnia, however, I was stalking sleep, not defenseless wayfarers. As a softy who is scarcely able to take a knife to a raw chicken—let alone hold it to a person's throat—I was surprised, embarrassed, and dismayed all at once. Her flight made me feel like an accomplice in tyranny. It also made it clear that I was indistinguishable from the muggers who occasionally seeped into the area from the surrounding ghetto. That first encounter, and those that followed, signified that a vast, unnerving gulf lay between nighttime pedestrians—particularly women—and me. And I soon gathered that being perceived as dangerous is a hazard in itself. I only needed to turn a corner into a dicey situation, or crowd some frightened, armed person in a foyer somewhere, or make an errant move after being pulled over by a policeman. Where fear and weapons meet—and they often do in urban America—there is always the possibility of death.

In that first year, my first away from my hometown, I was to become thoroughly familiar with the language of fear. At dark, shadowy intersections in Chicago, I could cross in front of a car stopped at a traffic light and elicit the *thunk, thunk, thunk, thunk* of the driver—black, white, male, or female—hammering down the door locks. On less traveled streets after dark, I grew accustomed to but never comfortable with people who crossed to the other side of the street rather than pass me. Then there were the standard unpleasantries with police, doormen, bouncers, cab drivers, and others whose business it is to screen out troublesome individuals *before* there is any nastiness.

I moved to New York nearly two years ago and I have remained an avid night walker. In central Manhattan, the near-constant crowd cover minimizes tense one-on-one street encounters. Elsewhere—visiting friends in SoHo, where sidewalks are narrow and tightly spaced buildings shut out the sky—things can get very taut indeed.

Black men have a firm place in New York mugging literature. Norman Podhoretz in his famed (or infamous) 1963 essay, "My Negro Problem—And Ours," recalls growing up in terror of black males; they "were tougher than we were, more ruthless," he writes—and as an adult on the Upper West Side of Manhattan, he continues, he cannot constrain his nervousness when he meets black men on certain streets. Similarly, a decade later, the essayist and novelist Edward Hoagland extols a New York where once "Negro bitterness bore down mainly on other Negroes." Where some see mere panhandlers, Hoagland sees "a mugger who is clearly screwing up his nerve to do more than just *ask* for money." But Hoagland has "the New Yorker's quick-hunch posture for broken-field maneuvering," and the bad guy swerves away.

I often witness that "hunch posture," from women after dark on the warrenlike streets of Brooklyn where I live. They seem to set their faces on neutral and, with their purse straps strung across their chests bandolier style, they forge ahead as though bracing themselves against being tackled. I understand, of course, that the danger they perceive is not a hallucination. Women are particularly vulnerable to street violence, and young black males are drastically overrepresented among the perpetrators of that violence. Yet these truths are no solace against the kind of alienation that comes of being ever the suspect, against being set apart, a fearsome entity with whom pedestrians avoid making eye contact.

It is not altogether clear to me how I reached the ripe old age of twenty-two without being conscious of the lethality nighttime pedestrians attributed to me. Perhaps it was because in Chester, Pennsylvania, the small, angry industrial town where I came of age in the 1960s, I was scarcely noticeable against a backdrop of gang warfare, street knifings, and murders. I grew up one of the good boys, had perhaps a half-dozen fist fights. In retrospect, my shyness of combat has clear sources.

Many things go into the making of a young thug. One of those things is the consummation of the male romance with the power to intimidate. An infant discovers that random flailings send the baby bottle flying out of the crib and crashing to the floor. Delighted, the joyful babe repeats those motions again and again, seeking to duplicate the feat. Just so, I recall the points at which some of my boyhood friends were finally seduced by the perception of themselves as tough guys. When a mark cowered and surrendered his money without resistance, myth and reality merged—and paid off. It is, after all, only manly to embrace the power to frighten and intimidate. We, as men, are not supposed to give an inch of our lane on the highway; we are to seize the fighter's edge in work and in play and even in love; we are to be valiant in the face of hostile forces.

Unfortunately, poor and powerless young men seem to take all this nonsense literally. As a boy, I saw countless tough guys locked away; I have since buried several, too. They were babies, really—a teenage cousin, a brother of twenty-two, a childhood friend in his mid-twenties—all gone down in episodes of bravado played out in the streets. I came to doubt the virtues of intimidation early on. I chose, perhaps even unconsciously, to remain a shadow—timid, but a survivor.

The fearsomeness mistakenly attributed to me in public places often has a perilous flavor. The most frightening of these confusions occurred in the late 1970s and early 1980s when I worked as a journalist in Chicago. One day, rushing into the office of a magazine I was writing for with a deadline story in hand, I was mistaken for a burglar. The office manager called security and, with an ad hoc posse, pursued me through the labyrinthine halls, nearly to my editor's door. I had no way of proving who I was. I could only move briskly toward the company of someone who knew me.

Another time I was on assignment for a local paper and killing time before an interview. I entered a jewelry store on the city's affluent Near North Side. The proprietor excused herself and returned with an enormous red Doberman pinscher straining at the end of a leash. She stood, the dog extended toward me, silent to my questions, her eyes bulging nearly out of her head. I took a cursory look around, nodded, and bade her good night. Relatively speaking, however, I never fared as badly as another black male journalist. He went to nearby Waukegan, Illinois, a couple of summers ago to work on a story about a murderer who was born there. Mistaking the reporter for the killer, police hauled him from his car at gunpoint and but for his press credentials would probably have tried to book him. Such episodes are not uncommon. Black men trade tales like this all the time.

In "My Negro Problem—And Ours," Podhoretz writes that the hatred he feels for blacks makes itself known to him through a variety of avenues—one being his discomfort with that "special brand of paranoid touchiness" to which he says blacks are prone. No doubt he is speaking here of black men. In time, I learned to smother the rage I felt at so often being taken for a criminal. Not to do so would surely have led to madness—via that special "paranoid touchiness" that so annoyed Podhoretz at the time he wrote the essay.

I began to take precautions to make myself less threatening. I move about with care, particularly late in the evening. I give a wide berth to nervous people on subway platforms during the wee hours, particularly when I have exchanged business clothes for jeans. If I happen to be entering a building behind some people who appear skittish, I may walk by, letting them clear the lobby before I return, so as not to seem to be following them. I have been calm and extremely congenial on those rare occasions when I've been pulled over by the police.

And on late-evening constitutionals along streets less traveled by, I employ what has proved to be an excellent tension-reducing measure: I whistle melodies from Beethoven and Vivaldi and the more popular classical composers. Even steely New Yorkers hunching toward nighttime destinations seem to relax, and occasionally they even join in the tune. Virtually everybody seems to sense that a mugger wouldn't be warbling bright, sunny selections from Vivaldi's *Four Seasons*. It is my equivalent of the cowbell that hikers wear when they know they are in bear country.

Speculations

1. "My first victim was a woman—white, well dressed, probably in her early twenties," Staples writes. Why does he choose to open his essay this way?
2. Staples talks about the "male romance with the power to intimidate" as a way of explaining why boys grow up to be young thugs. Describe what alternatives existed to bravado and street death other than "remain a shadow—timid, but a survivor"?

3. Staples describes the fear and intimidation which his presence on dark streets caused in others. How does his recognition of their fear help him understand himself and his relationship to others? What does he learn about himself from the ways others see him?

4. Have you either been the perpetrator or the victim in a situation similar to the ones that Staples describes? What happened? What factors created the fear and intimidation? How could the situation have been prevented? How did the experience change you?

5. Comparing the first three paragraphs of this essay with the last two paragraphs, describe the changes that take place in Staples's behavior.

6. How would you describe Staple's tone in this essay? Does he think the response that he receives (mostly from women) is funny? By adopting this particular stance, what is Staples implying about his purpose and his audience?

THE FRATERNAL BOND AS A JOKING RELATIONSHIP

Peter Lyman

A political scientist by training, Peter Lyman is a university librarian at the University of California, Berkeley. "I have a strange history," he told us. "I'm a political scientist by training. I studied anger for many years, anger in political and social movements. The women's anger I describe in 'The Fraternal Bond as a Joking Relationship' came from injustice, and it was my interest in anger that helped me to write the piece. I haven't done much research in gender, but my wife's a famous sociologist of gender (Barrie Thorne), and I've learned a lot from her about gender and power."

A native Californian, Lyman was born in San Francisco and grew up in Lake Oswego, Oregon. His professional interests include writing about computers and technology, an increasing trend in libraries throughout the country. Concerning "The Fraternal Bond," Lyman explained that "I just happened into the research setting. The essay is about how jokes are not just fun but how sex jokes are the way power is created in everyday life. I was trying to describe how this happens, rather than make moral judgments. It's probably the best thing I've ever written, and it was a complete accident." Accident or not, Lyman's essay provides a telling analysis of the ways that young men in group settings use "jokes" that demean and insult women in order to bond among themselves.

One evening during dinner, forty-five fraternity men suddenly broke into the dining room of a nearby campus sorority, surrounded the thirty women residents, and forced them to watch while one pledge gave a speech on Freud's theory of penis envy as another demonstrated various techniques of masturbation with a rubber penis. The women sat silently staring downward at their plates listening for about ten minutes, until a woman law student who was the graduate resident in charge of the house walked in, surveyed the scene, and demanded, "Please leave immediately!" As she later described that moment, "There was a mocking roar from the men, 'It's tradition.' I said, 'That's no reason to do something like this, please leave!' And they left. I was surprised. Then the women in the house started to get angry. And the guy who made the penis envy speech came back and said to us, 'That was funny to me. If that's not funny to you I don't know what kind of sense of humor you have, but I'm sorry.'"

That night the women sat around the stairwell of their house discussing the event, some angry and others simply wanting to forget the whole thing. They finally decided to ask the university to require that the men return to discuss the event. When university officials threatened to take action, the men agreed to the meeting. I was asked by both the men and the women involved to attend the discussion as a facilitator, and was given permission to write about the event as long as I concealed their identities.

In the women's view, the joke had not failed because of its subject; they considered sexual jokes to be a normal part of the erotic joking relationship between men and women. They criticized its emotional structure, the mixture of sexuality with aggression and the atmosphere of physical intimidation in the room. Although many of the men individually regretted the damage to their relationship with women friends in the group, they argued that the special group solidarity created by the initiation was a unique form of masculine friendship that justified the inconvenience caused the women.

Fraternal group bonding in everyday life frequently takes the form of *joking relationships,* in which men relate to each other by exchanging insults and jokes in order to create a feeling of solidarity that negotiates the latent tension and aggression they feel toward each other (Radcliffe-Brown, 1959). The humor of joking relationships is generally sexual and aggressive, and frequently consists of sexist or racist jokes. As Freud (1960:99) observed, the jokes men direct *toward* women are generally sexual, tend to be clever (like double entendres), and have a seductive purpose; but the jokes that men tell *about* women in the presence of other men tend to be sexist rather than intimate or erotic, and use hostile and aggressive rather than clever verbal forms. In this case study, joking relationships will be analyzed to uncover the emotional dynamics of fraternal groups and the impact of fraternal bonding upon relationships between men and women.

The Girls' Story

The women had frequently been the target of fraternity initiation rites in the past, and generally enjoyed this joking relationship with the men, if with a certain ambivalence. "There was the naked Christmas Carol event, they were singing 'We wish you a Merry Christmas,' and 'Bring on the hasty pudding' was the big line they liked to yell out. And they had five or six pledges who had to strip in front of the house and do naked jumping jacks on the lawn, after all the women in the house were lined up on the steps to watch." The women did not think these events were hostile because they had been invited to watch, and the men stood with them watching, suggesting that the pledges, not the women, were the targets of the joke. This defined the joke as sexual, not sexist, and part of the normal erotic joking relation between "guys and girls." Still, these jokes were ritual events, not real social relationships. One woman said, "We were just supposed to watch, and the guys were watching us watch. The men set up the stage and the women are brought along to observe. They were the controlling force, then they jump into the car and take off."

At the meeting with the men, two of the women spoke for the group while eleven others sat silently in the center, surrounded by about thirty men. The first woman began, "Your humor was pretty funny as long as it was sexual, but when it went beyond sexual to sexist, then it became painful. You were saying 'I'm better than you.' When you started using sex as a way of proving your superiority, it hurt me and made me angry."

The second woman said that the fraternity's raid had the tone of a rape. "I admit we knew you were coming over, and we were whispering about it. But it went too far, and I felt afraid to say anything. Why do men always think about women in terms of violating them, in sexual imagery? You have to understand that the combination of a sexual topic with the physical threat of all of you standing around terrified me. I couldn't move. You have to realize that when men combine sexuality and force, it's terrifying to women."

Many of the women began by saying, "I'm not a feminist, but ... ," to reassure the men that although they felt angry, they hoped to reestablish the many individual friendships that had existed between men and women in the two groups. In part the issue was resolved when the women accepted the men's construction of the event as a joke, although a failed joke, transforming a discussion about sexuality and force into a debate about good and bad jokes.

For an aggressive joke to be funny, and most jokes contain some hostility, the joke teller must send the audience a cue that says "this is meant as a joke." If accepted, the cue invokes special social rules that "frame" the hostile words that are typical of jokes, ensuring they will not be taken seriously. The men had implicitly sent such a cue when they stood *next* to the women during the naked jumping jacks. Verbal aggression mediated by the joke form will generally be without later consequences in the everyday world, and will be judged in terms of the formal intention of jokes, shared play and laughter.

In accepting the construction of the event as "just a joke" the women absolved the men of responsibility for their actions by calling them "little boys." One woman said, "It's not wrong, they're just boys playing a prank. They're little boys, they don't know what they're doing. It was unpleasant, but we shouldn't make a big deal out of it." In appealing to the rules of the joke form (as in saying "That was funny to me, I don't know what kind of a sense of humor you have"), the men sacrificed their personal friendships with the women in order to protect the feelings of fraternal solidarity it produced. In calling the men "little boys" the women were bending the rules of friendship, trying to preserve their relationships to the guys by playing a patient and nurturing role.

The Guys' Story

Aside from occasional roars of laughter, the men interrupted the women only once. When a woman began to say that the men had obviously intended to intimidate them, the men loudly protested that the women couldn't possibly judge their intentions, that they intended the whole event only as a joke, and the intention of a joke is, by definition, just fun.

At this point the two black men in the fraternity intervened to explain the rules of male joking relationships to the women. In a sense, they said, they agreed with the women, being the object of hostile jokes is painful. As they described it, the collective talk of the fraternity at meals and group events was entirely hostile joking, including many racist jokes. One said, "I've had to listen to things in the house that I'd have hit someone for saying if I'd heard them outside." The guys roared with laughter, for the fraternal joking relation consisted almost entirely of aggressive words that were barely contained by the convention that joke tellers are not responsible for what they say.

One woman responded, "Maybe people should be hit for saying those things, maybe that's the right thing to do." But the black speaker was trying to explain the rules of male joke culture to the women, "If you'd just ignored us, it wouldn't have been any fun." To ignore a joke, even though it makes you feel hurt or angry, is to be cool, one of the primary masculine ideals of the group.

Another man tried to explain the failure of the joke in terms of the difference between the degree of "crudeness" appropriate "between guys" and between "guys and girls." He said, "As I was listening to the speech I was both embarrassed and amused. I was standing at the edge of the room, near the door, and when I looked at the guys I was laughing but when I looked at the girls I was embarrassed. I could see both sides at the same time. It was too crude for your sense of propriety. We have a sense of crudeness you don't have. That's a cultural aspect of the difference between girls and guys."

The other men laughed as he mentioned "how crude we are at the house," and one of the black men added, "You wouldn't believe how crude it gets." Many of the men later said that although they individually found the jokes about women vulgar, the jokes were justified because they were necessary for the formation of the fraternal bond. These men thought that the mistake had been to reveal their crudeness to the women; this was "in bad taste."

In part the crudeness was a kind of "signifying" or "dozens," a ritual exchange of intimate insults that creates group solidarity. "If there's one theme that goes on it's the emphasis on being able to take a lot of ridicule, of shit, and not getting upset about it. Most of the interaction we have is verbally abusing each other, making disgusting references to your mother's sexuality, or the women you were seen with, or your sex organ, the size of your sex organ. And you aren't cool unless you can take it without trying to get back." Being cool is an important male value in other settings as well, like sports or work; the joking relationship is a kind of training that, in one guy's words, "teaches you how to keep in control of your emotions."

But the guys themselves would not have described their group as a joking relationship or fraternal bond, they called it friendship. One man said that he had found perhaps a dozen guys in the house who were special friends, "guys I could cry in front of." Another said, "I think the guys are very close, they would do nearly anything for each other, drive each other places, give each other money. I think when they have problems about school, their car, or something like that, they can talk to each other. I'm not sure they can talk to each other about problems with women though." Although the image of crying in front of the other guys was often mentioned as an example of the intimacy of the fraternal bond, no one could actually recall anyone in the group ever crying. In fact crying would be an admission of vulnerability which would violate the ideals of "strength" and "being cool."

The women interpreted the sexist jokes as a sign of vulnerability. "The thing that struck me the most about our meeting together," one said, "was when the men said they were afraid of trusting women, afraid of being seen as jerks." One of the guys added, "I think down deep all the guys would love to have satisfying relationships with women. I think they're scared of failing, of having to break away from the group they've become comfortable with. I think being in a fraternity, having close friendships with men is a replacement for having close relationships with women. It'd be painful for them because they'd probably fail." These men preferred to relate to women as a group at fraternity parties, where they could take women back to their rooms for quick sex without commitments.

Sexist jokes also had a social function, policing the boundaries of the group, making sure that guys didn't form serious relationships with girls and leave the fraternity (cf. Slater, 1963). "One of the guys just acquired a girlfriend a few weeks ago. He's someone I don't think has had a woman to be friends with, maybe ever, at least in a long time. Everybody has been ribbing him intensely the last few weeks. It's good natured in tone. Sitting at dinner they've invented a little song they sing to him. People yell questions about his girlfriend, the size of her vagina, does she have big breasts." Thus, in dealing with women, the group separated intimacy from sex, defining the male bond as intimate but not sexual (homosocial), and relationships with women as sexual but not intimate (heterosexual).

The Fraternal Bond in Men's Life Cycle

Men often speak of friendship as a group relationship, not a dyadic one, and men's friendships often grow from the experience of shared activities or risk, rather than from self-disclosing talk (cf. Rubin, 1983:130). J. Glenn Gray (1959:89–90) distinguishes the intimate form of friendship from the comradeship that develops from the shared experience of suffering and danger of men at war. In comradeship, he argues, the individual's sense of self is subordinated to a group identity, whereas friendship is based upon a specific feeling for another that heightens a sense of individuality.

In this case, the guys used joking relationships to suspend the ordinary rules and responsibilities of everyday life, placing the intimacy of the fraternal group in competition with heterosexual friendships. One of the men had been inexpressive as he listened to the discussion, but spoke about the fraternity in a voice filled with emotion, "The penis envy speech was a hilarious idea, great college fun. That's what I joined the fraternity for, a good time. College is a stage in my life to do crazy and humorous things. In ten years when I'm in the business world I won't be able to carry on like this [loud laughter from the men]. The initiation was intended to be humorous. We didn't think through how sensitive you women were going to be."

This speech gives the fraternal bond a specific place in the life cycle. The joking relationship is a ritual bond that creates a male group bond in the transition between boyhood and manhood: after the separation from the family where the authority of mothers limits fun, but before becoming subject to the authority of work. One man later commented on the transitional nature of the fraternal bond, "I think a lot of us are really scared of losing total control over our own lives. Having to sacrifice our individuality. I think we're scared of work in the same way we're scared of women." The jokes expressed hostility toward women because an intimate friendship with a woman was associated with "loss of control," namely the risk of responsibility for work and family.

Most, but not all, of the guys in the fraternity were divided between their group identity and a sense of personal identity that was expressed in private friendships with women. Some of the guys, like the one who could "see both sides" as he stood on the edge of the group during the initiation, had reached a point of leaving the fraternity because they couldn't reconcile the tension between his group identity and the sense of self that he felt in his friendships with women.

Ultimately the guys justified the penis envy joke because it created a special kind of male intimacy. But although the fraternal group was able to appropriate the guys' needs for intimacy and commitment it is not clear that it was able to satisfy those needs, because it defined strength as shared risk taking rather than a quality of individual character or personality. In Gray's terms, the guys were constructing comradeship through an erotic of shared activities with an element of risk, shared danger, or rule breaking such as sports, paramilitary games, wild parties, and hostile jokes. In these contexts, strength implied the substitution of a group identity for a personal code that might extend to commitment and care for others (cf. Bly 1982).

In the guys' world, aggression was identified with strength, and defined as loss of control only if it was angry. The fraternal bond was built upon an emotional balance between aggression and anger, for life of the group centered upon the mobilization of aggressive energies in rule-governed activities, especially sports and games. In each arena aggression was defined as strength (toughness) only when it was rule-governed (cool). Getting angry was called "losing control," and the guys thought they were most likely to lose control when they experienced themselves as personally dependent, that is, in relationships with women and at work. The sense of order within fraternal groups is based upon the belief that all members are equally dependent upon the rules, and that no *personal* dependence is created within the group. This is not true of the family or of relations with women, both of which are intimate, and, from the guys' point of view, are "out of control" because they are governed by emotional commitments.

The guys recognized the relationship between their male bond and the work world by claiming that "high officials of the University know about the way we act, and they understand what we are doing." Although this might be taken as evidence that the guys were internalizing their fathers' norms and thus inheriting the rights of patriarchy, the guys described their fathers as slaves to work and women, not as patriarchs. It is striking that the guys would not accept the notion that men have more power than women; to them it is not men who rule, but work and women that govern men.

Speculations

1. Lyman opens his essay with an account of a raid by forty-five fraternity men on a sorority house. Is this an effective way to begin this essay? Explain your response.
2. What is a "fraternal joking relationship"? What is its function? Is Lyman arguing that joking relationships are more characteristic of men than women? Do you think men and women use jokes and humor in different ways? Support your views with examples.
3. Explain what you think one of the women was getting at when she told the men:

   "Your humor was pretty funny as long as it was sexual, but when it went beyond sexual to sexist, then it became painful. You were saying 'I'm better than you.' When you started using sex as a way of proving your superiority, it hurt me and made me angry."

   What distinction is the woman drawing here?
4. Lyman divides his essay into "The Girls' Story" and "The Guys' Story." Is this an effective way to present the evidence about sexual and sexist behaviors? Or is Lyman further polarizing two irreconcilable perspectives?
5. One of the black men tells the girls, "I've had to listen to things in the house that I'd have hit someone for saying if I'd heard them outside." What point is he making here? How much difference does or should context make? Is it in some sense acceptable for people in a fraternity or sorority to make sexist or racist jokes?
6. Lyman asserts that the guys "would not accept the notion that men have more power than women; to them it is not men who rule, but work and women that govern men." Do you agree with them that men are ruled by work and women? Offer examples from reading or personal experience to support your point of view.

———————— **ASSIGNMENT SEQUENCES** ————————

Assignment One: Beauty and the Beholder

1. What are you willing to do to be attractive? In an essay, offer a description of the lengths you went to make yourself attractive for a date, a dance, an important family event, or other occasion. Focus on one particular experience. Offer as many details as you can. Decide also what kind of tone you want to take: serious, bemused, ironic, outraged, calm, celebratory, etc.

2. Now that you have written that essay, reflect on why being attractive was important (or unimportant). Explain to your readers where the various pressures come from—and how you respond to them. Why did being attractive matter? Did making yourself attractive make you into something you weren't? Was it an act of hypocrisy, superficiality, consideration, love? Was it worth it?

3. Choose two media personalities—one male and one female—that you find attractive. What particular qualities—physical, psychological, material—make these people attractive to you? Write an essay that defines "beauty" in terms of the two public figures that you choose. At the end of your essay, make sure that you define what you mean by "beauty" and why these two individuals embody that definition.

4. You discover that a woman friend is going on an extreme diet although she is already quite thin. Based on what you learned from reading Berman and Wolf, write her a letter in which you discuss the dangers involved. In your letter, consider the various societal values that are attached to thinness, particularly as they relate to women.

5. Consider that you have been asked by your campus newspaper to do a feature that explains and analyzes eating disorders. Here is what you know:

    > 8,000,000 people in the U.S. have anorexia (self-starvation) or bulimia (bingeing and purging)

    > 90% of those are women

    > 3–6% of those women die

    > The National Association of Anorexia Nervosa and Associated Disorders has recorded other cases in France, Germany, Italy, Japan, Africa, eastern Europe, and Canada.

The root cause of eating disorders is both social and psychological.

The information presented in the essays by Nina Berman and Naomi Wolf.

Write that feature. You should use quotations from both essays. Your essay should take a position—about why hunger disorders exist, what can be done about them, why they mostly affect women, how you can tell if you have a hunger disorder and so on.

6. Why don't men typically fall victim to eating disorders? In an essay that draws on Wolf, Lyman, Staples, and Greenstein describe some essential characteristics of maleness and some essential values within society that prevent most men from becoming anorexic or bulimic. What expectations, societal pressures, and cultural values (or the lack of them) shape men's views of their own bodies?

Sequence Two: Affirmation and Disapproval

1. Imagine that you are Maxine Hong Kingston's aunt, the "No Name Woman." You know that you are going to jump into the well, killing yourself and your child. Before you do, however, you decide you must write a letter to your descendants, explaining how you feel and what you think about the events that have transpired. Write the letter. You may be angry, defiant, woeful, disturbed, or contrite. You may analyze the situation, focusing on the psychology and motivations behind the culture that condemned you. You may try to understand and forgive those who have wronged you. You may ask for forgiveness and understanding. You may explain what really happened—the true story that nobody in the village (except perhaps your lover) knows. Choose your story and stick to it, remembering that someday, others may need to know what you thought and felt in those last moments.

2. "You must not tell anyone," my mother said, "what I am about to tell you. In China your father had a sister who killed herself." Thus does Maxine Hong Kingston begin "No Name Woman." In an essay, discuss the significance of Kingston's violating her mother's edict by focusing on the relationships between silence, obedience, power, and gender. In your essay, offer your own interpretations of why the aunt remained silent, why her lover remained silent, and why neither Kingston's mother nor Kingston herself maintained that silence. What points is Kingston making about what it means to be a woman?

3. Greenstein states that "Women make lousy screen heroes for the male viewer. They just aren't believable in the macho theme park of artificial violence." Choose three female screen heroes. In an essay analyze their popular appeal, their believability and attractiveness as screen persona. Your thesis is whether women make lousy screen heroes for males.

4. Now that you have considered women as screen heroes, invert the topic. Your next assignment is to choose three male screen heroes, analyze their appeal and attractiveness, and decide conversely if men make lousy screen heroes for females.

5. Consider that you are a parent of twins—a boy and a girl—and that you have just read Ben Greenstein's "Learning to be Superior." You sit down to write out a set of principles and promises on how you will raise your two children in terms of gender roles. Write out that statement. In your essay, be sure to include citations from Greenstein; you may also want to cite Wolf, Staples, and Lyman.

Assignment Sequence Three: Gendered Youth

1. In "Learning to be Superior," Ben Greenstein states that teachers reinforce gender stereotyping, that, for example, "teachers are more attentive to boys than they are to girls." Choose an event from your own past schooling and describe an event in which you perceived gender difference on the part of a teacher. What happened? Why did it happen? What effects did it have? What does your experience tell you about the system of unstated assumptions, values, and preferences that operate within society? Support your insights with appropriate quotations.

2. Brent Staples writes:

> Many things go into the making of a young thug. One of those things is the consummation of the male romance with the power to intimidate. . . . It is, after all, only manly to embrace the power to frighten and intimidate. We, as men, are not supposed to give an inch of our lane on the highway; we are to seize the fighter's edge in work and in play and even in love; we are to be valiant in the face of hostile forces.

In an essay, offer your own analysis of what it means to be "a man." What are the qualities of "manliness" that you most admire? How does one differentiate between the qualities that make up "manliness" and those that make up being a "young thug?" In your essay, draw upon quotations from Staples's "Just Walk On By" and other relevant essays.

3. Ben Greenstein, Brent Staples, and Peter Lyman offer accounts of differences between the ways that boys play and the ways that girls play. In an essay, discuss those differences and the results they have for boys and girls. Be sure to include relevant citations from the essays.

4. You are working in the administrative office of Tiptop University. Your job is to resolve conflicts among students. You arrive at work one day to learn that the incident that Peter Lyman describes has just occurred at Tiptop U. Your responsibility is to find common ground so that the two sides can get together and develop a more harmonious relationship. In a position paper, analyze the problem as you see it: its causes and consequences including who is at fault and who has responded unreasonably. Then offer a series of recommendations to help resolve the tension between the fraternity and the sorority.

FOCUS ON

Gay/Lesbian Identities

The metaphor of the closet is still dominant when one tries to talk about homosexuality—that is, what it means to be gay, lesbian, or bisexual. The closet is, of course, a place of concealment: it is where we hide our secrets, where we shove those embarrassing and self-incriminating actions that we want no one to see. The closet is dark, it is private, and it is almost always found in the bedroom. When we hide something there, we hope fervently that it will never see the light of day.

Yet what we hide possesses us and certainly can undermine our health and well-being. In *The Portrait of Dorian Gray*, Oscar Wilde presents a young man, who to the outside world remains handsome and ageless, but whose viciousness and corruption get inscribed on a portrait that hangs in a secured chamber in his house. A brilliant and flamboyant gay writer whose career—and life—were destroyed in large part because he was convicted of engaging in homosexual activity, Wilde here is invoking the closet metaphor, tracing the relationship between outward denial and inner suffering.

When gay/lesbian people talk about "outing," about "coming out of the closet," they are talking about bringing their sexual preference into the open. For those gays and lesbians, the hatred, alienation, and discrimination they often experience after "outing" is preferable to the burdens of secrecy and self-loathing they otherwise would carry. Even for them, however, the only hope for maintaining any semblance of a normal life is to remain at least partly closeted. As Eve Kosofsky Sedgwick writes in her important essay, "Epistemology of the Closet":

> Even at an individual level, there are remarkably few of even the most openly gay people who are not deliberately in the closet with someone personally or economically or institutionally important to them. . . . The gay closet is not a feature only of the lives of gay people. But for many gay people it is still the fundamental feature of social life; and there can be few gay people, however courageous and forthright by habit, however fortunate in the support of their immediate communities, in whose lives the closet is not still a shaping presence.

Sedgwick here reminds us that everyone occasionally hides something in the closet, but that for gays and lesbians, it is virtually impossible to live otherwise: for them, in contrast to the acceptance and freedom enjoyed by the heterosexual majority, identity must at least in part always remain buried.

Our intention in the following pages is to initiate discussion about gay and lesbian identities. In a small way, it is our attempt to bring this subject out of the closet and into the classroom. We realize that discussions about gay and lesbian identity can be difficult; some students may find this topic as difficult to consider as abortion or capital punishment. But we also strongly believe that students write best when they are forced to confront timely and significant issues—and in contemporary political terms, there are few issues as compelling as gay/lesbian civil and legal rights. Given our own experience teaching first-year composition, we think the following selections will provide material for thoughtful discussion and excellent writing.

HOMOPHOBIA AND HETEROSEXISM

Warren J. Blumenfeld and Diane Raymond

Warren J. Blumenfeld and Diane Raymond begin the second edition of their landmark book, *Looking at Gay and Lesbian Life,* with a brief account of some of the recent international legal victories for gay, lesbian, and bisexual people—victories that may come as a surprise to some American readers. For example:

> When Israel passed its gay rights law on January 1, 1992, it joined Denmark, France, Norway, Sweden, and some regions in Canada, Australia, and the United States in outlawing discrimination in housing and employment based on sexual orientation. In 1989, the Danish parliament legalized same-sex marriage, making Denmark the first country in the world to grant full rights to gay, lesbian, and bisexual people.

Those victories are important, but Blumenfeld and Raymond also acknowledge that "Hate crimes directed against those perceived as gay, lesbian, or bisexual continue to mount" and that "Gay, lesbian, and bisexual adolescents are at increased risk for suicide (Department of Human Services)—a fact which the Bush administration sought strenuously to hide."

Blumenfeld and Raymond have devoted much of their professional careers to bringing gay, lesbian, and bisexual lifestyles out of the closet and into public acceptance. *Looking at Gay and Lesbian Life* is a standard text in many courses throughout North America; it is used in classes ranging from philosophy and women's studies to anthropology and political science. Blumenfeld has authored two other texts addressing similar issues: *Homophobia: How We All Pay the Price* (1992) and *AIDS and Your Religious Community* (1991). Educated at San Jose State and Boston College, he is currently pursuing a doctorate in Social Justice at the University of Massachusetts-Amherst. Raymond is Department Chair of Philosophy at Simmons College and is active in both the reproductive rights and feminist movements. A lesbian mother, she is currently editing a book on the uses of existentialism in the classroom.

In the selection that follows, Blumenfeld and Raymond offer a grim account of the devastating effects of hatred and prejudice toward those who are marked "different" in terms of sexual orientation. As they make clear here and in the "Preface" to their book:

> *Everyone* has good reason to struggle against heterosexism and homophobia ... heterosexism is tied to rigid gender roles ... [and] linked to sex-negative attitudes and policies that rob us all of joyful sexual relationships and, in the era of AIDS, lead to an ignorance which is quite literally fatal; heterosexism and homophobia prevent all of us from understanding one another fully, and from recognizing the myriad and rich contributions gays, lesbians, and bisexuals have made to our culture.

The following selection charts out—in factual and committed fashion—a thoughtful basis for analyzing and responding to oppressive heterosexist attitudes toward gay/lesbian people.

Homophobia and Heterosexism

It is difficult for anyone living in the United States in the 20th century to avoid internalizing homophobic attitudes. All around are messages which defame lesbians, gays, and bisexuals.

A poll conducted by *Newsweek* magazine in 1983 estimated that 66 percent of the U.S. population feel that homosexuality is an unacceptable lifestyle. A Gallup poll (1982) found that 59 percent of those surveyed would exclude homosexuals from teaching grade school, while 51 percent would not permit them to enter the clergy. J.S. Simmons, in his book *Deviants*, states that homosexuals are considerably more disliked by the American public than ex-convicts, ex-mental patients, gamblers, and alcoholics.

A study of the sexual attitudes of over 1000 American teenagers (Coles & Stokes) found that 75 percent considered sex between two females to be "disgusting" and over 80 percent felt the same for sex between two males. Also, in this study, 32 percent of the males and 16 percent of the females said they would break off all ties with any same-sex friend discovered to be gay or lesbian.

Who Is Homophobic?

Who is most likely to have strong homophobic beliefs and reactions? Drawing from a large number of studies on this topic, Gregory Herek compiled a list of characteristics which appear to be common in people with such attitudes. Though there are of course scores of exceptions, Herek found that these people are generally:

1. less likely to have had personal contact with lesbians and gay men;

2. less likely to report having engaged in homosexual behaviors or to identify themselves as lesbian or gay;

3. more likely to perceive their peers as manifesting negative attitudes, especially if the respondents are males;

4. more likely to have resided in areas where negative attitudes are the norm (e.g., the Midwestern and Southern U.S., Canadian prairies, and in rural areas and small towns), especially during adolescence;

5. likely to be older and less well educated;

6. more likely to be religious, to attend church frequently, and to subscribe to a conservative religious ideology;

7. more likely to express traditional, restrictive attitudes about sex roles and to report more sex-negative attitudes (Dunbar);

8. less permissive sexually or manifesting more guilt or negativity about sexuality;

9. more likely to manifest high levels of authoritarianism and related personality characteristics;

10. more likely to label a man "homosexual" if he displays any qualities judged to be "feminine." (Dunbar)

These studies also suggest that heterosexuals have more negative attitudes toward homosexuals of their own sex, with stronger and deeper negative attitudes in males.

Irwin and Thompson found in their study that Roman Catholics and Protestants are less tolerant of homosexuality than Jews, members of other religions, and nonaffiliates.

Further, studies reveal that homophobia is not an isolated phenomenon detached from other forms of prejudice and discrimination. In fact, a number of studies, including Minnergerode, and Henley and Pincus, for example, reported a strong correlation between respondents' negative attitudes toward lesbians and gays and negative attitudes toward women in general. In addition, Henley and Pincus found that respondents holding negative attitudes toward gays and lesbians also exhibited negative attitudes toward blacks.

Finally, Gregory Herek found that people who are most apt to be accepting or supportive of sexual minorities include city-dwellers, people from Northeastern and Pacific Coastal regions of the U.S., younger persons whose peers' values reflect the changes of the 1960s and 1970s, the more educated, and people whose parents demonstrated support for human sexual diversity.

Heterosexism

Homophobia has a close ally—*heterosexism*. This is the system by which heterosexuality is assumed to be the only acceptable and viable life option. Very often heterosexism is quite subtle or indirect and may not even be apparent. Because this norm is so pervasive, heterosexism is difficult to detect.

When parents automatically expect that their children will marry a person of the other sex at some future date and will rear children within this union; when the only positive and satisfying relationships portrayed by the media are heterosexual; when teachers presume all of their students are straight and teach only about the contributions of heterosexuals—these are examples of heterosexism. It also takes the form of pity—when the dominant group looks upon sexual minorities as poor unfortunates who "can't help being the way they are." All this amounts to, in the words of author Christopher Isherwood, a "heterosexual dictatorship."

Heterosexism forces lesbians, gays, and bisexuals to struggle constantly against their own invisibility, and makes it much more difficult for them to integrate a positive sexual identity. This is not unlike the feeling of a Jew or a Muslim in a predominantly Christian country during Christmas time; a wheelchair user in a town with only stepped entrances to buildings; or an English-speaking visitor in a country in which English is not spoken. It also occurs when African Americans and Asians see only white faces in the media; when elder citizens reside in a land that values youthfulness; and when the young are told continually by adults that they are "not old enough."

Though not direct or overt, heterosexism is a form of discrimination. Its subtlety makes it somehow even more insidious because it is harder to define and combat. Heterosexism is discrimination by neglect, omission, and/or distortion, whereas often its more active partner—homophobia—is discrimination by intent and design.

Forms of Homophobia

> Macho men . . . need faggots. They've created faggots in order to act out a sexual fantasy on the body of another man and not take any responsibility for it. . . . The male homosexual . . . is a sexual target for other men and that is why he is despised and why he is called a faggot. (Baldwin in Goldstein.)

The Story of Charlie Howard
by Rev. Robert Wheatly

His name was Charles O. Howard, "Charlie" to most everyone, and described by his friends as a twenty-three-year-old gentle, flamboyant, happy sort of person.

In Bangor, Maine, Saturday night, July 7, 1984, he left a meeting of Interweave, a Unitarian-Universalist lesbian and gay support group that meets at the Unitarian Church, a little after 10:00 p.m., and was walking with a friend downtown, when the two of them were attacked by three youths, ages fifteen, sixteen, and seventeen.

His friend got away, but Charlie was not so lucky; he was kicked and beaten and thrown over the rail of a bridge over the Kenduskeag Stream canal, twenty feet down into ten-foot deep waters, despite his screams that he could not swim. His body was found the next day downstream.

Police said the teenagers charged with murdering Charlie bragged afterward to a friend that they "jumped a fag and beat the s—- out of him and then threw him into the stream."

Riding around town with two girl friends that night, they spotted Charlie and his friend, piled out of the car and chased them, beat Charlie and "picked him up and threw him over the railing." All three were released Monday, July 9, into the custody of their parents.

Lesbians and gay men in Bangor and throughout Maine were outraged at the treatment of those charged with Charlie's murder.

Thomas Goodwin, the assistant attorney general who will prosecute the case, said he recommended their release because they were "not a threat to the community," and that the youths did not necessarily intend to kill Charlie because "the evidence would suggest they didn't know he had drowned."

Sgt. Thomas Placella, the chief detective on the case, added, "I'm not trying to lessen the severity of the crime, but it's not like these were ax murderers. These people came from respectable families who own property in the city of Bangor."

That Monday night the Unitarian Church of Bangor was the setting of a memorial service led by its minister, the Rev. Richard Forcier, attended by some 200 persons who testified to their friendship with Charlie, expressed outrage at his murder, and marched to the police station for a candlelight vigil of protest.

Many told their own stories of harassment and violence at the hand of fag-bashers.

The same scene was repeated the following Friday night in the First Parish Society, Unitarian-Universalist, in Portland, Maine, in a service led by the Rev. Richard Hasty.

More than 400 persons memorialized Charlie Howard and participated in a protest march down Congress Street to the constant harassment of Bible-quoting fundamentalists who marched alongside.

Charlie was one of the effeminate ones—whose blond, soft looks, slender body, and graceful mannerisms could not hide the fact of his gayness, no matter how hard he tried to conceal them.

Christine Palmer, journalist with the *Bangor Daily News*, tells of watching him just six days before his death, at the morning worship service which he had begun attending regularly at the Unitarian Church, "Yes, he was bubbly and innocent and sweet and all those good things people said about him Monday night. But he was also a pain in the neck sometimes. He talked too much, listened too little, didn't do things *my* way."

"And isn't that exactly why, if we must find a reason, that he died? Charlie didn't do things the way others thought he should. He didn't conform."

He had learned to accept his gayness, had long since told his parents and family, and made "Glad to be Gay" his anthem, had moved beyond the shyness and self-doubt which haunted his childhood and, last week, told friends with a grin, "The fag-beaters were after me today, but they didn't get me."

Well, they did, they finally did. He was a sitting duck, a stereotypical target, the kind many love to hate. But as Christine Palmer said, "It doesn't make much sense that Charlie, whether he wanted to carry a purse or even if he had wanted to wear a dress, should be so hated."

I've known the embarrassment of which Christine speaks, for when the stereotypical gay male is envisioned, it is apt to be the swishy ones who come to mind—and that isn't me, I've convinced myself.

And yet, there it is—a Charlie Howard somewhere who carries the stigmata in my stead—and gets dumped over a bridge for it.

I am compelled once again to remember that it was the street queens in Greenwich Village who, in 1969, began the movement that resulted in my liberation, who shouted at the cops, "Hell, no, we won't go!" and locked up the police in Stonewall Bar: The Stonewall Rebellion. "Remind me, O Lord, of my debt to the street queens!"

. . . Members of the lesbian and gay group reached out in a supportive way to Charlie as did others, whose first reaction to him tended to be, "Oh no . . . !" but who came later to see and know more of his sweetness, his ingratiating ways, and thoughtful friendliness.

What the minister was saying, it seemed to me, was that the congregation had made an effort, intentionally, to become informed and knowledgeable about lesbian and gay people, had made them welcome users of its space, had taken time to know them as individuals, and were not locked into old stereotypes of who and what lesbians and gay men are like.

They had learned, as Rich Forcier put it, to become "extremely accepting." And all of this became evident when tragedy struck, when a time of need arose. (Wheatly.)

In large cities and small outlying villages, gays and lesbians continue to face harassment and physical abuse simply because of their sexual orientation, and Charlie Howard's case represents only one of a number of such assaults and murders each year. In this instance, as in the majority of cases involving anti-gay and lesbian violence, the assailants tend to be white males in their teens and early twenties who are acting out society's prejudices. The purpose of the assaults is not theft, though that sometimes is one by-product. Rather, some people choose to attack lesbians and gays simply because they do not like their lifestyles. Intimidation and humiliation are the means by which they make their beliefs known—beliefs which very often receive community sanction. There is a postscript to the Charlie Howard incident: the three teenagers accused of his murder did not go to trial. Instead, they accepted guilty pleas to reduced charges of manslaughter and were sent to the Maine Youth Center for a short time, after which they rejoined their families.

> The town's only major newspaper is still opposing gay-rights legislation or any other measures that would foster tolerance of gays. The fundamentalist preachers who dominate the town's clergy are still taking every opportunity to tell their parishioners that homosexuality is a sin and a danger to society. Bars and discos in the city are still expelling couples of the same sex who try to dance together. And high-school students are still issuing death threats to various members of the town's gay community. (Canellos.)

Six months following Howard's murder, a high school teacher in the neighboring town of Madison, Maine organized "Tolerance Day" to educate students about discrimination against people of color, Jews, ex-prisoners, elderly people, poor people, the physically challenged, and gays and lesbians. Though the school's faculty committee approved the proposal, and though 300 of 400 of the school's students signed a petition in favor of Tolerance Day, the Madison School Board unanimously voted to cancel the program on January 21, 1985, claiming the appearance of Dale McCormick, president of the Maine Lesbian and Gay Political Alliance, would threaten "safety, order, and security of the high school." The Kennebec County Superior Court upheld the School Board's cancellation of Tolerance Day, saying that lesbians and gay men have no "judicially enforceable" right to be protected from discrimination.

For lesbians, as for heterosexual women, sexual assault is a common form of violence directed against them. Abby Tallmer notes, however, that it would be wrong to conclude that lesbians and heterosexual women always are assaulted in the same ways. She suggests a number of patterns of attack in anti-lesbian violence including: anti-lesbian verbal harassment sometimes as a prelude to assault; attack outside lesbian-identified establishments by a man or gang outside a lesbian bar, for example, or by a cabdriver who parks near a lesbian bar and waits for a potential victim—this frequently results in rape; attack by a man who may follow a lesbian couple home and, following a forced entry, ties up one of the women and in clear view rapes the other; assault by a male ex-lover, ex-husband, or acquaintance stemming from the man's feelings of anger or rejection; or sexual assault by a heterosexual man who poses as gay to gain the woman's trust.

There was a new twist to anti-gay violence in the mid-1980s as the AIDS epidemic was used to rationalize and justify such attacks. Take, for example, an interview of an admitted gay-basher on the nationally televised Oprah Winfrey Show:

WINFREY: So, you admit that you used to do gay bashing?

GUEST: Yeah. Fag bashing. We used to go out driving in the car to [the] city—it has a strip of nightclubs, like go-go bars, and a strip of homosexual bars.

WINFREY: And why would you do this?

GUEST: We were young and full of goofiness and we just—there was nothing to do on a Friday or Saturday night.

WINFREY: And so, did that give you pleasure, doing that?

GUEST: At the time it was fun. Yes.

WINFREY: Where does this hostility, this hatred toward homosexuals come from?

GUEST: I think it came from the area I grew up in and in the household.

WINFREY: In your house?

GUEST: Yeah, in my household.

WINFREY: What does that mean?

GUEST: Well, I mean, my father—I don't think anybody really cared for homosexuals in my house, and spoke highly against them.

WINFREY: So, if someone in your house were to say, or to admit that they were gay, what would happen in your house to them?

GUEST: Well, I wouldn't talk to them no more.

WINFREY: So, you actually, you hate homosexuals.

GUEST: Right.

WINFREY: Why, though? Why?

GUEST: I think—

WINFREY: What has a homosexual ever done to you to cause you to have this kind of hatred? Where does it come from? I'm trying to understand.

GUEST: If God wanted homosexuals he would have made all one sex. You know. Why'd he make men and women? If homosexuals had their way, about 100 years from now, where would we be? There would be no more children. We'd be extinct.

WINFREY: And so, that's why you hate them. And so, that hatred carries over into what other areas of your life?

GUEST: I don't care to work—I won't work for them.

WINFREY: How do you know who is and who isn't?

GUEST: Well, sometimes you don't, but I mean if he's obvious or open about it, I wouldn't work for them.

WINFREY: If you see one on the street or in a restaurant—

GUEST: I'd get up and move to a different table.

WINFREY: See, in this society I think it's almost impossible not to encounter people who are homosexual ... from the time you get up and leave your house and go to work and do whatever you do—if you ever go to a restaurant, if you ever go out—you encounter gay people all the time, male and female. So, you must be really troubled living in a society where you have to encounter them all the time.

GUEST: Obviously, yes. I think, like, you go fishing, and you're fishing at the lake, and a mosquito bites a guy with AIDS, fishing down from you, and [the mosquito] comes and bites you.

WINFREY: (ironically) Yeah. I wonder how many times that's happened....

GUEST: Yeah. Could you get the AIDS from them?

WINFREY: Does that concern you?

GUEST: Yeah.

WINFREY: You fish a lot?

GUEST: Yeah. I fish often. But I mean—

WINFREY: . . . I think I understand what you're saying. And so, in your everyday—do you think about this a lot? Seriously. I mean, do you get up in the morning and think, "God, those gays. I'm out to get them."

GUEST: No. I don't get up in the morning like that, but when you get up in the morning and read the papers there's something on gay rights, or you see the gay parade, or AIDS. . . .

WINFREY: So, when you first heard about the AIDS virus what did you say?

GUEST: Well, at first I thought it would be all right.

WINFREY: Why?

GUEST: Because it was just affecting gays at that time. But now, you know, you see school children getting it from blood transfusions and now it's scary. It's very scary.

WINFREY: It's scary I think because a lot of people feel the way that you do. Do you have other friends who share this feeling?

GUEST: Yes.

WINFREY: And you get together and you talk about it and you say—

GUEST: Yeah. And a lot of people are scared.

WINFREY: So, does this fear come from you being afraid because of the AIDS virus or is it just a natural hatred that you have?

GUEST: I think it's some of both.

WINFREY: It's amazing you admit it. That's really honest of you.

Direct violence against lesbians and gays is a nationwide phenomenon. The National Gay and Lesbian Task Force published a study involving over two thousand lesbians and gay males in eight major U.S. cities (Atlanta, Boston, Dallas, Denver, Los Angeles, New York, St. Louis, and Seattle). The results showed that over 90 percent of the respondents experienced some form of victimization on account of their sexual orientation—greater than one out of three had been threatened directly with violence:

> More than one in five males, and nearly one in ten females, say they were "punched, hit, kicked, or beaten," and approximately the same ratios suffered some form of police abuse. Assaults with weapons are reported by one in ten males and one in twenty females. Many of those who report having been harassed or assaulted further state that incidents occurred multiple times. (NGLTF.)

Victimization was reported to have occurred at home, at school, and at other community locales. Approximately one-third of the respondents were assaulted verbally, while more than one in fifteen was physically abused by members of their own family.

The most widely publicized instance of anti-gay violence in recent years occurred on November 27, 1978, in San Francisco. On that day, a former policeman and city supervisor, Dan White, left his home in San Francisco, a .38 Smith & Wesson gun in hand, and headed for City Hall. Once there, he crawled through a window to avoid metal detectors. He then proceeded to Mayor George Moscone's office, where he shot him four times at close range, twice directly into his brain. He then walked down a hallway to the offices of gay City Supervisor Harvey Milk, where he unloaded five bullets into his body, killing him too.

Harvey Milk was a visible spokesperson for the rights of gay people and other disenfranchised minorities—and the mayor, though not gay himself, was an ally.

Their murderer, Dan White, was, on the other hand, a long-time foe of the lesbian and gay community. He was deeply disturbed by the relative political gains of this community during the years leading up to his violent actions.

Shortly following the shooting, White was captured and tried. The police and fire departments reportedly raised over $100,000 for his defense. (Shilts.) Graffiti soon appeared across the city with such epithets as: "Kill Fags: Dan White for Mayor," and "Dan White Showed You Can Fight City Hall."

White was convicted of a reduced charge of voluntary manslaughter and sentenced to a prison term of six years. Though he was convicted of the deaths of two elected city officials, he received a relatively mild sentence. Many believe that homophobia played a major role in the trial itself. Former policeman, white, husband and father, regular churchgoer, one-time high school athlete, distinguished military service record—Dan White in many ways personified the archetype of the "all-American boy." His crime included the killing of a gay man and his friend. It is likely that the sentence would have been much harsher if the elements of the case had been different: for example, if Milk had shot White or if White had shot only Moscone.

On January 7, 1984, Dan White was released from jail, having served only 5 1/2 years. On October 21, 1985 he committed suicide.

According to the National Gay and Lesbian Task Force, National Gay and Lesbian Anti-Gay/Lesbian Victimization Report, the number of reported incidents of violent acts is on the increase. Attacks included verbal harassment, intimidation, physical assault, vandalism, arson, rape, murder, and/or police abuse. In the year 1985 alone, the Task Force documented over two thousand such acts across the United States. That number increased to nearly five thousand in 1986, and a record 7,000 in 1987, and this is merely the tip of the iceberg because the majority of anti-gay/lesbian assaults are never reported due to victim's concern of "coming out" publicly, or lack of trust in the judicial system. Some reported incidents include:

In Jacksonville, Florida, arsonists twice set fire to the local Metropolitan Community Church, a Christian church serving the gay and lesbian community. Attacks against the church became so frequent that bullet-proof windows had to be installed.

Yelling "Sick Motherf———," two men threw a beaker of acid at a lesbian employee of the Los Angeles Gay and Lesbian Community Services Center. The victim sustained serious burns on her face and torso.

In Vermont, a gay man was stabbed to death by a man who later said, "I killed him because he looked like a fag."

In Portland, Maine, an assailant called three women anti-lesbian epithets and assaulted them, leaving one of the victims with a fractured jaw, several broken teeth, and bruised ribs. The other victims also sustained injuries that required medical attention.

Direct violence is simply the most visible means by which homophobia is expressed. However, as with other forms of prejudice and discrimination, homophobia appears in many forms and affects people's lives in a great number of ways.

Institutional Homophobia

Major institutions such as government, schools, businesses, and religion create all sorts of policies which dictate codes of behavior and reinforce attitudes and values. Institutions have tremendous power and social status, and, through penalties and rewards, disapproval and approval, create incentives for conformity to norms. Few contemporary institutions have policies supportive of homosexuals, and many actively work against gays. In fact, homosexuals and bisexuals are adversely affected by existing laws, codes, rules, and procedures of established political, social, business, and religious institutions.

Government.

Though a number of communities have enacted laws protecting the rights of lesbians and gay males, no such statute exists on the national level. In fact, same-sex eroticism is still illegal in many states. The language used in such laws to describe homosexual acts includes "crimes against nature," "sodomy," "buggery," "perversion," "fellatio," "unnatural intercourse," "unnatural and lascivious acts," "unnatural or perverted practices," "indecent or immoral practices," "perverse acts," and "deviate sexual conduct." (*The Challenge and Progress of Homosexual Law Reform.*) Penalties range from fines to short prison terms to life imprisonment. As one state legislator in the Florida House put it: "The homosexual deserves no better treatment than any other criminal," and he proposed new laws to the legislature because "homosexuality must be eliminated." (Phoenix.) In many places, laws which spell out the limits of sexual behavior apply also to heterosexuals but in practice are used chiefly to harass gays, lesbians, and bisexuals.

Sexual minorities are, in many instances, excluded from protections regulating fair employment practices, housing discrimination, rights of child custody, immigration, inheritance, security clearances, public accommodations, and police protection.

In employment, a person can be denied or fired from a position solely on the basis of sexual orientation. In those locales where equal protection is in effect, other reasons for termination have been given (e.g., incompatibility with co-workers or sloppy performance) to get around the law when no just cause exists. In most instances, it is difficult to prove discrimination on the basis of sexual orientation.

In housing, gays and lesbians may be evicted from rented or leased spaces. Some landlords and realtors refuse to show one-bedroom apartments to same-sex couples.

Having little protection under the law, gays are often the target of police entrapment and harassment through periodic raids on their bars and other social meeting places; frequently police respond slowly to a request for aid from a gay person and often refuse to respond at all. In addition, police often do not carry on a follow-up investigation of a complaint.

> In order to catch persons engaged in homosexual acts, the police have chosen to rely on two major techniques—both very expensive in time and money: "clandestine observation" which means spying through peepholes . . . or special mirrors, using hidden TV cameras, or secretly taking photographs; and trapping or "decoy operation," which means sending out plainclothesmen who dress, walk, talk and act as they think homosexuals do for the sole purpose of enticing a homosexual solicitation. (*The Challenge and Progress of Homosexual Law Reform*, p. 21.)

Police have entered gay and lesbian bars under the guise of inspecting for possible code violations, but in actuality have done so to intimidate and harass patrons. Police have arrested people for jaywalking and for minor traffic violations as they leave a bar.

Police departments have also compiled lists of suspected and known homosexuals and have made arrests on the charge of solicitation, loitering, disorderly conduct, lewd or indecent acts, indecent exposure, disturbing the peace, lewd vagrancy, assault, public nuisance, or being a lewd and wanton person. (*The Challenge and Progress of Homosexual Law Reform*.) Reports of the arrest of gays and lesbians have been sent to their employers and landlords. (Woetzel.)

One of the most famous cases involving police harassment of gays occurred in Boise, Idaho, in 1955. Police arrested sixteen gay men and charged five of them with committing homosexual acts with minors. The men were interrogated under questionable legal tactics and forced to give names of others. At the height of the scandal, the police collected over 500 names. Fear within the underground homosexual community ran rampant. Three men were convicted and handed prison sentences: one for seven years and two for five years each. It later came out that the "children" these men were alleged to have engaged in sex with were actually hardened street hustlers in their mid- to late teens—hardly the scenario of the older man seducing young innocent children as was portrayed in the press.

In the courts, gays and lesbians who have been victims of crime are often blamed for "provoking the crime." Perpetrators of anti-lesbian and-gay assault are often given light sentences or acquitted. In jails gays and lesbians are harassed, sexually assaulted, and sometimes murdered. Some states have castrated men for engaging in homosexual activity. Gays have been fair game to blackmailers, due to their illegal status.

There is no legal recognition of marriage vows taken by gay and lesbian couples, and hence they are not accorded the tax, medical, pension, and insurance breaks and other advantages accorded to heterosexual marriage partners. Rights of inheritance also do not extend to lesbians and gays.

In accordance with a widespread societal attitude that lesbians and gays should not have contact with children, many state and private child welfare agencies have stated or implied policies denying same-sex couples or individuals the right to adopt or serve as foster parents. In addition, gay fathers and lesbian mothers have repeatedly lost custody of their children in the courts primarily because of their sexual orientation.

Gay Foster Parenting: A Case Study

Donald Babets, age thirty-six, a senior investigator for the Boston Fair Housing Commission, and David Jean, age thirty-two, business manager of the Crittendon Hastings House, a multi-service women's health agency, applied to be foster parents. After spending twelve hours in training classes led by two social workers, having a routine police-record check and in-depth home study that included exhaustive interviews, they were approved for placement of children from two years nine months to nine years old. This whole process took almost a year, and involved the requisite four levels of approval from the home-finder to the area director. In addition, the application was sent to the regional office for review and then to the highest office—the central Department of Social Services—where it was finally approved.

Before these last two stages, this process was not so unlike other applications. But there was a key difference between Babets and Jean and other prospective foster parents: they were openly homosexual partners who had lived together for the past five years and were applying together to parent foster children.

Babets and Jean later received temporary custody of two children: a three-and-a-half-year-old boy and his twenty-two-month-old brother. Though the younger of the two was supposed to be placed in another foster home, the two men offered to keep them together, and later the social workers on the case agreed to the joint placement.

Soon after this, the *Boston Globe* newspaper ran a story about the case. Almost immediately after this story appeared, the children were removed from the home due in part to pressure from segments of the community. Yet friends had commented on the improvements in the children after just two weeks with Babets and Jean. Says Jean:

> Whatever happened to us, we can deal with that. It's the pain I saw in the two kids that we felt was unforgivable. . . . The older child was really angry. He wouldn't even talk to me. How do you explain to a kid who thinks you as an adult have control over things, that you have nothing to say about this? I saw the pain in him. I knew the pain in me. What could I say? What could I do? Nothing. (Jean, quoted in Diament, p. 88.)

This episode resulted in a change in the DSS's policy regarding placement of foster children. A joint legislative committee, following the lead of Massachusetts Governor Michael Dukakis, voted to pass a law stating that DSS should place children in homes where sexual orientation "presents no threat to the well-being of the child." This was claimed to be "nonspecific" language, but its effect was to bar lesbians and gay men from being foster parents.

On May 24, 1985, Philip Johnston, Massachusetts Secretary of Human Services, announced the following policy:

> This administration [that of Governor Dukakis] believes that foster children are served best when placed in traditional family settings— that is, with relatives or in families with married couples, preferably with parenting experience and with time available to care for foster children.

"Nontraditional" is taken to mean families where both parents work, households headed by a single person, unmarried couples, and homosexuals. Johnston indicated that any future placements with gays or lesbians were "highly unlikely."

Since the removal of the children from the home of Babets and Jean, the children have been moved in and out of three more foster homes. They were sexually abused by the foster parents in the last home in which they lived.

Another form of governmental homophobia occurred in the United States Postal Service which has employed the tactic of "mail covers"—drawing up lists of names and addresses—on people known to receive lesbian and gay publications and has handed such lists over to employers. The Postmaster General, on request from the Congress, finally ordered his department to terminate this practice. (*Newsweek,* 1966.)

Immigration laws have also been used against gays and lesbians. The United States Immigration and Naturalization Service has been given the authority to exclude certain aliens from entry into the country or to deny them U.S. citizenship. Throughout the twentieth century the Immigration and Nationality Act has been amended to extend such restrictions to anyone believed to engage in terrorism or who will attempt to overthrow the government, anyone with a "social psychopathic personality," "mental defect," or communicable disease, anyone whose political opinions or writings are deemed contrary to those of the government, or anyone suspected of engaging in "immoral sexual acts" (added to bar prostitutes).

In 1965 the law was further amended, under Section 212 (a)(4), adding the category of "sexual deviates" in an attempt to exclude homosexuals. The law has been used a number of times. Between 1971 and 1978 alone, thirty-one people were barred entry into the United States under the provisions of Section 212 (a)(4). (Sullivan.) Others have been denied citizenship and lesbians have been harassed by United States agents on the Canadian-U.S. border while trying to enter this country. Though the section has been challenged in the courts, it has been upheld as constitutional and remains in force.

Also on the governmental level, public schools and public libraries have limited or entirely restricted the purchasing of books, magazines, films, and recordings on lesbian, gay, and bisexual themes.

Military.

They gave me a medal for killing two men and a discharge for loving one. (Gay Vietnam veteran Leonard Matlovich)

Using the rationale that they would undermine effective operations and jeopardize security, the military bars homosexuals from enlisting in most branches of service. (In 1988, the Federal appeals court in San Francisco by a 2-to-1 vote ruled the Army's ban on homosexuals to be unconstitutional.) For those who remain silent about their sexual orientation and manage to get in, if discovered they can be placed in military stockades and/or given an undesirable discharge with all benefits suspended. In addition, students have been kicked out of college ROTC programs once their homosexuality becomes known. . . .

Conclusion

Virtually everyone has felt the effects of prejudice and discrimination in various forms sometime in life. From slavery, to the Black Codes and Jim Crow, to the Kerner Commission Report in 1968 stating that ". . . our nation is moving toward two societies, one black, one white—separate and unequal . . . ," to the present, African Americans have been excluded from many of the social and economic spheres of this country. U.S. territorial governments waged wars to systematically eradicate American Indian populations, confiscated their ancestral lands, and attempted to force them to abandon their cultural traditions. Today, as a group, American Indians are the poorest in the country. Chinese people were legally excluded from entering this country, from marrying whites, and from becoming U.S. citizens. Japanese people were prevented from owning land, from attending schools with whites, and were eventually forced during World War II to enter guarded camps or reservations where all personal rights were suspended. The Irish got off the boat only to find signs announcing, "Irish Need Not Apply." Over six million Jews were put to death under the Nazi regime and in this country Jewish synagogues have been torched and Jews, along with Catholics, have been banned from certain professions, prevented from attending many colleges, and restricted from membership in social organizations. Latin Americans still find it hard to move into many neighborhoods or obtain certain desirable jobs because of the prejudice around them. Southeast Asian Americans have been threatened and challenged when attempting to operate shops or to practice their traditional occupation of fishing. America's elder citizens are often forced into retirement while they remain capable and productive in the workplace. The physically challenged are barred from a number of buildings by architectural barriers and are denied housing, employment, and public accommodations. On average the earning power of women workers remains far less than that of men. Tasteless jokes and slurs abound for virtually every group. And though certain conditions have improved, lesbians, gays, and bisexuals continue to remain a despised minority.

Homosexuality has been called many things. Fascists say it's a sign of racial impurity, Communists blame it on Western bourgeois decadence, Westerners say it's a sign of deviance, and parents around the world blame themselves. Religious leaders call it sin and perversion and try to purge it, psychiatrists have called it illness and disturbance and have tried to cure it. Governments attempt to isolate and sometimes eradicate it, and school children learn from their elders to fear and hate it. In the face of all the subtle and extreme means that have been used to control it, though some people have internalized society's attitudes, many have acknowledged their homosexuality and have developed a sense of pride.

Prejudice is not only learned but it also serves many purposes. Homophobia—like racism, sexism, anti-Semitism, etc.—is a form of prejudice. It may be deliberate and blatant or unconscious and unintentional. But in the final analysis it is harmful not only to those who are victims of it, but also to those who hold it.

Works Cited

Canellos, Peter. "A City and Its Sins: The Killing of a Gay Man in Bangor." *The Boston Phoenix*, November 13, 1984.

The Challenge and Progress of Homosexual Law Reform. San Francisco: Council on Religion and the Homosexual, Daughters of Bilitis, Society for Individual Rights, Tavern Guild of San Francisco, 1968.

Coles, Robert, and Stokes, Jeffrey. *Sex and the American Teenager.* New York: Rolling Stone Press, 1985.

Diamant, Anita. "In the Best Interests of Children." *Boston Globe Magazine*, September 8, 1985, pp. 86–100.

Dunbar, John, Brown, Marvin, and Amoroso, Donald. "Some Correlates of Attitudes toward Homosexuality." *Journal of Social Psychology* (1973) 89:271–79.

Gallup Report #205. "Political, Social and Economic Trends: Americans Pro Equal Rights for Gays . . . but Hedge in Some Areas." Princeton, N.J.: The Gallup Poll, October 1982.

Goldstein, Richard. "Go the Way Your Blood Beats: An Interview with James Baldwin," *Village Voice*, June 26, 1984.

Henley, N.M., and Pincus, F. "Interrelationship of Sexist, Racist, and Antihomosexual Attitudes," *Psychological Reports*, 42, 1978, pp. 83–90.

Herek, Gregory. "Beyond 'Homophobia': A Social Psychological Perspective on Attitudes toward Lesbians and Gay Men." In *Bashers, Baiters, and Bigots: Homophobia in American Society.* New York: Harrington Park Press, 1985.

Irwin, P., and Thompson, N.L. "Acceptance of the Rights of Homosexuals: A Social Profile," *Journal of Homosexuality*, 3(2) 1977, pp. 107–121.

Minnergerode, F.A. "Attitudes toward Homosexuality: Feminist Attitudes and Social Conservatism." *Sex Roles*, 1, 1976, pp. 160–165.

National Gay and Lesbian Task Force. National Anti-Gay/Lesbian Victimization Report. New York: 1984.

Newsweek, "The Watch on the Mails," 67:24, June 13, 1966.

"Newsweek Poll on Homosexuality." *Newsweek*, August 9, 1983, p. 33.

Phoenix, 1:13, Sept.–Oct. 1966—quoting from the *Sun-Sentinel*.

Shilts, Randy. *The Mayor of Castro Street: The Life and Times of Harvey Milk.* New York: St. Martin's Press, 1982.

Simmons, J.S. *Deviants.* Boston: Glandessry Press, 1969.

Sullivan, Gerard. "A Bibliographic Guide to Government Hearings and Reports, Legislative Action, and Speeches Made in the House and Senate of the United States Congress on the Subject of Homosexuality." In *Bashers, Baiters and Bigots: Homophobia in American Society,* edited by John P. De Cecco. New York: Harrington Park Press, 1985.

Tallmer, Abby. "Anti-Lesbian Violence." National Gay and Lesbian Task Force Monograph Series, Violence Project, Washington, D.C.

Wheatly, Rev. Robert. "Candlelight Vigils Protest Killing of Gay Man." *Unitarian Universalist World,* August 15, 1984.

Oprah Winfrey Show. *Homophobia,* Transcript #8639. New York: Journal Graphics, Inc., Nov. 13, 1986.

Woetzel, Robert K. "Do Our Homosexuality Laws Make Sense?" *Saturday Review of Literature,* 48, p. 23–25. Oct. 9, 1965.

Speculations

1. What are the differences between "homophobia" and "heterosexism"? Do you agree that "a close ally" of homophobia is heterosexism? Do you agree that heterosexism "is a form of discrimination"?

2. In the epigraph to "Forms of Homophobia," Blumenfeld and Raymond quote an interview with the great black, gay writer, James Baldwin: "Macho men . . . need faggots. They've created faggots in order to act out a sexual fantasy on the body of another man and not take any responsibility for it." What do you think Baldwin is saying here? How do you respond to his use of the word "faggots"? Is it objectionable? Why does Baldwin use this word? Finally, why do you think Blumenfeld and Raymond begin with this statement?

3. "The Story of Charlie Howard" is written by a Reverend Robert Wheatly and was published in the *Unitarian Universalist World,* a church publication. Is the story effective? What is the rhetorical effect of the author being a representative of organized religion?

4. Blumenfeld and Raymond describe various consequences of Charlie Howard's murder. List two or three of these consequences and discuss their implications in terms of crime and punishment and civil rights. Was the school board right in canceling "Tolerance Day"? Should the three teenagers have been given stiffer sentences?

5. In this account of prejudice and discrimination against gay/lesbian and bisexual individuals, Blumenfeld and Raymond make use of a great deal of reported material: the Rev. Wheatly's narrative, the Oprah Winfrey transcript, news accounts of attacks against individuals. Is this technique useful and persuasive? Do Blumenfeld and Raymond have too many examples?

6. Blumenfeld and Raymond largely assume the role of somewhat distanced reporters and chroniclers: after the Oprah Winfrey

selection, for example, they make no comment other than "Direct violence against lesbians and gays is a nationwide phenomenon." Is this kind of objectivity useful and compelling? How does it affect your reading of this selection?

A MATTER OF DIFFERENCE

Martin Duberman

"There are times when I have trouble deciding which I am, historian or playwright," Martin Duberman has stated. Given the rich contributions he has made to both fields, it is no wonder Duberman feels some ambivalence. As a Distinguished Professor of History at The Graduate Center and Lehman College of the City University of New York, his research interests include nineteenth-century social and intellectual history, radical social movements, and the history of gender roles. He has authored a biography, *Charles Francis Adams, 1807–1886* (1961), edited and contributed to *The Antislavery Vanguard: New Essays on the Abolitionists* (1965), and earned grants and fellowships from Yale University and the American Council of Learned Societies.

On the American theatrical scene, Duberman is the author of numerous plays and screenplays including *In White America* (1963), "Mother Earth: The Life of Emma Goldman" (1971), and "Twelve Angry Men" in collaboration with Ossie Davis (1971). His plays were produced frequently in New York during the 1970s, and they have been anthologized in collections such as *The Best Short Plays of 1970, The Best Short Plays of 1972,* and *Readings in Human Sexuality* (1976).

As intellectual historian and social commentator, Duberman has published numerous essays and articles. He is a frequent contributor to the *New York Times,* the *Village Voice, New Republic, Harper's,* and other publications. His drama reviews have appeared in *Show* and *Partisan Review,* and he is a member of the editorial board of *Signs.* In the following essay published in *The Nation* in 1993, Duberman identifies with the gay community and calls for recognition of homosexual identity, history, and humanity as a fundamental step toward acknowledging the differences that are always present within society.

Virginia Woolf slept with Vita Sackville-West. Does that make her "lesbian"? Cary Grant had a long-standing affair with Randolph Scott. Does that make him "gay"? And what do we do with Colette, the lover of young men, once we learn of her involvement with the film star

Marguerite Moreno? And is there a category for Lord Byron, notorious for his many affairs with women *and* at one point madly in love with the choirboy John Edleston?

Queer theory has taught us to distrust categories as needless calcifications of what is purportedly our fluid, meandering erotic natures. We are told to move beyond Freud's notions of inherent bisexuality to posit a malleable sexuality that, if allowed to run free, would create all sorts of trisexual permutations. Most of us, alas, however attracted to the theory of infinite malleability, have been trained in a culture that regards sexual appetite as consisting of two, and only two, contrasting variations—gay or straight. And most of us have internalized that perhaps false dichotomy to such a degree that it has become as deeply imprinted in us—as immutable—as any genetically mandated trait.

Historians, often deeply conservative by temperament—who else would devote a lifetime to conserving the past?—tend to have little patience with the implicit injunction of queer theorists to reinvent ourselves constantly and dismiss such a view as utopian. Yet even historians cannot blink away much as they might wish, the ambiguities about human sexual nature that have arisen in the wake of the burgeoning scholarship on the gay and lesbian past.

A mere twenty years ago, the notion of a formal, scholarly, institutionalized inquiry into gay history would have been unthinkable, literally not nameable, yet there are now enough serious-minded scholars devoting their full-time efforts to its reclamation to fill conference rooms. Some are engaged in documenting the history of genital sex between members of the same gender. Others pursue evidence of passionate, romantic, *non*genital friendships. Yet another group of scholars is at work detailing the history of gender nonconformity and of cross-gender identifications in dress, speech, mannerisms and attitudes—studies that center on the phenomena of transvestism and transsexualism or, cross-culturally, on "third gender" figures like the Native American *berdache,* the Indian *hijra* and the Polynesian *mahu.* Finally, there are scholars whose primary inquiry is describing how and why cultural definitions of sexual and gender unorthodoxy have shifted over time; their interest is not in the nonconforming behavior itself but in understanding the shifting ways it has been regarded.

Although all these enterprises, and more, have swiftly accelerated in the past few years, their interconnections are not always clear, and the complex nature of the evidence being unearthed has often been difficult to interpret. To take just one example—the history of passionate friendship—scholars continue to debate earnestly, yet inconclusively, the connection of that phenomenon to the history of erotic arousal. Are they one and the same? Is passionate friendship best seen as an instance of erotic sublimation? Is overt sexuality a natural extension of

emotional closeness and should we therefore view its absence as an instance of cultural repression? And some would argue that the pursuit
of evidence of genital sex between two people of the same gender is itself a misguided enterprise, the "true" history of "gays" and "lesbians"
residing not in the record of same-gender erotic arousal but in the story
of gender nonconformity.

There is no question—to stay with the example of passionate friendship—but that many pairs of women in the United States and England
lived together during the latter part of the nineteenth and the early part
of the twentieth century in devoted partnerships, sharing all aspects of
their lives. Well, nearly all. Emotional intimacy—yes. Frequent hand-
holding, touching, even kissing—yes. But genital sexuality—apparently
no. Should we therefore refrain from calling them lesbians?

Perhaps the answer lies not in these women's (apparently) celibate
behavior but in their fantasy lives; perhaps these women secretly admitted to themselves what they were loath to act upon. Perhaps—but it is
unlikely we will ever know. We almost never have enough information
about the inner lives of people in the past to talk confidently about the
content of their subjective desires. Maps to the psychological interior (in
the form, say, of elaborate, unbridled diaries and letters) are almost always lacking for historical figures. In their absence, we form judgments
from *behavioral* evidence alone—itself not easy to gauge and interpret.

And what of the additionally complicating factor of *self*-definition?
Should we reserve the label "lesbian" (or "gay") for those who are sub-
jectively conscious of having a different sexuality, which they in turn
reify into a different "identity"? In regard to those pair-bonded women
involved in "Boston marriages" (as they were sometimes called in this
country), the historian Leila Rupp has concluded that they would most
probably have rejected the label "lesbian" for themselves.

Indeed, some of those women lived on into a more self-conscious
era when the terminology and categories "gay" and "lesbian," not earlier available, had come into common usage, and they often reacted
with angry disgust to the suggestion that *their* relationships could be so
characterized. True, their very vehemence can be taken as a classic instance of denial. But if we insist on that interpretation, we have placed
ourselves in the position of claiming to know the "truth" of a relationship better than the participants in it—to say nothing of placing ourselves in danger (one to which historians commonly succumb) of projecting *our* descriptive categories backward in time onto those who
might have neither understood nor approved of them.

The problem of interpreting "Boston marriages" is but one example of the conundrums facing those engaged in trying to unearth a us-
able past for today's lesbian and gay community, trying somehow to
lay claim to an extended history that can provide needed nourishment
and legitimacy. The large majority of gay men and lesbians share the

mainstream American view, common to most cultures, that legitimacy is predicated on the ability to lay claim to "roots"—to antecedents; to hoist the counter banner of being "something new under the sun" is tantamount to declaring impotence. Again like other mainstream Americans, most gay men and lesbians hanker after and rhetorically hallow the past even as they insist on its irrelevance.

In the case of gay people, the hankering takes on particular poignancy. Having been excluded from the textbooks, having been denied the kind of alternate, family-centered oral tradition available to other minorities, gay people long for some proof—some legitimizing evidence—that we have always existed, and in pretty much the same form as we currently do, and that we are therefore automatically entitled to the same status and rights other "official" minorities lay claim to.

Alas, we can never find *exact* precursors in the past, and any search for them is doomed to disappointment. This is no less true for heterosexuals than for homosexuals (as we have quaintly learned to call ourselves). Heterosexuality, too, has a history, a record of shifting definitions of what has been considered "healthy" or "authentic"—and therefore allowable—behavior. Women in this country and in England in the mid-nineteenth century, for example, were commonly viewed as passionless. Any woman who exhibited "undue" interest in sex was likely to be labeled disturbed—"neurasthenic"; she would be sent away for a rest cure and, should that fail, would become a candidate for a clitoridectomy. Yet a mere hundred years later a common feminist view is that women are "naturally" *more* sexual than men, capable of that indefinite number of orgasms and ever-heightened pleasure that the low-performing male can only fantasize about (and envy so furiously in the female that he invents the domestic lockup to curtail her).

Neither gays nor straights, in short, can hope to lay claim to any kind of history other than an endlessly changing one. We can never confirm our present images by citing lengthy lineages in the past. What the past *can* be said to confirm is that "human nature," far from being a constant, has taken on, under varying cultural imperatives, a wide range of shapes—the very starting point of queer theory.

Reclaiming the history of gender nonconformity—which some argue is conterminous if not wholly synonymous with the history of "gays" and "lesbians"—is also a way of confirming another truth of value to *all* human beings, regardless of their sexual orientation. And that is the demonstrable ability of people who are "different" to develop, in the face of denunciation and oppression, creative strategies for survival that then open up new possibilities for everyone. We are all far more different (though not necessarily in sexual ways) than most of us would care to admit in our conformist culture. The emerging history of lesbians and gay men has begun to provide empowering evidence for *anyone* insistent on allowing their differentness to emerge—and on it being respected.

Speculations

1. Duberman opens with a series of questions about some famous individuals. How do you answer them? Was Virginia Woolf, who was married to Leonard Woolf, a lesbian because she "slept with Vita Sackville-West"? What do you make of Cary Grant and Colette? What is Duberman's purpose in opening this way?

2. Explain the sudden interest on the part of historians and other scholars for studying gender, including gay/lesbian issues. Why now? Do you think this subject is worth studying in a careful and scholarly way? Explain your answers.

3. What conclusions can we draw from Leila Rupp's assertion that the participants in "Boston marriages" would themselves reject the label of "lesbian"? Does anyone else really know "the 'truth' of a relationship better than the participants in it"? Explain your response.

4. The language that Duberman uses might be said to be difficult and complex; it is characterized by long phrases and clauses and abstraction—and Duberman engages in a careful and close argumentative style. Is Duberman's essay accessible? Who is his audience? What is gained—and what is lost—by his writing in this manner?

5. Duberman writes: "We are all far more different (though not necessarily in sexual ways) than most of us would care to admit in our conformist culture." What does he mean by that? Offer your own assessment of the similarities and differences between human beings in this country. Why does Duberman make this assertion?

LESBIAN PARENTING 1986

Audre Lorde

While still in high school, Audre Lorde published a poem in *Seventeen* magazine that had been rejected by her high school newspaper for being too romantic. It was the beginning of an auspicious career: Audre Lorde went on to create important and significant works as a poet, novelist, essayist, and professor of English. Her work is filled with unflinching honesty. She writes with passion and integrity about relationships, race, motherhood, and social problems.

Born in 1934 during the Great Depression, Lorde earned a B.A. from Hunter College and a Masters in Library Science in 1961 from Columbia University. Working first as a librarian, Lorde then moved into the field of creative writing, teaching at City College in New York and John Jay College of Criminal Justice; she ultimately assumed the position of professor at Hunter College, her old alma mater. The mother of a son and daughter, proud of her African-American heritage, Lorde championed black, lesbian, and gay/feminist causes with her actions and her writings. Her published works include the bio-mythical novel, *Zami* (1982) and collections of poetry including *Coal* (1976), *The Black Unicorn* (1978), and *Our Dead Behind Us* (1986). In her major prose work, *The Cancer Journals* (1980), which is an account of her agonizing struggle to overcome breast cancer and mastectomy, Lorde discusses with characteristic directness her refusal to wear a prosthesis:

> Prosthesis offers the empty comfort of 'Nobody will know the difference.' But it is that very difference which I wish to affirm, because I have lived it, and survived it, and wish to share that strength with other women. If we are to translate the silence surrounding breast cancer into language and action against this scourge, then the first step is that women with mastectomies must become visible to each other.

Audre Lorde died of cancer in 1992.

Critics have seen in Lorde's poetry the figure of the mother as someone who resents her daughter, tries to make her conform to societal expectations, and ultimately withholds love and acceptance. As critic Joan Martin states, however, these ambivalent feelings about her mother "did not make [Lorde] bitter against her own children . . ." As is clear from the following essay, Lorde celebrates her lesbian motherhood and hopes that her children will live with integrity, honesty, and firm resolve in the face of likely social oppression.

These days it seems like everywhere I turn somebody is either having a baby or talking about having a baby, and on one level that feels quite benign because I love babies. At the same time, I can't help asking myself what it means in terms of where we are as a country, as well as where we are as people of Color within a white racist system. And when infants begin to appear with noticeable regularity within the Gay and Lesbian community, I find this occurrence even more worthy of close and unsentimental scrutiny.

We are Lesbians and Gays of Color surviving in a country that defines human—when it concerns itself with the question at all—as straight and white. We are Gays and Lesbians of Color at a time in that country's history when its domestic and international policies, as well as its posture toward those developing nations with which we share heritage, are so reactionary that self-preservation demands we involve ourselves actively in those policies and postures. And we must have some input and effect upon those policies if we are ever to take a responsible place within the international community of peoples of Color, a human community which includes two-thirds of the world's population. It is a time when the increase in conservatism upon every front affecting our lives as people of Color is oppressively obvious, from the recent appointment of a Supreme Court Chief Justice in flagrant disregard of his history of racial intolerance, to the largely unprotested rise in racial stereotypes and demeaning images saturating our popular media—radio, television, videos, movies, music.

We are Gays and Lesbians of Color at a time when the advent of a new and uncontrolled disease has carved wrenching inroads into the ranks of our comrades, our lovers, our friends. And the connection between these two facts—the rise in social and political conservatism and the appearance of what has become known in the general public's mind as the *gay* disease, AIDS—has not been sufficiently scrutinized. But we certainly see their unholy wedding in the increase of sanctioned and self-righteous acts of heterosexism and homophobia, from queer-bashing in our streets to the legal invasion of our bedrooms. Should we miss these connections between racism and homophobia, we are also asked to believe that this monstrously convenient disease—and I use *convenient* here in the sense of *convenient for extermination*—originated spontaneously and mysteriously in Africa. Yet, for all the public hysteria surrounding AIDS, almost nothing is heard of the growing incidence of CAIDS—along the Mexican border, in the Near East and in the other areas of industrial imperialism. Chemically Acquired Immune Deficiency Syndrome is an industrial disease caused by prolonged exposure to trichloroethylene. TCE is a chemical in wholesale use in the electronic sweatshops of the world, where workers are primarily people of Color, in Malaysia, Sri Lanka, the Philippines, and Mexico.

It is a time when we, Lesbians and Gays of Color, cannot ignore our position as citizens of a country that stands on the wrong side of every liberation struggle on this globe; a country that publicly condones and connives with the most vicious and systematic program for genocide since Nazi Germany—apartheid South Africa.

How do we raise children to deal with these realities? For if we do not, we only disarm them, send them out into the jaws of the dragon unprepared. If we raise our children in the absence of an accurate picture of the world as we know it, then we blunt their most effective weapons for survival and growth, as well as their motivation for social change.

We are Gays and Lesbians of Color in a time when race-war is being fought in a small Idaho town, Coeur D'Alene. It is a time when the lynching of two Black people in California within twenty miles of each other is called nonracial and coincidental by the local media. One of the two victims was a Black Gay man, Timothy Lee; the other was a Black woman reporter investigating his death, Jacqueline Peters.

It is a time when local and national funds for day care and other programs which offer help to poor and working-class families are being cut, a time when even the definition of family is growing more and more restrictive.

But we are having babies! And I say, thank the goddess. As members of ethnic and racial communities historically under siege, every Gay and Lesbian of Color knows deep down inside that the question of children is not merely an academic one, nor do our children represent a theoretical hold upon some vague immortality. Our parents are examples of survival as a living pursuit, and no matter how different from them we may now find ourselves, we have built their example into our definitions of self—which is why we can be here, naming ourselves. We know that all our work upon this planet is not going to be done in our lifetimes, and maybe not even in our children's lifetimes. But if we do what we came to do, our children will carry it on through their own living. And if we can keep this earth spinning and remain upon it long enough, the future belongs to us and our children because we are fashioning it with a vision rooted in human possibility and growth, a vision that does not shrivel before adversity.

There are those who say the urge to have children is a reaction to encroaching despair, a last desperate outcry before the leap into the void. I disagree. I believe that raising children is one way of participating in the future, in social change. On the other hand, it would be dangerous as well as sentimental to think that childrearing alone is enough to bring about a livable future in the absence of any definition of that future. For unless we develop some cohesive vision of that world in which we hope these children will participate, and some sense of our own responsibilities in the shaping of that world, we will only raise new performers in the master's sorry drama.

So what does this all have to do with Lesbian parenting? Well, when I talk about mothering, I do so with an urgency born of my consciousness as a Lesbian and a Black African Caribbean American woman staked out in white racist sexist homophobic america.

I gave birth to two children. I have a daughter and a son. The memory of their childhood years, storms and all, remains a joy to me. Those years were the most chaotic as well as the most creative of my life. Raising two children together with my lover, Frances, balancing the intricacies of relationship within that four-person interracial family, taught me invaluable measurements for my self, my capacities, my real agendas. It gave me tangible and sometimes painful lessons about difference, about power, and about purpose.

We were a Black and a white Lesbian in our forties, raising two Black children. Making do was not going to be a safe way to live our lives, nor was pretense, nor euphemism. *Lesbian* is a name for women who love each other. *Black* means of African ancestry. Our lives would never be simple. We had to learn and to teach what works while we lived, always, with a cautionary awareness of the social forces aligned against us—at the same time there was laundry to be done, dental appointments to be kept, and no you can't watch cartoons because we think they rot your feelings and we pay the electricity.

I knew, for example, that the rage I felt and kept carefully under lock and key would one day be matched by a similar rage in my children: the rage of Black survival within the daily trivializations of white racism. I had to discover ways to own and use that rage if I was to teach them how to own and use theirs, so that we did not wind up torturing ourselves by turning our rage against each other. It was not restraint I had to learn, but ways to use my rage to fuel actions, actions that could alter the very circumstances of oppression feeding my rage.

Screaming at my daughter's childish banter instead of standing up to a racist bus driver was misplacing my anger, making her its innocent victim. Getting a migraine headache instead of injecting my Black woman's voice into the smug whiteness of a Women's Studies meeting was swallowing that anger, turning it against myself. Neither one of these actions offered solutions I wanted to give my children for dealing with relationships or racism. Learning to recognize and label my angers, and to put them where they belonged in some effective way, became crucial—not only for my own survival, but also for my children's. So that when I was justifiably angry with one of them—and no one short of sainthood can live around growing children and not get angry at one time or another—I could express the anger appropriate to the situation and not have that anger magnified and distorted by all my other unexpressed and unused furies. I was not always successful in achieving that distinction, but trying kept me conscious of the difference.

If I could not learn to handle my anger, how could I expect the children to learn to handle theirs in some constructive way—not deny it or hide it or self-destruct upon it? As a Black Lesbian mother I came to realize I could not afford the energy drains of denial and still be open to my own growth. And if we do not grow with our children, they cannot learn.

That was a long and sometimes arduous journey toward self-possession. And that journey was sweetened by an increasing ability to stretch far beyond what I had previously thought possible—in understanding, in seeing common events in a new perspective, in trusting my own perceptions. It was an exciting journey, sweetened also by the sounds of their laughter in the street and the endearing beauty of the bodies of children sleeping. My daughter and my son made issues of survival daily questions, the answers to which had to be scrutinized as well as practiced. And what our children learned about using their own power and difference within our family, I hope they will someday use to save the world. I can hope for no less. I know that I am constantly learning from them. Still.

Like getting used to looking up instead of down. How looking up all the time gives you a slight ache in the back of the neck. Jonathan, at seventeen, asking, "Hey Ma, how come you never hit us until we were bigger'n you?" At that moment realizing I guess I never hit my kids when they were little for the same reason my father never hit me: because we were afraid that our rage at the world in which we lived might leak out to contaminate and destroy someone we loved. But my father never learned to express his anger beyond imaginary conversations behind closed doors. Instead, he stoppered it, denying me his image, and he died of inchoate rage at fifty-one. My mother, on the other hand, would beat me until she wept from weariness. But it was not me, the overly rambunctious child, who sold her rotting food and spat upon her and her children in the street.

Frances and I wanted the children to know who we were and who they were, and that we were proud of them and of ourselves, and we hoped they would be proud of themselves and of us, too. But I remember Beth's fifteen-year-old angry coolness: "You think just because you're lesbians you're so different from the rest of them, but you're not, you're just like all the other parents. . . ." Then she launched into a fairly accurate record of our disciplines, our demands, our errors.

What I remember most of all now is that we were not just like all the other parents. Our family was not just like all the other families. That did not keep us from being a family any more than our being Lesbians kept Frances and me from being parents. But we did not have to be just like all the rest in order to be valid. We were an interracial Lesbian family with radical parents in the most conservative borough of New York City. Exploring the meaning of those differences kept us all stretching and learning, and we used that exploration to get us from Friday to Thursday, from toothache through homework to who was going to babysit when we both worked late and did Frances go to PTA meetings.

There are certain basic requirements of any child—food, clothing, shelter, love. So what makes our children different? We do. Gays and Lesbians of Color are different because we are embattled by reason of our sexuality and our Color, and if there is any lesson we must teach our children, it is that difference is a creative force for change, that survival and struggle for the future is not a theoretical issue. It is the very texture of our lives, just as revolution is the texture of the lives of the children who stuff their pockets with stones in Soweto and quickstep all the way to Johannesburg to fall in the streets from tear gas and rubber bullets in front of Anglo-American Corporation. Those children did not choose to die little heroes. They did not ask their mothers and fathers for permission to run in the streets and die. They do it because somewhere their parents gave them an example of what can be paid for survival, and these children carry on the same work by redefining their roles in an inhuman environment.

The children of Lesbians of Color did not choose their Color nor their mamas. But these are the facts of their lives, and the power as well as the peril of these realities must not be hidden from them as they seek self-definition.

And yes, sometimes our daughter and son did pay a price for our insisting upon the articulation of our differences—political, racial, sexual. That is difficult for me to say, because it hurts to raise your children knowing they may be sacrificed to your vision, your beliefs. But as children of Color, Lesbian parents or no, our children are programmed to be sacrifices to the vision of white racist profit-oriented sexist homophobic america, and that we cannot allow. So if we must raise our children to be warriors rather than cannon fodder, at least let us be very clear in what war we are fighting and what inevitable shape victory will wear. Then our children will choose their own battles.

Lesbians and Gays of Color and the children of Lesbians and Gays of Color are in the forefront of every struggle for human dignity in this country today, and that is not by accident. At the same time, we must remember when they are children that they are children, and need love, protection, and direction. From the beginning, Frances and I tried to teach the children that they each had a right to define herself and himself and to feel his own and her own feelings. They also had to take responsibility for the actions which arose out of those feelings. In order to do this teaching, we had to make sure that Beth and Jonathan had access to information from which to form those definitions—true information, no matter how uncomfortable it might be for us. We also had to provide them with sufficient space within which to feel anger, fear, rebellion, joy.

We were very lucky to have the love and support of other Lesbians, most of whom did not have children of their own, but who loved us and our son and daughter. That support was particularly important at those times when some apparently insurmountable breach left us feeling isolated and alone as Lesbian parents. Another source of support and connection came from other Black women who were raising children alone. Even so, there were times when it seemed to Frances and me that we would not survive neighborhood disapproval, a double case of chickenpox, or escalating teenage rebellion. It is really scary when your children take what they have learned about self-assertion and nonviolent power and decide to test it in confrontations with you. But that is a necessary part of learning themselves, and the primary question is, have they learned to use it well?

Our daughter and son are in their twenties now. They are both warriors, and the battlefields shift: the war is the same. It stretches from the brothels of Southeast Asia to the blood-ridden alleys of Capetown to the incinerated Lesbian in Berlin to Michael Stewart's purloined eyes and grandmother Eleanor Bumpurs shot dead in the projects of New York. It stretches from the classroom where our daughter teaches Black and Latino third graders to chant, "I am somebody beautiful," to the college campus where our son replaced the Stars and Stripes with the flag of South Africa to protest his school's refusal to divest. They are in the process of choosing their own weapons, and no doubt some of those weapons will feel completely alien to me. Yet I trust them, deeply, because they were raised to be their own woman, their own man, in struggle, and in the service of all of our futures.

Speculations

1. This essay was written ten years ago. Are its views dated and irrelevant today? What issues and themes does Lorde address?

2. Lorde states that the "country defines human—when it concerns itself with the question at all—as straight and white." Is she right about this? In what ways do we see evidence for or against this proposition—in our schools, the media, literature, etc.?

3. This essay gives the reader a sense of eavesdropping on a conversation, as if Lorde is writing to a particular audience (i.e., the opening paragraph). As you reread, underline places in the essay that indicate that a special audience is being addressed and describe the relationship that is implied between Lorde and her audience.

4. Lorde states that "I believe that raising children is one way of participating in the future, in social change." Respond to this statement. Is Lorde in some manipulative way "using" her children? Does her view about child raising derive from her being both a lesbian and black? Explain your responses.

5. At one point, Lorde alludes to the possible difficulties that her children might encounter because their mother was a lesbian. She follows that by describing Beth's retort:

   "You think just because you're lesbians you're so different from the rest of them, but you're not, you're just like all the other parents. . . ." Then she launched into a fairly accurate record of our disciplines, our demands, our errors.

   Given this evidence, how would you characterize the relationship between Lorde and her daughter? Are Lorde and her daughter aware of the social stigma that can arise from being identified as a lesbian or a lesbian's daughter?

6. Lorde states that she and Frances gave the children access to "true information, no matter how uncomfortable it might be for us." What do you think she means by this? Do you think it is

typical for parents—straight, gay, or lesbian—to give their children this kind of information? Should they do so? Explain your position.

GENTLEMAN'S AGREEMENT

James B. Stewart

In 1983, while living and working in New York City, James B. Stewart started writing for the *Wall Street Journal*. He is now the *Journal*'s front-page editor. In 1988 he and Daniel Hertzberg were awarded the Pulitzer Prize for Explanatory Journalism for their news stories on the 1987 stock market crash and the insider trading scandal. As a result of his investigative journalism, Stewart has authored three books: *The Partners: Inside America's Most Powerful Law Firms* (1983), *The Prosecutors: Inside the Offices of the Government's Most Powerful Lawyers* (1987), and *Den of Thieves* (1991). *Den of Thieves* is a gripping account of how "insider" stock traders Ivan Boesky and Michael Milken robbed the securities market of hundreds of millions of dollars—which they never paid back—through bribery and secret deals that wound up victimizing all Americans, who consequently suffered from the collapsing financial markets and economic recession that followed the 1980s "decade of greed."

Having worked as a lawyer and assistant prosecutor in the State Attorney's Office in Quincey, Illinois, Stewart poignantly describes "working for a prosecutor as the only job I have held that drove me to tears of both pity and frustration" because "a first-time marijuana offender who was the sole support of his mother and sister [was] sentenced to prison" by a hard-line, anti-drug judge, while "the most hardened criminal I've met was a violent, racist fifteen-year-old" who was prosecuted as a juvenile, avoided prison altogether, and then continued to "wreak havoc" and destruction on innocent victims. Stewart's empathy with individuals who suffer because of poorly applied legal technicalities and stubborn moral attitudes is clearly revealed in this selection, in which he describes the clash between business life and personal choice, morality and ethics, employer mandates and employee rights.

On the morning of October 17, 1990, Donald L. DeMuth, of Donald L. DeMuth Professional Management Consultants, asked one of his employees, Daniel C. Miller, to step into his office. Miller wondered if DeMuth was going to raise the possibility of Miller's becoming a partner in the business, which specializes in financial matters for the medical and dental professions. DeMuth had never actually promised Miller a partnership, but he'd recently asked him if he wanted to invest with him in a new office building for the business, which is situated in Camp Hill, Pennsylvania, just across the Susquehanna River from Harrisburg. The two men had worked together for five years, and, as professional relationships go, they had become close. DeMuth occasionally asked Miller to join him at the Harrisburg Senators' baseball games (DeMuth is a baseball fan and used to be a co-owner of the Spartanburg, South Carolina, Phillies); they sometimes travelled together to professional conferences; and Miller often joined DeMuth and his wife for dinner. Over some fifteen years, DeMuth had had other employees who were candidates for partnership, but, according to someone who worked in the office, none had established the good rapport he had with Miller.

DeMuth's tone that morning indicated that something was wrong. "I'm sorry to have to do this," DeMuth began. Then he said, "I am terminating you."

"Why?"

"You know why," DeMuth replied. He said that Miller would get no severance pay and that his medical benefits were ended. He had to remove his belongings from the office before the end of the day.

Six weeks later, Dan Miller, after absorbing the shock—he had never got so much as a bad grade, let alone a summary discharge—opened his own office, across the river in Harrisburg. Several of his clients, baffled by his sudden departure, continued to send work his way. Some of them soon received a letter from DeMuth that said, in part, "Right now Dan is on his own. If he ever wants to grow, I question who he will be able to attract as an associate. While there may be other homosexual practice management consultants and C.P.A.s, to the best of my knowledge I've never met one." The letter continued, "It's well known that homosexuals are significantly at risk for AIDS. While I have no knowledge of Dan's medical condition, consider getting the results of a blood test from him, if you are considering using his services on a long-term basis."

When Dan Miller, a twenty-nine-year-old accountant, showed up in Don DeMuth's office in 1985, he seemed like a godsend. DeMuth's practice was flourishing, and the principal accountant who worked for him had just quit. Miller was not only a C.P.A., with experience at an important international firm in Harrisburg and several other companies, but also had an M.B.A. from Penn State. He made a good impression on DeMuth: thin, sandy-haired, and fair, and a tennis and basketball player, he is perhaps best described as "clean-cut." His hair is kept short and neatly parted and he always wears a white dress shirt to work. He keeps his desk immaculate. His parents and three sisters live in the Harrisburg area; his father, a former professional baseball player with Chicago White Sox farm teams, was an administrator at a local college, and his mother worked at Sears. He and his family regularly attend the Calgary United Methodist Church. There weren't a great many candidates for the job in central Pennsylvania who had Miller's credentials, especially the M.B.A.

DeMuth himself had an M.B.A. from Wharton, and he felt that the degree was a distinct advantage in attracting the kind of professionals, many of them doctors from the distinguished Hershey Medical Center, who were the mainstay of his practice. After graduating from Wharton, in 1976, DeMuth, too, had returned to the Harrisburg area to be near his family and the business opportunity he saw there. His father is a retired surgeon—a dean of the local medical establishment who seems to be revered both for professional competence and a kindly, gregarious personality. One of Don's younger brothers is also a highly regarded local practitioner.

Like his father and brother, DeMuth is generally described as pleasant and outgoing. An ardent jogger, he is trim and fit and looks a bit younger than his age, which is forty-three. His wife, Nancy, is a psychologist, and they have two sons, thirteen and eleven. In December, the DeMuths sometimes send Christmas cards showing photographs of the family posed before the fireplace, with the boys dressed in baseball uniforms. Baseball is DeMuth's passion. Not only was he part owner of a farm team but as a hobby he runs a mail-order business in minor-league baseball cards and plays catcher in the local over-thirty league. DeMuth attends the Second Presbyterian Church, in nearby Carlisle, and participates in adult Sunday-school classes there, but says he wouldn't describe himself as particularly religious. He is a Republican, as are many of his clients, and describes himself as conservative, though he has never been involved in any political activism or particular conservative causes.

Miller began working for DeMuth part time, but was soon doing so much work that he was billing more than forty hours a week, whereupon DeMuth offered to hire him full time, at a salary of $32,500. DeMuth asked Miller, as he asked all his employees, to sign an employment agreement that, among other things, would penalize Miller for leaving the firm and starting a competing practice. While this seemed reasonable to Miller if he quit voluntarily, it bothered him that he might not be able to earn a living in the area if he was fired—especially if he was fired unjustly. As he recalls it, he asked DeMuth, "What if you fire me and there's no valid reason?" DeMuth hadn't really pondered that, but agreed that the bar would take effect only if Miller should be fired "for cause." Still concerned, Miller asked him to spell out what he meant by "cause."

That evening, DeMuth wrote down what he deemed to be grounds for dismissal—something he says he'd never done before. He says he didn't consult his lawyer, because he didn't believe that he would ever need to enforce such a provision—especially with Miller, to whom it was most unlikely that any of DeMuth's objections would apply. "I listed about a dozen things, both personal and professional—things that I wouldn't want to be associated with," he recalls. In the agreement he finally offered Miller, he included the provision "Cause shall include, but is not limited to, moral turpitude, being charged with a felony, use of illicit drugs, intoxication while working, insulting Employer's family and clients, not working, intentionally working slowly, intentionally losing clients, engaging in sexual activities in the office, and homosexuality."

Outside the United States military, where homosexuality is specifically cited as a ground for discharge, that last provision appears to be exceedingly rare, and has rarely, if ever, been an issue in legal cases. But to DeMuth the logic of it seems so self-evident as hardly to call for explanation. "Homosexuality is not a big thing in my life," he says. "I'm not out stomping out homosexuality at every turn. I'm not a gay-basher." He included the provision partly out of concern for his business and partly out of his own repugnance. "Sodomy is what we're talking about," he says. "This is offensive. Why should I have to defend myself? My views are normal in America."

Miller was astounded when he saw DeMuth's clarification of the contract. He had been dating women, and had never had sex with a man. When he was in business school, he had spent a summer working in Manhattan, living in the East Village, yet had never set foot in a gay bar. Indeed, he'd come back to the Harrisburg area partly because he was dating a local woman and he thought there was a good chance they'd get married. There had been times when he questioned his sexuality. While studying for his M.B.A. at Penn State, he realized that he'd fallen in love with a male classmate who had become his best friend and had visited him during his summer in New York. That fall, hoping his feelings might be reciprocated, Miller mustered the courage to tell his friend that he "might" be gay. "I never want to speak to you again," his friend replied—and didn't. Miller seriously considered suicide, going as far as to buy razor blades and lock himself in his room. Another friend knocked on the door at that moment, reminding him that they had an intramural basketball game. He didn't want to let down the team, so he went. And he started dating a female friend who was in the stands watching the game.

Having asked for and got the clarification, Miller says, he felt he had no choice but to sign the employment agreement. When Susan Davis, DeMuth's secretary, typed the contract, she was surprised by the language, since no one else's contract had contained anything like it. "Doesn't this offend you?" she asked Miller.

"Yeah, it upsets me," he said.

"Is this legal?" Davis asked rhetorically. "I didn't know people could do this."

In Camp Hill, Pennsylvania, as in most of the country, there isn't any law protecting gays and lesbians from discrimination. Several large cities, including New York, Philadelphia, and Pittsburgh, have such ordinances. So does Harrisburg, but it doesn't extend across the river to Camp Hill. Eight states and the District of Columbia have enacted statutes forbidding employment discrimination on the basis of sexual orientation: California, Connecticut, Hawaii, Massachusetts, Minnesota, New Jersey, Vermont, and Wisconsin. Senator Edward Kennedy is currently preparing to sponsor similar federal legislation. To gain political support, the proposed bill is far less sweeping than similar statutes forbidding race discrimination; for example, it would exempt all religious organizations, and it would apply only to large businesses (and thus would not have had any effect on DeMuth and Miller). Nevertheless, it is given scant chance of passage. Indeed, the most heated recent battles have focussed on efforts to roll back those laws that already exist, on the ground that homosexuals shouldn't be given "special treatment." Miller therefore made no effort to protest the contract. . . .

After signing the contract, Miller heard nothing further from De-Muth on the subject of homosexuality. Except for telling the odd joke based on sexist or ethnic stereotypes, DeMuth didn't offer many opinions on politics and social issues at the office. For four years, Miller was asked to renew his contract, with a salary increase each time, and each contract contained the homosexuality clause. Then, as Miller began his fifth year, no contract materialized. Either DeMuth had forgotten or he no longer cared, Miller figured. Either way, it was a good sign.

In January of 1986, after Miller began working for DeMuth but before he signed the contract, he and his girlfriend were at a supermarket, buying taco ingredients for a Mexican dinner, when Miller, flipping through an issue of *Newsweek* displayed at the checkout counter, was startled by a photograph of two young men of about his age, one with his arm around the other. They seemed like regular guys; they even looked a lot like him, he thought. The headline was "GROWING UP GAY."

Miller's relationship with his girlfriend had reached a plateau short of marriage. They had vacationed together in Colorado and, though they had had a good time, something romantic seemed to be missing, at least for Miller. They continued to date steadily, but they didn't move in together. When Miller asked himself if she was the person he wanted to spend the rest of his life with, he began to think that the answer was no. It took the magazine article—which, among other things, described a quasi-marital relationship between the men in the picture—to crystallize his thinking. "That's what I wanted," Miller says.

In the phone book, Miller found a number for a gay-and-lesbian switchboard. He called it, and learned that there was a gay volleyball game in Harrisburg every Tuesday and Friday. He was nervous, but on Friday he went. It was a revelation. He met dozens of gay men at the game. Afterward, they took him to a gay bar. He arranged to go out with a man he met there that night.

The next evening, he told his girlfriend. She seemed hurt and angry, and told their mutual friends what had happened. Miller felt that they were giving him the cold shoulder. Several weeks later, he told one of his sisters, and she said she couldn't keep it a secret from their family. Two nights later, he went to his parents' house, and found them watching an episode of "Dynasty." Miller joined them in front of the TV just as one of the show's characters, Steve Carrington, confronted his father with the fact that he was gay. "I'm here to tell you the same thing," Miller burst out. His parents, astonished, looked at him and said nothing. "Turn the TV off," he urged, and then his confession poured out. When he was done, his mother hugged him. "We still love you," she said. Two days later, his three sisters joined his parents to discuss his being gay, and everyone cried.

Eventually, Miller did get the relationship he'd begun dreaming about when he read the issue of *Newsweek*. During the summer of 1990, at a pool party given by a high-school classmate, he met Carl Bechdel, a lawyer who worked for a large bank and who was recently divorced, with two children. Since 1991, they have lived together in a Victorian house they restored in central Harrisburg. Carl attends all the Miller family gatherings, and Miller has pictures of Carl's children on his desk.

As Miller widened the circle of people who knew he was gay, he gained confidence. He thought less and less of the employment agreement. While he was circumspect at the office—DeMuth remained oblivious of the transformation in Miller's personal circumstances—on some level Miller seems to have wanted the truth to emerge. Over the years he worked there, he and Susan Davis had become close friends, and she often shared with him details of her life outside the office. Davis is attractive and soft-spoken, and at the time she was divorced, with two children. "He listened to all my troubles," she says of Miller. "We were best friends." But they had been working together for three years before Davis, one Monday, asked Miller how he'd spent the weekend. Miller figured that she had guessed. They got coffee and sat down in his office, and Miller told her he was gay. She seemed to take the news in stride. It was only on the following Friday that she really reacted, pulling him aside to say, "When you told me, I was floored. I've been thinking about it all week." She seemed worried, anxious. "Don't ever tell Don," she said. "He'll fire you."

Davis says that the warning was prompted as much by her intuition about DeMuth as by the contract. "He'd say 'That queer got bashed' after seeing something in the paper or on the news," she says of De-Muth. "The tone suggested that the person deserved to be bashed." But Miller didn't pay much attention to her warning. "I thought, I've been here five years," he says. "I could do everything. I was a second DeMuth. He knew me. What difference did it make if I was gay?"

Miller had grown up in a Republican family and had twice voted for Ronald Reagan, but otherwise had given almost no thought to politics, let alone social causes. In college, he had been elected a student senator on a nonpartisan platform. But now his personal situation took on a political dimension. He had become a regular player in the gay volleyball league, and at a volleyball fundraiser the co-chairman of the switchboard asked if he'd like to volunteer. Pleased to have been asked, and having benefitted from the switchboard's existence himself, he agreed. A year later, when a chairman died of AIDS, Miller, something of a natural administrator, thanks to his financial skills, was elected to the position.

During the summer of 1990, with public awareness of the AIDS crisis building, there were several gay-bashings in Harrisburg. Angry calls came in to the switchboard, complaining about the atmosphere of violence and inadequate police investigation. A "town meeting" was convened at a local gay bar to discuss the situation, and Miller, in his capacity as chairman of the switchboard, felt obliged to attend. He and about ten other people showed up early to organize the meeting and discovered that someone had alerted the local press. Though activists might have been expected to welcome press attention, the fledgling gay community in Harrisburg was hardly ready for it. None of the organizers, including Miller, wanted to be identified by name or to appear on television. Not one person was willing to speak out publicly. "We were afraid," Miller says. "We were asking victims"—of gay-bashings—"to go to the police and speak out, but we couldn't even speak to the media." Finally, Miller stepped forward. Though he wasn't willing to be filmed, he made a statement. He was quoted by name in the next day's issue of the Harrisburg *Patriot-News*.

Miller was extremely nervous at the office that week. How would DeMuth react? But nothing happened. DeMuth gave no sign of having read the paper.

A month later, on September 25th, the Harrisburg City Council was scheduled to take up the issue of the outbreak of violence against gays and lesbians, but dropped the matter from its agenda. A friend from the switchboard asked Miller to meet her by the council chamber that evening to find out what was going on. When he arrived, television crews were standing outside the meeting. Miller spoke to an arriving council member, unaware at first that their conversation was being taped by the media.

Then everything happened so fast that he couldn't think about the consequences. With microphones suddenly thrust before him, and told he was already on videotape, Miller spoke out, advocating more police protection for gays and lesbians. It didn't seem a very radical thing to say, and he was careful not to say that he himself was gay.

Still, it was with considerable trepidation that he returned home and, with Bechdel beside him, tuned in the local eleven-o'clock news. He was appalled. He was on every local telecast, including public television. Worse, he was identified as "Daniel Miller, gay-rights activist."

"It was done, it was over," Miller says. "Carl was holding me. I was afraid of what would happen the next day. I was scared."

As before, nothing happened. This time, Miller thought, DeMuth had to know. Perhaps his silence meant that he didn't care.

The day after the television broadcasts, DeMuth was on the phone with a client. "I saw Dan on TV last night," the client remarked. DeMuth said he hadn't seen any of the news programs. "He was on as a spokesman for the gay-lesbian coalition, or something," the client continued matter-of-factly, and went on to other topics.

"I nearly dropped my socks," DeMuth says. "I was shocked and stunned." As the week went on, several other clients and friends mentioned having seen Miller on TV. But no one seemed particularly concerned, or even interested. "Nobody said, 'Why are you foisting off a homosexual on us?'" DeMuth says. "They just happened to bring it up. A couple of people asked, 'Did you know?' Others just mentioned that they happened to see it."

But DeMuth himself was reeling: "We were close. In this office, with four full-time employees, it would be hard not to be close. I considered him as much a friend as any employee I've had. But I knew what I had in the contract. I knew I had to act." DeMuth says that he was especially concerned about what others might think of *him*. "I thought to have a homosexual in my firm would imply an acquiescence, an acceptance." After all, he and Miller had often shared a room while travelling. "There was absolutely nothing sexual. Separate beds," he says. "But the appearance would not look good. I was sharing a room with a homosexual who decided to proclaim this to the world. How did it look?" Similarly, he says he once spent the night at Miller's house, purely for logistical reasons. "That didn't bolster my reputation. Had I known he was a homosexual, I wouldn't have shared his room or stayed in his house." And the more he thought about it, the more he became convinced that his practice hadn't been growing as fast as it had grown before Miller joined him. Were people hesitant to refer business because they believed Miller to be homosexual? DeMuth wasn't sure. No one had ever expressed any concern. But DeMuth considered it a distinct possibility. And, on another level, DeMuth was angry and felt defrauded because Miller didn't conform to any gay stereotypes. "I felt duped, used," he says. "There were at least three women he appeared to be dating. I thought he was a regular single guy."

DeMuth called his lawyer, Samuel L. Andes, and together they worked out a strategy for firing Miller. On Andes' advice, DeMuth said only that he was firing Miller for "going public on a controversial issue that reflected poorly on the firm," even though DeMuth freely concedes that that wasn't the issue—that "his being a homosexual was the issue." But DeMuth didn't act immediately on his decision to fire Miller. One of the things about the affair that most irked him was the timing—just when a number of retirement-plan tax returns were due. Miller had worked on many of those and was, DeMuth had to concede, indispensable. "As soon as those were out the door," DeMuth says, "he'd be gone, too."

Thus it wasn't until October 17th, three weeks after the broadcast, that DeMuth called Miller into his office. After breaking the news that Miller was fired, DeMuth asked Miller what he wanted him to tell the clients. DeMuth says he was just trying to be helpful, since he assumed that the last thing Miller wanted was any mention of homosexuality. But DeMuth's attempt to render what he considered a kindness seemed to trigger an explosion in the hitherto composed Miller. "Tell them I was dismissed because you're a bigot!" Miller yelled. "Tell them the truth! Tell them you fired me because I'm gay!" As the other employees sat in astonished silence, Miller walked out and slammed the door.

Bechdel was at work in Harrisburg when Miller arrived at his office that morning. He looked shaken. He had never come to Bechdel's office before. Miller told him that he'd been fired and that DeMuth wouldn't tell him why. Miller didn't know how he'd support himself.

Susan Davis was at home on maternity leave when she got a call from DeMuth. He said he wanted her to know that he'd fired Miller.

"Why?" she asked.

"I don't think he was a good asset for us," he replied. "He's no longer an asset to the business." She pressed him for more, but he said they'd have to discuss it when she returned to work. A few minutes later, Miller arrived at her front door. When he told her what had happened, Davis said she was so angry that she would start looking for a new job herself. She didn't want to work for DeMuth if Miller wasn't going to be there.

Miller decided to start his own practice, and rented some space in Harrisburg. Because he had trouble sleeping, he'd get up at 2 A.M. and type letters to prospective clients. He had filed for unemployment insurance, but DeMuth had challenged that move, arguing that Miller had been fired for misconduct and thus didn't merit any benefits. (The board ruled against DeMuth, but delayed Miller's payments for weeks while the matter was being resolved.) Once, Miller wouldn't have dreamed of mentioning his personal life to clients. Now he told them point blank that he had been fired because he was gay. He saw no reason to mince words. He didn't worry much about the non-compete clause in his contract with DeMuth, since a similar provision had been ruled not to apply when DeMuth sued one of his predecessors who had left. In any event, Miller didn't see any choice short of leaving the Harrisburg area.

DeMuth had assumed Miller would go to work for the state government in Harrisburg, "where they tolerate that sort of thing," he says. He had not expected Miller to solicit potential clients in what he deemed to be blatant disregard of their agreement. And he certainly hadn't expected some of his clients to take Miller's side in the affair. "If you asked me, 'Name one thing you could do or say that would destroy your business in a day,' I'd say, 'Come out and say you're a homosexual,'" DeMuth says. But the first client who called, the same day DeMuth fired Miller, told DeMuth he wanted Miller to take his files with him, because Miller would be doing his firm's work in the future. "Wait a minute," DeMuth countered. "Let's talk. We don't just hand out client files." DeMuth says he tried to explain the situation, but the client insisted on taking his work to Miller.

Within a matter of days, the business manager for one of DeMuth's largest clients, a medical group, called to say that he, too, wanted to follow Miller. Miller had visited him personally, explaining why he'd been fired. Like many of DeMuth's clients, he sought to follow Miller for reasons having little or nothing to do with why Miller had been fired. "I wanted Dan to succeed for selfish reasons," he says. "We rely on Dan on an almost daily basis. He was, in fact, doing almost all our work. He understood the technology, the computer system. Don didn't even have a fax. We'd grown quite a bit since we started using Don, and a lot had changed. I didn't want to go back to Don."

DeMuth "didn't take this lying down," the client says, and went directly to the group's doctors. One of the senior practitioners, in particular, who was a close friend of DeMuth's father, demanded an explanation from the business manager, but he seemed satisfied when he learned of Miller's automation skills. "Dan's preference—is that the word?—didn't come up then," the business manager says, adding that the only time it did was when Miller sent clients a newsletter mentioning tax planning for same-sex couples. The manager says he asked

Miller not to mention homosexual issues in future newsletters—at least, not if he was sending them to clients' home addresses.

DeMuth's letter to clients disclosing Miller's homosexuality and raising the possibility that he might have AIDS seems to have been prompted by such defections. Of the letter, DeMuth says, "I decided I would be more active when I was in a situation with somebody out there trying to take my clients. He knew who the good clients were. I think Dan wanted to take business to get at me." Copies of the letter were soon circulating among the local medical profession, and some were sent on to Miller. "I would have thought they would keep it in confidence," DeMuth says. "I regret the way the letter sounds. I made a number of true statements in a colorful manner that certainly didn't make him look good." Nor, apparently, did it make DeMuth look good. The letter was "the nail in DeMuth's coffin, as far as we were concerned," the business manager who followed Miller says. DeMuth's views on homosexuality were his own business. But now "it began to seem like some kind of phobia," this man says.

Miller might have been more upset by the letter if it had seemed to have any effect. But, somewhat to his surprise, the client defections accelerated. Eventually, nearly a third of DeMuth's practice, accounting for about a hundred thousand dollars a year in billings, followed Miller. He felt confident enough to buy a vintage office building in downtown Harrisburg, to begin renovating it, and to hire an associate of his own. He also hired Susan Davis, who was still working with DeMuth, to do some typing during the evenings. One Sunday afternoon, DeMuth called her at home. "I don't want you coming back to work" he said, and fired her.

"Why?" she asked.

"You know why," DeMuth said. The only explanation Davis received came when she applied for unemployment insurance and DeMuth lodged his opposition on the basis of "inability to separate business and personal life."

In the summer of 1991 Miller applied for membership in the Society of Medical-Dental Management Consultants, which was having its annual meeting in Chicago. DeMuth attended the meeting and succeeded in getting the issue of Miller's membership on the agenda. He made an impassioned speech arguing that homosexuals—and Miller specifically—should be barred from membership. "I feel our clients have a right to know the moral character of people coming to them," DeMuth says. Someone in the audience asked if a client had ever complained about Miller's sexual orientation. DeMuth said no. Another asked if Miller's sexuality had ever affected his work. Again, DeMuth said no. Miller was admitted to membership with only one dissenting vote—DeMuth's.

Soon after being fired, Miller had consulted a lawyer, James W. Evans, about the possibility of suing DeMuth. Discussions of the subject had continued, but as the anniversary of Miller's discharge neared, and his practice seemed be taking off, he decided he wanted put the whole affair behind him. On Monday, November 25th, he called his lawyer and said he'd decided to let the matter drop. Then, just two days later, he arrived at his office to find a summons and complaint taped to the door. DeMuth had sued *him.*

The trial of DeMuth v. Miller began on Monday, June 21, 1993, before Judge Kevin A. Hess of the Cumberland County Court of Common Pleas, in Carlisle. DeMuth was suing for breach of contract—specifically, breach of the non-compete prohibition. By this time, Miller had countersued for wrongful discharge, defamation, and interference with his efforts to earn a living. The jury consisted of ten men and two women, among them a truck driver, an office supervisor, a retired military man, and a reporter for the *Patriot-News.*

As jury trials go, it was remarkably straightforward and to the point. DeMuth, conservatively dressed in a tan suit and seeming self-assured, was the first witness. His wife, Nancy, sat in the courtroom, avoiding Miller's gaze. (Indeed, she never spoke to him after his dismissal, even though Miller had considered her a friend.) A fair amount of time was spent establishing that there was no signed contract at the time Miller was fired, and why, and also establishing the client billings that DeMuth had lost to Miller's new firm. The earlier employment agreements had called for Miller to pay DeMuth a hundred and twenty-five per cent of the amount of any client billings obtained in violation of the non-compete clause. Then DeMuth's lawyer, Samuel Andes, asked him to describe Miller's termination.

"I indicated that I was sorry that things hadn't worked out, that I was terminating his employment, that he knew why I was doing this, and I remember Dan objecting to my use of the term sexual preference. He indicated that it was a sexual orientation of his that he could no more change than the color of his eyes."

"Did you tell him at that time that he was fired because he was homosexual?"

"In so many words, no. I indicated to him that he knew why, and I think that it was obvious from the nature of our conversation that he knew why."

DeMuth testified several times that Miller's work was satisfactory and that he was on track to becoming a partner, culminating in this exchange with Miller's lawyer, Dan Sullivan:

"Now, as of October 17, 1990, Mr. Miller was properly discharging his duties?"

"I consider homosexuality as cause that incapacitated him from properly discharging his duties."

"Was he properly discharging his duties with respect to his services as a professional financial consultant as of October 17, 1990?"

"Not if he's a homosexual, as far as I'm concerned."

The next day, Miller took the stand. His testimony paralleled DeMuth's, for there had never been any serious disagreement over the facts. On being asked why he had signed the employment agreement after DeMuth inserted the homosexuality clause, Miller explained, "I felt I didn't have much of a choice."

Sullivan asked Miller for his version of his termination.

"I went to work like I regularly went to work," Miller said. "And Don called me into his office. And I went over. It was not unusual. And he said sit down. And he said, 'I am terminating you.' It was just, it was very, you know, just very blunt."

Under further questioning, Miller testified, "Well, as I said, I was very stunned about this. We had a good relationship professionally and personally. The thing I remember most vividly is we were having this discussion, and finally Don says to me, he says, 'Well, Dan, what do you want me to tell the clients?'

"And I said, Don, just tell them the truth. I said, tell them that I am gay. At that point Don responded, 'No, no, no! It is not that. It is that you appeared on television. And you made your sexual preference known there.' And, you know, I remember that just like it was yesterday, because I was so angry at him, and him trying to insinuate that I was embarrassed about who I was."

Before the jury could consider Miller's counterclaim of wrongful discharge, Judge Hess dismissed it. "The argument that a person is protected in Pennsylvania from either being a homosexual and announcing it in public, that may be the law someday," the judge announced. "Someday the legislature may create such a set of legal principles. But as I understand the law to be at this point in time there is no such protection." He then granted the motion by DeMuth's lawyer to dismiss Miller's claim.

That narrowed the case to three points: whether Miller breached a contract that was in effect; whether Miller misappropriated confidential information from DeMuth; and whether DeMuth defamed Miller by raising the issue of AIDS in his letter. The judge said in his charge to the jury, "Mr. Miller cannot avoid the consequences of a contract between himself and Mr. DeMuth simply by claiming that he did not intend to be bound by it. An agreement need not be reduced to writing to be enforceable. Oral or verbal agreements between the parties are valid. And the law will enforce them."

The jurors deliberated a day and a half. "The gay issue was discussed," recalls Mary Warner, the reporter for the Harrisburg *Patriot-News* who was on the jury. "People were concerned about the contract, more than I would have expected. I heard concerns expressed about the unfairness of the contract. I feel some people would have liked to take steps to come out on Miller's side. But they didn't feel they could, because of the structure of the case. Some people were quiet. No one said, as I expected someone might, that a person has a right to keep those kind of people out."

Warner herself felt "a certain amount of outrage about the nature of that contract," she says. "I can remember feeling physically sick when DeMuth was asked what was the problem, and he said, 'Just his being gay was enough.' I wasn't the only one who felt that way." But in the end Warner's was the lone vote in Miller's favor. (In Pennsylvania, civil cases do not require unanimous verdicts.) Once the jurors had narrowed the issue in accordance with the judge's instructions, they concluded that there was a contract providing that homosexuality was cause for firing, that Miller was a homosexual and thus was in breach of the contract, and that he had taken clients from DeMuth—all facts that really weren't at issue. Little time was spent on either the misappropriation claim—it was moot given the jury's view that the contract had been breached—or the defamation claim, since DeMuth had never actually said that Miller had AIDS. The damages were just a matter of mathematics. As Warner later wrote in the *Patriot-News*, explaining the result, "I know that the jurors whose votes prevailed deliberated carefully, even agonizingly, and concluded with good reason that their verdict followed from the law they were given."

Warner was watching DeMuth as the verdict was read; it awarded him $126,648. A triumphant smile spread across his face.

Before the judge released the jury, he thanked them for their efforts. "This could prove to be a significant case," he told them. He said he hoped they understood that he could not let them consider whether the contract was fair, or whether DeMuth should have been allowed to fire Miller for being gay. "If we'd done that, we would have been making law," he said. "It is not for this court to make law."

After the verdict, Miller borrowed most of the money for his bond—a hundred and fifty-six thousand dollars (the amount of the verdict plus interest)—from Bechdel, his family, and his friends. He sold all his personal assets except his real estate, which was heavily mortgaged. He couldn't afford to keep paying his lawyers, whom he owed forty-four thousand dollars, and had to negotiate a reduction in their fees for the trial. At first, he felt like giving up. "He was so wrung out he just wanted to pay and get on with his life," Bechdel says. "But I knew that eventually he'd be ready for a good fight."

A group of people in Harrisburg organized a defense fund to raise money for an appeal, and at the same time Miller got in touch with both the American Civil Liberties Union and the Lambda Legal

Defense Fund, asking for help. The A.C.L.U. turned down the request. At first, Lambda refused to help, but then, somewhat to Miller's surprise, Lambda agreed to take the case.

Beatrice Dohrn, Lambda's legal director, who is one of the lawyers representing Miller in the appeal, says that Lambda rarely accepts cases at the trial level. Lambda is now convinced, however, that Miller's case has far-reaching significance. Reasoning from Shelley v. Kraemer, a famous Supreme Court case, which held that a court cannot enforce a racially discriminatory agreement, she says, "Basic fairness suggests that a court should not enforce such a blatantly discriminatory contract," and she goes on, "Even if we lose—and we shouldn't lose—this should highlight the fact that gays and lesbians need protection. People should wake up."

The appeal, which is scheduled for June 21st, is taking a narrower approach than Miller's lawyers did at the trial. Miller is no longer arguing that it was unlawful to fire him simply because he is gay. "I'm sorry to say that there is no remedy in Pennsylvania law for that," Dohrn concedes. "If DeMuth had stopped at that, we wouldn't have a case." But DeMuth went several steps further, invoking the state court system to enforce the contract and extract damages. That, Dohrn will argue, involves state, rather than private, action. Ultimately, the case could wind up in the Supreme Court.

"I expected to be vindicated, and I was," DeMuth says now of the verdict. "It was gratifying." But he's not entirely satisfied. "I'm still waiting to see the first cent" of the damages, he complains. "I'd be better off financially if this matter had never come up," what with attorneys' fees and lost client revenues. "But I said at the time, 'If I knew that every client would leave me, would I still fire Dan?' The answer is yes."

DeMuth's convictions on the subject of homosexuality, reinforced by his victory in the lawsuit, seem to have deepened. He consulted his minister about the lawsuit and the Presbyterian Church's stand on homosexuality, and the minister told him, "The church welcomes homosexuals as well as everyone else." But, DeMuth points out, "it does not ordain homosexuals as ministers. What does that tell you?" (In fact, the Presbyterian Church will not accept gays as elders, or even deacons.)

Recently, DeMuth read about a so-called "gay gene" and has been pondering the implications. "Could this be biological?" he wonders. "Wouldn't it be good if we could test for this in utero, like Down's syndrome? There aren't many parents who'd be happy knowing they had a fetus they had reason to believe would be a homosexual, any more than they'd be happy to know it would have Down's syndrome."

It is impossible to know how DeMuth came to feel about these questions as strongly as he does. His demeanor as he expounds his views remains eminently calm and reasonable, as though he were patiently explaining the fine points of the tax code to one of his doctor clients. And, given the surge in violence against gays and lesbians, the public outcry about gays in the military, and the vehement rhetoric of recent voter initiatives against gay rights, his views hardly seem isolated.

But why would DeMuth fire and pursue Miller to the point that his own business has suffered? DeMuth seems puzzled by such a question. As he sees it, his beliefs stem not from prejudice but from principle: he stands in a long line of Americans who have stood up for what they believed in, however harshly history may ultimately have judged many of their causes. DeMuth is a man of conviction, and he is proud of that.

Miller, once afraid to phone the gay switchboard, is now a leader of the gay community in Harrisburg. During the summer of 1991, the *Patriot-News* did a Sunday feature headlined "GAY IN THE '90s." On the paper's front page, in a one-column photograph, are Miller and Bechdel, smiling, dressed in shirts and ties, with Bechdel's hand resting on Miller's atop a desk. Like the issue of *Newsweek* that had once inspired Miller, the Sunday paper was displayed at the supermarket checkout counter.

That same summer, Miller organized a Gay and Lesbian Pride festival in Harrisburg—a picnic with live entertainment in a local park—to mark the June anniversary of the Stonewall riots in New York. About a thousand people showed up. The following year, the crowd doubled. Miller has also organized a Harrisburg chapter of the Pennsylvania Justice Campaign, a statewide organization that has as its goal extending Pennsylvania's human-rights law to cover sexual orientation. (Prospects do not look favorable.) Last year, Miller co-wrote a guide for gay and lesbian voters in Harrisburg, which got him the attention of local Democratic Party officials. His local state representative, Ron Buxton, and his councilwoman, Peggy Grove, encouraged him to run for the post of ward committeeman. This spring, Miller, the former Republican, ran as a Democrat and was elected.

But Miller is ambivalent about his transformation into an activist. He feels that his new role has been thrust upon him. "Once I had a normal life," he says almost wistfully. "I went to a job, I went home, I had friends and a social life. There are days when I feel like I don't want to be gay anymore. I just want to go back to living the way I did. Now I have a business I have to keep afloat. I have to work continuously. I'm the most visible gay person in Harrisburg. That's a heavy responsibility." But, he says, "I'm free. I can be myself."

Speculations

1. What "personal and professional" reasons does Donald L. DeMuth list for firing an employee? Which of these reasons do you agree are fair and which unfair? Explain your response.
2. Explain DeMuth's motivations for firing Daniel Miller and writing the letter about the danger of AIDS to Miller's business clients. Explain why you think DeMuth was right or wrong in these actions.
3. Imagine yourself to be in Miller's position at the gay rights demonstration when the TV cameras arrived—though you might imagine another cause you feel strongly about such as animal rights, civil rights, pro-life, pro-choice, or even the right to protest itself. What would you do in this situation if you knew your career and job would be threatened? Would you speak up or disappear? Explain your response.
4. When asked why he signed the employment agreement that said homosexuals could be fired, Miller replied "I felt I didn't have much of a choice." Why does he believe this? Do you agree? Explain your response.
5. What was the final verdict of the judge and what were the actual consequences for both parties, both legally and personally? Explain whether you think the verdict and its consequences were just or fair.
6. Do you feel that Stewart has portrayed each of the individuals, DeMuth and Miller, in this story fairly and sympathetically? Or does the story seem to favor one individual over the other? Explain your response.

CONDUCT UNBECOMING: THE "COPY" BERG STORY

Randy Shilts

Journalist, gay activist, and author of many articles and essays, Randy Shilts was the first openly gay establishment journalist in California. He is perhaps best known for his masterful account of the beginning of the AIDS epidemic, *And the Band Played On: Politics, People, and the AIDS Epidemic* (1987), which was ultimately transformed into an HBO movie in 1994, the same year that Shilts died of AIDS. *And the Band Played On* garnered many awards for Shilts including the Silver

Medal for best nonfiction author from the Commonwealth Club (1987) and the Outstanding Communicator award from the Association for Education in Journalism and Mass Communication (1988); he was also named Outstanding Author of 1988 by the American Society of Journalists and Authors.

Shilts was born in Davenport, Iowa, in 1951, the son of working class parents. He attended the University of Oregon, earning a B.S. in 1975 after switching majors from English to Journalism, but he had no luck finding employment in Oregon. As Shilts stated to *Contemporary Authors:*

> I couldn't get a job when I came out of journalism school, even though I was managing editor of the campus paper and I'd won more awards than anybody else at the University of Oregon in years and was at the very top of my class. I'd been very open about being gay.... That became well known around the state.... Other people who weren't as active as I was in journalism or didn't have the awards or the grades were getting job offers in Oregon. I wasn't, so I sort of took the hint.

Shilts moved to San Francisco and began work on *The Advocate,* a gay publication. Ultimately, he moved into broadcast journalism, reported on the political scene surrounding George Moscone and Harvey Milk, and wrote many essays and articles for a wide range of publications including *Christopher Street,* the *Washington Post,* the *Village Voice,* the San Francisco *Chronicle* and *Examiner,* and the *Columbia Journalism Review.* In 1982, he wrote *The Mayor of Castro Street: The Life and Times of Harvey Milk,* a biography of Harvey Milk, the charismatic and powerful gay activist and member of the Board of Supervisors in San Francisco who was assassinated in 1978.

Shilts stated that his writing style was greatly influenced by television "in terms of being highly image-oriented. Whenever I'm writing a story or a book, I tend to lean on very visual scenes." That ability to visualize, to introduce drama and image into his work, can be seen as well in the following excerpt from *Conduct Unbecoming: Gays and Lesbians in the U.S. Military* (1993). It is worth noting that Shilts conducted interviews with more than 1,100 gay men and women in the U.S. military as part of the research for this provocative and important book.

George Washington Hotel
Washington, D.C.

Though she was still young and pretty, her show-business career had certainly known better days, it was clear. That undoubtedly was why she was dressed up in a cowboy hat, a satin cowboy dress with fringe, and had toy six-shooters strapped to her hips. Her husband hovered nearby, looking officious and shouting orders, but the woman looked lonely and a little sad sitting backstage knitting, waiting to appear. Everybody else knew Anita Bryant from her orange-juice commercials on television, but this was how Copy Berg always remembered her, looking lonesome and a little lost backstage at the George Washington Hotel.

It was one of the perks of being in the Glee Club of the United States Naval Academy that you got to meet celebrities wherever you went. This was how winners lived, and as he lined up with the other Annapolis cadets to back up Anita Bryant on her trademark song, "The Battle Hymn of the Republic," Navy Midshipman Copy Berg had no doubt that he was a winner.

Vernon E. Berg III was the eldest son of Navy Commander Vernon E. Berg, Jr., one of the most respected officers in the Navy's chaplain corps. The senior Berg had been equally revered in the civilian ministry, as a preacher who touched people's souls. His sermons changed lives, they said of Vernon E. Berg; he was charismatic, and no one could believe how much his namesake resembled his father. Their childhood photographs were indistinguishable. As young Vernon grew into his full five-foot-nine-inch frame and his hair turned sandy blond, he was still the carbon copy of his dad, right down to the deep blue eyes and second-tenor voice, which was why they called him Copy. And they were extraordinarily close, to the point that Copy knew what his father was thinking just by looking at him, as if they were the same person. They did virtually everything together until the commander went to Vietnam in 1967 to minister to the Marines.

Copy began establishing his own track record of being a winner then. He was not just another track letterman at Frank W. Cox High School; he was also student body president. At Boy's State, he was not just a delegate, he was a candidate for governor. At Boy Scout Troop 422, he was not simply another Life Scout, he was Alowat Sikima, Chief of Fire, the top position of the elite Order of the Arrow fraternity for the entire Chesapeake Bay area. Whenever local chapters of the Lion's or Rotary or Optimist's Clubs needed a *good* teenager to speak, they trotted out Copy Berg.

There was a creative side to Copy, and he excelled in music and art. Later, he regretted he did not apply to Juilliard to develop his artistic talent earlier, but Copy Berg lived in Virginia Beach, Virginia, one of the communities that circles the elaborate network of Navy installations centered around Norfolk. In Virginia Beach, nobody went to Juilliard; few had even heard of it. Winners went to the United States Naval Academy at Annapolis. In the Cox High class of 1969, a dozen graduates went, and Copy Berg was among them.

Only in his sexual attractions did his confidence waver. He liked women and had had plenty of sexual experiences with them in high school and after. But he also liked men. In Troop 422, he had begun a four-year relationship with another Boy Scout that endured through his senior year at Cox. They had good sex, too. He was not plagued by guilt over this, but he knew he was not supposed to be having these kinds of attractions and he also knew instinctively he was not supposed to talk about it. Commander Berg had a number of books about sexuality in his library, and one day Copy looked up homosexuality. The book offered "case studies of deviate sexual behavior," which relieved Copy. Homosexuals wore dresses and wanted to be women; Copy was not like that, so obviously he was not one of them.

But in the year he spent at the Naval Academy Preparatory School in advance of his first year at Annapolis, there were rumors. One friend finally asked, "Why is it everyone thinks you're a homo?"

"Because I'm thin," Copy said, which seemed reasonable enough.

On weekends, Berg went from the preparatory school to New York City, and occasionally had sex with men he met at Times Square or on the subway. But for him, these encounters were play; they did not comprise an identity.

Copy never wanted for dates with girls. He was active in the Annapolis drama program, where he met and began dating the daughter of Admiral William Mack, the superintendent of the Naval Academy. The admiral was pleased. Copy Berg was the kind of man you wanted your daughter to date. All this was diverting, but Copy sometimes felt that somehow, in his romantic life, he was missing the point. By the autumn of his sophomore year at Annapolis, he was thinking more about his identity and becoming aware that his attractions were drifting toward males. Lord knew, he could not expect to pursue a Navy career with such extracurricular activities; they threw people like that in the brig.

With no one to talk to about them, his conflicts grew. The Naval Academy did not offer many opportunities to explore one's feelings and Annapolis was not an environment that gave a twenty-year-old any venue in which to discuss his confusion over sexual identity. Any such discussion would be the end not only of a Navy career but the Academy's college education, as well. One night, standing at the head of the stairs in Bancroft Hall, the huge redbrick Academy dormitory, Copy Berg stared down the open stairwell toward the lobby, eight floors below, and wondered what it would be like to throw himself down.

The 1972 Democratic National Convention had marked a number of pivotal points for emerging constituency groups. There was the first, though unsuccessful, attempt to obtain a gay-rights plank to the party platform. Women, for the first time, received a substantial role in the proceedings, comprising 40 percent of the total delegates, compared to just 13 percent four years earlier. Though these advances were significant for gays and women, it must also be noted that the convention was a prelude to disaster for the Democratic party.

A political realignment took shape in the 1972 election, a shift that would define presidential politicking for the next two decades. Democrat McGovern based his campaign in large part on an extremely liberal domestic agenda and the promise to withdraw troops from Vietnam.

Henry Kissinger assured the public in the last days of the campaign that "peace is at hand." That left McGovern with a domestic agenda demanding more change from a public weary and fearful of all the changes that had been foisted on it in the past decade.

Many of the fears were unspoken, but Republicans were learning to play on them just the same. President Nixon talked about his opposition to school busing as a means of achieving racial integration in schools and about the need for law and order. To a public fearful of African Americans and of crime and economic dislocation, these were powerful code words. Jim Foster and Gloria Steinem did not speak to those fears; often they exacerbated them. And so the Republicans could paint the Democratic party as a radical fringe, outside the mainstream. Vice President Agnew called them the party of the three A's: acid, abortion, and amnesty for draft dodgers. Blue-collar workers, who had found a new spokesman on the wildly popular new television show "All in the Family," retreated into the nostalgic rhetoric of Archie Bunker and deserted the Democrats. Most crucially, the Republicans pursued a "southern strategy" of alienating conservative southern voters from their century-old alliance with the Democrats. All of this culminated in one of the largest landslides in American history, meaning that come January 20, 1973, Copy Berg and the Naval Academy Chorus would be singing for the inauguration of Richard Nixon to a second term as President.

There was one respite from Berg's growing personal turmoil at the Naval Academy: singing second tenor in the Glee Club. Every other month, the Glee Club toured to promote the Academy, and it was on one of these tours at a meeting of the International Truckers' Association that Berg saw Bryant in her cowboy outfit. Copy felt sorry for her, so he and a friend grabbed a vase of roses sitting on the side of the stage and passed them out among the entire Glee Club. One by one, the white-uniformed men walked up to the singer and handed her a rose. She seemed almost shy as she put aside her knitting and gave each of the cadets a kiss on the cheek as he handed her a blossom: for every rose, a kiss from Anita Bryant.

Copy Berg's window on a new world opened unexpectedly during his junior year when he tried out for the part of Senex in *A Funny Thing Happened on the Way to the Forum*. The part was outrageously campy and, since the twenty-one-year-old midshipman always had had more nerve than talent onstage, it suited Berg's disposition perfectly. It was during auditions that Copy met Lawrence Gibson, a private grade-school teacher who was choreographer and director for the play. Bald and bearded, not especially handsome, Gibson was fifteen years older than Copy. He was, by most accounts, a bit stuffy; he always wore a three-piece suit and was not what you would call, in the lingo of the day, laid-back. None of this mattered to Copy, however, because Gibson also was many things that Copy Berg had never seen before in another person, someone he had never met in base towns like Virginia Beach or among the squared-away, buttoned-down instructors at the Naval Academy. Gibson was the first person Copy had ever met who he knew was gay. Copy aggressively invited himself to dinner at Gibson's apartment and the two began an affair.

Lawrence Gibson introduced Copy to a new world. The older man knew about good wines and antiques, the latest books and theater. He was not married, nor did he have children, something Copy just assumed he would have to do one day, because he had no idea there was any other way to live. On trips to Washington, Gibson introduced Berg to a vast network of gay men. Berg, who was barely old enough to go to bars, had been vaguely aware that such a subculture existed, but he never considered it something that related to him. This was not the gay world of, say, the Gay Liberation Front or even the Mattachine Society. This was more like life in the play *The Boys in the Band,* full of shrewd one-liners, aging opera aficionados, and stuffy bureaucrats, all extremely closeted.

By the middle of Copy Berg's senior year, in December 1973, he had decided that he would not make a career of the Navy as his dad had. There was a free world outside the rigid confines of the Navy, one in which he did not have to hide. The past year had shown Copy how to navigate in these waters. On his summer cruise aboard the *USS Kennedy,* he had gone to Majorca and realized how easy it was to meet like-minded men.

Back in the United States there was also a palpable hostility toward anything military. Midshipmen were advised not to walk around the streets in their uniforms. When the Academy Glee Club toured other cities, people would shout out, "How many babies have you burned?" These Glee Club members were college students; they had not killed any babies. This was not the career for Copy. His future was clear to him. He would do the five years he owed the Navy for his education, then leave.

For Midshipman Vernon "Copy" Berg, the graduation ceremony at the Naval Academy seemed somehow representative of the times. President Nixon, just two months away from resignation, was the commencement speaker. Copy's family photo album commemorated the day: There was Copy's sister in a black miniskirt, his younger brother in a Fu Manchu mustache, and Berg's lover, Lawrence Gibson.

His time together with Gibson seemed about to end. Copy had known for several months that his first duty station would be in Gaeta, Italy, with the Sixth Fleet. He had been excited about striking out on his own, but Gibson seemed crestfallen to him. Copy had ignored the older man's entreaties that he could not live without Berg, until the night before graduation, when he went to Gibson's apartment and found him dazed and stumbling, apparently suffering from what looked to Berg like a drug overdose. Years later, Gibson would not discuss this period of his past, but to Berg it looked as if he had attempted suicide. It was enough to make the twenty-two-year-old midshipman feel terrible about leaving Gibson behind.

Okay, Berg recalls finally agreeing, Gibson could join him in Italy the following year when Berg had completed his technical training in the San Francisco Bay Area. The next morning Gibson joined Midshipman Vernon E. Berg III, Berg's father, the commander, and the rest of the family for the commencement at Annapolis.

Newspaper accounts of the graduation ceremony mentioned that the day reflected the tensions of the times. A month earlier, the House Judiciary Committee had begun hearings on whether to impeach Nixon. Already, a host of administration officials had been indicted, including two former Attorneys General. Calls for Nixon's resignation mounted. The President had long ago stopped making public appearances where he might encounter a hostile audience, which was just about everywhere in the country; now he spoke mainly in foreign countries or on military bases. If Nixon thought Annapolis would be an entirely friendly site, however, he was mistaken. Some midshipmen refused to stand for the Commander in Chief. When each company mounted the stage for the customary presentation of a gift to the commencement speaker, the President found himself accepting such items as a rubber lizard. Ignited by the unpopular war and accelerated by the distrust in public institutions that the Watergate scandal had caused, the questioning of authority that had begun years ago in the Summer of Love reached even here.

The topic that loomed larger even than President Nixon at the Naval Academy, however, was whether women should be admitted to Annapolis in years to come. In February, the United States Merchant Marine Academy on Long Island had enrolled its first two female "midshippersons." The first WACs had begun training to be military police; in August 1974, the Army opened its first coed barracks. Meanwhile, after Congress ordered it to admit women for the first time in its 184-year history, the Coast Guard was trying to figure out how to adapt what had always been an all-male service. As Chief Boatswain Mate Royce Jones, an eighteen-year veteran in charge of the new women recruits, told the *New York Times*, "We don't want to take the woman out of the women. Maybe you've seen movies of the old Marine woman sergeants. This is not what we're looking for. We don't want them acting like a bunch of Russians. We hope we never have to have the women on the front lines in this country, but they certainly are nice to have behind you."

The other service academies were still adamant in refusing admission to women. Major General James Allen, the superintendent of the Air Force Academy, went on record as being firmly opposed to women cadets. West Point superintendent Major General Sidney Berry also vowed women would never attend the Army academy. At the Naval Academy, the idea that women might one day inhabit their beloved Bancroft Hall horrified Copy Berg's classmates.

June 5, 1975
Suez Canal
Egypt

Ensign Vernon "Copy" Berg stood on the bridge of the USS *Little Rock,* snapping pictures of Egyptians berserk with joy. The Suez Canal, devastated by the Six-Day War in 1967, had been reopened at last. Thousands lined the banks, climbed up phone poles, piled into little boats, and waved from the roofs of buildings. The USS *Little Rock,* the flagship of the Sixth Fleet, in "full-dress ship," would lead all other ships through the narrow channel of water into the Red Sea.

The mid-1970s was not an ideal time to be part of the United States military stationed overseas. The Vietnam War had been even more unpopular in Europe than in the United States, and American ships found themselves unwelcome in the ports of such traditional allies as Greece, Spain, and France. The *Little Rock* was home-ported in Gaeta, Italy, near Naples, a pit of a town with no base or facilities. Morale among the sailors and their families was low. Of the five ensigns on the *Little Rock,* Berg was the only Academy graduate, which presaged jealousies. But his positive attitude saw him through his service, and he managed to have a pretty good time aboard the "Show Boat," as he called the *Little Rock,* though he formed no intimate relationships. There had been a close encounter when a journalist second class named Laurent John Crofwell showed interest. Crofwell even went to Berg's villa one night and was about to spend the night, but he left abruptly, before any physical contact, as Berg recalled. He thought Crofwell was struggling just as Berg had years earlier. He did not think much more of it and over the ensuing weeks the two resumed a normal working relationship on the *Little Rock.*

Meanwhile, Berg looked forward to Lawrence Gibson's imminent arrival. Gibson would arrive while the *Little Rock* was visiting Yugoslavia, so Berg left notes for his lover throughout the apartment. It was at about this time, while Berg was still in Yugoslavia and Gibson had not yet arrived, that Berg's sister came early for a visit. Another ensign's wife, a dour Mormon as it turned out, let her into Berg's apartment, where they found the little notes everywhere, with affectionate allusions obvious to anyone who saw them, all addressed to Lawrence.

By then, however, Berg was already under investigation, as he had been for several months.

July 29, 1975
Aboard USS Little Rock
Gaeta, Italy

As an officer, Ensign Copy Berg frequently interacted with agents from the Naval Investigative Service, so he did not consider it unusual when NIS agent Parker called him into his office on a sunny day while the ship was at port. From Parker's office, Berg was escorted to an old apartment house that the Navy had converted into a warren of offices and classrooms. Once there, Parker introduced another NIS agent. "We're here to talk about your homosexuality," he said.

"What homosexuality?" Berg asked.

The NIS later said it could not locate Agent Parker for an interview, but the way Berg recalled the afternoon, the agents alternated their questions. One was confrontational and hostile; Parker was kind and understanding.

"You can tell us everything," Parker said. The NIS already had the names of all the Naval Academy officers, midshipmen, and faculty members with whom Berg had had sex and the dates when these assignations had taken place. They knew everything already, he said. He recited a long list of names. Berg recognized some as Academy faculty members, but he had never even met most of them. He refused to admit to anything.

The interview continued by the script, the good cop/bad cop dialogue, the crudely detailed questions about Berg's sexuality. When Berg still would not respond, the pair played their trump card.

"Mr. Gibson says that you did have sexual relations," the belligerent agent said, and then described a particular intimate act as Gibson had presumably described it to him. "Do you deny it?" he asked.

That morning, Lawrence Gibson had been removed from his classroom aboard the USS *Little Rock* as he prepared to teach his second class and was escorted to a small room where he met with two agents of the NIS.

According to Gibson's later account of the morning, one agent, who identified himself as R. W. Bartlett, was hostile; the other, S. I.

Eisenson, was understanding. Neither Bartlett nor Eisenson were later made available to give their versions of what happened that morning, but Gibson said he held out for a while, through Bartlett's crude insinuations and impertinent questions, through Eisenson's assurances that anything he said about Berg would be held in the strictest confidence—they weren't after Gibson. He was Civil Service and the NIS had no jurisdiction over the Civil Service. They were simply trying to ensure national security.

Bartlett read Gibson a list of a dozen or more names from the Naval Academy—civilian teachers, midshipmen, senior officers—and said Ensign Berg had had sex with all of them, according to Gibson. Agent Eisenson asked Gibson how he had liked Annapolis. Wasn't it a beautiful setting? Bartlett wanted to know who fucked whom. Who was the "inserter" and who was the "insertee"?

Eventually, they broke Gibson down. He admitted that he was gay and that he and Berg were having a sexual relationship.

But this was not enough. Precisely when had they engaged in oral copulation? Anal copulation? How many times? When? The agents also wanted all correspondence between the two men. When Gibson refused, they asked him to sign a statement reiterating all he had told them. He refused again, pointing out that Agent Bartlett had taken copious notes all morning. He did agree to take an oath attesting to the truth of what he had said. They then asked him to sign a waiver allowing them to search his apartment. It was his "patriotic duty" to sign the waiver; Berg might have documents that would compromise national security. Gibson would not. Finally, he was permitted to leave.

The NIS agents told Berg what Gibson had said, including a number of specifics that convinced Berg that Gibson had indeed talked to them. Nothing Berg had learned at the Naval Academy had prepared him for this kind of interrogation. Gay issues had never even been discussed in his education. Now, with Gibson's confession, Berg saw no use in denying that he was gay. It seemed more significant that innocent names from the Naval Academy were being bandied about. It appeared that scores of careers were threatened. To define what was not true, Berg admitted to what was.

At the end of the interrogation, Berg figured his Navy career was over. He was very surprised, therefore, when he returned to the *Little Rock* and Vice Admiral F. C. "Fox" Turner's chief of staff asked him to replace the head of public affairs, who was going on vacation. They would sail for North Africa the next morning. Berg was to report aboard the *Little Rock* at 0730. There was no need to revoke his security clearance or to do anything "unusual" until further orders came from Washington.

It was the most responsible post Berg had ever held during his Navy career: managing public affairs for the fifty ships of the Sixth Fleet. But then, no one was questioning Berg's ability to do his job.

Berg was still not home when Gibson made his way back to the villa they shared. He was still waiting for Copy when Lieutenant Thompson appeared at the apartment door to summon Gibson to the office of the ship's executive officer, Commander Kent Siegel. Siegel ordered Gibson to pack up his books and get off the ship within a half hour, Gibson later recalled. "You're never to set foot on this ship again," he ordered and demanded Gibson submit his letter of resignation and return to the United States immediately. Gibson noted that he worked for the Civil Service, not the Navy, and that he would do nothing without talking to a lawyer first. He told Siegel that his "uncivil manners" were a discredit to the Navy, then left the stateroom.

The sun was blazing when Berg returned to the villa late in the afternoon. Blackness greeted him inside. Gibson had closed all the shutters and drawn the drapes. His bravado had been just that; he was convinced their lives were over.

But after all the years of hiding his homosexuality, Berg was ready to let the world know, if it really cared. The younger man went through the house pulling back the drapes, throwing open the shutters, letting the sunlight flood in. Just think, he said, they would not have to hide anymore. To Berg's eyes, Gibson did not seem reassured. Copy had long known that there was something in Lawrence that hearkened from generations past, from an era when it seemed as if homosexuals suffered almost eagerly to expiate their guilt. Copy had never felt particularly guilty and did not believe in suffering. In truth, he felt relieved.

The next morning, Gibson took Berg on the back of the couple's Vespa scooter down Mount Orlando and into Gaeta for the departure of the USS *Little Rock.* Gibson was grave. Berg was filled with optimism. He could get on with his life now, maybe move to New York and go to art school. His life was beginning again.

August 30, 1975
Norfolk, Virginia

Ensign Vernon Berg and Lawrence Gibson arrived back in Virginia in the sultriest summer weather. Berg had hoped the Navy would move quickly for his separation, but, instead of ordering a hearing, it had transferred him to the staff of Rear Admiral Richard Rumple, commander of the Fifth Fleet in Norfolk. But no charges were pressed. All Berg could do was wait.

Time crept by. It was while he drifted in this netherworld that Berg wandered into The Cue, a gay bar in Norfolk, and saw a face that looked familiar. That was Technical Sergeant Leonard Matlovich, someone explained. He looked familiar because Leonard Matlovich in his crisp blue Air Force uniform was on the cover of *Time* magazine, over the bold headline I AM A HOMOSEXUAL. His picture could be seen at every checkout stand and magazine rack in the country.

It marked the first time the young gay movement had ever made the cover of a major newsweekly. To a cause still struggling for legitimacy, the event was a major turning point.

Columbia University
New York City

A gay conference? It had never occurred to Ensign Vernon Berg that there were such things. His only experience with the gay community was what he knew through his older lover: Georgetown cocktail parties, where sly but vaguely bitchy witticisms were bandied about. But here at Columbia University were people like himself, *winners*, who were doing more than mouthing clever bon mots, who diligently pondered how to refashion the world and eliminate prejudice and discrimination.

Berg and Lawrence Gibson had come to New York City to see whether some of the gay activists there could help them with Copy's increasingly problematical relationship with the Navy. Somebody mentioned a gay symposium at Columbia University that weekend. The conference was a mélange of what was old and what was new in the burgeoning gay movement. In some rooms, participants engaged in "rap sessions" in which they discussed the traumas of coming out to families that could not understand. Every gay man, it seemed, had thrown out his battered copy of Gore Vidal's *City and the Pillar* and was now reading the new book in vogue, *Society and the Healthy Homosexual*. The new word of the hour, introduced in the volume, was *homophobia*, meaning an irrational fear of and prejudice against homosexuality. Every gay woman, meanwhile, had discarded the former lesbian Bible, the depressing *Well of Loneliness*, and was quoting from Rita Mae Brown's sassy *Rubyfruit Jungle*. Such sessions, throwbacks to the early movement's borrowing from feminist consciousness-raising, were now supplemented by new seminars favoring more prosaic political strategizing. What was the best way to lobby the legislature for sodomy repeal? What approach was most effective in getting a city council to enact a gay-rights ordinance? What legal strategy would best win civil rights guarantees in the state and federal courts?

Throughout the day, Copy Berg listened as the gay conference unfolded. For the past six months, he had considered his interrogation and pending discharge as a singular ordeal, something just between himself and the Navy. Suddenly, he understood that there was more to his case than his Navy career. His story had to do with the relationship of all gay people to the military, and, in a broader sense, with the question of where homosexuals fit into American life as a whole.

At the end of the conference, as the sun set across the Hudson River and a winter chill settled over Manhattan, in a crowded classroom where the subject of discussion was discrimination against gays in the military, Copy Berg stood and told the assemblage that he was in the process of being thrown out of the Navy for being gay. And then he said he had decided to fight it. The crowd burst into spontaneous applause. An attorney from a new gay advocacy group called Lambda Legal Defense and Education Fund slipped Copy his card; they would help him with a lawyer, he said. And Copy Berg, a Naval officer who was the son of a career Naval officer, knew that from that moment on his life would be very different.

In July, Berg would have been happy enough to have had his resignation accepted and to have quietly left the service. Why the Navy did not immediately accept the resignation would become a matter of some conjecture. Perhaps it hoped to find evidence of a judicial offense for which it could prosecute Berg criminally. Perhaps the Navy simply wanted to make Berg's life difficult as their punishment for his being homosexual. Certainly the Navy believed it could decide Berg's fate in its own time and in its own manner. After all, no officer in the history of the United States Navy had ever picked a public fight over this issue before.

In the beginning, after his return to Norfolk from Italy, Copy had confidently taken weekend trips to New York and New Jersey to apply for jobs. He hoped to have a decent position waiting for him when he was discharged. The country was gripped by a recession, but Copy's Annapolis education made him an enviable catch for a number of corporations. Invariably, though, a prospective employer asked precisely when Copy Berg would be leaving the Navy, and since the Navy had still not set a date for a discharge hearing, Berg could not even guess.

Nor was there an easy answer for why, just one year after graduating from Annapolis, Berg was exiting so abruptly. Every employment application also asked about the character of discharge for an ex-military applicant. This was when Copy began to understand the long-term implications of even a general discharge. He needed an honorable discharge, and it was increasingly clear that the Navy had no intention of issuing such a separation. Copy's frustration had been mounting for months before the gay conference in New York. But he had certainly not gone expecting to make his case a cause célèbre. By the end of his first day in Manhattan, though, his impromptu announcement at the Columbia University conference had accomplished just that.

A few hours after Berg left the Columbia campus, he and Gibson were talking about the case with Bruce Voeller, executive director of the National Gay Task Force, at Voeller's apartment. Though many of the older hands of the gay movement had cut their political teeth in the antiwar movement and were reluctant to take up the cause of allowing gays into the military, Voeller had appreciated the potential influence of the issue from the start.

Gays such as Leonard Matlovich and Copy Berg were precisely the people for whom reformers like Voeller were scouting, responsible homosexuals with impeccable credentials. Though *Time* magazine had originally planned to use a photo of Voeller and his lover on the cover of its 1975 gay issue, it was Voeller himself who had argued for Matlovich's, sensing a stronger public-relations coup if a serviceman's image was used. The evening after Berg's dramatic announcement at the Columbia conference, Voeller was excited at what Berg's case might accomplish. But he did not minimize the problems or the risks.

Voeller described the custody battle he himself was fighting against his wife for visitation rights to his three children. Most state courts were so steeped in the notion that homosexuals were child molesters, he noted, that few would allow gays any form of parental rights, even to their own children. Voeller's lover, meanwhile, was the unnamed plaintiff in a lawsuit, *Doe* v. *Commonwealth's Attorney*, making its way through the federal courts. Already, a federal judge had decided that the Commonwealth of Virginia had every constitutional right to punish homosexuals with three years of prison every time they made love. No matter what changes had transpired in the past several years, acknowledged gay people could not expect meaningful redress against discrimination for many years to come, Voeller warned Berg.

Much to Voeller's relief, none of these arguments deterred Berg. As far as Berg was concerned, his life could not get any worse than it was now, his future clouded by the prospect of a less than honorable discharge. Lawrence Gibson, still indignant at his treatment by the NIS and Civil Service, was ready to fight, too.

Berg and Gibson spent the weekend at Voeller's refurbished brownstone on Spring Street and West Broadway, taking in the Manhattan gay scene, which still astounded Copy. They visited gay restaurants and gay discos crowded with thousands of successful young gay men. It was a world Berg had never imagined in his days as a lonely Academy student.

When Copy returned to Norfolk, he wrote a brief letter to the Chief of Naval Personnel, withdrawing his resignation and requesting a hearing on the matter of his separation. "I have compiled in my six years of service a record of which I am proud," he wrote. "I feel strongly that I bring to the Navy talents which are versatile and unique . . . Upon reflection on my actions I now feel that my submission of a letter of resignation was neither in the best interest of the naval service nor myself. My actions were completed naively with undue haste while under duress."

Two days later, Berg contacted a reporter for the *Newport News Daily Press.* The Navy would be forced to give him a fair hearing if they knew the media were watching, Copy thought, and he wanted the case to be scrutinized from now on. The *Daily Press* story immediately went over the Associated Press national wire. "Ensign Vernon E. Berg III, a homosexual, may be forced out of uniform," the story reported. "Berg, 24, a 1974 graduate of the U.S. Naval Academy, has become the latest serviceman—and the first officer—to fight the military's traditional ban on homosexuals."

After months of drifting aimlessly, Copy felt a new resolve, his optimism renewed. Though his lawyers cautioned that it would be unprecedented for an acknowledged gay officer to be retained, he believed that he could win a fair fight with the Navy on the issue. All he had to do was present the facts of his case. In a few months, he believed, his Navy career might be back on track.

December 21, 1975
Virginia Beach, Virginia

The Navy set a January hearing date for Copy Berg's separation board. Copy assembled a team of five lawyers, including an Air Force lawyer from Langley Air Force Base who was familiar with the gay regulations from the Matlovich case, a Navy attorney, and E. Carrington Boggan, a gay ACLU attorney who had been brought on board by Lambda Legal Defense and Education Fund. There was one key piece to Copy's case that was not yet in place, however, even as the hearing neared. He wanted his father at his side, in uniform, during the hearing.

Four days before Christmas, during a monsoonlike rainstorm, Commander Vernon Berg, Jr., and his wife drove their camper van from Chicago, where the elder Berg served as senior chaplain for the

Services School Command at the Great Lakes Naval Training Center. From the beginning, the commander had encouraged his son to fight the discharge, largely because he assumed Copy had been falsely accused. Copy had dated girls all through high school and through much of his Naval Academy career, his father knew, in spite of Lawrence Gibson, who he felt was obviously the cause of all Copy's problems. Meanwhile, Copy's mom wandered through the tiny house the two men shared, came upon the one bedroom with its one bed, and burst into tears.

When his parents left, nothing had been decided. Copy did not know whether his father would stand with him or not. Over the next days, Copy bore down on his case with his attorneys. The Navy planned to introduce new evidence in the hearing: a statement from Journalist Second Class Laurent Crofwell asserting that Berg had made a pass at him the previous February. Then on Christmas Eve, the NIS released a new five-page report indicating that it had used "confidential informants" to spy on Berg while he was aboard the USS *Little Rock.*

One informant, identified only as GAP-ı in the report, was clearly another officer, most probably another ensign. GAP-ı had told the NIS that he had noticed Berg writing numerous letters to Gibson before the latter's arrival in Gaeta and that he had actually read the letters and seen that they included "various romantic endearments." The fact that at least one other officer had read Copy's private correspondence was troubling enough, but the report also noted that GAP-ı was aware of "some additional letters further indicating a homosexual relationship between subject and Gibson," which told Berg that the ensign had rifled through his private residence to find evidence for the NIS investigators. Copy's lawyers moved to delay the hearing to investigate this breach, which again raised questions as to how the Berg probe had begun, but their request was denied.

While the attorneys dug into their law books, Copy worried about whether his father would make the trip to Norfolk when the separation hearing began. His lawyers were unanimously opposed to having the senior Berg appear. No one was sure what he would say. He could hurt Berg's case if he came down on the side of the anti-gay regulation.

Copy did not think his father would hurt his case. On one level, he appreciated the significance of walking into the hearing alongside his father, a career Navy man like those who would be judging him. This, however, was an almost trivial consideration in comparison with the main issue. He could stand losing his bond with the service, but he could not stand losing his father. It would be like losing a part of himself.

As the date of the hearing neared, he awaited word from Chicago; finally it came. When did the hearing start? Commander Vernon Berg asked Ensign Vernon Berg when he finally called. He wanted to be there.

The witness who garnered the most press strode into Building SP-64 on the fourth day of the Berg hearing. He was well known in the Navy—the honors awarded him during his decades of service included the Bronze Star, the Silver Star, and the Legion of Merit. Vice Admiral William P. Mack had retired from the Navy five months earlier with the pithy observation that both political and military leaders were responsible for the Vietnam debacle. Coming from a man who had served years in both the Pentagon—including a stint as Deputy Assistant Secretary of Defense—and on the battlefield—including a tour as Commander of the Seventh Fleet—the candid remarks had caused no small embarrassment to the military establishment. So would his comments at the Berg hearing.

Mack remembered Berg from the days when the midshipman had dated his daughter. He had personally commissioned Berg as an officer in the United States Navy in a private ceremony seventeen months earlier, and it was clear that even given the events of the past year he had no regrets about his action. Between his academic performance and his extracurricular activities, Berg had been in "the top ten percent" of Academy students, Mack testified. Though he understood that Berg now identified himself as a homosexual, he added that he did not believe his separation should be mandatory and that "each case should be determined on its own merits." As far as he was concerned, Ensign Berg still "was capable of performing as a Naval officer."

Board president Gibson pressed Mack about this conclusion. Mack admitted that he had never opposed the Navy's gay policies in the past and that the regulations being enforced against the ensign were no different from when he commanded the Seventh Fleet. That did not make them right, however, Mack said. "The country is changing," he said, "the Navy is not."

Berg next took the stand in his own defense. Just listing all his extracurricular activities at Annapolis consumed two hours. When prosecutor Wallace finally asked him about the crucial evening in his apartment in Gaeta, Berg said any contact between himself and Crofwell was "insignificant in consequence."

The climax of the eight-day hearing occurred the next morning when a sandy-haired Navy commander took the stand. His dress blue uniform only highlighted the striking resemblance the man bore to the defendant. On his chest, among all the other ribbons Commander Vernon Berg, Jr., had accumulated during the course of his career, was the

Bronze Star he had won when he almost died ministering to Marines during the Tet offensive. In the middle of the red, white, and blue ribbon was the letter *V*—for valor. Berg's Navy lawyer, Lieutenant John Montgomery, asked the chaplain about his experiences with gay sailors.

"A person is a person," Berg began. "I really have felt strained in this whole hearing about people saying homosexuals have different problems. They have the same problems as anybody else. A homosexual can perform badly or spectacularly well. Homosexuals that I have known in the military have done extremely well, getting to extremely high ranks after I first met them."

"Are you saying that you know of homosexuals who are officers in the United States Navy today?" Montgomery asked.

"Certainly," the chaplain answered.

"Do you know any of them of the rank of commander?"

"Certainly."

"The rank of captain?" Montgomery asked.

"Certainly."

"The rank of rear admiral?"

"Yes, sir," Berg said. The room fell utterly silent while the chaplain continued. "Therefore, I would like to interject that I think it behooves all of us to look at what we do. We condemn blindly with prejudice and, you know, we must be careful whom we condemn."

When Montgomery asked about Berg's experience as a chaplain to Marine units in Vietnam, the commander said that at least once a week one or another Marine would come to him and admit to being gay. He also acknowledged, somewhat painfully, what he would have done not too long before if a commander had sent him a gay soldier.

"This week has been a learning experience for me," the elder Berg said, "and I'm sure it has been for all of us. I'm a product of Navy society also, and, sadly to say, years ago in 1960, '61, '62, I would have told him carte blanche, 'If you are a homosexual, you had better get out.'"

The world was changing, he added, looking toward his son. "We are advancing into an age of enlightenment. Hopefully, that will make such inquisitions unnecessary in the future."

Berg's statements about Marines clearly rankled the board's most junior member, Lieutenant Herbert Artis. Artis was a *mustang*, the Navy term for an enlisted man who later became an officer. At thirty-eight, Artis had twenty years in the Navy, including his thirteen years in enlisted service, and was the most outspoken board member against Berg. Copy thought it was ironic considering Artis was also the board's only African-American member.

"Getting back to the Marines," Artis said to the commander. "You say you served with the Marines in Vietnam and it came to light that certain Marines were homosexuals and their buddies knew about them. From my experience, they were not accepted. They were sort of outcasts."

"In the Marines, we're talking about a Marine unit," Berg answered. "When one of those guys in that small unit finds their buddy is a homosexual, and if anybody else tells on him, watch out. They will protect him."

"Why?" asked Artis.

"Knowing Marines as I do," Berg said, "why would a given unit of Marines, once they know a man, live with him, fight with him, watch friends die with him, what do they care about what he does in his bedroom? It becomes unimportant, like color, or like male or female. Gosh, who cares? Sometimes, even in combat, I have had all sorts of men come to me and say, 'Gee, why can't the real world be like this? Why can't we all sit down and have communion together and drink wine together? Why can't we all love each other as human beings and accept each other as we are?'"

Another board member, Charles Erwin, interrupted Berg. "I'm having difficulty in trying to interpret homosexual behavior and tendencies," he said. "What is normal homosexual behavior that makes it identifiable?"

"When I hold a dying Marine in my arms and cry because he is dying, and I stroke his face and kiss him on the head, am I a homosexual?" Berg asked. Tears appeared in his eyes. He paused briefly while he brought his hands up to cover his face.

"Pardon me," he said. "When I talk about Vietnam, I get out of control. When I talk about Marines I get out of control, because I love them. Does that make me a homosexual?" He looked at the board. "What is a homosexual?" he asked. "Where does emotion and love stop and perversity take up?"

Lieutenant Artis cut the commander short. "The way I read the SECNAV instructions," Artis said, "it clearly states it is the policy of the Secretary of the Navy to dismiss homosexuals. It says, 'Prompt separation is essential.'"

The board had no more interest in listening to Chaplain Berg's musings. Before Berg could utter another word, the board president, Gibson, said, "Chaplain, you may be excused."

The elder Berg walked down the aisle of the hearing room as Lieutenant Artis began reading from the Navy's regulations on homosexuals again: "Under 'Policy,' paragraph four, it's very clear, very insistent, the way I read it. . . ."

The voice faded into background noise as Copy watched his father walk from the stand. Commander Berg had rarely discussed his Vietnam experiences, and now Copy could see why. A part of the chaplain still grieved for the dying Marines he had held in his arms. Copy had never seen his dad so emotional; he had never seen him so mortal; he had never loved him more.

When Copy focused again on the proceeding, he was consumed with resentment that the officers could so roundly ignore what his father had just said and so easily slip back into quoting SECNAV instructions. There were many things that would long anger Copy Berg about the hearing, but nothing more than a board that asked a man to resurrect the most painful moments of his life and then answered him with quotes from a rule book.

There was a second painful understanding Copy came to that day. He had learned for the first time what his father thought of homosexuals there, in a hearing room in answer to a lawyer's questions, because he had not had the courage to ask such questions himself.

For the Navy, the first four days of Copy Berg's hearings were a public-relations disaster. The first public cracks in military support for the gay exclusion policy were apparent with the statements of Vice Admiral Mack and the testimony of Commander Berg. When the hearings entered the second week, the Navy launched its own counteroffensive against the gay ensign.

The first phase of the Navy's retaliation became apparent outside of the hearing room when Lawrence Gibson happened to run into Special Agent Parker of the Naval Investigative Service at the Norfolk Navy installation. Parker seemed embarrassed to see Gibson and hurried away. Gibson was stunned to see Parker, knowing that Berg's lawyers had pleaded that he be brought from Gaeta to Norfolk to testify in the hearings. His testimony could go a long way toward answering questions about the legality of the secret informant's search of Berg's apartment and the manipulated confession from Gibson. The Navy had refused to make Parker available. He was not in Norfolk to appear at the hearing; he was here to brief the press on the NIS investigation of Berg, reading to them from the extensive NIS files.

Such briefings are illegal. The NIS acts only as an investigatory agency for the Navy; materials from their probes are for release solely to Navy officials. Attorney Boggan moved that the charges against Berg be dismissed "on the grounds of the gross misconduct of the United States government." The motion was denied.

That afternoon, the Navy called the Norfolk base commander to testify at the hearing. His testimony seemed cursory; the commander merely reiterated support for the Navy's prohibition of gay sailors. All homosexuals, he said, should be kicked out. Just why he appeared to restate obvious Navy policy mystified Berg's lawyers—until Copy pointed out that the captain was also one of the board members' commanding officer.

To ensure that all board members got the point, the region's highest-ranking naval officer, Admiral Richard Rumble, appeared on television that afternoon to reiterate his position: The Navy should rid itself of all homosexuals. The comments of Vice Admiral Mack, he added, were "taken out of context," and any change in the gay policy "is going to be a long time coming."

By the time Commander Vernon Berg left Norfolk, his relationship with his son had been renewed and strengthened. There were to be repercussions, however. At the hearings, Copy had, of course, noted the presence of Commander T. J. Hilligan, Admiral Rumble's staff lawyer. Hilligan had sat through the entire proceedings and taken copious notes. Occasionally, a board member would glance his way before answering a question during the voir dire process. Even out of the courtroom, the admiral's men were never far away. Every time Copy or his father had talked to a reporter, a uniformed member of the admiral's staff seemed somewhere within earshot.

It was several years later, after Berg's attorneys had successfully obtained reams of memoranda under the provisions of the Freedom of Information Act, that Berg discovered that the reports Rumble's staff had forwarded to Washington each day contained notes on Commander Berg as well as on Ensign Berg. Two men, it turned out, saw their Navy careers end that week.

May 28, 1976
Norfolk Naval Station
Norfolk, Virginia

Ever since Ensign Berg had gone public about his fight with the Navy seven months earlier, he had been assigned the most obscure job the brass could find, which meant working in the Naval base's Civilian Personnel Office. His coworkers were largely civilians who had been extraordinarily supportive of him throughout the hearings. When the Navy set May 28 as the date of Copy's discharge, they planned a going-away party. Legal delays postponed the discharge for several days, but the party went on as scheduled. The secretarial pool awarded him a civilian shirt and a large sheet cake inscribed, "Good Luck, Copy! We'll Miss You."

It was odd to be partying, given the other than honorable discharge the Navy had handed him. This decision meant no benefits for his education. The Veterans Administration listed homosexuals in the same category as mutineers, spies, and convicted felons when deciding who should receive benefits. The Navy had also decided to withhold substantial back pay Berg had accrued from unpaid leave.

On June 1, Judge Gerhard Gesell refused to issue a temporary restraining order to bar Berg's discharge. As he had in Leonard Matlovich's case seven months earlier, Gesell made it clear he would hear arguments against the Navy's policy but that he could find no legal reason for obstructing that policy now. With that, the Navy ordered Copy Berg to be gone by midnight the next day.

As Berg was being processed out the next afternoon, a cluster of reporters gathered around him to ask whether he would continue to fight—he said he would—and to ask about his plans. A slight rain had begun to fall when Lieutenant Commander C. W. Albaugh broke through the circle of reporters and ordered Berg to remove the base sticker from his car. "Make sure I get it before you leave the base," Albaugh said.

The drizzle turned into a heavy downpour, many of the reporters scattered, and Copy Berg spent his last minutes in the United States Navy scraping the blue parking sticker from the rubber bumper of his station wagon. It was an automobile-age version of ripping the shoulder boards off a disgraced officer's jacket, one reporter joked. The ordeal delivered the desired humiliation. By the time he had returned the pulpy remains of a parking sticker to Albaugh and was ready to leave the base for the last time, Copy was soaked, his dress white uniform splattered with mud.

In the months that followed, Berg granted endless interviews and appeared on countless talk shows to advance his cause. There were two striking things about Copy's surge into media prominence during those months. First, he had the words to articulate ideas that he could barely have conceived of just a year earlier. Second, there were people ready to listen.

Copy Berg's experience was not singular. Across the nation in the second half of the 1970s, people were taking the gay-rights movement more seriously. It was not a widespread acceptance, to be sure, but gay demands were being discussed with earnestness in some quarters, which was a remarkable achievement considering that just a few years earlier gay activism had seemed an utterly fringe cause.

Speculations

1. What kind of student was Copy Berg? What were his achievements in high school? Why do you think Shilts mentions these achievements?

2. Commander Berg makes two statements about his own love for Marines. He says, "When I hold a dying Marine in my arms and cry because he is dying, and I stroke his face and kiss him on the head, am I a homosexual?" Then later he states, "When I talk about Marines I get out of control, because I love them. Does that make me a homosexual?" How would you answer these two questions? Why does he ask them? How important are the answers?

3. Did the Navy violate Copy Berg's civil rights? Did the Navy violate Lawrence Gibson's civil rights? Did Copy Berg violate Navy regulations? As you read through this account, how do you assess the rights and wrongs of the case? Make sure you use references from the selection to support your views.

4. Shilts uses a journalistic and narrative style to tell the Copy Berg story, dividing the story into scenes, settings, and vignettes. What effect does this style have on you? Do you feel as though you are reading a novel or newspaper article—or like you are seeing a documentary film? Does Shilts communicate his own perspective? If so, how—and what is it?

5. Considering what you learn from this article, on what basis has the Navy determined that homosexuals are unfit to serve? On what basis, if any, should Copy Berg have been allowed to continue to serve in the military?

6. Shilts concludes this account of Copy Berg with two paragraphs that describe a change in Berg and a change in the tenor of the debate about gay rights. What is Shilts's point? How has the Navy's determination to drive out homosexuals been counterproductive to the Navy's position?

ASSIGNMENT SEQUENCES

Sequence One: Heterosexism and Homophobia

1. Your job this week is to watch two popular sitcoms. As of this writing, they might be "Married with Children," "The Simpsons," "Seinfeld," "Frasier," "Roseanne" "Ellen," "Home Improvement"—the kinds of shows that get watched and talked about by many Americans during the week. If you are able, make a tape of the programs so that you can watch them several times. Then, write down the various assumptions these shows are making about gender. What is considered "normal" gender behavior? What references, if any, do they make concerning heterosexuality or homosexuality? Are they heterosexist or homosexist? In a largely descriptive essay, explore the values these shows explicitly and implicitly express.

2. Now consider that you have been made the producer for one of these shows—and that the network has asked you to produce a show that is "not heterosexist." In an essay, explain what kinds of changes you would make and how these changes would affect the character, humor, situation, message, and overrall success of the show.

3. One of the more famous TV sitcom episodes is the lesbian kiss that took place on an episode of "Roseanne." Assume that you are the producer of that show, and that you have received a great many letters expressing outrage that "Roseanne" would show a lesbian kiss on the air. In an essay, respond to the charges being raised that you and your show are immoral, irresponsible, and trying to capitalize on sensationalism. You can decide whether your decision to feature that kiss was right, wrong, or somewhere in between. Be sure to include citations from the essays you have read to support your viewpoint.

4. Many people in the United States find serious discussion of sexual preference difficult if not impossible. For one thing, many people claim that heterosexuality is normal and homosexuality is abnormal, that heterosexuals are good and homosexuals are bad, that heterosexuals are healthy and vigorous while homosexuals are sick and diseased. Martin Duberman complicates this oversimplified view by arguing that sexual preference exists along a spectrum. According to Duberman, many individuals don't fall into one single category, which makes such labeling destructive and distorting. Offer your own views on this subject in a reasonable and thoughtful manner. Why does it matter so much if a person is straight or gay? What difference does a person's sexual orientation make to her or his friends, family, or society at large?

5. The 1993 comic strip "For Better or For Worse" series featured a young teenage boy who declared that he was gay—and a number of newspapers in America temporarily or permanently cancelled publication of the strip because of the subject matter. For this essay, we ask that you step back in time. It is 1993 and this particular "For Better or For Worse" strip is about to be released to newspapers. Your local newspaper has suspended publication of the strip for six weeks—until the story is completed. You feel strongly that the newspaper is either doing the right or wrong thing by suspending publication, and you decide to write a commentary to be published on the editorial page of the newspaper concerning this issue. Write that commentary. Instead of focusing on First Amendment rights, you want to raise questions concerning what the comic strip is

advocating: whether children should be reading about a young man's declaration of homosexuality, whether our society should encourage explicit discussion (even in comic-strip format) of a homosexual lifestyle. Remember as you write this essay that thoughtful people exist who hold different views; offer your position in a reasonable manner and support your positions with references from the readings you have done, personal examples, etc.

Sequence Two: Civil and Moral Rights

1. What is a civil right? Who grants it? Who benefits by it? How does an individual or a group obtain such a right? How does an individual or a group lose such a right? What is the difference between a civil right and a moral or legal right? Although you may want to consult a reference book for this assignment (we recommend something other than a dictionary), explore this subject in your own terms as well. What civil and moral rights do you enjoy? What responsibilities come with them?

2. James Stewart's "Gentleman's Agreement" raises some important questions. According to national statistics, approximately 5–10% of all Americans identify themselves as gay or lesbian. In a country of 200 million people, that means 10 to 20 million American citizens are homosexual. What civil rights do these individuals have? What guarantees should they have in terms of "life, liberty, and the pursuit of happiness"? To what extent should they be able to

    marry,

    live in the neighborhoods of their choice,

    raise families,

    share health care coverage,

    and otherwise lead the same kinds of lives as heterosexual individuals?

    What kinds of rights should be theirs, and what kinds of rights should not be theirs—and why? Offer your views in a reasonable and thoughtful manner.

3. Some people consider that the gay/lesbian civil rights movement is parallel to the civil rights movements that focused on equality for blacks and women. All three groups, after all, consider(ed) themselves to be oppressed by mainstream society. In

an essay, offer your own assessment of the gay/lesbian pride movement. Can the gay/lesbian community lay claim to the same justifications as those offered by blacks and women? Are all three of these movements about basic civil rights, or do they distort basic American values? This is a challenging essay to write, so be sure to reason carefully and support your statements with appropriate quotations from at least three or four readings. However you choose to argue, remember that there are reasonable people who are positioned in a variety of ways on every issue.

If you are working on gay/lesbian rights in comparison to the black civil rights movement, you might wish to read selections by Martin Luther King, Jr., Malcolm X, Stephen Carter, Ellis Cose, and Brent Staples. If you are working on gay/lesbian rights in comparison to women's rights, you might want to read selections by Marion Meade, Nina Berman, Naomi Wolf, Susan Faludi, and Susan Fraker.

4. "The Copy Berg Story" raises a central question about gays and the military: Should an individual's sexual preference determine whether he or she can be a member of one of our armed services? Offer your views in a reasonable and thoughtful manner. Is the military justified in taking so firm a stance concerning the sexual orientation of those serving in the Armed Forces? What arguments do you see on both sides of this question? Which arguments do you find most compelling?

5. In describing herself and her partner, Audre Lorde writes "We were a Black and a white Lesbian in our forties, raising two Black children. Making do was not going to be a safe way to live our lives, nor was pretense, nor euphemism. *Lesbian* is a name for women who love each other. *Black* means of African ancestry. Our lives would never be simple." Even aside from the issue of mixed race, there is no doubt that the children of gay or lesbian parents are likely to face different challenges than the children of heterosexual parents. In a carefully reasoned essay, discuss the essential qualities you think parents should possess—and whether gay/lesbian parents can have those qualities. You might also want to consider whether children should be allowed to be raised by their biological parent, if that parent is gay. To simplify matters, do not focus on whether gay and lesbian parents should be allowed to adopt; instead, focus on the situation that Lorde describes—that is, raising her own children while maintaining (in her case) a lesbian relationship.

As you write, remember that reasonable people have various views on this subject—and that it is your job to develop a logical, coherent, thoughtful position supported by information, fact, and careful reasoning.

6. You are the principal of the Kim Biddle Memorial High School. You have heard that a graduating senior has declared himself gay and plans to attend the prom and dinner dance with his male date. Several parents have called to express their concern; they want you to deny him the right to bring a same-sex partner. Other parents have called to express their concern; they want you to allow him to bring a same-sex partner. You have to make a decision based on your own interpretation of what is right and what best represents the principles and values of Kim Biddle Memorial High School. Write out your decision along with the reasons. Be aware that you will have to send your decision and rationale to the Kim Biddle School Board Meeting where, no matter what you decide, you expect serious opposition.

Sequence Three: In and Out of the Closet

1. All of us keep some secrets—from our parents, our friends, our family, our teachers. As Eve Sedgwick reminds us, we all have secrets that we prefer to keep hidden in the closet. Write an essay in which you consider the concept of keeping something secret. Are secrets necessary, useful, good? How does keeping something important about ourselves hidden from view affect our character, psychological growth, and well being? In writing this essay, you can draw on personal experience but do not reveal some terrible secret about yourself—unless you are willing to share it with your instructor and the rest of the class.

2. In another part of their book, Blumenfeld and Raymond write:

> Where heterosexual couples might kiss in public, embrace at the airport, walk arm in arm, wear wedding bands, and talk about their most recent "date," similar behavior in same-sex couples is judged quite differently. This form of discrimination has important repercussions for gays and lesbians who fear negative reactions from other members of society and as a result are made to think constantly about even the most casual forms of behavior.

Consider that you have a very close relative or friend who is gay or lesbian—and that this person comes to you for advice about how to act in public with his/her partner. What advice would you give? Why would you give it? In an essay, offer your response and then analyze it in terms of the assumptions and concerns that lie behind it.

3. Just as we prepare these pages, we are reading about the case of the "outing" of Jann Wenner, the founder of *Rolling Stone* magazine, by the *Wall Street Journal*, a conservative, business-oriented newspaper. Rumors had circulated for weeks about Wenner's personal affairs. While other newspapers and magazines agonized over whether to reveal that Wenner left his wife of 26 years to live with a former male model, the *Journal* ran a front-page lead story about the possible breakup of Wenner's business empire—a story which detailed Wenner's choice of a gay lover in the third paragraph. Paul Steiger, the managing editor of the *Journal*, stated that "Ordinarily we don't pay attention to people's sexual orientation. In this case it was relevant to the business issues."

   Consider that you are the managing editor of a newspaper that did not run this story—and now you have been scooped by the *Wall Street Journal*. Your publisher is furious with you for not breaking this story. In a well-reasoned essay, defend your decision. Why do you think it important to maintain silence about Wenner's gender preference? Have you violated or upheld the unwritten code of journalistic ethics?

4. Now let's consider that you are the managing editor of the *Wall Street Journal* who decided to run the Wenner story. You are being attacked by other newspaper editors and gay/lesbian organizations for "outing" Jann Wenner. In an essay, defend your decision. Why did you think it was important to present this fact publicly? How have you upheld the unwritten code of journalistic ethics?

5. Let's look at this problem from one more angle. You are in the U.S. Navy. One evening, you happen to see another sailor coming out of a gay bar with one arm wrapped around the shoulders of another person of the same sex. In an essay, decide what you would do and why. Would you report this incident to your commanding officer? Would you speak to the sailor first, last, or not at all? On what basis would you make your decision?

6. Write an editorial in which you take a stand on "coming out of the closet." Are such decisions self-affirming and socially liberating, or

self-destructive and damaging to society? Is sexual preference best left in the closet, no matter whether one is heterosexual or homosexual? Is the outing of a homosexual a political act? Offer your own views, based on the readings and discussions that you have had in this course.

5

STRUGGLING

TOWARD SUCCESS

A college degree has for many decades been viewed as the key to professional and financial success in the United States. During the past thirty years, higher education has leaned toward vocational-technical curricula, as suggested by schools of nursing, engineering, business, and health. Many requirements have all but disappeared (foreign language, physical education, and literature, to name three), and have been replaced by preprofessional courses and intensive concentration in a single area of expertise. For many students, college is a means to an end—and that end is largely bound up in finding a job and making enough money to afford a house and some comforts.

In recent years, the demand for greater technical specialization has increased in the job market, yet only about 20 percent of U.S. citizens receive a college degree. At the same time, the number of skilled labor jobs has shrunk while the number of service-oriented, low-skilled, part-time jobs has increased. In a 1995 speech at the National Press Club in Washington, D.C., Gary Chapman, a researcher from the University of Texas at Austin, painted this bleak picture of inequality in the U.S. employment scene:

> In the last few years, New England alone has seen over 40,000 computer specialists laid off. . . . Microsoft, the largest, most influential computer software company in the world, having a stock value greater than General Motors, employs only 7,000 people. New industries, touted as the hope of the future, don't generate many jobs. We hear a lot of talk about the information super highway, but communications companies fixated on this concept are now laying off people by the thousands. . . . The U.S. now has a greater income inequality than any nation in the industrialized world. In 1970, corporate owners made about 50 times the wage of their average workers, now it is about 150 times the wages of their average workers. . . . Real wages in America have been falling for most Americans since the 1970's. Men in the lowest wage-earning category in the U.S. earn half of what their counterparts earn in Italy and women in that category make even less. . . . So while parents of middle-class families are working two jobs just to make ends meet, we have people like Michael Eisner of Walt Disney, Inc. taking home hundreds of millions of dollars a year—more money than anybody could spend even if you spent money 24 hours a day.

What are some of the effects of America's problems with work and wealth? According to a feature in *Mother Jones* (May/June, 1991):

> Families headed by women comprised 23% of all poor families in 1959; by 1988 that number had increased to 53%. Children in single-parent families are 5 times more likely to be poor as children born to married couples.
>
> For young minority men and women, the jobless rate is close to 30%.

Federally funded job-training programs have been cut by 69% since 1981.

Nearly one out of two black children is defined as poor by federal poverty standards.

Fewer than half of U.S. 17-year-olds in high school have the reading, math, and science skills they need to perform entry-level jobs.

Against this background, we have gathered selections from authors who explore how work gets done, how it gets rewarded, and how individuals advance up the ladder of success. The essays gathered here raise substantive and complex questions concerning fair employment practices and the ethics and values of work. We hope they provide you with an opportunity to enter a dialogue about how the democratic principle of equal opportunity, the time-honored ethos of "hard work," and the policy of "fair pay for a fair day's labor" are revealed in contemporary America.

MCDONALD'S—WE DO IT ALL FOR YOU

Barbara Garson

Barbara Garson, who characterizes herself as a "socialist agitator and educator," caused a great deal of controversy when her play *MacBird* was produced Off-Broadway in New York in 1967. The play became a hit, was produced over three hundred times, and has been translated into French, Portuguese, and Spanish. *MacBird* is a parody of modern politics and propaganda, converting President Lyndon Johnson and *Macbeth* to its own uses and exposing the absurd pronouncements of extreme left-wing and right-wing politicians as little more than cartoon-like imitations of popular truths. The play demonstrates how pop art and propaganda can be stirred together with hot emotions to satirize the times.

Garson was born in Brooklyn, New York, and attended the University of California. Her children's play "The Dinosaur Door" won an Obie award. In addition to writing four successful plays, her articles have appeared in *Harper's,* the *New York Times, Ms., Ramparts, Liberation, Mother Jones, McCall's,* and the *Washington Post.*

Garson demonstrates an ability to create a sense of place and dialogue that shapes an argument and persuades readers. Her book *All the Livelong Day: The Meaning and Demeaning of Routine Work* was described by *Newsweek* as a "loving book" that "celebrates man's vitality and ingenuity." Similarly, this essay from *The Electronic Sweatshop: How Computers Are Transforming the Office of the Future into the Factory of the Past* provides a sense of diverse working people whose insights speak about the struggles in the modern workplace.

Jason Pratt:

"They called us the Green Machine," says Jason Pratt, recently retired McDonald's griddleman, "'cause the crew had green uniforms then. And that's what it is, a machine. You don't have to know how to cook, you don't have to know how to think. There's a procedure for everything and you just follow the procedures."

"Like?" I asked. I was interviewing Jason in the Pizza Hut across from his old McDonald's.

"Like, uh," the wiry teenager searched for a way to describe the all-encompassing procedures. "O.K., we'll start you off on something simple. You're on the ten-in-one grill, ten patties in a pound. Your basic burger. The guy on the bin calls, 'Six hamburgers,' So you lay your six pieces of meat on the grill and set the timer." Before my eyes Jason conjures up the gleaming, mechanized McDonald's kitchen. "Beep-beep, beep-beep, beep-beep. That's the beeper to sear 'em. It goes off in twenty seconds. Sup, sup, sup, sup, sup, sup." He presses each of the six patties down on the sizzling grill with an imaginary silver disk. "Now you turn off the sear beeper, put the buns in the oven, set the oven timer and then the next beeper is to turn the meat. This one goes beep-beep-beep, beep-beep-beep. So you turn your patties and then you drop your re-cons on the meat, t-con, t-con, t-con." Here Jason takes two imaginary handfuls of reconstituted onions out of water and sets them out, two blops at a time, on top of the six patties he's arranged in two neat rows on our grill. "Now the bun oven buzzes [there are over a half dozen different timers with distinct beeps and buzzes in a McDonald's kitchen]. "This one turns itself off when you open the oven door so you just take out your crowns, line 'em up and give 'em each a squirt of mustard and a squirt of ketchup." With mustard in his right hand and ketchup in his left, Jason wields the dispensers like a pair of six-shooters up and down the lines of buns. Each dispenser has two triggers. One fires the premeasured squirt for ten-in-ones—the second is set for quarter-pounders.

"Now," says Jason, slowing down, "now you get to put on the pickles. Two if they're regular, three if they're small. That's the creative part. Then the lettuce, then you ask for a cheese count ('cheese on four please'). Finally the last beep goes off and you lay your burger on the crowns."

"On the *crown* of the buns?" I ask, unable to visualize. "On top?"

"Yeah, you dress 'em upside down. Put 'em in the box upside down too. They flip 'em over when they serve 'em."

"Oh, I think I see."

"Then scoop up the heels [the bun bottoms] which are on top of the bun warmer, rake the heels with one hand and push the tray out from underneath and they land (plip) one on each burger, right on top of the re-cons, neat and perfect. [The official time allotted by Hamburger Central, the McDonald's headquarters in Oak Brook, Ill., is ninety seconds to prepare and serve a burger.] It's like I told you. The procedures makes the burgers. You don't have to know a thing."

McDonald's employs 500,000 teenagers at any one time. Most don't stay long. About 8 million Americans—7 per cent of our labor force—have worked at McDonald's and moved on.[1] Jason is not a typical ex-employee. In fact, Jason is a legend among the teenagers at the three McDonald's outlets in his suburban area. It seems he was so fast at the griddle (or maybe just fast talking) that he'd been taken back three times by two different managers after quitting.

But Jason became a real legend in his last stint at McDonald's. He'd been sent out the back door with the garbage, but instead of coming back in he got into a car with two friends and just drove away. That's the part the local teenagers love to tell. "No fight with the manager or anything . . . just drove away and never came back. . . . I don't think they'd give him a job again."

"I would never go back to McDonald's," says Jason. "Not even as a manager." Jason is enrolled at the local junior college. "I'd like to run a real restaurant someday, but I'm taking data processing to fall back on." He's had many part-time jobs, the highest-paid at a hospital ($4.00 an hour), but that didn't last, and now dishwashing (at the $3.35 minimum). "Same as McDonald's. But I would never go back there. You're a complete robot."

"It seems like you can improvise a little with the onions," I suggested. "They're not premeasured." Indeed, the reconstituted onion shreds grabbed out of a container by the unscientific-looking wet handful struck me as oddly out of character in the McDonald's kitchen.

"There's supposed to be twelve onion bits per patty," Jason informed me. "They spot check."

"Oh come on."

"You think I'm kiddin'. They lift your heels and they say, 'You got too many onions.' It's portion control."

"Is there any freedom anywhere in the process?" I asked.

"Lettuce. They'll leave you alone as long as it's neat."

---

[1] These statistics come from John F. Love, *McDonald's Behind the Golden Arches* (New York: Bantam, 1986). Additional background information in this chapter comes from Ray Kroc and Robert Anderson, *Grinding It Out* (Chicago: Contemporary Books, 1977), and Max Boas and Steve Chain, *Big Mac* (New York: Dutton, 1976).

"So lettuce is freedom; pickles is judgment?"

"Yeah but you don't have time to play around with your pickles. They're never gonna say just six pickles except on the disk. [Each store has video disks to train the crew for each of about twenty work stations, like fries, register, lobby, quarter-pounder grill.] What you'll hear in real life is 'twelve and six on a turn-lay.' The first number is your hamburgers, the second is your Big Macs. On a turn-lay means you lay the first twelve, then you put down the second batch after you turn the first. So you got twenty-four burgers on the grill, in shifts. It's what they call a production mode. And remember you also got your fillets, your McNuggets. . . ."

"Wait, slow down." By then I was losing track of the patties on our imaginary grill. "I don't understand this turn-lay thing."

"Don't worry, you don't have to understand. You follow the beepers, you follow the buzzers and you turn your meat as fast as you can. It's like I told you, to work at McDonald's you don't need a face, you don't need a brain. You need to have two hands and two legs and move 'em as fast as you can. That's the whole system. I wouldn't go back there again for anything."

June Sanders:

McDonald's french fries are deservedly the pride of their menu: uniformly golden brown all across America and in thirty-one other countries. However, it's difficult to standardize the number of fries per serving. The McDonald's fry scoop, perhaps their greatest technological innovation, helps to control this variable. The unique flat funnel holds the bag open while it aligns a limited number of fries so that they fall into the package with a paradoxically free, overflowing cornucopia look.

Despite the scoop, there's still a spread. The acceptable fry yield is 400 to 420 servings per 100-lb. bag of potatoes. It's one of the few areas of McDonald's cookery in which such a range is possible. The fry yield is therefore one important measure of a manager's efficiency. "Fluffy, not stuffy," they remind the young workers when the fry yield is running low.

No such variation is possible in the browning of the fries. Early in McDonald's history Louis Martino, the husband of the secretary of McDonald's founder Ray Kroc, designed a computer to be submerged in the fry vats. In his autobiography, *Grinding It Out*, Kroc explained the importance of this innovation. "We had a recipe . . . that called for pulling the potatoes out of the oil when they got a certain color and grease bubbles formed in a certain way. It was amazing that we got them as uniform as we did because each kid working the fry vats would have his own interpretation of the proper color and so forth. [The word "kid" was officially replaced by "person" or "crew person" in McDonald's management vocabulary in 1973 in response to union organizing attempts.] Louis's computer took all the guesswork out of it, modifying the frying to suit the balance of water to solids in a given batch of potatoes. He also engineered the dispenser that allowed us to squirt exactly the right amount of catsup and mustard onto our pre-measured hamburger patties. . . ."

The fry vat probe is a complex miniature computer. The fry scoop, on the other hand, is as simple and almost as elegant as the wheel. Both eliminate the need for a human being to make "his own interpretation," as Ray Kroc puts it.

Together, these two innovations mean that a new worker can be trained in fifteen minutes and reach maximum efficiency in a half hour. This makes it economically feasible to use a kid for one day and replace him with another kid the next day.

June Sanders worked at McDonald's for one day.

"I needed money, so I went in and the manager told me my hours would be 4 to 10 P.M." This was fine with June, a well-organized black woman in her early twenties who goes to college full time.

"But when I came in the next day the manager said I could work till 10 for that one day. But from then on my hours would be 4 P.M. to 1 A.M. And I really wouldn't get off at 1 because I'd have to stay to clean up after they closed. . . . Yes it was the same manager, a Mr. O'Neil.

"I told him I'd have to check first with my family if I could come home that late. But he told me to put on the uniform and fill out the forms. He would start me out on french fries.

"Then he showed me an orientation film on a TV screen all about fries. . . . No, I still hadn't punched in. This was all in the basement. Then I went upstairs, and *then* I punched in and went to work. . . . No, I was not paid for the training downstairs. Yes, I'm sure."

I asked June if she had had any difficulty with the fries.

"No, it was just like the film. You put the french fries in the grease and you push a button which doesn't go off till the fries are done. Then you take them out and put them in a bin under a light. Then you scoop them into the bags with this thing, this flat, light metal—I can't really describe it—scoop thing that sits right in the package and makes the fries fall in place."

"Did they watch you for a while?" I asked. "Did you need more instruction?"

"Someone leaned over once and showed me how to make sure the fry scooper was set inside the opening of the bag so the fries would fall in right."

"And then?"

"And then, I stood on my feet from twenty after four till the manager took over my station at 10:35 P.M.

"When I left my legs were aching. I knew it wasn't a job for me. But I probably would have tried to last it out—at least more than a day—if it wasn't for the hours. When I got home I talked it over with my mother and my sister and then I phoned and said I couldn't work there. They weren't angry. They just said to bring back the uniform. . . . The people were nice, even the managers. It's just a rushed system."

"June," I said, "does it make any sense to train you and have you work for one day? Why didn't he tell you the real hours in the first place?"

"They take a chance and see if you're desperate. I have my family to stay with. That's why I didn't go back. But if I really needed the money, like if I had a kid and no family, I'd have to make arrangements to work any hours.

"Anyway, they got a full day's work out of me."

Damita:

I waited on line at my neighborhood McDonald's. It was lunch hour and there were four or five customers at each of the five open cash registers. "May I take your order?" a very thin girl said in a flat tone to the man at the head of my line.

"McNuggets, large fries and a Coke," said the man. The cashier punched in the order. "That will be—".

"Big Mac, large fries and a shake," said the next woman on line. The cashier rang it up.

"Two cheeseburgers, large fries and a coffee," said the third customer. The cashier rang it up.

"How much is a large fries?" asked the woman directly in front of me.

The thin cashier twisted her neck around trying to look up at the menu board.

"Sorry," apologized the customer, "I don't have my glasses."

"Large fries is seventy-nine," a round-faced cashier with glasses interjected from the next register.

"Seventy-nine cents," the thin cashier repeated.

"Well how much is a *small* fries?"

As they talked I leaned over the next register. "Say, can I interview you?" I asked the clerk with glasses, whose line was by then empty.

"Huh?"

"I'm writing a story about jobs at fast-food restaurants."

"O.K. I guess so."

"Can I have your phone number?"

"Well . . . I'll meet you when I get off. Should be sometime between 4 and 4:30."

By then it was my turn.

"Just a large fries," I said.

The thin cashier pressed 'lge fries.' In place of numbers, the keys on a McDonald's cash register say "lge fries," "reg fries," "med coke," "big mac," and so on. Some registers have pictures on the key caps. The next time the price of fries goes up (or down) the change will be entered in the store's central computer. But the thin cashier will continue to press the same button. I wondered how long she'd worked there and how many hundreds of 'lge fries' she'd served without learning the price.

Damita, the cashier with the glasses, came up from the crew room (a room in the basement with lockers, a table and a video player for studying the training disks) at 4:45. She looked older and more serious without her striped uniform.

"Sorry, but they got busy and, you know, here you get off when they let you."

The expandable schedule was her first complaint. "You give them your availability when you sign on. Mine I said 9 to 4. But they scheduled me for 7 o'clock two or three days a week. And I needed the money. So I got to get up 5 in the morning to get here from Queens by 7. And I don't get off till whoever's supposed to get here gets here to take my place. . . . It's hard to study with all the pressures."

Damita had come to the city from a small town outside of Detroit. She lives with her sister in Queens and takes extension courses in psychology at New York University. Depending on the schedule posted each Friday, her McDonald's paycheck for a five-day week has varied from $80 to $114.

"How long have you worked at McDonald's?" I asked.

"Well, see I only know six people in this city, so my manager from Michigan . . . yeah, I worked for McDonald's in high school . . . my manager from Michigan called this guy Brian who's the second assistant manager here. So I didn't have to fill out an application. Well, I mean the first thing I needed was a job," she seemed to apologize, "and I knew I could always work at McDonald's. I always say I'm gonna look for something else, but I don't get out till 4 and that could be 5 or whenever."

The flexible scheduling at McDonald's only seems to work one way. One day Damita had arrived a half hour late because the E train was running on the R track.

"The assistant manager told me not to clock in at all, just to go home. So I said O.K. and I left."

"What did you do the rest of the day?" I asked.

"I went home and studied, and I went to sleep."

"But how did it make you feel?"

"It's like a humiliating feeling 'cause I wasn't given any chance to justify myself. But when I spoke to the Puerto Rican manager he said it was nothing personal against me. Just it was raining that day, and they were really slow and someone who got here on time, it wouldn't be right to send them home."

"Weren't you annoyed to spend four hours traveling and then lose a day's pay?" I suggested.

"I was mad at first that they didn't let me explain. But afterwards I understood and I tried to explain to my sister: 'Time waits for no man.'"

"Since you signed on for 9 to 4," I asked Damita, "and you're going to school, why can't you say, 'Look, I have to study at night, I need regular hours'?"

"Don't work that way. They make up your schedule every week and if you can't work it, you're responsible to replace yourself. If you can't stay they can always get someone else."

"But Damita," I tried to argue with her low estimate of her own worth, "anyone can see right away that your line moves fast, yet you're helpful to people. I mean, you're a valuable employee. And this manager seems to like you."

"Valuable! $3.35 an hour. And I can be replaced by any [pointing across the room] kid off the street." I hadn't noticed. At a small table under the staircase a manager in a light beige shirt was taking an application from a lanky black teenager.

"But you know the register. You know the routine."

"How long you think it takes to learn the six steps? Step 1. Greet the customer, 'Good morning, can I help you?' Step 2. Take his order. Step 3. Repeat the order. They can have someone off the street working my register in five minutes."

"By the way," I asked, "on those cash registers without numbers, how do you change something after you ring it up? I mean if somebody orders a cheeseburger and then they change it to a hamburger, how do you subtract the slice of cheese?"

"I guess that's why you have step 3, repeat the order. One cheeseburger, two Cokes, three . . ."

"Yeah but if you punched a mistake or they don't want it after you get it together?"

"Like if I have a crazy customer, which I do be gettin' 'specially in this city, and they order hamburger, fries and shake, and it's $2.95 and then they just walk away?"

"I once did that here," I said. "About a week ago when I first started my research. All I ordered was some french fries. And I was so busy watching how the computer works that only after she rang it up I discovered that I'd walked out of my house without my wallet. I didn't have a penny. I was so embarrassed."

"Are you that one the other day? Arnetta, this girl next to me, she said, 'Look at that crazy lady going out. She's lookin' and lookin' at everything and then she didn't have no money for a bag of fries.' I saw you leaving, but I guess I didn't recognize you. [I agreed it was probably me.] O.K., so say this crazy lady comes in and orders french fries and leaves. In Michigan I could just zero it out. I'd wait till I start the next order and press zero and large fries. But here you're supposed to call out 'cancel sale' and the manager comes over and does it with his key.

"But I hate to call the manager every time, 'specially if I got a whole line waiting. So I still zero out myself. They can tell I do it by the computer tape, and they tell me not to. Some of them let me, though, because they know I came from another store. But they don't show the girls here how to zero out. Everybody thinks you need the manager's key to do it."

"Maybe they let you because they can tell you're honest," I said. She smiled, pleased, but let it pass. "That's what I mean that you're valuable to them. You know how to use the register. You're good with customers."

"You know there was a man here," Damita said, a little embarrassed about bragging, "when I was transferred off night he asked my manager, 'What happened to that girl from Michigan?'"

"Did your manager tell you that?"

"No, another girl on the night shift told me. The manager said it to her. They don't tell you nothing nice themselves."

"But, see, you are good with people and he appreciates it."

"In my other McDonald's—not the one where they let me zero out but another one I worked in Michigan—I was almost fired for my attitude. Which was helping customers who had arthritis to open the little packets. And another bad attitude of mine is that you're supposed to suggest to the customer, 'Would you like a drink with that?' or 'Do you want a pie?'—whatever they're pushing. I don't like to do it. And they can look on my tape after my shift and see I didn't push the suggested sell item."

McDonald's computerized cash registers allow managers to determine immediately not only the dollar volume for the store but the amount of each item that was sold at each register for any given period. Two experienced managers, interviewed separately, both insisted that the new electronic cash registers were in fact slower than the old mechanical registers. Clerks who knew the combination—hamburger, fries, Coke: $2.45—could ring up the total immediately, take the cash and give change in one operation. On the new register you have to enter each item and may be slowed down by computer response time. The value of the new registers, or at least their main selling point (McDonald's franchisers can choose from several approved registers), is the increasingly sophisticated tracking systems, which monitor all the activity and report with many different statistical breakdowns.

"Look, there," said Damita as the teenage job applicant left and the manager went behind the counter with the application. "If I was to say I can't come in at 7, they'd cut my hours down to one shift a week, and if I never came back they wouldn't call to find out where I was.

"I worked at a hospital once as an X-ray assistant. There if I didn't come in there were things that had to be done that wouldn't be done. I would call there and say, 'Remember to run the EKGs.' Here, if I called and said, 'I just can't come by 7 no more,' they'd have one of these high school kids off the street half an hour later. And they'd do my job just as good."

Damita was silent for a while and then she made a difficult plea. "This might sound stupid, I don't know," she said, "but I feel like, I came here to study and advance myself but I'm not excelling myself in any way. I'm twenty years old but—this sounds terrible to say—I'm twenty but I'd rather have a babysitting job. At least I could help a kid and take care. But I only know six people in this city. So I don't even know how I'd find a babysitting job."

"I'll keep my ears open," I said. "I don't know where I'd hear of one but. . . ."

Damita seemed a little relieved. I suppose she realized there wasn't much chance of babysitting full-time, but at least she now knew seven people in the city.

Jon DeAngelo:
Jon DeAngelo, twenty-two, has been a McDonald's manager for three years. He started in the restaurant business at sixteen as a busboy and planned even then to run a restaurant of his own someday. At nineteen, when he was the night manager of a resort kitchen, he was hired away by McOpCo, the McDonald's Operating Company.

Though McDonald's is primarily a franchise system, the company also owns and operates about 30 percent of the stores directly. These McOpCo stores, including some of the busiest units, are managed via a chain of command including regional supervisors, store managers and first and second assistants who can be moved from unit to unit. In addition, there's a network of inspectors from Hamburger Central who make announced and unannounced checks for QSC (quality, service, cleanliness) at both franchise and McOpCo installations.

Jon was hired at $14,000 a year. At the time I spoke with him his annual pay was $21,000—a very good salary at McDonald's. At first he'd been an assistant manager in one of the highest-volume stores in his region. Then he was deliberately transferred to a store with productivity problems.

"I got there and found it was really a great crew. They hated being hassled, but they loved to work. I started them having fun by putting the men on the women's jobs and vice versa. [At most McDonald's the

women tend to work on the registers, the men on the grill. But everyone starts at the same pay.] Oh, sure, they hated it at first, the guys that
is. But they liked learning all the stations. I also ran a lot of register
races."

Since the computer tape in each register indicates sales per hour,
per half hour or for any interval requested, the manager can rev the
crew up for a real "on your mark, get set, go!" race with a printout
ready as they cross the finish line, showing the dollars taken in at each
register during the race.

The computer will also print out a breakdown of sales for any particular menu item. The central office can check, therefore, how many
Egg McMuffins were sold on Friday from 9 to 9:30 two weeks or two
years ago, either in the entire store or at any particular register.

This makes it possible to run a register race limited to Cokes for instance, or Big Macs. Cashiers are instructed to try suggestive selling
("Would you like a drink with that?") at all times. But there are peri-
ods when a particular item is being pushed. The manager may then
offer a prize for the most danish sold.

A typical prize for either type of cash register race might be a
Snoopy mug (if that's the current promotion) or even a $5 cash bonus.

"This crew loved to race as individuals," says Jon of his troubled
store, "but even more as a team. They'd love to get on a production
mode, like a chicken-pull-drop or a burger-turn-lay and kill themselves
for a big rush.

"One Saturday after a rock concert we did a $1,900 hour with ten
people on crew. We killed ourselves but when the rush was over everyone said it was the most fun they ever had in a McDonald's."

I asked Jon how managers made up their weekly schedule. How
would he decide who and how many to assign?

"It comes out of the computer," Jon explained. "It's a bar graph
with the business you're going to do that week already printed in."

"The business you're *going* to do, already printed in?"

"It's based on the last week's sales, like maybe you did a $300 hour
on Thursday at 3 P.M. Then it automatically adds a certain percent, say
15 percent, which is the projected annual increase for your particular
store. . . . No, the person scheduling doesn't have to do any of this calculation. I just happen to know how it's arrived at. Really, it's simple,
it's just a graph with the numbers already in it. $400 hour, $500 hour.
According to Hamburger Central you schedule two crew members per
$100 hour. So if you're projected for a $600 hour on Friday between 1
and 2, you know you need twelve crew for that lunch hour and the
schedule sheet leaves space for their names."

"You mean you just fill in the blanks on the chart?"

"It's pretty automatic except in the case of a special event like the
concert. Then you have to guess the dollar volume. Scheduling under

could be a problem, but over would be a disaster to your crew labor productivity."

"Crew labor productivity?"

"Everything at McDonald's is based on the numbers. But crew labor productivity is pretty much *the* number a manager is judged by."

"Crew labor productivity? You have to be an economist."

"It's really simple to calculate. You take the total crew labor dollars paid out, divide that into the total food dollars taken in. That gives you your crew labor productivity. The more food you sell and the less people you use to do it, the better your percentage. It's pretty simple."

Apparently, I still looked confused.

"For example, if you take an $800 hour and you run it with ten crew you get a very high crew labor percent."

"That's good?"

"Yes that's good. Then the manager in the next store hears Jon ran a 12 percent labor this week, I'll run a 10 percent labor. Of course you burn people out that way. But . . ."

"But Jon," I asked, "if the number of crew you need is set in advance and printed by the computer, why do so many managers keep changing hours and putting pressure on kids to work more?"

"They advertise McDonald's as a flexible work schedule for high school and college kids," he said, "but the truth is it's a high-pressure job, and we have so much trouble keeping help, especially in fast stores like my first one (it grossed $1.8 million last year), that 50 percent never make it past two weeks. And a lot walk out within two days.

"When I was a first assistant, scheduling and hiring was my responsibility and I had to fill the spots one way or another. There were so many times I covered the shifts myself. Times I worked 100 hours a week. A manager has to fill the spaces on his chart somehow. So if a crew person is manipulable they manipulate him."

"What do you mean?"

"When you first sign on, you give your availability. Let's say a person's schedule is weeknights, 4 to 10. But after a week the manager schedules him as a closer Friday night. He calls in upset, 'Hey, my availability isn't Friday night.' The manager says 'Well the schedule is already done. And you know the rule. If you can't work it's up to you to replace yourself.' At that point the person might quit, or he might not show up or he might have a fight with the manager."

"So he's fired?"

"No. You don't fire. You would only fire for cause like drugs or stealing. But what happens is he signed up for thirty hours a week and suddenly he's only scheduled for four. So either he starts being more available or he quits."

"Aren't you worried that the most qualified people will quit?"

"The only qualification to be able to do the job is to be able physically to do the job. I believe it says that in almost those words in my regional manual. And being there is the main part of being physically able to do the job."

"But what about your great crew at the second store? Don't you want to keep a team together?"

"Let me qualify that qualification. It takes a special kind of person to be able to move before he can think. We find people like that and use them till they quit."

"But as a manager don't you look bad if too many people are quitting?"

"As a manager I am judged by the statistical reports which come off the computer. Which basically means my crew labor productivity. What else can I really distinguish myself by? I could have a good fry yield, a low M&R [Maintenance and Repair budget]. But these are minor."

As it happens, Jon is distinguished among McDonald's managers in his area as an expert on the computerized equipment. Other managers call on him for cash register repairs. "They say, 'Jon, could you look at my register? I just can't afford the M&R this month.' So I come and fix it and they'll buy me a beer."

"So keeping M&R low is a real feather in a manager's cap," I deduced.

"O.K., it's true, you can over spend your M&R budget; you can have a low fry yield; you can run a dirty store; you can be fired for bothering the high school girls. But basically, every Coke spigot is monitored. [At most McDonald's, Coke doesn't flow from taps that turn on and off. Instead the clerk pushes the button "sm," "med" or "lge," which then dispenses the premeasured amount into the appropriate-size cup. This makes the syrup yield fairly consistent.] Every ketchup squirt is measured. My costs for every item are set. So my crew labor productivity is my main flexibility."

I was beginning to understand the pressures toward pettiness. I had by then heard many complaints about slight pilferage of time. For instance, as a safety measure no one was allowed to stay in a store alone. There was a common complaint that a closer would be clocked out when he finished cleaning the store for the night, even though he might be required to wait around unpaid till the manager finished his own nightly statistical reports. At other times kids clocked out and then waited hours (unpaid) for a crew chief training course (unpaid).

Overtime is an absolute taboo at McDonald's. Managers practice every kind of scheduling gymnastic to see that no one works over forty hours a week. If a crew member approaching forty hours is needed to close the store, he or she might be asked to check out for a long lunch. I had heard of a couple of occasions when, in desperation, a manager scheduled someone to stay an hour or two over forty hours. Instead of paying time-and-a-half, he compensated at straight time listing the extra hours as miscellaneous and paying through a fund reserved for things like register race bonuses. All of this of course to make his statistics look good.

"There must be some other way to raise your productivity," I suggested, "besides squeezing it out of the kids."

"I try to make it fun," Jon pleaded earnestly. "I know that people like to work on my shifts. I have the highest crew labor productivity in the area. But I get that from burning people out. Look, you can't squeeze a McDonald's hamburger any flatter. If you want to improve your productivity there is nothing for a manager to squeeze but the crew."

"But if it's crew dollars paid out divided by food dollars taken in, maybe you can bring in more dollars instead of using less crew."

"O.K., let me tell you about sausage sandwiches."

"Sausage sandwiches?" (Sounded awful.)

"My crew was crazy about sausage sandwiches. [Crew members are entitled to one meal a day at reduced prices. The meals are deducted from wages through a computerized link to the time clocks.] They made it from a buttered English muffin, a slice of sausage and a slice of cheese. I understand this had actually been a menu item in some parts of the country but never here. But the crew would make it for themselves and then all their friends came in and wanted them.

"So, I decided to go ahead and sell it. It costs about 9¢ to make and I sold it for $1.40. It went like hotcakes. My supervisor even liked the idea because it made so much money. You could see the little dollar signs in his eyes when he first came into the store. And he said nothing. So we kept selling it.

"Then someone came from Oak Brook and they made us stop it.

"Just look how ridiculous that is. A slice of sausage is 60¢ as a regular menu item, and an English muffin is 45¢. So if you come in and ask for a sausage and an English muffin I can still sell them to you today for $1.05. But there's no way I can add the slice of cheese and put it in the box and get that $1.40.

"Basically, I can't be any more creative than a crew person. I can't take any more initiative than the person on the register."

"Speaking of cash registers and initiative," I said . . . and told him about Damita. I explained that she was honest, bright and had learned how to zero out at another store. "Do you let cashiers zero out?" I asked.

"I might let her in this case," Jon said. "The store she learned it at was probably a franchise and they were looser. But basically we don't need people like her. Thinking generally slows this operation down.

"When I first came to McDonald's, I said, 'How mechanical! These kids don't even know how to cook.' But the pace is so fast that if they didn't have all the systems, you couldn't handle it. It takes ninety seconds to cook a hamburger. In those seconds you have to toast the bun, dress it, sear it, turn it, take it off the grill and serve it. Meanwhile you've got maybe twenty-four burgers, plus your chicken, your fish. You haven't got time to pick up a rack of fillet and see if it's done. You have to press the timer, drop the fish and know, without looking, that when it buzzes it's done.

"It's the same thing with management. You have to record the money each night before you close and get it to the bank the next day by 11 A.M. So you have to trust the computer to do a lot of the job. These computers also calculate the payrolls, because they're hooked into the time clocks. My payroll is paid out of a bank in Chicago. The computers also tell you how many people you're going to need each hour. It's so fast that the manager hasn't got time to think about it. He has to follow the procedures like the crew. And if he follows the procedures everything is going to come out more or less as it's supposed to. So basically the computer manages the store."

Listening to Jon made me remember what Ray Kroc had written about his own job (head of the corporation) and computers:

> We have a computer in Oak Brook that is designed to make real estate surveys. But those printouts are of no use to me. After we find a promising location, I drive around it in a car, go into the corner saloon and the neighborhood supermarket. I mingle with the people and observe their comings and goings. That tells me what I need to know about how a McDonald's store would do there.[2]

By combining twentieth-century computer technology with nineteenth-century time-and-motion studies, the McDonald's corporation has broken the jobs of griddleman, waitress, cashier and even manager down into small, simple steps. Historically these have been service jobs involving a lot of flexibility and personal flair. But the corporation has systematically extracted the decision-making elements from filling french fry boxes or scheduling staff. They've siphoned the know-how from the employees into the programs. They relentlessly weed out all variables that might make it necessary to make a decision at the store level, whether on pickles or on cleaning procedures.

It's interesting and understandable that Ray Kroc refused to work that way. The real estate computer may be as reliable as the fry vat probe. But as head of the company Kroc didn't have to surrender to it. He'd let the computer juggle all the demographic variables, but in the end Ray Kroc would decide, intuitively, where to put the next store.

---

[2] Ray Kroc and Robert Anderson, *Grinding It Out* (Chicago: Contemporary Books, 1977), p. 176.

Jon DeAngelo would like to work that way, too. So would Jason, June, and Damita. If they had a chance to use some skill or intuition at their own levels, they'd not only feel more alive, they'd also be treated with more consideration. It's job organization, not malice, that allows (almost requires) McDonald's workers to be handled like paper plates. They feel disposable because they are.

I was beginning to wonder why Jon stayed on at McDonald's. He still yearned to open a restaurant. "The one thing I'd take from McDonald's to a French restaurant of my own is the fry vat computer. It really works." He seemed to have both the diligence and the style to run a personalized restaurant. Of course he may not have had the capital.

"So basically I would tell that girl [bringing me back to Damita] to find a different job. She's thinking too much and it slows things down. The way the system is set up, I don't need that in a register person, and they don't need it in me."

"Jon," I said, trying to be tactful, "I don't exactly know why you stay at McDonald's."

"As a matter of fact, I have already turned in my resignation."

"You mean you're not a McDonald's manager any more?" I was dismayed.

"I quit once before and they asked me to stay."

"I have had such a hard time getting a full-fledged manager to talk to me and now I don't know whether you count."

"They haven't actually accepted my resignation yet. You know I heard of this guy in another region who said he was going to leave and they didn't believe him. They just wouldn't accept his resignation. And you know what he did? One day, at noon, he just emptied the store, walked out, and locked the door behind him."

For a second Jon seemed to drift away on that beautiful image. It was like the kids telling me about Jason, the crewman who just walked out the back door.

"You know what that means to close a McDonald's at noon, to do a zero hour at lunch?"

"Jon," I said. "This has been fantastic. You are fantastic. I don't think anyone could explain the computers to me the way you do. But I want to talk to someone who's happy and moving up in the McDonald's system. Do you think you could introduce me to a manager who . . ."

"You won't be able to."

"How come?"

"First of all, there's the media hotline. If any press comes around or anyone is writing a book I'm supposed to call the regional office immediately and they will provide someone to talk to you. So you can't speak to a real corporation person except by arrangement with the corporation.

"Second, you can't talk to a happy McDonald's manager because 98 percent are miserable.

"Third of all, there is no such thing as a McDonald's manager. The computer manages the store."

Speculations

1. Why did Jason Pratt become a legend among the teenagers in his neighborhood? How would you describe his values and response to working at McDonald's?
2. What did you learn about McDonald's from this article that you did not know before? What surprised you or was most striking about this description of how McDonald's works?
3. How do you interpret the title of this essay?
4. How would you describe Garson's tone in this essay? How does her tone reinforce her role as an interviewer and researcher?
5. How would you compare the data in this article to your own perspective and experience of McDonald's? How has this article changed your view of McDonald's? Are you more sympathetic with the employees and less sympathetic with the corporation itself now? Explain why.
6. Using examples from your own work experience, describe how your values and goals as an employee resemble or differ from the values and goals of one or more of the working people interviewed in this essay.

GREETINGS FROM THE ELECTRONIC PLANTATION

Roger Swardson

Born in Cincinnati in 1934, Roger Swardson grew up in Ohio and received his B.A. in English from Ohio University. Having a talent for writing insightfully about everyday life, he took a job as a police reporter for *The Cincinnati Inquirer*. His journalism career got interrupted when Swardson moved into the world of blue collar labor and started working in steel mills, factories, and a variety of other industrial jobs. Since 1991, he has worked as a temporary telephone services representative at a well-known national mail order company—an experience he describes vividly in the following selection.

Returning to his journalism career as a free-lance writer in recent years, Swardson has published in *The Washington Post*, the *San Francisco Chronicle*, St. Paul-Minneapolis's *City Pages*, and the *Utne Reader*, in which this selection appeared in 1993. He writes mainly about the working poor and expects to publish a book on this subject in late 1995. "Greetings from the Electronic Plantation" provides an insider's view of what it's like to work long hours for low pay at one of the many repetitive, monotonous jobs recently created in the service sector of the U.S. economy. Drawing a troublesome picture of temporary employees who have no benefits and an unstable future, Swardson suggests that rather than revitalizing the economy, the computer revolution has combined with corporate cost cutting to produce a new class of working poor who have no chance at advancement nor any promise of financial success. In an interview with *Speculations*, Swardson, who has three sons and two daughters, said, "I would give young writers the same advice that I give my own children about getting an education: Don't specialize. Learn what used to be called the liberal arts. Learn how the world works and how to think. That's all you need to know. You learn that by reading the great thinkers."

Out in the economic sector where you work all week but can't make a living, lots of us are fastened like barnacles to the bottom of the computer revolution. Soldering tiny leads on circuit boards. Plugging data into terminals. All sorts of things that tend to share one characteristic: repetition. Some of the jobs, like mine, consist of sitting in a chair while, all day long, people call you from all over the country to buy things like T-shirts that read "Compost Happens."

Just after 9 a.m., a tireless recorded voice in my headset tips me off. A catalog shopper is coming my way from across the continent. I press the appropriate key and say, "Good morning, welcome to Wireless. My name is Roger. How can I help you?"

Wireless is one of five direct-mail catalogs operated by Rivertown Trading Company, a shirttail relation of Minnesota Public Radio, the spawning ground of Garrison Keillor.

This morning I walk through a new industrial park to the clusters of smokers hanging around the lone door in the block-long wall of a warehouse. Once inside I show my picture ID to the guard behind the glass window and stick another plastic card in the time clock.

I initial the sheet that tells me when to take my morning and afternoon 15-minute breaks and half-hour lunch period. I nod good morning to two women at the group leader station that overlooks the room. They smile and nod back. Both are concentrating on computer terminals that identify scores of telephone service representatives (TSRs) like me who have logged onto the system this morning. The screens tell the group leaders exactly what all the TSRs are doing in the system and for how many seconds they have been doing it. In a seven-day period prior to Christmas 1991, despite the lousy economy, about 300 of us in two shifts wrote 87,642 mail or credit card orders, up 47 percent from the year before.

One supervisor in a headset has a distant look on her face. She's monitoring a TSR, tapping into a customer call to check on two dozen points that must be covered. The TSR will be told the results later in the day.

I fill up my coffee mug and check the printout taped to the wall next to the time card rack. The printout summarizes the results of our weekly monitorings. Ideally we should get 24 pieces of information from the customer (like home phone, work address, whether or not they want to be on our mailing list) during the course of the conversation. During the monitorings, we are graded according to how much of the data we have gotten, which is a difficult task when you've got a customer on the other end of the line who just wants to make a purchase and hang up without being asked a bunch of questions. We are expected to maintain an average above 90 percent. The names of all TSRs in the 90s have been highlighted with a blue marker. I'm at 89.6 percent. It has been suggested that I could use additional training.

I head down a double row of 20 stalls where the backsides of seated people stick out like the rumps of Guernsey cows. The room is done in tones of gray, and merchandise is pinned to white walls. The 80 stalls I can see are mostly occupied. There is a continuous yammer like audience noise before a concert. On two walls electronic scoreboards flash the number of calls completed for each of five catalogs. The total is around 2,200. A busy morning. Must have been a big catalog mailing.

I find an open stall, adjust the chair height, get my headset on, and log onto the phone and computer systems, using my password. An orange light on my console indicates that there are callers on hold.

I bring up the initial screen of the order process and tap the button on my phone to signal that I'm ready to take a customer call. A recorded voice instantly says "Wireless."

I swing right into it. "Good morning. Welcome to Wireless. My name is Roger. How can I help you?"

A woman from New Jersey is distressed.

"You have to help me."

"Sure, what's the problem?"

"I ordered a ring for my husband for our anniversary. Last night we went out and I gave it to him before dinner. Well, he's put on a little weight and it didn't fit. The poor man was so upset he couldn't eat his dinner. Today he's out there running around the neighborhood and getting red in the face."

"That's terrible. What can I do?"

"Well, I looked at the ring this morning and I ordered a size too small."

"Send it back. We'll send you another one right away."

"How long will it take?"

"If you want to pay extra I can send it overnight air. Regular delivery is 10 working days."

"Make it the 10-day. It won't kill him."

"Interface" is a word that tells millions of American workers where we fit. We are devices between you and a computer system. Various terms further identify the device: data entry, customer service, word processing, telemarketing, and others. We take reservations. We do market research. We sell people aluminum siding the minute they sit down to dinner. Every night we update computer records so that multinational corporations can begin the day on top of things. We type most of today's business communications. We do all those mundane tasks that provide computer systems with the raw data that makes them useful.

Even so, most of us are among the more than 14 million Americans who work every week but are still classified by the government as poor. The people Ross Perot talks about when he says, "I suppose when they are up to six bucks an hour in Mexico and down to six bucks here, American corporations will again begin creating jobs in this country."

Here's another way we are classified. The first sentence of my employee handbook tells me that the company "believes in the practice of employment at will, which means that employment is terminable by either the employee or the company at any time, for any reason." We are devices that accommodate the economic needs of our era. Flexible. Disposable.

Even recyclable.

Say a company is "downsizing" or "delayering" or whatever other term describes job cuts. Through a combination of early retirement, attrition, and layoffs they manage to take 200 current semi-skilled employees off the payroll over the course of a year. Say those employees were paid an average of $12 an hour with full benefits. The company then hires a temporary agency to fill openings as they occur. The agency may even have an office in the company's building. Job qualifications are determined, and the agency finds the people and trains them if necessary. The jobs will pay from $5 to $7 an hour. Even with the agency's commission, the company has just saved around $2 million annually in wages and benefits.

Improbable? A want ad placed by a temporary employment agency in my St. Paul newspaper lists four major corporations that need temporary workers. The agency is offering a $25 bonus to people with prior experience with any of the listed companies. Today, through the wonders of current economic policy, it is possible to replace yourself at a bargain rate.

Here's another way the system works. You have a data entry barn where the job routine is easy and repetitive. The problem is that your volume is changeable, with big bulges around some of the holidays. A permanent work force would be awkward, so you have a standing order with three temporary agencies.

When your temporaries show up, they are told their hours will vary as necessary with one week's advance notice. The temps will rarely get a full week's work. They can be sent home any time during the day or let go permanently for any reason. They will receive no benefits. They are subject to a probationary period and can be dropped with a call to the agency. In a relatively short time you have a high-performance, completely flexible work force. You can even offer the best of them permanent part-time jobs, again with no benefits but with a raise in pay. (This actually amounts to a savings, since you no longer have to pay the agency commission.)

Look at the costs and problems you have eliminated. Look how easy the system is to manage. All you have to do is keep weeding.

This is the employment system of the 1990s, made possible by a bankrupt economy and an increasingly desperate work force.

We are the vocational descendants of the dapper clerks in the better stores who knew your sizes and decided when your son ought to be ready for his first suit. Our voices, regardless of how we happen to look or feel that day, are fresh and animated and friendly. We just happen to be sitting here in jeans and a sweatshirt talking into a little foam ball.

After a while you get into a rhythm. You learn to judge how the calls will go. Women in California invariably say they have shopped with us before when they have not, men everywhere say they have no idea whether they've shopped with us before though many of them are repeaters.

Southern women sign off with "Ba-Ba" except for Texans, who just say "Ba," and people from Alaska sound like friends you can rely on, which seems fortunate in that kind of country. I never heard a shrill voice from Alaska.

You can easily tell people who are ordering with a purpose and people who love to shop or do it to feel better. One day a woman browsed through the catalog for 18 minutes and ordered more than 3,000 bucks' worth of stuff. I had a pretty good idea the order wouldn't go through, but she had a wonderful time.

This two-week pay period I'm able to get in 74 hours at $6 an hour. My take-home, after federal and state taxes and Social Security, is $355.48. With another good pay period plus the 5 percent commission I make by selling merchandise on the specials list, I could net $800 this month.

On this particular day I take 57 calls from 23 states. I write $4,096.59 in orders. The biggest is from a guy in California for a selection of videotapes that includes complete sets of the British television shows *Reilly, Ace of Spies* and *Rumpole of the Bailey*.

In just over eight months, working at a pace where I am either available for or taking orders more than 90 percent of the time I am logged on, I have taken 4,462 orders and booked nearly $300,000.

Even so, many jobs like mine, especially in urban America, are at risk. Workers in American cities cost more than elsewhere simply because it costs more to live here. As a result, there is a kind of ongoing economic cleansing. Software "upgrades" constantly eliminate some jobs, data barns move to cheaper rural locations, and the Caribbean and Mexico are claiming jobs.

In the meantime, take that $6-an-hour job that provides about $800 a month if you can get 40 hours a week in, and then add up rent, utilities, phone, food, and transportation. Then try adding a family.

It doesn't add up.

"Recovery" is a wishful term. It is also a word that means something understandable. Most of us can tell whether we are recovering. Thirty-eight million people below the poverty line is not a persuasive definition of an economic "recovery."

Leading economic indicators are used by economists to describe conditions as they may be six to nine months in the future. How, if the present constantly worsens, can the future remain perpetually bright? Even schoolchildren can see that that's denial.

How else could "downsizing" be heralded for improving corporate profits and aiding the "recovery"? Fewer livelihoods mean "recovery"? For whom?

The same with "diminished expectations" or lesser livelihoods. That must mean those economic refugees from companies that let $12-an-hour people go and replaced them with $6 temporaries. These resettled workers are a non-statistical phenomenon. They are employed. But because millions of dollars have been hacked out of their paychecks, they no longer qualify for mortgages, car loans, or credit cards no matter what the interest rate. Who will spend us into the "recovery"?

Workers are getting pushed farther down the economic ladder as laid-off skilled workers and recent college graduates secure even the menial jobs. And, on the bottom, public assistance is breaking its seams.

Surely, the term "recovery" has become a mockery of the way millions of Americans now live.

The rest of us come and go. The young. Men without jobs. People picking up some extra money. But women between 40 and 60 are always there, plugging away at countless uninspiring jobs that need doing day in and day out, year in and year out.

On break they sit together eating homemade food out of Tupperware while the rest of us use the vending machines. They show each other craft handiwork. They bring packets of photos. They take work seriously and talk about the merchandise and what kind of a day they're having. They do well at jobs many make fun of or would not do. And they succeed at life as it is.

I left a temp job at an insurance company at dusk. A woman was sitting at a terminal in word processing wearing a smock. I said something sprightly like "Working late, huh?" And that started a conversation. It happens easily with night-shift people.

Her husband put in 27 years on the production line of a company that went broke and then cheated him out of his pension. She worked for a small office-equipment firm and the same thing happened. He is now a part-time security guard. She holds down two temporary jobs. Their jobs don't provide health insurance, and they can't afford it. They put in a lifetime working, raising their kids, and they must continue working indefinitely. I was enraged but she passed it off. Gave me a brownie. Then in the lighted corner of the darkened office floor she went to work, producing letters from dictation. As I left I could hear the tape of some dayside junior exec talking through his nose about yet another intolerable situation that had come to his attention.

The caller's voice does not hold together well. I can tell he is quite old and not well. He is calling from Maryland.

"I want four boxes of the Nut Goodies," he rasps at me after giving me his credit card information in a faltering hurry.

"There are 24 bars in each box" I say in case he doesn't know the magnitude of his order. Nut Goodies are made here in St. Paul and consist of a patty of maple cream covered with milk chocolate and peanuts. Sort of a Norwegian praline.

"OK, then make it five boxes but hurry this up before my nurse gets back."

He wants the order billed to a home address but sent to a nursing home.

"I've got Parkinson's," he says. "I'm 84."

"OK, sir. I think I've got it all. They're on the way." I put a rush on it.

"Right. Bye," he says, and in the pause when he is concentrating God knows how much energy on getting the receiver back in its cradle, I hear a long, dry chuckle.

One hundred and twenty Nut Goodies.

Way to go, buddy.

During our time together I am not sucking cough drops and scratching for rent money and she, with her mellow alto, is not calling from a condo at Sea Island. We are two grandparents talking over the selection of videos for her grandson's seventh birthday. We settle on classics, among them *The Red Balloon, Old Yeller,* and *Fantasia.*

I say "we" because when I'm on the phone I identify with the people I speak with; I'm no longer an electronic menial. And it's not just me. We all do it. I can hear my neighbors. You'd think we were at a Newport garden party.

We identify with wealth because none of us, moneyless, think of ourselves as poor. We'll be on this plantation another month. Maybe two. That $10 job will come through. That ominous feeling around the tooth will go away. The car won't break again. We'll be on our way presently.

Except there's a feeling these days that's hard to pin down. A detachment that comes out now and then as rage or despair. Many of the people I work with are bone-tired from just trying to make it week by week. A lot of people have just plain stopped believing any politician.

For years the working poor in this country have felt they had a pact with the powerful. Work hard and you'll be OK. Do your job well and you'll have the basics and a chance to move up. The rich and powerful, because they run the system, have been stewards of that promise. It means when the chips are down, the preservation of opportunity is supposed to come before the cultivation of privilege.

On the bus and in the break room today there is a great deal of frustration. The promise has been broken and people don't really know what they can do about it. Another system has taken the place of the old pact. Those who have found a secure place in the suburbs, in government, in the corporations, in wealth, have redefined the country under a different set of rules. It is a smug new club. And those riding the bus and sitting in the break room need not apply.

At the end of my shift I log off the computer and phone system, nod good-bye to the two women at the supervisory station, punch out, open my backpack for the guard so he knows I'm not stealing anything, and head for the bus.

Not a bad day. Remarkably like yesterday.

Speculations

1. What is the significance of Roger Swardson's title, "Greetings from the Electronic Plantation"? What kind of images does it conjure up and what kind of tone does it set for the article?
2. How does Swardson's narrative reproduce the experience of an actual day on the job? What does this narrative make you feel towards the work he describes?

3. Who are the "working poor" and what specific "devices" are used to perpetuate their labor status?

4. How do the actual voices of Swardson's co-workers and other individuals in this piece contrast with the anonymous, repetitious, and mundane work he has to perform? Compare Swardson's description of the work and the people in this essay with your own work experiences.

5. Swardson argues that "'Recovery' is a wishful term." What is his argument and how does he support it? Do you agree or disagree with his prognosis? Explain your answer.

6. What "promise" does Swardson describe at the end of his article and what moral point does he make about it? Do you agree or disagree? Explain your answer.

MIKE LEFEVRE, STEELWORKER

Studs Terkel

"Next to Richard Nixon, the person whose life has been most dramatically affected by the tape recorder is Studs Terkel," according to a *Time* magazine book review. Terkel's particular genius has been his ability to interview a vast cross section of Americans. He has chronicled Americans talking about how they see themselves and their work in more than seven books.

Studs Terkel was born Louis Terkel in 1912 in New York City, but his roots are in Chicago. He grew up there, earned his law degree from the University of Chicago, worked for years on radio in Chicago, and took his nickname from the fictional Chicago character, Studs Lonigan. An enthusiastic liberal, Terkel credits blacklisting in the 1950s with ending his television career and starting his writing career. He was blacklisted for petitioning for rent control and social security and for petitioning against Jim Crow laws and poll taxes.

His first book was a collection of revealing, first-person narratives about the Depression called *Division Street: America and Hard Times*, which he followed up with *Hard Times: An Oral History of the Great Depression*. His next book, *Working: People Talk about What They Do All Day and How They Feel about What They Do*, is perhaps his best-known work, a compendium of over fifty interviews from Americans in all walks of life. In 1985 he won a Pulitzer Prize for *The Good War: An Oral History of World War II*, and in 1992 he published his most recent book, *Race: How Blacks and Whites Think and Feel About the American Obsession*.

Terkel's interviews are with "real people." "I celebrate the non-celebrated," the author once said. "I've found that average people want to talk about themselves, their hopes, dreams, aspirations, provided they sense that you're interested in what they're saying." In a talk to the Friends of Libraries U.S.A., Terkel said,

> The key ingredient in democracy is not saluting a flag or standing tall. It is the aware citizenry. . . . And behind each informed citizen, there is a book. . . . It may not be a major work, but some piece of reading or some story told by a grandmother or by an old stranger. And that is what enriches the life and gives that person a kind of insight.

It is a two-flat dwelling, somewhere in Cicero, on the outskirts of Chicago. He is thirty-seven. He works in a steel mill. On occasion, his wife Carol works as a waitress in a neighborhood restaurant; otherwise, she is at home, caring for their two small children, a girl and a boy.

At the time of my first visit, a sculpted statuette of Mother and Child was on the floor, head severed from body. He laughed softly as he indicated his three-year-old daughter: "she Doctor Spock'd it."

I'm a dying breed. A laborer. Strictly muscle work . . . pick it up, put it down, pick it up, put it down. We handle between forty and fifty thousand pounds of steel a day. (Laughs.) I know this is hard to believe—from four hundred pounds to three- and four-pound pieces. It's dying.

You can't take pride any more. You remember when a guy could point to a house he built, how many logs he stacked. He built it and he was proud of it. I don't really think I could be proud if a contractor built a home for me. I would be tempted to get in there and kick the carpenter in the ass (laughs), and take the saw away from him. 'Cause I would have to be part of it, you know.

It's hard to take pride in a bridge you're never gonna cross, in a door you're never gonna open. You're mass-producing things and you never see the end result of it. (Muses.) I worked for a trucker one time. And I got this tiny satisfaction when I loaded a truck. At least I could see the truck depart loaded. In a steel mill, forget it. You don't see where nothing goes.

I got chewed out by my foreman once. He said, "Mike, you're a good worker but you have a bad attitude." My attitude is that I don't get excited about my job. I do my work but I don't say whoopee-doo. The day I get excited about my job is the day I go to a head shrinker. How are you gonna get excited about pullin' steel? How are you gonna get excited when you're tired and want to sit down?

It's not just the work. Somebody built the pyramids. Somebody's going to build something. Pyramids, Empire State Building—these things just don't happen. There's hard work behind it. I would like to see a building, say, the Empire State, I would like to see on one side of it a foot-wide strip from top to bottom with the name of every brick-layer, the name of every electrician, with all the names. So when a guy walked by, he could take his son and say, "See, that's me over there on the forty-fifth floor. I put the steel beam in." Picasso can point to a painting. What can I point to? A writer can point to a book. Everybody should have something to point to.

It's the not-recognition by other people. To say a woman is *just* a housewife is degrading, right? Okay. *Just* a housewife. It's also de-grading to say *just* a laborer. The difference is that a man goes out and maybe gets smashed.

When I was single, I could quit, just split. I wandered all over the country. You worked just enough to get a poke, money in your pocket. Now I'm married and I got two kids . . . (trails off). I worked on a truck dock one time and I was single. The foreman came over and he grabbed my shoulder, kind of gave me a shove. I punched him and knocked him off the dock. I said, "Leave me alone. I'm doing my work, just stay away from me, just don't give me the with-the-hands business."

Hell, if you whip a damn mule he might kick you. Stay out of my way, that's all. Working is bad enough, don't bug me. I would rather work my ass off for eight hours a day with nobody watching me than five minutes with a guy watching me. Who you gonna sock? You can't sock General Motors, you can't sock anybody in Washington, you can't sock a system.

A mule, an old mule, that's the way I feel. Oh yeah. See. (Shows black and blue marks on arms and legs, burns.) You know what I heard from more than one guy at work? "If my kid wants to work in a facto-ry, I am going to kick the hell out of him." I want my kid to be an ef-fete snob. Yeah, mm-hmm. (Laughs.) I want him to be able to quote Walt Whitman, to be proud of it.

If you can't improve yourself, you improve your posterity. Other-wise life isn't worth nothing. You might as well go back to the cave and stay there. I'm sure the first caveman who went over the hill to see what was on the other side—I don't think he went there wholly out of curiosity. He went there because he wanted to get his son out of the cave. Just the same way I want to send my kid to college.

I work so damn hard and want to come home and sit down and lay around. *But I gotta get it out.* I want to be able to turn around to some-body and say, "Hey, fuck you." You know? (Laughs.) The guy sitting next to me on the bus too. 'Cause all day I wanted to tell my foreman to go fuck himself, but I can't.

So I find a guy in a tavern. To tell him that. And he tells me too. I've been in brawls. He's punching me and I'm punching him, because we actually want to punch somebody else. The most that'll happen is the bartender will bar us from the tavern. But at work, you lose your job.

This one foreman I've got, he's a kid. He's a college graduate. He thinks he's better than everybody else. He was chewing me out and I was saying, "Yeah, yeah, yeah." He said, "What do you mean, yeah, yeah, yeah. Yes, *sir*." I told him, "Who the hell are you, Hitler? What is this '*Yes, sir*' bullshit? I came here to work, I didn't come here to crawl. There's a fuckin' difference." One word led to another and I lost.

I got broke down to a lower grade and lost twenty-five cents an hour, which is a hell of a lot. It amounts to about ten dollars a week. He came over—after breaking me down. The guy comes over and smiles at me. I blew up. He didn't know it, but he was about two seconds and two feet away from a hospital. I said, "Stay the fuck away from me." He was just about to say something and was pointing his finger. I just reached my hand up and just grabbed his finger and I just put it back in his pocket. He walked away. I grabbed his finger because I'm married. If I'd a been single, I'd a grabbed his head. That's the difference.

You're doing this manual labor and you know that technology can do it. (Laughs.) Let's face it, a machine can do the work of a man; otherwise they wouldn't have space probes. Why can we send a rocket ship that's unmanned and yet send a man in a steel mill to do a mule's work?

Automation? Depends how it's applied. It frightens me if it puts me out on the street. It doesn't frighten me if it shortens my work week. You read that little thing: What are you going to do when this computer replaces you? Blow up computers. (Laughs.) Really. Blow up computers. I'll be goddamned if a computer is gonna eat before I do! I want milk for my kids and beer for me. Machines can either liberate man or enslave 'im, because they're pretty neutral. It's man who has the bias to put the thing one place or another.

If I had a twenty-hour workweek, I'd get to know my kids better, my wife better. Some kid invited me to go on a college campus. On a Saturday. It was summertime. Hell, if I had a choice of taking my wife and kids to a picnic or going to a college campus, it's gonna be the picnic. But if I worked a twenty-hour week, I could go do both. Don't you think with that extra twenty hours people could really expand? Who's to say? There are some people in factories just by force of circumstance. I'm just like the colored people. Potential Einsteins don't have to be white. They could be in cotton fields, they could be in factories.

The twenty-hour week is a possibility today. The intellectuals, they always say there are potential Lord Byrons, Walt Whitmans, Roosevelts, Picassos working in construction or steel mills or factories. But I don't think they believe it. I think what they're afraid of is the potential Hitlers and Stalins that are there too. The people in power fear the leisure man. Not just the United States. Russia's the same way.

What do you think would happen in this country if, for one year, they experimented and gave everybody a twenty-hour week? How do they know that the guy who digs Wallace today doesn't try to resurrect Hitler tomorrow? Or the guy who is mildly disturbed at pollution doesn't decide to go to General Motors and shit on the guy's desk? You can become a fanatic if you had the time. The whole thing is time. That is, I think, one reason rich kids tend to be fanatic about politics: They have time. Time, that's the important thing.

It isn't that the average working guy is dumb. He's tired, that's all. I picked up a book on chess one time. That thing laid in the drawer for two or three weeks, you're too tired. During the weekends you want to take your kids out. You don't want to sit there and the kid comes up: "Daddy, can I go to the park?" You got your nose in a book? Forget it.

I know a guy fifty-seven years old. Know what he tells me? "Mike, I'm old and tired *all* the time." The first thing happens at work: When the arms start moving, the brain stops. I punch in about ten minutes to seven in the morning. I say hello to a couple of guys I like, I kid around with them. One guy says good morning to you and you say good morning. To another guy you say fuck you. The guy you say fuck you to is your friend.

I put on my hard hat, change into my safety shoes, put on my safety glasses, go to the bonderizer. It's the thing I work on. They rake the metal, they wash it, they dip it in a paint solution, and we take it off. Put it on, take it off, put it on, take it off, put it on, take it off. . . .

I say hello to everybody but my boss. At seven it starts. My arms get tired about the first half-hour. After that, they don't get tired any more until maybe the last half-hour at the end of the day. I work from seven to three thirty. My arms are tired at seven thirty and they're tired at three o'clock. I hope to God I never get broke in, because I always want my arms to be tired at seven thirty and three o'clock. (Laughs.) 'Cause that's when I know that there's a beginning and there's an end. That I'm not brainwashed. In between, I don't even try to think.

If I were to put you in front of a dock and I pulled up a skid in front of you with fifty hundred-pound sacks of potatoes and there are fifty more skids just like it, and this is what you're gonna do all day, what would you think about—potatoes? Unless a guy's a nut, he never thinks about work or talks about it. Maybe about baseball or about getting drunk the other night or he got laid or he didn't get laid. I'd say one out of a hundred will actually get excited about work.

Why is it that the communists always say they're for the working-man, and as soon as they set up a country, you got guys singing to tractors? They're singing about how they love the factory. That's where I couldn't buy communism. It's the intellectuals' utopia, not mine. I cannot picture myself singing to a tractor, I just can't. (Laughs.) Or singing to steel. (Singsongs.) Oh whoop-dee-doo, I'm at the bonderizer, oh how I love this heavy steel. No thanks. Never happen.

Oh yeah, I daydream. I fantasize about a sexy blonde in Miami who's got my union dues. (Laughs.) I think of the head of the union the way I think of the head of my company. Living it up. I think of February in Miami. Warm weather, a place to lay in. When I hear a college kid say, "I'm oppressed," I don't believe him. You know what I'd like to do for one year? Live like a college kid. Just for one year. I'd love to. Wow! (Whispers.) Wow! Sports car! Marijuana! (Laughs.) Wild, sexy broads. I'd love that, hell yes, I would.

Somebody has to do this work. If my kid ever goes to college, I just want him to have a little respect, to realize that his dad is one of those somebodies. This is why even on—(muses) yeah, I guess, sure—on the black thing. . . . (Sighs heavily.) I can't really hate the colored fella that's working with me all day. The black intellectual I got no respect for. The white intellectual I got no use for. I got no use for the black militant who's gonna scream three hundred years of slavery to me while I'm busting my ass. You know what I mean? (Laughs.) I have one answer for that guy: Go see Rockefeller. See Harriman. Don't bother me. We're in the same cotton field. So just don't bug me. (Laughs.)

After work I usually stop off at a tavern. Cold beer. Cold beer right away. When I was single, I used to go into hillbilly bars, get in a lot of brawls. Just to explode. I got a thing on my arm here (indicates scar). I got slapped with a bicycle chain. Oh, wow! (Softly.) Mmm. I'm getting older. (Laughs.) I don't explode as much. You might say I'm broken in. (Quickly.) No, I'll never be broken in. (Sighs.) When you get a little older, you exchange the words. When you're younger, you exchange the blows.

When I get home, I argue with my wife a little bit. Turn on TV, get mad at the news. (Laughs.) I don't even watch the news that much. I watch Jackie Gleason. I look for any alternative to the ten o'clock news. I don't want to go to bed angry. Don't hit a man with anything heavy at five o'clock. He just can't be bothered. This is his time to relax. The heaviest thing he wants is what his wife has to tell him.

When I come home, know what I do for the first twenty minutes? Fake it. I put on a smile. I got a kid three years old. Sometimes she says, "Daddy, where've you been?" I say, "Work." I could have told her I'd been in Disneyland. What's work to a three-year-old kid? If I feel bad, I can't take it out on the kids. Kids are born innocent of everything but birth. You can't take it out on your wife either. This is why you go to a tavern. You want to release it there rather than do it at home. What does an actor do when he's got a bad movie? I got a bad movie every day.

I don't even need the alarm clock to get up in the morning. I can go out drinking all night, fall asleep at four, and bam! I'm up at six—no matter what I do. (Laughs.) It's a pseudo-death, more or less. Your whole system is paralyzed and you give all the appearance of death.

It's an ingrown clock. It's a thing you just get used to. The hours differ. It depends. Sometimes my wife wants to do something crazy like play five hundred rummy or put a puzzle together. It could be midnight, could be ten o'clock, could be nine thirty.

What do you do weekends?

Drink beer, read a book. See that one? *Violence in America.* It's one of them studies from Washington. One of the committees they're always appointing. A thing like that I read on a weekend. But during the weekdays, gee . . . I just thought about it. I don't do that much reading from Monday through Friday. Unless it's a horny book. I'll read it at work and go home and do my homework. (Laughs.) That's what the guys at the plant call it—homework. (Laughs.) Sometimes my wife works on Saturday and I drink beer at the tavern.

I went out drinking with one guy, oh, a long time ago. A college boy. He was working where I work now. Always preaching to me about how you need violence to change the system and all that garbage. We went into a hillbilly joint. Some guy there, I didn't know him from Adam, he said, "You think you're smart," I said, "What's your pleasure?" (Laughs.) He said, "My pleasure's to kick your ass." I told him I really can't be bothered. He said, "What're you, chicken?" I said, "No, I just don't want to be bothered." He came over and said something to me again. I said, "I don't beat women, drunks, or fools. Now leave me alone."

The guy called his brother over. This college boy that was with me, he came nudging my arm, "Mike, let's get out of here." I said, "What are you worried about?" (Laughs.) This isn't unusual. People will bug you. You fend it off as much as you can with your mouth and when you can't, you punch the guy out.

It was close to closing time and we stayed. We could have left, but when you go into a place to have a beer and a guy challenges you—if you expect to go in that place again, you don't leave. If you have to fight the guy, you fight.

I got just outside the door and one of these guys jumped on me and grabbed me around the neck. I grabbed his arm and flung him against the wall. I grabbed him here (indicates throat), and jiggled his head against the wall quite a few times. He kind of slid down a little bit. This guy who said he was his brother took a swing at me with a garrison belt. He just missed and hit the wall. I'm looking around for my junior Stalin (laughs), who loves violence and everything. He's gone. Split. (Laughs.) Next day I see him at work. I couldn't get mad at him, he's a baby.

He saw a book in my back pocket one time and he was amazed. He walked up to me and he said, "You read?" I said, "What do you mean, I read?" He said, "All these dummies read the sports pages around here. What are you doing with a book?" I got pissed off at the kid right away. I said, "What do you mean, all these dummies? Don't knock a man who's paying somebody else's way through college." He was a nineteen-year-old effete snob.

Yet you want your kid to be an effete snob?

Yes. I want my kid to look at me and say, "Dad, you're a nice guy, but you're a fuckin' dummy." Hell yes, I want my kid to tell me that he's not gonna be like me. . . .

If I were hiring people to work, I'd try naturally to pay them a decent wage. I'd try to find out their first names, their last names, keep the company as small as possible, so I could personalize the whole thing. All I would ask a man is a handshake, see you in the morning. No applications, nothing. I wouldn't be interested in the guy's past. Nobody ever checks the pedigree on a mule, do they? But they do on a man. Can you picture walking up to a mule and saying, "I'd like to know who his granddaddy was"?

I'd like to run a combination bookstore and tavern. (Laughs.) I would like to have a place where college kids came and a steelworker could sit down and talk. Where a workingman could not be ashamed of Walt Whitman and where a college professor could not be ashamed that he painted his house over the weekend.

If a carpenter built a cabin for poets, I think the least the poets owe the carpenter is just three or four one-liners on the wall. A little plaque: Though we labor with our minds, this place we can relax in was built by someone who can work with his hands. And his work is as noble as ours. I think the poet owes something to the guy who builds the cabin for him.

I don't think of Monday. You know what I'm thinking about on Sunday night? Next Sunday. If you work real hard, you think of a perpetual vacation. Not perpetual sleep. . . . What do I think of on a Sunday night? Lord, I wish the fuck I could do something else for a living.

I don't know who the guy is who said there is nothing sweeter than an unfinished symphony. Like an unfinished painting and an unfinished poem. If he creates this thing one day—let's say, Michelangelo's Sistine Chapel. It took him a long time to do this, this beautiful work of art. But what if he had to create this Sistine Chapel a thousand times a year? Don't you think that would even dull Michelangelo's mind? Or if da Vinci had to draw his anatomical charts thirty, forty, fifty, sixty, eighty, ninety, a hundred times a day? Don't you think that would even bore da Vinci?

Way back, you spoke of the guys who built the pyramids, not the pharaohs, the unknown. You put yourself in their category?

Yes. I want my signature on 'em, too. Sometimes, out of pure meanness, when I make something, I put a little dent in it. I like to do something to make it really unique.

Speculations

1. What shapes Mike LeFevre's attitude toward his work? What does he feel he is missing and how has it created his attitude?
2. How would you describe the problems that haunt LeFevre with regard to automation and the workplace? How would you respond to his question, "Why can we send a rocket ship that's unmanned [into space] and yet send a man in a steel mill to do a mule's work?"
3. Explain why you agree or disagree with LeFevre's assertion that if people had more time "to expand," they would upset the balance of political power because "The people in power fear the leisure man. Not just the United States. Russia's the same way."
4. What speaking style dominates LeFevre's description of work and his relationships at work? How does his way of speaking change when he talks about his family?
5. How would you characterize LeFevre's politics? Use specific examples and statements he makes about political figures and political movements. What motivates his view?

THE WAGES OF THE BACKLASH: THE TOLL ON WORKING WOMEN

Susan Faludi

In the introduction to *Backlash: The Undeclared War Against American Women*, Susan Faludi asks the following questions:

> If American women are so equal, why do they represent two-thirds of all poor adults? Why are nearly 75 percent of full-time working women making less than $20,000 a year, nearly double the male rate? Why are they still far more likely than men to live in poor housing and receive no health insurance, and twice as likely to draw no pension? Why does the average working woman's salary still lag as far behind the average man's as it did twenty years ago? Why does the

average female college graduate today earn less than a man with no more than a high school diploma (just as she did in the '50s)—and why does the average female high school graduate today earn less than a male high school dropout? Why do American women, in fact, face one of the worst gender-based pay gaps in the developed world?

Faludi's book addresses these issues in what she calls the "backlash" effect, which has eroded women's economic position while trumpeting their supposed equality.

Faludi, a Pulitzer Prize-winning writer, has been nominated for a National Book Award. A reporter for the *Wall Street Journal*, America's most prestigious business newspaper, Faludi's essays and articles have also appeared in *West,* the Sunday magazine of the *San Jose Mercury News.*

Faludi describes herself as a "female writer with strong convictions . . . I write so forcefully because I speak so tentatively." She recalls how as editor of her high school newspaper she would speak out against injustices in print but would seldom speak during class discussions: "We saw what happened to the girls who argued in class. The boys called them 'bitches,' and they sat home Saturday nights. Popular girls raised their voices only at pep squad."

As a popular public speaker because of *Backlash,* Faludi has learned that "the writer asserts herself from behind the veil of the printed page . . . [but] until you translate personal words on a page into public connections with other people, you aren't really part of a political movement. . . ."

The backlash against women's rights would be just one of several powerful forces creating a harsh and painful climate for women at work. Reaganomics, the recession, and the expansion of a minimum-wage service economy also helped, in no small measure, to slow and even undermine women's momentum in the job market.

But the backlash did more than impede women's opportunities for employment, promotions, and better pay. Its spokesmen kept the news of many of these setbacks from women. Not only did the backlash do grievous damage to working women—it did it on the sly. The Reagan administration downplayed or simply shelved reports that revealed the extent of working women's declining status. Corporations claimed women's numbers and promotions were at record highs. And the press didn't seem to mind. As the situation of working women fell into increasing peril in the '80s, the backlash media issued ever more upbeat reports—assuring that women's only problem at work was that they would rather be home.

Many myths about working women's "improving" circumstances made the rounds in the '80s—while some discouraging and *real* trends that working women faced didn't get much press. Here are just a few examples.

The trend story we all read about women's wages:
PAY GAP BETWEEN THE SEXES CLOSING!

The difference between the average man's and woman's paycheck, we learned in 1986, had suddenly narrowed. Women who work full-time were now said to make an unprecedented 70 cents to a man's dollar. Newspaper editorials applauded and advised feminists to retire their "obsolete" buttons protesting female pay of 59 cents to a man's dollar.

The trend story we should have seen:
IT'S BACK! THE '50S PAY GAP

The pay gap did *not* suddenly improve to 70 cents in 1986. Women working full-time made only 64 cents to a man's dollar that year, actually slightly *worse* than the year before—and exactly the same gap that working women had faced in *1955*.

The press got the 70-cent figure from a onetime Census Bureau report that was actually based on data from another year and that departed from the bureau's standard method for computing the gap. This report artificially inflated women's earnings by using weekly instead of the standard yearly wages—thus grossly exaggerating the salary of part-time workers, a predominantly female group, who don't work a full year. Later, the Census Bureau calculated the pay gap for 1986 using its standard formula and came up with 64 cents. This report, however, managed to elude media notice.

By that year, in fact, the pay gap had only "improved" for women by less than five percentage points since 1979. And as much as half of that improvement was due to men's falling wages, not women's improving earnings. Take out men's declining pay as a factor and the gap had closed only three percentage points.

By 1988, women with a college diploma could still wear the famous 59-cent buttons. They were still making 59 cents to their male counterparts' dollar. In fact, the pay gap for them was now a bit worse than five years earlier. Black women, who had made almost no progress in the decade, could wear the 59-cent buttons, too. Older and Hispanic women couldn't—but only because their pay gap was even worse now than 59 cents. Older working women had actually fared better in *1968*, when they had made hourly wages of 61 cents to a man's dollar; by 1986, they were down to 58 cents. And Hispanic women, by 1988, found their wages backsliding; they were now making an abysmal 54 cents to a white man's dollar.

The pay gap was also getting worse in many occupations, from social work to screenwriting to real estate management, as U.S. Labor Department data detail. By 1989, the pay gap for women in all full-time managerial jobs was growing worse again; that year, while the average male manager enjoyed a four-percent income boost, his average female counterpart received none. And the gap was widening most in the very fields where female employment was growing most, a list that includes food preparation and service supervisory jobs, waiting tables, and cleaning services. In public relations, where women doubled their ranks in the decade, the pay gap grew so massively that communications professor Elizabeth Lance Toth, who tracks women's status in this profession, reported, "In a forty-year career, a woman will lose $1 million on gender alone."

The trend story we all read about integrating the workplace:
WOMEN INVADE MAN'S WORLD!

Women, we learned, charged into traditional "male" occupations. A sea of women in their dress-for-success suits and stride-to-work sneakers abandoned the "pink-collar" ghettos and descended on Wall Street, law firms, and corporate suites. Still other women laced up army boots, slapped on hard hats, and barged into the all-male military and blue-collar factories.

The trend story we should have seen:
MORE AND MORE, WOMEN STUCK IN SECRETARIAL POOL

While the level of occupational segregation between the sexes eased by 9 percent in the 1970s—the first time it had improved in the century—that progress stalled in the '80s. The Bureau of Labor Statistics soon began projecting a more sex-segregated work force. This was a bitter financial pill for women: as much as 45 percent of the pay gap is caused by sex segregation in the work force. (By one estimate, for every 10 percent rise in the number of women in an occupation, the annual wage for women drops by roughly $700.) A resegregating work force was one reason why women's wages fell in the '80s; by 1986, more working women would be taking home poverty-level wages than in 1973.

Women were pouring into many low-paid female work ghettos. The already huge proportion of working women holding down menial clerical jobs climbed to nearly 40 percent by the early '80s, higher than it had been in 1970. By the late '80s, the proportion of women consigned to the traditionally female service industries had grown, too. A long list of traditionally "female" jobs became *more* female-dominated, including salesclerking, cleaning services, food preparation, and secretarial, administrative, and reception work. The proportion of bookkeepers who were women, for example, rose from 88 to 93 percent between 1979 and 1986. Black women, especially, were resegregated into such traditional female jobs as nursing, teaching, and secretarial and social work. And the story was the same at the office of the nation's largest employer, the federal government. Between 1976 and 1986, the lowest job rungs in the civil service ladder went from 67 to 71 percent female. (At the same time at the top of the ladder, the proportion of women in senior executive services had not improved since 1979—it was still a paltry 8 percent. And the rate of women appointed to top posts had declined to the point that, by the early '80s, less than 1 percent of the G.S. 13 and 14 grade office holders were women.)

In the few cases where working women did make substantial inroads into male enclaves, they were only admitted by default. As a job-integration study by sociologist Barbara Reskin found, in the dozen occupations where women had made the most progress entering "male" jobs—a list that ranged from typesetting to insurance adjustment to pharmaceuticals—women succeeded only because the pay and status of these jobs had fallen dramatically and men were bailing out. Computerization, for example, had demoted male typesetters to typists; the retail chaining of drugstores had turned independent pharmacists into poorly paid clerks. Other studies of women's "progress" in bank management found that women were largely just inheriting branch-manager jobs that men didn't want anymore because their pay, power, and status had declined dramatically. And still another analysis of occupational shifts concluded that one-third of the growth of female employment in transportation and half of the growth in financial services could be attributed simply to a loss of status in the jobs that women were getting in these two professions.

In many of the higher-paying white-collar occupations, where women's successes have been most heavily publicized, the rate of progress slowed to a trickle or stopped altogether by the end of the decade. The proportion of women in some of the more elite or glamorous fields actually shrank slightly in the last half of the '80s. Professional athletes, screenwriters, commercial voice-overs, producers and orchestra musicians, economists, geologists, biological and life scientists were all a little *less* likely to be female by the late '80s than earlier in the decade.

The breathless reports about droves of female "careerists" crashing the legal, medical, and other elite professions were inflated. Between 1972 and 1988, women increased their share of such professional jobs by only 5 percent. In fact, only 2 percent more of all working women were in professional specialties in 1988 than fifteen years earlier—and that increase had been largely achieved by the early '80s and barely budged since.

Hardly any progress occurred in the upper echelons of corporations. In fact, according to scattered studies, in the top executive suites in many industries, from advertising to retailing, women's already tiny numbers were beginning to fall once more by the end of the decade. The rate of growth in numbers of women appointed to Fortune 1000 boards slacked off by the late '80s, after women's share of the director chairs had reached only 6.8 percent. Even the many reports of the rise of female "entrepreneurs" founding their own companies masked the nickel-and-dime reality: the majority of white female-owned business-es had sales of less than $5,000 a year.

Under Reagan, women's progress in the military soon came under fire. In the mid-'70s, after quota ceilings on female recruits had been lifted and combat classifications rewritten to open more jobs to women, women's ranks in the armed services had soared—by 800 per-cent by 1980. But shortly after Reagan's election, the new army chief of staff declared, "I have called a pause to further increases in the number of army women"—and by 1982, the army had revised combat classifications to bar women from an additional twenty-three career occupations. All the services reined in their recruitment efforts, subse-quently slowing female employment growth in the military through-out the '80s.

The blue-collar working world offered no better news. After 1983, as a Labor Department study quietly reported to no fanfare, women made *no* progress breaking into the blue-collar work force with its bet-ter salaries. By 1988, the tiny proportions of women who had squeezed into the trades were shrinking in a long list of job categories from elec-tricians and plumbers to automotive mechanics and machine opera-tors. The already tiny ranks of female carpenters, for example, fell by half, to 0.5 percent, between 1979 and 1986. Higher up the ladder, women's share of construction inspector jobs fell from 7 to 5.4 percent between 1983 and 1988.

Where women did improve their toeholds in blue-collar jobs, the increments were pretty insubstantial. The proportion of women in con-struction, for example, rose from 1.1 to 1.4 percent between 1978 and 1988. Women made the most progress in the blue-collar professions as motor vehicle operators—more than doubling their numbers between 1972 and 1985—but that was only because women were being hired to drive school buses, typically a part-time job with the worst pay and benefits of any transportation position.

The trend story we all read about equal opportunity:
DISCRIMINATION ON THE JOB: FADING FAST!

Corporations, we read, were now welcoming women. "Virtually all large employers are now on [women's] side," *Working Woman* as-sured female readers in 1986. Discrimination was dropping, mistreat-ment of female workers was on the wane—and any reports to the con-trary were just "propaganda from self-interested parties," as *Forbes* asserted in 1989—in its story on the "decline" of sexual harassment on the job.

The trend story we should have seen:
NOW MORE THAN EVER! INEQUITY AND INTIMIDATION

Reports of sex discrimination and sexual harassment reached record highs in the decade—by both private and federal employees.

Women's sex discrimination complaints to the Equal Employment Opportunity Commission (EEOC) climbed by nearly 25 percent in the Reagan years—and by 40 percent among federally employed women just in the first half of the '80s. Complaints of exclusion, demotions, and discharges on the basis of sex rose 30 percent. General harassment of women, excluding sexual harassment, more than doubled. And while the EEOC's public relations office issued statements claiming that sexual harassment in corporate America was falling, its own figures showed that annual charges of sexual harassment nearly doubled in the decade.

Throughout much of the '80s, women were also far more likely than men to lose their jobs or get their wages cut—and legal challenges to remedy the imbalance went nowhere in the courts. Press accounts to the contrary, the mass layoffs of the '80s actually took a greater toll on female service workers than male manufacturing workers—the service sector accounted for almost half of the job displacement in the decade, nearly 10 percentage points more than manufacturing. And even among blue-collar workers, women suffered higher unemployment rates than men. In the federal "reductions in force" in the early '80s, too, women who held higher-paid civil-service jobs (G.S. 12 and above) got laid off at more than twice the average rate. Far more working women than men were also forced into the part-time work force and expanding "temp" pools of the '80s, where women faced an extraordinary pay gap of 52 cents to a man's dollar and labored with little to no job security, insurance, benefits, or pension. Even among displaced workers who managed to get rehired, women had it worse. Women in service jobs who were reemployed had to settle for pay reductions of 16 percent, nearly double the reductions borne by their male counterparts.

If we heard less about discrimination in the '80s workplace, that was partly because the federal government had muzzled, or fired, its equal-employment investigators. At the same time that the EEOC's sex discrimination files were overflowing, the Reagan administration was cutting the agency's budget in half and jettisoning its caseload. The year Reagan came into office, the EEOC had twenty-five active class-action cases; a year later, it had none. The agency scaled back the number of suits it pursued by more than 300 percent. A House Education and Labor Committee report found that in the first half of the '80s, the number of discrimination victims receiving compensation fell by two-thirds. By 1987, a General Accounting Office study found that EEOC district offices and state equal-employment agencies were closing 40 to 80 percent of their cases without proper, or any, investigation.

A similar process was taking place in the other federal agencies charged with enforcing equal opportunity for women and minorities. At the Office of Federal Contract Compliance (OFCC), for example, back-pay awards fell from $9.3 million in 1980 to $600,000 in 1983; the number of government contractors that this agency barred from federal work because of discrimination fell from five in the year before Reagan took office to none a year after his inauguration. In fact, in a 1982 study, every OFCC staff member interviewed said that they had never found a company *not* to be in compliance. This wasn't because American corporations had suddenly reformed: the majority of federal contractors polled in the same study said they just felt no pressure to comply with the agency's affirmative action requirements anymore.

An exhaustive study of women's occupational patterns in the '80s would be outside the scope of this book. But it is possible to tell the stories of some women in key representative employment areas—from the white-collar media to the pink-collar sales force to the most embattled blue-collar universe. These are women who, one way or another, set themselves against the backlash in the work force and, in the process, ran up against the barriers built by employers, male peers, judges, government officials, and even "feminist" scholars. They had to face ridicule, ostracism, threats and even physical assaults—as they simply tried to make a living.

Diane Joyce: Women in the Blue-Collar World

It would take Diane Joyce nearly ten years of battles to become the first female skilled crafts worker ever in Santa Clara County history. It would take another seven years of court litigation, pursued all the way to the U.S. Supreme Court, before she could actually start work. And then, the real fight would begin.

For blue-collar women, there was no honeymoon period on the job; the backlash began the first day they reported to work—and only intensified as the Reagan economy put more than a million blue-collar men out of work, reduced wages, and spread mounting fear. While the white-collar world seemed capable of absorbing countless lawyers and bankers in the '80s, the trades and crafts had no room for expansion. "Women are far more economically threatening in blue-collar work, because there are a finite number of jobs from which to choose," Mary Ellen Boyd, executive director of Non-Traditional Employment for Women, observes. "An MBA can do anything. But a plumber is only a plumber." While women never represented more than a few percentage points of the blue-collar work force, in this powder-keg situation it only took a few female faces to trigger a violent explosion.

Diane Joyce arrived in California in 1970, a thirty-three-year-old widow with four children, born and raised in Chicago. Her father was a tool-and-die maker, her mother a returned-goods clerk at a Walgreen's warehouse. At eighteen, she married Donald Joyce, a tool-and-die maker's apprentice at her father's plant. Fifteen years later, after working knee-deep in PCBs for years, he died suddenly of a rare form of liver cancer.

After her husband's death, Joyce taught herself to drive, packed her children in a 1966 Chrysler station wagon and headed west to San Jose, California, where a lone relative lived. Joyce was an experienced bookkeeper and she soon found work as a clerk in the county Office of Education, at $506 a month. A year later, she heard that the county's transportation department had a senior account clerk job vacant that paid $50 more a month. She applied in March 1972.

"You know, we wanted a man," the interviewer told her as soon as she walked through the door. But the account clerk jobs had all taken a pay cut recently, and sixteen women and no men had applied for the job. So he sent her on to the second interview. "This guy was a little politer," Joyce recalls. "First, he said, 'Nice day, isn't it?' before he tells me, 'You know, we wanted a man.' I wanted to say, 'Yeah, and where's my man? I am the man in my house.' But I'm sitting there with four kids to feed and all I can see is dollar signs, so I kept my mouth shut."

She got the job. Three months later, Joyce saw a posting for a "road maintenance man." An eighth-grade education and one year's work experience was all that was required, and the pay was $723 a month. Her current job required a high-school education, bookkeeping skills, and four years' experience—and paid $150 less a month. "I saw that flier and I said, 'Oh wow, I can do that.' Everyone in the office laughed. They thought it was a riot. . . . I let it drop."

But later that same year, every county worker got a 2 to 5 percent raise except for the 70 female account clerks. "Oh now, what do you girls need a raise for?" the director of personnel told Joyce and some other women who went before the board of supervisors to object. "All you'd do is spend the money on trips to Europe." Joyce was shocked. "Every account clerk I knew was supporting a family through death or divorce. I'd never seen Mexico, let alone Europe." Joyce decided to apply for the next better-paying "male" job that opened. In the meantime, she became active in the union; a skillful writer and one of the best-educated representatives there, Joyce wound up composing the safety language in the master contract and negotiating what became the most powerful county agreement protecting seniority rights.

In 1974, a road dispatcher retired, and both Joyce and a man named Paul Johnson, a former oil-fields roustabout, applied for the post. The supervisors told Joyce she needed to work on the road crew first and handed back her application. Johnson didn't have any road crew experience either, but his application was accepted. In the end, the job went to another man.

Joyce set out to get road crew experience. As she was filling out her application for the next road crew job that opened, in 1975, her supervisor walked in, asked what she was doing, and turned red. "You're taking a man's job away!" he shouted. Joyce sat silently for a minute, thinking. Then she said, "No, I'm not. Because a man can sit right here where I'm sitting."

In the evenings, she took courses in road maintenance and truck and light equipment operation. She came in third out of 87 applicants on the job test; there were ten openings on the road crew, and she got one of them.

For the next four years, Joyce carried tar pots on her shoulder, pulled trash from the median strip, and maneuvered trucks up the mountains to clear mud slides. "Working outdoors was great," she says. "You know, women pay fifty dollars a month to join a health club, and here I was getting paid to get in shape."

The road men didn't exactly welcome her arrival. When they trained her to drive the bobtail trucks, she says, they kept changing instructions; one gave her driving tips that nearly blew up the engine. Her supervisor wouldn't issue her a pair of coveralls; she had to file a formal grievance to get them. In the yard, the men kept the ladies' room locked, and on the road they wouldn't stop to let her use the bathroom. "You wanted a man's job, you learn to pee like a man," her supervisor told her.

Obscene graffiti about Joyce appeared on the sides of trucks. Men threw darts at union notices she posted on the bulletin board. One day, the stockroom storekeeper, Tony Laramie, who says later he liked to call her "the piglet," called a general meeting in the depot's Ready Room. "I hate the day you came here," Laramie started screaming at Joyce as the other men looked on, many nodding. "We don't want you here. You don't belong here. Why don't you go the hell away?"

Joyce's experience was typical of the forthright and often violent backlash within the blue-collar work force, an assault undisguised by decorous homages to women's "difference." At a construction site in New York, for example, where only a few female hard-hats had found work, the men took a woman's work boots and hacked them into bits. Another woman was injured by a male co-worker; he hit her on the head with a two-by-four. In Santa Clara County, where Joyce worked, the county's equal opportunity office files were stuffed with reports of ostracism, hazing, sexual harassment, threats, verbal and physical abuse. "It's pervasive in some of the shops," says John Longabaugh, the county's equal employment officer at the time. "They mess up their tools, leave pornography on their desks. Safety equipment is made difficult to get, or unavailable." A maintenance worker greeted the first women in his department with these words: "I know someone who would break your arm or leg for a price." Another new woman was ordered to clean a transit bus by her supervisor—only to find when she climbed aboard that the men had left a little gift for her: feces smeared across the seats.

In 1980, another dispatcher job opened up. Joyce and Johnson both applied. They both got similarly high scores on the written exam. Joyce now had four years' experience on the road crew; Paul Johnson only had a year and a half. The three interviewers, one of whom later referred to Joyce in court as "rabble-rousing" and "not a lady," gave the job to Johnson. Joyce decided to complain to the county affirmative action office.

The decision fell to James Graebner, the new director of the transportation department, an engineer who believed that it was about time the county hired its first woman for its 238 skilled-crafts jobs. Graebner confronted the roads director, Ron Shields. "What's wrong with the women?" Graebner asked. "I hate her," Shields said, according to other people in the room. "I just said I thought Johnson was more qualified," is how Shields remembers it. "She didn't have the proficiency with heavy equipment." Neither, of course, did Johnson. Not that it was relevant anyway: dispatch is an office job that doesn't require lifting anything heavier than a microphone.

Graebner told Shields he was being overruled; Joyce had the job. Later that day, Joyce recalls, her supervisor called her into the conference room. "Well, you got the job," he told her. "But you're not qualified." Johnson, meanwhile, sat by the phone, dialing up the chain of command. "I felt like tearing something up," he recalls later. He demanded a meeting with the affirmative action office. "The affirmative action man walks in," Johnson says, "and he's this big black guy. He can't tell me anything. He brings in this minority who can barely speak English. . . . I told them, 'You haven't heard the last of me.'" Within days, he had hired a lawyer and set his reverse discrimination suit in motion, contending that the county had given the job to a "less qualified" woman.

In 1987, the Supreme Court ruled against Johnson. The decision was hailed by women's and civil rights groups. But victory in Washington was not the same as triumph in the transportation yard. For Joyce and the road men, the backlash was just warming up. "Something like this is going to hurt me one day," Gerald Pourroy, a foreman in Joyce's office, says of the court's ruling, his voice low and bitter. He stares at the concrete wall above his desk. "I look down the tracks and I see the train coming toward me."

The day after the Supreme Court decision, a woman in the county office sent Joyce a congratulatory bouquet, two dozen carnations. Joyce arranged the flowers in a vase on her desk. The next day they were gone. She found them finally, crushed in a garbage bin. A road foreman told her, "I drop-kicked them across the yard."

Several months after the court's verdict, on a late summer afternoon, the county trucks groan into the depot yard, lifting the dust in slow, tired circles. The men file in, and Joyce takes their keys and signs them out. Four men in one-way sunglasses lean as far as they can over the counter.

"Well, well, well, Diii-ane. How the hell are you?"

"Hey, Diane, how the fuck are you?"

"Oh, don't ask her. She don't know that."

"Yeah, Diane, she don't know nothing."

Diane Joyce continues to smile, thinly, as she collects the keys. Some of the men drift over to the Ready Room. They leaf through dog-eared copies of *Guns* magazine and kick an uncooperative snack vending machine. When asked about Diane Joyce, they respond with put-downs and bitterness.

"She thinks she is high class now that she's got her face on TV," one of the men says. "Like we are dirt or something."

"Now all a girl has got to do is say, Hey, they're discriminating, and she gets a job. You tell me how a man's supposed to get a promotion against something like that."

"She's not qualified for ninety-nine percent of the jobs, I'll tell you that right now. I bet next foreman's job opens up, she'll get it just because she's female. I've been a road maintenance worker sixteen years. Now you tell me what's fair?"

Paul Johnson has since retired to the tiny fishing town of Sequim, Washington. From there, he dispatches an "Open Letter to the White Males of America" to newspaper offices across the country: "Fellow men," he writes, "I believe it is time for us to object to OUR suppression." His wife Betty, Johnson explains, helped compose and typed the letter. Her job at a bank also helped pay the bills—and underwrote much of his reverse discrimination lawsuit.

Women's numbers in the Santa Clara County's skilled-crafts jobs, after the Supreme Court ruling, increased by a paltry two to three a year. By the end of 1988, while the total number of available craft slots had grown from 238 to 468, the number of women rose only to 12. This was not because women had lost interest in these jobs. They were enrolling in union craft apprenticeship programs in the area in record numbers. And a county survey of its own female employees (who were still overwhelmingly relegated to the clerical pool) found that 85 percent of these women were interested in higher-paying "men's" jobs. Moreover, 90 percent of the women surveyed said they believed they knew the reason why they weren't getting these higher-paying positions: discrimination.

Lady Bench-Hands and Gentlemen Testers

The Supreme Court would ultimately undercut Diane Joyce's legal victory, too—only two years after she "won" in Washington. Within ten days in June 1989, the U.S. Supreme Court rolled back two decades of landmark civil rights decisions in four separate rulings. The court opened the way for men to challenge affirmative action suits, set up new barriers that made it far more difficult to demonstrate discrimination in court with statistics, and ruled that an 1866 civil rights statute doesn't protect employees from discrimination that occurs after they are hired.

One of the four cases that summer, *Lorance* v. *AT&T Technologies*, dealt a particularly hard blow to blue-collar women. The court ruled that women at AT&T's electronics plant in Illinois couldn't challenge a 1979 seniority system that union and company officials had openly devised to lock out women. The reason: the women had missed the 180-day federal filing deadline for lodging unfair employment practices. The court made this ruling even though five past court rulings had all allowed employees to file such challenges after the deadline had passed. And ironically enough, that very same day the court ruled that a group of white male firefighters were not too late to file *their* reverse discrimination suit—against a settlement of an affirmative action case filed in *1974*.

In the economically depressed town of Montgomery, Illinois, forty miles outside Chicago, nearly all the jobs pay minimum wage—except at the Western Electric plant, where circuit boards are assembled and tested for AT&T. As long as anyone at the plant can remember, the factory had been rigidly divided by sex: the women had virtually all the lowly "bench-hand" jobs (assembling and wiring switching systems by hand) and the men had virtually all the high-paying "testing" jobs (checking the circuit boards). So it had remained until 1976, when three women decided, without so much as a nudge from affirmative action recruiters, to cross the gender line.

Pat Lorance was one of the first to ford the divide. She had been working since adolescence, ever since her father had deserted the family and left her mother with no job and five children to raise. She joined the plant in 1970 as a bench-hand; after nine years she was weary of the tedious work and even wearier of the low pay. When she heard that the local community college was offering courses to qualify as a tester, Lorance decided to give it a try. She brought two women, both bench-hands, with her.

"In the beginning, it was a little intimidating because the teacher, who was from Western Electric, told us, 'You know, women don't usually finish.' But by the fourth course, we won his respect." She eventually completed sixteen courses, including electronic circuitry, computer programming, and "AC/DC fundamentals." To fit it all in, Lorance worked the five A.M.—or sometimes even the three A.M.—shift, studied in the afternoon, and attended class until 9:30 at night.

Officials at Western Electric–AT&T were closely, and uneasily, following the women's efforts. At the time, the EEOC was pursuing its highly visible round of class-action suits against industrial employers, including other divisions of AT&T, and the company's managers knew that if the women at the plant began raising questions publicly about the company's equal employment record, they could well be the next target. In 1976, as employees at the time recall, the personnel office suddenly began calling in some of the female bench-hands, one by one, and offering them a deal. As several women who got the summons remember, a personnel manager informed them that the company had "mistakenly" overlooked them for some job openings. They could now receive a check of several hundred dollars as "compensation"; all they had to do in return was sign a statement promising never to sue the company for discrimination. The women say they were also instructed not to discuss the matter with their co-workers. "Some of the girls wanted to know what the jobs were," recalls one woman, a bench-hand, who, like the others, asked that her name not be used for fear she will lose her job. "Some didn't want to take the money. But it was like, 'Take the money or you are out the door.' I got over $600." (Company officials say they have no record of these sessions in the personnel office. "We have found no facts to support such claims," the company's attorney Charles Jackson says.)

By the fall of 1978, Lorance had all the academic credentials she needed and she applied for the first vacancy in testing. Company officials accepted her for the job—then, a week later, told her the job had been eliminated. Then she heard that the company had hired three men as testers that same week. She protested to the union, and after a struggle, finally became the company's first female tester.

By the end of 1978, about fifteen of the two hundred testers were women. To the men in the shops, that was fifteen too many. "They made these comments about how women were dumb and couldn't do the job," Lorance recalls. "I have a pretty good personality and I just shrugged it off, figured they'd get over it." But as the number of women rose, so did the men's resentment.

Some of the men began sabotaging women's test sets, hooking up the wires the wrong way while the women were on their breaks or spilling ink on their schematic notebooks. They tacked up a series of humiliating posters around the plant. A typical example: a picture of a grotesquely fat woman standing on a table with her nylons down around her calves and money spilling out of her shoes. The men wrote on it: "Yesterday I couldn't spell tester. Today I are a tester."

In 1980, Jan King joined the second round of women to break into the tester ranks. She had worked at the company as a bench-hand since 1966, starting at $1.97 an hour. King desperately needed the extra money: her husband, a violent alcoholic, spent most of the money he earned on drink and gambling, and she had a child to support. "I looked around at the plant one day and I realized I had just accepted what I saw there," she says. "I thought I wasn't any good in math because that's what they said about women. But part of my brain said, Wait a minute, if they can do it, I can. Just because I was brought up to be a certain way, that doesn't mean I have to stay that way."

King had to fight for the job on two fronts, work and home. "My husband said, 'You are not going to go to school for this. It's a waste of time.'" First he threatened her. Then, when she went to class anyway, "he'd do stuff like five minutes before it was time for me to leave, he'd announce that he wasn't going to baby-sit. But I just kept at it because there was this little voice in the back of my mind saying, 'You are going to end up taking care of your daughter by yourself.' I knew if he left, he was the kind of guy who was not going to be paying child support."

The company officials weren't any more helpful. As King recalls, "The whole attitude at the company was, women can't do it. Women can't do math, women can't do electronics." As women began applying to become testers, the company suddenly issued a new set of training and examination requirements. Some of the tactics were peculiar. One of the top managers tried to require that female testers be sent home if they didn't carry see-through purses, a strategy supposedly to discourage thieving.

When some of the men who were testers heard that twelve more female bench-hands had signed up for training at the community college, they decided matters had gone far enough. The younger men were the most upset; because they had the least seniority, they knew that the bench-hand women who had worked at the plant for years would be ahead of them for advancement—and behind them for layoffs. In the winter of 1978, the men organized a secret union meeting; when Lorance heard about it, she and a female co-worker made a surprise appearance.

"They weren't real happy to see us," she recalls. Lorance sat in the union hall and listened. She discovered they were drafting a new seniority system that would prevent women from counting their years as bench-hands in calculating their length of employment. If approved, it would mean that women would take the brunt of any layoff in the testing department. Lorance and her friend went back and spread the word to the other female testers.

At the union meeting to vote on the new seniority proposal, ninety men gathered on one side of the hall, fifteen women on the other. One man after another stood up to speak on behalf of the proposed seniority plan: "I have a family to feed. Do you know how much a loaf of bread costs now?" Then the women stood up, to say that many of them were divorced mothers with families to feed, too; their ex-husbands weren't paying any child support. "This is a man's job," one of the men yelled. "Yes, but this is a woman's factory," a woman retorted, pointing out that more women than men were on the company payroll; he just didn't notice them because they were tucked away in the lowest-paying jobs.

In the end, the men won the vote; in the testing universe, anyway, they still had numbers on their side. The union officialdom assured Lorance and the other women at the time that the seniority plan would have no effect on downgrades or layoffs, just advancement. Company officials, who had helped design the new seniority system and quickly approved it, made similar promises about layoffs. The women accepted their guarantees—and didn't file suit. As Lorance points out, no one was being laid off in 1978, so "why cause trouble when you don't have to?" None of the women wanted to risk losing the jobs they had fought so hard to get.

Jan King, for one, needed her paycheck more than ever; she was facing even more problems at home. "It was like every step I took toward improving myself, every step forward, he saw it as a rejection of him," she says of her husband. "As long as he could keep me dependent on him, then he could think that I would stay." Her husband turned even more violent; he began dragging her out of bed by the hair, beating and, ultimately, raping her. Whenever she made a move toward divorce, he would threaten murder. "If you leave me, you're dead," he told her. "If I can't have you, no one can."

When the recession hit in 1982, the women discovered that the union and company officials had misled them; the seniority plan did apply to layoffs, and the women were the first ones out the door. Eventually, women with nearly twenty years' experience would lose their jobs. Even women who weren't let go were downgraded and shunted back to the bench-hand side of the plant, a demotion that cost some women more than $10,000 in yearly wages.

Lorance was downgraded immediately. She went to a superior she trusted and asked for an explanation. He spoke to his bosses, then came back and told her, "I'm sorry, Patty, but they told me I have to write you up [for a reprimand]." But what, she asked, had she done? He explained that she had "asked a question." Then he pulled her aside and said he suspected the real reason was they hoped this would discourage her from taking legal action. "Well, you know what that made me do," Lorance says. The next day she pulled out the *Yellow Pages* and started dialing lawyers.

Ultimately, Lorance and three other female testers filed suit against the company. (One of the women later dropped out, after her husband forbade her to pursue the litigation.) Bridget Arimond, a Chicago attorney who specializes in sex discrimination law, took the case, which was promptly derailed in the courts over a technical debate about the filing deadline for unfair employment practices. The company contended that the clock started running in 1978, when the seniority system was first adopted, and their complaints constituted "stale claims." "The ladies hadn't exercised their legal rights at the appropriate time," Charles Jackson, Western Electric's counsel on the case, asserts later. "It was really their fault." The women maintained the clock started when they were fired; how could they have known until then that the policy was unfair? "The irony of it all," Arimond says, "was that the whole fight in court came down to whether women who had no background in the law didn't file on time. Yet, the judge [in the lower court] waited over a year to rule on the motion." That judge: John Nordberg of the Sears case.

Meanwhile, Pat Lorance kept getting laid off and rehired. Finally, on March 31, 1989, she was laid off for good. She had to take a job as a bartender. Two months later, when she turned on the television set one night to watch the news, she learned that she had lost the ruling. "I was very disappointed," she says. "I don't think the court gave it a fair look. None of us were screaming. We just wanted to right a wrong, that's all."

King wasn't surprised by the decision. "You could see, the way the court had been going, we weren't in good water." The ruling was financial disaster for King, who was now a single mother. Her violent husband had been killed in a street brawl in 1983. After his death, she took a leave of absence to pull herself together. While she was away, the company fired her, maintaining she had failed to notify the personnel office at the appropriate time of her return date. Desperate for work to support her two children, King cleaned houses, then took a job as a waitress. She lost all her benefits. "Today I cleaned the venetian blinds at work," she says. "I make $2.01 an hour and that's it, top pay. It's demeaning, degrading. It makes you feel like you are not worthwhile."

As she scrapes gravy from diners' plates, King replays the scenes that led her to this dismal point. "Whenever I'm thinking about it, the feeling I get is of all these barricades, the ones with the yellow lights, and every time you try to take a step, they throw another barricade at you." But in spite of everything, she says—the legal defeat, her late husband's reign of terror, the humiliating descent to dishwasher—she has never regretted her decision to ask for more. "If it gets someone fired up enough to say, 'We've got to turn this thing around,' then it's been worth it," she says.

That same year, back at the "Breakthroughs and Backlash" media conference in California, some of the most influential female journalists and women's rights leaders were busy recoiling from conflict. They were pondering the question of whether women really wanted "male" jobs and "male" power. Jan King, who likes to say, "Just call me one of those women's libbers," would have doubtless found such proceedings strange and depressing—even shameful. She hasn't lost sight of what she and many other economically deprived women want, and she is still willing to rush the backlash barricades to get it. "I don't believe you have to accept things the way they are," she says. "I'll never change my mind about that."

Speculations

1. Susan Faludi states that:

   > ... the backlash did more than impede women's opportunities for employment, promotions, and better pay. Its spokesmen kept the news of many of these setbacks from women. Not only did the backlash do grievous damage to working women—it did it on the sly.

   Does Faludi offer sufficient evidence to make her case? Cite other evidence that either proves or disproves her statement.

2. How would you describe Faludi's rhetoric in this essay? That is, what kinds of images, metaphors, diction, facts and figures, and people's attitudes and sentiments does she use to get her point across?

3. Respond to the treatment of either Diane Joyce, Pat Lorance, or Jan King by their male co-workers. Is this behavior justified by the men? What is their rationale? What would you have done if you were trying to secure a better job?

4. In describing the effect of the backlash on working women, Faludi presents several case studies that reveal what happened to specific women in specific jobs and in specific court cases. Is this an effective way of exemplifying her argument? Do you find yourself persuaded by Faludi? Why or why not?

5. What assumptions about society, work, and money are revealed in Faludi's essay? What basic assumptions does it reveal about women in the workforce, at least as Faludi describes their situation?

6. Based on your personal experience and insights as a working man or a working woman, give specific examples of how you have witnessed the psychology and mechanisms of the backlash against women's rights operating in the workplace.

WHY WOMEN AREN'T GETTING TO THE TOP

Susan Fraker

In 1984, "Why Women Aren't Getting to the Top" appeared in *Fortune* magazine. It was introduced by the following statement:

> No women are on the fast track to the chief executive's job at any *Fortune* 500 corporation. That's incongruous, given the number of years women have been working in management. The reasons are elusive and tough for management to deal with.

Susan Faludi (see "Backlash: The Toll on Working Women" in this section) and others have written about the problems women face in the workforce—the glass ceiling that prevents women from rising to the higher echelons of the corporate culture. According to a 1990 poll of *Fortune* 1000 companies, eighty percent of corporate executives said that sex discrimination was preventing women from achieving their career goals—but less than one percent agreed that their personnel departments should actively intervene in ending such discrimination. Such polls reinforce Fraker's main argument.

At the time Fraker's essay was published, she was an associate editor at *Fortune*, where she had been since 1983. Before that, she served as a senior editor at *Newsweek*. Fraker is a graduate of Carleton College and holds an M.S. in journalism from Columbia University. In 1973, she was awarded the Pulitzer Traveling Fellowship.

Ten years have passed since U.S. corporations began hiring more than token numbers of women for jobs at the bottom rung of the management ladder. A decade into their careers, how far up have these women climbed? The answer: not as far as their male counterparts. Despite impressive progress at the entry level and in middle management, women are having trouble breaking into senior management. "There is an invisible ceiling for women at that level," says Janet Jones-Parker, executive director of the Association of Executive Search Consultants Inc. "After eight or ten years, they hit a barrier."

The trouble begins at about the $75,000 to $100,000 salary level, and seems to get worse the higher one looks. Only one company on *Fortune*'s list of the 500 largest U.S. industrial corporations has a woman chief executive. That woman, Katharine Graham of the Washington Post Co. (No. 342), readily admits she got the job because her family owns a controlling share of the corporation.

More surprising, given that women have been on the ladder for ten years, is that none currently seems to have a shot at the top rung. Executive recruiters, asked to identify women who might become presidents or chief executives of *Fortune* 500 companies, draw a blank. Even companies that have women in senior management privately concede that these women aren't going to occupy the chairman's office.

Women have only four of the 154 spots this year at the Harvard Business School's Advanced Management Program—a prestigious 13-week conclave to which companies send executives they are grooming for the corridors of power. The numbers aren't much better at comparable programs at Stanford and at Dartmouth's Tuck School. But perhaps the most telling admission of trouble comes from men at the top. "The women aren't making it," confessed the chief executive of a *Fortune* 500 company to a consultant. "Can you help us find out why?"

All explanations are controversial to one faction or another in this highly charged debate. At one extreme, many women—and some men—maintain that women are the victims of blatant sexism. At the other extreme, many men—and a few women—believe women are unsuitable for the highest managerial jobs: they lack the necessary assertiveness, they don't know how to get along in this rarefied world, or they have children and lose interest in—or time for—their careers. Somewhere in between is a surprisingly large group of men and women who see "discrimination" as the major problem, but who often can't define precisely what they mean by the term.

The discrimination they talk about is not the simple-minded sexism of dirty jokes and references to "girls." It is not born of hatred, or indeed of any ill will that the bearer may be conscious of. What they call discrimination consists simply of treating women differently from men. The notion dumbfounds some male managers. You mean to say, they ask, that managerial women don't want to be treated differently from men in any respect, and that by acting otherwise—as I was raised to think only decent and gentlemanly—I'm somehow prejudicing their chances for success? Yes, the women respond.

"Men I talk to would like to see more women in senior management," says Ann Carol Brown, a consultant to several *Fortune* 500 companies. "But they don't recognize the subtle barriers that stand in the way." Brown thinks the biggest hurdle is a matter of comfort, not competence. "At senior management levels, competence is assumed," she says. "What you're looking for is someone who fits, someone who gets along, someone you trust. Now that's subtle stuff. How does a group of men feel that a woman is going to fit? I think it's very hard."

The experience of an executive at a large Northeastern bank illustrates how many managerial women see the problem. Promoted to senior vice president several years ago, she was the first woman named to that position. But she now believes it will be many years before the bank appoints a woman executive vice president. "The men just don't feel comfortable," she says. "They make all sorts of excuses—that I'm not a banker [she worked as a consultant originally], that I don't know the culture. There's a smoke screen four miles thick. I attribute it to being a woman." Similarly, 117 to 300 women executives polled recently by UCLA's Graduate School of Management and Korn/Ferry International, an executive search firm, felt that being a woman was the greatest obstacle to their success.

A common concern among women, particularly in law and investment banking, is that the best assignments go to men. "Some departments—like sales and trading or mergers and acquisitions—are considered more macho, hence more prestigious," says a woman at a New York investment bank. "It's nothing explicit. But if women can't get the assignments that allow them to shine, how can they advance?"

Women also worry that they don't receive the same kind of constructive criticism that men do. While these women probably overestimate the amount of feedback their male colleagues receive, even some men acknowledge widespread male reluctance to criticize a woman. "There are vast numbers of men who can't do it," says Eugene Jennings, professor of business administration at Michigan State University and a consultant to a dozen large companies. A male banking executive agrees: "A male boss will haul a guy aside and just kick ass if the subordinate performs badly in front of a client. But I heard about a woman here who gets nervous and tends to giggle in front of customers. She's unaware of it and her boss hasn't told her. But behind her back he downgrades her for not being smooth with customers."

Sometimes the message that has to be conveyed to a woman manager is much more sensitive. An executive at a large company says he once had to tell a woman that she should either cross her legs or keep her legs together when she sat. The encounter was obviously painful to him. "She listened to me and thanked me and expressed shock at what she was doing," he recalls, with a touch of agony in his voice. "My God, this is something only your mother tells you. I'm a fairly direct person and a great believer in equal opportunity. But it was damn difficult for me to say this to a woman whom I view to be very proper in all other respects."

Research by Anne Harlan, a human resource manager at the Federal Aviation Administration, and Carol Weiss, a managing associate of Charles Hamilton Associates, a Boston consulting firm, suggests that the situation doesn't necessarily improve as the number of women in an organization increases. Their study, conducted at the Wellesley College Center for Research on Women and completed in 1982, challenges the theory advanced by some experts that when a corporation attained a "critical mass" of executive women—defined as somewhere between

30% and 35%—job discrimination would vanish naturally as men and women began to take each other for granted.

Harlan and Weiss observed the effects of different numbers of women in an organization during a three-year study of 100 men and women managers at two Northeastern retailing corporations. While their sample of companies was not large, after their results were published, other companies said they had similar experiences. Harlan and Weiss found that while overt resistance drops quickly after the first few women become managers, it seems to pick up again as the number of women reaches 15%. In one company they studied, only 6% of the managers were women, compared with 19% in the second company. But more women in the second company complained of discrimination, ranging from sexual harassment to inadequate feedback. Could something other than discrimination—very different corporate cultures, say—have accounted for the result? Harlan and Weiss say no, that the two companies were eminently comparable.

Consultants and executives who think discrimination is the problem tend to believe it persists in part because the government has relaxed its commitment to affirmative action, which they define more narrowly than some advocates do. "We're not talking about quotas or preferential treatment," says Margaret Hennig who, along with Anne Jardim, heads the Simmons College Graduate School of Management. "That's stupid management. We just mean the chance to compete equally." Again, a semantic chasm separates women and men. Women like Hennig and Jardim think of affirmative action as a vigorous effort on the part of companies to ensure that women are treated equally and that sexist prejudices aren't permitted to operate. Men think the term means reverse discrimination, giving women preferential treatment.

Legislation such as the Equal Employment Opportunity Act of 1972 prohibits companies from discriminating against women in hiring. The laws worked well—indeed, almost too well. After seven or eight years, says Jennings of Michigan State, the pressure was off and no one pushed hard to see that discrimination was eliminated in selecting people for senior management. Jennings thinks the problem began in the latter days of the Carter administration, when the economy was lagging and companies worried more about making money than about how their women managers were doing. The Reagan administration hasn't made equal opportunity a priority either.

What about the belief that women fall behind not because of discrimination, but because they are cautious, unaggressive, and differently motivated than men—or less motivated? Even some female executives believe that women derail their careers by choosing staff jobs over high-risk, high-reward line positions. One woman, formerly with a large consumer goods company and now president of a market research firm, urges women to worry less about sexism and more about whether the jobs they take are the right route to the top. "I spent five years thinking the only reason I didn't become a corporate officer at my former company was because of my sex," she says. "I finally had to come to grips with the fact that I overemphasized being a woman and underemphasized what I did for a living. I was in a staff function—the company didn't live and die by what I did."

Men and women alike tend to believe that because women are raised differently they must manage differently. Research to support this belief is hard to come by, though. The women retail managers studied by Harlan and Weiss, while never quarterbacks or catchers, had no trouble playing on management teams. Nor did they perform less well on standardized tests measuring qualities like assertiveness and leadership. "Women don't manage differently," Harlan says flatly.

In a much larger study specifically addressing management styles, psychologists Jay Hall and Susan Donnell of Teleometrics International Inc., a management training company, reached the same conclusion. They matched nearly 2,000 men and women managers according to age, rank in their organization, kind of organization, and the number of people they supervised. The psychologists ran tests to assess everything from managerial philosophies to the ability to get along with people, even quizzing subordinates on their views of the boss. Donnell and Hall concluded, "Male and female managers do not differ in the way they manage the organization's technical and human resources."

Data on how women's expectations—and therefore, arguably, their performance—may differ from men's are more confusing. Stanford Professor Myra Strober studied 150 men and 26 women who graduated from the Stanford Business School in 1974. When she and a colleague, Francine Gordon, polled the MBAs shortly before graduation, they discovered that the women had much lower expectations for their peak earnings. The top salary the women expected during their careers was only 60% of the men's. Four years later the ratio had fallen to 40%.

Did this mean that women were less ambitious or were willing to take lower salaries to get management jobs? Strober doesn't think so. She says a major reason for the women's lower salary expectations was that they took jobs in industries that traditionally pay less, but which, the women thought, offered opportunities for advancement. Almost 20% of the women in her sample went into government, compared with 3% of the men. On the other hand, no women went into investment banking or real estate development, which each employed about 6% of the men. Strober points out, however, that investment banking and big-time real estate were all but closed to women in the early 1970s. "One way people decide what their aspirations are," she says, "is to look around and see what seems realistic. If you look at a field and see no women advancing, you may modify your goals."

Some of what Mary Ann Devanna found in her examination of MBAs contradicts Strober's conclusions. Devanna, research coordinator of the Columbia Business School's Center for Research in Career Development, matched 45 men and 45 women who graduated from the Columbia Business School from 1969 to 1972. Each paired man and woman had similar backgrounds, credentials, and marital status. The starting salaries of the women were 98% of the men's. Using data collected in 1980, Devanna found a big difference in the salaries men and women ultimately achieved, though. In manufacturing, the highest paying sector, women earned $41,818 after ten years vs. $59,733 for the men. Women in finance had salaries of $42,867 vs. $46,786 for the men. The gap in the service industries was smallest: $36,666 vs. $38,600. She then tested four hypotheses in seeking to explain the salary differences: (1) that women are less successful because they are motivated differently than men, (2) that motherhood causes women to divert attention from their careers, (3) that women seek jobs in low-paying industries, and (4) that women seek types of jobs—in human resources, say—that pay less.

Devanna found no major differences between the sexes in the importance they attached to the psychic or monetary rewards of work. "The women did not expect to earn less than the men," she says. Nor did she find that motherhood led women to abandon their careers. Although several women took maternity leaves, all returned to work full time within six months. Finally, Devanna found no big differences in the MBAs' choice of industry or function, either when they took their first jobs or ten years later.

Devanna concluded that discrimination, not level of motivation or choice of job, accounted for the pay differences. Could the problem simply have been performance—that the women didn't manage as well as men? Devanna claims that while she couldn't take this variable into account specifically, she controlled for all the variables that should have made for a difference in performance—from family background to grades in business school.

In their discussions with male executives, researchers like Devanna hear a recurrent theme—a conviction that women don't take their careers seriously. Even though most female managers were regarded as extremely competent, the men thought they would eventually leave—either to have children or because the tensions of work became too much. Both are legitimate concerns. A woman on the fast track is under intense pressure. Many corporate types believe that she gets much more scrutiny than a man and must work harder to succeed. The pressures increase geometrically if she has small children at home.

Perhaps as a result, thousands of women have careers rather than husbands and children. In the UCLA-Korn/Ferry study of executive women, 52% had never married, were divorced, or were widowed, and

61% had no children. A similar study of male executives done in 1979 found that only 5% of the men had never married or were divorced and even fewer—3%—had no children.

Statistics on how many women bear children and then leave the corporation are incomplete. Catalyst, a nonprofit organization that encourages the participation of women in business, studied 815 two-career families in 1980. It found that 37% of the new mothers in the study returned to work within two months; 68% were back after 4 1/2 months; 87% in eight months. To a company, of course, an eight-month absence is a long time. Moreover, the 10% or so who never come back—most males are convinced the figure is higher—represent a substantial capital investment lost. It would be naive to think that companies don't crank this into their calculation of how much the women who remain are worth.

Motherhood clearly slows the progress of women who decide to take long maternity leaves or who choose to work part time. But even those committed to working full time on their return believe they are sometimes held back—purposely or inadvertently. "Men make too many assumptions that women with children aren't free to take on time-consuming tasks," says Gene Kofke, director of human resources at AT&T. Karen Gonçalves, 34, quit her job as a consultant when she was denied challenging assignments after the birth of her daughter. "I was told clearly that I couldn't expect to move ahead as fast as I had been," she says. Later, when Gonçalves began working at the consulting firm of Arthur D. Little, Inc. in Cambridge, Massachusetts, she intentionally avoided discussions of family and children: "I didn't keep a picture of my daughter in the office, and I would travel anywhere, no matter how hard it was for me."

Sometimes pregnancy is more of an issue for the men who witness it than for the women who go through it. Karol Emmerich, 35, now treasurer of Dayton Hudson Corp., was the first high-level woman at the department-store company to become pregnant. "The men didn't really know what to do," she recalls. "They were worried when I wanted to take three months off. But they wanted to encourage me to come back. So they promoted me to treasurer when I was seven months pregnant. Management got a lot of good feedback." Emmerich's experience would please Simmons Dean Anne Jardim, who worries that most organizations aren't doing enough to keep women who want to have children. "It's mind-boggling," she argues. "Either some of the brightest women in this country aren't going to reproduce or the companies are going to write off women in whom they have a tremendous investment."

To the corporation it may seem wasteful to train a woman and then be unable to promote her because she won't move to take the new job.

The Catalyst study found that 40% of the men surveyed had moved for their jobs, vs. only 21% of the women. An argument can be made that an immobile executive is worthless to the corporation—and hence may be paid less.

Where women frequently do go is out of the company and into business for themselves. "When the achievements you want aren't forthcoming, it makes going out on your own easier," says a woman who has set up her own consultancy. "I was told I wouldn't make it into senior management at my bank. Maybe I just didn't have it. But the bank never found any woman who did. They were operating under a consent decree and they brought in a lot of women at the vice president level. Every single one of them left." Karen Gonçalves left Arthur D. Little to do part-time teaching and consulting when she was pregnant with her second child. "I didn't think I would get the professional satisfaction I wanted at ADL," she says.

From 1977 to 1980, according to the Small Business Administration, the number of businesses owned by women increased 33%, compared with an 11% increase for men—though admittedly the women's increase started from a much smaller base. While it's not clear from the numbers that women are entering the entrepreneurial ranks in greater numbers than they are joining corporations, some experts think so. "It's ironic," says Strober of Stanford. "The problem of the 1970s was bringing women into the corporation. The problem of the 1980s is keeping them there."

A few companies, convinced that women face special problems and that it's in the corporation's interest to help overcome them, are working hard at solutions. At Penn Mutual Life Insurance Co. in Philadelphia, where nearly half the managers are women, executives conducted a series of off-site seminars on gender issues and sex-role stereotypes. Dayton Hudson provides support (moral and financial) for a program whereby women in the company trade information on issues like personal financial planning and child care.

What women need most, the experts say, are loud, clear, continuing statements of support from senior management. Women have come a long way at Merck, says B. Lawrence Branch, the company's director of equal employment affairs, because Chairman John J. Horan insisted that their progress be watched. Merck has a program that identifies 10% of its women and 10% of minorities as "most promising." The company prepares a written agenda of what it will take for them to move to the next level. Progress upward may mean changing jobs or switching functions, so Merck circulates their credentials throughout the company. "We have a timetable and we track these women carefully," says Branch. Since 1979 almost 40% of the net growth in Merck's managerial staff has been women.

Sensitive to charges of reverse discrimination, Branch explains that Merck has for years singled out the best employees to make sure they get opportunities to advance. Women, he notes, were consistently underrepresented in that group. In his view the tracking program simply allows women to get into the competition with fast-track men. Others might not be so charitable. Any company that undertakes to do something on behalf of its managerial women leaves itself open to the charge that it too is discriminating—treating women and men differently.

What everyone may be able to agree on is that opening corporations to competition in the executive ranks is clearly good for performance and profits. But how can a company do this? It can try to find productive part-time work for all employees who want to work part time—even managers. It can structure promotions so that fewer careers are derailed by an absence of a few months or the unwillingness to relocate. It can make sure that the right information, particularly on job openings, reaches everyone. Perhaps most importantly, it can reward its managers for developing talent of all sorts and sexes, penalize them if they don't, and vigilantly supervise the process.

Speculations

1. What arguments does Susan Fraker provide in response to the title of her essay, "Why Women Aren't Getting to the Top"?
2. After reading Fraker's essay, how would you define discrimination against women as managers in U.S. corporations? Provide examples of the types of discrimination that support your definition.
3. Do you think women should be treated differently from men in the workplace? Explain your position and support your argument with specific examples from your own experience and from Fraker's essay.
4. What do you think Fraker's position is about women and the workplace? How does her even-handed and moderate tone serve her argument? How would you compare her tone to that of Susan Faludi in "Backlash"?
5. Based on Fraker's perspective, do you think corporations should support pregnancy leaves? How do you respond to the view that women's commitment to having children implies that they do not take their careers seriously?

ASSIGNMENT SEQUENCES

Sequence Number One: Exploring the Values of Work

1. In an essay, describe a work experience—at a fast food restaurant, a convenience store, a supermarket, baby-sitting, doing housework for an allowance—any experience that paid a wage or salary. What

did you learn from working? Did working make you more aware of the value of money, more responsible, flexible, cooperative? Did you have a positive or negative experience? What did you learn about employer/employee relations, bosses, the value (or meaningless-ness) of an education? Are you glad you worked? Would you rec-ommend it to high school and college students? As you write this essay, describe in rich detail the nature of your work—and reflect on what that work taught you about yourself and others.

2. When talking to Barbara Garson, ex-McDonald's employee Jason Pratt says:

> You follow the beepers, you follow the buzzers and you turn your meat as fast as you can. It's like I told you, to work at Mc-Donald's you don't need a face, you don't need a brain. You need to have two hands and two legs and move 'em as fast as you can. That's the whole system. I wouldn't go back there again for any-thing.

Pratt may be expressing the point of view of a disgruntled ex-em-ployee or he may be offering a more generalized criticism of the McDonald's working philosophy. In an essay, write an answer to Pratt. What kinds of explanations might an administrator from McDonald's offer after reading this essay? What's *right* about McDonald's? The restaurant chain is a great success story. What positive values, lessons, principles about working at McDonald's may Jason be overlooking?

3. Both Barbara Garson and Roger Swardson describe a specific ethos—assumed values, beliefs, and attitudes—that exist among employees and employers in the work situations they describe. Write an essay that compares these two work situations and how the ethos of the workplace influences the workers and their notions of success. Evaluate the positive and negative aspects of working in each environment and include an analysis of the attitudes and goals you think would be most effective for getting ahead in either environment.

4. Roger Swardson asserts in his essay that "For years the working poor in this country have felt they had a pact with the powerful. Work hard and you'll be OK. Do your job well and you'll have the basics and a chance to move up." In what ways does he argue that this pact has been broken? Drawing on Swardson and other de-scriptions of working people in this section, write a reflective essay in which you offer your own views about the value—or lack of value—of such work. Is Swardson being too idealistic? Is work such as he describes meaningful and dignified—or is it exhausting, monotonous, and dreary? In whose interest is it performed? Where

and in what circumstances is it done? Supplement examples from this section with your own experience doing a difficult job and the real and ideal affects it had on you.

5. In an invitation to give a speech to college students, the president of the local chapter of an undergraduate English Honors Society asks:

> We understand that you have been reading and thinking about the relationship of work to success and to social concerns. Many of our undergraduates are worried about the kind of work available to them and their opportunities for advancement. Questions our members have include: What kinds of jobs are available in today's service economy? What are the opportunities for women to advance in the business world or other nontraditional careers? What is the impact of computers and telecommunications on the workplace? What social concerns do employers and employees share? Please come to our next meeting as a guest speaker.

Write the speech: serious, satiric, political, or social. Your speech must in some very specific ways respond to the questions asked, but you are not limited to them.

6. Imagine a conversation between two or three workers that you have read about in this section (Jason Pratt, Roger Swardson, Mike LeFevre, Diane Joyce, Pat Lorance or Jan King). Those individuals are talking about the current employment situation and how people like themselves can get to the top. They discuss the kinds of values they encounter in the workplace and how those values impede or further their work and success. Write that conversation.

Sequence Number Two: Individuality and Success

1. Is Garson right—is McDonald's an "electronic sweatshop"? Is she also correct that a good bit of work in America increasingly exists within an "electronic sweatshop" atmosphere? Support a point of view based on research and observation of local employment practices in your neighborhood. To do this research, interview at least two or three people who work in the food industry. Try to include at least one who works in a fast food environment like McDonald's. Ask questions that specifically develop a picture of the work environment, the employee's attitude, and the kinds of pressures that employees as well as managers face. What inside knowledge do these people have that the public does not see or hear about? Write up profiles of each of the individuals in a paper which includes your analysis, speculations, and conclusions about the main issues, problems, and values represented within the food industry.

2. Notice that Mike LeFevre's description of his work describes the oppression and exhaustion that he feels. LeFevre argues that people in power "fear the leisure man" and he suggests that keeping workers tired is the best way to rule them and keep them in their place. Write an essay that examines politics, power, work, and the working class. As evidence for your ideas, use perspectives offered in this selection, other essays from this section, and your own work experience.

3. In "Mike LeFevre, Steelworker," Studs Terkel reports LeFevre as saying: "Picasso can point to a painting. What can I point to? A writer can point to a book. Everybody should have something to point to." Explore this notion of work in an essay. What does LeFevre want? Why does he want it? Compare his views to those expressed by other workers represented in this section.

4. Create a profile of a worker, such as Studs Terkel's, based on an interview. To create such a profile, follow the steps below.

   1. Choose a profession/job/vocation that you are interested in learning more about. Find someone within your immediate community who works in your specific area of interest. Arrange to have an interview with that person.
   2. In small class groups, create a list of questions to ask the individual. Share your questions with other members of the class. Begin the interview with at least 25 questions.
   3. Talk over (in small groups and in the entire class) interview procedures. Discuss various options: open vs. closed interview questions, interview style, use of a tape recorder, importance of the interview setting, time constraints, and so on.
   4. Interview your subject.
   5. Transcribe or paraphrase or summarize the entire interview, omitting useless digressions, and so on.
   6. Organize the profile—thinking through what major qualities or points you want to emphasize about your subject and their vocation.
   7. Write a first draft, incorporating many quotations. A second interview may be necessary; if so, schedule it right away. If your chosen subject has no time, try for a brief follow-up interview over the phone. Additional library research may provide other relevant information.
   8. In a workshop in class, discuss the draft.
   9. Complete the profile.
   10. Present several profiles by class members, perhaps as a published anthology of essays on work and wealth.

5. Write an in-depth description of a former boss, a former co-worker, or a work situation that typifies at least one aspect of what you think is wrong with the workplace in America. Use specific examples and details about the person or place you describe to argue

your case. What assumptions about work, wealth, and personal values lie behind your analysis and critique? Make specific proposals or recommendations to change the situation.

Sequence Number Three: The Gendered Workplace

1. Susan Fraker says that most men and women agree that discrimination is a major problem for women in U.S. corporations, but that the term covers a range of meanings and that most people "often can't define precisely what they mean by the term." After reviewing both Susan Fraker's and Susan Faludi's articles, write an essay that defines and explores the range of meanings associated with sexual discrimination in the workplace. In your essay include the most significant ways that men and women compete, succeed, or fail in the work place. You may also include personal experiences of discrimination or unfairness which seemed especially meaningful because of your individual perspective as a man or as a woman.

2. Reread Susan Faludi's essay "The Wages of the Backlash: The Toll on Working Women," paying close attention to the case of Pat Lorance, the woman who went back to school and qualified as a tester at Western Electric. Imagine that you are the male supervisor, whom Pat Lorance trusts and goes to after her demotion and to air the broken promises made by the union and management. As Pat Lorance's supervisor, you have been told to "write her up for a reprimand," an act they hope will discourage her from taking legal action against the company. Decide what you would do in this situation. Your job may be on the line if you do not follow orders. Write one of the following: a) a reprimand of Lorance which deals as fairly as possible with the company's goal and Lorance's complaint; b) a formal letter to Pat Lorance explaining your personal and professional feelings; c) a formal letter to the company explaining your view of the situation and what you recommend should be done now. Write your response as a protest, as a compromise position, as an apology, or as a way of rationalizing the company's position. The goal is to examine the ethics of the situation and to come to a conclusion. Support your opinion or argument with facts from the case, recognizing that whatever is written may be used in a future lawsuit.

3. As the personnel manager of a large U.S. corporation, you have recently attended a seminar at which the two keynote speakers were Susan Faludi and Susan Fraker, who read their essays from this section. The president of the corporation is sympathetic to Faludi's and Fraker's views and wants the company to promote more women to top management positions. In your company mostly men are in top management positions, and the women

are employed largely in clerical positions. A very small percentage of women are in lower management positions, even fewer are in middle management, and none whatsoever are in top management jobs. The president assigns you the job of writing a three-to-five-page analysis and policy statement that will initiate change by stating how women managers should be treated and encouraged in this company. Include a summary of the kinds of discrimination potential women managers have traditionally faced at corporations in general and a description of the changes in perceptions, attitudes, policies, and personnel training that you believe will improve the situation, including a policy on pregnancy and family leave. Since several influential men in middle and upper management are uncomfortable with and even hostile toward the changes you have been asked to initiate, write as persuasively as possible to all the employees and managers.

4. Susan Fraker offers many explanations as to why women are not getting to the top. Interview either a man or a woman who is at or near the top of an organization. You might want to interview the president or vice president of a company, a department chairperson or key administrator within the university—some person who has risen to a position of considerable influence and power. In your interview, focus on what it took for that person to rise to the top. What kinds of educational, social, and political preparation were necessary? What were the most important attributes or events that led to that person's rise to the top? Then, in a well-reasoned essay that draws upon the research Fraker reports, discuss the extent to which that person's success was dependent on gender. Was that person's rise to the top facilitated or impeded by his or her gender? What bearing, if any, did gender play?

5. Susan Faludi builds her case by producing considerable research: interviews, research summaries, statistics, expert testimony. Following the Faludi model, investigate a specific economic area which affects women's employment by finding at least three authoritative sources of information—and then produce a report card on women in the workplace. For example, you might want to investigate whether there are more women in the media than there were thirty years ago or the extent to which businesses are providing services such as child care, family leave, and so on. Use library resources and write an assessment of women in a specific work area in the 1990s.

FOCUS ON

Opportunity and Otherness

One of the most contentious issues confronting America is affirmative action, quotas, and preferential hiring. At first glance, nothing could seem simpler: if everyone has an equal opportunity to go to school and to work, then we need no laws that allow one race, gender, or class to be preferred over another. Why should cities be required to give contracts to minority firms? Why should public and private businesses, governmental agencies, and educational institutions be required to reward women more than men, people of color more than whites, poor people more than the middle class? Why should a student with lower grades and test scores receive a full scholarship because of race or gender, when a better student of a different race or gender is given no money at all?

Even as we go to press, the U.S. Congress is embroiled in debates about curtailing affirmative action, cutting back on governmental interference, and limiting government mandates. At the same time, we find reports like that of the bipartisan federal Glass Ceiling Commission which spent three years studying this issue. Early in 1995, they delivered their report entitled "Good for Business: Making Full Use of the Nation's Human Capital." Their conclusions:

> Efforts to eliminate the "glass ceiling" that blocks advancement for women and minorities are "disappointingly slow," even though the majority of corporate executives believe the problem has already been solved, at least for women.
>
> Of the senior managers employed at the Fortune 1000 industrial corporations, 97% are white and male.
>
> Of the top managers at Fortune 2000 industrial and service companies, 5% are women—this despite the work force being nearly 60% female.

The Commission cited numerous studies which made clear "that the glass ceiling exists because of the perception of many white males that as a group they are losing—losing the corporate game, losing control and losing opportunity." Even though these male managers possess the same odds of reaching the top as they did 30 years ago, they perceive that they are losing out to "others"—namely women and minorities.

By highlighting the conclusions of the Commission, we do not intend to suggest that affirmative action is the answer to America's inequities; clearly it cannot be, and it may well have run out of political capital. What we do mean to suggest is that there are no easy answers concerning how—or even whether—to socially engineer solutions to prejudice, bigotry, and discrimination. The arguments raised by Hacker, Carter, Cose, Magnet, and Rodriguez represent a broad spectrum debate on the problems and justifications for legislating solutions for women, minorities, and other marginalized groups. There is no easy answer, especially as America struggles to maintain economic viability in the face of a ballooning national deficit and increasing competition from abroad. We invite you to participate in a debate that almost certainly will affect the rest of your working life.

BEING BLACK IN AMERICA

Andrew Hacker

Born in 1929 in New York City, Andrew Hacker received his B.A. from Amherst College (1951), M.A. from Oxford University (1953), and Ph.D. from Princeton University (1955). After teaching at Cornell University, Hacker went to Queens College of the City University of New York in 1971, where he became a full professor of Political Science. Having received fellowship awards from both the Social Science Research Council and the Ford Foundation, he has written nine books, co-authored or edited four additional books, and published in numerous periodicals, including: *Atlantic, Harper's,* and the *New York Times Magazine.* His best known works are *U/S: A Statistical Portrait of the American People* (1983) and *Two Nations: Black and White, Separate, Hostile, and Unequal* (1992)—books that have been praised for presenting a statistical profile of race relations in America that is both accessible and interesting to a wide audience. David Gates, a book critic for *Newsweek,* enthusiastically described Hacker's writing in *Two Nations,* the book from which this selection was taken:

> Andrew Hacker is a political scientist known for doing with statistics what Fred Astaire did with hats, canes, and chairs. . . . In his new book on race relations in America, he doesn't crunch numbers: he makes them live and breathe.

"Being Black in America" turns an unblinking eye on the realities of racial difference by placing the reader uncomfortably at the center of facts about race relations that no one wants to examine closely. In so doing, Hacker forces us to question our assumptions about America's "progress" toward leveling the playing field for all people in our democracy regardless of their racial heritage.

Most white Americans will say that, all things considered, things aren't so bad for black people in the United States. Of course, they will grant that many problems remain. Still, whites feel there has been steady improvement, bringing blacks closer to parity, especially when compared with conditions in the past. Some have even been heard to muse that it's better to be black, since affirmative action policies make it a disadvantage to be white.

What white people seldom stop to ask is how they may benefit from belonging to their race. Nor is this surprising. People who can see do not regard their vision as a gift for which they should offer thanks. It may also be replied that having a white skin does not immunize a person from misfortune or failure. Yet even for those who fall to the bottom, being white has a worth. What could that value be?

Let us try to find out by means of a parable: suspend disbelief for a moment, and assume that what follows might actually happen:

THE VISIT

You will be visited tonight by an official you have never met. He begins by telling you that he is extremely embarrassed. The organization he represents has made a mistake, something that hardly ever happens.

According to their records, he goes on, you were to have been born black: to another set of parents, far from where you were raised.

However, the rules being what they are, this error must be rectified, and as soon as possible. So at midnight tonight, you will become black. And this will mean not simply a darker skin, but the bodily and facial features associated with African ancestry. However, inside you will be the person you always were. Your knowledge and ideas will remain intact. But outwardly you will not be recognizable to anyone you now know.

Your visitor emphasizes that being born to the wrong parents was in no way your fault. Consequently, his organization is prepared to offer you some reasonable recompense. Would you, he asks, care to name a sum of money you might consider appropriate? He adds that his group is by no means poor. It can be quite generous when the circumstances warrant, as they seem to in your case. He finishes by saying that their records show you are scheduled to live another fifty years—as a black man or woman in America.

How much financial recompense would you request?

When this parable has been put to white students, most seemed to feel that it would not be out of place to ask for $50 million, or $1 million for each coming black year. And this calculation conveys, as well as anything, the value that white people place on their own skins. Indeed, to be white is to possess a gift whose value can be appreciated only after it has been taken away. And why ask so large a sum? Surely this needs no detailing. The money would be used, as best it could, to buy protections from the discriminations and dangers white people know they would face once they were perceived to be black.

Of course, no one who is white can understand what it is like to be black in America. Still, were they to spend time in a black body, here are some of the things they would learn.

In the eyes of white Americans, being black encapsulates your identity. No other racial or national origin is seen as having so pervasive a personality or character. Even if you write a book on Euclidean algorithms or Renaissance sculpture, you will still be described as a "black author." Although you are a native American, with a longer lineage than most, you will never be accorded full membership in the nation or society. More than that, you early learn that this nation feels no need or desire for your physical presence. (Indeed, your people are no longer in demand as cheap labor.) You sense that most white citizens would heave a sigh of relief were you simply to disappear. While few openly propose that you return to Africa, they would be greatly pleased were you to make that decision for yourself.

Your people originated in Africa, and you want to feel pride in your homeland. After all, it was where humanity began. Hence your desire to know more of its peoples and their history, their culture and achievements, and how they endure within yourself. W. E. B. Du Bois said it best: "two thoughts, two unrecognizable stirrings, two warring ideals in one black body."

Yet there is also your awareness that not only America, but also much of the rest of the world, regards Africa as the primal continent: the most backward, the least developed, by almost every modern measure. Equally unsettling, Africa is regarded as barely worth the world's attention, a region no longer expected to improve in condition or status. During its periodic misfortunes—usually famine or slaughter—Africa may evoke compassion and pity. Yet the message persists that it must receive outside help, since there is little likelihood that it will set things right by itself.

Then there are the personal choices you must make about your identity. Unless you want to stress a Caribbean connection, you are an American and it is the only citizenship you have. At the same time, you realize that this is a white country, which expects its inhabitants to think and act in white ways. How far do you wish to adapt, adjust, assimilate, to a civilization so at variance with your people's past? For example, there is the not-so-simple matter of deciding on your diction. You know how white people talk and what they like to hear. Should you conform to those expectations, even if it demands denying or concealing much of your self? After all, white America gives out most of the rewards and prizes associated with success. Your decisions are rendered all the more painful by the hypocrisy of it all, since you are aware that even if you make every effort to conform, whites will still not accept you as one of their own.

So to a far greater degree than for immigrants from other lands, it rests on you to create your own identity. But it is still not easy to follow the counsel of Zora Neale Hurston: "Be as black as you want to be." For one thing, that choice is not always left to you. By citizenship and birth, you may count as an American, yet you find yourself agreeing with August Wilson when he says "We're a different people." Why else can you refer to your people as "folks" and "family," to one another as "sisters" and "brothers," in ways whites never can?

There are moments when you understand Toni Morrison's riposte, "At no moment in my life have I ever felt as though I were an American." This in turn gives rise to feelings of sympathy with figures like Cassius Clay, H. Rap Brown, Lew Alcindor, and Stokely Carmichael, who decided to repatriate themselves as Muhammad Ali, Jamil Abdullah al-Amin, Kareem Abdul-Jabbar, and Kwame Touré.

Those choices are not just for yourself. There will be the perplexing—and equally painful—task of having to explain to your children why they will not be treated as other Americans: that they will never be altogether accepted, that they will always be regarded warily, if not with suspicion or hostility. When they ask whether this happens because of anything they have done, you must find ways of conveying that, no, it is not because of any fault of their own. Further, for reasons you can barely explain yourself, you must tell them that much of the world has decided that you are not and cannot be their equals; that this world wishes to keep you apart, a caste it will neither absorb nor assimilate.

You will tell your children this world is wrong. But, because that world is there, they will have to struggle to survive, with scales weighted against them. They will have to work harder and do better, yet the result may be less recognition and reward. We all know life can be unfair. For black people, this knowledge is not an academic theory but a fact of daily life.

You find yourself granting that there are more black faces in places where they were never seen before. Within living memory, your people were barred from major league teams; now they command the highest salaries in most professional sports. In the movies, your people had to settle for roles as servants or buffoons. Now at least some of them are cast as physicians, business executives, and police officials. But are things truly different? When everything is added up, white America still prefers its black people to be performers who divert them as athletes and musicians and comedians.

Yet where you yourself are concerned, you sense that in mainstream occupations, your prospects are quite limited. In most areas of employment, even after playing by the rules, you find yourself hitting a not-so-invisible ceiling. You wonder if you are simply corporate wallpaper, a protective coloration they find it prudent to display. You begin to suspect that a "qualification" you will always lack is white pigmentation.

In theory, all Americans with financial means and a respectable demeanor can choose where they want to live. For over a generation, courts across the country have decreed that a person's race cannot be a reason for refusing to rent or sell a residence. However, the law seems to have had little impact on practice, since almost all residential areas are entirely black or white. Most whites prefer it that way. Some will say they would like a black family nearby, if only to be able to report that their area is integrated. But not many do. Most white Americans do not move in circles where racial integration wins social or moral credit.

This does not mean it is absolutely impossible for a black family to find a home in a white area. Some have, and others undoubtedly will. Even so, black Americans have no illusions about the hurdles they will face. If you look outside your designated areas, you can expect chilly receptions, evasive responses, and outright lies: a humiliating experience, rendered all the more enraging because it is so repeated and prolonged. After a while, it becomes too draining to continue the search. Still, if you have the income, you will find an area to your liking; but it will probably be all black. In various suburbs and at the outer edges of cities, one can see well-kept homes, outwardly like other such settings. But a closer view shows all the householders to be black.

This is the place to consider residential apartheid—and that is what it is—in its full perspective. Black segregation differs markedly from that imposed on any other group. Even newly arrived immigrants are more readily accepted in white neighborhoods.

Nor should it be assumed that most black householders prefer the racial ratios in areas where they currently reside. Successive surveys have shown that, on average, only about one in eight say they prefer a neighborhood that is all or mostly black, which is the condition most presently confront. The vast majority—some 85 percent—state they would like an equal mixture of black and white neighbors. Unfortunately, this degree of racial balance has virtually no chance of being realized. The reason, very simply, is that hardly any whites will live in a neighborhood or community where half the residents are black. So directly or indirectly, white Americans have the power to decide the racial composition of communities and neighborhoods. Most egregious have been instances where acts of arson or vandalism force black families to leave. But such methods are exceptional. There are other, less blatant, ways to prevent residential integration from passing a certain "tipping" point.

Here we have no shortage of studies. By and large, this research agrees that white residents will stay—and some new ones may move in—if black arrivals do not exceed 8 percent. But once the black proportion passes that point, whites begin to leave the neighborhood and no new ones will move in. The vacated houses or apartments will be bought or rented by blacks, and the area will be on its way to becoming all black.

What makes integration difficult if not impossible is that so few whites will accept even a racial composition reflecting the overall national proportion of 12 or 13 percent. In this regard, one or two attempts have been made to impose ceilings on the number of black residents in housing projects and developments, so as not to frighten away whites. Starrett City in New York has used this strategy, as has Atrium Village in Chicago. According to some legal readings these procedures are unconstitutional, since they treat racial groups differently. Those administering such "benign quotas" have found they must maintain two sets of waiting lists. This has been necessary to ensure that the next families chosen for vacant apartments will preserve the prevailing racial ratio. Given the preference of most blacks for integrated housing, quite a few tend to apply, and they invariably outnumber the whites on the list. The result is that black applicants have to wait longer, and are less likely to get their first choice of accommodation.

Whites and blacks who want to achieve and maintain interracial housing—itself a rarity—find they are forced to defend "benign quotas" that are biased against some blacks, since there are fewer "black" places. Racial quotas also tend to put blacks on the spot. On the one hand, few are willing to publicly support a ceiling for people of their race. Even so, most of the black householders already in residence would prefer that the racial ratio remain stabilized. After all, they themselves underwent a wait because they wanted to live in a racially integrated setting. Yet preserving the equation pits them against other blacks impatient to get in.

If many whites say they support racial integration in principle, even if this only means a token black neighbor, at least as many do not want any blacks living near them at all. One question, certainly, is how far this resistance is based solely on race, or whether the reasons have more to do with culture or class. White people themselves vary in income and other signals of status, and every section of the nation has hierarchies among white neighborhoods. Even in an area where everyone earns essentially the same income, many residents would not want a homosexual couple on their block, or a neighbor who parked a business van ("PARAGON PEST CONTROL") in his driveway every night. Simply being a fellow white is not enough to make a person a desired neighbor.

This granted, we can try to isolate the element of race by positing some "ideal" black neighbors: persons with professional credentials or those who hold administrative positions in respected organizations. Give them sophisticated tastes; make them congenial in demeanor; and have them willing to care about their property and the area as a whole. And allow, further, that a fair number of whites might not object to having one or two such households nearby. Why, then, would such open-minded neighbors start worrying if the number of black families—granting that all of them are impeccably middle class—seems to be approaching a racial "tipping" point?

The first reason is that there is no assurance that the black proportion will stay below the "tipping" figure. Word gets around among black families when a "white" neighborhood appears willing to accept a measure of integration. Rental and real estate agents are also quick to note this fact and begin recommending the area to black customers. As a result, whenever homes and apartments become vacant, a visible number of those coming to look at them appear to be black. Nor should this be surprising. Some black Americans want more interracial exposure for themselves and their children. Others may not share this wish, but they know that better schools and safer streets are more apt to be where whites are.

Longitudinal studies, based on tracing census tracts, show that whites begin to move out once the black proportion reaches somewhere between 10 and 20 percent. Moreover, this happens even when the blacks who move in have the same economic and social standing as the white residents. What is it, then, that makes white Americans unwilling to risk having black neighbors? Some of the reasons are familiar and openly stated. Others involve fears less easily articulated or admitted.

To the minds of most Americans, the mere presence of black people is associated with a high incidence of crime, residential deterioration, and lower educational attainment. Of course, most whites are willing to acknowledge that these strictures do not apply to all blacks. At the same time, they do not want to have to worry about trying to distinguish blacks who would make good neighbors from those who would not. To which is added the suspicion that if more black families arrive, it would take only one or two undesirables to undermine any interracial amity.

Even if all one's black neighbors were vouchsafed to be middle class or better, there may still be misgivings about their teenaged children. To start, there is the well-known wariness of white parents that their children—especially their daughters—could begin to make black friends. Plus the fear that even less intimate contacts will influence the vocabulary and diction, even the academic commitments, of their own offspring. And if white parents are already uneasy over the kinds of music their children enjoy, imagine their anxieties at hearing an even greater black resonance. Along with the worry that some of the black youths on the block might display a hostile demeanor, clouding the congenial ambience most Americans seek.

Americans have extraordinarily sensitive antennae for the colorations of neighborhoods. In virtually every metropolitan area, white householders can rank each enclave by the racial makeup of the residents. Given this knowledge, where a family lives becomes an index of its social standing. While this is largely an economic matter, proximity to blacks compounds this assessment. For a white family to be seen as living in a mixed—or changing—neighborhood can be construed as a symptom of surrender, indeed as evidence that they are on a downward spiral.

If you are black, these white reactions brand you as a carrier of contaminations. No matter what your talents or attainments, you are seen as infecting a neighborhood simply because of your race. This is the ultimate insult of segregation. It opens wounds that never really heal and leaves scars to remind you how far you stand from full citizenship.

Except when you are in your own neighborhood, you feel always on display. On many occasions, you find you are the only person of your race present. You may be the only black student in a college classroom, the only black on a jury, the sole black at a corporate meeting, the only one at a social gathering. With luck, there may be one or two others. You feel every eye is on you, and you are not clear what posture to present. You realize that your presence makes whites uncomfortable; most of them probably wish you were not there at all. But since you are, they want to see you smile, so they can believe that you are being treated well. Not only is an upbeat air expected, but you must never show exasperation or anger, let alone anything that could look like a chip on your shoulder. Not everyone can keep such tight control. You don't find it surprising that so many black athletes and entertainers seek relief from those tensions.

Even when not in white company, you know that you are forever in their conversations. Ralph Ellison once said that to whites, you are an "invisible man." You know what he meant. Yet for all that, you and your people have been studied and scrutinized and dissected, caricatured, and pitied or deplored, as no other group ever has. You see yourself reduced to data in research, statistics in reports. Each year, the nation asks how many of your teenagers have become pregnant, how many of your young men are in prison. Not only are you continually on view; you are always on trial.

What we have come to call the media looms large in the lives of almost all Americans. Television and films, newspapers and magazines, books and advertising, all serve as windows on a wider world, providing real and fantasized images of the human experience. The media also help us to fill out our own identities, telling us about ourselves, or the selves we might like to be.

If you are black, most of what is available for you to read and watch and hear depicts the activities of white people, with only rare and incidental allusions to persons like yourself. Black topics and authors and performers appear even less than your share of the population, not least because the rest of America doesn't care to know about you. Whites will be quick to point out that there have been successful "black" programs on radio and television, as well as popular black entertainers and best-selling authors. Yet in these and other instances, it is whites who decide which people and productions will be underwritten, which almost always usually means that "black" projects will have to appeal to whites as well. You sometimes sense that much that is "black" is missing in artists like Jessye Norman and Toni Morrison, Paul Robeson, and Bill Cosby, who you sense must tailor their talents to white audiences. You often find yourself wishing they could just be themselves, among their own people.

At the same time, you feel frustration and disgust when white America appropriates your music, your styles, indeed your speech and sexuality. At times, white audiences will laud the originality of black artists and performers and athletes. But in the end, they feel more comfortable when white musicians and designers and writers—and athletic coaches—adapt black talents to white sensibilities.

Add to this your bemusement when movies and television series cast more blacks as physicians and attorneys and executives than one will ever find in actual hospitals or law firms or corporations. True, these depictions can serve as role models for your children, encouraging their aspirations. At the same time, you do not want white audiences to conclude that since so many of your people seem to be doing well, little more needs to be done.

Then there are those advertisements showing groups of people. Yes, one of them may be black, although not too black, and always looking happy to be in white company. Still, these blacks are seldom in the front row, or close to the center. Even worse, you think you have detected a recent trend: in advertisements that include a person of color, you see Asians being used instead of blacks.

To be sure, textbooks and lesson plans now include allusions to "contributions" made by Americans of many ancestries. Children are taught how the Chinese built the railroads, and that Hispanics have a vibrant and varied culture. Even acknowledging these nods, the curriculums of the nation's schools and colleges focus mainly on the achievements of white people. The emphasis is on English origins, and that those settlers brought their institutions and ideas from the British

Isles. Most Americans with European ancestors can identify with this "Anglo-Saxon" past. Descendants of slaves do not find it as easy. Whether black children are alienated by the content of the curriculum is a matter of controversy, which will be considered later on. At this point, it can be said that few teachers attempt to explain how the human beings consigned to slavery shaped the structure and sensibilities of the new nation. Apart from brief allusions to a Sojourner Truth or a Benjamin Banneker, your people appear as passive victims and faceless individuals.

In much the same vein, white children can be led to see how the travails of Shakespeare's heroes shed light on the human condition. Or that Jane Austen's heroines have messages for Americans of today. Nor is this impossible for black Americans. Ralph Ellison, raised in rural Alabama, recalled that reading Ezra Pound and Sigmund Freud give him a broader sense of life. Jamaica Kincaid has cited Charlotte Brontë as her first literary influence. Yet no matter how diligently you think about these authors and their ideas, you find that much of your life is not reflected in European learning. You often feel that there is a part of yourself, your soul, that Europe cannot reach. As in Countée Cullen's lines:

> What is Africa to me:
> Copper sun or scarlet sea,
> Jungle star or jungle track,
> Strong bronzed men, or regal black,
> Women from whose loins I sprang
> When the birds of Eden sang?

Whether you would like to know more white people is not an easy question to answer. So many of the contacts you have with them are stiff and uneasy, hardly worth the effort. If you are a woman, you may have developed some cordial acquaintances among white women at your place of work, since women tend to be more relaxed when among themselves. Still, very few black men and women can say that they have white "friends," if by that is meant people they confide in or entertain in their homes.

Of course, friendships often grow out of shared experiences. People with similar backgrounds can take certain things for granted when with one another. In this respect, you and white people may not have very much in common. At the same time, by no means all your outlooks and interests relate to your race. There probably are at least a few white people you would like to know better. It just might be that some of them would like to know you. But as matters now stand, the chances that these barriers will be broken do not appear to be very great.

Societies create vocabularies, devising new terms when they are needed, and retaining old ones when they serve a purpose. Dictionaries list words as obsolete or archaic, denoting that they are no longer used or heard. But one epithet survives, because people want it to. Your vulnerability to humiliation can be summed up in a single word. That word, of course, is "nigger."

When a white person voices it, it becomes a knife with a whetted edge. No black person can hear it with equanimity or ignore it as "simply a word." This word has the force to pierce, to wound, to penetrate, as no other has. There have, of course, been terms like "kike" and "spic" and "chink." But these are less frequently heard today, and they lack the same emotional impact. Some nonethnic terms come closer, such as "slut" and "fag" and "cripple." Yet, "nigger" stands alone with its power to tear at one's insides. It is revealing that whites have never created so wrenching an epithet for even the most benighted members of their own race.

Black people may use "nigger" among themselves, but with a tone and intention that is known and understood. Even so, if you are black, you know white society devised this word and keeps it available for use. (Not officially, of course, or even in print; but you know it continues to be uttered behind closed doors.) Its persistence reminds you that you are still perceived as a degraded species of humanity, a level to which whites can never descend.

You and your people have problems, far more than your share. And it is not as if you are ignorant of them, or wish to sweep them under a rug. But how to frame your opinions is not an easy matter. For example, what should you say about black crime or addiction or out-of-wedlock pregnancies? Of course, you have much to say on these and other topics, and you certainly express your ideas when you are among your own people. And you can be critical—very critical—of a lot of behavior you agree has become common among blacks.

However, the white world also asks that black people conduct these discussions in public. In particular, they want to hear you condemn black figures they regard as outrageous or irresponsible. This cannot help but annoy you. For one thing, you have never asked for white advice. Yet whites seem to feel that you stand in need of their tutelage, as if you lack the insight to understand your own interests. Moreover, it makes sense for members of a minority to stand together, especially since so many whites delight in magnifying differences among blacks. Your people have had a long history of being divided and conquered. At the same time, you have no desire to be held responsible for what every person of your color thinks or does. You cannot count how many times you have been asked to atone for some utterances of Louis Farrakhan, or simply to assert that he does not speak for you. You want to retort that you will choose your own causes and laments. Like other Americans, you have no obligation to follow agendas set by others.

As it happens, black Americans can and do disagree on racial matters, not to mention a host of other issues. Thus a survey conducted in 1990 found that 78 percent of those polled said they preferred to think of themselves as "black," and another 20 percent chose "African-American," while the remaining 2 percent stayed with "Negro." Another study by a team of black social scientists found that less than a quarter of the blacks they polled felt that black parents should give their children African names. Indeed, on a wide range of matters, there is no fixed, let alone official, black position. Yet it is amazing how often white people ask you to tell them how "black people" think about some individual or issue.

Then there are the accusations of inconsistency. As when you seem to favor taking race into consideration in some areas, but not in others. Or that you support a double standard, which allows separate criteria to be used for blacks in employment or education. Well, as it happens, you do believe:

- That discrimination against blacks remains real and calls for radical remedies; yet you cannot take seriously the argument that these compensatory actions will cause whites to suffer from "reverse" discrimination.

- That blacks have every right to attend dominantly white schools; yet once they are there, they should not be taken to task for spending much of their time with classmates of their own race.

- That it is important to preserve historically black colleges; yet you would feel entitled to object if some other schools were to designate themselves as "historically white."

- That racism is often the key reason why white voters rally behind white candidates; yet when blacks support a candidate of their own race, you do not see this as expressing racism.

- That while you reject censorship, you would prefer that a book like *Huckleberry Finn* not be assigned in high school classes, since its ubiquitous use of "nigger" sustains a view of blacks that can only hurt your people. Nor are you persuaded that the typical teacher can make clear Mark Twain's intentions, or put them in perspective, for white teenagers.

It will often seem to you as if black people's opinions are constantly under scrutiny by the white world. Every time you express an opinion, whites seem to slap it on their dissecting table, showing that blacks want the best of both ways. In fact, you have answers on these issues, but whites take so much delight in citing alleged "inconsistencies" that they hardly hear what you have to say.

You may, by a combination of brains and luck and perseverance, make it into the middle class. And like all middle-class Americans, you will want to enjoy the comforts and pleasures that come with that status. One downside is that you will find many white people asking why you aren't doing more to help members of your race whom you have supposedly left behind. There is even the suggestion that, by moving to a safer or more spacious area, you have callously deserted your own people.

Yet hardly ever do middle-class whites reflect on the fact that they, too, have moved to better neighborhoods, usually far from poorer and less equable persons of their own race or ethnic origins. There is little evidence that middle-class whites are prepared to give much of themselves in aid of fellow whites who have fallen on misfortune. Indeed, the majority of white Americans have chosen to live in sequestered suburbs, where they are insulated from the nation's losers and failures.

Compounding these expectations, you find yourself continually subjected to comparisons with other minorities or even members of your own race. For example, you are informed that blacks who have emigrated from the Caribbean earn higher incomes than those born in the United States. Here the message seems to be that color by itself is not an insurmountable barrier. Most stinging of all are contrasts with recent immigrants. You hear people just off the boat (or, nowadays, a plane) extolled for building businesses and becoming productive citizens. Which is another way of asking why you haven't matched their achievements, considering how long your people have been here.

Moreover, immigrants are praised for being willing to start at the bottom. The fact that so many of them manage to find jobs is taken as evidence that the economy still has ample opportunities for employment. You want to reply that you are not an immigrant, but as much a citizen as any white person born here. Perhaps you can't match the mathematical skills of a teenager from Korea, but then neither can most white kids at suburban high schools. You feel much like a child being chided because she has not done as well as a precocious sister. However, you are an adult, and do not find such scolding helpful or welcome.

No law of humanity or nature posits a precise format for the family. Throughout history and even in our day, households have had many shapes and structures. The same strictures apply to marriage and parental relationships. All this requires some emphasis, given concerns expressed about "the black family" and its presumed disintegration. In fact, the last several decades have seen a weakening of domestic ties in all classes and races.

Black Americans are fully aware of what is happening in this sphere. They know that most black children are being born out of wedlock and that these youngsters will spend most of their growing years with a single parent. They understand that a majority of their marriages will dissolve in separation or divorce, and that many black men and women will never marry at all. Black Americans also realize that tensions between men and women sometimes bear a violence and bitterness that can take an awful toll.

If you are black, you soon learn it is safest to make peace with reality: to acknowledge that the conditions of your time can undercut dreams of enduring romance and "happily ever after." This is especially true if you are a black woman, since you may find yourself spending many of your years without a man in your life. Of course, you will survive and adapt, as your people always have. Central in this effort will be joining and sustaining a community of women—another form of a family—on whom you can rely for love and strength and support.

If you are a black woman, you can expect to live five fewer years than your white counterpart. Among men, the gap is seven years. Indeed, a man living in New York's Harlem is less likely to reach sixty-five than is a resident of Bangladesh. Black men have a three times greater chance of dying of AIDS, and outnumber whites as murder victims by a factor of seven. According to studies, you get less sleep, are more likely to be overweight, and to develop hypertension. This is not simply due to poverty. Your shorter and more painful life results, in considerable measure, from the anxieties that come with being black in America.

If you are a black young man, life can be an interlude with an early demise. Black youths do what they must to survive in a hostile world, with the prospect of violence and death on its battlefields. Attitudes can turn fatalistic, even suicidal: gladiators without even the cheers of an audience.

When white people hear the cry, "the police are coming!" for them it almost always means, "help is on the way." Black citizens cannot make the same assumption. If you have been the victim of a crime, you cannot presume that the police will actually show up; or, if they do, that they will take much note of your losses or suffering. You sense police officials feel that blacks should accept being robbed or raped as one of life's everyday risks. It seems to you obvious that more detectives are assigned to a case when a white person is murdered.

If you are black and young and a man, the arrival of the police does not usually signify help, but something very different. If you are a teenager simply socializing with some friends, the police may order you to disperse and get off the streets. They may turn on a searchlight, order you against a wall. Then comes the command to spread your legs and empty out your pockets, and stand splayed there while they call in your identity over their radio. You may be a college student and sing in a church choir, but that will not overcome the police presumption that you have probably done something they can arrest you for.

If you find yourself caught up in the system, it will seem like alien terrain. Usually your judge and prosecutor will be white, as will most members of the jury, as well as your attorney. In short, your fate will be decided by a white world.

This may help to explain why you have so many harsh words for the police, even though you want and need their protection more than white people do. After all, there tends to be more crime in areas where you live, not to mention drug dealing and all that comes in its wake. Black citizens are at least twice as likely as whites to become victims of violent crimes. Moreover, in almost all of these cases, the person who attacks you will be black. Since this is so, whites want to know, why don't black people speak out against the members of their race who are causing so much grief? The reason is partly that you do not want to attack other blacks while whites are listening. At least equally important is that while you obviously have no taste for violence, you are also wary of measures that might come with a campaign to stamp out "black crime." These reasons will receive fuller consideration in a later chapter. At this point you might simply say that you are not sure you want a more vigorous police presence, if those enforcers are unable to distinguish between law-abiding citizens and local predators. Of course, you want to be protected. But not if it means that you and your friends and relatives end up included among those the police harass or arrest.

The national anthem sings of America as "the land of the free." The Pledge of Allegiance promises "liberty and justice for all." The Declaration of Independence proclaims that all human creatures are "created equal."

If you are black, you cannot easily join in the anthem's refrain, reciting the pledge, or affirming that your country is committed to equality. While you grant that the United States is "your" country, you may define your citizenship as partial and qualified. It is not that you are "disloyal," if that means having your first allegiance elsewhere. Rather, you feel no compelling commitment to a republic that has always rebuffed you and your people.

We know from surveys that during the Cold War era, black Americans felt less antipathy toward nations then designated as our enemies, since they saw themselves less threatened by the Soviet Union or Cuba or China than did most white Americans. Nor were they so sure why they or their children were asked to risk their lives fighting people of color in places like Vietnam and Panama and the Middle East. And if the United States finds itself increasingly at odds with Islamic countries or other movements in the Third World, even more black Americans may find themselves wondering where their own allegiances lie.

As you look back on the way this nation has treated your people, you wonder how so many have managed to persevere amid so much adversity. About slavery, of course, too much cannot be said. Yet even within living memory, there were beaches and parks—in the North as well as in the South—where black Americans simply could not set foot. Segregation meant separation without even a pretense of equal facilities. In Southern communities that had only a single public library or swimming pool, black residents and taxpayers could never borrow a book or go for a swim. Indeed, black youths were even forbidden to stroll past the pool, lest they catch a glimpse of white girls in their bathing costumes.

How did they endure the endless insults and humiliations? Grown people being called by their first names, having to avert their eyes when addressed by white people, even being expected to step off a sidewalk when whites walked by. Overarching it all was the terror, with white police and prosecutors and judges possessing all but total power over black lives. Not to mention the lynchings by white mobs, with victims even chosen at random, to remind all blacks of what could happen to them if they did not remain compliant and submissive.

You wonder how much that has changed. Suppose, for example, you find yourself having to drive across the country, stopping at gasoline stations and restaurants and motels. As you travel across the heart of white America, you can never be sure of how you will be received. While the odds are that you will reach your destination alive, you cannot be so sure that you will not be stopped by the police or spend a night in a cell. So you would be well advised to keep to the speed limit, and not exceed it by a single mile. Of course, white people are pulled over by state troopers; but how often are their cars searched? Or if a motel clerk cannot "find" your reservation, is it because she has now seen you in person? And are all the toilet facilities at this service station really out of order?

The day-to-day aggravations and humiliations add up bit by bitter bit. To take a depressingly familiar example, you stroll into a shop to look at the merchandise, and it soon becomes clear that the clerks are keeping a watchful eye on you. Too quickly, one of them comes over to inquire what it is you might want, and then remains conspicuously close as you continue your search. It also seems that they take an unusually long time verifying your credit card. And then you and a black friend enter a restaurant, and find yourselves greeted warily, with what is obviously a more anxious reception than that given to white guests. Yes, you will be served, and your table will not necessarily be next to the kitchen. Still, you sense that they would rather you had chosen some other eating place. Or has this sort of thing happened so often that you are growing paranoid?

So there is the sheer strain of living in a white world, the rage that you must suppress almost every day. No wonder black Americans, especially black men, suffer so much from hypertension. (If ever an illness had social causes, this is certainly one.) To be black in America means reining in your opinions and emotions as no whites ever have to do. Not to mention the forced and false smiles you are expected to contrive, to assure white Americans that you harbor no grievances against them.

Along with the tension and the strain and the rage, there come those moments of despair. At times, the conclusion seems all but self-evident that white America has no desire for your presence or any need for your people. Can this nation have an unstated strategy for annihilating your people? How else, you ask yourself, can one explain the incidence of death and debilitation from drugs and disease; the incarceration of a whole generation of your men; the consignment of millions of women and children to half-lives of poverty and dependency?* Each of these debilities has its causes; indeed, analyzing them has become a minor industry. Yet with so much about these conditions that is so closely related to race, they say something about the larger society that has allowed them to happen.

This is not to say that white officials sit in secret rooms, plotting the genocide of black America. You understand as well as anyone that politics and history seldom operate that way. Nor do you think of yourself as unduly suspicious. Still, you cannot rid yourself of some lingering mistrust. Just as your people were once made to serve silently as slaves, could it be that if white America begins to conclude that you are becoming too much trouble, it will find itself contemplating more lasting solutions?

Speculations

1. Hacker asks at the beginning of this essay how individuals might benefit from being white and what real differences it makes to them. How does he get us to stop and think about this question? Is his technique effective for you? Explain your response.

2. What is "residential apartheid" in America and what factors contribute to sustaining this apartheid?

---

* In 1990, when a sample of black Americans were asked if they thought that the government was deliberately encouraging drug use among black people, 64 percent felt that this might be true. When asked if they suspected that AIDS had been purposely created by scientists to infect black people, 32 percent believed there might be some truth in this view.

3. What is the "racial tipping point" and what role does it play in reversing the racial make-up of a neighborhood?
4. Hacker refers to Ralph Ellison's image of the "invisible man" as a way of describing how blacks are "invisible" to whites. What does he mean by this and how does he support this idea with examples from the media and textbooks?
5. According to Hacker, what specific problems does a black person worry about and encounter when driving across America? Imagine yourself repeatedly confronted with such difficulties: How would you respond? Why?
6. Is Hacker's use of statistics effective? Do his facts and figures persuade you that he is right? Explain your responses.

THE BEST BLACK

Stephen L. Carter

Born in 1954 into a professional and academic family, Stephen L. Carter grew up in Washington D.C. and received a B.A. from Stanford University and a law degree from Yale University. After working as a clerk for renowned Supreme Court Justice Thurgood Marshall, he returned to teach at Yale, where he became one of the youngest faculty members to receive tenure and was soon named the William Nelson Cromwell Professor of Law. A frequent contributor to many law journals and other publications such as *The New Republic* and *The New York Times Book Review,* Carter has become a central figure in a new breed of American intellectuals through his publication of three important books: *Reflections of an Affirmative Action Baby* (1991), from which this selection has been taken, *The Culture of Disbelief: How American Law and Politics Trivialize Religious Devotion* (1993), and *The Confirmation Mess: Cleaning Up the Federal Appointments Process* (1994).

Having built his intellectual reputation through a capacity to lucidly analyze controversial issues and empathize with people who do not share his political or religious views, Carter's style of argument is quiet, reasoned, and iconoclastic. He begins *Reflections of an Affirmative Action Baby* with the simple statement "I got into law school because I am black," and then argues that although affirmative action in university admissions is justifiable, "When the time comes for entry into the job market, I think it is quite clear that among professionals, the case for preference evaporates . . . The time has come for one to stand or fall on what one has actually achieved." As a writer and a teacher, he says simply "I write to spark a dialogue" and warns that it is all too easy "to be smug, to be sure that we in our academic niches, with our libraries and our computers, have found the right answers." In this selection, Carter asks hard questions about the history, purpose, and effects—both intentional and unintentional—of affirmative action and its viability as a tool for social justice.

Affirmative action has been with me always. I do not mean to suggest that I have always been the beneficiary of special programs and preferences. I mean, rather, that no matter what my accomplishments, I have had trouble escaping an assumption that often seems to underlie the worst forms of affirmative action: that black people cannot compete intellectually with white people. Certainly I have not escaped it since my teen years, spent mostly in Ithaca, New York, where the presence of Cornell University lends an air of academic intensity to the public schools. At Ithaca High School in the days of my adolescence, we had far more than our share of National Merit Scholars, of students who scored exceptionally well on standardized tests, of students who earned advanced placement credits for college, and of every other commodity by which secondary schools compare their academic quality.

My father taught at Cornell, which made me a Cornell kid, a "fac-brat," and I hung out with a bunch of white Cornell kids in a private little world where we competed fiercely (but only with one another— no one else mattered!) for grades and test scores and solutions to brain teasers. We were the sort of kids other kids hated: the ones who would run around compiling lists of everyone else's test scores and would badger guidance counselors into admitting their errors in arithmetic (no computers then) in order to raise our class ranks a few notches. I held my own in this bunch, although I was forced by the norms of the fac-brat community to retake the Mathematics Level II achievement test to raise a humiliating score of 780 to an acceptable 800. (No one had yet told me that standardized tests were culturally biased against me.) Like the rest of the fac-brats, I yearned for the sobriquet "brilliant," and tried desperately to convince myself and everyone else who would listen that I had the grades and test scores to deserve it.

And yet there were unnerving indications that others did not see me as just another fac-brat, that they saw me instead as that black kid who hung out with the Cornell kids. There was, for example, the recruiter from Harvard College who asked to see those he considered the brightest kids in the school; I was included, so a guidance counselor said, because I was black. And when I decided that I wanted to attend Stanford University, I was told by a teacher that I would surely be admitted because I was black and I was smart. Not because I was smart and not even because I was smart and black, but because I was black and smart: the skin color always preceding any other observation.

But the worst of it came at National Merit Scholarship time. In those days (this was the early 1970s), the National Merit Scholarship Qualifying Test was a separate examination, not combined with the

Preliminary Scholastic Aptitude Test as it later would be. When the qualifying scores came in, I was in heaven. Mine was the second highest in the school. I saw my future then—best fac-brat!—and awaited my National Merit Scholarship. Instead, well before the National Merit Scholarships were announced, I received a telephone call informing me that I had been awarded a National Achievement Scholarship, presented, in the awkward usage of the day, to "outstanding Negro students." Well, all right. If one wants more black students to go to college, one had better provide the necessary resources. So I wasn't insulted. College is expensive and money is money. But—I inquired politely as I saw my "best fac-brat" status slipping away—what about my possible National *Merit* Scholarship? The one not for the best black students, but for the *best* students?

The caller responded, a bit coldly, that she knew nothing about that. Well, I pressed on, if I accepted this, could I still be considered for that? Oh, no, of course not, she said. It was one or the other. And did I have to decide now? Well, yes. In a few days, anyway. But I was not to worry, she told me; I wouldn't win a National Merit Scholarship anyway. Oh, I said sadly. The decision is already made, then. Well, no, she responded. But the people who get National Achievement Scholarships are never good enough to get National Merit Scholarships.

I was stunned—the more so when, later, a number of white students who had lower test scores than mine and, I was sure, similar grades were awarded National Merit Scholarships. Could I have had one too? I will never know. What I do know is that I was faced with a bizarre rule under which, in order to receive a National Achievement Scholarship, I was required to forfeit any claim to a National Merit Scholarship. The lesson was clear: the smartest students of color were not considered as capable as the smartest white students, and therefore would not be allowed to compete with them, but only with one another.

I call it the "best black" syndrome, and all black people who have done well in school are familiar with it. We are measured by a different yardstick: *first black, only black, best black.* The best black syndrome is cut from the same cloth as the implicit and demeaning tokenism that often accompanies racial preferences: "Oh, we'll tolerate so-and-so at our hospital or in our firm or on our faculty, because she's the best black." Not because she's the best-qualified candidate, but because she's the best-qualified *black* candidate. She can fill the black slot. And then the rest of the slots can be filled in the usual way: with the best-*qualified* candidates.

This dichotomy between "best" and "best black" is not merely something manufactured by racists to denigrate the abilities of professionals who are not white. On the contrary, the durable and demeaning stereotype of black people as unable to compete with white ones is reinforced by advocates of certain forms of affirmative action. It is reinforced, for example, every time employers are urged to set aside test scores (even, in some cases, on tests that are good predictors of job performance) and to hire from separate lists, one of the best white scorers, the other of the best black ones. It is reinforced every time state pension plans are pressed to invest some of their funds with "minority-controlled" money management firms, even if it turns out that the competing "white" firms have superior track records.[1] It is reinforced every time students demand that universities commit to hiring some pre-set number of minority faculty members. What all of these people are really saying is, "There are black folks out there. Go and find the best of them." And the best black syndrome is further reinforced, almost unthinkingly, by politicians or bureaucrats or faculty members who see these demands as nothing more than claims for simple justice.

Successful black students and professionals have repeatedly disproved the proposition that the best black minds are not as good as the best white ones, but the stereotype lingers, even among the most ardent friends of civil rights. In my own area of endeavor, academia, I hear this all the time from people who should know better. It is not at all unusual for white professors, with no thought that they are indulging a demeaning stereotype, to argue for hiring the best available professors of color, whether or not the individuals on whom that double-edged mantle is bestowed meet the usual appointment standards. I put aside for the moment the question of the fairness of the standards, for the white people I am describing have few doubts about *that;* I have in mind white people who argue with straight face for the hiring of black people *they themselves* do not believe are good enough to be hired without extra points for race. For example, one prominent law professor, a strong and sincere proponent of racial diversity, sent me a list of scholars in his field who might be considered for appointment to the Yale faculty. The first part of the list set out the names of the best people in the field; the second part, the names of people who were so-so; and the last part, the names of the leading "minorities and women" in the field, none of whom apparently qualified (in his judgment) for even the "so-so" category, let alone the best. I know that my colleague acted with the best of intentions, but the implicit invitation offered by this extraordinary document was to choose between diversity and quality. I suspect that to this day he is unaware of any insult and actually believes he was advancing the cause of racial justice.

"No responsible advocate of affirmative action," argues Ira Glasser, "opposes merit or argues . . . that standards should be reduced in order to meet affirmative action goals."[2] Perhaps not; but the language of standards and merit is slippery at best. I am reminded of a conversation I had some years ago with a veteran civil rights litigator who, concerned at charges that affirmative action sometimes results in hiring unqualified candidates, drew a sharp distinction between *unquali-*

fied and *less qualified.* An employer, he mused, does not have to hire the *best* person for the job, as long as everyone hired is *good enough* to do the job. Consequently, he reasoned, it is perfectly fine to require employers to hire black applicants who are less qualified than some white applicants, as long as the black candidates are capable of doing the job. A tidy argument in its way, but, of course, another example of an almost unconscious acceptance of a situation in which an employer is made to distinguish between the best black candidates and the best ones.

Even our sensible but sometimes overzealous insistence that the rest of the nation respect the achievements of black culture might reinforce the depressing dichotomy: if we insist, as often we must, that others appreciate "our" music and "our" literature, we should not be surprised if those others come to think of the best of our music and the best of our literature as distinct from the best music and the best literature. Indeed, this is the implication of Stanley Crouch's vigorous argument (on which I here express no view) that white critics accept a level of mediocrity from black artists, filmmakers, and writers that they would never tolerate from creative people who are white.[3]

The best black syndrome creates in those of us who have benefited from racial preferences a peculiar contradiction. We are told over and over that we are among the best black people in our professions. And in part we are flattered, or should be, because, after all, those who call us the best black lawyers or doctors or investment bankers consider it a compliment. But to professionals who have worked hard to succeed, flattery of this kind carries an unsubtle insult, for we yearn to be called what our achievements often deserve: simply the best—no qualifiers needed! In *this* society, however, we sooner or later must accept that being viewed as the best blacks is part of what has led us to where we are; and we must further accept that to some of our colleagues, black as well as white, we will never be anything else.

II

Despite these rather unsettling pitfalls, many of us resist the best black syndrome less than we should, and one of the reasons is surely that it can bestow considerable benefits. Racial preferences are perhaps the most obvious benefit, but there are others. In high school, for example, I quickly stood out, if only because I was the lone black student in any number of honors and advanced placement courses. Perhaps my intellect was not unusually keen; although I did as well as anyone, I have always thought that with proper training, scoring well on standardized tests is no great trick. Nevertheless, other students and, eventually, teachers as well concluded that I was particularly sharp. These perceptions naturally fed my ego, because all I really wanted from high school was to be considered one of the best and brightest.

What I could not see then, but see clearly now, two decades later, is that while the perceptions others had of my abilities were influenced in part by grades and test scores, they were further influenced by the fact that students and teachers (black and white alike) were unaccustomed to the idea that a black kid could sit among the white kids as an equal, doing as well, learning as much, speaking as ably, arguing with as much force. In their experience, I was so different that I had to be exceptional. But exceptional in a specific and limited sense: the best black.

College was not much different. My college grades were somewhat better than average, but at Stanford in the era of grade inflation, good grades were the norm. Nevertheless, I quickly discovered that black students with good grades stood out from the crowd. Other students and many of my professors treated me as a member of some odd and fascinating species. I sat among them as an equal in seminars, my papers were as good as anyone else's, so I had to be exceptionally bright. In their experience, it seemed, no merely ordinarily smart black person could possibly sit among them as an equal.

In law school, the trend continued. I was fortunate enough to come early to the attention of my professors, but all I was doing was playing by the rules: talking in class with reasonable intelligence, exhibiting genuine interest in questions at the podium later, and treating papers and examinations as matters of serious scholarship rather than obstacles to be overcome. Lots of students did the same—but, in the stereotyped visions of some of my professors, not lots of black students. Here was the best black syndrome at work once more: I was not just another bright student with an enthusiastic but untrained intellect; I was a bright *black* student, a fact that apparently made a special impression.

The stultifying mythology of racism holds that black people are intellectually inferior. Consistent survey data over the years indicate that this stereotype persists.[4] Such incidents as those I have described, however, make me somewhat skeptical of the familiar complaint that because of this mythology, black people of intellectual talent have a harder time than others in proving their worth. My own experience suggests quite the contrary, that like a flower blooming in winter, intellect is more readily noticed where it is not expected to be found. Or, as a black investment banker has put the point, "Our mistakes are amplified, but so are our successes."[5] And it is the amplification of success that makes the achieving black student or professional into the best black.

When people assign to a smart black person the status of best black, they do so with the purest of motives: the curing of bewilderment. There must be an explanation, the reasoning runs, and the explanation must be that this black person, in order to do as well as white people, is exceptionally bright. What I describe is not racism in the sense of a design to oppress, but it is in its racialist assumption of inferiority every bit as insulting and nearly as tragic. The awe and celebration with which our achievements are often greeted (by black and white people alike) suggest a widespread expectation that our achievements will be few. The surprise is greater, perhaps, when our achievements are intellectual, but other achievements, too, seem to astonish. The astonishment, moreover, takes a long time to fade: even, or perhaps especially, in the era of affirmative action, it seems, the need to prove one's professional worth over and over again has not receded.

III

Affirmative action, to be sure, did not create this particular box into which black people are routinely stuffed. Throughout the long, tragic history of the interaction between white people and people of color in America (it is too often forgotten that there were people of color here before there were white people), the society has treated white as normal and color as an aberration that must be explained or justified or apologized for. Black people have always been the target of openly racist assumptions, perhaps the worst among these being that we are a stupid, primitive people. Every intellectual attainment by black people in America has been greeted with widespread suspicion. When the American Missionary Association and other abolitionist groups established black colleges in the South after the Civil War and determined to offer to the freed slaves and their progeny classical educations (Eurocentric educations, I suppose they would be called on today's campuses), emulating those available at the best Northern schools, editorialists had a field day. By the turn of the century, a standing joke had it that when two black students met on the campus of one of these colleges, the first greeted the second with, "Is yo' done yo' Greek yet?" The joke has faded from national memory, but its import, I fear, remains part of the nation's swirling racial consciousness.

Small wonder, then, that every black professional, in our racially conscious times, is assumed to have earned his or her position not by being among the best available but by being among the best available blacks. Any delusions to the contrary I might have harbored about my own achievements were shattered a few months after I was voted tenure at the Yale Law School. Late one night, a reporter for the campus newspaper called my home to say that the paper was doing a story about my promotion. Why was that? I wanted to know. Lots of law professors earn tenure, I said. Oh, I know, said the reporter, unabashed. Still, wasn't it true that I was the first black one? But that was the luck of the draw, I protested. It could as easily have been someone else. And besides, I wanted to shout, but dared not; besides, that isn't why I was promoted! (I hope.)

My protests mattered not a jot, and the newspaper ran its story. A banner headline on the front page screamed that the law faculty had, for the first time, voted to promote a black professor to tenure. The tone of the article—years of lily-whiteness in the academy was its theme—suggested that my promotion was simple justice. But justice of a special sort: not the justice of earned reward for a job well done, but the justice due me as a professor who happens to be black. Whether I was a strong scholar or a weak one, a creative thinker or a derivative one, a diligent researcher or a lazy one, a good teacher or a bad one, mattered less to the newspaper than the fact that I was a black one. Evidently I had finally arrived, had I but the gumption to acknowledge it, as one of the best blacks.

I muted my protest, however. I did not complain, to the newspaper or to others, that I felt oppressed by this vision of tenure as an extension of affirmative action. Like many other black professionals, I simply wanted to be left alone to do my work. My hope, then as now, was that if I earned a place in the academic world, it would be for the seriousness of my research and the thoughtful contributions I hoped to make to legal knowledge—not for the color of my skin. Most of the scholarship I have committed has related to the separation of powers in the federal government, the regulation of intellectual property,* and the relationship of law and religion—to the lay person, perhaps not the most thrilling of topics, but, for me, intellectually engaging and lots of fun. I have always relished the look of surprise in the eyes of people who, having read my work in these areas, meet me for the first time. My favorite response (this really did happen) came at an academic conference at the University of Michigan Law School, where a dapper, buttoned-down young white man glanced at my name tag, evidently ignored the name but noted the school, and said, "If you're at Yale, you must know this Carter fellow who wrote that article about thus-and-so." Well, yes, I admitted. I did know that Carter fellow slightly. An awkward pause ensued. And then the young man, realizing his error, apologized with a smile warm enough to freeze butter.

"Oh," he said, "*you're* Carter." (I have since wondered from time to time whether, had I been white and the error a less telling one, his voice would have been inflected differently: "You're *Carter*." Think about it.) Naturally, we then discussed the article, which happened to be about the separation of powers, and by way of showing the sincerity of his apology, he gushed about its quality in terms so adulatory that a casual observer might have been excused for thinking me the second coming of Oliver Wendell Holmes or, more likely, for thinking my interlocutor an idiot. (That gushing is part of the peculiar relationship between black intellectuals and the white ones who seem loath to criticize us for fear of being branded racists—which is itself a mark of racism of

---

* Intellectual property is the field of law governing rights in intangible creations of the mind and includes such subjects as patents, copyrights, and trademarks.

a sort.) I suppose I should have been flattered, although, if the truth is told, I quickly gained the impression that he was excited more by the political uses to which my argument might be put than by the analysis in the article itself.

But there it was! The Best Black Syndrome! It had, as they say, stood up and bitten me! Since this young man liked the article, its author could not, in his initial evaluation, have been a person of color. He had not even conceived of that possibility, or he would have glanced twice at my name tag. No, if the work was of high quality, the author had to be white—there was no room for doubt! The best blacks don't do this stuff!

And if you're black, you can't escape it! It's everywhere, this awkward set of expectations. No matter what you might accomplish (or imagine yourself to have accomplished), the label follows you. A friend of mine who works in the financial services field—I'll call him X—tells the story of his arrival at a client's headquarters. The client had been told that a supervisor was on the way to straighten out a particularly knotty problem. When my friend arrived, alone, and gave his name, the client said, "But where is the supervisor? Where is Mr. X?" With my friend standing right in front of him, name already announced! My friend, being black, could not possibly be the problem solver who was awaited. He was only . . . THE BEST BLACK! The winner of the coveted prize!

And that's the way it works. You don't even need to worry about a National Merit Scholarship—you've got a program of your own! This is the risk some critics see in setting up Afro-American Studies departments: Isn't there a good chance that the school will dismiss the professors in the department as simply the best blacks, saying, in effect, don't worry about the academic standards the rest of us have to meet, you've got your own department? The answer is yes, of course, the school might do that—but that isn't an argument against Afro-American studies as a discipline, any more than it's an argument against hiring black faculty at all. It's just an admission that this is the way many of the white people who provide affirmative action programs and other goodies tend to think about them: there's Category A for the smart folks, and Category B for the best blacks. It's also a reminder to all people of color that our parents' advice was true: we really do have to work twice as hard to be considered half as good.

This is an important point for those who are trapped by the best black syndrome. We cannot afford, ever, to let our standards slip. There are too many doubters waiting in the wings to pop out at the worst possible moment and cry, "See? Told you!" The only way to keep them off the stage is to make our own performances so good that there is no reasonable possibility of calling them into question. It isn't fair that so much should be demanded of us, but what has life to do with fairness? It was the artist Paul Klee, I believe, who said that one must adapt oneself to the contents of the paintbox. This is particularly true for upwardly mobile professionals who happen to be people of color, for people of color have had very little say about what those contents are.

So we have to adapt ourselves, a point I finally came to accept when I was in law school. In those days, the black students spent lots of time sitting around and discussing our obligations, if any, to the race. (I suppose black students still sit around and hold the same conversation.) In the course of one such conversation over a casual lunch, I blurted out to a classmate my driving ambition. It infuriated me, I said, that no matter what we might accomplish, none of us could aspire to anything more than the role of best black. What we should do for the race, I said, was achieve. Shatter stereotypes. Make white doubters think twice about our supposed intellectual inferiority.

A few years later, I foolishly imagined that I had attained my goal. It was the fall of 1981, and I was a young lawyer seeking a teaching position at a law school. I had, I was certain, played my cards right. In my law school years, I had managed to get to know a professor or two, and some of them liked me. I had compiled the right paper record before setting out to hunt for a job: my résumé included practice with a well-regarded law firm, good law school grades, service on the *Yale Law Journal,* and a spate of other awards and honors, including a clerkship with a Justice of the Supreme Court of the United States. One might have thought, and I suppose I thought it myself, that someone with my credentials would have no trouble landing a teaching job. But what people told me was that any school would be happy to have a black professor with my credentials. (Did a white professor need more, or did white professors just make their schools unhappy?) In the end, I was fortunate enough to collect a flattering set of job offers, but the taste was soured for me, at least a little, by the knowledge that whatever my qualifications, they probably looked more impressive on the résumé of someone black.

There is an important point here, one that is missed by the critics who point out (correctly, I think) that affirmative action programs tend to call into question the legitimate achievements of highly qualified black professionals. Yes, they do; but that is not the end of the story. A few years ago, in a panel discussion on racial preferences, the economist Glenn Loury noted that the Harvard Law School had on its faculty two black professors who are also former law clerks for Justices of the Supreme Court of the United States. (As I write, I believe that the number is three.) It isn't fair, he argued, that they should be dismissed as affirmative action appointments when they are obviously strongly qualified for the positions they hold. He is right that it isn't fair to dismiss them and he is right that they are obviously qualified, but it is also true that there are nowadays literally dozens of similarly qualified candidates for teaching positions every year. It is no diminution of the achievements of the professors Loury had in mind to point out that there is no real way to tell whether they would have risen to the top if not for the fact that faculties are on the lookout for highly qualified people of color. The same is surely true for many black people rising to the top of political, economic, and educational institutions.

There is a distinction here, however, that even the harshest critics of affirmative action should be willing to concede. Hiring to fill a slot that must be filled—the black slot, say—is not the same as using race to sort among a number of equally qualified candidates. Put otherwise, yes, it is true that the result of racial preferences is sometimes the hiring of black people not as well qualified as white people who are turned away, and preferences of that kind do much that is harmful and little that is good. But preferences can also be a means of selecting highly qualified black people from a pool of people who are all excellent. True, employers will almost always claim to be doing the second even when they are really doing the first; but that does not mean the second is impossible to do. And if an employer undertakes the second method, a sorting among the excellent, then although there might be legitimate grounds for concern, a criticism on the ground of lack of qualification of the person hired cannot be among them.

Ah, but are our analytical antennae sufficiently sensitive to detect the difference? I am not sure they are, and the sometimes tortured arguments advanced by the strongest advocates of affirmative action (I include the argument for viewpoint diversity discussed in chapter 2) occasionally leave me with a bleak and hopeless sense that all people of color who are hired for the tasks for which their intellects and professional training have prepared them will be dismissed, always, as nothing more than the best blacks. And I draw from all of this two convictions: first, that affirmative action will not alter this perception; and, second, that white Americans will not change it simply because it is unjust. Consequently change, if change there is to be, is in *our* hands—and the only change for which we can reasonably hope will come about because we commit ourselves to battle for excellence, to show ourselves able to meet any standard, to pass any test that looms before us, in short, to form ourselves into a vanguard of black professionals who are simply too good to ignore.

And that, I suppose, is why I relish the reactions of those who have liked my work without knowing I am black: in my mind, I am proving them wrong, as I promised I would at that lunch so many years ago. No doubt my pleasure at the widened eyes is childish, but it is sometimes a relief to be sure for once that it is really the work they like, not the-unexpected-quality-of-the-work-given-the-naturally-inferior-intellects-of-those-with-darker-skins. It is a commonplace of social science, a matter of common sense as well, that an observer's evaluation of a piece of work is frequently influenced by awareness of the race of the author. Happily, I have found that people who like my work before they learn that I am black do not seem to like it less once they discover my color.*

And when those who read my work *do* know that I am black? Well, any prejudices that the readers might bring to bear are, at least, nothing new. John Hope Franklin, in his sparkling essay on "The Dilemma of the American Negro Scholar," details the struggles of black academics during the past century to have their work taken seriously by white scholars.[6] Although progress has obviously been made, the struggle Franklin describes is not yet ended, which means I have to face the likelihood that many white scholars who read my work will judge it by a different standard than the one they use to judge the work of white people. Perhaps the standard will be higher, perhaps the standard will be lower, perhaps the standard will simply involve different criteria—but whatever the standard, all I can do is try to carry out the instruction that black parents have given their children for generations, and make the work not simply as good as the work of white scholars of similar background, but better. Sometimes I succeed, sometimes I fail; but to be a professional is always to strive. And while I am perfectly willing to concede the unfairness of a world that judges black people and white people by different standards, I do not lose large amounts of sleep over it. A journalist friend recently told my wife and me that he is tired of hearing black people complain about having to work twice as hard as white people to reach the same level of success. He says that if that's what we have to do, that's what we have to do, and it would not be a bad thing at all for us as a race to develop that habit as our defining characteristic: "Oh, you know those black people, they always work twice as hard as everybody else." If you can't escape it, then make the most of it: in my friend's racial utopia, it would no longer be taken as an insult to be called by a white colleague the best black.

IV

My desire to succeed in the professional world without the aid of preferential treatment is hardly a rejection of the unhappy truth that the most important factor retarding the progress of people of color historically has been society's racism. It is, rather, an insistence on the opportunity to do what the National Merit Scholarship people said I would not be allowed to, what I promised at that fateful lunch I would:

---

* Often, however, they do suddenly assume that I must possess a special expertise in the most sophisticated quandaries and delicately nuanced esoterica of civil rights law, areas that take years of careful study to master, no matter the contrary impression given by the sometimes simpleminded reporting on civil rights law in the mass media.

to show the world that we who are black are not so marked by our history of racist oppression that we are incapable of intellectual achievement on the same terms as anybody else.

In a society less marked by racist history, the intellectual achievements of people of color might be accepted as a matter of course. In *this* society, however, they are either ignored or applauded, but never accepted as a matter of course. As I have said, however, the general astonishment when our achievements are intellectual carries with it certain benefits. Perhaps chief among these is the possibility of entrée to what I call the "star system." The characteristics of the star system are familiar to anyone who has attended college or professional school or has struggled upward on the corporate ladder, and it has analogues in sports, the military, and other arenas. Early in their careers, a handful of individuals are marked by their teachers or supervisors as having the potential for special success, even greatness. Thereafter, the potential stars are closely watched. Not every person marked early as a possible star becomes one, but the vast majority of those who are never marked will never star. Even very talented individuals who lack entrée to the star system may never gain attention in the places that matter: the hushed and private conference rooms (I can testify to their existence, having sat in more than a few) where money is spent and hiring and promotion decisions are made.

Getting into the star system is not easy, and the fact that few people of color scramble to the top of it should scarcely be surprising. The reason is not any failing in our native abilities—although it is true that only in the past decade have we been present as students in numbers sufficient to make entry more plausible—but the social dynamics of the star system itself. Entrée is not simply a matter of smarts, although that helps, or of working hard, although that helps, too. The star system rewards familiarity, comfort, and perseverence. It usually begins on campus, and so do its problems. One must get to know one's professors. Most college and professional school students are far too intimidated by their professors to feel comfortable getting to know them well, and for many students of color, already subject to a variety of discomforts, this barrier may seem especially high. When one feels uneasy about one's status in the classroom to begin with, the task of setting out to get to know the professor personally may seem close to insuperable. The fact that some students of color indeed reap the benefits of the star system does not alter the likelihood that many more would never dream of trying.

Exclusion from the star system is costly. Anyone left out will meet with difficulties in being taken seriously as a candidate for entry-level hiring at any of our most selective firms and institutions, which is why the failure of people of color to get into the star system makes a difference. Still, there is an opportunity here: because so little is expected of students of color, intellectual attainment is sometimes seen as a mark of genuine brilliance. (None of the merely ordinarily smart need apply!) So the best black syndrome can have a salutary side effect: it can help those trapped inside it get through the door of the star system. Certainly it worked that way for me. (Who *is* this character? my professors seemed to want to know.) The star system, in turn, got me in the door of the academy at the entry level. (From the doorway, I would like to think, I made the rest of the journey on my own; my achievements ought to speak for themselves. But in a world in which I have heard my colleagues use the very words *best black* in discussions of faculty hiring, I have no way to tell.) So, yes, I am a beneficiary of both the star system and the best black syndrome. Yet I hope it is clear that I am not a fan of either. The star system is exclusionary and incoherent; the best black syndrome is demeaning and oppressive. Both ought to be abandoned.

Consider the so-called glass ceiling, the asserted reluctance of corporations to promote people of color to top management positions. If indeed the glass ceiling exists, it is very likely a function of the star system. If people of color tend to have trouble getting in good, as the saying goes, with their professors, they are likely to have as much or more trouble getting in good with their employers. And if, once hired, people who are not white face difficulties in finding mentors, powerful institutional figures to smooth their paths, then they will naturally advance more slowly. Oh, there will always be some black participants in the star system, not as tokens but as people who have, as I said, taken to heart the adage that they must be twice as good. (One need but think of Colin Powell or William Coleman.) Still, plenty of people of color who are merely as good as or slightly better than white people who are inside the star system will find themselves outside. The social turns do not work for them, and their advancement on the corporate ladder will be slow or nonexistent.

To be sure, the star system cannot get all of the blame for the dearth of people who are not white in (and, especially, at the top of) the professions. That there is present-day racism, overt and covert, might almost go without saying, except that so many people keep insisting there isn't any. But one should not assume too readily that contemporary discrimination explains all of the observed difference. Groups are complex and no two groups are the same. With cultural and other differences, it would be surprising if all group outcomes were identical. When the nation's odious history of racial oppression is grafted onto any other differences that might exist, the numbers are less surprising still. What would be surprising would be if we as a people had so successfully shrugged off the shackles of that history as to have reached, at this relatively early stage in the nation's evolution, economic and educational parity.

But the star system is not exactly blameless, either. Any system that rewards friendship and comfort rather than merit will burden most heavily those least likely to find the right friends.[7] It is ironic, even awkward, to make this point in an era when the attack on meritocracy is so sharply focused, but the claims pressed by today's critics in that attack—bigotry, unconscious bias, corrupt and malleable standards, social and cultural exclusion—are among the reasons that led other ethnic groups in the past to insist on the establishment of measurable systems for rewarding merit. The star system is a corrupt and biased means for circumventing the meritocratic ideal, but its corruption should not be attributed to the ideal itself.

V

None of this means that affirmative action is the right answer to the difficulties the star system has spawned. Among the group of intellectuals known loosely (and, I believe, often inaccurately) as black conservatives, there is a widely shared view that the removal of artificial barriers to entry into a labor market is the proper goal to be pursued by those who want to increase minority representation. The economist Walter Williams often cites the example of cities like New York that limit the number of individuals permitted to drive taxi-cabs. No wonder, he says, there are so few black cabdrivers: it's too difficult to get into the market. Consequently, says Williams, New York should abolish its limits and, subject only to some basic regulatory needs, open the field to anyone. This, he says, would automatically result in an increase in black drivers—assuming, that is, that there are black people who want to drive cabs.

Other strategies, too, are easy to defend. For example, it is difficult to quarrel with the idea that an employer concerned about diversity—whatever its needs and hiring standards—should be as certain as possible that any candidate search it conducts is designed to yield the names of people of color who fit the search profile. After centuries of exclusion by design, it would be a terrible tragedy were black and other minority professionals excluded through inadvertence. Mari Matsuda has argued that a serious intellectual ought to make an effort to read books by members of groups not a part of his or her familiar experience, and I think she is quite right.[8] It is in the process of that determined reading—that searching—that the people who have been overlooked will, if truly excellent, eventually come to light.

The example can be generalized. Searching is the only way to find outstanding people of color, which is why all professional employers should practice it. Although the cost of a search is not trivial, the potential return in diversity, without any concomitant lowering of standards, is enormous—provided always that the employer is careful to use the search only to turn up candidates, not as a means of bringing racial preferences into the hiring process through the back door. For it is easy, but demeaning, to conflate the goal of searching with the goal of hiring, and to imagine therefore that the reason for the search is to ensure that the optimal number of black people are hired. It isn't. The reason for the search is to find the blacks among the best, not the best among the blacks.

If this distinction is borne firmly in mind, then an obligation to search will of course provide no guarantee that the statistics will improve. But I am not sure that a guarantee is what we should be seeking. People of color do not need special treatment in order to advance in the professional world; we do not need to be considered the best blacks, competing only with one another for the black slots. On the contrary, our goal ought to be to prove that we can compete with anybody, to demonstrate that the so-called pool problem, the alleged dearth of qualified entry-level candidates who are not white, is at least partly a myth. So if we can gain for ourselves a fair and equal chance to show what we can do—what the affirmative action literature likes to call a level playing field—then it is something of an insult to our intellectual capacities to insist on more.

And of course, although we do not like to discuss it, the insistence on more carries with it certain risks. After all, an employer can hire a candidate because the employer thinks that person is the best one available or for some other reason: pleasing a powerful customer, rewarding an old friend, keeping peace in the family, keeping the work force all white, getting the best black. When the employer hires on one of these other grounds, it should come as no surprise if the employee does not perform as well as the best available candidate would have. There will be times when the performance will be every bit as good, but those will not be the norm unless the employer is a poor judge of talent; and if the employer consistently judges talent poorly, a second, shrewder judge of talent will eventually put the first employer out of business.[9] That is not, I think, a web in which we as a people should want to be entangled.

Racial preferences, in sum, are not the most constructive method for overcoming the barriers that keep people of color out of high-prestige positions. They are often implemented in ways that are insulting, and besides, they can carry considerable costs. Although there are fewer unfair and arbitrary barriers to the hiring and retention of black professionals than there once were, many barriers remain, and the star system, although some few of us benefit from it, is prominent among them. But if the barriers are the problem, then it is the barriers themselves that should be attacked. Should the star system be brushed aside, our opportunities would be considerably enhanced because many of the special advantages from which we are excluded would vanish.

Getting rid of the star system will not be easy. I have discovered through painful experience that many of its most earnest white defenders—as well as many of those who pay lip service to overturning it but meanwhile continue to exploit it—are also among the most ardent advocates of hiring black people who, if white, they would consider second-rate. They are saying, in effect, We have one corrupt system for helping out our friends, and we'll be happy to let you have one for getting the numbers right. Faced with such obduracy, small wonder that racial preferences seem an attractive alternative.

But people of color must resist the urge to join the race to the bottom. The stakes are too high. I am sensitive to Cornell University Professor Isaac Kramnick's comment that even if a school hires some black professors who are not first-rate, "it will take till eternity for the number of second-rate blacks in the university to match the number of second-rate whites."[10] Point taken: one can hardly claim that elite educational institutions have been perfect meritocracies. However, the claim that there are incompetent whites and therefore incompetent blacks should be given a chance is unlikely to resonate with many people's visions of justice. Because of the racial stereotyping that is rampant in our society, moreover, any inadequacies among second-rate white professionals are unlikely to be attributed by those with the power to do something about it to whites as a whole; with black professionals, matters are quite unfairly the other way around, which is why the hiring of second-rate black professionals in any field would be detrimental to the effort to break down barriers.

The corruption of the meritocratic ideal with bias and favoritism offers professionals who are not white an opportunity we should not ignore: the chance to teach the corrupters their own values by making our goal excellence rather than adequacy. Consider this perceptive advice to the black scholar from John Hope Franklin, one of the nation's preeminent historians: "He should know that by maintaining the highest standards of scholarship he not only becomes worthy but also sets an example that many of his contemporaries who claim to be the arbiters in the field do not themselves follow."[11] The need to beat down the star system should spur us not to demand more affirmative action but to exceed the achievements of those who manipulate the system to their advantage.

Besides, the star system does not taint every institution to an equal degree. Some hiring and promotion processes actually make sense. If we rush to graft systems of racial preference onto hiring processes rationally designed to produce the best doctors or lawyers or investment bankers or professors, we might all hope that the professionals hired because of the preferences turn out to be as good as those hired because they are expected to be the best, but no one should be surprised if this hope turns to ashes. Painful though this possibility may seem, it is consistent with a point that many supporters of affirmative action tend to miss, or at least to obscure: racial preferences that make no difference are unimportant.

Racial preferences are founded on the proposition that the achievements of their beneficiaries would be fewer if the preferences did not exist. Supporters of preferences cite a whole catalogue of explanations for the inability of people of color to get along without them: institutional racism, inferior education, overt prejudice, the lingering effects of slavery and oppression, cultural bias in the criteria for admission and employment. All of these arguments are most sincerely pressed, and some of them are true. But like the best black syndrome, they all entail the assumption that people of color cannot at present compete on the same playing field with people who are white. I don't believe this for an instant; and after all these years, I still wish the National Merit Scholarship people had given me the chance to prove it.

NOTES

1. See, for example, the account of the debate in Maryland in *Bond Buyer*, 31 July 1990, p. 32.

2. Ira Glasser, "Affirmative Action and the Legacy of Racial Injustice," in *Eliminating Racism: Profiles in Controversy*, ed. Phyllis A. Katz and Dalmas A. Taylor (New York: Plenum Press, 1988), pp. 341, 350.

3. Stanley Crouch, *Notes of a Hanging Judge* (New York: Oxford University Press, 1990).

4. The most recent General Social Survey, a regular report of the widely respected National Opinion Research Center, found that 53 percent of white respondents consider black people generally less intelligent than white people. ("Whites Retain Negative View of Minorities, a Survey Finds," *New York Times*, 10 January 1991, p. B10.) Prior surveys through the late 1960s had shown a decline in the percentage of white respondents who consider black people less intelligent. Historical polling results on the attitudes of white Americans about black Americans are collected in National Research Council, *A Common Destiny: Blacks and American Society* (Washington, D.C.: National Academy Press, 1989), pp. 120–23. For a more detailed discussion of data collected during the 1980s, see Lee Sigelman and Susan Welch, *Black Americans' Views of Racial Inequality* (Cambridge: Cambridge University Press, 1991), esp. pp. 85–100.

5. Quoted in Colin Lemster, "Black Executives: How They're Doing," *Fortune*, 18 January 1988, p. 109.

6. John Hope Franklin, "The Dilemma of the American Negro Scholar," in *Race and History: Selected Essays 1938–1988* (Baton Rouge: Louisiana State University Press, 1989), p. 295. The essay was originally published in 1963.

7. My description of the star system might usefully be compared to the French sociologist Pierre Bourdieu's analysis of the role of "cultural capital" and "social capital" in the maintenance of the class structure: Pierre Bourdieu, "Cultural Reproduction and Social Reproduction," in *Power and Ideology in Ed-*

ucation, ed. J. Karabel and A. H. Halsey (New York: Oxford University Press, 1977), p. 487. I am less sure than Bourdieu is that the system works principally to the benefit of the children of those already part of it; my concern with the star system is that it is exclusionary and at the same time a distortion of the meritocratic ideal.

8. Mari Matsuda, "Affirmative Action and Legal Knowledge: Planting Seeds in Plowed-up Ground," *Harvard Women's Law Journal* 11 (Spring 1988): 5–6.

9. Although it is sometimes said that racial discrimination serves the interests of capitalism, the inefficiency of prejudice in the market is well understood in economics. The classic analysis of the market costs of discrimination on the basis of race is Gary S. Becker, *The Economics of Discrimination* (Chicago: University of Chicago Press, 1957). Much of the analysis in Becker's book is mathematical and may be inaccessible to the lay reader. A recent and more accessible treatment of the same issue is Thomas Sowell, *Preferential Policies: An International Perspective* (New York: William Morrow, 1990), esp. pp. 20–40. For a discussion of the way that racial discrimination following the Civil War retarded the growth of the Southern economy, see Roger L. Ransom and Richard Sutch, *One Kind of Freedom: The Economic Consequences of Emancipation* (Cambridge: Cambridge University Press, 1977).

10. Quoted in Adam Begley, "Black Studies' New Era: Henry Louis Gates Jr.," *New York Times Magazine,* 1 April 1990, p. 24.

11. Franklin, "The Dilemma of the American Negro Scholar," p. 305.

Speculations

1. What fundamental argument does Stephen L. Carter make when he begins by saying "Affirmative action has been with me always. . . . I have had trouble escaping an assumption . . . that black people cannot compete intellectually with white people." How does this statement provide coherence and consistency for his entire argument?
2. What is the "best black syndrome"? Why does Carter find it so damaging for blacks?
3. Explain Carter's use of the analogy from Paul Klee, who said, "one must adapt oneself to the contents of the paintbox." How does this analogy apply to your own experience and how is that experience different from or similar to Carter's?
4. Carter describes two instances of mistaken identity—one when he was mistaken for not being "this Carter fellow who wrote that article" and a second in which the authority of his friend in financial services was not recognized. What point is Carter making? Do you believe these mistakes are typical? Why do you think people make such mistakes?
5. What is the "star system" Carter describes? How does it work and what is bad about it in his opinion? Do you agree? Explain your answer.

AFFIRMATIVE ACTION AND THE DILEMMA OF THE "QUALIFIED"

Ellis Cose

Born in 1951 in Chicago, Ellis Cose received his B.A. from University of Illinois at Chicago Circle (1972) and M. A. in Science, Technology, and Public Policy from George Washington University (1978). He began his journalism career as a columnist and reporter for the *Chicago Sun-Times* in 1970, where he worked for seven years before becoming a senior fellow and director of energy policy studies at the Joint Center for Political Studies in Washington D.C. (1977–1979) and a member of the advisory committee of the U.S. Department of Energy. Returning to his journalism career in 1979, Cose worked as an editorial writer for the *Detroit Free Press* and as a special writer for *USA Today*, and in 1983 he became president of the Institute for Journalism Education.

In addition to winning five outstanding awards for newswriting, Cose has published five books, including: *Energy and the Urban Crisis* (1973), *Energy and Equity: Some Social Concerns* (1979), *Decentralizing Energy Decisions: The Rebirth of Community Power* (1983), *Employment and Journalism* (1986), and *The Rage of the Privileged Class* (1994), which contains this selection on the problems associated with affirmative action. Cose's familiarity with the social dimensions, the emotional distortions, and the statistical arguments about who benefits and who gets hurt from affirmative action offer a spirited defense of this governmental program at a time when it is increasingly under fire.

When the talk turns to affirmative action, I often recall a conversation from years ago. A young white man, a Harvard student and the brother of a close friend, happened to be in Washington when the Supreme Court ruled on an affirmative action question. I have long since forgotten the question and the Court's decision, but I remember the young man's reaction.

He was not only troubled but choleric at the very notion that "unqualified minorities" would dare to demand preferential treatment. Why, he wanted to know, couldn't they compete like everyone else? Why should hardworking whites like himself be pushed aside for second-rate affirmative action hires? Why should he be discriminated against in order to accommodate *them*? His tirade went on for quite a while, and he became more indignant by the second as he conjured up one injustice after another.

When the young man paused to catch his breath, I took the occasion to observe that it seemed more than a bit hypocritical of him to rage on about preferential treatment. A person of modest intellect, he had gotten into Harvard largely on the basis of family connections. His first summer internship, with the White House, had been arranged by a family member. His second, with the World Bank, had been similarly arranged. Thanks to his nice internships and Harvard degree, he had been promised a coveted slot in a major company's executive training program. In short, he was already well on his way to a distinguished career—a career made possible by preferential treatment.

My words seemed not to register, and that did not surprise me. Clearly he had never thought of himself as a beneficiary of special treatment, and no doubt never will. Nor is it likely that either his colleagues or his superiors would be inclined to look down on him as an undeserving incompetent who got ahead on the basis of unfair advantage and was keeping better-qualified people out of work. Yet that assumption is routinely made about black beneficiaries of "affirmative action."

In February 1993, for instance, *Forbes* magazine published an article purporting to demonstrate "how affirmative action slows the economy." The authors referred approvingly to a 1984 poll that "found one in ten white males reporting they had lost a promotion because of quotas." They went on to argue that the poll "was quite possibly accurate. Indeed, it could be an underestimate."

It's impossible from the article to be certain just what poll *Forbes* is citing, but it appears to be a never-published telephone survey by Gordon S. Black Corporation for *USA Today* in which one-tenth of white males answered yes to a much broader question: "Have you yourself ever lost a job *opportunity* or educational *opportunity* at least *partially* as a result of policies and programs aimed at promoting equal opportunity for minorities?" (Emphasis mine.) That, of course, is a very different question from the one *Forbes* reported.

In 1993, *Newsweek* magazine commissioned a national poll that framed the question more narrowly. That poll, interestingly, found even more white males claiming to have been victimized by affirmative action. When asked, "Have you ever been a victim of discrimination or reverse discrimination in getting a promotion?" 15 percent of white males said that they had—the same percentage reporting such discrimination in "getting a job."

Let's assume for the sake of discussion that the *Forbes* figure is correct, and that ten percent of white males do indeed believe that some quota-driven minority person has snatched a position that would otherwise have gone to them. Let's further assume that the ratio holds across occupational categories, so that one out of ten white men in managerial and professional jobs (which, after all, is the group *Forbes* caters to) believes he was unfairly held back by a black or Hispanic colleague's promotion.

Blacks and Hispanics make up 10 percent of the total employees in such jobs, and white males make up 46 percent. So if one out of every ten white males has been held back by a black or Hispanic, that would mean that nearly half of those blacks and Hispanics received promotions they didn't deserve at the expense of white men. (If the *Newsweek* numbers are right, and if we assume that racial and ethnic minorities were the beneficiaries of the "reverse discrimination" suffered by whites, the percentage of minorities who have been unfairly promoted is even higher.) Yet if so many minorities are being promoted ahead of whites, why do black and Hispanic professionals, on average, earn less and hold lower positions than whites? It could be that despite their unfair advantage, minority professionals are so incompetent that whites still manage to get ahead of them on merit. Or it could be that white males who think minorities are zooming ahead of them are way off the mark. *Forbes*, for whatever reason, chose not to consider that possibility. Just as it chose not to consider that the alternative to a system based on "quotas" is not necessarily one based on merit. Or that affirmative action might conceivably result in some competent people getting jobs. Instead, the *Forbes* writers simply assumed such problematic possibilities away. Indeed, like many arguments against affirmative action, their article was not a reasoned analysis at all, but an example of pandering to the anger and anxieties of white males who believe they and their kind are being wronged. And the editors of *Forbes* have plenty of company.

In April 1991, for example, a white Georgetown University law student, Timothy Maguire, set off a tempest in Washington's scholarly and legal communities by questioning the academic quality of blacks admitted to the law school. In an article entitled "Admissions Apartheid," written for a student-controlled paper, Maguire charged that the black law students were in general not as qualified as the whites. The blacks, he said, had lower average scores on the Law School Admissions Tests and lower grade point averages—an allegation based on documents he perused, apparently surreptitiously, while working as a file clerk in the student records office.

The article polarized the campus. On one side were those who demanded that Maguire be expelled for unethical behavior in reading and publishing confidential information. They also raised questions about his mastery of statistics, pointing out that the "random sample" on which he based his conclusions was nothing of the sort, since the files he rifled were only a small selection and included the scores of many applicants who had not been admitted. On the other side were those who saw Maguire as a champion of free speech, a courageous young man who—at risk of public censure—had undertaken to disseminate information that deserved to be debated in a public arena. Maguire apparently saw himself as a victim of leftist ideologues, declaring at one point, according to the *Washington Post*, "It's painful not being politically correct."

In the midst of the ruckus, and after a leak focused attention on Maguire's own academic background, he admitted that his own LSAT scores were below the median for Georgetown students. Interestingly, in light of his charges, coverage of the controversy did not highlight the fact that Maguire got into Georgetown through a special screening program for "low testers," people who would not have been admitted on the basis of their scores but were in effect given extra credit for showing other evidence of promise, dedication, or commitment. In Maguire's case, the fact that he had been a Peace Corps volunteer in Africa weighed heavily in his favor. In short, he was every bit as much a beneficiary of special preference as the black students he scorned.

Shortly after it began, the uproar died down. And despite the protests of the black student organization and others, Maguire was permitted to graduate with his class. Though he was formally reprimanded for violating confidentiality, an agreement worked out by attorneys specifically barred the reprimand from becoming part of his official transcript. Maguire, in short, was allowed to resume a normal life and to put both the controversy and his need for special preference behind him.

Unlike the black students he assailed, who will find their careers haunted by the specter of affirmative action, and who will often be greeted by doubts about their competence whatever their real abilities, Maguire is not likely to suffer because he got into law school on grounds other than academic performance. In other words, he will never be seen as an affirmative action man but simply as a lawyer— entitled to all the recognition conferred by his prestigious degree and all the privileges granted to those presumed to be professionally "qualified."

Why should the presumption of competence differ for black and white graduates of the same school? One answer may be that blacks should be scrutinized more carefully because they are more likely to have met lower admission standards. While that is true in many cases, it is far from true that every black student admitted to a selective school is academically inferior (in any sense of the word) to every white student admitted. Nor is it true, as Maguire's case illustrates, that whites do not receive special treatment in academia. Just as Maguire benefited from a program for "low testers," others benefit from "diversity" policies in East Coast schools that favor residents of Wyoming over those of Connecticut, or from policies that favor relatives of alumni (or children of faculty members, donors, and other influential figures) over those with no family connections. Sometimes universities wish to attract mature students or veterans, or to nurture relationships with certain high schools by admitting their graduates.

One reason for such policies, as virtually any admissions officer will attest, is that prior academic performance is a far from perfect predictor of who will succeed in any specific school, much less who will succeed in life. And that rationale is apparently accepted even by many fervent opponents of affirmative action, since nonracial preferences never seem to elicit anything like the animosity provoked by so-called racial quotas. And even if we grant that many blacks who gain admission with the help of affirmative action are not objectively "qualified," precisely the same can be said about certain children of alumni or about the student who caught the admissions committee's eye because he spent a year on a mission of mercy in Malaysia.

Moreover, determining what it means to be "qualified" is not as easy as it is often made to seem. Ted Miller, who was associate dean of admissions at Georgetown Law at the time of the Maguire imbroglio, points out that many older white professors there—"if they were being honest"—would admit that they could not have met the standards exceeded by the school's typical black student today. As the number of applicants escalated during the 1940s, notes Miller, law schools turned to the LSAT as "an artificial means" to help them sift through applications. And as the numbers continued to increase, the minimum score needed to get into the more exclusive schools (the "qualified threshold") rose. Yet many of those who met the lower standards of the past nonetheless turned out to be distinguished lawyers. Obviously, they were not "unqualified," even if their test results would not win them admission to a prestigious law school today. By the same token, reasons Miller, as long as black students are capable of doing the work, who is to say they are "unqualified"?

Whatever one thinks of Miller's argument, it is unlikely that hostility to affirmative action programs would suddenly vanish if it could be established that "quota" recruits are in fact "qualified." If that were the only issue, programs favoring the children of alumni, say, would provoke the same animus directed at affirmative action. So the primary cause of the hostility must lie elsewhere. And the most logical place to look for it is in American attitudes about race.

In a country largely stuck in a state of denial, any such inquiry is fraught with peril. For one thing, and for any number of reasons, Americans have a devil of a time being honest (even with ourselves) when it comes to race. And because determining what our basic attitudes are is so difficult, agreeing on what those attitudes mean may well be impossible.

Not to put too fine a point on it, some people lie—almost reflexively under certain circumstances—about their attitudes regarding race, as public opinion experts have long known. Moreover, the phrasing of the question and the race of the interviewer can make a huge difference in what people say.

In 1989, for instance, pollsters for ABC News and the *Washington Post* asked a random sample of whites, "Do you happen to have a close friend who is black?" When the question was asked by a black, 67 percent of respondents answered yes. When a white asked, the percentage dropped to 57. Conversely, 67 percent of blacks told a black caller they had a close friend who was white, while 79 percent gave the same answer to a white interviewer.

On the question of whether the problems faced by blacks were "brought on by blacks themselves," the variation in responses was even greater. When interviewed by whites, 62 percent of whites said yes. When the same question was asked by blacks, the number dropped to 46 percent. Similarly, when whites were asked by blacks whether it was "very important" for children to attend racially mixed schools, 39 percent said yes, compared to 29 percent who thought so when asked by whites. In all, ABC/*Washington Post* pollsters found that answers varied significantly on more than half of the thirty-three race-related questions in the survey, depending on the race of the interviewer. The disparity might well have been greater if the interviewees could have been absolutely certain of the race of the person on the other end of the telephone line.

Even when the race of the interviewer is not an issue, when people know (or assume) they are talking to someone of their own racial stock, honesty is hardly assured—certainly not in morally charged areas, and especially not when people sense that what they feel is "politically incorrect." Hence, any poll on race must be taken with more than a few grains of salt. When pollsters ask, in one way or another, "Are you a racist?" people know what they are supposed to say. As a consequence, polling has proven to be problematic in political campaigns that pit black and white candidates against each other, because a gap exists between those who say they will vote for a candidate of another race and those who actually will in the privacy of the voting booth. There is no real reason to believe that polls measuring racial attitudes in general are any more accurate. The presumption, instead, should be that they understate the dimensions of racial bias and disharmony. If that presumption is true, the statistics reported below are all the more stunning for what they reveal about the pervasiveness and perdurability of racial stereotypes.

In 1990, 62 percent of whites across America told pollsters for the University of Chicago's National Opinion Research Center (NORC) that they believed blacks were lazier than whites. Fifty-one percent thought blacks likely to be less patriotic. Fifty-three percent said blacks were less intelligent. On every relevant measure of merit or virtue, blacks were judged inferior to whites. What the survey means, in short—despite a widespread belief to the contrary—is that America remains a color-struck society; and there is an abundance of data corroborating that finding.

Two less ambitious polls patterned in part on the National Opinion Research Center's study—in Wisconsin and Los Angeles—yielded results that were strikingly similar. New Yorkers polled in 1992 for the American Jewish Committee rated blacks less intelligent and lazier than the Irish and Italians. Another survey, of 185 employers in the Chicago area, found that those responsible for hiring tended to associate blacks—at least blacks in the central city—with crime, illiteracy, drug use, and a poor work ethic. Many employers had developed strategies (such as recruiting in suburbs and predominantly white schools and advertising in neighborhood and ethnic publications) that allowed them to avoid large numbers of black job applicants. The study, conducted by University of Chicago sociologists Kathryn Neckerman and Joleen Kirschenman, did not focus specifically on firms hiring for professional or executive positions, so its relevance to highly educated blacks is a matter of conjecture; but other research by the same scholars has found that many employers generalize stereotypes of the black underclass to all black applicants.

Not surprisingly, people who see blacks as lazier than whites tend to be among those most strongly opposed to affirmative action. To Tom Smith, director of NORC's general social survey, the reason is obvious: "Negative images lead people to conclude these groups don't deserve this special help." Indeed, it's fairly easy to understand why anyone might have a hard time with the idea that lazy, unintelligent, violence-prone people (whom Americans believe to be disproportionately black and Hispanic) deserve any special consideration at all.

Imagine, for a moment, a society in which there are no different races or ethnic groups, in which everyone sounds and looks essentially the same in terms of color, hair texture, etc. But at birth everyone is branded on the forehead with one of two large letters: either U or W, depending on the letters on their parents' heads. In the case of children of mixed parentage, the child is branded with a U—though a smaller U than children of pure lineage. And if in time that child marries someone wearing the W brand, the mark on their offspring will be smaller yet.

Now imagine that though the two groups are officially equal, a gigantic propaganda campaign is mounted, with the full (if unacknowledged) assistance of the government, to convince everyone that "Unworths" (those with the U brand) are congenitally stupid, lazy, ugly, and unpatriotic, that they make poor neighbors and worse leaders, that in just about every way they are inferior to the "Worths."

Assume that more than 60 percent of the population (including a majority of the Unworths themselves) swallows at least part of the propaganda, so that whenever an Unworth walks into a classroom or office, or tries to buy a home, he or she confronts someone who believes Unworths to be—well, unworthy. Now assume that after an outbreak of violent protests, society decides to eliminate discrimination against Unworths.

The republic passes laws not only guaranteeing access to its institutions but in many cases encouraging preferential treatment of the Unworths. The people who believe in the stereotypes created by the propaganda (in other words, the majority of the population) develop ingenious ways to get around the laws. And they feel virtuous in doing so because they consider any law awarding special privileges to the Unworths patently unfair. Many Unworths, fully accepting the stereotypes of inferiority, shrink from competing with Worths in intellectual or business pursuits. And those Unworths who do manage to get prestigious positions find their right to keep them constantly questioned, and discover that although the number of successful Unworths is very small, the Worths still think there are too many.

Some Unworths become so frustrated by the constant doubting of their competence that they blame the special privileges for their plight—and the Worths strongly encourage them to do so. Indeed, the Worths lavishly praise and promote the books of Unworths who advance such a premise; they put them up for tenured professorships and maybe even name one of them to a special Unworth seat on the highest court of the land. From the perspective of the Worths of the world, given the well-known attributes of Unworths, it is much better to require that individual Unworths prove themselves worthy than to continue to reward so many lazy, unintelligent, and generally unmeritorious people with jobs that belong to the more deserving. And what better allies for the Worths in such an enterprise than articulate Unworths who help make the case.

Now imagine a different scenario. Envision another society where children are branded at birth. But in this society there is only one brand, and it only goes to a very select group: the letter B is impressed on the heads of all children who pass a special test. The test is rather mysterious. No one quite knows how it works, but anyone who passes it is certified to be among the best and the brightest in our imaginary world. Let's assume further that the test was cobbled together by a brilliant prankster who died before he could let the world in on his joke, and that it really doesn't measure anything, that the scores it generates are in fact random. Nonetheless, society accepts the test as perfect, and whoever achieves the requisite score gets to wear the B for life.

Since B-kids are special, society develops them with the utmost care. They are sent to special schools and receive advance placement in the nation's top universities. Even if they prove to be incompetent students, they continue as objects of veneration. Their academic inadequacies are made into virtues. Clearly their true potential cannot be unlocked in the dry and irrelevant world of books but only in the real world of important affairs. Upon completion of schooling, they are assured countless job offers, many leading directly to the top of the corporate pyramid. Indeed, they find it easy to rise to the top of virtually any field they enter, for everywhere they go they are recognized as the best. And everyone takes that as proof of the meritocracy at work.

Whenever B's walk into a building or a store, they are treated with the greatest respect. Whenever they say something stupid, it is assumed that they were misunderstood, or perhaps were using a vernacular only comprehensible to the elite. And whenever they make decisions with catastrophic results, they are shielded from the consequences—in some cases with multimillion dollar settlements. For everyone understands, that whatever mistakes may have been made, these are extremely deserving individuals.

Their entire lives, in short, are played out as a series of special privileges. And they wear the B as a badge of pride. Very few people resent them. Instead, ordinary folks are delighted to travel in their circles. Even if the high court were to rule that no special treatment be given them, people would defer to them anyway. After all, as everyone can see, they deserve it. They are B's.

The point here is obvious. One cannot honestly and intelligently discuss hostility to preferential treatment without examining attitudes toward those who benefit from the treatment. Well before affirmative action came along, a substantial number of people considered blacks deficient—morally, aesthetically, and (especially) intellectually. And if survey findings are any indication, that continues to be the case. It does not mean that *nothing* has changed or that race relations have not improved. It does mean that things have not changed quite as much as many people like to think—and that even in the 1990s, even in the most enlightened of places, black people regularly encounter attitudes that make even the most thick-skinned cringe.

A black woman who had recently graduated from Harvard Law School, for instance, told me she had found her educational experience unsettling, largely because she had not anticipated that she would be treated so differently from whites. She noticed in class that blacks tended to be called on less, but every so often a professor would begin calling on one black student after another—as if the professor had suddenly realized that he was neglecting an important segment of the student body and had resolved to make amends. Whether blacks were called on repeatedly or not at all, she concluded, they were never treated like whites.

A one point, she recalls, a fellow black student went to argue with a professor about a grade. The young man had received a B minus and thought he deserved something better. Instead of arguing the merits of the case or telling the student how to improve his work, the professor assured him that there was absolutely nothing wrong with a B minus. "He would not tell that to a white person," the woman said, "but they would tell a black man that a B minus was a good grade. That he should be satisfied."

Such encounters convinced her that professors expected a very different level of work from blacks, that in general they felt that blacks "just don't have the intellectual horsepower." It was "very rare for a black person to be taken seriously as an intellectual," she said. "It was never like the normal thing." The observation bothered her, for she had not expected to leave Harvard thinking that. But while her inclination was to assume "that race is not the explanation for everything," she had seen enough to persuade her that even at Harvard it explained more than she had supposed.

One could argue that the woman's experience is a perfect example of why affirmative action is ill-advised; that were it not for an "inclusive" admissions policy, certain black females would not be at Harvard Law School and therefore would run a substantially smaller risk of being exposed to people (at least to *Harvard* people) who questioned their "intellectual horsepower." Though the woman's complaint may indeed illuminate a serious problem with affirmative action, that does not dispose of the question of underlying attitudes—and what effect they may have on any policy designed to integrate blacks into institutions historically predisposed to doubt their basic abilities.

Ella Bell, of MIT's Sloan School of Management, is among those who defend affirmative action, but she understands why others of her background might not. "I think it's very difficult once we have achieved, and we have good educations, and we know we're good, we know we have the skills, and we run up against this brick wall. . . . We've got to have a way to rationalize that brick wall. And one of the ways I think that we have begun to rationalize [it] is to say, 'Well, this is because I came in under affirmative action. If I had come in just like John Doe, I would not be running into this brick wall. The only reason they can't see my talent and my skill and all the things that I bring . . . is because I came in under affirmative action.' . . . What we forget in this dialogue is the whole issue of white racism. And it's very hard to call people on that, because nobody wants to think they're prejudiced. They reject it. They reject it instantly. So we wind up doing this whole rationalization thing, where we're winding up talking about dismantling affirmative action. . . . But affirmative action is a bridge to get us over racist attitudes. . . . It's a necessary mechanism. And it's not about past days . . . from history. This is everyday reality."

"Nobody wants to be perceived as being a victim of racism, or prejudice. It hurts. It hurts deeply," adds Bell, but she does not think that eliminating affirmative action would ease the pain. "No matter what I do, I will still be perceived as a token until you bring in a significant number [of blacks]."

Sharon Collins, the sociologist from the University of Illinois, notes that very few blacks moved into upper management even when affirmative action was in full flower. If that is how blacks fare in a "very supportive environment," she asks, why would anyone presume they would do better if that support were taken away?

One answer, of course, is that it's difficult to conceive of blacks doing much worse under *any* system, that even in the era when affirmative action enjoyed its broadest support, it carried a heavy stigma—one that so undermined the credibility of African-American managers that it virtually guaranteed the results we see today, where less than 1 percent of senior executives at Fortune 500 firms are black.

Without question, many who were hired to fill "minority" slots were never viewed in the same light as other managers. Ulric Haynes, who ran a management recruiting firm in the 1960s (initially specializing in placing minority executives), says the work often left him exasperated. "The most threatening thing that I could do in my minority search activities," he recalls, "was to present a candidate whose qualifications were better than those of the person responsible for recruiting him. They couldn't handle it. . . . If I would present three candidates . . . the predominantly white corporation would invariably select the weakest of the three, not the strongest. . . . They certainly didn't want anybody whose academic preparation was as good as theirs, who spoke English as well as they did, who dressed as well as they did, who moved with grace and ease in their world. . . . They wanted somebody who, by and large, they could sort of feel a little bit sorry for, who would be so happy to have the position that he was entering into [that he] would not cause them any problems in terms of professional advancement."

Not that any client ever said as much to Haynes; he doesn't even think they were cognizant of what they were doing. "This was an unwritten practice. . . . It was so unconscious they weren't even aware of it. But they felt more comfortable with the least qualified than they did with the most qualified." Haynes had not expected to encounter such attitudes, which made the work "discouraging" despite his initial enthusiasm for placing blacks in corporate management.

Only if you assume that (even at some unconscious level) Haynes's corporate clients never expected blacks to shoulder the same responsibilities as white executives does the behavior he describes make sense. For if blacks were not being hired to perform a "white man's job," they would not need a white executive's skills. In fact, possessing such skills (or even obvious competence and excellent credentials) could be a distinct disadvantage—not only because accomplished and confident blacks might demand more power, money, and rank than they could realistically expect, but because it would be much easier to rationalize maintaining the status quo if blacks selected for management were by some set of standards clearly inferior. I cannot vouch for the accuracy of Haynes's recollections; but it's certainly possible that in the 1960s, when black executives were being hired almost exclusively (in truth, if not in title) for "black" jobs, employers gravitated toward those without the savvy, standing, or inclination to advance or rock the boat.

Such strange behavior can be seen less as the fault of white employers than as the natural result of attitudes that place more emphasis on getting minorities into visible jobs than on making the best use of all available talent. In that light, such practices become a powerful argument against any kind of racial preference—especially in the 1990s, when companies can no longer afford to keep people just for show. If affirmative action creates so many problems—even for those it was designed to benefit—could a society that eschewed it conceivably do any worse?

Stephen Carter, author of *Reflections of an Affirmative Action Baby*, argues that people of color might be much better served by the free market than by any explicit scheme of racial preferences. "Left to itself, the market isn't racist at all," he writes, "and if highly qualified minority scholars or lawyers or doctors are a more valuable commodity than white ones, a free market will naturally bid up their price. That is what markets do (at least in the absence of regulation) when valuable commodities are in short supply; outstanding professionals who are members of desirable minority groups are expensive for the same reason that gold or diamonds are expensive. And that is evidently the result that the market currently produces, at least at the top end."

How is one to square Carter's view with Haynes's lament that the top ranks of Fortune 500 companies remain all but closed to African Americans, and that even large companies not on the Fortune 500 list have locked the CEO's office to blacks (except a conspicuous few, such as the late Reginald Lewis, who bought TLC Beatrice International Holdings in 1987, and Richard Parsons, who was named chief executive officer of Dime Savings Bank in 1990). "Certainly, given the fact that the first wave of minority group executives entered Fortune 500 companies in the late 1960s, certainly by now one would have made it, at least to be one of the top three executives in a Fortune 500 company," says Haynes. "I can't think of anyone who's made it to the top. By the law of averages, one of us, even if we didn't stay there, should have gotten to be chief financial officer."

One reason Haynes and Carter disagree is that they are looking at different markets. The market for law partners or university faculty members is considerably larger than the market for Fortune 500 CEOs. To put it another way, a law firm with one hundred partners or a university with two hundred faculty slots might easily see how they could profit by naming blacks to a few of those posts. A firm with only one CEO, however, is likely to view things differently. In my profession, there is considerable evidence of Carter's market theory in action. It is generally accepted among newspaper executives that a big-city daily needs at least some minority journalists in order to do an adequate job. As a result, the bidding for black, Hispanic, and Asian reporters considered topnotch can sometimes get furious. A few years ago, Ben Bradlee, then editor of the *Washington Post,* became so annoyed that the *New York Times* was trying to recruit his best black reporters that he wrote a note to the *Times* editor volunteering to send him a list of them. Despite the intense competition for black reporters, however, the top tier of newspaper management remains overwhelmingly white. None of the nation's biggest and most prestigious papers (or the three major news magazines) has installed an African American as its principal editor.

There are reasons for the scarcity of blacks at the top, some having to do with race and some not, but anyone who sees newspapers and other large organizations as nothing more than economic units in a gigantic market is bound to miss many of them. Newspapers in the real world are not elegant abstractions full of people with perfect knowledge and perfect access, driven purely by a desire to maximize profit. They are much more (for lack of a better word) *human* than that.

Even economists these days don't hew to the view that the "market" always knows what is best. Economist Herbert Stein, for instance, tells the story of two men, one an economist and one not, who were out for a stroll when the noneconomist stopped dead in his tracks and exclaimed, "Look, there's a $20 bill lying on the sidewalk!" The economist responded, "No, there can't be. If there had been, it would already have been picked up."

People don't always know where the money lies in life, and as a result they don't always make decisions that maximize their wealth, even if that is their intention. And often that is *not* their intention. Human beings, after all, are not bloodless calculators. They often act in romantic, altruistic, or merely mysterious ways. The same sort of emotional attachment that can lead a father to try to fulfill his dreams through his son, or a mother to sacrifice everything, including life itself, for the welfare of her family, operate—though generally in much milder ways— in the work environment, which is as much a social organization as an economic one. So decisions get made, and people get accepted (and rapidly promoted), for reasons that have nothing to do in a direct way with profit maximization. Perhaps a corporate officer sees a younger version of himself in the appearance and style of a certain young man. Or maybe a subordinate shares a passion for an exotic sport, or for a particular kind of after-hours entertainment. And even for competent people, especially blacks, such social bonding can present a problem. As Edward Jones observes: "The kinds of social relationships, the kinds of acceptance by others [needed to advance], are not within your control. You can't make somebody love you or root for you."

Moreover, however much corporate mandarins like to think of themselves as risk-seeking entrepreneurs, most senior executives of established firms avoid risk whenever they can—not only looking out for their own economic welfare by negotiating compensation packages that never go down, regardless of their performance, but by rejecting any personnel move that seems a radical departure from the norm. And in many conservative corporate cultures, moving a black person into a sensitive job would be seen as an unacceptable risk, irrespective of that person's abilities. As [a] *New York Times* executive insinuated in explaining his hesitation to promote a certain black man, the very fact that a black had never previously held the post constituted part of the argument as to why one should not. Only after the "first black" managed to succeed would that particular barrier be removed.

The hesitation to move blacks along may have nothing to do with personal prejudice, but with a perception that putting a black person in a visible slot might have economic consequences—a perception that makes sense if one assumes (whatever the reality) that some segments of the market or some players who influence the market might be disturbed to see a black person in a job where only whites are normally seen. In assessing the comfort level of whites with very visible blacks, most executives have only assumptions to guide them, and those assumptions tend to be conservative, often to the point of rigidity. Until very recently, for instance, one big-city paper had an explicit policy against running more than one minority op-ed columnist a day, regardless of the columns' subject matter, perspectives, or quality. The assumption apparently was that while whites were comfortable with one nonwhite pictured in the commentary section of the newspaper, they would not be comfortable with more. So the editor had taken it upon himself to protect his readers from encountering too many minority writers.

Even if there were no explicit racial criteria at work, the market model would have obvious limits. Assuming that a market existed for "good people" and that it was to the economic advantage of the firm to make sure that such people were allowed, relative to others in the organization, to go as far as their abilities could take them, how would the organization recognize the best talent? To many, the answer seems obvious. That is exactly what they assume corporations are already doing. Isn't it self-evident that simply out of economic self-interest, a firm would do everything within its power to ensure that the best people were in the most appropriate jobs? Yet, . . . many people (perhaps most) end up in jobs for reasons that seem to have little to do with merit. Edward Irons and Gilbert Moore, in their research on black bankers, were surprised to find that "virtually 100 percent of the interviewees indicated that the most important criterion for promotion was 'who you know,' or 'being plugged into the political system.'" Technical competence, in their eyes, counted for little.

Perhaps we can dismiss the bankers interviewed by Irons and Moore as extremists of some sort, but it's much more difficult to dismiss the mountain of academic studies, personal narratives, and anecdotal evidence that reveals the workplace as a social institution run largely on the basis of favoritism, stereotypes, and unexamined (often incorrect) suppositions. While affirmative action may have aggravated the problem, for all we know it has not. It may just be that *that is the way the workplace works*—or at least the way it has worked so far.

Hence, one is not quite sure what to make of Stephen Carter's declaration of war on racial preferences, or of the fact that he apparently expects an army of black professionals to join his crusade. The time will come, he speculates, when "we, the professionals who are people of color, decide to say that we have had enough—enough of stereotyping, enough of different standards, enough of the best-black syndrome." But Carter's stirring rhetoric obscures an important question. If in fact affirmative action does not account for all the problems he so eloquently pinpoints, then what, upon reflection, should be the response? If stereotyping, double standards, and professional ceilings exist quite independently of formal racial preference programs, how eager should we be to join the movement to abolish affirmative action? And if we assume that people in general, and employers in particular, tend to be marginally competent in assessing merit and potential irrespective of race, what are we to think of Carter's desire "to show the world that we who are black are not so marked by our history of racist oppression that we are incapable of intellectual achievement on the same terms as anybody else."

The problem he addresses is a real one. Yet the presumption of lesser competence is a cross borne not only by blacks who were "affirmative action hires," but at one time or another by many blacks who were not; by most blacks, in fact, who have ever found themselves working for a major American institution. That presumption is difficult, if not impossible, to overcome, which raises the obvious question of exactly what proof it would take to "show the world" that blacks are capable of real intellectual achievement.

I suspect that those inclined to believe in the possibility of genuine black achievement will accept that proposition even in the absence of absolute proof; or will note that blacks throughout history have already accomplished so much that yet another demonstration is unnecessary; or will point out that blacks, as Americans, deserve to be treated as individuals and equals without having to prove their worth first. On the other hand, those not inclined to believe that blacks are capable of any real intellectual achievement will reject "proof" of it with one of several responses. They may praise the black person who finally "shows" them as an "exception," and therefore not really black. Or they may claim that whatever feat of genius a black person performs, it is a simple intellectual parlor trick that demonstrates nothing at all. Or they may accept the proffered proof but then demand that blacks pass yet another test, that black professionals, for instance, make the black crime rate equal the white crime rate before they presume the right to be treated as equals. Common sense, in short, dictates that there is no such thing as proving such a proposition to a world unwilling to believe it, and no need to prove it to a world disposed to accept it.

To expect that abolishing affirmative action would make black intellectual capability easier to prove strikes me as more than a little naïve. Just as to argue, as Carter does, that "affirmative action has done nothing at all for the true victims of racism" strikes me as myopic. Putting aside the question of whether affirmative action has truly benefited most members of any class, who exactly are these "true victims of racism"? Presumably, in Carter's mind, they are the poor souls who populate the underclass. Yet if you believe the volumes of evidence that show racial problems and racial stereotypes percolating through every level of American society, you could argue that just about every American, whatever his or her race, is a true victim of racism.

For all my problems with Carter's analysis, I believe he has a compelling point: that affirmative action or racial preference programs will never bring blacks into parity with whites. And I'm sure that others who might disagree with much of what he says would not disagree with him on that. Roosevelt Thomas, founder of the American Institute for Managing Diversity, comes to a similar conclusion about affirmative action from a different set of premises. "Sooner or later, affirmative action will die a natural death. Its achievements have been stupendous, but if we look at the premises that underlie it, we find assumptions and priorities that look increasingly shopworn," he wrote in 1990 in the *Harvard Business Review*.

I will return to Thomas later. Suffice it to say here that like many black professionals, I find myself profoundly ambivalent on the question of affirmative action. I don't believe that it works very well, nor that it can be made to satisfy much of anyone. Moreover, I believe that programs based on racial preferences are inherently riddled with the taint and the reality of unfairness. I don't, however, believe that such programs belong on any list of the most odious things to have befallen America. And I certainly don't believe—despite the anguished cries of untold numbers of white men—that such programs have had much to do with the inability of any but a handful of whites to get hired or promoted. I believe, rather, that affirmative action has been made the scapegoat for a host of problems that many Americans simply don't wish to face up to; and that while a huge and largely phony public debate has raged over whether affirmative action is good or bad, the reality is much more nuanced and complex. In recent days, that debate has sometimes pitted so-called black conservatives against so-called black liberals. Yet I doubt that if pressed to the wall, the two sides would find themselves in much disagreement—at least over the essential bankruptcy of affirmative action as a policy to foster workplace equality. Where their more fundamental disagreement lies is in their assessment of the virtues of whites. Would whites treat everyone more equally if affirmative action wasn't gumming up the works? Without the millstone of affirmative action, would corporations and other large organizations be more capable of judging people on performance, potential, and merit rather than on preconceptions and office politics? Would acceptance as full members of the American family come easier if the prod were taken away? One side, in effect, says yes, and the other says no.

These are not questions of fact, for the future, by definition, is unknown. They are essentially questions of faith—of whether one believes in the ability and willingness of those whites who still control the majority of important institutions in America to do what they have not done thus far: ensure that no group is systematically penalized as a consequence of color.

In March 1961, when John F. Kennedy signed Executive Order 10925, which created the President's Committee on Equal Employment Opportunity and brought the phrase affirmative action into common usage, he apparently had little more than that in mind: "The contractor will not discriminate against any employee or applicant for employment because of race, creed, color or national origin . . . [and] will take affirmative action to ensure that applicants are employed, and that employees are treated during employment, without regard to their race, creed, color, or national origin." The difficulty companies had in carrying out that simple injunction is a story much too tangled and complicated even to begin to detail here; but the fact that they in large measure did not carry it out explains both why we are still debating affirmative action more than three decades later and why so many blacks are reluctant to take a leap of faith.

Imagine a brown, unpopular child who wants more than anything to be a runner. His classmates refuse to let him run with them, or even to practice on *their* track. When he dares to go near it, they taunt him, and then they push him away. A kindly official, noticing the harassment, decides to give the boy a break. He declares that even if the other children will not let the brown kid practice with them, they must let him run in every scheduled public race. Moreover, since the boy is at a disadvantage because he has not been allowed to practice with them, the official orders all the other boys to give him a five-yard head start.

As the first race approaches, the boy is both apprehensive and elated. He is unsure of his own abilities but delighted that he will finally have a chance to show all the other kids what he can do, and he is comforted by the thought that once he does they will finally accept him as a peer. On the day of the race, however, an unexpected thing happens. Even before he starts to run, the crowd pelts him with garbage and stones. When the race begins, he stumbles and the other kids catch up with him. Some pass him with looks of concern and sympathy, others pass with looks of scorn, and a few even elbow him or kick him as they scamper on their way.

The experience repeats itself race after race; and as the child struggles to understand why he is being treated so, he learns that the people in the crowd suffer from a strange affliction, that though they can see him well enough to abuse him, no one up there can really see what he is going through. Those in the stands can see, at most, a fraction of the objects that fly his way; and those who are hurling them can't understand their force. He learns that many of the onlookers pity him, that some refuse to throw stones and even whisper words of encouragement, but that most deeply resent the fact that the other kids had to let him into the race, and that they resent his five-yard head start even more.

Though the official has given a very public and heartfelt explanation for the special treatment, loudmouths in the bleachers focus increasingly on the unfairness of the brown kid's head start. Why is it necessary? If he must run, why can't he start with the other kids? Could he be genetically inferior? If so, why is he running at all? And why in the blazes can't he ever win even with a head start? Could he have a psychological problem? Is he lazy? Is he stupid? Is something in his culture keeping him from keeping up?

Soon the questions have reached such a pitch that the mere sight of the kid on the track is enough to whip the crowd into a frenzy. The child, as he comes to understand the anger of the mob, realizes that even with a five-yard head start, he will never win. And he doesn't know whether he should ask for a bigger lead, give up the one he has, or simply abandon the race.

Speculations

1. What connection is there between Cose's opening description of his young, white, male friend at Harvard and his description of the responses given by most white male respondents to the *Forbes* and *Newsweek* polls? How does Cose use statistics to respond to the polls and what is his argument about them?
2. Do you agree with those who sided with Timothy Maguire or those who criticized him? Why? Support your responses.

3. What facts and examples does Cose use to support his claim that some Americans consistently lie about their racial attitudes? How would you account for these facts?

4. What does Cose mean when he says, "America remains a color-struck society" and how does his allegory of the "Unworths" and the "Worths" account for this claim? Are you persuaded by his account? Explain your response.

5. Describe the difference between the positions represented by Eric Haynes and Stephen Carter concerning minority hiring and affirmative action. How does Cose explain the differences in their positions?

6. Cose eventually confesses that, "I find myself profoundly ambivalent on the question of affirmative action." Explain his ambivalence and the reasons he gives for it. Do you share his ambivalence or do you have a stronger opinion on one side or the other? Explain your response.

RACE AND REPARATIONS

Myron Magnet

Born in 1944 in Springfield, Massachusetts, Myron Magnet earned undergraduate degrees from Columbia and Cambridge Universities and a Ph.D. from Columbia University (1977). A contributor to popular magazines, he began writing for *Fortune* in 1980 and is now on that magazine's editorial board. Currently living in New York City with his wife and two children, Magnet is a senior fellow at the Manhattan Institute for Policy Research and the author of *Dickens and the Social Order* (1985) and *The Dream and the Nightmare: The Sixties Legacy to the Underclass* (1993), from which the following selection has been taken.

Magnet believes something terrible has gone wrong in American society during the past thirty years. As the introduction to *The Dream and the Nightmare* explains, the wealthy are implicated in the suffering of the poor: "This book's central argument is that the Haves are implicated because over the last thirty years they radically remade American culture, turning it inside out and upside down to accomplish a cultural revolution whose most mangled victims turned out to be the Have-Nots." Closely examining social programs created by well-intentioned people for honorable reasons, he asserts that "the War on Poverty, welfare benefits, court-ordered school busing, more public housing projects, affirmative action, [and] job-training programs" have become ultimately destructive attempts to engineer a more "equal" society. According to Magnet, these programs have instead produced more poverty, more dependency, and more inequality.

Extending his critique to include virtually all Americans, Magnet writes in his last chapter: "Even though the children of the sixties have left cultural mayhem behind them, they can seem generous-minded and life-affirming by comparison with the self-interested opportunism that characterizes so many young people of this age" (p. 220). Greatly concerned about the future of American society and desiring a renewed emphasis on hard work, morality, individual responsibility, and an end to ill-considered government hand-outs, Magnet argues that economic success is now possible for all Americans—irrespective of race—and that we need to rethink current forms of welfare, reparation, and economic assistance.

Poverty and race are inseparable issues in America. To talk about the poor is often to talk in code, with poor blacks on one's mind if not on one's lips. Concern about the "victimized" poor, especially, repeatedly turns out to be a proxy for anxiety, and guilt, over racial injustice.

The numbers partly explain why. Nearly one out of every three poor Americans is black; nearly one black in three is poor. Of the long-term American poor, blacks account for a disproportionate 65 to 90 percent, depending on age. The poorer and younger the long-term poor, the higher the percentage of blacks.

Behind the numbers lies a yet more telling history. If uneasiness about the poor is implicitly concern about the black poor, then the Haves' worry that the poor are victims is not baseless. Two centuries of slavery and another of discrimination and segregation did indeed produce victims on a world-historical scale. Today's black poverty is the most visible reminder of a history filled with equal measures of pain and shame on the subject of race.

Little wonder if, in the aftermath, the issues of poverty, racism, and victimization have become inextricably jumbled together. And the civil rights movement collapsed them together even further. It brought to many of the Haves their starkest glance into poverty, disclosing to them that the black poor were the heart of America's poverty problem. At least since 1963, when a quarter of a million blacks marched on Washington to protest poverty along with racial discrimination, poverty has explicitly been a civil rights issue rather than a purely economic one.

But the confusion of racial and economic matters in the idea of the victimized poor has created a tangle of further confusions. Yes, injustice and victimization long kept blacks poor, but the injustice was racism, not some recondite economic inequity such as Michael Harrington or Kevin Phillips describe. Blacks are not Marx's "industrial reserve army," barred from regular employment by the very structure of capitalism, as white radicals and (more recently) black civil rights leaders have imagined. To escape victimization, poor blacks didn't need a vast remaking of the economic order. They needed something large but more specific: an end to the pervasive racial discrimination that limited economic opportunity, along with so many other opportunities to share in the full resources of American society.

The crucial barriers have fallen. They fell years ago, giving way before the force of the civil rights movement and the 1964 Civil Rights Act, as thinkers as politically disparate as Thomas Sowell, Shelby Steele, and William Julius Wilson have argued. Not by any means has racism been expunged from the fabric of American life—and possibly the increasingly rancorous tone of racial politics has pushed that goal further off into the future. But institutionalized racism has dramatically abated.

Only think that in the forties, two-thirds of whites told pollsters that they believed in school segregation, and the majority of whites thought blacks inferior. By contrast, by the start of the eighties, four out of five whites believed blacks to be fully their equals, and by 1990, 95 percent of whites backed school desegregation. White attitudes on social mixing had grown, and were continuing to grow, correspondingly more accepting, and white acceptance of intermarriage, 4 percent in 1958, had risen to 40 percent by the mid-eighties. In 1958, 38 percent of Americans told pollsters they'd vote for a black for president; 84 percent said they would in 1990.

Attitudes about economic equality improved most dramatically of all. It's a huge shift from the majority white view in the forties that whites should get job preference to the 1972 poll data showing that almost all whites support equality of economic opportunity for blacks. All this has meant that for years blacks have not been barred from the economic mainstream. What other conclusion can be drawn from the proliferation of the black middle class in the last quarter century? Though doors still remain to be unlocked, as a general principle opportunity is open for whoever wishes to seek it.

But the idea of the victimized poor didn't allow the Haves to rest content with overturning the barriers of institutionalized discrimination. In the grip of that notion, many Haves tacitly assumed that oppression and exclusion had damaged blacks enough so that some were defective, like Harrington's sharecroppers adrift in the bewildering city. Mere equality wasn't justice enough for such victims; it wasn't adequate to solve their problem.

For such violation they deserved reparations, a view still powerfully held. In 1989, for example, Representative John Conyers moved to have a congressional committee decide whether blacks should get financial reparations for their ancestors' sufferings under slavery. The following year, columnist Charles Krauthammer suggested in *Time* magazine paying $100,000 cash reparations to each black family. A sign waved by black demonstrators during New York's 1991 Crown Heights disturbances demanded "Reparations Now."

For the Haves, the idea of reparations often went hand in hand with the idea that blacks needed to be insulated from a reality whose demands some were not quite competent to meet, having been damaged by racism's long history. White assumptions about victimization and reparations, in other words, contained a measure of unacknowledged, guilt-inducing contempt.

And these ideas produced much more harm than good. They subverted in three key ways the liberation offered by the Civil Rights Act by holding poor blacks back from seizing the opportunities newly opened to them.

The first subversion was accomplished by the reparations that were duly paid. For they were paid—most notably, in the form of welfare. As Michael Harrington had asserted in the early sixties, the poor got welfare as appropriate compensation for their victimization, as a matter of justice, not charity. Since the structure of the economy and the legacy of oppression have kept them from earning an adequate living, the government must provide it instead.

Persuaded by this line of argument, and impelled by a sincere intention to do good, the Haves hugely expanded the welfare system in the sixties, so that today the whole welfare package provides a living often equal in economic terms to a $20,000-a-year job, payable, if not quite on demand, then very nearly so. For three decades the Haves have proudly asserted the justice of this arrangement, with an increasingly breathtaking denial of its nightmarish results for the Have-Nots and for society as a whole. Indeed, it is hardly news that welfare corrupts. Lao-tzu knew it in 500 B.C., two and a half millennia before Charles Murray: "The more subsidies you have, the less self-reliant people will be." Some truths are universal.

Certainly welfare shields its recipients from the demands and obligations of the ordinary world, as the Haves thought reparations should do. Even with the recent, largely cosmetic workfare reforms, the obligations imposed by AFDC are minimal and easily evaded, especially since mothers with very young children—by definition welfare's core clientele—are exempt. As we wait for workfare to perform its wished-for therapeutic mission of gradually, supportively leading these women into the work force and mainstream life, it looks as if we will be waiting for generations yet to come.

But the very name "welfare" is a cruel satire. It's hard to say whose welfare it has promoted or which of its long-term recipients has been made better by it. Veteran welfare mothers are right to speak of it as a trap. Available, ease-inducing, will-dissolving, insinuatingly easy to get hooked on, welfare is the social policy equivalent of hard drugs, capable of taking over one's entire life and blighting it. To change the image, it has turned out to be the thalidomide of social policy, humanely therapeutic in design but engendering monstrous deformity instead.

A Gulliver, transported to the Robert Taylor Homes or the Castle Hill Houses to see the fruits of the welfare system in all their exotic strangeness, would reel in stunned amazement at a central, vast, fundamental irrationality, no less glaringly obvious than it is destructive. Here is a society lamenting its plague of intergenerational poverty, crime, and the whole host of attendant social pathologies that define the underclass. And yet in welfare it has created a machine for perpetuating that very underclass, by encouraging the least competent women—with the least initiative, the worst values, and the most blighted family structures—to become the mothers of the next generation and pass along their legacy of failure.

A naïve Gulliver might expect that something called Aid to Families with Dependent Children wouldn't go out of its way to multiply the weak families that produce children doomed to remain in the underclass. But not only does AFDC increase the number of *poor* families by offering an income to impoverished women if only they will have a child, it also increases the number of poor, *weak* families by giving that income to unmarried mothers. To be sure, strong-minded single women who try hard certainly can raise children successfully, but the overwhelming conclusion of study after study is that two-parent families do the job more dependably.

Even putting aside the cockeyed notion of the Haves that welfare is reparations or an "entitlement"—a notion without which the welfare culture couldn't exist—the idea that society ought to give an income to the single mothers of illegitimate children and set them up in apartments, without a hint of stigma, is curious enough from a historical perspective to require comment. It gained acceptance just when the Haves were too enthralled by their own sexual revolution to condemn the sexual license of others, however irresponsible—when, in the service of their own "liberation" and "self-realization," the Haves suspended judgment on sexual and family matters, lest they be judged.

At that moment, as the divorce rate more than doubled from 10.3 per thousand in 1950 to 22.6 in 1980, the epidemic of divorce and remarriage and open marriage and redivorce among the Haves signaled the fraying of the ideal that people should work at marriage with tolerance and forbearance because, among other benefits, stable two-parent families are good for kids. At that time, of course, the prevailing wisdom was that children resiliently recover from the loss and pain of divorce in no time. But that was before Judith Wallerstein and Sandra Blakeslee's research, reported in *Second Chances: Men, Women, and Children a Decade After Divorce,* demonstrated to their dismay and contrary to their preconceptions that for children the wound of divorce never heals.

In other words, the welfare mess became as bad as it has become partly because America's sexual revolution so devalued the traditional family that public opinion was willing to treat unmarried single-mother families as in essence no less functional than real families. I worry as I write this that such talk about the value of the traditional family might sound extremist: that anxiety is a gauge of how much the status of this primary social institution has sagged. In the cultural devaluation of the family, the two great liberations of our generation—the personal liberation of the Haves and the social liberation of the Have-Nots—came together to produce failure.

For the Haves, the idea of what a family *is* has grown remarkably fuzzy in the last decade or more. For instance, under the headline "Family Redefines Itself, And Now the Law Follows," *The New York Times* reports a New York court ruling that a homosexual couple is legally a family, so the survivor can't be evicted from the pair's shared apartment. Citing that ruling, a New York teacher went to court claiming that his homosexual lover, like any family member, should be entitled to coverage under his health insurance policy. In Los Angeles, reports *The New York Times* as another example of the family "redefining itself," city employees who officially register their "domestic partnerships" are entitled to paid bereavement leave and unpaid leave to tend their ill partner.

By recognizing such households as families, these authorities weaken the authority and status of traditional families related by blood and marriage, demoting them to one alternative out of several. Indeed, the *Times* slightly dismisses the traditional family as a "stereotype"— something hackneyed, conventional, simpleminded, and not quite in tune with today's enlightened reality.

The social policy goal ought to be to encourage and strengthen traditional, two-parent families in every way as the essential socializing institution. No other institution has proved so successful at equipping people with the values and habits necessary for productive, meaningful lives as this one, itself based on the willingness of individuals to turn their most basic impulses and energies to accomplishing some larger social purpose beyond their individual imperatives. At a time when most public institutions, especially the schools, fail to articulate and convey values, the weakening of this primary value-transmitting institution is doubly a disaster.

Behind *The New York Times*'s headline lies the assumption that social institutions evolve in some organic way, just as a language evolves, slowly changing as individuals randomly, experimentally modify existing practices. The law, like the dictionary, simply registers what has already occurred. In this view it is as if social and cultural changes of such magnitude had nothing to do with will and choice and intense struggle among competing values—as if judges and great newspapers and other key spokesmen for the official, institutional culture did not make changes by endorsing certain developments, treating them as natural and inevitable, while rejecting others.

Such a view allows one to endorse change without responsibly discussing what its consequences might be or, more fundamentally, whether it is right or wrong. Such questions are bound to seem beside the point anyway if you believe that the family in some mysterious way is "remaking *itself*," rather than being remade by human agents according to their own values and interests.

For the poor, the consequences of the steady unfocusing of the norm of what a family is have been far-reaching. Since the Haves could no longer make a ringing defense of the traditional, two-parent family, they could see no grounds for objection when the government gave increasing amounts of taxpayers' money to expanding numbers of unmarried mothers with illegitimate children. They had nothing to reply when black advocates for the poor and their white radical supporters began to assert, as they now formulaically do, that there is nothing wrong with the single-parent family, that children thrive in it, that it is a time-tested, historically sanctioned form of the black family that functions admirably because it is suspended in a richly nurturing web of kinship relationships beyond the nuclear family.

No matter that the historian Herbert Gutman has shown conclusively in *The Black Family in Slavery and Freedom, 1750–1925* that such an account of the black family is utterly mythical, that until very recent times blacks clung with upright tenacity to the ideal of the stable, two-parent family, even under slavery's hardship. If all families are alike, if the differences between single-parent families and traditional families are mere matters of taste and style, then the question of what works best for children and for society at large is dismissed even before it is asked.

Yet considering the overwhelming reality of the families whose proliferation the welfare system abets and fosters—the poor health of the children resulting from parental incompetence, the school failure rooted in parental neglect, the destructive behavior, the emotional deformity and intellectual stunting, the failure of the children as adults—what response can there be but condemnation of that system?

Or consider the underworld of foster care, which reveals from another vantage point the damage welfare entails. Here are legions of hurt children summoned into existence by the welfare culture only to be neglected or abused, so that now they are motherless as well as fatherless. In New York, 87.5 percent of the 45,000 children in foster care have been plucked out of welfare families. Is this evidence of a system that protects the welfare of the child, or rather of one that encourages unfit women to be mothers?

With examples of welfare's blighted harvest of failure in mind, one remembers with horrified incredulity the movement for welfare rights in the mid-sixties—as if breeding illegitimate children at the expense of one's working neighbors were a proud right of the citizens of a free democracy rather than a matter for shame and censure. One recalls too that the angry sit-ins under the aegis of the National Welfare Rights Organization, coupled with the ugly mau-mauing of welfare offices to demand expanded welfare benefits, succeeded all too well in tripling New York City's welfare caseload and, in only one year, almost quadrupling the amount the city paid out in supplemental welfare benefits.

Even today, assertions are made that all is as it should be in welfare's unwholesome world, where young women grow middle-aged as wards of the state. In the brutal housing projects that are our soviet socialist republics, welfare mothers live under a grim socialism, a comprehensive system that gives them a meager, dreary living if they accept the most shrunken scope for choice and free will, the lowest horizon of hope for the future, the narrowest possibilities for self-realization. But in a recent *New York Times* op-ed article that could have been written by Lewis Carroll, political scientist Frances Fox Piven, a founder of the National Welfare Rights Organization, and Barbara Ehrenreich, cochair of the Democratic Socialists, argue against adding any workfare requirements to the existing welfare system: "Welfare recipients are already making a contribution to society: they are rearing children, and they are doing so under the adverse conditions of extreme poverty and single parenthood. Why is a job flipping hamburgers or working in a K-mart a greater contribution than caring for the next generation of citizens?"

If only they *were* rearing citizens, in the full meaning of that word, rather than another underclass generation, incapable of real participation in the civic life. And don't most nonwelfare mothers work, rearing much better citizens than welfare mothers, without support from the state?

Unhappily the welfare system, malignant at the core, will work its mischief for time to come: from the evidence so far, workfare seems most unlikely to come to grips with AFDC's real defects.

True, researchers have found that if welfare clients are required to seek jobs, some will try and succeed, and total welfare costs will decline. The same researchers report that more ambitious workfare programs—those that try to regenerate the worst-off of the Have-Nots with training programs and restore them to the world of citizenship and work—also show positive results. But very lukewarmly positive— a mere $271 gain in annual earnings for the average single mother who participated in the program's first year. These results are as tepidly positive as the Job Corps, which after all the shouting increased the average trainee's earnings less than $200 a year; or as trivially positive as the job training programs of the Manpower Development and Training Act, which raised participants' earnings a scanty $150 to $600 a year, with the increase dwindling to half that meager figure within five years.

Champions of workfare and training programs will argue, reasonably, that any positive result, however paltry, is not to be sneezed at. Yet even with workfare, the system will still make it easy for poor single women not to worry about the consequences of getting pregnant.

Such a huge problem cries for more basic reform. In an ideal world, there doubtless would be no welfare; and if the policymakers who brought AFDC into the world and those who expanded it in the sixties could have foreseen what it would bring forth, they would have hesitated, appalled. But in the world that we have, welfare is an obdurate fact. Charles Murray may be right that it ultimately would be a gain in human happiness to scrap the entire system of welfare, Medicaid, food stamps, and so on, leaving no recourse but the job market; but even those who suspect he *is* right have little inclination to conduct the experiment and find out, since they fear the casualties would be too great. For most other Americans, so strong is the cultural revolution's belief in the justice and necessity of welfare that the political likelihood of abolishing it is zero.

The practical question for now, then, is how to change the existing bad system so that it does the least possible mischief. To begin with, it has been a mistake to concentrate on the mothers. Unfortunately, not much can be done to regenerate the great mass of underclass mothers, to release them from the shrunken and self-defeating version of humanity in which they are imprisoned. Work requirements—if inflexible enough to be unavoidable—will spark a transformation for a few, but most will go through the motions with all the sullenness of Moscow street sweepers. It will be just another "program" to be shirked and outwitted.

But though most long-term welfare mothers won't be saved by work requirements, workfare—as long as it is *work* rather than endless preparatory courses in how to work—has the advantage of eliminating the corrupting option of an indolent life on welfare, with an income equal to what a low-paid worker makes. The salutary, culture-altering message for all would be that work is valued, that everyone is responsible for his or her fate, and that everyone is part of the community, because, among other things, everyone works.

The real focus belongs on the children, though, not the mothers. That means, first, changing the welfare incentives so that women who are unmarried, too young to begin families, and too poor or unskilled to support them are not encouraged to have them. I'm sure I will be accused of all sorts of things for suggesting that people likely to be incompetent parents shouldn't be abetted in having babies to be supported by the state. But looking out at the mournful prospect of the underclass, I find it cruelty to induce the bringing into the world of children who will be so badly nurtured as most of these, and who will grow up with so many of their human excellences unawakened.

New Jersey's proposal not to raise welfare payments to mothers who have a second welfare child is a step in the right direction: a high proportion of families with more than one welfare child are likely to be dysfunctional underclass families, and this provision discourages the production of new underclass recruits. I would suggest three further reforms of this kind.

First, *unmarried* mothers should not be set up in their own apartments, an attraction of the current welfare system to teenage girls unhappy at home. Instead, they would have to live in group shelters with rules of behavior. Coupled with a work requirement, this provision would make getting pregnant and having a baby a much less attractive option for poor young unmarried women.

Moreover, it would make a wholesome distinction between the widowed and divorced mothers of dependent children—women who have made a public, legal commitment to the ideal of a stable family but who have lost their husbands—and those women, generally very young, who have embarked on motherhood with no such sense of responsibility or commitment. If the state is to promote the strong families that are best for children, it must once again distinguish between these two kinds of families when dispensing benefits.

The purpose of these shelters would be to try to strengthen the families and, most particularly, the children who live in them. Accordingly, my second proposal is to require resident single mothers to attend daily workshops on child care and child rearing. These would begin with child development truisms, unknown to many welfare mothers: babies cry because they need something, not because they are being "bad," for instance; or children need to be talked to and responded to, not ignored, not threatened, not hit.

Finally—and this is the most important point—preschool children would be cared for during working hours in day care centers in the shelters, where, from the beginning, a Head Start-style program would ensure that they felt valued, and that they learned cause and effect, big and little, before and after, similar and dissimilar, good and naughty, friendly and unfriendly, the names of colors and feelings and animals, and the whole array of cognitive and moral categories that underclass children don't adequately acquire and without which it is hard to learn and think.

From such seemingly modest efforts dramatic results can flow, as the High/Scope Educational Foundation proved with the celebrated early education project it began for underclass three- and four-year-olds in Ypsilanti, Michigan, in 1962. After dividing children randomly into one group that went through its two-year program and a control group that didn't, researchers then followed all but four children in both groups from the time the project ended until 1990. As of 1984, the latest year for which the data have been analyzed, two-thirds of the program kids finished high school, compared to half the control group. Thereafter, nearly twice as many program kids went on to college or job training, and by the time they were out of their teens they were dramatically more law-abiding and self-supporting than the control group kids, who were twice as likely to have illegitimate children and be on welfare.

If you can make such a difference in averting the underclass fate starting with three- and four-year-olds, it's certain you can make a more profound difference if you start much earlier, at an even more crucial developmental stage, and if in addition you teach and motivate the mothers to further the child's early learning. It isn't just intelligence that is at issue in this development; it is the qualities that come under the rubric of character—patience, perseverance, pride in a job well done, respect for others, determination, loyalty, and so on.

What will happen to the children if welfare mothers don't choose to participate in this new scheme? If mothers decide instead that they are willing and able to support themselves and their children, even by flipping hamburgers, so much the better for the children to live in families that take part in the mainstream world of work instead of being enmeshed in welfare's marginal existence. But if mothers refuse to enter the group homes and fail to support the children, then the state will intervene to take the children away, as it does now.

Welfare was the first subversion of the liberation promised by the Civil Rights Act. The second major way that liberation was subverted was that the culture of the Haves withdrew respect from the humble but decent working life in the process of embracing the idea that the poor were victims of an unfair society. Seen through the distorting lens of this idea, a poor person who doesn't work deserves sympathy and compassion, not harsh judgment; his idleness is imposed upon him by the structure of the economy, by the lack of opportunity, not by irresponsibility and moral failure. If he takes welfare, he should not be stigmatized: welfare is no more than his right.

At that moment, the very thing that gives a hardworking poor person his decisive moral superiority over the nonworking poor person starts to dissolve, as Charles Murray has movingly written. Whether a poor person works or not grows morally neutral. If it is not blameworthy *not* to work, no definitive praise attaches to someone who works and supports his family. A growing disdain for the working class at large as benighted "hard hats" and Archie Bunkers, all beer and bigotry, hastened that withdrawal of respect.

A breadwinner's income itself becomes less meaningful, since it no longer greatly distinguishes him economically from the nonworking poor person to whom a beefed-up welfare system provides an equivalent income. The low-income worker is shunted to the side, out of view of the larger culture, while the culture's official spokesmen overwhelm his or her nonworking neighbor with compassion and understanding.

He is shunted aside in a more important way, too. According to the ideology of victimization, by working in his low-wage job, he is not a fellow participant in the community but a victim of an unjust, unequal economy that makes the Haves richer while keeping him on a lower plane at an ever greater disadvantage. Seen in this way, he is no longer part of the same universe as the Haves: a fellow wage earner, a family man, a citizen. In one perverse sense, he is even less worthy of respect than the nonworkers. They at least are smart enough to know that the available low-wage work is exploitation and victimization. Too canny to be hoodwinked, they have enough dignity to refuse to participate in their own victimization. They resist; they hold themselves inviolate.

Most families don't rise from poverty to neurosurgery or mergers and acquisitions in one generation. It goes by stages, it takes time, and it often starts humbly. But if cleaning houses, making up hotel rooms, cutting meat, or cooking french fries is being a sap—if it makes the person doing it feel himself in a demeaning, false position, earning "chump change" in a "dead-end job," rather than being decent and honest—then it is that much harder to put a foot on the bottom of the ladder. Perhaps that's why getting started is easier for immigrants: they are detached enough from the larger society not to hear its messages clearly, and they come with values and goals strong enough to turn their menial jobs into a liberation rather than a servitude.

The new taint of indignity upon low-wage work undermined blacks especially. Even though closed opportunities had kept many blacks in menial low-wage work for generations, within those unjust limits blacks had made lives of dignity and rectitude and had preached the mainstream values by which they lived to their children. But right at the moment when the Civil Rights Act genuinely opened opportunity, when those values of work and self-respecting propriety could have fueled real economic advancement, they came under assault.

Prompted by the culture of the Haves, children of upright black workers were quick to see their parents' admirable attitudes as a badge of servility and inferiority. Didn't their parents know that they were trapped in jobs that led nowhere, that merely exploited and oppressed them, as the majority culture was insisting? Didn't they know that the right attitude wasn't dutiful effort and hopeful patience? When Black Power demagogues charged that such a life was Uncle Tomism, unworthy of respect, they were only intensifying a message that the culture of the Haves had already voiced.

It wasn't just white teenagers who rejected their parents' values all through the sixties. But when black adolescents of that era spurned the "straight" values of their parents as passive and politically naïve, the consequences were especially harsh. Before they even gave themselves a chance, legions from an entire generation smothered within themselves the outlook on life that could have brought them success, adopting instead a defiant resentment that locked them out and helped form the underclass.

Finally, the idea of victimization paralyzed the black poor in the face of opportunity precisely by encouraging them to think of themselves as the helpless victims. This vigorous fanning of already smoldering feelings caused the conviction of victimization to blaze up to a higher pitch of self-destructiveness just when those feelings most needed damping down.

For paradoxically the success of the civil rights movement often intensified the sense of victimization instead of assuaging it. The civil rights movement's enflaming of white guilt with a stark display of the wrongs done to blacks made victimhood a means of extracting benefits, as essayist Shelby Steele has pointed out, and thus it wedded blacks more firmly to the victim's identity. But while giving blacks a sense of strength as a group, victimhood simultaneously made them feel all the more helpless as individuals, unable to advance by personal effort but only by collective protest.

More important, the Civil Rights Act's opening of opportunity flooded blacks with anxiety and self-doubt. They were free to succeed—but also to fail, as Steele remarks. To deny the very existence of such unwanted feelings, many blacks clung all the more fiercely to their sense of victimization. If blacks fail, they vociferated, white racism is to blame, not individual blacks. Blacks can't be held responsible when the whole society is stacked against them. Hence while racism was dramatically abating, charges of racism grew more shrill.

Out of fear that the newly open mainstream society might reject them *personally,* based on their individual merits or demerits, reject them more deeply and woundingly than when whites simply rejected all blacks because of the color of their skin, blacks often tended preemptively to reject white society. The more they feared failure, the angrier they became, for anger is easier to bear than fear and vulnerability.

Fear transmuted into anger led some blacks to see oppression that wasn't there, and the imaginary oppression grew to monstrous, truly delusional proportions. At the more modest end of the scale is poet and playwright Amiri Baraka, formerly LeRoi Jones, who publicly likened the Rutgers University English professors who voted not to give him tenure to Nazis and Klansmen. At the extreme, a dismaying number of blacks today are ready to believe that the government itself is conspiring to kill them.

Look at a recent poll of blacks of all classes in New York. Was it true, could it possibly be true, that the government purposely strives to discredit black officials like Marion Barry, the crack-smoking ex-mayor of Washington, D.C.? Over three quarters of those interviewed said yes. Washington blacks believe it so firmly that they call the imagined conspiracy "the Plan."

Was it true, could it possibly be true, that the government deliberately makes drugs easy to get in the ghetto, in order to harm blacks? Yes indeed, said three out of every five respondents to the poll. Even more ominous in the wildness of paranoia it suggests, 29 percent said it was true or possibly true that the AIDS virus was created in a laboratory expressly to infect and destroy blacks.

When you believe that the government or the whole white race is waging genocidal biological warfare against you, how can you possibly see that opportunity is open before you? If you believe the government is *forcing* blacks into such self-destructive acts as taking drugs and sharing dirty needles, how can you possibly think that you have either the power or the responsibility to forge your own fate?

So strongly did fear of freedom lead many blacks to assert their victimhood, so much store did they put in victimhood as a source of collective power, that increasingly they came to define black identity in terms of victimization, as Shelby Steele argues. To be black is to be a victim—to be poor, ghettoized, marginal. "The purest black was the poor black," in Steele's formulation. Blacks who wanted to retain their sense of racial solidarity had only that downtrodden stereotype with which to identify.

For purposes of upward mobility, it is a hopeless model. It takes for granted, as Steele once explained to me in an interview, that any attempt to enter the mainstream, to declare yourself a full-fledged American, to rise into the middle class, is a racial betrayal—what blacks mean when they accuse each other of "acting white." It's why one mostly black high school had to have its academic awards ceremony at night, semiclandestinely, since jeering at the winners had become all but universal among the rest of the students.

Nor is it a helpful model for maintaining a viable community. A schoolteacher friend told me how her mostly black class sneered at her as being not authentically black for telling them to throw their candy wrappers in the trash cans, not on the street.

Such a limiting ideal confronts middle-class and solid working-class blacks with a painful conflict. What does it mean for them to be true to themselves? True to what? To the mainstream ideals and values that made them what they are, or to the poor, downtrodden, passive, resentful identity that they hope might make them feel whole as blacks but that is antithetical to their entire life's achievement?

What should they tell their children? "If you're raising your children encouraging them to be black and to identify with the mass of black people—and you make this a crucial element of their lives—then in effect you're conditioning them, almost, to be poor, to not subscribe to the same values that you yourself are living by," Steele told me.

So basic a conflict helps explain such painful happenings as the well-known self-destruction of Edmund Perry, a promising Harlem teenager, the pride of his neighborhood, who won a scholarship to Exeter, the elite New England prep school. After graduation, with a coveted acceptance to Stanford in his pocket, he came home for the summer before starting college.

Yes, his years at Exeter had been full of strain; he never really fit in; he was left with a sense of bitterness. Yes, he mirrored the divisions that raged inside his high-strung mother—a woman both angry and ambitious, wanting mainstream success for him yet seething with resentment at the insults and injuries that she believed the oppressive mainstream world had inflicted upon her. Yes, he often spouted what his Exeter classmates took as militant politics steeped in black rage, but which an older black friend of his rightly recognized as a badly needed "psychological defense mechanism" against the strains and rejections of life in the high white world. But despite the sharp and painful conflicts, the world really did lie all before him.

At the heart of the conflicts raging within him lay his sense that the journey to the world of Exeter had estranged him from the world—and the identity—with which he'd grown up, a world he appeared implicitly to reject and betray by leaving it, by his effort to meet the different standards of his new community. You can't simultaneously belong to the mainstream and to a world that defines itself by its rebellious, often nihilistic, rejection of mainstream values.

A young woman who knew Perry, and who also had made the dislocating odyssey from a New York ghetto to a New England prep school, spoke about the resulting sense of alienation to journalist Robert Anson, who wrote about the Perry case. "What's even harder than going to one of those schools . . . is coming home from one," she said. "You really aren't a part of th[e] neighborhood any more." Your horizons have widened; your perspective has shifted. But you feel acutely the need to show that you still belong, that you haven't inwardly rejected your community, thereby betraying your race and falsifying your identity.

How? "You gotta snort more coke, smoke more reefer, shoot more baskets, and give up more poontang," she explained. "You've got a week to prove you are black, before you're on that bus Monday morning, heading back for class."

Perry evidently felt the need to give that proof, most likely to himself above all. One June night in 1985, wanting movie money, he and his older brother tried to mug a young man near the Columbia University campus. The man, it happened, was a plainsclothes cop. In the struggle, he killed Edmund Perry with a shot in the belly, resolving with terrible finality the youth's inner clash between the mainstream world in which he felt so misplaced and the ghetto world he had left behind but died trying to show he still belonged to.

Whether or not this story fulfills Aristotle's criteria, to my mind it counts as a modern tragedy, painful beyond expression. And it has such power to appall because both the tragic fate and the inner flaw that sparked it have a social significance beyond the merely personal.

The identification with victimhood has ever-expanding evil consequences. It engenders rage and resentment that seem amply justified and worth acting upon; it rejects responsibility; it falsifies reality. At its outer reaches, it can explode catastrophically; within its more ordinary bounds, it can sap and sabotage, causing those who believe it to become their own victimizers, fulfilling their own prophecy, which comes true only because they believe in it.

The poet William Blake spoke of "mind-forg'd manacles"—the ideas engendered from within one's own imagination that one invests with power enough to enslave oneself. Victimization is one such idea. Because it has such malign power over the black poor, the Haves must not endow this idea with even more power, as they have so relentlessly been doing. They should not give the black poor the message that they are damaged souls who require reparations. In acknowledging and deploring the injustice that blacks have suffered, the Haves must add that the injustice must now be transcended. One mustn't forget it; one must acknowledge how one's history has made one who one is; but to remain obsessed with past injustice is to remain forever in its thrall.

I know this is easy to say, and one can dismissively reply that only those who have been at the receiving end of racism should pronounce on it. I know that blacks still chronically suffer racial slights and insults, and so one doesn't need high-falutin psychological explanations to account for black anger. But how different are the insults of today from the injuries of yesterday, when opportunity for blacks was radically more limited. Even though millennial perfection hasn't arrived, opportunity is now open, and the great question is how many of the once-excluded will seize it, despite their scars. The culture of the Haves needs to tell them that they *can* do it—not that, because of past victimization, they cannot.

Speculations

1. Magnet asserts that "The crucial barriers" to economic opportunity for blacks "have fallen." Do you agree? If economic barriers have fallen, what holds minorities back from progress? Explain your responses.
2. According to Magnet, what attitudes on the part of the "Haves" have resulted in a redefinition of the family? What impact has this redefining had on the "Have Nots" and American moral expectations about poor families?
3. What three proposals does Magnet recommend to correct the problems he sees with "welfare mothers" and "welfare children"? Do you agree that these proposals are reasonable and would solve the problems? Explain your response.
4. What does Magnet mean when he says "Whether a poor person works or not grows morally neutral"? In his view, how has respect for certain types of work changed? Based on your work experience or the jobs you've seen available to youths and to poor people, explain whether you agree with Magnet's argument.
5. Explain the tragedy of Edmund Perry. Based on your experience with peer pressure and your perceptions of social and racial differences, why did this tragedy occur?
6. Magnet concludes by invoking the metaphor of "mind-forg'd manacles" from William Blake's poem "London," which describes a closed vision of urban despair in a blighted city. What does this metaphor mean for Magnet and how does he use it to summarize his argument about victimization?

COMPLEXION

Richard Rodriguez

Alienation—the alienation of self and language, self and family, self and society—is the theme that dominates Richard Rodriguez's work. Rodriguez sees *his* alienation, however, as a necessary precondition to becoming a writer and journalist.

A Mexican-American, Rodriguez was born in 1944 in San Francisco. His choice to master English and abandon Spanish is sensitively chronicled in his autobiography, *Hunger of Memory*, published in 1982. As a self-described "scholarship boy," he earned a B.A. at Stanford University in 1967 and did graduate work at the University of California at Berkeley and at London's Warburg Institute as a Fulbright fellow from 1972–1973. He refused to accept offers to teach at the university level because, as he told *New York Times* critic Le Anne Schreiber, "he could not withstand the irony of being counted a 'minority' when he was, in fact, a fully assimilated member of the majority." Instead, he began writing. In 1994, he published his most recent book, *Days of Obligation: An Argument with My Mexican Father.*

Rodriguez has been criticized for his conservative and unpopular views concerning bilingualism. In a *Publishers Weekly* interview with Suzanne Dalezal, he said that teachers

> [H]ave an obligation to teach a public language. Public language isn't just English or Spanish. . . . It is the language of public society. . . . For Appalachian children who speak a fractured English or black children in a ghetto, the problem is the same. . . . My argument has always been that the imperative is to get children away from those languages that increase their sense of alienation from public society.

As Rodriguez explained in an interview with *Contemporary Authors:*

> I see myself straddling two worlds of writing, journalism and literature. . . . It takes me a very long time to write. What I try to do when I write is break down the line separating the prosaic world from the poetic word. I try to write about everyday concerns—an educational issue, say, or the problems of the unemployed—but to write about them as powerfully, as richly, as well as I can.

This excerpt is taken from his autobiography, *Hunger of Memory.*

Visiting the East Coast or the gray capitals of Europe during the long months of winter, I often meet people at deluxe hotels who comment on my complexion. (In such hotels it appears nowadays a mark of leisure and wealth to have a complexion like mine.) Have I been skiing? In the Swiss Alps? Have I just returned from a Caribbean vacation? No. I say no softly but in a firm voice that intends to explain: My complexion is dark. (My skin is brown. More exactly, terra-cotta in sunlight, tawny in shade. I do not redden in sunlight. Instead, my skin becomes progressively dark; the sun singes the flesh.)

When I was a boy the white summer sun of Sacramento would darken me so, my T-shirt would seem bleached against my slender dark arms. My mother would see me come up the front steps. She'd wait for the screen door to slam at my back. "You look like a *negrito*," she'd say, angry, sorry to be angry, frustrated almost to laughing, scorn. "You know how important looks are in this country. With *los gringos* looks are all that they judge on. But you! Look at you! You're so careless!" Then she'd start in all over again. "You won't be satisfied till you end up looking like *los pobres* who work in the fields, *los braceros.*"

(*Los braceros:* Those men who work with their *brazos,* their arms; Mexican nationals who were licensed to work for American farmers in the 1950s. They worked very hard for very little money, my father would tell me. And what money they earned they sent back to Mexico to support their families, my mother would add. *Los pobres*—the poor, the pitiful, the powerless ones. But paradoxically also powerful men. They were the men with brown-muscled arms I stared at in awe on Saturday mornings when they showed up downtown like gypsies to shop at Woolworth's or Penney's. On Monday nights they would gather hours early on the steps of the Memorial Auditorium for the wrestling matches. Passing by on my bicycle in summer, I would spy them there, clustered in small groups, talking—frightening and fascinating men— some wearing Texas *sombreros* and T-shirts which shone fluorescent in the twilight. I would sit forward in the back seat of our family's '48 Chevy to see them, working alongside Valley highways: dark men on an even horizon, loading a truck amid rows of straight green. Powerful, powerless men. Their fascinating darkness—like mine—to be feared.)

"You'll end up looking just like them."

Regarding my family, I see faces that do not closely resemble my own. Like some other Mexican families, my family suggests Mexico's confused colonial past. Gathered around a table, we appear to be from separate continents. My father's face recalls faces I have seen in France. His complexion is white—he does not tan; he does not burn. Over the years, his dark wavy hair has grayed handsomely. But with time his face has sagged to a perpetual sigh. My mother, whose surname is inexplicably Irish—Moran—has an olive complexion. People have frequently wondered if, perhaps, she is Italian or Portuguese. And, in fact, she looks as though she could be from southern Europe. My mother's face has not aged as quickly as the rest of her body; it remains smooth and glowing—a cool tan—which her gray hair cleanly accentuates. My older brother has inherited her good looks. When he was a boy people would tell him that he looked like Mario Lanza, and hearing it he would smile with dimpled assurance. He would come home from high school with girl friends who seemed to me glamorous (because they were) blonds. And during those years I envied him his skin that burned red and peeled like the skin of the *gringos.* His complexion never darkened like mine. My youngest sister is exotically pale, almost ashen. She is delicately featured, Near Eastern, people have said. Only my older sister has a complexion as dark as mine, though her facial features are much less harshly defined than my own. To many people meeting her, she seems (they say) Polynesian. I am the only one in the family whose face is severely cut to the line of ancient Indian ancestors. My face is mournfully long, in the classical Indian manner; my profile suggests one of those beaknosed Mayan sculptures—the eaglelike face upturned, open-mouthed, against the deserted, primitive sky.

"We are Mexicans," my mother and father would say, and taught their four children to say whenever we (often) were asked about our ancestry. My mother and father scorned those "white" Mexican-Americans who tried to pass themselves off as Spanish. My parents would never have thought of denying their ancestry. I never denied it: My ancestry is Mexican, I told strangers mechanically. But I never forgot that only my older sister's complexion was as dark as mine.

My older sister never spoke to me about her complexion when she was a girl. But I guessed that she found her dark skin a burden. I knew that she suffered for being a "nigger." As she came home from grammar school, little boys came up behind her and pushed her down to the sidewalk. In high school, she struggled in the adolescent competition for boyfriends in a world of football games and proms, a world where her looks were plainly uncommon. In college, she was afraid and scornful when dark-skinned foreign students from countries like Turkey and India found her attractive. She revealed her fear of dark skin to me only in adulthood when, regarding her own three children, she quietly admitted relief that they were all light.

That is the kind of remark women in my family have often made before. As a boy, I'd stay in the kitchen (never seeming to attract any notice), listening while my aunts spoke of their pleasure at having light children. (The men, some of whom were dark-skinned from years of working out of doors, would be in another part of the house.) It was the woman's spoken concern: the fear of having a dark-skinned son or daughter. Remedies were exchanged. One aunt prescribed to her sisters the elixir of large doses of castor oil during the last weeks of pregnancy. (The remedy risked an abortion.) Children born dark grew up to have their faces treated regularly with a mixture of egg white and lemon juice concentrate. (In my case, the solution never would take.) One Mexican-American friend of my mother's, who regarded it a special blessing that she had a measure of English blood, spoke disparagingly of her husband, a construction worker, for being so dark. "He doesn't take care of himself," she complained. But the remark, I noticed, annoyed my mother, who sat tracing an invisible design with her finger on the tablecloth.

There was affection too and a kind of humor about these matters. With daring tenderness, one of my uncles would refer to his wife as *mi negra*. An aunt regularly called her dark child *mi feito* (my little ugly one), her smile only partially hidden as she bent down to dig her mouth under his ticklish chin. And at times relatives spoke scornfully of pale, white skin. A *gringo's* skin resembled *masa*—

baker's dough—someone remarked. Everyone laughed. Voices chuckled over the fact that the *gringos* spent so many hours in summer sunning themselves. ("They need to get sun because they look like *los muertos*.")[1]

I heard the laughing but remembered what the women had said, with unsmiling voices, concerning dark skin. Nothing I heard outside the house, regarding my skin, was so impressive to me.

In public I occasionally heard racial slurs. Complete strangers would yell out at me. A teenager drove past, shouting, "Hey, Greaser! Hey, Pancho!" Over his shoulder I saw the giggling face of his girl friend. A boy pedaled by and announced matter-of-factly, "I pee on dirty Mexicans." Such remarks would be said so casually that I wouldn't quickly realize that they were being addressed to me. When I did, I would be paralyzed with embarrassment, unable to return the insult. (Those times I happened to be with white grammar school friends, *they* shouted back. Imbued with the mysterious kindness of children, my friends would never ask later why I hadn't yelled out in my own defense.)

In all, there could not have been more than a dozen incidents of name-calling. That there were so few suggests that I was not a primary victim of racial abuse. But that, even today, I can clearly remember particular incidents is proof of their impact. Because of such incidents, I listened when my parents remarked that Mexicans were often mistreated in California border towns. And in Texas. I listened carefully when I heard that two of my cousins had been refused admittance to an "all-white" swimming pool. And that an uncle had been told by some man to go back to Africa. I followed the progress of the southern black civil rights movement, which was gaining prominent notice in Sacramento's afternoon newspaper. But what most intrigued me was the connection between dark skin and poverty. Because I heard my mother speak so often about the relegation of dark people to menial labor, I considered the great victims of racism to be those who were poor and forced to do menial work. People like the farmworkers whose skin was dark from the sun.

After meeting a black grammar school friend of my sister's, I remember thinking that she wasn't really "black." What interested me was the fact that she wasn't poor. (Her well-dressed parents would come by after work to pick her up in a shiny green Oldsmobile.) By contrast, the garbage men who appeared every Friday morning seemed to me unmistakably black. (I didn't bother to ask my parents why Sacramento garbage men always were black. I thought I knew.) One morning I was in the backyard when a man opened the gate. He

---

[1] Dead people. [Eds.]

was an ugly, square-faced black man with popping red eyes, a pail slung over his shoulder. As he approached, I stood up. And in a voice that seemed to me very weak, I piped, "Hi." But the man paid me no heed. He strode past to the can by the garage. In a single broad movement, he overturned its contents into his larger pail. Our can came crashing down as he turned and left me watching, in awe.

"*Pobres negros*," my mother remarked when she'd notice a headline in the paper about a civil rights demonstration in the South. "How the *gringos* mistreat them." In the same tone of voice she'd tell me about the mistreatment her brother endured years before. (After my grandfather's death, my grandmother had come to America with her son and five daughters.) "My sisters, we were still all just teenagers. And since *mi pápa* was dead, my brother had to be the head of the family. He had to support us, to find work. But what skills did he have! Twenty years old. *Pobre.* He was tall; like your grandfather. And strong. He did construction work. 'Construction!' The *gringos* kept him digging all day, doing the dirtiest jobs. And they would pay him next to nothing. Sometimes they promised him one salary and paid him less when he finished. But what could he do? Report them? We weren't citizens then. He didn't even know English. And he was dark. What chances could he have? As soon as we sisters got older, he went right back to Mexico. He hated this country. He looked so tired when he left. Already with a hunchback. Still in his twenties. But old-looking. No life for him here. *Pobre.*"

Dark skin was for my mother the most important symbol of a life of oppressive labor and poverty. But both my parents recognized other symbols as well.

My father noticed the feel of every hand he shook. (He'd smile sometimes—marvel more than scorn—remembering a man he'd met who had soft, uncalloused hands.)

My mother would grab a towel in the kitchen and rub my oily face sore when I came in from playing outside. "Clean the *graza* off of your face!" (*Greaser!*)

Symbols: When my older sister, then in high school, asked my mother if she could do light housework in the afternoons for a rich lady we knew, my mother was frightened by the idea. For several weeks she troubled over it before granting conditional permission: "Just remember, you're not a maid. I don't want you wearing a uniform." My father echoed the same warning. Walking with him past a hotel, I watched as he stared at a doorman dressed like a Beefeater. "How can anyone let himself be dressed up like that? Like a clown. Don't you ever get a job where you have to put on a uniform." In summertime neighbors would ask me if I wanted to earn extra money by mowing their lawns. Again and again my mother worried: "Why did they ask *you*? Can't you find anything better?" Inevitably, she'd relent. She knew I needed the money. But I was instructed to work after dinner. ("When the sun's not so hot.") Even then, I'd have to wear a hat. *Un sombrero de* baseball.

(*Sombrero.* Watching gray cowboy movies, I'd brood over the meaning of the broad-rimmed hat—that troubling symbol—which comically distinguished a Mexican cowboy from real cowboys.)

From my father came no warnings concerning the sun. His fear was of dark factory jobs. He remembered too well his first jobs when he came to this country, not intending to stay, just to earn money enough to sail on to Australia. (In Mexico he had heard too many stories of discrimination in *los Estados Unidos.* So it was Australia, that distant island-continent, that loomed in his imagination as his "America.") The work my father found in San Francisco was work for the unskilled. A factory job. Then a cannery job. (He'd remember the noise and the heat.) Then a job at a warehouse. (He'd remember the dark stench of old urine.) At one place there were fistfights; at another a supervisor who hated Chinese and Mexicans. Nowhere a union.

His memory of himself in those years is held by those jobs. Never making money enough for passage to Australia; slowly giving up the plan of returning to school to resume his third-grade education—to become an engineer. My memory of him in those years, however, is lifted from photographs in the family album which show him on his honeymoon with my mother—the woman who had convinced him to stay in America. I have studied their photographs often, seeking to find in those figures some clear resemblance to the man and the woman I've known as my parents. But the youthful faces in the photos remain, behind dark glasses, shadowy figures anticipating my mother and father.

They are pictured on the grounds of the Coronado Hotel near San Diego, standing in the pale light of a winter afternoon. She is wearing slacks. Her hair falls seductively over one side of her face. He appears wearing a double-breasted suit, an unneeded raincoat draped over his arm. Another shows them standing together, solemnly staring ahead. Their shoulders barely are touching. There is to their pose an aristocratic formality, an elegant Latin hauteur.

The man in those pictures is the same man who was fascinated by Italian grand opera. I have never known just what my father saw in the spectacle, but he has told me that he would take my mother to the Opera House every Friday night—if he had money enough for orchestra seats. ("Why go to sit in the balcony?") On Sundays he'd don Italian silk scarves and a camel's hair coat to take his new wife to the polo matches in Golden Gate Park. But one weekend my father stopped going to the opera and polo matches. He would blame the change in his life on one job—a warehouse job, working for a large corporation which today advertises its products with the smiling faces of children. "They made me an old man before my time," he'd say to me many years later. Afterward, jobs got easier and cleaner. Eventually, in middle age, he got a job making false teeth. But his youth was spent at the warehouse. "Everything changed," his wife remembers. The dapper young man in the old photographs yielded to the man I saw after dinner: haggard, asleep on the sofa. During "The Ed Sullivan Show" on Sunday nights, when Roberta Peters or Licia Albanese would appear on the tiny blue screen, his head would jerk up alert. He'd sit forward while the notes of Puccini sounded before him. ("Un bel dí.")

By the time they had a family, my parents no longer dressed in very fine clothes. Those symbols of great wealth and the reality of their lives too noisily clashed. No longer did they try to fit themselves, like paper-doll figures, behind trappings so foreign to their actual lives. My father no longer wore silk scarves or expensive wool suits. He sold his tuxedo to a second-hand store for five dollars. My mother sold her rabbit fur coat to the wife of a Spanish radio station disc jockey. ("It looks better on you than it does on me," she kept telling the lady until the sale was completed.) I was six years old at the time, but I recall watching the transaction with complete understanding. The woman I knew as my mother was already physically unlike the woman in her honeymoon photos. My mother's hair was short. Her shoulders were thick from carrying children. Her fingers were swollen red, roughened by housecleaning. Already my mother would admit to foreseeing herself in her own mother, a woman grown old, bald and bowlegged, after a hard lifetime of working.

In their manner, both my parents continued to respect the symbols of what they considered to be upper-class life. Very early, they taught me the *propria* way of eating *como los ricos*. And I was carefully taught elaborate formulas of polite greeting and parting. The dark little boy would be invited by classmates to the rich houses on Forty-fourth and Forty-fifth streets. "How do you do?" or "I am very pleased to meet you," I would say, bowing slightly to the amused mothers of classmates. "Thank you very much for the dinner; it was very delicious."

I made an impression. I intended to make an impression, to be invited back. (I soon realized that the trick was to get the mother or father to notice me.) From those early days began my association with rich people, my fascination with their secret. My mother worried. She warned me not to come home expecting to have the things my friends possessed. But she needn't have said anything. When I went to the big houses, I remembered that I was, at best, a visitor to the world I saw there. For that reason, I was an especially watchful guest. I was my parents' child. Things most middle-class children wouldn't trouble to notice, I studied. Remembered to see: the starched black and white uniform worn by the maid who opened the door; the Mexican gardeners—their complexions as dark as my own. (One gardener's face, glassed by sweat, looked up to see me going inside.)

"Take Richard upstairs and show him your electric train," the mother said. But it was really the vast polished dining room table I'd come to appraise. Those nights when I was invited to stay for dinner, I'd notice that my friend's mother rang a small silver bell to tell the black woman when to bring in the food. The father, at his end of the table, ate while wearing his tie. When I was not required to speak, I'd skate the icy cut of crystal with my eye; my gaze would follow the golden threads etched onto the rim of china. With my mother's eyes I'd see my hostess's manicured nails and judge them to be marks of her leisure. Later, when my schoolmate's father would bid me goodnight, I would feel his soft fingers and palm when we shook hands. And turning to leave, I'd see my dark self, lit by chandelier light, in a tall hallway mirror.

Complexion. My first conscious experience of sexual excitement concerns my complexion. One summer weekend, when I was around seven years old, I was at a public swimming pool with the whole family. I remember sitting on the damp pavement next to the pool and seeing my mother, in the spectators' bleachers, holding my younger sister on her lap. My mother, I noticed, was watching my father as he stood on a diving board, waving to her. I watched her wave back. Then saw her radiant, bashful, astonishing smile. In that second I sensed that my mother and father had a relationship I knew nothing about. A nervous excitement encircled my stomach as I saw my mother's eyes follow my father's figure curving into the water. A second or two later, he emerged. I heard him call out. Smiling, his voice sounded, buoyant, calling me to swim to him. But turning to see him, I caught my mother's eye. I heard her shout over to me. In Spanish she called through the crowd: "Put a towel on over your shoulders." In public, she didn't want to say why. I knew.

That incident anticipates the shame and sexual inferiority I was to feel in later years because of my dark complexion. I was to grow up an ugly child. Or one who thought himself ugly. (*Feo.*) One night when I was eleven or twelve years old, I locked myself in the bathroom and carefully regarded my reflection in the mirror over the sink. Without any pleasure I studied my skin. I turned on the faucet. (In my mind I heard the swirling voices of aunts, and even my mother's voice, whispering, whispering incessantly about lemon juice solutions and dark, *feo* children.) With a bar of soap, I fashioned a thick ball of lather. I began soaping my arms. I took my father's straight razor out of the medicine cabinet. Slowly, with steady deliberateness, I put the blade against my flesh, pressed it as close as I could without cutting, and moved it up and down across my skin to see if I could get out, somehow lessen, the dark. All I succeeded in doing, however, was in shaving my arms bare of their hair. For as I noted with disappointment, the dark would not come out. It remained. Trapped. Deep in the cells of my skin.

Throughout adolescence, I felt myself mysteriously marked. Nothing else about my appearance would concern me so much as the fact that my complexion was dark. My mother would say how sorry she was that there was not money enough to get braces to straighten my teeth. But I never bothered about my teeth. In three-way mirrors at department stores, I'd see my profile dramatically defined by a long nose, but it was really only the color of my skin that caught my attention.

I wasn't afraid that I would become a menial laborer because of my skin. Nor did my complexion make me feel especially vulnerable to racial abuse. (I didn't really consider my dark skin to be a racial characteristic. I would have been only too happy to look as Mexican as my light-skinned older brother.) Simply, I judged myself ugly. And, since the women in my family had been the ones who discussed it in such worried tones, I felt my dark skin made me unattractive to women.

Thirteen years old. Fourteen. In a grammar school art class, when the assignment was to draw a self-portrait, I tried and I tried but could not bring myself to shade in the face on the paper to anything like my actual tone. With disgust then I would come face to face with myself in mirrors. With disappointment I located myself in class photographs— my dark face undefined by the camera which had clearly described the white faces of classmates. Or I'd see my dark wrist against my long-sleeved white shirt.

I grew divorced from my body. Insecure, overweight, listless. On hot summer days when my rubber-soled shoes soaked up the heat from the sidewalk, I kept my head down. Or walked in the shade. My mother didn't need anymore to tell me to watch out for the sun. I denied myself a sensational life. The normal, extraordinary, animal excitement of feeling my body alive—riding shirtless on a bicycle in the warm wind created by furious self-propelled motion—the sensations that first had excited in me a sense of my maleness, I denied. I was too ashamed of my body. I wanted to forget that I had a body because I had a brown body. I was grateful that none of my classmates ever mentioned the fact.

I continued to see the *braceros*, those men I resembled in one way and, in another way, didn't resemble at all. On the watery horizon of a Valley afternoon, I'd see them. And though I feared looking like them, it was with silent envy that I regarded them still. I envied them their physical lives, their freedom to violate the taboo of the sun. Closer to home I would notice the shirtless construction workers, the roofers, the sweating men tarring the street in front of the house. And I'd see the Mexican gardeners. I was unwilling to admit the attraction of their lives. I tried to deny it by looking away. But what was denied became strongly desired.

In high school physical education classes, I withdrew, in the regular company of five or six classmates, to a distant corner of a football field where we smoked and talked. Our company was composed of bodies too short or too tall, all graceless and all—except mine—pale. Our conversation was usually witty. (In fact we were intelligent.) If we referred to the athletic contests around us, it was with sarcasm. With savage scorn I'd refer to the "animals" playing football or baseball. It would have been important for me to have joined them. Or for me to have taken off my shirt, to have let the sun burn on my skin, and to have run barefoot on the warm wet grass. It would have been very important. Too important. It would have been too telling a gesture—to admit the desire for sensation, the body, my body.

Fifteen, sixteen. I was a teenager shy in the presence of girls. Never dated. Barely could talk to a girl without stammering. In high school I went to several dances, but I never managed to ask a girl to dance. So I stopped going. I cannot remember high school years now with the parade of typical images: bright drive-ins or gliding blue shadows of a Junior Prom. At home most weekend nights, I would pass evenings reading. Like those hidden, precocious adolescents who have no real-life sexual experiences, I read a great deal of romantic fiction. "You won't find it in your books," my brother would playfully taunt me as he prepared to go to a party by freezing the crest of the wave in his hair with sticky pomade. Through my reading, however, I developed a fabulous and sophisticated sexual imagination. At seventeen, I may not have known how to engage a girl in small talk, but I had read *Lady Chatterley's Lover*.

It annoyed me to bear my father's teasing: that I would never know what "real work" is; that my hands were so soft. I think I knew it was his way of admitting pleasure and pride in my academic success. But I didn't smile. My mother said she was glad her children were getting their educations and would not be pushed around like *los pobres*. I heard the remark ironically as a reminder of my separation from *los braceros*. At such times I suspected that education was making me effeminate. The odd thing, however, was that I did not judge my classmates so harshly. Nor did I consider my male teachers in high school effeminate. It was only myself I judged against some shadowy, mythical Mexican laborer—dark like me, yet very different.

Language was crucial. I knew that I had violated the ideal of the *macho* by becoming such a dedicated student of language and literature. *Machismo* was a word never exactly defined by the persons who used it. (It was best described in the "proper" behavior of men.) Women at home, nevertheless, would repeat the old Mexican dictum that a man should be *feo, fuerte, y formal.* "The three F's," my mother called them, smiling slyly. *Feo* I took to mean not literally ugly so much as ruggedly handsome. (When my mother and her sisters spent a loud, laughing afternoon determining ideal male good looks, they finally settled on the actor Gilbert Roland, who was neither too pretty nor ugly but had looks "like a man.") *Fuerte,* "strong," seemed to mean not physical strength as much as inner strength, character. A dependable man is *fuerte. Fuerte* for that reason was a characteristic subsumed by the last of the three qualities, and the one I most often considered—*formal.* To be *formal* is to be steady. A man of responsibility, a good provider. Someone *formal* is also constant. A person to be relied upon in adversity. A sober man, a man of high seriousness.

I learned a great deal about being *formal* just by listening to the way my father and other male relatives of his generation spoke. A man was not silent necessarily. Nor was he limited in the tones he could sound. For example, he could tell a long, involved, humorous story and laugh at his own humor with high-pitched giggling. But a man was not talkative the way a woman could be. It was permitted a woman to be gossipy and chatty. (When one heard many voices in a room, it was usually women who were talking.) Men spoke much less rapidly. And often men spoke in monologues. (When one voice sounded in a crowded room, it was most often a man's voice one heard.) More important than any of this was the fact that a man never verbally revealed his emotions. Men did not speak about their unease in moments of crisis or danger. It was the woman who worried aloud when her husband got laid off from work. At times of illness or death in the family, a man was usually quiet, even silent. Women spoke up to voice prayers. In distress, women always sounded quick ejaculations to God or the Virgin; women prayed in clearly audible voices at a wake held in a funeral parlor. And on the subject of love, a woman was verbally expansive. She spoke of her yearning and delight. A married man, if he spoke publicly about love, usually did so with playful, mischievous irony. Younger, unmarried men more often were quiet. (The *macho* is a silent suitor. *Formal.*)

At home I was quiet, so perhaps I seemed *formal* to my relations and other Spanish-speaking visitors to the house. But outside the house—my God!—I talked. Particularly in class or alone with my teachers, I chattered. (Talking seemed to make teachers think I was bright.) I often was proud of my way with words. Though, on other occasions, for example, when I would hear my mother busily speaking to women, it would occur to me that my attachment to words made me like her. Her son. Not *formal* like my father. At such times I even suspected that my nostalgia for sounds—the noisy, intimate

Spanish sounds of my past—was nothing more than effeminate yearning.

High school English teachers encouraged me to describe very personal feelings in words. Poems and short stories I wrote, expressing sorrow and loneliness, were awarded high grades. In my bedroom were books by poets and novelists—books that I loved—in which male writers published feelings the men in my family never revealed or acknowledged in words. And it seemed to me that there was something unmanly about my attachment to literature. Even today, when so much about the myth of the *macho* no longer concerns me, I cannot altogether evade such notions. Writing these pages, admitting my embarrassment or my guilt, admitting my sexual anxieties and my physical insecurity, I have not been able to forget that I am not being *formal*.

So be it.

I went to college at Stanford, attracted partly by its academic reputation, partly because it was the school rich people went to. I found myself on a campus with golden children of western America's upper middle class. Many were students both ambitious for academic success *and* accustomed to leisured life in the sun. In the afternoon, they lay spread out, sunbathing in front of the library, reading Swift or Engels or Beckett. Others went by in convertibles, off to play tennis or ride horses or sail. Beach boys dressed in tank-tops and shorts were my classmates in undergraduate seminars. Tall tan girls wearing white strapless dresses sat directly in front of me in lecture rooms. I'd study them, their physical confidence. I was still recognizably kin to the boy I had been. Less tortured perhaps. But still kin. At Stanford, it's true, I began to have something like a conventional sexual life. I don't think, however, that I really believed that the women I knew found me physically appealing. I continued to stay out of the sun. I didn't linger in mirrors. And I was the student at Stanford who remembered to notice the Mexican-American janitors and gardeners working on campus.

It was at Stanford, one day near the end of my senior year, that a friend told me about a summer construction job he knew was available. I was quickly alert. Desire uncoiled within me. My friend said that he knew I had been looking for summer employment. He knew I needed some money. Almost apologetically he explained: It was something I probably wouldn't be interested in, but a friend of his, a contractor, needed someone for the summer to do menial jobs. There would be lots of shoveling and raking and sweeping. Nothing too hard. But nothing more interesting either. Still, the pay would be good. Did I want it? Or did I know someone who did?

I did. Yes, I said, surprised to hear myself say it.

In the weeks following, friends cautioned that I had no idea how hard physical labor really is. ("You only *think* you know what it is like to shovel for eight hours straight.") Their objections seemed to me challenges. They resolved the issue. I became happy with my plan. I decided, however, not to tell my parents. I wouldn't tell my mother because I could guess her worried reaction. I would tell my father only after the summer was over, when I could announce that, after all, I did know what "real work" is like.

The day I met the contractor (a Princeton graduate, it turned out), he asked me whether I had done any physical labor before. "In high school, during the summer," I lied. And although he seemed to regard me with skepticism, he decided to give me a try. Several days later, expectant, I arrived at my first construction site. I would take off my shirt to the sun. And at last grasp desired sensation. No longer afraid. At last become like a *bracero*. "We need those tree stumps out of here by tomorrow," the contractor said. I started to work.

I labored with excitement that first morning—and all the days after. The work was harder than I could have expected. But it was never as tedious as my friends had warned me it would be. There was too much physical pleasure in the labor. Especially early in the day, I would be most alert to the sensations of movement and straining. Beginning around seven each morning (when the air was still damp but the scent of weeds and dry earth anticipated the heat of the sun), I would feel my body resist the first thrusts of the shovel. My arms, tightened by sleep, would gradually loosen; after only several minutes, sweat would gather in beads on my forehead and then—a short while later—I would feel my chest silky with sweat in the breeze. I would return to my work. A nervous spark of pain would fly up my arm and settle to burn like an ember in the thick of my shoulder. An hour, two passed. Three. My whole body would assume regular movements; my shoveling would be described by identical, even movements. Even later in the day, my enthusiasm for primitive sensation would survive the heat and the dust and the insects pricking my back. I would strain wildly for sensation as the day came to a close. At three-thirty, quitting time, I would stand upright and slowly let my head fall back, luxuriating in the feeling of tightness relieved.

Some of the men working nearby would watch me and laugh. Two or three of the older men took the trouble to teach me the right way to use a pick, the correct way to shovel. "You're doing it wrong, too fucking hard," one man scolded. Then proceeded to show me—what persons who work with their bodies all their lives quickly learn—the most economical way to use one's body in labor.

"Don't make your back do so much work," he instructed. I stood impatiently listening, half listening, vaguely watching, then noticed his work-thickened fingers clutching the shovel. I was annoyed. I wanted to tell him that I enjoyed shoveling the wrong way. And I didn't want to learn the right way. I wasn't afraid of back pain. I liked the way my body felt sore at the end of the day.

I was about to, but, as it turned out, I didn't say a thing. Rather it was at that moment I realized that I was fooling myself if I expected a few weeks of labor to gain me admission to the world of the laborer. I would not learn in three months what my father had meant by "real work." I was not bound to this job; I could imagine its rapid conclusion. For me the sensations of exertion and fatigue could be savored. For my father or uncle, working at comparable jobs when they were my age, such sensations were to be feared. Fatigue took a different toll on their bodies—and minds.

It was, I know, a simple insight. But it was with this realization that I took my first step that summer toward realizing something even more important about the "worker." In the company of carpenters, electricians, plumbers, and painters at lunch, I would often sit quietly, observant. I was not shy in such company. I felt easy, pleased by the knowledge that I was casually accepted, my presence taken for granted by men (exotics) who worked with their hands. Some days the younger men would talk and talk about sex, and they would howl at women who drove by in cars. Other days the talk at lunchtime was subdued; men gathered in separate groups. It depended on who was around. There were rough, good-natured workers. Others were quiet. The more I remember that summer, the more I realize that there was no single *type* of worker. I am embarrassed to say I had not expected such diversity. I certainly had not expected to meet, for example, a plumber who was an abstract painter in his off hours and admired the work of Mark Rothko. Nor did I expect to meet so many workers with college diplomas. (They were the ones who were not surprised that I intended to enter graduate school in the fall.) I suppose what I really want to say here is painfully obvious, but I must say it nevertheless: The men of that summer were middle-class Americans. They certainly didn't constitute an oppressed society. Carefully completing their work sheets; talking about the fortunes of local football teams; planning Las Vegas vacations; comparing the gas mileage of various makes of campers—they were not *los pobres* my mother had spoken about.

On two occasions, the contractor hired a group of Mexican aliens. They were employed to cut down some trees and haul off debris. In all, there were six men of varying age. The youngest in his late twenties; the oldest (his father?) perhaps sixty years old. They came and they left in a single old truck. Anonymous men. They were never introduced to the other men at the site. Immediately upon their arrival, they would follow the contractor's directions, start working—rarely resting— seemingly driven by a fatalistic sense that work which had to be done was best done as quickly as possible.

I watched them sometimes. Perhaps they watched me. The only time I saw them pay me much notice was one day at lunchtime when I was laughing with the other men. The Mexicans sat apart when they ate, just as they worked by themselves. Quiet. I rarely heard them say much to each other. All I could hear were their voices calling out sharply to one another, giving directions. Otherwise, when they stood briefly resting, they talked among themselves in voices too hard to overhear.

The contractor knew enough Spanish, and the Mexicans—or at least the oldest of them, their spokesman—seemed to know enough English to communicate. But because I was around, the contractor decided one day to make me his translator. (He assumed I could speak Spanish.) I did what I was told. Shyly I went over to tell the Mexicans that the *patrón* wanted them to do something else before they left for the day. As I started to speak, I was afraid with my old fear that I would be unable to pronounce the Spanish words. But it was a simple instruction I had to convey. I could say it in phrases.

The dark sweating faces turned toward me as I spoke. They stopped their work to hear me. Each nodded in response. I stood there. I wanted to say something more. But what could I say in Spanish, even if I could have pronounced the words right? Perhaps I just wanted to engage them in small talk, to be assured of their confidence, our familiarity. I thought for a moment to ask them where in Mexico they were from. Something like that. And maybe I wanted to tell them (a lie, if need be) that my parents were from the same part of Mexico.

I stood there.

Their faces watched me. The eyes of the man directly in front of me moved slowly over my shoulder, and I turned to follow his glance toward *el patrón* some distance away. For a moment I felt swept up by that glance into the Mexicans' company. But then I heard one of them returning to work. And then the others went back to work. I left them without saying anything more.

When they had finished, the contractor went over to pay them in cash. (He later told me that he paid them collectively "for the job," though he wouldn't tell me their wages. He said something quickly about the good rate of exchange "in their own country.") I can still hear the loudly confident voice he used with the Mexicans. It was the sound of the *gringo* I had heard as a very young boy. And I can still hear the quiet, indistinct sounds of the Mexican, the oldest, who replied. At hearing that voice I was sad for the Mexicans. Depressed by their vulnerability. Angry at myself. The adventure of the summer seemed suddenly ludicrous. I would not shorten the distance I felt from *los pobres* with a few weeks of physical labor. I would not become like them. They were different from me.

After that summer, a great deal—and not very much really—changed in my life. The curse of physical shame was broken by the sun; I was no longer ashamed of my body. No longer would I deny myself the pleasing sensations of my maleness. During those years when middle-class black Americans began to assert with pride, "Black is beautiful," I was able to regard my complexion without shame. I am today darker than I ever was as a boy. I have taken up the middle-class sport of long-distance running. Nearly every day now I run ten or fifteen miles, barely clothed, my skin exposed to the California winter rain and wind or the summer sun of late afternoon. The torso, the soccer player's calves and thighs, the arms of the twenty-year-old I never was, I possess now in my thirties. I study the youthful parody shape in the mirror: the stomach lipped tight by muscle; the shoulders rounded by chin-ups; the arms veined strong. This man. A man. I meet him. He laughs to see me, what I have become.

The dandy. I wear double-breasted Italian suits and custom-made English shoes. I resemble no one so much as my father—the man pictured in those honeymoon photos. At that point in life when he abandoned the dandy's posture, I assume it. At the point when my parents would not consider going on vacation, I register at the Hotel Carlyle in New York and the Plaza Athenée in Paris. I am as taken by the symbols of leisure and wealth as they were. For my parents, however, those symbols became taunts, reminders of all they could not achieve in one lifetime. For me those same symbols are reassuring reminders of public success. I tempt vulgarity to be reassured. I am filled with the gaudy delight, the monstrous grace of the nouveau riche.

In recent years I have had occasion to lecture in ghetto high schools. There I see students of remarkable style and physical grace. (One can see more dandies in such schools than one ever will find in middle-class high schools.) There is not the look of casual assurance I saw students at Stanford display. Ghetto girls mimic high-fashion models. Their dresses are of bold, forceful color; their figures elegant, long; the stance theatrical. Boys wear shirts that grip at their overdeveloped muscular bodies. (Against a powerless future, they engage images of strength.) Bad nutrition does not yet tell. Great disappointment, fatal to youth, awaits them still. For the moment, movements in school hallways are dancelike, a procession of postures in a sexual masque. Watching them, I feel a kind of envy. I wonder how different my adolescence would have been had I been free. . . . But no, it is my parents I see—their optimism during those years when they were entertained by Italian grand opera.

The registration clerk in London wonders if I have just been to Switzerland. And the man who carries my luggage in New York guesses the Caribbean. My complexion becomes a mark of my leisure. Yet no one would regard my complexion the same way if I entered such hotels through the service entrance. That is only to say that my complexion assumes its significance from the context of my life. My skin, in itself, means nothing. I stress the point because I know there are people who would label me "disadvantaged" because of my color. They make the same mistake I made as a boy, when I thought a disadvantaged life was circumscribed by particular occupations. That summer I worked in the sun may have made me physically indistinguishable from the Mexicans working nearby. (My skin was actually darker because, unlike them, I worked without wearing a shirt. By late August my hands were probably as tough as theirs.) But I was not one of *los pobres*. What made me different from them was an attitude of *mind*, my imagination of myself.

I do not blame my mother for warning me away from the sun when I was young. In a world where her brother had become an old man in his twenties because he was dark, my complexion was something to worry about. "Don't run in the sun," she warns me today. I run. In the end, my father was right—though perhaps he did not know how right or why—to say that I would never know what real work is. I will never know what he felt at his last factory job. If tomorrow I worked at some kind of factory, it would go differently for me. My long education would favor me. I could act as a public person—able to defend my interests, to unionize, to petition, to speak up—to challenge and demand. (I will never know what real work is.) I will never know what the Mexicans knew, gathering their shovels and ladders and saws.

Their silence stays with me now. The wages those Mexicans received for their labor were only a measure of their disadvantaged condition. Their silence is more telling. They lack a public identity. They remain profoundly alien. Persons apart. People lacking a union obviously, people without grounds. They depend upon the relative good will or fairness of their employers each day. For such people, lacking a better alternative, it is not such an unreasonable risk.

Their silence stays with me. I have taken these many words to describe its impact. Only: the quiet. Something uncanny about it. Its compliance. Vulnerability. Pathos. As I heard their truck rumbling away, I shuddered, my face mirrored with sweat. I had finally come face to face with *los pobres*.

Speculations

1. Rodriguez describes how he was intrigued by "the connection between dark skin and poverty." How does he describe this connection and what notable examples does he use to describe it? What examples of your own can you think of?
2. Rodriguez's mother warns his sister against wearing a maid's uniform, and his father reacts negatively when he sees a doorman in uniform, saying "Don't you ever get a job where you have to put on a uniform." What does the uniform symbolize? What other symbols related to "lightness" and "darkness" of skin are his parents concerned about?
3. Rodriguez went to the rich houses of his wealthy classmates. He writes:

   > I made an impression. I intended to make an impression, to be invited back. (I soon realized that the trick was to get the mother or father to notice me.) From those early days began my association with rich people, my fascination with their secret.

   How would you describe Rodriguez's motivation? What does he want? What is his own attitude toward this desire as revealed in the tone of this writing?
4. Have you ever felt like an alien, that is, so out of place that you felt you had no way to talk with others around you? Describe the situation and where it occurred—at a party, in a store, in a foreign country. Explain how it came about and what you felt and experienced as an "alien."
5. Rodriguez's experience as a construction worker had a major impact on him. What does the experience teach him about himself, about the other workers, the contractor, the Mexican aliens?
6. Toward the end of the excerpt, Rodriguez describes himself as a "dandy," as someone who tempts "vulgarity to be reassured," as someone successful, leisured, yet distanced from himself, even a bit cynical about his own pretensions. He contrasts himself with the Mexican laborers who are lacking "a public identity," silent, and "profoundly alien." Evaluate Rodriguez's attitude toward his accomplishments. How does he see himself in comparison to the Mexicans? How do you sort out Rodriguez's point of view?

ASSIGNMENT SEQUENCES

Sequence One: Arguing about Opportunity and Affirmative Action

1. Andrew Hacker describes how driving across America, blacks "can never be sure how they will be received" and goes on to de-

scribe situations in which they are impeded or harassed on the highway, in service stations, restaurants, and motels. Imagine that you are with a group of blacks or even another ethnic minority that is treated this way. At the end of your journey, everyone in the group agrees that someone should write about this. You decide to write an essay that tries to account for this social situation and why it is harmful or troublesome to you. Using Hacker as a source, write the essay.

2. Several pieces in this section deal with the problem of affirmative action; some emphasize how it doesn't work, while others emphasize why it is still a viable and important idea. Take your own position on this subject and write an essay using examples, quotes, statistics, and arguments from the authors in this section to support your position.

3. Ellis Cose describes several polls taken of people concerning their reactions to affirmative action. Devise your own poll of several questions about affirmative action, including several of the specific questions that Cose talks about in the polls he discusses. You might wish to use quotations from Hacker, Carter, Cose, or Magnet about the issues surrounding affirmative action and ask people why they agree or disagree. Administer your poll to at least a dozen people, which might include friends, family members, classmates, and other people on campus, such as teachers, administrators, and office workers. Make sure you get a variety of respondents among this group. Analyze the responses to the poll and compare them to what Cose and others have to say in this section. Write an essay evaluating your results and reflecting on the significance of those results. Explain how the results confirm or change your own thoughts on this issue.

4. Using the authors' ideas in this section, draw up a list of the four or five most critical issues you think relate to affirmative action and equal opportunity in hiring. Interview the Chair of the English Department, the Affirmative Action Officer or representative for your college, and the Dean or Assistant Dean of your school. Ask them to describe their primary concerns about the issues you have listed, problems the school has faced, and solutions they have found. Take notes or tape record your interviews and write up your findings in an essay on how your school has dealt with affirmative action.

5. Myron Magnet argues that welfare and a sense of victimization have been destructive to an individual's sense of self-worth and motivation to get ahead: "The identification with victimhood has ever-expanding evil consequences. It engenders rage and resent-

ment that seem amply justified and worth acting upon; it rejects responsibility; it falsifies reality." Perhaps everyone at some point has felt victimized, and in many cases the sense of victimization is clearly much more justified than in other cases. Write an essay evaluating Magnet's definition of victimization, how it works on the psyche, and describing an example of victimization from your experience. Explain in your essay why you agree or disagree with Magnet's evaluation of victimization and how your experience is similar or different.

6. Drawing on the assignments you have written above, write a letter to the editor of your local newspaper arguing for either keeping affirmative action in place, for abolishing it altogether, or for altering it to make the policy more fair. Support your argument with what you have learned from reading and writing about this section.

Sequence Two: Opportunity and Difference

1. Andrew Hacker and Stephen Carter describe what it is like to be different and the difficulties it causes for black people relating to the larger society in which they find themselves. Write an essay that analyzes the perspectives of these authors and describes their differences in approach to this problem. Which arguments and approaches of authors do you find most compelling? Explain why in your essay. To focus your essay, select any one issue or approach from either Carter's or Hacker's essay.

2. For this assignment, work with a partner in your class. Interview each other and then write biographies or profiles of one another. Ask your partner about the community values, cultural background, and school experiences that shaped his or her sense of belonging to social groups outside of his or her immediate family. Include any significant events, activities, or life changes that this person experienced. Write your profiles and exchange them with each other. Respond in writing, adding information, making suggestions, and commenting on ways that you think will improve the profile and make it more accurate or meaningful. Then, incorporating your partner's comments and suggestions, rewrite the profile.

3. Richard Rodriguez has frequently been attacked by members of the American Hispanic community for his views, for being against bilingualism and advocating that all children in this country should learn English (as opposed to learning both English and Spanish). He has been criticized for abandoning Hispanic culture

and the Hispanic community. During a television interview with Bill Moyers, the following exchange occurred:

RODRIGUEZ: You can be born again in this country. You can become a new man. You can even change your name. You can dye your hair. You can go to Muscle Beach and get a new body.... People always accuse me of having lost my culture, as though it was a little suitcase that I left in some train station back there. And I suppose I have, in the sense that I'm not my father. But that's inevitable I think. I belong to a different time. I belong to your culture.

MOYERS: What do you mean "my culture"?

RODRIGUEZ: That is to say, I'm an American. You know, I'm not a Mexican. I think of myself now as having been converted to America, and in that sense, I'm not a missionary from Mexico.... The pity of America I think is always that we don't understand just how enormously seductive we are to the world.... [America] is a culture. It is an idea. It is an advertisement. It's a lipstick. It's a Coke bottle.

Having read "Complexion" and other essays in this book by authors from a variety of cultural backgrounds, respond to Rodriguez and his critics in an essay that considers the relationship of self to American culture—and to other individuals within that culture. How should one maintain oneself in American culture? What is American culture anyway? Focus your essay on one aspect of American culture that has been important to you, your family, or your friends.

4. As a follow-up to assignment 3, focus specifically on the issue of race. Rodriguez's essay describes how his dark skin created a constant awareness of himself as different from white society. Andrew Hacker and Stephen Carter similarly provide many examples of what it is like to constantly be reminded of their difference from the white majority and how that affects where they can live or how others treat them. Ellis Cose provides the allegory of the "Unworths" versus the "Worths" and the story of the "B-kids." In each case, he shows how being marked in this way determines opportunities in life and how people think of people who are so marked. Using these authors' observations and examples from other essays in this section (and other sections), write an essay which discusses your understanding of racial difference in our society and how it creates a sense of otherness. Identify what is learned from that otherness—as made evident in a specific situation comedy on television: you might write about "The Cosby Show" or "In Living

Color" or "All in the Family." Consider the roles that race and racial difference play in the ways that people are represented and the ways that self and society are represented on these shows, and then respond with your own evaluation of these shows based on what you've learned from the essays in this section.

5. As a follow-up to assignment 4 imagine that you are a television producer who wants to create a television show on some issue of "race" and "other." You decide that the selections in this book offer more than enough possibilities. Choose one and offer a rationale for why you have chosen it and a brief description of what the show would be like, who would star in it, its setting, message, appeal, and so on. Write so as to persuade a television network to put your show on prime time.

6. Rodriguez discusses in detail three words that define the "proper" attributes of a man in Mexican culture. They are *feo* (rugged handsomeness), *fuerte* (inner strength and character), and *formal* (being responsible, sober, and a good provider). Write an essay in which you identify three or more terms in American culture that typically define what you think it means to be a successful working man or a successful working woman. You may want to discuss how these terms are personalized for you by your individual cultural or ethnic background or how these terms either coincide or conflict with those of the larger society. Give a full explanation of why these terms are essential to your definition.

ACKNOWLEDGMENTS

MARTIN LUTHER KING, JR. "Letter from the Birmingham Jail" from *Why We Can't Wait* by Martin Luther King, Jr. Copyright © 1963, 1964 by Martin Luther King, Jr.; copyright renewed 1991, 1992 by Coretta Scott King. Reprinted by arrangement with The Heirs to the Estate of Martin Luther King, Jr., c/o Joan Daves Agency as agent for the Proprietor.

MAXINE HONG KINGSTON "No Name Woman" from *The Woman Warrior: Memoirs of a Girlhood Among Ghosts* by Maxine Hong Kingston. Copyright © 1975, 1976 by Maxine Hong Kingston. Reprinted by permission of Alfred A. Knopf, Inc., a subsidiary of Random House, Inc.

JONATHAN KOZOL "Concealment" from *Rachel and Her Children* by Jonathan Kozol. Copyright © 1987 by Jonathan Kozol. Reprinted by permission of Crown Publishers, Inc.

MICHAEL KRASNY "Passing the Buck in Tinsel Town." Copyright © 1993 by the Foundation for National Progress. Reprinted with permission from *Mother Jones* Magazine (July/August 1993).

JOHN LEONARD "TV and the Decline of Civilization." Copyright © The Nation Company, L. P. Reprinted from *The Nation* magazine.

AUDRE LORDE "Turning the Beat Around: Lesbian Parenting 1986" from *A Burst of Light* by Audre Lord. Copyright © 1988 by Audre Lorde. Reprinted with permission of Firebrand Books, Ithaca, New York.

PETER LYMAN "The Fraternal Bond as a Joking Relationship" from *Changing Men: New Directions in Research on Man and Masculinity* by Michael Kimmel. Copyright © by Sage Publications. Reprinted by permission of Sage Publications.

MYRON MAGNET "Race and Reparations" from *The Dream and the Nightmare* by Myron Magnet. Copyright © 1993. Reprinted by permission of William Morrow and Company, Inc.

MIKE MALES "Public Enemy Number 1." Copyright © 1993 by *In These Times*. Reprinted from *In These Times*, a biweekly newsmagazine published in Chicago.

MARION MEADE "The Degradation of Women." Copyright © 1971 by The New York Times Company. Reprinted by permission.

JESSICA MITFORD "The Criminal Type" from *Kind and Unusual Punishment* by Jessica Mitford. Copyright © 1973 by Jessica Mitford. Reprinted by permission of Alfred A. Knopf, Inc.

CAMILLE PAGLIA "Rape and Modern Sex War." Copyright © 1991 by Camille Paglia. Originally published in *New York Newsday*. Reprinted by permission of the author.

ELAYNE RAPPING "In Praise of Roseanne." Copyright © 1994 by *The Progressive*. Reprinted by permission of *The Progressive*, 409 East Main Street, Madison, WI 53703.

RICHARD RODRIGUEZ "Complexion" from *Hunger of Memory* by Richard Rodriguez. Copyright © 1992 by Richard Rodriguez. Reprinted by permission of David R. Godine, Publisher, Inc.

KATIE ROIPHE "Date Rape's Other Victim," from *The Morning After* by Katie Roiphe. Copyright © 1992 by Katherine Anne Roiphe. By permission of Little, Brown and Company.

RANDY SHILTS "The Copy Berg Story" from *Conduct Unbecoming* by Randy Shilts. Copyright © 1993 by Randy Shilts. Reprinted by permission of St. Martin's Press, Inc.

INDEX OF AUTHORS
AND
TITLES